W. Mudge

An account of the operations carried out for accomplishing a trigonometrical survey of England and Wales

W Mudge

An account of the operations carried out for accomplishing a trigonometrical survey of England and Wales

ISBN/EAN: 9783741166532

Manufactured in Europe, USA, Canada, Australia, Japa

Cover: Foto ©Thomas Meinert / pixelio.de

Manufactured and distributed by brebook publishing software (www.brebook.com)

W. Mudge

An account of the operations carried out for accomplishing a trigonometrical survey of England and Wales

AN

ACCOUNT OF THE OPERATIONS

CARRIED ON FOR ACCOMPLISHING

A TRIGONOMETRICAL SURVEY

OF

ENGLAND AND WALES,

CONTINUED FROM THE YEAR 1797,

TO THE END OF THE YEAR 1799.

BY CAPTAIN WILLIAM MUDGE,

OF THE ROYAL ARTILLERY, F. R. S.

VOL. II.

ILLUSTRATED WITH SEVEN COPPER PLATES.

FROM THE

PHILOSOPHICAL TRANSACTIONS.

LONDON:

PRINTED BY W. BULMER AND CO. CLEVELAND-ROW, ST. JAMES'S,
FOR W. FADEN, GEOGRAPHER TO HIS MAJESTY,
AND TO HIS ROYAL HIGHNESS THE PRINCE OF WALES,
CHARING CROSS.
1801.

CONTENTS.

TRIGONOMETRICAL SURVEY, 1797—1799.

b

b 2

PLATES.

N. B. The Numbers affixed to the above Plates have not been altered since Impressions were taken from them for the Philosophical Transactions.

AN

ACCOUNT OF THE OPERATIONS

CARRIED ON FOR ACCOMPLISHING

A TRIGONOMETRICAL SURVEY.

By William Mudge.

Read before the ROYAL SOCIETY, *July* 3, 1800.

INTRODUCTION.

Having interspersed in the following Paper, with as much attention to brevity as the subject admits, every intelligence relating to the Trigonometrical Survey, I think it unnecessary to swell the bulk of the communication, by giving a long prefatory account of its progress since the year 1796.

The contents of the work now meeting the public eye, are important and numerous: I have divided it into sections. The first contains the calculations of the sides of the principal and secondary triangles extended over the country in 1797, 1798; and 1799; together with an account of the measurement of a new base line on Sedgemoor, and a short historical narrative of each year's operation. The second section contains the computed latitudes and longitudes of those places, on the western coast, intersected in 1795 and 1796, and also such others, since determined, as lie conveniently situated to the newly-observed meridians. This section also contains the directions of those meridians; one on Black Down, in Dorsetshire; another on Butterton Hill, in Devonshire; and another on St. Agnes Beacon, in Cornwall. Among the contents are likewise to be numbered the bearings, distances, &c. of the stations and intersected objects, from the parallels and meridians

The third and last section contains the triangles which have been carried over Essex, the western part of Kent, and portions of the counties joining the former, Suffolk and Hertfordshire. It is with satisfaction I am enabled to state, that Mr. GARDNER, the chief Draftsman, with his assistants, has almost completed the Survey of this extensive tract, which, no doubt, like the map of Kent, will be given to the public: the materials for these different surveys are ample, and will be found in this section, which concludes with the altitudes of the stations and mean refractions.

Before I had advanced far in my work, I entertained ideas of condensing all the *data* in my possession, and distributing them in it; but, when I found my paper would, in that case, be too large for the Philosophical Transactions, I desisted, contenting myself with presenting little more than a moiety: it is even now, of inconvenient magnitude, but I could not, with propriety, still farther abridge it, for I have, in several instances, rejected important matter. I shall, therefore, take an early opportunity of compiling a fourth account, in which will be given the latitudes and longitudes of those places, in Essex, Kent, &c. found in the last section.

It is right, I should observe that, knowing from experience, how liable surveyors are to mistake the names of places, and also, how utterly impracticable it is to detect errors, till the interiors of the great triangles have been *filled up*, I have been cautious to give only the distances of such objects as could not be easily mistaken. I do not mean to insinuate that, among

the great number now published, instances may not be found
of misnomers, or even wrong bearings; but I rely with great
confidence on their general accuracy, and particularly on those
constituting the surveys of Essex and the northern shore of the
Thames, as the whole of them have been *verified* by Mr. GARDNER.
Indeed this is to be understood as holding good throughout the
last section, in which are 375 triangles. In our former accounts
of this survey, we were particularly guarded in not intermixing
their contents with distances determined from numerous doubtful
intersections; and experience has hitherto not detected above
three or four errors arising from wrong bearings or misnomers.
Previously, indeed, to the compilation of them, a great part of
the objects in Sussex, Hampshire, and the Isle of Wight, were
verified by Mr. GARDNER, in process of an extensive survey, carried on by the order, and performed for the service, of the Board
of Ordnance. This gentleman will also have it in his power to
detect any errors, if such exist, in the names of places to the
westward; as the Master General has been pleased to issue his
directions for the survey of Devonshire, and as much of Somersetshire and Cornwall as will *square* the work.

I have mentioned, in the body of the account, that the President and Council of the Royal Society, were pleased to accede
to the request made by the Honorable Board of Ordnance, to en-
trust to my care, the circular instrument used by the late Major
General ROY, in his well known operation. It has already been
found highly useful, and will shortly prove to be still more so,
as one theodolite will be employed in carrying the above orders
of Marquis CORNWALLIS into effect, while the other is used
in carrying a meridional line through the country; an undertaking begun, and partly executed.

B

Before I close this Introduction, I am to announce, that Mr. Isaac Dalby, no longer able to endure the fatigues incident to the service, has retired from it; and it would be a matter of injustice, if I were not to acknowledge the extent of his services, his unremitted labour, and attention. But, whilst I lament the loss of a man so perfectly calculated to assist me in this arduous undertaking, I derive every consolation from a knowledge, founded on experience, of the talents and abilities of Mr. Simon Woolcot, his successor.

SECTION FIRST.

1. *Particulars relating to the Operations of the Year* 1797.

The principal object proposed to be accomplished this year, was the determination of the directions of meridians at proper stations, in order to afford the necessary *data* for computing the latitudes and longitudes of places intersected in the surveys of 1795 and 1796.

From errors which are the result of computations made on the supposition of the earth's surface being a plane, it is expedient that new directions of meridians should be observed, when the operations are extended, in eastern or western directions, over spaces of sixty miles from fixed meridians. The distance from Dover to the Land's End being upwards of 300 miles, it becomes necessary, on this principle, that four directions of meridians should be observed; which, with that of Greenwich, amounts to five, dividing this space into six nearly equal parts.

Whatever be the stations farther to the westward, which offer

themselves as fit places for these observations, Dunnose in the
Isle of Wight presents itself as highly eligible, not only because
it is removed the necessary distance from the meridian of
Greenwich, but also because it commands a most extensive
view of the western coast : therefore, as the direction of the meridian was observed on this station in 1793, (see Philosophical
Transactions for 1795, p. 517.) it became necessary to fix on
three places only.

In the selection of these stations, it was our wish to have
found such as should lie nearly in the same parallel, each intermediate one being visible from those east and west of it; by which
means, the differences of latitude between their respective parallels would be accurately determined.

When the party was at Dunnose, in the year 1793, a hill at a
very considerable distance, in a direction very nearly west, was
seen just rising out of the horizon. It then occurred to us that
this spot would, at some future period, be a very proper one for
a station whereon a new direction of the meridian might be observed. Experience, in the Survey of 1795, led us to believe
this hill was actually Black Down in Dorsetshire; therefore it was
determined that our operations should commence at that station,
and the event verified the truth of our suppositions.

The party took the field early in April, as observations on the
Pole Star, for the purpose in question, are made with superior
advantage at this season of the year, because the star comes to
its greatest elongations from the meridian at those times, when
the sun produces little tremor in the air, by which means, the
staff to which the Pole Star is referred, in good weather, is easily
perceived.

As the high land in the vicinity of Teignmouth, in Devonshire, cuts off all view of the southern extremity of Dartmoor from Black Down, the necessary alternative was, the firing of lights on some remote station, communicating with Butterton. Rippin Tor was quickly discovered to be the most proper spot; and that eminence would, in every point of view, be a most eligible one for a new direction of the meridian, if the hills in the middle of the moor were not considerably higher. It was, therefore, chosen only with a view of being subservient to the purpose of finding the latitude of Butterton.

In making observations on the Pole Star, the same precautions were taken to ensure accuracy, as were observed at Dunnose and Beachy Head in the year 1799; (see Phil. Trans. for 1795, p. 460.) I shall, therefore, not enumerate them, but content myself with observing, that no pains were spared in this performance.

From Black Down, the party removed to Butterton; at which place but few observations were made, the weather being either tempestuous or hazy, during the greatest part of the time we were at that station: they were, however, made under favourable circumstances, in other respects, and are therefore likely to afford accurate results.

As in the case of Rippin Tor, with respect to Black Down, so Hensbarrow, in Cornwall, was selected as the spot for connecting St. Agnes Beacon with the station on Butterton; for these latter are not visible from each other, the high land about St. Austle, on the northern part of which is situated Hens or Hengist barrow, being higher and intermediate. The staff to which the lights and star were referred, was placed on a hill called Hemmerdon Ball, a secondary station in the series of 1795.

On the 1st of May, the party proceeded to St. Agnes Beacon; at which place the observations were completed on the 8th. 'The staff for connecting the observations made on the Pole Star with those made on the lights fired at Hensbarrow, was placed near Puranzabulo; which spot is laid down in the plan, Pl. XXVII.

After these directions of meridians were determined, we proceeded with the survey, and from St. Agnes Beacon repaired to Trevose Head, a promontory on the northern coast of Cornwall. The ascent from the sea to the station on this headland being very gradual and unobstructed, we took the opportunity of finding its altitude by means of the transit instrument. The levelling was begun on the 30th of May, and finished the following day; from which operation, it was found that the height of the station above low water-mark was 274,2 feet; which is, probably, within six inches of the truth. This base of altitude, will afford the means of computing the heights of the stations in the north of Devon, and also of verifying those in the western part of Cornwall. (See Phil. Trans. for 1797, p. 471.)

In giving an account of this and similar articles, it is my intention merely to set forth the order in which the different parts of the survey have been performed. It would be prolix, and perhaps, unnecessary, to assign the reasons for the choice of each station. In the present instance, however, it may not be improper to observe, that a station called Black Down, near Lydford, was selected for the purpose of carrying distances into the north of Devon, by means of the side formed by that station and Carraton Hill. The difficulty of running up the series of triangles from the west, (and it might have been also added, towards the north,) is mentioned in the account of 1797. A tract of country exists in Cornwall, possessing the same characteristic features with Dartmoor, and has thrown in our way equal embarrassments. The station called Carraton Hill, is situated on its southern extremity, from which no part of the north of Cornwall can be seen : it, therefore, became expedient to erect a staff on the top of the rugged hill Brown Willy, (a spot not accessible to the instrument,) and afterwards to content ourselves with *surveying round it*. This resolution became the more necessary, as by means of it, the triangles in the west of Devon will be hereafter connected with those in the north of Cornwall, in a shorter and more direct way than from the sides in the more southern country. In order, therefore, to observe the staff erected on this station, the instrument was taken a second time to Bodmin Down. The station named Cadon Barrow, near Camelford, and those on St. Stephen's Down, near Launceston, were also visited ; at which time it was judged expedient to discontinue the operations in Devonshire.

In proceeding along the southern coast, in the years 1795 and 1796, with a single chain of triangles, we acted in conformity with our instructions. It was, in many points of view, the most eligible mode of proceeding; and particularly in that which regarded an early determination of the latitudes and longitudes of the great head-lands in the channel, and also of the Scilly Isles.

When the operations above spoken of were completed, and those instructions carried into full execution, (ample materials being provided for ascertaining the situations of every remarkable point on the English side of the channel,) the want of a spot in the southern part of Cornwall, for the measurement of a base, was felt and regretted; we were, therefore, unwilling to introduce errors, if any should exist, from the sides in Cornwall, into the north of Devon : our operations were consequently discontinued.

From Devonshire we proceeded to the eastward, for the purpose of carrying on a second series of triangles. These were necessarily intended to originate from the side which connects the station on Beacon Hill, near Amesbury, with that on Wingreen Hill, near Shaftesbury.

In the month of July, the observations were completed at the station on the Mendip Hills, after which the instrument was taken to Bradley Knoll; Dundry Beacon, near Bristol; Lansdown and Farley Down; the station on Lansdown being chosen rather for a secondary than a principal place of observation.

From Bradley Knoll, to which place the instrument was carried from Farley Down, we proceeded to Westbury Down, and from thence to Beacon Hill, near Amesbury; because it was necessary that a new point on the range near Marlborough, commonly named St. Ann's Hills, should be observed. The station formerly chosen at the eastern extremity of this range, and observed in 1794, (see Phil. Trans. 1795, p. 471.) was this year found to be useless, as the high land, on the same range, prevented it from being seen at Lansdown: two others were, therefore, selected to the westward of the former, and observed from Beacon Hill; one for the purpose of connecting with Lansdown, and a station near Symmond's Hall, in Gloucestershire; and the other with Inkpin Beacon. The particular circumstances of this range, both as to situation and height, have thrown great impediments in the way of the survey, and are the means of cutting off, in a considerable degree, the connection between the southern triangles and those which have been since carried on in the midland of the kingdom. From Amesbury the party proceeded to Inkpin Beacon, near Hungerford, where the operations terminated.

The stations chosen and observed this year, but not visited with the instrument, were Monymoor, near Penhow; the mountain Twymbawlin, near Newport; and Scilly Point, in Glamorganshire. These stations in South Wales will connect with three in Somersetshire, also selected this season; one on Bleak Down, which is situated on the western extremity of the Mendip range; a second on Brent Beacon; and a third on the Quantock Hills.

Subsequent to the operations on Salisbury Plain, enquiries had been often made after a spot on which a third base might be measured. Experience had almost convinced us that, if Sedgemoor were excepted, the southern part of England did not contain one of sufficient extent for a base of three miles. Aware, therefore, of the imperfect state in which our work must rest, without a fresh base, Mr. DALBY and myself passed over into South Wales, and examined the extensive level between the new Passage House and Cardigan. After, however, a very diligent search, we could not find any spot, four miles in length, sufficiently unobstructed. The advantages which the situation itself holds out, are so great, that we should not have scrupled to dispense with a desideratum, heretofore required, of the base being one continued line. So much, however, is this flat cut up with *rhynes* and ditches, that we were not able to find any point from which two right lines might be measured, and so inclined to each other as to afford, by means of an including angle, a third side of five miles in length: necessity, therefore, compelled us to think of measuring a base on Sedgemoor, which we immediately examined. That which relates to this situation, will be found in an ensuing article: it is now only necessary to observe, that we concluded the operations of 1797, after the practicability of measuring a base upon it had been decided in the affirmative.

ART. II. *Angles taken in the Year 1797.*

At Black Down.

Between				° ′ ″	Mean.
Dunnose and Abbotsbury staff	•	•	•	164 26 33.75 / 37	} 35.25
Rippin Tor and Abbotsbury staff	•	-	-	3 8 51.75 / 52.75	} 52.5
Pilsden and Abbotsbury staff	•	•	•	45 16 15 / 13	} 14, bot 13 preferred.
Pole star and Abbotsbury staff, April 17, morning	•	104 19 16.75	
	18, morning	-	••	104 19 19.25	
	19, morning	•	104 19 33	
	19, afternoon	•	98 42 47	
	20, morning	•	104 19 25.25	
	20, afternoon	•	98 42 35.5	

At Butterton.

				° ′ ″	
Hemmerdon Ball and Rippin Tor	-	-	•	113 17 7.25 / 8.5	} 7.75
Hemmerdon Ball and Hensbarrow	•	•	•	1 52 2.75 / 6.25	} 4.5
Pole star and staff on Hemmerdon Ball, May 6, afternoon	•	91 29 13.75	
	7, morning	•	97 4 14	
	7, afternoon	-	91 29 12	

On St. Agnes Beacon.

				° ′ ″	
Hensbarrow and Trevose Head	•	•	47 10 0.75	
Hensbarrow and Peranzabulo staff	•	-	•	31 50 55.5 / 56.25	} 56, but 55.5 pref.
Pole star and Peranzabulo staff, May 10, afternoon	•	44 0 45.75	
	11, afternoon	-	44 0 44.75	
	11, morning	•	38 26 1.5	
	11, afternoon	-	44 0 33.25	
	13, morning	•	38 26 9	

At Trevose Head.

			° ′ ″	
St. Agnes Beacon and Hensbarrow	-	•	65 43 43.75 / 47 / 50	} 47

C

Between								Mean
Hensbarrow and Bodmin Down	·			·	34	17	45 46	} 45.5
Bodmin Down and Cadon Barrow	·			·	42	33	43 46,5	} rejected.
							51,75 52,75	} 52

At Hensbarrow.

St. Agnes Beacon and Trevose Head	·	·		·	67	6	13,25 13,25	} 13.25
Bodmin Down and Trevose Head	·	·		·	77	20	17.75 19,25	} 18.5

At Bodmin Down.

Hensbarrow and Trevose Head	·	·		·	68	21	57,25 59.5	} 58.25
Trevose Head and Cadon Barrow	·	·		·	71	55	26,75 27	} 27
Carraton Hill and staff on Brown Willy	·	·			52	3	59.5 4 1,25 4.5	} 1.75
Carraton Hill and picket on Brown Willy	·	·			52	36	11 11	} 11
Cadon Barrow and staff on Brown Willy	·	·		·	30	58	13 13	} 13
Cadon Barrow and picket on Brown Willy	·	·			31	26	0,25 1,25 3,25	} 1.75

On Cadon Barrow.

Trevose Head and direction post on Bodmin Down		·			68	7	53,75 54 54,25 54.75	} 54.25
Direction post on Bodmin Down and staff on Brown Willy	·				41	11	37.5 39 41	} 39.25
Direction post on Bodmin Down and picket on Brown Willy		·			40	40	36 36,75	} 35.25
Tresparrot Down and staff on Brown Willy		·		·	100	20	51,25 55 57	} 54.75
Tresparrot Down and picket on Brown Willy		·			100	53	1 1 ·	} 1

At St. Stephen's Down.

Staff on Brown Willy and Warbstow	·	·		·	41	18	24.25 25,5	} 25

Between				Mean.
Warbstow Beacon and Brendon Moor	•	19 41	18,5 / 18,75 / 19 }	18,75
Brendon Moor and Broadbury Down	• • •	90 0	40,75 / 41 }	41
Broadbury Down and Black Down	- • •	15 34	36 0 / 41,75 / 43 }	42,25
Black Down and Carraton Hill	• • -	91 18	12,85 / 13,5 }	12,75
Carraton Hill and Kit Hill	- • •	37 1	56	
Black Down and Kit Hill	• • • -	54 16	13	

At Maker.

Carraton Hill and Black Down	- • •	53 4	28 / 30,5 }	29,25

At Carraton Hill.

Black Down and Maker Heights	• • •	74 5	21,5 / 22,75 }	22,5
Trevose Head and Redmin Down	• • -	77 10	17,75 / 19,25 }	18,5

At Black Down.

Maker Heights and Carraton Hill	- • •	52 50	7,75 / 11,75 }	9,75
Carraton Hill and St. Stephen's Down	- • •	39 44	37,25 / 40,75 }	39
St. Stephen's Down and Broadbury Down	• •	66 49	57,5 / 58,25 }	58
Carraton Hill and Kit Hill	• • • •	13 18	58	

On the Mendip Hills.

Dundon Beacon and Bleak Down	- •	85 15 / 16	59,25 / 59,75 / 1,5 / 4,5 }	1,25
Bleak Down and Brent Knoll	•	19 11	35,75 / 38 / 41,25 / 41,75 }	39,25
Bleak Down and Dundry Beacon	•	33 39	30,5 / 30,5 }	30,5

C 2

Between	°	,	,	Mean.
Dundry Beacon and Lansdown	41	3	58,5 / 58,75	} 58,5
Lansdown and Farley Down	19	31	16,5 / 17	} 16,75
Farley Down and Westbury Down	38	55	17 / 18,25	} 17,5
Westbury Down and Bradley Knoll	37	47	57 / 57,75 / 58,75 / 59 / 48 0,25	} 58,5
Farley Down and Dundry Beacon	60	36	15 / 15,75	} 15,5
Farley Down and Bradley Knoll	76	43	14 / 18,5 / 21	} 19,75

At Dundry Beacon.

	°	,	,	Mean.
Tickenham Down and Grey Hill	37	44	2,25 / 3 5 / 6,25	} 3,75
Tickenham Down and Kingweston	60	5	27,25 / 90	} 28,75
Kingweston and Grey Hill	22	19	23,5 / 27,75	} 25,75
Bleak Down and Grey Hill	120	0	23 / 24 / 26	} 25
Lansdown and station on the Mendip Hills	83	34	16,25 / 19,75	} 18
Farley Down and Mendip Hills	69	51	21 / 23	} 22
Mendip and Bleak Down	54	34	24 / 25,75	} 25,5

At Lansdown.

	°	,	,
Kingweston and Dundry	36	31	29

On Farley Down.

	°	,	,	Mean.
St. Ann's Hill and Westbury Down	51	44	10,75 / 11 / 11,25 / 13,75	} 11,75
Westbury Down and Bradley Knoll	37	5	30,75 / 31 / 34 / 34,25	} 32,5

Between		°	'	"	Mean.
Westbury Down and Mendip Hills	- -	77	11	51,75 }55,75	}53,75
Bradley Knoll and Mendip Hills	- -	40	16	23 }23,75	}23,5
Mendip Hills and Dundry Beacon	- -	49	31	15,25 }21,5	}rejec- ted.
				25 }23,75	}23,5

On *Bradley Knoll.*

Mendip Hills and Westbury Down	- - -	101	23	56,5 }57,75 }59
		24	0	1,75
Westbury Down and Beacon Hill	- -	42	43	29,25 }30,5 }29,75
St. Ann's Hill and Westbury Down	- -	7	28	44 }45,25 }45 }46,5
Westbury Down and Milk Hill	- -	10	12	49,5 }53,25 }51,5
Beacon Hill and Wingreen	- -	57	50	38,25
Beacon Hill and Bull Barrow	- -	98	34	31 }33,5 }32,5 }34
Wingreen and Bull Barrow	- - - -	40	43	51,25 }52,75 }52
Bull Barrow and Ash Beacon	- -	45	43	3,25 }3,75 }3,5
Ash Beacon and Mendip Hills	- -	71	34	54,75 }55,25 }55
Mendip Hills and Parley Down	- - -	63	0	21,5 a

At *Bull Barrow.*

Ash Beacon and Mintern	- - -	51	26	41 }41,75 }42 }43
Bradley Knoll and Wingreen	-	41	55	32,75

At *Pilsden Hill.*

Mintern and Ash Beacon	- -	35	2	59 }3,25 } 2 }3

At Mintern.

Between						Mean.
Pilsden and Ash Beacon	-	•	•	95 35	21,25 22,5	} 22
Ash Beacon and Bull Barrow	•	•	•	94. 14, 22 24		} 23

On *Westbury Down*.

						Mean.
Beacon Hill and Bradley Knoll	•	•	•	114 12	18,25 18,5 18,75	} 18,5
Bradley Knoll and Mendip Hills				40 48	1 1,75 1,75	} 1,75
Mendip Hills and Farley Down				63 42	50,5 52	} 51,25
Farley Down and St. Ann's Hill				88 50	2 3 48	} 4,75
St. Ann's Hill and Beacon Hill	•	•	•	52 26	42,25 43,25	} 42,75
Beacon Hill and Milk Hill	•	•	•	48 7	31 36	} 33,5

Beacon Hill (*Amesbury*.)

					Mean.
Bradley Knoll and Westbury Down	•	•	•	23 4	15
Inkpin Down and Milk Hill	•	•	•	66 14	58
Inkpin Down and St. Ann's Hill	•	•	•	70 51	57,5 57,75	} 57,75
Westbury Down and Milk Hill	•	•	51 11	9	
Westbury Down and St. Ann's Hill	•	•	48 54	6 9,25	} 7,75

On *Inkpin Down*.

					Mean.
White Horse Hill and Highclere	•	•	133 27	57,25 57,5	} 57,5
Highclere and Beacon Hill	•	•	•	106 16	52,25 54,25	} 53,25
Beacon Hill and Hewish	•	•	•	52 53	32,25 32,5 35	} 33,25

ART. III. *Particulars relating to the Operations of the Year* 1798.

The object first attained this year, consisted in a trigonometrical survey of the counties adjacent to the northern and southern shores of the Thames.

In the last communication it will be seen, that the survey of Kent had been carried on from the sea-coast, till it reached the range which runs eastward from Wrotham through Hollingbourn, and there terminated. The country to the northward could not be surveyed, because the view from General Roy's station at Wrotham is almost entirely cut off, in that direction. In order, therefore, to obtain a base for the purpose, when the party arrived at Wrotham, a new station was chosen, to the eastward of the former one, and the distance between them accurately measured; by which means, together with the included angle at the old station, and the distance of it from Severndroog Tower, on Shooter's Hill, a new distance was found, which became a base for the survey proposed.

The chief draftsmen and surveyors belonging to the Drawing-room in the Tower, attended our operations in this county, and also those afterwards carried on in Essex. It was, indeed, for their immediate service, that we renewed the survey in this quarter, as the Master-General had given directions to prepare ample materials for completing the map which meets the public eye with this article.

The stations in Kent, besides that of Wrotham, were Gravesend, Gad's Hill, and the Isle of Sheppey; those in Essex were Hadleigh, South End, and Prittlewell. Observations made from these places afforded *data* for the proposed survey: after they were completed, the small circular instrument supplied the place of the great one, and was used, with good effect, in carrying on the subsequent operations in this quarter.

In our Paper published in the Philosophical Transactions for 1795, an observation is made, of the necessity then existing for the measurement of a base on Salisbury Plain, in consequence of resolutions taken to inclose Sedgemoor: an act for which purpose was passed a few years ago, and partly carried into execution in 1797. At this time, however, King's Sedgemoor was only set out into parochial allotments, as exhibited in Plate XXVIII. accompanying this Account. The ditches, represented by lines on this plan, were generally ten feet broad, and five feet deep; but the principal and secondary drains were much wider, the first being thirty, and the last twenty-five, feet in breadth. The subdivisions on the Moor, or the individual allotments of it, were not traced out in the Somerton quarter, at this time, the task being deferred till the latter part of the following year. The measurement, therefore, of this base, in an early part of the season, became necessary, because fewer obstacles were then expected to present themselves.

As it appeared that many instances would probably occur, in which a chain of 50 feet in length would be useful, if not absolutely necessary, one was provided by Mr. RAMSDEN, in the winter; its make and form being precisely similar to those of the larger chains, used in the measurement of our former bases. Such a chain did, indeed, prove highly serviceable in the subsequent operation; as the handles of the 100-feet chain would very often have had their places in ditches, or been so situated on their banks, as to leave imperfect means of correctly placing the register heads under the handles.

The apparatus for the measurement, consisting of the tressels belonging to the Royal Society, pickets, iron heads, and a new set of coffers, were sent to Somerton, after Mr. GARDNER had been furnished with the means of proceeding with the survey before spoken of.

The measurement was begun in July, and finished in August; in the course of which, very little interruption arose from any inclemency of weather. It is unnecessary to enter minutely into a description of the difficulties which arose from the frequent intervention of ditches; let it suffice to observe, that, possessed of the 50-feet chain, these were rendered less material than they would otherwise have been.

When we arrived at that point which ends with the 114th chain, an *offset* was taken, and 19 chains measured, in a direction perfectly parallel to that of the base, at the extremity of which we returned into the base itself, and continued the measurement. This interruption proceeded from an accidental and unforeseen circumstance; a great ditch having been excavated in a direction coincident with that of the base, while the measurement was going on at the upper end of it. This, however, cannot be the means of introducing any sensible inaccuracy; for, to proceed in this matter correctly, when it became necessary to take an offset, a silver wire was let fall from the register head, having a plummet, under the point of which a small dot was made, on a stake driven firmly into the ground. *The great theodolite* was then placed over the stake, *and the instrument accurately adjusted over the dot.* A diaphragm, whose aperture was $\frac{1}{4}$ an inch, was then put over the object-glass of the transit telescope, which was afterwards directed towards the staff at Lugshorn Corner, and then moved round, till it exactly made a right angle with the base. The telescope being sufficiently

D

depressed, a peg was driven into the ground, with its centre nearly under the cross wires; after which, a pin was moved on the surface of the peg, as directed by a person looking through the telescope, till it came to that point at which it bisected the angle formed by the cross wires. The measurement was then carried on, in this new direction, a space of 19 chains, at the end of which, the same operations were repeated, and the old direction pursued. It does not seem probable, that an error amounting to more than $\frac{1}{15}$ of an inch, can have resulted from this procedure.

King's Sedgemoor being sufficiently level, the base was measured horizontally; an advantageous circumstance; but, from the soft texture of the soil, the pickets could not be driven into the ground so firmly as to be without some small degree of motion, in case a person stood close to them. Therefore, those who attended the handles of the chains, either used long stools, or placed themselves so as to divide the pressure arising from the weights of their bodies equally on each side of the pickets. The disturbances to which the register-heads were liable, did not discover themselves till a mile of the base had been measured; and, although it became probable that small errors only had resulted from the want of those precautions we afterwards followed, yet we considered what we had done as erroneous, and recommenced the measurement, with the advantage of experience. At present, I shall content myself with observing, that due attention was paid to all necessary minutiæ in this measurement, and refer those who are desirous of being more particularly informed, to the Philosophical Transactions for 1795, as the mode of proceeding on the present occasion was perfectly similar to that on Hounslow Heath.

After the conclusion of this operation, we proceeded to select such stations in the neighbourhood of the base, as might afford means of connecting it with the triangles carried on in the preceding year. The two chosen for this purpose, were Dundon Beacon, and a spot near the village of Moor Lynch; both nearer to their respective ends of the base than we wished to have found them; yet, as small rods of only an inch in diameter were placed on those stations, when they were observed from Dundon Beacon and Moor Lynch, and the same erected at the ends of the base, when they were observed from those stations, it becomes probable that very trifling errors resulted from this proceeding.

The station at Ash Beacon was visited subsequent to these just spoken of, and afterwards that on the Mendip Hills, for the purpose of taking the angle between Moor Lynch and Dundon Beacon. The operations of 1798 then terminated with a diligent search after some spot in Cornwall, for a base of only two or three miles in length: this search, however, was fruitless, as in fact we had reason to imagine it would prove to be; but we were not willing to relinquish the hope, that a piece of ground might be discovered proper for so confined a purpose. The contrary, however, being the case, the party returned to London in October.

ART. IV. *Angles taken in the Year* 1798.

At Wrotham. Station of 1787.

Between		° ′ ″	Mean.
New Station and staff on Severndroog Tower	-	94 19 30	

Station of 1798.

		° ′ ″	
Severndroog Tower and Gravesend	- -	62 54 36.5 36.5 39.5 }	38

At Gravesend.

Between	°	'	"	Mean.
Severndroog Tower and Wrotham	82	39	41	} 41
			21	
Severndroog Tower and Langdon Hill	95	53	56	} 59
			59.25	
		54	1.25	
Langdon Hill and Hadleigh	34	31	49.5	} 53
			52.5	
		54		
			57.5	
Halstow and Hadleigh	30	24	17	} 19
			19.75	
			20.5	
Halstow and Gad's Hill	31	38	19.75	} 22
			22.25	
Severndroog Tower and Hadleigh	130	25	50	} 50.75
			51.5	

Isle of Sheppey.

	°	'	"	Mean.
Gad's Hill and Halstow	18	18	1.5	} 3
			3	
			3.5	
Halstow and Hadleigh	31	18	23	} 24.25
			24.5	
			25	
Langdon Hill and Hadleigh	16	26	30	
Langdon Hill and Rayleigh	27	4	46	

At Halstow.

	°	'	"	Mean.
Gad's Hill and Gravesend	24	18	21.25	} 21.25
			21.25	
Gravesend and Hadleigh	107	49	5.25	} 5.25
			5.25	
Hadleigh and Sheppey	99	18	4	} 6
			7.5	
Gravesend and centre of Rayleigh Tower	111	20	14	
Sheppey and Rayleigh Tower	95	46	57	

At Hadleigh.

	°	'	"
Sheppey and South End	38	43	29
Sheppey and Halstow	49	23	33.5
Gravesend and Halstow	42	46	32
Langdon Hill and Gravesend	43	31	52

Between	o	,	,	Mean.
Gravesend and Severndroog Tower • •	26	16	56.75 / 57.75 }	57.25
Langdon Hill and Sheppey • • •	131	11	55	

At South End.

Sheppey and Hadleigh • • •	119	20	5

At Langdon Hill.

Gravesend and Severndroog • • •	53	47	15
Centre of Rayleigh Tower and Gravesend •	121	2	46
Station on Rayleigh Tower and centre of the same Tower •	0	0	37
Station on Rayleigh Tower and Danbury Spire •	43	18	1
Severndroog Tower and Frierning • •	95	15	0
Frierning Tower and Station on Rayleigh Tower •	88	44	19
Frierning and Danbury Spire • • •	45	16	17
Severndroog Tower and Brentwood Spire • •	66	16	39

At Triptree Heath. 1st Station.

Tillingham Tower and Station on Rayleigh Tower •	66	18	58
Tillingham and Danbury Spire • • •	100	28	21
Station on Rayleigh Tower and Langdon Hill •	51	15	14
Station on Rayleigh Tower and Frierning Tower •	47	8	50

At Lugsborn Corner.

Greylock's Foss and Dundon Beacon • •	107	44	30.75 / 31.25 }	31
Greylock's Foss and Moor Lynch • •	15	51	58.5 / 59 / 59.75 }	59
Moor Lynch and Dundon Beacon • •	93	51	33.75	

At Greylock's Foss.

Moor Lynch and Lugsborn Corner • • •	114	9	58.25 / 59.75 }	59
Lugsborn Corner and Dundon Beacon • •	8	29	59.75 / 30 0.5 }	0
Dundon Beacon and Moor Lynch • • •	105	40	0 / 0.5 }	0.25

Near Moor Lynch Windmill.

Between		°	′	″	Mean
Greylock's Foss and Dundon Beacon	• • •	59	58	12.5	
Greylock's Foss and Lugshorn Corner	• • •	51	58	2.25 4.25	} 3.25
Lugshorn Corner and Dundon Beacon	• • •	8	0	10 10.25	} 10.25
Dundon Beacon and Mendip Hills	• •	54	38	50 50	} 50
Mendip Hills and Ash Beacon	•	54	3	80 23.5 23.75	} 22.5
Ash Beacon and Pilsden Hill	• •	57	19	2.5 3.75 4.5	} 3.5
Dundon Beacon and Pilsden Hill	• •	56	43	36.25 36.5 37.25	} 36.75
Pilsden and Quantock Hills	• •	87	15	6 7	} 6.5
Quantock Hills and Brent Knoll	• •	71	38	57.75 58.5 58.5	} 58.25
Brent Knoll and Bleak Down	•	46	1	38.75 35.25 39	} 35.75
Bleak Down and Mendip Hills	•	43	44	43.5 45 45.25 40.75	} 45.25
Brent Knoll and Mendip Hills	• • •	89	43	19.5 20.5 24	} 21.25

On Dundon Beacon.

Between		°	′	″	Mean
Lugshorn Corner and Moor Lynch	• • •	78	7	14.75 14.5	} 14.5
Lugshorn Corner and Greylock's Foss	• • •	63	45	28.5 29.5	} 29
Greylock's Foss and Moor Lynch	• • •	108	1	51.25 53	} 52.25
Moor Lynch and Bleak Down	• • •	58	42	10 10.25	} 10.25
Moor Lynch and Mendip Hills	• • •	101	22	54.25 55	} 54.5

At Ash Beacon.

Between.					° ′ ″	Mean.
Moor Lynch and Mendip Hills	-	-	-	56 29	50 52.25 52.25	} 51.5
Mendip Hills and Bradley Knoll		-	-	50 8	45.25 45.75	} 45.5
Bradley Knoll and Bull Barrow		-	-	93 38	10.5 13 14	} 12.5
Bull Barrow and Pilsden	-		-	83 40	33.5 35.5	} 34.5
Mintern Hill and Pilsden	-		-	49 21	35.75 39.75 39.75	} 38.25
Pilsden and Quantock Hills	-	-	-	59 34	40.5 42.25	} 41.5
Quantock Hills and Mendip Hills	-	-	-	72 57	49.75	

On the Mendip Hills.

				° ′ ″	Mean.
Bradley Knoll and Ash Beacon	-	-	58 16	20 21.5 24.25	} 22
Ash Beacon and Moor Lynch	-		69 26	46.5 49 49.25	} 48.25
Dundon Beacon and Moor Lynch		-	83 58	16.5 17.75	} 17

ART. V. *Particulars relating to the Operations of the Year* 1799.

I have shewn in the preceding articles, that sufficient materials are now in my possession, for calculating the latitudes and
longitudes of those places whose bearings and distances from
given stations are found in the Account of 1797. I have also
pointed out the direction which the survey has subsequently
taken; and given a short account of the measurement of a new
base in Somersetshire. The operations of 1799 now remain to
be spoken of.

In very early stages of the work, I had frequent opportunities of observing, that eminent advantages would accrue to the service, were the survey prosecuted on a more extensive scale. The consideration of a grand instrument being laid up in the apartments of the Royal Society, suggested the propriety of obtaining it; therefore, when my appointment to my present situation gave me the means of effecting former ideas, I lost no time in applying to the President and Council, for the loan of their large theodolite, the excellence of which had been incontestibly demonstrated by the late Major General Roy. The distinguished services which the Royal Society have rendered this branch of the public service, leave it almost unnecessary for me to observe how readily they granted my request. The instrument was, accordingly, put into the hands of Mr. RAMSDEN, early in the month of January, for the purpose of being examined, and also of having new microscopes fixed to it; the former ones being much inferior, in construction, to those attached to the instrument belonging to Government.

To carry on so extensive a survey as that which is now the subject of this Paper, much consideration is necessary. I have endeavoured to give it the best effect, both as to design, and celerity of execution. What degree of success has attended my endeavours, the public, in possession of this Paper, can readily determine. In the present stage of the survey, I have been sufficiently impressed with just ideas, as to the importance of the task, and responsibility of my situation. The difficulties which start up, in prosecuting a survey of this kind, become more numerous as it becomes more extensive. In the earliest part of it, when few objects only were in view, speedy execution followed the design; but, circumstances now require every exertion, as the triangles are branched out into several parts of the kingdom.

Were the length of a degree of the meridian, in these latitudes, accurately known, the most eligible method of carrying on the survey would be, that of working between any two determined parallels of latitude, till the space between them was completed. Yet this mode would manifestly be subject to some slight innovations, from the necessity of measuring bases in certain stages of the work : it would be right, however, to adopt the principle for general practice. Under this idea, it would have been proper to have commenced the operations of this year in Somersetshire, and to have carried on the triangles from the neighbourhood of the new base into the north of Devon.

It is mentioned in one of the former Accounts, that a zenith sector was formerly bespoken of Mr. RAMSDEN, by his Grace the Duke of RICHMOND, for the purpose of aiding the design of measuring the length of a degree of latitude in this country. The pressure of other business caused Mr. RAMSDEN to lay aside this instrument, after he had considerably advanced in its construction. The real necessity, however, for our being supplied with an instrument of this description being made known to him, he resolved to take it in hand again, and complete it. Relying on the strength of his assurances to this effect, I determined to relinquish the intention of proceeding to the westward; and resolved to commence this year's operations, with running up a series of triangles along the meridian of Blenheim. As it is probable my next communication will contain the result of this interesting part of the survey, I shall now confine myself to such particulars as relate to the subject under consideration.

In a former article, I have observed, that the chief Draftsman,

MDCCC. E

Mr. GARDNER, has been furnished with materials for surveying the northern shore of the Thames, and the north of Kent : these proved ample, as the map, thence compiled, will sufficiently demonstrate. As the Master-General issued directions, at this time, to survey Essex, and parts of the adjoining counties, in the same manner, and for the same purpose, as Kent has been, I was obliged to suspend, for a short time, my intention of proceeding with the measurement of a meridional degree, and to devise the best means for carrying his Lordship's instructions into execution.

For this purpose, therefore, before any stations were chosen in Essex, the county was very minutely examined ; when it appeared, that insuperable difficulties would occur, if the survey were prosecuted with the large theodolite only. The range commencing at Havering Bower, and running to Gallywide Common, cuts off a regular communication between the stations subsequently chosen in the southern and northern parts of Essex. The difficulty resulting from this circumstance, was made still greater, from the want of success in our endeavours to find one spot on this range, proper for a station. The eastern part was, in some degree, found more favourable ; but it was discovered that, even here, the small instrument must frequently be used as a substitute for the large one. Under these disadvantages, the survey commenced in March; the large theodolite being taken to a station on Hampstead Heath.

The base chosen for carrying on the distances towards the north, was that constituted by Severndroog Tower on Shooter's Hill and the new station on Hampstead Heath ; which distance, although it has not, perhaps, been obtained so correctly as many others, yet is determined with sufficient accuracy for the matter in hand. When the observations were made on Severndroog Tower, in the year 1787, the angle between Hanger Hill Tower and the cross on the dome of St. Paul's was taken: this was now made use of, in order to get the angle between Hanger Hill Tower and Hampstead Heath; because the former station could not be discovered, on account of the wind blowing the thick and darkened atmosphere of London between the stations, when the instrument this year was carried to Shooter's Hill.

For the purpose of connecting the eastern and western triangles with each other, a station was chosen on Southweald Tower, accessible only to the small instrument. Brentwood Spire was also found to be conveniently situated for carrying on the distances: this will be readily perceived by the plan. Langdon Hill was also selected; which, with the former station at Gravesend, were to become the means of connecting the triangles. A station on Epping Forest was judged necessary: but no spot could be found fit for general purposes, the view towards the north being confined. One was, however, fixed on, called Highbeech, from which a high building near Berkhamstead was found to be visible, by means of which, the distances in the north of Essex could be verified, as the station on the top of it would connect with Bushy Heath, near Watford, and a point on the elevated range near Dunstable.

From Hampstead, the instrument and portable scaffold were carried to Langdon Hill, and from thence to Triptree Heath, near Malden; from whence the party repaired to Highbeech, leaving the remainder of the county to be surveyed with the small circular instrument; which seems to have been done with considerable accuracy.

After the necessary observations were made at Highbeech, I

proceeded to Shotover Hill, in Oxfordshire; and, before May elapsed, had reconnoitred the country. As the distance between Inkpin Hill and Highclere, appeared to be shorter than was necessary for a base on which the northern triangles were to rest, it became certain, that their sides would depend on the base on Hounslow Heath. The only means by which the series now proposed to be carried westwards, (for the double purpose of forwarding the survey, and also of finding a portion of the meridional arc,) could be properly connected with the triangles in the neighbourhood of Salisbury Plain, was the side just spoken of; for the high land in the vicinity of Calne, intercepted the view of the stations on the Marlborough range, from White Horse Hill. In order, however, to make a connection, although imperfect, an intermediate station was chosen on this high intercepting land.

When the ground about Nettlebed was formerly examined by us, it appeared difficult to carry on the triangles from Bagshot Heath towards the northward; because no spot could be found near the former, from which the Chiltern range could be seen. I now, therefore, departed from the usual practice of choosing stations on the ground, and selected Pen Church Tower; by means of which, I found a connection might be made between the triangles carried round the Chiltern range, from White Horse Hill and Nuffield, with those in Hertfordshire.

At Shotover Hill the party separated, each having its instrument. I shall close this article, without entering minutely into the reasons which operated with me for the choice of all the stations selected this year. I shall content myself with enumerating the names of the stations visited and observed, and mentioning that Shotover Hill and Cumner Hill, in Oxfordshire, were selected principally with a view of ascertaining the situations of the observatories at Oxford and Blenheim. The names of the stations were, Nuffield, White Horse Hill, and Scutchamfly, in Berkshire. Shotover Hill, Cumner Hill, Whiteham Hill, Crouch Hill, and Epwell Hill, all in Oxfordshire. Those in Gloucestershire were, Pen, Cleave, Broadway Beacon, and the Malvern Hills. The Lecky Hills, in Worcestershire. Corley and Nuneaton, in Warwickshire. Bardon Hill, Naseby Field and Barrow Hill, in Leicestershire. Arbury Hill, and Souldrop, in Northamptonshire. Quainton, Brill, Wendover, and Bow Brickhill, in Buckinghamshire. Woburn Park, and Lidlington, in Bedfordshire. Kinsworth, Lillyhoe, Berkhamstead, Tharfield, and Bushy Heath, in Hertfordshire. From the last mentioned station, the party returned to London, in October.

ART. VI. *Angles taken in the Year* 1799.

On Hampstead Heath.

Between	° ′ ″	Mean.
Hanger Hill Tower and Stanmore	50 51 15.75 / 17	16.25
Highbeech and Shooter's Hill	70 6 35.5 / 34.5	35
Highbeech and St. Paul's, London	83 1 17.25 / 22.75	20
Severndroog Tower on Shooter's Hill, and Hanger Hill Tower	117 22 13 / 11	12

At Langdon Hill.

	° ′ ″
Gravesend and Severndroog Tower	53 47 25
Centre of Rayleigh Steeple and Gravesend	122 2 46
Station on Rayleigh Steeple and centre of the same	0 0 27
Station on Rayleigh Steeple and Danbury Spire	43 18 2
Severndroog Tower and Frierning Steeple	95 25 0
Frierning Steeple and Station on Rayleigh Steeple	88 14 19
Frierning Steeple and Danbury Spire	45 26 17
Severndroog Tower and Brentwood Spire	66 26 29

At Triptree Heath.

Between		°	'	"	Mean.
Tillingham Steeple and Station on Rayleigh Steeple	-	68	18	58	"
Tillingham Steeple and Danbury Spire	•	100	18	11	
Station on Rayleigh Tower and Langdon Hill	•	21	15	14	
Station on Rayleigh Tower and Frierning Steeple	-	67	1	50	

At Highbeerb.

		°	'	"	Mean.
Severndroog Tower and Brentwood Spire	•	71	16	43 / 45	} 44
Severndroog Tower and Southweald	•	44	34	17 / 19	} 18
Severndroog Tower and Hampstead	•	58	18	18 / 18	} 18
Cross on the Dome of St. Paul's and Hampstead	•	83	1	11	
Berkhamstead Gazebo and Hampstead	•	118	19	57 / 10 0	} 58,5

At Shotover Hill.

		°	'	"	Mean.
Nuffield and White Horse Hill	•	81	53	27.75 / 29.75	} 28,75
Scutchamfly Barrow and White Horse Hill	•	26	8	7.75 / 7.75 / 8.25	} 8
White Horse Hill and Whitcham Hill	•	48	5	31.25 / 34.75 / 33.75	} 32,75
Wendover and Scutchamfly Barrow	•	117	30	55 / 57.25	} 56

On Whitebam Hill.

		°	'	"	Mean.
Shotover Hill and White Horse Hill	•	114	54	34.75 / 34.75	} 34.75
Shotover Hill and Cumner Hill	•	55	52	34.5 / 35.5	} 35
Staff over the Quadrant at Blenheim and White Horse Hill	131	25	34.5 / 38.5	} 36,5

On Cumner Hill.

		°	'	"	Mean.
Whitebam Hill and Shotover Hill	•	99	19	47 / 49.5	} 48,5
Shotover Hill and Atlas on the Top of the Observatory at Oxford }	-	29	23	34 / 34	} 30

On *White Horse Hill.*

Between	°	′	″	Mean.
Nuffield and Shotover Hill	35	34	22.25 / 23.75	} 23.25
Nuffield and Brill	38	48	11.5 / 15.25	} 13.25
Scutchamfly Barrow and Shotover Hill	111	47	50	
Whiteham Hill and Staff on Blenheim Observatory	10	30	43.5 / 43.5	} 43.5
Brill and Stow on the Wold	64	45	42.75 / 44.75	} 43.75
Station near Calne and Inkpin	67	10	28.5 / 32.5	} 30.5
Highclere and Inkpin	12	4	11.25 / 11.5	} 11.5
Highclere and Nuffield	63	7	53.25 / 53.5	} 53.25

At *Nuffield.*

	°	′	″	
Bagshot Heath and Highclere	78	17	16.5 / 17.75 / 18.75 / 19.75	} 18.25
Highclere and White Horse Hill	53	33	49.5 / 49.75	} 49.5
White Horse Hill and Shotover Hill	62	38	3.5 / 4.5 / 6.5 / 7	} 5.25
White Horse Hill and Brill	16	4	15.75 / 16 / 17	} 16.25

On *Scutchamfly Barrow.*

	°	′	″	
White Horse Hill and Shotover Hill	111	47	50	
Shotover Hill and Wendover	34	26	50 / 50.75 / 52.75 / 54.5	} 52

At *Stow on the Wold.*

	°	′	″	
Cleave and Broadway Beacon	54	24	54.5 / 54.5 / 57 / 57	} 55.75

Between			°	′	″	Mean.
Broadway Beacon and Epwell	•	•	73	31	48,5 49 50,5	} 49.5
Epwell and Brill	•	•	60	56	6 6,5	} 6,25
White Horse Hill and Cleave	•		109	40	36,25 36,75 37 37,75	} 37

At Broadway Beacon.

			°	′	″	
Epwell and Stow	•	•	69	10	50,75 51,5 51,75	} 51.75
Stow and Cleave	•	•	78	53	6 8 9,5	} 7.75
Cleave and Malvern Hills	•	•	60	28	12,5 17,75 18	} 16
Malvern and Lecky Hills	•	•	53	53	19,5 20	} 19.75

At Epwell.

			°	′	″	
Stow and Broadway Beacon	•	•	38	20	43,25 43,5 44 44,25 44,5	} 44
Stow and Brill	•		86	29	13 13,5 13,75	} 13.5
Brill and Arbury Hill		•	85	0	16,5 20,5	} 18,5
Arbury Hill and Corley		•	54	55	17, 5 19 20,25	} 18,75

At Corley.

		°	′	″	
Bardon Hill and Nuneaton Common	•	49	54	50,75 53	} 51.75
Nuneaton and Arbury Hill	•	110	20	52 52,5 52,75 53	} 52.75

Between				°	′	″	Mean
Arbury Hill and Epwell	-	-	-	35	17	34.75	
						35.75	
						36.25	
						36.25	} 36.75
						38	
						39.25	
Epwell and Broadway Beacon		-		28	2	46.75	
						50	} 49.75
						53	
Nuneaton and Lechy Hills	-	-	-	133	25	11.5	} 11.5
						11.5	
Nuneaton and Station near Birmingham	-	-	49	54	50.75	} 51
						53	

At Arbury Hill.

Quainton and Brill	-	-	-	16	12	37.25	
						37.5	
						40.5	} 40
						41.5	
						41.75	
Brill and Epwell	-		-	-	60	35	43	
						43.25	
						44.5	
						45	} 45.5
						46.5	
						48.5	
						48.5	

Near Brill on the Hill.

White Horse Hill and Stow	-	-	-	50	14	44	
						44.5	} 44.5
						44.75	
Nuffield and White Horse Hill		-		55	7	33	} 33.5
						34	
Stow and Epwell	-		-		32	34	42.5	
						43.5	
						43	} 43
						43.25	
Epwell and Arbury Hill	-	-	-	34	23	58.5	} 58.5
						58.75	
Arbury Hill and Bow Brickhill	-	-	-	68	20	7.75	
Bow Brickhill and Wendover	-	-	-	57	25	1 2	} 1.5
Wendover and Shotover Hill	-	-	-	108	5	22	} 22.75
						23.5	
Quainton and Wendover	-	-	-	51	34	33.25	} 33
						32.75	

Near Wendover.

Scutchamfly Barrow and Shotover Hill	-	-	28	8	12.75	

F

Between	°	′	″	Mean.
Brill and Quainton	33	16	4⅛ 4⅜ 48,25	} 48⅜
Brill and Bow Brickhill	80	11	8,25 10,25	} 9,25
Brill and Shotover Hill	23	13	56,25 58,75	} 57.5
Bow Brickhill and Stanmore	102	22	29	
Pen Tower and Stanmore	38	13	16,25 19,75	} 18

Near Quainton.

	°	′	″	Mean.
Bow Brickhill and Wendover	94	23	49,25 52,25	} 50,25
Wendover and Brill	94	50	36 38	} 37

At Bow Brickhill.

	°	′	″	Mean.
Brill and Arbury Hill	68	42	55,5 56,75 57,5 58,75	} 56,75
Brill and Wendover	42	23	50,5 51	} 50,75
Wendover and Kinsworth	46	18	4,25 5,75 9,25 14	} 8,25
Kinsworth and Quainton	85	9	51,75 53,75	} 52,75
Kinsworth and Lillyhoe	42	10	33,25 38,5 39	} 38,25
Kinsworth and Lidlington	80	39	37,25	
Trusler Hill and Lillyhoe	14	54	38,75 43,5 45,5	} 42,5
Trusler Hill and Arbury Hill	45	49	41,75 44	} 43

At Kinsworth.

	°	′	″	Mean.
Brill and Bow Brickhill	62	55	35,25 38,5 39 42	} 38,75
Quainton and Bow Brickhill	52	17	56,25 57,25 57	} 56,75

Between	°	′	″	Mean.
Bow Brickhill and Lillyhoe	82	50	26	} 30,5
			30	
			35	
Lillyhoe and Tharfield Tower · ·	12	11	39.75	} 40,75
			42	
Tharfield and Station on Gazebo at Berkhamstead ·	50	2	55,5	} 53,25
			56	
		3	0,5	
		1		
Stanmore and Berkhamstead ′	42	15	56,5	} 57,25
			57.75	
Bow Brickhill and Stanmore · · ·	173	37	43	} 44
			45	

Near Lillyhoe.

Bow Brickhill and Kinsworth · ·	54	58	52,5	} 59
			52,5	
			52,5	
			53.75	
Lidlington and Bow Brickhill · · ·	83	59	30	} 31
			32	
Bow Brickhill and Trusler Hill · · ·	5	52	11,5	
Station on the Ground near Tharfield Tower and Kinsworth	166	4	44,5	} 46,25
			48	

At Lidlington.

Kinsworth and Bow Brickhill · · ·	68	16	19	} 22,25
			22,75	
			25,25	

At Crouch Hill.

Brill and Epwell · · · ·	145	23	25,75	} 26,25
			27	

At Stanmore.

Wendover and Kinsworth · · ·	37	41	39,25	} 41
			43	
Pen Tower and Wendover · · ·	23	4	47,5	} 48,5
			47,5	
			47.75	
			49,25	
			49,25	
Bagshot and Pen Tower · ·	49	32	19,5	
Bagshot Heath and Hanger Hill Tower ·	59	55	54,25	} 54
			53.75	

F 2

Between			°	′	″	Mean.

Between

Hampstead Heath and Hanger Hill Tower   ‒   •   45   25   51

51.5
51.5 } 51.75
52.75

On *Busby Heath.*

Wendover and Kinsworth   -   •   -   38   22   8.5 } 6.75

On *Bagshot Heath.*   *Station of* 1794.

Highclere and Nuffield   -   -   •   55   38   25.5

25.75 } 16
26.75

Nuffield and Pen Tower   48   47   11

12.75 } 12.5
12.75

Pen Tower and St. Ann's Hill   -   -   •   70   30   37.25

39 } 39.25
40

ART. 7. *Situations of the Stations.*

Trevose Head. The station on this point of land, which is about four miles from Padstow, in Cornwall, is situated on the southern part of it, and is about forty feet from the declivity. The ground seems a little higher than any other part of the Head.

Cadon Barrow. The station is on the centre of the Barrow; which is a very remarkable one, and well known about the country. It is about two miles from Tintagel, being in a field lying south of the road leading from that town to Camelford.

Brown Willy. The staff is erected on the highest part of this mountain, which is about nine miles southward of Camelford.

St. Stephen's Down. The station is about 150 feet from the eastern part of the building erected on this Down. It lies south-west from the corner of it, and about twenty feet from the road.

Mendip. The station is in a field on the top of the down, being about two miles north of *Shepton Mallet.* The field is next to the road leading from that place to Bristol, and lies west of it: it is also north of the road which goes from Wells to Frome.

This road crosses the former at right angles. The station is 20 feet north of the southern hedge, and about 200 from the eastern one. The ground round the station is rather higher than any other part of the field.

Dundry. The station is on the down, close to, but west of, the town so called. The down is full of holes and pits, from which stones have been taken for the purposes of building. The station, however, may easily be found, as it is situated on a rising which has the appearance of having been a barrow.

Lansdown. This place is well known, and near Bath. The station is on the highest part of the broken ground called CROMWELL's *Camp*, which is near Mr. GRANVILLE's monument.

Furley Down. The station on this Down is 5 feet north of the stone wall, and about 150 feet eastward of the plantation.

Bradley Knoll. This is a remarkable hill, very near Maiden Bradley. The highest part of the hill is towards the west, on which there is a small ring, exhibiting an appearance of a ruined plantation. The station is a few feet to the northward of this ring.

Westbury Down. There are no objects on this Down, of any kind ; therefore, the station cannot be found from measurements. It is, however, just above the *White horse* cut out in the side of the hill.

Ash Beacon. This eminence is about four miles north of Sherborne : on the top of it there is a small plantation, round which is a circular wall. The station is 65 feet east of it.

Dundon Beacon. This is an insulated hill, at the eastern extremity of King's Sedgemoor ; upon it are the remains of a barrow, probably the site of the ancient beacon. The station is about 4 feet eastward of the small cavity in the centre of it.

Lugsborn Corner, the eastern extremity of King's Sedgemoor.
There is a small rivulet, which separates the moor from the cultivated ground on the Somerton side, and, close to a particular
part of it, is a passage called *Somerton Gate*. About a quarter of
a mile eastward of this entrance, and in the second field, north
of the stream, is the station called *Lugsborn Corner*, one of the
ends of the base. The spot is 5 feet from the ditch, and 19
from the gateway. There were but three fields in this part of
the moor, at the time the base was measured.

Greylock's Foss. This is towards the western extremity of the
moor: a causeway leads from *Middlezoy* to *Greinton*, over it.
In the second field from the bridge, near the latter, is the other
extremity of the base. The station is about 10 feet from the
ditch, running parallel to the Foss, and is in the angle formed
by the ditch contiguous to the road and the second ditch north
of the drain.

Nuffield. The station is in the field opposite to the church:
it is in the south-west corner of it, 14 feet from the *stile*, and
10 feet from the hedge.

Scutchamfly. A very remarkable Barrow, on the Berkshire
downs, situated near Little Hendred. The station is on the
south-west part of it, and can easily be found.

White Horse Hill. This is a well known eminence in Berkshire. The station is on the eastern side of the Saxon work,
and on the top of the small parapet surrounding the ditch.

Shotover Hill, near Oxford. The station is 150 feet from the
hedge eastward of it, and 60 feet from that southward of it; but,
when the traces of our former operations are obliterated, it will
be difficult to recover this station.

Stow on the Wold. The station bearing this name, is in a

field 2 miles eastward of the town: it lies on the north side of the road leading from Stow to Burford, and may be easily distinguished, being that particular field which affords the most commanding view. The station is 32 feet west of the corner of the hedge which forms a right angle with another abruptly running out: it is also 279 feet from the ridge which divides the field.

Broadway Beacon. This is a very high and remarkable spot, near the village of Broadway, in Gloucestershire. The station is about 20 feet south-east of the foundation of a building proposed to be erected by the Earl of COVENTRY.

Corley, a village in Warwickshire. The station is in the second field eastward of the church, being 180 feet from the eastern hedge, and 230 feet from the stile in the corner of it.

Epwell, a village in Oxfordshire. The station is on the apex of the hill, and may easily be found, by measuring 17 feet from the stile, and 14 feet from the hedge which runs across the hill. N. B. The station is west of the hedge.

Brill on the Hill, Buckinghamshire. The station is on *Muzzle Hill,* near the town. There is but one field on this hill: it is on the highest part of it. The station is situated in the centre of the field, and in the middle of a rising, once the site of a windmill.

Arbury Hill. This hill is still surrounded with the remains of an ancient fortification. The station is on the north-west corner of it, and near the brow, but cannot be easily found, from the want of proper objects to which measurements may be made.

Wendover, Buckinghamshire. The station is on the down south of the town, and contiguous to the village of Ellesborough. A road from Wendover, to Sir JOHN RUSSELL's seat, Checquers, runs over the down: but, as there are no marks on it, its pre-

else situation cannot be easily pointed out by measurement. It may, however, be observed, that it is 14 feet southwards, from the decayed parapet on the top of the hill.

Quainton, Buckinghamshire. The station is on the high ground, north of this town. It cannot very easily be found, because the hill is destitute of objects; yet it may, probably, be discovered, by looking for it on the *green ridge* which divides the land : it is in the middle of that boundary, and about 200 feet westward of the pathway.

Kinsworth, a village near Dunstable. The station is on the summit of a hill, about half a mile north of the village. A hedge runs across the hill, from which the station is 40 feet north-west : it is likewise *close* to the road.

Lillyboe, Hertfordshire. The station is on a commanding eminence, having the *Icknield way* at the foot of it. There are no objects on this hill, therefore the precise situation cannot be pointed out by means of measurement : it is towards the north-west corner of the hill.

Stanmore. This station is on the southern extremity of the range above the town : it is near the trees, and a little to the westward of the broken ground.

Busby Heath, near Stanmore. The station cannot be easily found : it is about 1000 feet from the road, but there are no objects near enough to determine it by measurement.

Wrotham. This station is 205½ feet north-east of the old station : it may be easily found, with the assistance of a theodolite, Severndroog Tower making an angle of 94° 19′ with the new station.

Gravesend. The station is on Windmill Hill, and on the western side of it : it is about 50 feet south of the stile, and near the brow.

Gad's Hill, Kent. The station is very easily found, being in the middle of the *tumulus*.

Sheppey, Isle of. The station is on the bare hill, westward of, and contiguous to, the high range : it cannot be found through means of measurement.

Hampstead. The station is on the heath, but cannot easily be found, on account of the rugged and broken ground which surrounds it : it is situated 40 feet from the road, and among the sand holes.

Langdon Hill, Essex. The station is in the middle of the field on the top of this hill : it is about 400 feet from either of the stiles.

Hadleigh. The station is on a remarkable hill, in shape very like a barrow, and is about a mile south-west of the town.

Southend. The station is in the second field westward from the terrace : it cannot be easily found.

Interior Stations.

Hope's Nose, the north projecting point of Torbay. The only spot fit for a station in this part is the one chosen : it can easily be found, for it is the high and bare rising, just above the Nose.

Ball's Obelisk. This object is on the eastern part of Great Haldon, in Devonshire. The station can be easily found, for it is close to the gate of the inclosure, and on the only spot not covered with heath.

Evercrutch, in Somersetshire. The hill on which the station is, commands an extensive view, and is not far from the town of Evercrutch. Bruton is also near it. The station is in the middle of the flat place on the top of the hill.

Crouch Hill, near Banbury, in Oxfordshire. The hill is well

G

known, and the station easily found; for the apex of the hill appears as if it were truncated, and in the middle of the smooth part is the station.

Cumner Hill, near Oxford. The station is about 130 feet westward from the centre of the clump of trees.

Whitebam Hill, Oxfordshire. There are a few trees contiguous to the station, which bear eastward from it, and are about 80 feet distant. The station is on the highest and smoothest part of the hill.

Lidlington, a village near Ampthill in Bedfordshire. This station can easily be found, for a tumulus, whose centre is the station, has been erected, to render it conspicuous.

Trusler Hill, in Woburn Park. The station is on a tumulus likewise; and can be found without any difficulty.

Stations in *Essex, Suffolk, and Hertfordshire.*

Prittlewell Steeple.

Rayleigh Steeple. The station is in the north-east corner, 20 inches from the north parapet, and 4 feet from the eastern one.

Danbury Steeple. The instrument was placed in the four angles of the Steeple, as circumstances rendered it necessary. The points are readily found, as there is scarcely room in the corners to place an instrument. Stations were also selected on the following Steeples, &c.

Canewden Steeple.	West Mersea St.	Little Beatley St.
Frierning St.	Colchester, St. Mary's Staircase.	Wordbridge St.
Tillingham St.	Tattingstone St.	Dutely St.
Thorp St.	Rushmere St.	Orley St.
Stoke St.	Great Tey St.	Henley St.
Dover Court St.	St. Osyth Priory, Flagstaff.	Falkenham St.
Peldon St.	Shœbury Ness, Staff.	Copdock St.

Naughton St.	Beauchamp Roding St.	Wenham St.
Lavenham St.	Hornchurch St.	Barking, Staircase.
Bulmer St.	Naseing St.	Berkhampstead, Ga-
Glemsford St.	Henham on the Mount St.	zebo.
Toppesfield St.	Thorley St.	Gallywood Common.
Twinested St.	Albury St.	Purfleet Cliff.
Southweald St.	Elmdon St.	Babraham Mount.
Pleshley St.	Rickling St.	Epping Mill, Base.
High Easter St.	Thaxted St.	Brentwood Spire, sur-
Hatfield Broad Oak St.	Dalsham St.	veyed round.

Stations in Kent.

Frant Steeple. Station of 1787.	Seal Chart.	Ash St.
Botley Hill. Do.	Tunbridge St.	North Fleet St.
Chiddingstone St.	Oxford Mount.	Stockbury St.
Mount Sion.	Silverden Farm.	Hernhill St.
East Peckham St.	Well Hill.	
Tudely St.	Crayford St.	

The stations chosen for the survey of Essex, and parts of the adjoining counties, as also for completing the survey of Kent, are mostly towers, as may be seen from the above. When the tops of the towers have been smooth and even, the stations were always in the centres of them; but, when they were covered with roofs, or had spires upon them, stations were chosen in the most convenient places, and staffs always erected. I have omitted giving the measurements by which the stations may be exactly found, Rayleigh and Prittlewell excepted, in order to avoid swelling this article to an inconvenient length.

ART. VIII. *Particulars relating to the Base on King's Sedgemoor, and the Reduction of that Base.* Plate XXVIII.

Comparisons of the Chains.

As the chains, after the measurement on Salisbury Plain, were oiled, and laid up in the Tower, no apprehensions were entertained that either of them was elongated by the rusting of the joints. It was, however, our wish to have compared them with each other, previous to the commencement of this operation, and attempts were made, but rendered unsatisfactory, from the want of sufficient firmness in the soil. It was not till we arrived at the 70th chain, that a good opportunity presented itself: the measuring chain A, was then compared with the standard B, and found to be thirteen divisions of the micrometer head, attached to the brass scale, in excess. In these trials, the temperature remained constant; the mercury in FAHRENHEIT's thermometer being at 66¼°.

The 50-feet chain, spoken of in a former article, came from the hands of Mr. RAMSDEN without being very accurately measured; therefore it now became proper to ascertain its length, by means of the standard chain. This was accordingly done at the present time; when B was found to exceed twice the length of the 50-feet chain, by 14 divisions of the micrometer screw; the thermometer, at the time of trial, standing at 69¼°.

At the conclusion of the measurement, the chains were again compared, when the working chain A, was found to exceed the standard, 17¼ divisions on the micrometer head: this was after 279 chains were measured. Now, when 70 chains only had been measured, the difference between A and B was 13 of those divisions; consequently $17\frac{1}{4} - 13, = 4\frac{1}{4}$ divisions, was the wear of B, in measuring 203 chains. Therefore, the whole wear is found by this proportion, *viz.* $203 : 4\frac{1}{4} :: 273 : 5,223$ divisions, $= \frac{1}{100}$ of an inch; which very inconsiderable quantity, like the wear on Salisbury Plain, no doubt, arose from the pivots and pivot holes of the joints being polished by continual use. This supposition seems just; as the wear of the chain, after the measurement on Hounslow Heath, was found to be much greater.

The length of the chain A, as well as that of the standard B, was accurately ascertained by Mr. RAMSDEN, in the year 1793, as particularly shewn in the Philosophical Transactions for 1795. In the temperature of 54°, A was found to exceed 100 feet, $\frac{1421}{100000}$ of an inch; therefore, adding the wear which took place on Salisbury Plain, *viz.* $\frac{1}{100}$ part of an inch, we get the length of A at the commencement of the measurement on Sedgemoor $= 100,01009$ feet.

From repeated trials, as before observed, the standard B was found to exceed the length of twice that of the new fifty-feet chain, $1\frac{1}{4}$ divisions of the micrometer head; and, *after* the measurement, the same chain fell short of A, $17\frac{1}{4}$ of those divisions: hence, A exceeds twice the length of the 50-feet chain, $31\frac{1}{4}$ divisions. Therefore the length of the short chain, in the temperature of 54°, may be taken at $50,00075$ feet.

ART. IX. *Table of the Measurement of the Base of Verification on King's Sedgemoor.*

Days.	Spaces measured. Yards.	Mean temp. by thermom.	Days.	Spaces measured. Yards.	Mean temp. by thermom.	Days.	Spaces measured. Yards.	Mean temp. by thermom.
July	100	69,7		5100	79,27	6	6300	92,26
	200	65,56		5300	78,90		6400	86,73
11	300	67,75	25	3400	82,06		6500	66,30
	400	67,40		3500	85,90		66..0	82,06
	500	65,10	26	3600	67,65		6700	91,06
12	600	65,50		3700	64,83		6800	89,76
	700	73,40	27	3800	67,72		6900	93,43
	800	69,36		3900	75,53	8	7000	75,94
	900	68,06		4000	71,40		7100	81,57
13	1000	66,03		4100	71,25		7200	81,93
	1100	70,30		4200	67,14		7300	79,36
	1200	69,33	31	4300	66,56		7400	68,20
	1300	62,83	Aug. 1	4400	71,16	9	7500	78,18
14	1400	63,93	2	4500	64,60		7600	76,50
	1500	61,40		4600	65,26		7700	71,26
	1600	57,03		4700	68,16		7800	72,13
16	1700	66,36		4800	70,16		7900	70,8
	1800	63,80		4900	76,25	13	8000	71,5
	1900	71,03		5000	70,66		8100	8,4
17	2000	75,70		5100	64,83		8200	84,53
	2100	80,43	3	5200	81,40		8300	76,17
	2200	77,53		5300	65,96		8400	69,50
18	2300	65,90		5400	65,86		8500	66,05
	2400	69,79		5500	67,13	14	8600	85,53
	2500	69,58	4	5600	78,53		8700	85,73
	2600	68,16		5700	71,84		8800	85,87
19	2700	68,19		5800	66,93		8900	76,46
	2800	71,66		5900	65,86		9000	78,36
	2900	69,03		6000	61,50	15	9100	73,27
21	3000	70,76		6100	76,48	16	9225.4943	83,90
	3100	79,68		6200	84,76			

ART. x. *Reduction of the Base.*

Feet.

The overplus of the 273d chain was measured
by Mr. RAMSDEN, and found to be 23,517 feet;
wherefore, the apparent length of the base was - 27676,4830
From the measurement in the Riding-house of
his Grace the Duke of MARLBOROUGH, the chain
A was found to exceed 100 feet, in the temperature
of 54°, 0,11425 parts of an inch; to which, adding the wear by the measurement on Salisbury
Plain, *viz.* $\frac{1}{316}$, and also *half* the wear by the
measurement of this base, *viz.* $\frac{1}{108}$ part of an inch,
we get $\frac{0.1191}{12}$ for the excess of the chain's length
above 100 feet; therefore, $\frac{0.1191}{12}$ x 272,8 = 2,7075
feet; which add - - - - +2,7075
The sum of all the degrees shewn by the ther-
mometer was 98511; wherefore, $\frac{\overline{98511}}{5}$ — 54° x 272,8
x $\frac{0.0075}{12}$ = 3,1069 feet; which also add - +3,1069
Again, from the comparison of the 50-feet chain
with the standard B, it appeared that the excess
above 50 feet, in the temperature of 54°, was 0,09075
parts of an inch; therefore, $\frac{0.09075}{12}$ x 8 = 0,0605
parts of a foot. This likewise add - +0,0605
The sum of all the degrees shewn by the thermometers placed by the sides of the 50-feet chain,
was 1372; therefore $\frac{\overline{1372}}{5}$ — 54° x 4 x $\frac{.0075}{12}$ = 0,0365
parts of a foot: and this add - - +0,0365
                                                    27682,3944

$$27682,3944$$

And, for the reduction of the base to the temperature of 62°, *viz.* for 8° on the brass scale, we have

$$\frac{0,01037 \times 171.8 \times 1^m}{12} = 2,2497 \text{ feet}; \text{ which subtract} \qquad -2,2497$$

Therefore, the length of the base is - - - feet 27680,1447
which, neglecting decimals, may be taken at 27680 feet.

As to the probable error of the above conclusion, I know not how to form a just opinion. On ground sufficiently hard, and otherwise favourable, I think a base of 5 miles might be measured so accurately, as to afford a result not differing from the truth more than three inches : but, on this occasion, I should not suppose the error can be less than six, nor more than nine inches. Motives for adopting this supposition, have been related in a foregoing article.

ART. XI. *Calculation of the Sides of certain principal Triangles in Cornwall and Devonshire.* Plate XXVII.

Distance from Hensbarrow to St. Agnes Beacon. 97084,8 Feet. Phil. Trans. 1797. p. 461.

No. of triangles	Names of stations.	Observed angles.	Diff.	Spherical excess.	Error.	Angles corrected for calculation.	Distances.
		° ' "	' "	"	"	° ' "	Feet.
1.	St. Agnes Beacon	47 10 2,75	—0,15			47 10 3,25	
	Hensbarrow - -	67 6 13,25	—0,58			67 6 13	
	Trevose Head -	65 43 47	—0,57			65 43 43,75	
		180 0 1		1,31	—0,31		
	Trevose Head from { St. Agnes Beacon					·	98108,1
	Hensbarrow					· ·	78099,9

Distance from Hensbarrow to Bodmin Down, 47137,2 Feet. Phil. Trans. 1797. p. 460.

No. of triangles	Names of stations.	Observed angles.	Diff.	Spherical excess.	Error.	Angles corrected for calculation.	Distances.
							Feet.
ii.	Hensbarrow - -	77 60 18,5	—0,50	•	•	77 30 17,5	
	Bodmin Down -	68 21 58,25	—0,38			68 21 57,25	
	Trevose Head -	34 17 45,5	—0,25			34 17 45,25	
		180 0 2,25		0,86	+1,39		

Trevose Head from { Bodmin Down - - | 81967,6
{ Hensbarrow - - | 78093

Mean distance from Hensbarrow to Trevose Head, 78096,4 feet.

iii.	Trevose Head -	42 33 52	—0,35			42 33 51,25	
	Bodmin Down -	71 55 27	—0,45			71 55 26,75	
	Cadon Barrow -	. . .				65 30 42,0	

Cadon Barrow from { Trevose Head - - | 85615
{ Bodmin Down - - | 60915

iv.	Bodmin Down -	30 58 13	—0,03			30 58 12,75	
	Cadon Barrow - -	43 49 50,5	—0,04			43 49 50	
	Brown Willy - -	. . .				105 11 57,25	

Brown Willy from { Bodmin Down - - | 43722
{ Cadon Barrow - - | 52482

Distance from Carraton Hill to Maker Heights, 61600,3 feet. Phil. Trans. 1797. p. 452.

v.	Carraton Hill - -	74 5 22,5	—0,60			74 5 21,75	
	Maker Heights -	53 4 29	—0,48			53 4 28,75	
	Black Down - -	52 50 9,75	—0,48			52 50 9,5	
		180 0 1,25		1,57	—0,32		

Black Down from { Maker Heights - - | 99680
{ Carraton Hill - - | 82860,4

H

No. of triangles	Names of stations.	Observed angles.	D.ff	Spherical excess.	Error.	Angles corrected for calculation	Distances.
vi.	Carraton Hill - -	48 57 8.25	—8.24			48 57 9.05	Feet.
	Black Down - -	39 44 39	—0.32			39 44 38.5	
	St. Stephen's Down	91 18 12.75				91 18 12.85	
		180 0 0		0.89	—0.89		

St. Stephen's Down from { Carraton Hill - -   52991.3
                      { Black Down - -   62506.7

Distance from Carraton Hill to Kit Hill, 33407 feet. Phil. Trans. 1797. p. 459.

vii.	Carraton Hill - -	70 15 32	—0.14			70 15 32.85	
	St. Stephen's Down	37 1 56	—0.11			37 1 55.75	
	Kit Hill - -	. . .				72 42 32	

St. Stephen's Down from { Carraton Hill - - -   52994
                      { Kit Hill - - -   52240.4

Mean distance from St. Stephen's Down to Carraton Hill, 52992.7 feet.

viii.	St. Stephen's Down	54 16 13	—0.29			54 16 12.5	
	Black Down	52 57 37	—2.19			52 57 36.5	
	Kit Hill -	. . .				72 46 11	

Black Down from { Kit Hill - - -   53228
                    { St. Stephen's Down -   62509.2

Hence the mean distance from Black Down to St. Stephen's Down, is 62508 feet.

In the third triangle, the angle at Cadon Barrow is supplementary. When the observations were made at that station, a direction-post at Bodmin Down was mistaken for the staff, (to which it was similar in shape,) erected at no great distance from it. This error was not detected till long after: and, although it has been a maxim to which we have generally adhered, of observing all the angles of each triangle, yet, for the reasons assigned in the preface, I have chosen to depart from it on the present occasion. In another principal triangle, the angle at Brown Willy is also supplementary: it has already been mentioned, that an instrument cannot be got on the top of it. As to the angles at Kit Hill, in the two last triangles, being inferred ones, it may be proper to mention, that Black Down was chosen for a station, after the observations were made at the former. To have visited Kit Hill a second time would have been unnecessary, because there are not any distances, except to interior objects, which depend upon those triangles.

ART. XII. *Calculation of the Sides of a Set of principal Triangles, carried on from the Side which joins the Stations on Beacon Hill, near Amesbury, and Wingreen Hill, near Shaftsbury, towards the Base of Verification on King's Sedgemoor.* Plate XXIX.

Distance from Beacon Hill to Wingreen Hill, 114522.4 Feet. Phil. Trans. 1795. p. 501.

No. of triangles	Names of station.	Observed angles.	Diff.	Spherical excess.	Error.	Angles corrected for calculation.	Distances.
11.	Wingreen Hill Beacon Hill Bradley Knoll	89 57 37.75 —0.97 32 11 43.25 —0.48 57 50 38.25 —0.48				89 57 37 32 11 43 57 50 40	Feet.
		179 59 39.25		1.93	—2.68		
	Bradley Knoll from {			Wingreen Beacon Hill			72074 155272.5
12.	Bradley Knoll Wingreen Bull Barrow	40 43 52 —0.26 96 20 37 —0.65 42 55 32.75 —0.25				40 43 51.5 96 20 36.25 42 55 32.25	
		180 0 1.75		1.16	+0.55		
	Bull Barrow from {			Bradley Knoll Wingreen			105580 82053.6

In the Philosophical Transactions for 1797. p. 455, the distance from Bull Barrow to Wingreen is said to be 69056, being 4½ feet greater than the above conclusion.

No of triangles	Names of stations.	Observed angles.	Diff.	Spherical excess.	Error.	Angles corrected for calculation.	Distances.
xI.	Bull Barrow	40 58 47.75	—0,28	"	'	40 58 45.25	Feet.
	Bradley Knoll	45 43 3.5	—0,22			45 43 3.25	
	Ash Beacon	93 38 12.5	—0,65			93 38 11.5	
		180 0 3.75		1,25	+2,50		
	Ash Beacon from { Bradley Knoll					-	68650,6
	Bull Barrow					-	73451
xII.	Beacon Hill	23 4 15	—0,08			23 4 14.75	
	Bradley Knoll	42 43 29.75	+0,07			42 43 28.85	
	Westbury Down	114 12 18,5	—0,97			114 12 17	
		180 0 3.25		1,17	+2,08		
	Westbury Down from { Beacon Hill					-	100625,1
	Bradley Knoll					-	58118,2
xIII.	Westbury Down	40 42 1,75	—0,12			40 42 1.75	
	Bradley Knoll	101 23 59	—0,48			101 23 59.75	
	Mendip Hills	37 47 38,5	—0,16			37 47 38.5	
		179 59 59.25		0,77	—1,52		
	Mendip Hills from { Westbury Down					-	92954,0
	Bradley Knoll					-	61981,1

Base of verification.—Greylock's Foss to Lugshorn Corner, 27680 feet.

xIV.	Lugshorn Corner	107 44 31				107 44 31	
	Greylock's Foss	8 30 0				8 30 0	
	Dundon Beacon	63 45 29				63 45 29	
		180 0 0			0		
	Dundon Beacon from { Lugshorn Corner					-	4561,5
	Greylock's Foss					-	29393

No. of triangles	Names of stations.	Observed angles.	Diff.	Spherical excess.	Error.	Angles corrected for calculation.	Distances
							Feet.
XV.	Greylock's Foss -	105 40 0,25				105 40 0,5	
	Moor Lynch -	59 58 14				59 58 14,5	
	Dundon -	14 21 44.75				14 21 45	
		179 59 59			—1,0		
		Moor Lynch from { Greylock's Foss -					8421,5
		Dundon Beacon -					32088,7
XVI.	Lugshorn Corner -	13 51 58				13 51 58,75	
	Greylock's Foss -	114 9 59				114 9 58,5	
	Moor Lynch -	51 58 3.25				51 58 2,75	
		180 0 1,25			+1,25		
		Moor Lynch from { Lugshorn Corner -					31061,9
		Greylock's Foss -					8421,8
XVII.	Lugshorn Corner -	93 58 33.75				93 58 34,25	
	Moor Lynch -	8 0 10,25				8 0 10,75	
	Dundon Beacon -	78 7 14.5				78 7 15	
		179 59 58.5			—1,5		
		Dundon Beacon from { Lugshorn Corner -					4561,5
		Moor Lynch -					31689,0

Hence the mean distance from Moor Lynch to Dundon Beacon is 31688,85 feet.

XVIII.	Moor Lynch -	54 38 50	—0,07			54 38 49,5	
	Dundon Beacon -	101 22 54,5	—0,38			101 22 53,75	
	Mendip Hills -	23 58 17	—0,10			23 58 16,75	
		180 0 1,5		0,5	+1,0		
		Mendip Hills from { Moor Lynch - -					78876,8
		Dundon Beacon -					65622,7

No. of Triangles	Names of stations.	Observed angles.	Diff.	Spherical excess.	Error.	Angles corrected for calculation.	Distances.
11X.	Moor Lynch	54 3 22,5	—0,42			54 3 22	Feet.
	Mendip Hills	69 26 48,25	—0,49			69 26 47	
	Ash Beacon	56 29 51,5	—0,42			56 29 51	
		180 0 2,25		1,33 +0,92			
	Ash Beacon from { Moor Lynch						88571
	Mendip Hills						76851
22.	Mendip Hills	58 16 22	—0,30			58 16 23,5	
	Ash Beacon	50 8 45,5	—0,28			50 8 45,25	
	Bradley Knoll	71 34 55	—0,56			71 34 54,25	
		180 0 2,5		0,95 +1,55			
	Bradley Knoll from { Mendip Hills						61963,5
	Ash Beacon						68653,6

The distance from Bradley Knoll to the station on Mendip Hills, and also to that on Ash Beacon, is given in the preceding triangles, independent of the above values. The first is 61961,1, and the second 68650,6 feet: these distances have their origin in the base on Salisbury Plain. The other distances are 61963,5, and 68653,6 feet: and these depend on the base of verification on King's Sedgemoor. There is, therefore, a difference of $2\frac{4}{10}$ feet between the values of one distance, (12 miles nearly,) and 3 feet between those of the other, which is about 13 miles in length. If the computations had been carried on from one base to another, the difference between the measured base on Sedgemoor and the computed base, would have appeared to be *one foot nearly*. I have already delivered it as my opinion, that an error of nine inches may exist in the new base: therefore, these results must be considered as satisfactory enough. A different correction of the observed angles, or another selection of

the angles themselves, might afford a closer agreement; but I can-
nee no just reason for making any alterations in one or the other.
I shall now take the means of the distances, as derived from both
bases, and consider 68652,2 feet as the true distance from Ash
Beacon to Bradley Knoll; and 61962,9 feet for that between Bradley
Knoll and the station on Mendip Hills.

In one of the foregoing triangles, (Bull Barrow, Bradley Knoll,
and Ash Beacon,) the distance between Ash Beacon and Bull Barrow
is found to be 75451 feet. If the *mean distance* between Bradley.
Knoll and Ash Beacon, *viz.* 61962,3 feet, be now used, 75452,7
feet becomes the distance between those stations; and this I shall
use, in computing the sides of the two triangles which immediately
follow.

No. of triangle	Names of stations.	Observed angles.	Diff.	Spherical excess.	Error.	Angles corrected for calculation.	Distances.
		° ′ ″	″	′	″	° ′ ″	Feet.
121.	Ash Beacon	34 18 56,25	—0,14			34 18 55,75	
	Bull Barrow	51 26 42	—0,13			51 26 41,75	
	Mintern	94 14 23	—0,31			94 14 22,5	
		180 0 1,25		0,59	+0,66		
	Mintern from { Ash Beacon						59166,6
	{ Bull Barrow						42653,7
122.	Pilsden	35 3 1	—0,24			35 3 0,75	
	Ash Beacon	49 21 38,25	—0,26			49 21 38	
	Mintern	95 35 22	—0,60			95 35 21,25	
		180 0 1,25		1,08	+0,17		
	Pilsden from { Ash Beacon						102535
	{ Mintern						78177,6

In our last account, (see Phil. Trans. 1797. p. 455 and 456,) the distance from Bull Barrow
to Mintern was found to be 42653,4 feet; and the distance from Pilsden to Mintern 78177
feet. The distances derived from the above triangles are very nearly the same; a difference
of a few inches only existing between them.

No. of triangles	Names of stations.	Observed angles	Diff.	Spherical excess	Error	Angles corrected for calculation.	Distances.
		° ′ ″				° ′ ″	Feet.
XXIII.	Moor Lynch	57 19 1,5	−0,64			57 19 2,5	
	Ash Beacon	76 1 16,5	−0,39			76 1 36	
	Pilsden	. . .				46 38 21,5	
	Pilsden from Moor Lynch				−	−	118130

But Pilsden was also observed from Dundon Beacon; from which, and the angle observed at Moor Lynch, between Dundon Beacon and Pilsden, results the following triangle.

XXIV.	Moor Lynch	56 43 36,75	+0,03			56 43 36,5	
	Dundon Beacon	108 1 51	−0,64			108 1 51,75	
	Pilsden	. . .				15 14 31,75	
	Pilsden from Moor Lynch		−	−	−	−	118033,6

Hence, the mean distance from Moor Lynch to Pilsden is 118131,8 feet; and this is the side from which the series about to be carried on, for the survey of the north of Devonshire, is to originate.

In the triangle formed by the stations on Mendip Hills, Bradley Knoll, and Westbury Down, the distance between the first and last is 99954,0 feet; but, computing with the mean distance from Mendip to Bradley Knoll, (61962,3 feet,) as found from both bases, the distance from Mendip to Westbury Down proves to be 99955,9 feet; which distance is used in the remaining principal triangles in this quarter.

XXV.	Farley Down	77 21 53.75	−0,44			77 21 53.75	
	Westbury Down	63 41 51,85	−0,34			63 41 49.75	
	Mendip Hills	38 55 17,5	−0,32			38 55 17.5	
		180 0 1,5		1,10	+1,40		
	Mendip from { Farley Down				−	−	85412,2
	{ Westbury Down				−	−	91911,9

No. of triangles.	Names of stations.	Observed angles	Diff.	Spherical excess.	Error.	Angles corrected for calculation.	Distances.
XXVI.	Mendip - - - Dundry - - - Farley Down -	60 36 14,5 69 52 22 49 31 23,5	—0,40 —0,44 —0,37			60 36 15 69 52 22 49 31 23	Feet.
		180 0 1		1,21	—0,21		
	Dundry from { Farley Down - - - Mendip - - -						79255,3 69196
XXVII.	Mendip - - Dundry - - Lansdown - -	41 3 58,5 83 34 18 . . .	—0,25 —0,40			41 3 58,25 83 34 17,5 55 21 44,25	
	Lansdown from { Mendip - - - Dundry - - -						83573,2 55249,2
XXVIII.	Dundry - - Farley Down - Lansdown - -	13 41 16,25 27 5 27,5 . . .	—0,09 —0,11			13 41 16 27 5 27,25 139 12 36,75	
	Lansdown from { Farley Down - - - Dundry - - -						187304 55248,7

Wherefore, the mean distance from Dundry to Lansdown is 52248.9 feet.

ART. XIII. *Calculation of the sides of certain principal Triangles, carried on from the side Bagshot Heath and Highclere, towards the north.* Plate XXXI.

Distance from Bagshot Heath to Highclere, 142952,6 feet. Phil. Trans. 1795. p. 496.

XXIX.	Bagshot Heath - Highclere - Nuffield - -	55 32 26 46 10 18,25 78 17 18,25	—0,89 —0,83 —1,20			55 32 25,25 46 10 17,75 78 17 17	
		180 0 2,5		2,94	—0,43		
	Nuffield from { Bagshot Heath - - Highclere - -						105321,2 180374

I

No. of triangles.	Names of stations.	Observed angles	Diff.	Spherical excess	Error.	Angles corrected for calculation	Distances.
xxx.	White Horse Hill	63 7 53,85	—0,94			63 7 53,5	feet.
	Highclere - -	63 18 18,75	—0,94			63 18 17	
	Nuffield - -	53 33 49,5	—0,86			63 33 49,5	
		179 59 59,5		8,74	—3,84		

White Horse Hill from { Nuffield - - -   120557,7
Highclere - - -   108563,1

Distance from Beacon Hill to Highclere, 98694,4 feet.   Phil. Trans. 1795. p. 497.

xxxi.	Beacon Hill - -	17 41 38,5	—0,11			17 41 38,15	
	Highclere - -	56 0 29,75	+0,08			56 0 29,15	
	Inkpin Hill - -	106 16 53,85	—0,47			106 16 52,5	
		180 0 1,5		0,50	+1,0		

Inkpin Hill from { Highclere - - 51276,8
Beacon Hill - - 85247,9

xxxii.	Highclere - -	34 27 50,75	+0,38			34 27 50,75	
	Inkpin Hill -	133 27 57,5	—0,91			133 27 58	
	White Horse Hill	12 4 11,5	+0,04			12 4 11,25	
		179 59 59,75		0,49	—1,24		

White Horse Hill from { Highclere - - 108565,5
Inkpin - - 84047,1

In the following computations, I shall use 120557,7 feet for the distance between White Horse Hill and Nuffield: this is derived from the base on Hounslow Heath. By the last triangle, White Horse Hill, from Highclere, is distant 108565,5 feet; which is computed from the base on Salisbury Plain. The distance between those stations, found by the second of the above triangles, is 108563,1 feet. Therefore, whether the distance between White Horse Hill and Nuffield be founded on the base measured on Salisbury Plain, or Hounslow Heath, nearly the same conclusion is derived: the difference will not amount to four feet; a small quantity in a side of three-and-twenty miles. I shall, however, use 120557.7, because I think it the most accurate determination.

No. of triangles.	Names of stations.	Observed angles.	Diff.	Spherical excess.	Error.	Angles corrected for calculation.	Distances.
		° ′ ″		″	″	° ′ ″	Feet
XXXIII.	White Horse Hill	38 48 13.25	−0.67			38 48 12.5	
	Nuffield	86 4 16.25	−1.21			86 4 15	
	Brill	55 7 33.5	−0.71			55 7 32.5	
		180 0 3		2.6	+0.4		
	Brill from { White Horse Hill						146603.8
	{ Nuffield						92085.5
XXXIV.	Brill	50 14 44.5	−1.18			50 14 45	
	White Horse Hill	64 45 43.75	−1.31			64 45 42.5	
	Stow on the Wold	64 59 32	−1.35			64 59 45	
		180 0 0.25		3.88	−3.63		
	Stow from { White Horse Hill						124365.6
	{ Brill						146326.3
XXXV.	Brill	32 34 43	−0.61			32 34 42.25	
	Stow	60 56 6.25	−0.64			60 56 5.5	
	Epwell	86 29 13.5	−1.11			86 29 12.25	
		180 0 2.25		6.37	+0.38		
	Epwell from { Stow						78938.2
	{ Brill						128140
XXXVI.	Epwell	38 10 44	−0.85			38 10 42.75	
	Stow	72 38 49.5	−0.34			72 38 47.5	
	Broadway Beacon	69 10 31.75	−0.32			69 10 29.75	
		180 0 5.25		0.92	+4.33		
	Broadway Beacon from { Stow						51203.2
	{ Epwell						80611.4

I 2

No. of triangles	Names of stations	Observed angles	Diff.	Spherical excess	Error	Angles corrected for calculation	Distances
XXXVII.	Broadway Beacon	56 32 45	—0,34	"	"	56 32 44.75	Tot.
	Epwell -	95 36 85.85	—1,62			95 34 84.75	
	Corley - -	27 52 49.75	—0,61			27 52 50.5	
		180 0 0		1,58	—1,58		
		Corley from Broadway Beacon - -					171568
XXXVIII.	Brill - -	34 23 58.5	—0,65			34 23 57.9	
	Epwell -	85 0 18.5	—1,10			85 0 17.5	
	Arbury Hill -	60 35 45.3	—0,70			60 35 57.5	
		180 0 2.5		2,46	—0,04		
		Arbury Hill from { Epwell / Brill } - -					8308,4 / 145570
XXXIX.	Arbury Hill -	89 57 6.5	—1,14			89 57 5.3	
	Epwell -	54 45 18.75	—0,57			54 45 18.25	
	Corley -	35 17 36.75	—0,57			35 17 36.25	
		180 0 0		1,89	—1,89		
		Corley from { Arbury Hill / Epwell } - -					117463 / 143857,8

By the triangle Broadway Beacon, Epwell, Corley, (see the above) the distance from Corley to Broadway Beacon is the only distance computed; and this has been obtained through the means of two observed angles only. When the observations were made at Broadway Beacon, it was not imagined Corley could be seen; and the contrary was not known till the party arrived at the latter place. In so large a triangle, it would certainly be right to observe all the angles: but I have given the angles as they now stand, because the distance from Epwell to Corley comes out 143831 feet, which determination differs only three feet from the same distance found by the last triangle.

No. of triangles	Names of stations	Observed angles	Diff.	Spherical excess	Error	Angles corrected for calculation	Distances
XL.	Bow Brickhill -	68 11 56.75	—1,21			68 11 59	
	Arbury Hill -	43 16 55.5	—0,99			43 16 54.5	
	Brill - -	68 10 7.75	—1,22			68 10 6.5	
		180 0 0		3,43	—3,43		
		Bow Brickhill from { Arbury Hill / Brill } - -					144481 / 108058,9

It will now be expedient to compute the distance from Bow Brick-hill to Brill, by means of another set of triangles. And it was for the express purpose of verifying this distance found by the last triangle, that Scutchamfly Barrow, in Berkshire, and the station above Wendover, were chosen. The base on which these triangles are to rest, is the distance between Nuffield and White Horse Hill, *viz.* 180557,7 feet.

No. of triangle	Names of stations.	Observed angles.	Diff.	Spherical excess.	Error.	Angles corrected for calculation.	Distances.
XLI.	Nuffield -	62 32 5.25	—0,53	"	"	62 32 0	Feet.
	White Horse Hill	35 34 22.25	—0.47			35 34 24	
	Shotover Hill -	81 53 29.75	—0.74			81 53 30	
		179 59 58.25		1.75	—3.5		
	Shotover Hill from { White Horse Hill -						108050,2
	{ Nuffield - -						70842,5
XLII.	Shotover Hill -	26 8 8	—0,13			26 8 8	
	White Horse Hill	42 4 2	—0,04			42 4 2	
	Scutchamfly Barrow	111 47 50	—0.70			111 47 50	
		180 0 0		0,86	—0,86		
	Scutchamfly Barrow from { White Horse Hill -						51161,9
	{ Shotover Hill - -						77968,3
XLIII.	Shotover Hill -	117 30 56	—1,41			117 30 55,25	
	Scutchamfly Barrow	34 26 52	—0,03			34 26 52	
	Wendover -	28 2 12,75	—0,09			28 2 12,75	
		180 0 0,75		1,52	—0,77		
	Wendover from { Scutchamfly Barrow -						147113,3
	{ Shotover - -						93822,6

No. of triangles	Names of Stations	Observed angles.	Diff.	Spheri-cal excess.	Error.	Angles corrected for calculation.	Distances
XLIV.	Wendover	23 23 57.5	0,11		a	23 23 57,25	Feet.
	Shotover Hill	48 30 39.75	0,04			48 30 40,5	
	Brill	. . .				108 5 82,25	
				1,21			

Brill from { Wendover   73940.}
         Shotover Hill   39000,2

XLV.	Wendover	80 11 9.25	—0,67			80 11 8,5	
	Brill	57 25 1,5	—0,47			57 25 0,75	
	Bow Brickhill	42 23 50,75	—0,44			42 23 50,75	
		180 0 1,51		1,58	—0,07		

Bow Brickhill from { Wendover   92400,7
         Brill   108055

According to the first determination, the distance from Bow Brickhill to Brill is 108058,9 feet, and by the last, 108855 feet. There is, therefore, a difference of 4 feet nearly; a quantity which must be deemed inconsiderable; hence, 108056,9 feet may be taken for the true distance.

XLVI.	Kinsworth	62 55 38,75				62 55 38,5	
	Bow Brickhill	88 42 0				88 41 59,25	
	Brill	. . .				28 22 22,25	

Kinsworth from { Brill   131328,5
         Bow Brickhill   57608

XLVII.	Wendover	33 26 45				33 26 49	
	Quainton	94 58 37				94 58 38	
	Brill	51 34 33				51 34 33	
		179 59 58		0,55	—2,55		

Quainton from { Brill   40908
         Wendover   58146,4

No. of triangles	Names of Stations.	Angles observed.	D.S.	Spheri-cal excess.	Error.	Angles corrected for calculation.	Distances.
XLVIII	Bow Brickhill	38 51 40,75	"	"	"	38 51 40,75	Feet.
	Wendover	45 44 29,5				45 44 29,25	
	Quainton	94 23 50,25				94 23 50	
		180 0 1,25		0,83	+0,42		
	Quainton from { Wendover						58146,9
	{ Bow Brickhill					-	67491,3

In the above triangle, I have computed the distances of Wendover and Bow Brickhill from Quainton with 92400,7 feet, the side Wendover and Bow Brickhill, as determined in a former triangle.

XLIX	Bow Brickhill	85 9 52,75				85 9 52	
	Kinsworth	52 17 56,75				52 17 56	
	Quainton	. . .				42 32 12	
	Quainton from { Kinsworth					-	84997
	{ Bow Brickhill					-	67490,3

Therefore, 67490 may be considered as nearly the true distance, in feet, between Quainton and Bow Brickhill.

L.	Bow Brickhill	41 10 36,75				41 10 36,5	
	Kinsworth	83 50 30,5				83 50 30	
	Lillyhoe	44 38 53				54 38 53,5	
		180 0 0,25		1,26	—1,50		
	Lillyhoe from { Kinsworth					-	47278,7
	{ Bow Brickhill					-	69867

As the stations Lidlington, Trusler Hill, together with Cronch Hill, Cwmmer Hill, and Whiteham Hill, have been used for purposes of greater importance than secondary ones have been generally applied to, I shall insert the triangles formed by their intersections in this article.

No of triangles	Names of stations	Observed angles	Diff.	Spherical excess.	Error.	Angles corrected for calculation.	Distances
ɪ.ɪ.	Kinsworth -	31 4 5				31 4 4	Feet
	Bow Brickhill -	80 39 37.25				80 39 54.75	
	Lidlington -	68 16 82.25				68 16 81.25	
		180 0 4.5			0.41 +4.91		
	Lidlington from { Bow Brickhill -						38035.6
	Kinsworth -						61255.3
ɪ.ɪɪ.	Lillyhoe - -	78 58 16				78 58 16	
	Kinsworth -	51 46 22				51 46 22	
	Lidlington -	. . .				49 15 22	
	Lillyhoe from { Kinsworth - -						47280
	Lidlington -						49015

The distance from Lillyhoe to Kinsworth, as found in a former triangle, is 47278.1 feet, and by the last 47280 feet; therefore, 47279.3 may be taken for the true distance in feet.

ɪ.ɪɪɪ.	Bow Brickhill -	38 28 56				38 28 56	
	Lillyhoe - -	23 59 31				23 59 31	
	Lidlington -	. . .				117 31 33	
	Lillyhoe from { Lidlington - -						49027.3
	Bow Brickhill - -						69869

And this triangle, with that preceding it, gives the mean distance between Lillyhoe and Lidlington = 49026.1 feet; and, with the triangle Lillyhoe, Kinsworth, and Bow Brickhill, it assigns 69868 feet for the mean distance between Lillyhoe and Bow Brickhill.

ɪ.ɪv.	Lillyhoe - -	5 58 11.5				5 58 11.5	
	Bow Brickhill -	14 54 42.75				14 54 42.75	
	Trusler Hill -	. . .				159 13 5.75	
	Trusler Hill from { Bow Brickhill -						101387
	Lillyhoe - -						50673.6

No. of triangle.	Names of stations.	Observed angles.	Diff.	Spherical excess.	Error.	Angles corrected for calculation.	Distances.
LIV.	Crouch Hill	145 23 26,25				145 23 26	Feet.
	Epwell	27 3 10				27 3 10	
	Brill	. . .				7 33 24	
		Crouch Hill from { Brill / Epwell					107608 / 29668,1

Distance from White Horse Hill to Shotover Hill 108050,8 feet.

LV.	Shotover Hill	48 5 32,75				48 5 32,25	
	White Horse	16 59 53,75				16 59 53,25	
	Whitcham Hill	114 54 34,75				114 54 34,5	
		180 0 1,25					
		Whitcham Hill from { White Horse Hill / Shotover Hill					83661,2 / 34827,4

LVI.	Whitcham Hill	55 52 38				55 52 36	
	Shotover Hill	24 37 36				24 37 37	
	Cumner Hill	99 29 48,5				99 29 47	
		179 59 59,5					
		Cumner Hill from { Shotover Hill / Whitcham Hill					19231,5 / 14714,3

And, because the Observatory of his Grace the Duke of MARL-
BOROUGH, at Blenheim, together with that at Oxford, have been
observed with the same care and attention as the principal stations,
and also because precise determinations of the situations are of
great importance, I shall here insert the triangles formed by their
intersections.

K

No. of tr angle	Names of stations	Observed angles	Diff	Spheri cal excess	Error	Angles corrected for calculation	Distances
LVII.	Shotover Hill - - Cumner Hill - - The Atlas on the top of the Observatory at Oxford	23 11 5 29 23 33 . . .	.	.	.	23 11 5 29 23 33 127 25 22	*Feet.*
	Oxford Observatory from { Cumner Hill - - { Shotover Hill - -						14491 18065.1
LVIII.	Whitcham Hill - White Horse Hill - Blenheim Observatory	131 25 36.5 10 30 43.5 . . .					131 25 35.5 10 30 43.75 38 3 40.75	
	Blenheim Observatory from { White Horse Hill - { Whitcham Hill - -						107851.9 26237.6

ART. XIV. *Triangles for connecting the Series carried on from Scut-chamfly Barrow and White Horse Hill, in Berkshire, into Buckingbamshire and Bedfordshire, with the Series carried on for the Survey of Essex.*

The angle at St. Ann's Hill, between the station on Hanger Hill Tower and Hampton Poor House, inferred from General Roy's Account, is 25° 33′ 58″,5. In 1793, the angle between the staff on Pen Church Tower and Hampton Poor House was taken, and found = 95° 57′ 34″,5; therefore, the angle between Pen Tower and Hanger Hill is 70° 23′ 36″.

The distance from St. Ann's Hill to Pen is determined by

the following triangle, in which the distance between St. Ann's
Hill and Bagshot Heath, *viz.* 46955,3 feet, (see Phil. Trans.
for 1795, p. 496,) is used for the base.

No. of triangles	Names of stations.	Observed angles.	Diff.	Spherical excess.	Error.	Angles corrected for calculation.	Distances.
		° ′ ″				° ′ ″	Feet.
LIX.	St. Ann's Hill	80 43 48				80 43 48	
	Bagshot - -	70 30 37				70 30 37	
	Pen Tower -	. . .				88 45 35	

Pen Tower from { St. Ann's Hill - - 92000,5
{ Bagshot Heath - - 96318

The distance from St. Ann's Hill to Hanger Hill Tower is
68895,8 feet: this is derived from the *mean* length of the base
on Hounslow Heath. This side, together with St. Ann's Hill
and Pen, using the included angle at St. Ann's Hill, as found
above, give 94640,5 feet, for the distance between Pen and
Hanger Hill Towers.

The angle at St. Ann's Hill, between Bagshot Heath and
Hanger Hill Tower, is 151° 7′ 24″,25: this, with the sides
Bagshot Heath and St. Ann's, St. Ann's and Hanger Hill,
give 17° 13′ 48″, for the angle at Bagshot Heath, between
Hanger Hill Tower and St. Ann's Hill: hence we have the
following triangle.

Bagshot Heath - - 16° 45′ 43″
Hanger Hill - - 103 18 23
Stanmore - - 59 55 54

K 2

Which triangle gives 37431 feet, for the distance between Stanmore and Hanger Hill Tower.

The angle at the station on Bow Brickhill, (see the preceding article,) between Wendover and Kinsworth, is 46° 18′ 8″,5; and the distances from it to these stations are 94402,2 feet, and 57668 feet respectively: these give the following triangle.

Bow Brickhill   -   46° 18′ 8″,5
Wendover   -   -   98 25 21,25
Kinsworth   -   -   95 16 30,25

From which the distance between Wendover and Kinsworth is found = 67090,7 feet. The observed angle at Wendover, between Bow Brickhill and Stanmore, is 102° 22′ 29″; from which, subtracting 38° 25′ 21″,25, the angle between Bow Brickhill and Kinsworth, we get 63° 57′ 7″,75, for the angle between Kinsworth and Stanmore. Again, the observed angle at Kinsworth, between Bow Brickhill and Stanmore, is 179° 57′ 44″; from which, subtracting the angle between Bow Brickhill and Wendover, we get 78° 21′ 13″,75, for the angle between Stanmore and Wendover. If these *computed* angles are actually such as might be observed, were Kinsworth and Wendover visible from each other, the angle at Stanmore between those stations ought to be 37° 41′ 39″, nearly: but the observed angle was 37° 41′ 41″,75; which is so nearly the computed one, as to leave little doubt of the accuracy of those *data* from which the angles are derived. The distance from Wendover to Kinsworth is 67090,7 feet.

Wendover   -   63 57 7,75 ⎫
Kinsworth   -   78 21 13,75 ⎬ which, corrected for calcula-
Stanmore   -   - 37 41 41,75 ⎭ tion, becomes,
                       180 0 3,25

Wendover - 69 57 7

Kinsworth - 78 21 12

Stanmore - 37 41 41   which triangle gives

the distance of Stanmore from $\begin{Bmatrix} \text{Wendover} = 107464,1 \\ \text{Kinsworth} = 98577,5 \end{Bmatrix}$ feet.

In consequence of Bushy Heath intercepting the view towards the east from Stanmore, it became necessary to choose a station on the former. To determine the distance, the angles at the two stations were taken very accurately; they were as follows,

Stanmore - 42 11 21,5

Bushy Heath 135 35 40,5

Kinsworth,   . . .   which gives 5489,3 feet for the required distance.

To determine the distance of the station on Pen Church Tower, we have two angles in the following triangle, *viz.*

Wendover - 38 19 18 } which, corrected for calcula-

Stanmore - 23 44 48 } tion, becomes,

Pen Tower - 118 1 54 }

Wendover - 38 19 18,25

Stanmore - 23 44 48,25

Pen Tower - 118 1 54,5   which triangle gives

the distance of Pen from $\begin{Bmatrix} \text{Wendover} = 49027 \\ \text{Stanmore} = 75325,4 \end{Bmatrix}$ feet.

With this distance of Stanmore from Pen, found from the last triangle, and also that between Stanmore and Hanger Hill, derived from the triangle, Bagshot Heath, Hanger Hill, and Stanmore, together with the included angle at Stanmore, *viz.* 109' 28' 22",5, we get the distance of Pen to Hanger Hill Tower = 94631,8 feet. The same distance has been found before, in a shorter and more direct way, being 94640,5 feet: the difference is only 8,7 feet; a sufficient proof that the distances given for the survey of this intricate and woody country, are sufficiently correct. It will be more convenient to show how these triangles are connected with those to the eastward, when I arrive at that part of the work which treats of the survey of Essex, than at present. I shall, therefore, proceed to the following article, after observing, that by the help of Harrow Spire, (the situation of which has been determined by General Roy,) and by observations hereafter to be made with the small instrument on Pen Tower, less difficulty will occur in the interior survey than was at first expected.

ART. XV. *Triangles formed by the intersections of Churches, Windmills, and other Objects.*

Triangles.	Angles observed.	Distances of the Stations from the intersected Objects.	
Little Haldon - - Ball's Obelisk - - - Great Haldon, secondary station	43 54 50 132 41 8	} Great Haldon -	Feet 18971 19366
Great Haldon from Ball's Obelisk 19366 feet.			
Great Haldon - - Ball's Obelisk - - Topsham Steeple	68 0 35 71 31 30	} Topsham Steeple -	18316 17679
Little Haldon from Furland 71776 feet.			
Little Haldon - - Furland - - - Hope's Nose, secondary station	18 2 2 18 42 53	} Hope's Nose -	37656 39028
Bodmin from Trevose 81967,6 feet.			
Bodmin - - Trevose - - St. Minvern Steeple	15 48 43 21 28 36	} St. Minvern Steeple -	45935 36866
Bodmin - - Trevose - - St. Minvern Windmill	12 5 33 8 46 51	} St. Minvern Windmill -	34852 48478

Trevose from Cadon Barrow 85684,8 feet.

Triangles.	Angles observed.	Distances of the stations from the intersected objects.	
Trevose Cadon Barrow St. Issy Steeple	55 38 59 19 15 48	} St. Issy Steeple -	{ 19856 73216
Trevose Cadon Barrow St. Merian Steeple	58 41 39 6 38 22	} St. Merian Steeple -	{ 10894 80504

Black Down from St. Stephen's 63506,7 feet.

Black Down St. Stephen's Down Werrington Steeple	4 46 17 74 20 14	} Werrington Steeple -	{ 61889 5301
Black Down St. Stephen's Boyton Steeple	15 18 49 104 53 9	} Boyton Steeple -	{ 69897 19101
Black Down St. Stephen's St. Stephen's Steeple	1 8 22 30 7 22	} St. Stephen's Steeple -	{ 60448 2395
Black Down St. Stephen's North Petherwin Steeple	5 31 36 153 13 23	} North Petherwin Steeple	{ 77698 16610

Carraton from St. Stephen's 52994 feet.

Carraton St. Stephen's Stokeclimsland Steeple	50 40 15 38 21 4	} Stokeclimsland Steeple	{ 32886 40997
Carraton St. Stephen's Launceston Steeple	6 11 7 55 31 16	} Launceston Steeple -	{ 47613 6483
Carraton St. Stephen's Launceston Chapel	5 58 26 53 7 37	} Launceston Chapel -	{ 49404 6427

Long Knoll from Westbury 58118,8 feet.

Long Knoll Westbury Frome Steeple	45 5 0 34 53 50	} Frome Steeple -	{ 33765 41793

Lansdown from Farley Down 28730.4 feet.

Triangles.	Angles observed.	Distances of the stations from the interceted objects.	
Lansdown - - Farley Down - - - Cold Aston	56 63 16 28 2 35	} Cold Aston - {	Feet. 13563 24180

Moor Lynch from Dundon 31688.8 feet.

Triangles.	Angles observed.	Distances of the stations from the interceted objects.	
Moor Lynch - - Dundon - - - Walton Windmill	15 54 56 83 11 6	} Walton Windmill - {	20406 14213
Moor Lynch - - Dundon - - Westonzoyland Steeple	123 0 11 19 18 55	} Westonzoyland Steeple {	17688 44848
Moor Lynch - - Dundon - - Middletoy Steeple	91 5 56 85 18 0	} Middletoy Steeple - {	15691 30530
Moor Lynch - - Dundon - - Chedzoy Steeple	153 58 50 9 39 13	} Chedzoy Steeple - {	19454 29550
Moor Lynch - - Dundon - - Highham Windmill	39 10 18 40 30 22	} Highham Windmill {	84457 16518
Moor Lynch - - Dundon - - Highbam Steeple	36 25 56 39 51 57	} Highham Steeple - {	21567 19981
Moor Lynch - - Dundon - - Bridgewater Spire	147 57 0 16 15 14	} Bridgewater Spire - {	33656 03708
Moor Lynch - - Dundon - - Burton Pynsent Obelisk	69 52 39 63 18 39	} Burton Pynsent Obelisk {	40063 43101
Moor Lynch - - Dundon - - Somerton Steeple	18 18 41 149 45 57	} Somerton Steeple - {	40792 11281

Dundry from Lansdown 55248,9 feet.

Triangles.	Angles observed.	Distances of the various from the interested objects	Feet.
Dundry Lansdown *Puckle Church Steeple*	22 7 16 85 25 0	} Puckle Church Steeple {	57757 21819
Dundry Lansdown *Westleigh Steeple*	30 37 18 46 18 39	} Westleigh Steeple - {	61842 31566
Dundry Lansdown *Bristol Cathedral*	51 19 11 22 25 3	} Bristol Cathedral - {	21920 41935
Dundry Lansdown *Redcliff Steeple*	44 18 9 21 82 84	} Redcliff Steeple - {	22096 48346
Dundry Lansdown *Long Aston Steeple*	78 18 19 14 52 8	} Long Aston Steeple - {	13883 54168
Dundry Lansdown *Clifden Windmill*	67 33 51 13 17 8	} Clifden Windmill - {	12860 51735
Dundry Lansdown *Blaze Castle*	76 37 25 39 7 35	} Blaze Castle - {	38591 58932
Dundry Lansdown *Penpole Park Gazebo*	89 10 18 32 52 56	} Penpole Park Gazebo {	35391 65180
Dundry Lansdown *St. George's Steeple*	32 16 31 51 49 58	} St. George's Steeple - {	32391 38795
Dundry Lansdown *Duke of Beaufort's House, Stoke*	44 54 50 48 5 1	} Duke of Beaufort's House {	41168 39064
Dundry Lansdown *Harfield Steeple*	57 15 32 39 14 57	} Harfield Steeple - {	35182 46773

L

Triangles.	Angles observed.	Distances of the Stations from the surveyed Objects	
			Feet.
Dundry Lansdown Durbom Steeple	13 58 0 150 8 3	} Durham Steeple -	{ 66541 18573
Dundry Lansdown Knowle Steeple	63 45 11 59 9 55	} Knowle Steeple -	{ 56512 59050
Dundry Lansdown Mangotsfield Steeple	29 42 10 59 59 41	} Mangotsfield Steeple -	{ 47845 87376
Dundry Lansdown Winterbourn Steeple	46 12 31 66 38 49	} Winterbourn Steeple -	{ 50045 43280

Mendip from Dundry 69196 feet.

Triangles.	Angles observed.	Distances	
Dundry Mendip Leigh Steeple on Mendip	15 0 54 104 10 15	} Leigh Steeple on Mendip	{ 76847 20533
Dundry Mendip Dundry Steeple	90 22 22 1 10 21	} Dundry Steeple -	{ 1417 69221

Mendip from Long Knoll 61962.3 feet,

Triangles.	Angles	Distances	
Long Knoll Mendip Doulting Spire	7 20 84 25 41 22	} Doulting Spire -	{ 49286 14517

Farley Down from Westbury 59849.5 feet,

Triangles.	Angles	Distances	
Westbury Farley Down Devizes Steeple	81 15 20 46 6 53	} Devizes Steeple -	{ 51197 72726

Whitehorse from Scutchamfly 51261.9 feet.

Triangles.	Angles	Distances	
Whitehorse Scutchamfly Abingdon Spire	32 55 51 104 3 27	} Abingdon Spire -	{ 72898 40852

Triangles.	Angles observed.	Distances of the Stations from the intersected Objects.	
Whitehorse Scutchamdy *Wallingford Steeple*	10 39 30 158 52 86	} Wallingford Steeple -	Feet. { 101693 52185
Whitehorse Scutchamdy *Great Coxwell Windmill*	121 19 10 81 7 0	} Great Coxwell Windmill	{ 30895 71834
Whitehorse Scutchamdy *Highworth Steeple*	153 24 7 11 21 56	} Highworth Steeple -	{ 38448 87355
Whitehorse Scutchamdy *Drayton Steeple*	18 6 9 99 45 35	} Drayton Steeple -	{ 63991 70586
Whitehorse Scutchamdy *Radley Steeple*	34 8 57 109 33 86	} Radley Steeple -	{ 81618 48614
Whitehorse Scutchamdy *Buckland Steeple*	75 85 57 44 15 50	} Buckland Steeple -	{ 41189 57115
Whitehorse Scutchamdy *Witney Steeple*	81 19 11 61 34 49	} Witney Steeple -	{ 57889 82007
Whitehorse Scutchamdy *Bampton Steeple*	90 57 40 48 27 50	} Bampton Steeple -	{ 58991 78799

Whiteham from Brill 68000,1 feet.

Whiteham Brill *Islip Steeple*	19 47 5 14 55 46	} Islip Steeple - -	{ 28983 36073
Whiteham Brill *Woodstock Steeple*	78 47 7 25 3 58	} Woodstock Steeple -	{ 27956 64785
Whiteham Brill *Kidlington Spire*	38 39 85 18 59 28	} Kidlington Spire -	{ 24677 47375

L 2

Whitehorse from Brill 146603,2 feet.

Triangles.	Angles observed.	Distances of the stations from the intersected Objects.	
Whitehorse - - - Brill - - - - - Witchwood Forest Beacon	48 10 15 40 32 9	} Witchwood Forest Beacon {	Feet 95439 105936

Broadway from Epwell 80611,4 feet.

Broadway - - - Epwell - - - - - Warwick Steeple	46 51 21 85 48 34	} Warwick Steeple - {	109337 79491
Broadway - - - Epwell - - - - - St. Martin's Spire, Coventry	49 43 19 100 10 39	} St. Martin's, Coventry - {	158205 126627
Broadway - - - - Epwell - - - - - Soleyhull Spire	71 17 32 74 13 55	} Soleyhull Spire - {	142027 139806

Corley from Arbury Hill 117463 feet.

Corley - - - - Arbury - - - - - Dun Church Windmill	10 17 47 18 1 45	} Dun Church Windmill {	70611 44249
Corley - - - - Arbury - - - - - Gazebo on Bardon Hill, Leicestershire	107 11 9 34 10 2	} Gazebo on Bardon Hill {	106471 180344
Corley - - - - Arbury - - - - - Markfield Windmill	100 41 54 36 37 10	} Markfield Windmill - {	103373 170170
Corley - - - - Arbury - - - - - Newnham Windmill	8 45 41 101 33 35	} Newnham Windmill - {	118771 5845

Corley from Broadway 171570 feet.

Broadway - - - - Corley - - - - - Building on Breedon Hill	96 31 27 14 13 9	} Building on Breedon Hill {	46201 192682

Epwell from Crouch Hill 29668.8 feet.

Triangles.	Angles observed	Distances of the stations from the intersected Objects.	
Epwell Crouch Hill Deddington Steeple	24 43 28 124 5 31	} Deddington Steeple · {	Feet. 47493 24000
Epwell Crouch Hill Bloxham Spire	21 1 57 69 57 20	} Bloxham Spire · {	3168; 11971
Epwell Crouch Hill Aynoe Steeple	12 41 59 155 28 33	} Aynoe Steeple · {	60070 31802
Epwell Crouch Hill Adderbury Spire	12 45 23 143 29 30	} Adderbury Spire · {	43823 16265
Epwell Crouch Hill Farthingo Steeple	9 33 29 162 29 20	} Farthingo Steeple · {	64520 35605

Epwell from Arbury Hill 83098.4 feet.

Epwell Arbury Hill Round House, Edge Hills	27 30 1 8 9 43	{ Round House, Edge Hills {	20235 65816
Epwell Arbury Hill St. Martin's, Coventry	50 9 8 87 15 6	} St. Martin's, Coventry {	122636 94802
Epwell Arbury Hill Round House Windmill, Edge Hills	28 31 46 7 34 6	} Round House Windmill {	18576 87304

Brill from Quainton 40908,5 feet.

Brill Quainton Wingrove Steeple	19 36 51 140 7 47	} Wingrove Steeple · {	75747 39605
Brill Quainton Hardwick Steeple	26 25 48 128 12 5	} Hardwick Steeple · {	55539 ? 19989.

Triangles.	Angles observed.	Distances of the Stations from the intersected Objects.	
			Feet.
Brill - - - - - Quainton - - - - *Luggersal Steeple*	18 42 12 4 24 16	} Luggersal Steeple -	{ 8710 11664
Brill - - - - Quainton - - - - *Granborough Steeple*	8 30 43 144 20 28	} Granborough Steeple -	{ 51166 13270
Brill - - - - Quainton - - - - *Bicester Steeple*	105 7 30 32 10 53	} Bicester Steeple -	{ 32152 58210
Brill - - - - Quainton - - - - *Centre of the Great Mouse at Wooton*	17 37 18 9 58 57	} House at Wooton -	{ 14793 87181

Stow from Broadway 52203,2 feet.

Stow - - - - Broadway - - - *Saruden Chapel*	113 23 50 19 25 13	} Saruden Chapel -	{ 18710 79115
Stow - - - - Broadway - - - *Walford Spire*	56 10 43 49 34 47	} Walford Spire -	{ 41895 45063
Stow - - - - Broadway - - - *Bourton Chapel*	14 3 44 31 32 40	} Bourton Chapel -	{ 18926 21786

Stow from Epwell 78938,2 feet.

Stow - - - - Epwell - - - - *Stow on the Wold Steeple*	60 30 30 6 37 9	} Stow on the Wold -	{ 9876 74573

Wendover from Brill 92400,7 feet.

Brill - - - - Wendover - - - *Pitchcot Windmill*	43 30 18 46 37 4	} Pitchcot Windmill -	{ 53739 50901

Triangles.	Angles observed.	Distances of the Stations from the intersected Objects.	
Brill Wendover Ivinghoe Spire	84 15 12 111 33 40	} Ivinghoe Spire	{ 9566 3 43571
Brill Wendover Padbury Steeple (doubtful)	66 36 4 46 31 33	} Padbury Steeple	{ 71943 91401
Brill Wendover Quainton Steeple	46 40 52 31 1 48	} Quainton Steeple	{ 39003 55056

Wendover from Quainton 72889.4 feet.

| Wendover
Quainton
Wing Steeple | 34 46 37
43 9 20 | } Wing Steeple | { 52487
42330 |
| Wendover
Quainton
Crindon Windmill | 44 58 11
61 9 54 | } Crindon Windmill | { 66472
53626 |

Quainton from Bow Brickhill 67400,6 feet.

| Quainton
Bow Brickhill
Souther Obelisk, Stow Park, Bucks | 75 15 34
47 19 1 | } Southern Obelisk | { 58876
77449 |
| Quainton
Bow Brickhill
Northern Obelisk, Stow Park | 71 4 46
69 13 49 | } Northern Obelisk | { 61881
78942 |

Wendover from Kinsworth 84563 feet.

| Kinsworth
Wendover
Leighton Buzzard Spire | 69 56 52
31 6 26 | } Leighton Buzzard | { 55317
84215 |

Kinsworth from Quainton 84996,3 feet.

| Kinsworth
Quainton
Aylesbury Steeple | 17 49 12
51 5 23 | } Aylesbury Steeple | { 70886
27879 |

Bow Brickhill from Lidlington 32035,6 feet.

Triangles.	Angles observed.	Distances of the Stations from the intersected Objects.	
			Feet.
Bow Brickhill Lidlington *North Crawley Spire*	57 43 11 65 40 39	} North Crawley Spire	{ 34968 32444
Bow Brickhill Lidlington *Pavenham Spire*	45 8 47 118 13 11	} Pavenham Spire	{ 77064 59014
Bow Brickhill Lidlington *St. Paul's Spire, Bedford*	24 15 15 137 19 11	} St. Paul's, Bedford	{ 68717 41652
Bow Brickhill Lidlington *Sharnbrook Spire*	48 2 42 111 8 15	} Sharnbrook Spire	{ 84080 67038
Bow Brickhill Lidlington *Woburn Market House*	38 42 47 19 39 30	} Woburn Market House	{ 10636 11533
Bow Brickhill Lidlington *Ridgemont Station*	5 3 35 10 8 1	} Ridgemont Station	{ 21484 10804
Bow Brickhill Lidlington *Wootton Spire*	15 51 19 116 31 15	} Wootton Spire	{ 46919 22869
Bow Brickhill Lidlington *Cranfield Spire*	36 40 14 64 51 16	} Cranfield Spire	{ 19599 19526

Lillyhoe from Lidlington 49026,1 feet.

Lillyhoe Lidlington *Pollux Hill Spire*	3 1 15 3 1 16	} Pollux Hill Spire	{ 24804 24469
Lillyhoe Lidlington *Bow Brickhill Steeple*	23 13 13 119 15 11	} Bow Brickhill Steeple	{ 70124 31738
Lillyhoe Lidlington *Colmworth Spire*	49 54 3 100 30 33	} Colmworth Spire	{ 97617 75944

Triangles.	Angles observed.	Distances of the stations from the intersected objects.	
Lillyhoo · · · · Lidlington · · · *Silsoe Spire*	83 57 30 12 4 36	} Silsoe Spire -	{ 25599 27658
Lillyhoe · · · Lidlington · · · *Flitton Steeple*	11 46 83 17 18 29	} Flitton Steeple -	{ 30008 20580
Lillyhoe · · · Lidlington · · · *Shillington Steeple*	57 56 38 19 37 7	} Shillington Steeple	{ 16857 42549
Lillyhoe · · · Lidlington · · · *Westoning Steeple*	14 35 14 24 29 56	} Westoning Steeple -	{ 32142 29586
Lillyhoe · · · Lidlington · · · *Wrest Garden Obelisk*	83 40 47 19 18 12	} Wrest Garden Obelisk	{ 23770 28880
Lillyhoe · · · Lidlington · · · *St. Neot's Steeple*	63 39 11 88 31 51	} St. Neot's Steeple -	{ 105026 94147

Kinsworth from Lidlington 61855.3 feet.

Triangles.	Angles observed.	Distances of the stations from the intersected objects.	
Kinsworth · · · Lidlington · · *Harlington Steeple*	17 4 20 83 33 2	} Harlington Steeple -	{ 37666 27565
Kinsworth · · · Lidlington · · *Maulden Steeple*	17 24 11 87 3 13	} Maulden Steeple »	{ 63165 18888
Kinsworth · · · Lidlington · · *Millbrook Steeple*	5 13 24 73 16 9	} Millbrook Steeple -	{ 60167 42622
Kinsworth · · · Lidlington · · · *Streatly Steeple*	36 15 30 33 41 7	} Streatly Steeple -	{ 36167 38567
Kinsworth · · · Lidlington - · · *Hanslop Spire*	34 29 11 166 4 4	} Hanslop Spire -	{ 111928 70552

M

Kinworth from Bow Brickhill 57668 feet.

Triangles.	Angles observed.	Distances of the Stations from the Intersected Objects.	
Bow Brickhill Kinsworth Souldrope Spire	131 31 20 30 17 44	} Souldrope Spire	Feet. 93229 138367
Bow Brickhill Kinsworth Sauldon Windmill	91 22 55 28 24 55	} Sauldon Windmill	31623 66434
Bow Brickhill Kinsworth Stewbley Windmill	70 9 33 33 17 4	} Stewbley Windmill	32706 55812
Bow Brickhill Kinsworth Tharfield Windmill	61 57 57 93 36 13	} Tharfield Windmill	139137 123073
Bow Brickhill Kinsworth Tottenhoe Station	4 13 44 14 47 37	} Tottenhoe Station	43177 13049
Bow Brickhill Kinsworth Chalgrave Steeple	22 55 14 43 21 54	} Chalgrave Steeple	43590 23699
Bow Brickhill Kinsworth Lidlington Windmill	85 34 3 27 23 29	} Lidlington Windmill	28814 62442
Bow Brickhill Kinsworth Keysoe Spire	116 44 10 41 6 4	} Keysoe Spire	10727 5 141830

Lillyhoe from Trodler Hill 50673.6 feet.

Lillyhoe Trodler Hill Knotting Green Elm Tree	51 56 21 103 29 55	} Knotting Green Elm Tree	118536 99981
Lillyhoe Trodler Hill Sundon Windmill	36 45 37 37 4 1	} Sundon Windmill	25602 33790

Bow Brickhill from Trusler Hill 20138,7 feet.

Triangles.	Angles observed.	Distances of the stations from the intersected objects.	
Bow Brickhill Trusler Hill *Crawley Steeble*	25 13 54 50 10 12	} Crawley Steeple -	{ 15998 8867
Bow Brickhill Trusler Hill *Moulsbor Steeple*	93 18 15 49 17 46	} Moulshoe Steeple -	{ 25136 33101
Bow Brickhill Trusler Hill *Woburn Steeple*	13 27 17 19 46 14	} Woburn Steeple -	{ 12432 8552

Bow Brickhill from Lillyhoe 69867 feet.

Bow Brickhill Lillyhoe *Renhold Steeple*	50 57 17 62 43 59	} Renhold Steeple -	{ 84608 79373
Bow Brickhill Lillyhoe *Ravensden Steeple*	64 55 32 66 41 24	} Ravensden Steeple -	{ 85925 84646

Kinsworth from Lillyhoe 47278,7 feet.

Kinsworth Lillyhoe *Fulwich Steeple*	43 44 48 71 53 53	} Fulwick Steeple -	{ 19849 35264

M 2

SECTION SECOND.

Determination of the Latitudes and Longitudes of the Stations on Black Down, in Dorsetshire, Butterton, in Devonshire, and St. Agnes Beacon, in Cornwall.

Art. xvi.—*Calculation of the Distance between Black Down and Dunnose in the Isle of Wight.*

To complete this distance, I shall have recourse to the xxvith and xxviith triangles, published in the Philosophical Transactions of 1795, and liiid and livth of the Trans. for 1797, together with the observations made at Black Down, in the latter year. (See also Pl. XXX. Fig. 1.).

The most eligible method of calculating with these *data,* seems to be that of first finding the *cross-distance* between Black Down and Dean Hill. To do this, we have the angle at Nine Barrow Down, between Black Down and Dean Hill, and the respective distances from the first to the latter stations, together with the newly observed angle between Dunnose and Nine Barrow Down; from which we obtain the angles of a triangle, constituted by Dunnose, Nine Barrow Down, and Black Down.

The distance from Nine Barrow Down to Dean Hill is 166497 feet, and, from the same station to Black Down, the distance is 106782 feet, (see Phil. Trans. for 1795, p. 502, and for 1797, p. 455,) and the angle comprehended by those distances = 110° 30′ 13″,25. The difference between the horizontal angle and that formed by the chords is 3″,25, which, substracted from 110° 30′ 13″,25, leaves 110° 30′ 10″: computing with this

angle and the sides spoken of, there results the following triangle, viz.

Nine Barrow Down -   110° 30' 10"
Black Down - -   40 6 54,75
Dean Hill - - - 29 22 55,75

This, using the side Nine Barrow and Dean Hill, (166497
feet,) gives 240236,7 feet, for the distance between Black Down
and Dean Hill.

The angle at Dean Hill, between Nine Barrow Down and
Dunnose, is 64° 50' 19", (see Phil. Trans. for 1795. p. 501,) and
the angle between Black Down and Nine Barrow, as just found,
is 29° 22' 55",75, which, increased by the proper correction for
the difference between the chord and horizontal angles, becomes
29° 22' 57",5. The sum of these angles ,94° 13' 16",5, is the horizontal angle between Black Down and Dunnose.

The angle at Black Down, between Dunnose and Nine Barrow Down, deduced from observations made in 1797, is found
to be 4° 30' 25",75: this, subtracted from the angle between
Dean Hill and Dunnose, leaves 35° 56' 29", for the angle at
Black Down; which, corrected for the purpose of reduction
to their respective chord angles, become 94° 13' 11",5, and 35°
56' 25",75, from whence we get the angle at Dunnose = 50°
10' 22",75. We have, therefore, the following triangle, viz.

Dean Hill - - - 94° 13' 11,5"
Black Down - - 35 56 25,75
Dunnose - - - 50 10 22,75

The distance between Dean Hill and Dunnose is 183496,2
feet, (Phil. Trans. for 1795, p. 501,) and that between Black
Down and Dean Hill, according to the foregoing computation, is
240236,7 feet: these, applied to the angles of the above triangle,

give 314309,6, and 314305,4 feet, respectively, for the distance between Black Down and Dunnose: wherefore, the mean 314307,5 feet, = 59,528 miles, may be considered as the true distance between those stations.

Direction of the Meridian at Black Down.

On the 18th of April, in the forenoon, the angle between the Pole Star, when at its greatest apparent elongation from the meridian, was observed, and found to be   -   104° 19′ 19″,25
And on the 19th, in the afternoon   -   98 42 47
Half their sum is the angle between the meridian and Abbotsbury staff - -   101 31 3
On the 20th of April, in the forenoon, the angle between the Pole Star, when at its greatest apparent elongation from the meridian, was observed, and found to be   -   104 19 25,25
And on the 19th, in the afternoon   -   98 42 35,5
Half their sum is the angle between the meridian and Abbotsbury staff   - -   101 31 0,5
Therefore, 101° 31′ 2″ may be taken for the angle between the meridian and Abbotsbury staff.

ART. XVII.—*Latitude and Longitude of Black Down.*

The angle between Dunnose and the Abbotsbury Staff was observed, and found = 164° 26′ 35″25; and the angle between the meridian and the same staff, by double azimuths of the Pole Star, 101° 31′ 2″. Wherefore their sum, subtracted from 360°, leaves 94° 2′ 22″,75, the angle which Dunnose makes with the meridian.

. In Fig. 4. Plate XXX, let Z be the zenith, B the station on Black Down, and ZBA its meridian; also, let D be Dunnose, and ZD its meridian; likewise, suppose BC to be an arc of a great circle, perpendicular to the meridian at B, and DA another arc of a great circle, perpendicular to the meridian at D, BF and ED being the parallels of latitude at Black Down and Dunnose.

In the spherical triangle BZD, the angles at B and D are given, the first being 94° 8′ 22″,75; and the second 84° 54′ 53″; therefore, in the triangle ABD the angle at B is 85° 57′ 36″,75, and, in the triangle BDC, the angle at D = 84° 54′ 53″ : hence, the angles of these triangles, when reduced to those formed by the chords, are as follows :

$$
\text{In the triangle BDC} \left\{
\begin{array}{l}
\text{BDC} = 84° 54′ 52,5″ \\
\text{CDB} = 91° \ 2 \ 44,75 \\
\text{CBD} = \ 4 \ \ 2 \ 22,75
\end{array}
\right.
$$

$$
\text{And in the triangle ABD} \left\{
\begin{array}{l}
\text{ABD} = 85 \ 57 \ 36,75 \\
\text{BAD} = 88 \ 57 \ 16,25 \\
\text{BDA} = \ 5 \ \ 5 \ \ 7
\end{array}
\right.
$$

Now the distance between Black Down and Dunnose, BD, has been already found to be 314307,5 feet; therefore, using the above angles with that distance, (after the proper corrections are applied for reducing the horizontal angles to those formed by the chords,) we get,

$$
\text{In the triangle BCD} \left\{
\begin{array}{l}
\text{BC} = 313128 \\
\text{CD} = 311476,9
\end{array}
\right\} \text{feet.}
$$

$$
\text{And in the triangle ABD} \left\{
\begin{array}{l}
\text{AD} = 313581,2 \\
\text{AB} = 27864,5
\end{array}
\right\} \text{feet.}
$$

Again, in the two small triangles formed by the parallels BF and ED, the perpendiculars B and DA, and the small arcs CF and AE, we have the angles at C and A given, the first being 91° 2' 45",75, and the last 88° 57' 15"; which angles, however, are augmented by the addition of the differences between the horizontal angles and those formed by the chords, We have therefore,

In the triangle BCF $\begin{cases} BCF = 91° \ 2' \ 45,75'' \\ BFC = 88 \ 25 \ 51,5 \\ FBC = 0 \ 31 \ 22,75 \end{cases}$

And in the triangle AED $\begin{cases} EAD = 88 \ 57 \ 17 \\ AED = 90 \ 31 \ 21,5 \\ ADE = 0 \ 31 \ 21,5 \end{cases}$

And, using BC and AD, as found above, we get

$\begin{cases} CF = 2859,1 \\ \text{And } EA = 2859,8 \end{cases}$ feet.

Therefore FD = DC + CF = 22146,9 + 2859,1 = 25006 feet. And BE = BA = EA = 27864,5 — 2859,8 = 25004,7 feet. The mean, 25005,3 feet, may be considered as very nearly the true distance between the parallels of Black Down and Dunnose. This method is the same as that made use of in the Phil. Trans. for 1795, p. 521, and affords the means of very accurately determining the distance between the parallels of latitude of the two stations, when the angles were observed with precision, and the direction in which the stations lie, is not much removed from east and west.

This small space, 25004,7 feet, corresponds to 4' 6",5, in which I use 60851 fathoms for the length of a degree of the meridian in 50° 41'. See Phil. Trans. for 1795, p. 537.

Now the latitude of Dunnose is 50° 37' 7",3, and its longitude 1° 11' 36"; (Phil. Trans. for 1795, p. 536;) therefore, 50° 37' 7"3 + 4' 6",5 = 50° 41' 13",8, is the latitude of Black Down.

This method of finding the latitude seems to be more correct than by spherical computation; yet, by this latter, nearly the same conclusion is derived; for, the bearing of Black Down west of Dunnose being 84° 54′ 52″,5, we get the distance of that station from the meridian of the latter = 313072 feet, and from the perpendicular, 27861 feet; which, converted into parts of an arch, according to the lengths of their respective degrees, gives 50° 41′ 14″ for the latitude, and 1° 20′ 46″,4 for the longitude west of Dunnose. According to the troublesome yet ingenious method recommended by M. SEJOUR, in his *Traité Analytique des Mouvemens apparens des Corps Célestes*, the latitude of Black Down comes out 50° 41′ 13″,9, and the longitude 1° 20′ 45″,75. We may, therefore, admitting the supposition of Dunnose being situated in 50° 37′ 7″,9, safely take 50° 41′ 13″,8 for the latitude, and 2° 32′ 22″,4 for the longitude, of Black Down; that of Dunnose being 1° 11′ 36″ west of the meridian of Greenwich.

ART. XVIII. *Calculation of the Distance between the Stations on Black Down, in Dorsetshire, and Rippin Tor, in Devonshire.*

For the calculation of this distance, we must have recourse to the XLVIIth, XLVIIIth, XLIXth, and Lth triangles. (See Philosophical Transactions for 1797, and Plate XXX, Fig. 1 of this Volume.) In the two first, we have the whole angle at Pilsden, between Dumpdon and Black Down = 152° 37′ 27″,25, which, reduced to the angle formed by the chords, becomes 152° 37′24″,25. The sides forming this angle, are Dumpdon and Pilsden, Pilsden and Black Down: the distance between the two first stations being 78459,3 feet, and between the two last 79110,7 feet. From these *data*, the distance between Dumpdon and Black Down is found to be 153095,7 feet, the triangle for computation being,

N

     Pilsden -   -   152° 37' 24",25
     Black Down -   13 37 50 ,5
     Dumpdon -   - 13 44 45 ,25

But this side may be also found, by computing with the whole angle at Charton Common, which angle, when reduced to the plane of the chords, becomes 141° 33' 53",75. The two sides are 58 1012,5 feet, and 103345 feet; which *data* give the following triangle:

     Charton -   -   141° 33' 53",5
     Dumpdon   -   24 48 39 ,25
     Black Down   -   13 37 27 ,25; from whence we find the distance from Dumpdon to Black Down = 153094,6 feet. Wherefore, the mean, 153095,2 feet, may be considered to be very nearly the true distance.

In the Lth triangle, (Cawsand Beacon, Dumpdon, and Little Haldon) the angle at Cawsand Beacon is 43° 14' 21",25; and in the LIst, (Rippin Tor, Cawsand Beacon, and Little Haldon) the angle at the same station is 25° 30' 39",75: their sum is 68° 45' 1", and, adding 1" for the necessary correction, it becomes 68° 45' 2". Computing with this angle, and the including sides, (64020,5 and 18394 feet,) we obtain the following triangle:

     Rippin Tor -   -   90° 34' 35"
     Cawsand Beacon   -   68 45 2
     Dumpdon -   -   20 40 23, which gives the distance from Dumpdon to Cawsand Beacon = 16901,4 feet.

In the XLIXth triangle, the observed angle at Dumpdon is found to be 86° 39' 8",5 and, by adding to it the horizontal angle at Dumpdon, between Rippin Tor and Little Haldon, and also that between Black Down and Charton Common, we get 125° 51' 30",5, for the horizontal angle between Rippin

Tor and Cawsand Beacon. To reduce this angle to that formed by the chords, 6" must be subtracted; therefore, 125° 54' 24".5 is the angle for computation. The sides Dumpdon and Rippin Tor, Dumpdon and Black Down, (16901 and 153095,2 feet,) with this angle, give the following triangle:

Rippin Tor - - 25° 26' 4",5
Dumpdon - 125 54 24.5
Black Down - 28 29 31, which gives the distance from Rippin Tor to Black Down = 286973,9 feet.

On referring to the observations made in 1797, on Black Down, it will be seen that the angle between Rippin Tor and the staff erected near Abbotsbury, was 3° 8' 52".5, and the angle between Pilsden and the same staff 45° 16' 13"; their difference, 42° 7' 20".5, is the angle between Rippin Tor and Pilsden. Now, if the angles of the triangles, five in number, used in finding the distance between Rippin Tor and Black Down have been observed correctly, and the calculations properly made, the computed angle at Blackdown, between those stations, should be, of course, the same; but the angle formed by the chords of the arcs between Blackdown and Pilsden and Dumpdon, has been found = 13° 37' 50".5, (which is very nearly the same as the horizontal one,) and the angle between Dumpdon and Rippin Tor = 28° 29' 31", which it is also unnecessary to correct: their sum is 42° 7' 21".5, the very angle observed. It is not, perhaps, proper to dismiss this consideration, without observing that this agreement affords a strong proof of the excellence of our instrument, as the triangles, from their magnitude and nature, are not so disposed as to favour the comparison. · ·

N 2

ART. XIX. *Latitude and Longitude of Rippin Tor.*

The angle at Blackdown, between the staff at Abbotsbury and the meridian, has been found = 101° 31′ 1″,5, nearly, and that between Rippin Tor and the same staff = 3° 6′ 52″,5; therefore, 98° 22′ 8″ is the angle which Rippin Tor makes with the meridian, and this, taken from 180°, leaves 81° 37′ 52″, the bearing of Rippin Tor SW from Black Down.

This angle, with the distance found above, gives 28585,3 feet, for the distance of Rippin Tor from the meridian of Black Down, and 56086,0 feet, for that from its perpendicular ; therefore, the latitude is 50° 33′ 59″,1, and the longitude west from Black Down, 1° 13′ 3″,8 ; consequently, its longitude west of Greenwich is 3° 45′ 26″,2.

Direction of the Meridian at Butterton Hill.

On the 6th of May, in the afternoon, the angle between the Pole Star, when at its greatest apparent elongation from the meridian, and the staff on Hemmerdon Ball was observed, and found to be   -   -   -   -   -   91° 29′ 13″75

And on the 7th, in the afternoon   -   -   97 4 14

Half their sum is the angle between the meridian and the staff on Hemmerdon Ball   -   94 16 44

Again, on the 7th, in the afternoon, the angle between the Pole Star, when at its greatest apparent elongation from the meridian, and the staff on Hemmerdon Ball was observed, and found to be   -   -   -   -   -   93 29 12

Half the sum of this, and the angle observed

in the forenoon of the same day, $(97° 4' 14'')$

is   -   -   -   -   - $94° 16' 43''$

Hence, $94° 16' 44''$ may be considered as the true angle between the meridian and the staff on Hemmerdon Ball.

The angle between the station on Rippin Tor and Hemmerdon Ball, is $121° 17' 7'',75$; therefore, $121° 17' 7'',75 - 94° 16' 44'' = 27° 0' 23'',75$, is the bearing of Rippin Tor, north-east of Butterton. This angle, with 62951 feet, gives $28585,2$ feet, and $56086,6$ feet, for the distance of Rippin Tor from the meridian and perpendicular; which, using 61182 and 60847 fathoms, for the lengths of degrees on the meridian and perpendicular, respectively become $4' 40'',9$, and $9' 13''$. Therefore, in the right angled spherical triangle BPT, (Plate XXX, Fig. 2,) in which B is Butterton, P the pole, T Rippin Tor, and R the point where the parallel to the perpendicular cuts the meridian, we have the co-latitude of T, or Rippin Tor, $= 39° 26' 0'',9$, and RT $= 4'$ $40'',3$, We have, consequently, cosine $4' 40'',3$: radius :: cosine $39° 26' 0'',9$: cosine $39° 26' 0'',7$, the co-latitude of the point R. So PR $=$ PR $+$ RT $= 39° 26' 0'',7 + 9' 13'' = 39° 35' 13'',7$; therefore, the latitude of Butterton is $50° 24' 46'',3$, and its longitude west from Greenwich, $3° 52' 47'',5$.

Art. xx. *Calculation of the Distance between Hensbarrow and Butterton.*

The most convenient, as well as the most accurate means of computing this distance, will be by referring to the LVIth, LVIIth, and LXIVth triangles, in the series of 1796, where the sum of the observed angles at Carraton Hill is $136° 52' 43''$. The correction for reducing this angle to that formed by the chords, is $4''$; therefore, $136° 52' 39''$ is the proper angle for computation.

The distance from Hensbarrow to Carraton Hill, is 100416 feet, and from Butterton to that station 131576 feet. (See Phil. Trans. for 1797, p. 458, 460.) These *data* give the following triangle, viz.

Carraton Hill	- -	136° 52' 39"
Hensbarrow	- -	24 35 57.5
Butterton	- -	18 31 23.5,

which gives 21602 feet, for the distance between Hensbarrow and Butterton Hill.

The angle between Carraton Hill and Rippin Tor was observed in 1796, and found = 101° 3' 44",25. (See Phil. Trans. 1797.) The angle between Hensbarrow and Rippin Tor is 119° 35' 3",25; therefore, 18° 31' 19" is the angle between Hensbarrow and Carraton. The difference between the horizontal and chord angle is 0",25 nearly; this, added to 18° 31' 23",5, gives 18° 31' 23",75, which is nearly the same as the observed angle. This agreement proves, that the angles of the triangles connecting Butterton and Hensbarrow have been observed correctly.

ART. XXI. *Latitude and Longitude of Hensbarrow.*

The angle between Hensbarrow and Hemmerdon, (see Observations made at Butterton,) was 1° 52' 4",5; therefore, as the angle between the latter and the meridian = 94° 16' 44", we get 92° 24' 39",5, for the angle which Hensbarrow makes with the same meridian. The distance from Hensbarrow to Butterton, as found above, is 21602 feet; this, with the angle 92° 24' 39",5, gives the distance of Hensbarrow from the meridian = 215871 feet, and from the perpendicular 9089 feet; these, converted into parts of degrees, become 35' 17",1, and 1' 29",62. Therefore, the latitude of Hensbarrow is 50° 23′ 3″,3, and its longitude, west of Butterton, 55′ 20″,2 ; consequently, its longitude, west of Greenwich, is 3° 52′ 47″,5 + 55′ 20″,2 = 4° 48′ 7″,7.

ART XXII.   *Direction of the Meridian at St. Agnes Beacon.*

On the 22d of May, in the forenoon, the angle between the Pole Star, when at its greatest elongation from the meridian, and the staff near Peranzabulo, was observed, and found to be   -   -   -   -   -   38° 26′ 1″,5
And on the 22d, in the afternoon   -   44 0 33,25
Half their sum is the angle between the meridian and staff   -   -   -   41 13 17,5

The angle between the staff at Peranzabulo and the station Hensbarrow, was also observed at the same station, and found to be 31° 50′ 55″,5 ; wherefore, 41° 13′ 17″,5 + 31° 50′ 55″,5 = 73° 4′ 13″, is the angle between Hensbarrow and St. Agnes Beacon.

ART. XXIII.   *To find the Latitude and Longitude of St. Agnes Beacon.*

In Plate XXX. Fig. 3. Let A be the station at St. Agnes, P the pole, H Hensbarrow, and B the point where the parallel to the meridian of St. Agnes cuts that meridian, BHP being a right angled spherical triangle on the earth's surface.

PH has been already found = 39° 36′ 56″,7 ; and, as BH, the distance of Hensbarrow from the meridian, = 92878, and AB, the distance from the perpendicular, = 28271, we get BH = 15′ 10″,9, and AB = 4′ 38″,8; which arcs are found by using 61182 and 60845 fathoms, for the length of their respective degrees. From these *data*, the latitude of the point B is easily derived; for cosine 15′ 10″,9 : radius :: cosine 39° 36′ 56″,7 : cosine 39° 36′ 54″,2, the co-latitude of B; hence 39° 36′ 54″,2 + 4′ 38″,8 = 39° 41′ 33″,0 the co-latitude of A; hence 50° 18′ 27″ is the latitude of St. Agnes. Its longitude, west from Hensbarrow, is also found by a simple proportion; sine 39° 36′ 54″,2 : radius :: sine 15′ 10″,9 : sine 0° 23′ 48″; therefore, 4° 48′ 7″,7 + 0° 23′ 48″ = 5° 11′ 55″,7, is the longitude of St. Agnes, west of Greenwich.

ART. XXIV.—*Remarks.*

I have shewn, with attention to minuteness, the manner in which the latitudes and longitudes of the stations on which directions of meridians have been observed are determined. It now remains to be considered, how far the uncertain state in which we remain, with respect to the figure of the earth, may affect the accuracy of those conclusions.

If the earth were homogeneous, it would necessarily be an ellipsoid; and, were its diameters known, the longitudes and latitudes of places on its surface might be accurately computed, provided their geodetical situations were correctly ascertained, and the latitude of one station in the series of triangles truly determined.

As there is, however, great reason to suppose that the earth is not any regular geometrical figure, from the impossibility of reconciling the results of the various measurements for ascertaining the lengths of degrees of latitude, some uncertainty must remain with respect to our deductions; but there seems to be reasons for supposing the errors, thence resulting, are confined within moderate limits.

In making computations on a given hypothesis of the earth's figure, the truth of the conclusions, as well as the ease with which they are found, materially depends on the distances of the objects from their respective fixed meridians.

If the difference of longitude approaches nearly to, or exceeds 9°, to compute that longitude, and also the latitude, it is necessary the precise figure should be understood; because the analogy does not hold good, in that case, between the equality of the sums of the angles of spherical and spheroidical triangles on the earth's surface. With regard to latitudes, more particularly when the distances are diminished by means of frequent new directions of meridians, a knowledge of the exact length of a degree of a great circle is not necessary; because the determination of those latitudes, by means of spherical computation, being true as to sense, the cosines of those small arcs will remain the same.

As there cannot be a doubt justly entertained of the latitude of Greenwich being very accurately determined, as particularly set forth by the Astronomer Royal in his reply to M. Cassini, it is reasonable to suppose, that if any errors do exist in the latitudes of those stations, they can only have arisen from the computations being made with erroneous lengths of degrees on the meridian.

In our former Papers on this subject, we have taken it for granted, that the length of a degree of the meridian at the middle point between Greenwich and Paris, (50° 10',) is 60842 fathoms, (which supposition may be considered just, provided the latitude of Paris, 48° 50' 14", be as near the truth as 51° 28' 40" is to that of Greenwich,) and afterwards added 9 fathoms,

O

making it 60851, in order to get the length of the degree in
50° 41'; (see Phil. Trans. 1795, p. 537;) these 9 fathoms,
however, were not arbitrarily assumed, but computed. If the
latitude of Paris be 48° 50' 15", (*Conn. des Tems,* 1797-98,
p. 373,) the length of the degree will be about 7 fathoms
greater, which will make the degree in 50° 41', 60849 instead
of 60849 fathoms.

The latitude of the station on Beachy Head, 50° 44' 23",7,
was found by using 60861 fathoms for the length of a degree
on the meridian in 51° 6'; but, if it be true that 48° 50' 15" is
the latitude of Paris, the latitude of Beachy Head will be about
one-third of a second greater. This seems to be the limit of the
probable error in the computed latitude of this station; since its
proximity to the meridian of Greenwich, obviates any doubt of
the conclusions being affected by any uncertainty respecting the
length of the degree of the great circle perpendicular to the
meridian.

The latitude of Dunnose was determined by computing the
distance between the parallels of that station and Beachy Head;
(see Phil. Trans. for 1795, p. 312;) which method is very exact,
and preferable to any other, since the small space between the
parallels was determined with great accuracy, leaving not a
doubt of a greater error than 9 feet, a quantity corresponding
to about $\frac{1}{17}$d part of a second. And, since the same method
has been adopted to find the difference of latitude between
Black Down and Dunnose, it is highly probable that the latitude of the former station is not removed more than $\frac{1}{10}$ths of a
second from the true one, that of Beachy Head being supposed
= 50° 44' 23",7.

It would have been fortunate, had the difference of latitude between Black Down and Butterton, and Butterton and St. Agnes Beacon, been determined in the same manner, since the latitudes of all these important stations would, in that case, have been found with evident accuracy; but, whoever has leisure and inclination to go through these calculations, will find that, by means of the directions of meridians at Butterton and St. Agnes Beacon, the latitudes of those stations may be found to within half a second. By this I mean, that, allowing the latitude of Black Down to be 50° 41′ 19″,8, the latitude of Butterton, 50° 24′ 46″,3, will not deviate more than half a second from the truth; and the same may be said with respect to the latitude of St. Agnes, that of Butterton being admitted as correct. Supposing, therefore, the latitude of Greenwich to be 51° 28′ 40″, we may rely on the assurance of the latitude of St. Agnes Beacon being determined within 1½″ of the truth.

With respect to the longitudes of these stations, their accuracy entirely depends on the observations made at Dunnose and Beachy Head, for determining the length of a degree of a great circle perpendicular to the meridian. The truth of the deduction drawn from those observations rests on their accuracy; and it can scarcely be deemed presumptuous to assert, that an error of more than 1″ cannot have existed in either of the angles. On this account, therefore, I should suppose, that the difference of longitude between those stations, has been found so nearly as to leave no greater error than 1″. The whole of the operation to which I now allude, was performed with great care; the directions of the meridians having been determined by means of double azimuths of the Pole Star, confirmed by computed azimuths. In returning to the consideration of this sub-

ject, I do not perceive any source of error likely to affect the
conclusions, unless it be that to which all astronomical observations, made with instruments adjusted by plumb-lines or levels,
are liable. In determining differences of longitude through these
means, the direction in which any lateral attraction must act,
to produce *a maximum* of error, is at right angles to the meridian. If the attraction be *in the plane of it*, it is obvious the
double azimuth, although the telescope of the theodolite does
not move in a vertical, will nevertheless give, almost exactly,
the true direction of the meridian.

The high lands about St. Catherine's Light-House, in the Isle
of Wight, are about six miles from Dunnose, and nearly west
of it; but it does not appear that the effect of their lateral attraction can have produced any sensible error; since it may be
shewn, that the plumb-line of the sector at Schehallien would
have deviated only a small part of a second from the true vertical, had the sector itself been placed at that distance from
the hill. Beachy Head is situated at the eastern extremity of
the South Downs; *a defect* of matter towards the east immediately taking place. This circumstance renders the observations liable to some small errors, on account of the superior
lateral attraction in the opposite direction; but, notwithstanding
it is very probable that an error induced by either of these
attractions, is so very small as to render the subject scarcely
worth consideration, yet, as both lie *the same way*, it is satisfactory to consider that they mutually tend to correct the errors
which may result from either; we may, therefore, safely conclude, that 1° 11' 36" is very nearly the true longitude between
the station on Beachy Head and that on Dunnose. Under this
persuasion, I consider it probable that the longitude of Black

Down cannot err in excess or defect more than 3″; that of Butterton 5″; and that of St. Agnes Beacon 6″.

The latitudes and longitudes of these important stations, brought under one point of view, will be as follows :

	Latitude.	Longitude west from Greenwich.	
		In degrees.	In time.
Black Down -	50° 41′ 13″,8	2° 32′ 22″,4	10′ 9″,5
Butterton Hill -	50 24 46,3	3 52 47,5	15 31,2
St. Agnes Beacon	50 18 27	5 11 55,7	20 47,7

Note. It may probably be expected, that I should determine the directions of the meridians at Black Down, Butterton Hill, and St. Agnes Beacon, by calculation, and afterwards compare them with the observed ones. I have desisted from the measure in the body of the work, and reserved the little I have to say for this note.

If the earth were a perfect sphere, or an ellipsoid of known diameters, the direction of the meridian, at any station not very remotely situated from the parallel of another, might be determined, provided the direction of the meridian at that station were observed, and the value of the arc subtended by the space between them pretty accurately ascertained, and also the latitude of the station, at which the angle is given, nearly obtained.

Thus, if it be required to find the angle at Dunnose, between Beachy Head and the meridian, from the observed angle at the latter station, and the arc between them, we shall have 39° 15′ 36″,3, the co-latitude of Beachy Head, and 55′ 28″,7 for the oblique arc. These data (two sides and an included angle) give 1° 26′ 48″,4, for the difference of longitude between Beachy Head and Dunnose, and 81° 56′ 52″,6, for the angle which the meridian at the latter makes with the former station. The difference of longitude found in a rather more correct way, has been heretofore shewn to be 1° 26′ 47″,93, (see Philos. Trans. 1795. p. 523.) and the angle at Dunnose was also shewn to be 81° 56′ 55″, from observation, which may be considered the same with that found by this mode of computation. In all cases in which the data were equally correct, no doubt the direction of meridians might be computed, without fear of the results deviating much from the truth ; but, if it be required to find the angle at Black Down, from the observed direction of the meridian at Dunnose, a different method must be used. It is, however, less accurate than the former one, and it has been expressly for this reason, that I have not introduced this subject into the account.

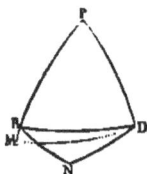

In the adjoining diagram, suppose B, Black Down; D, Dunnose; and, N, Nine Barrow Down: also, let PB, the meridian of Black Down, be prolonged to M, and DM be drawn, PM being = PD. Then we shall have three spherical triangles BPD, BND, and BMD. Now, the angle NBD was found from observations to be 4° 30′ 28″, and BND 172° 27′ 33″.5; these give the angle BDN = 3° 1′ 59″.5, nearly, because the excess of the three angles above 180° is 1″. The observed angle at D, Dunnose, between Nine Barrow Down and the meridian DP, or PDN, was 87° 56′ 53′; therefore, 87° 56′ 53′ — 3° 1′ 59″.5 = 84° 54′ 53″.5, is the angle at D, between the meridian and the station on Black Down.

Now, the difference of longitude between B and D, or the angle at P, has been already found = 1° 20′ 46″.4 ; and, since BP is very nearly = PD, and BD is small, we shall have rad. : tang. ½P :: cosine DP : cosine BMD = 8.° 26′ 47″. But the angle PDB has been found = 84° 54′ 53″.5 ; therefore, 85° 28′ 47″ — 84° 54′53″.5 = 4° 33′ 53″.5, the angle BDM ; hence, 180° 0′ 0″ — 94° 2′ 40″.5 = 85° 57′ 81″.5, or MBD ; therefore, 94° 2′ 38″.5, or DBP, is the angle at Black Down obtained in this way, which differs nearly 16″ from the observed one, viz. 94° 2′ 28″.75. It is probable, some portion of this arises from defects in the observation made at Dunnose, on the lights fired at Nine Barrow Down : only two lights were seen; and, as the observations differed 5″ from each other, some degree of doubt exists, as to the accuracy of the angle. The angle at Nine Barrow Down, between Black Down and Dunnose, is not absolutely to be depended on for purposes of this kind, although there can be no doubt of its being sufficiently near the truth, for that to which it has been before applied. In the correction of the angles at that station, in our former accounts, we proceeded on the supposition of their being less satisfactory than the other angles of the triangles to which Nine Barrow Down is a common station. For these reasons, I am of opinion the computed angle cannot be applied as a test to the observed one ; and it also appears to me, that greater objections lie against similar comparisons between the computed and observed angles at Butterton and St. Agnes; as those stations could not be seen from each other, nor the latter from Black Down. Although the computed directions of the meridians differ some seconds from the observed ones, I am by no means doubtful of the truth of the latter ; as the double azimuths of the Pole Star, found from computation, agree very satisfactorily with those which have been used in obtaining the directions of the several meridians.——In finding the value of the oblique arc, or the line which joins Black Down and Dunnose, as used in the first method of computation, I have had recourse to the following correct expression, viz.

$$d = \frac{p\,m}{p + m - p \cdot s}$$; where d is the length of the required degree, p that of the great circle perpendicular to the meridian, m that of a degree of the meridian itself, and s the sine of the angle constituted by the oblique arc and the meridian.

ART. XXV. *Bearings of the Stations in the Series of 1795 and 1796, from the Parallels to the Meridians of Black Down, Butterton Hill, and St. Agnes Beacon; likewise their Distances from those Meridians, and from their Perpendiculars.*

Meridian of Black Down.

Bearings from the Parallel to the Meridian.		Distance from merid.	Distance from perp.
		Feet.	Feet.
Bull Barrow -	Black Down	41 4 30 N E	53643.1	59489.7
Minterne - · · ·	10 36 33 N E	10996.8	58709
Pilsden - · · ·	56 14 48 N W	65775.6	43955.4
Charton Common - · ·	83 30 3 N W	102681	11697.5
Dumpdon - Charton Common	45 4 0 N W	143749	52670.9
Rippin Tor - · ·	81 37 52 6 W		

Meridian of Butterton.

			Distance from merid.	Distance from perp.
Rippin Tor · -	Butterton	27 0 23 N E	18585.3	56086.6
Furland · · ·	78 37 39 S E	78966.3	15883
Bolt Head · ·	14 49 48 S E	18551.3	70065.4
Maker Heights - ·	70 36 9 S W	71407.9	25264.3
Kit Hill - · ·	67 13 17 N W	93081.9	39121.7
Carraton Hill - · · ·	73 53 22 N W	126408.9	36511.3
Cawsand Beacon - Rippin Tor	35 35 19 N W	86744.4	108147.5
Little Haldon - Furland	4 15 3 N E	84571.4	56676.8
Biodown - · Maker	70 4 48 N W	52926.6	19180.1
Hensbarrow - · ·	87 35 18 S W	92878.0	28271.0

Meridian of St. Agnes Beacon.

Hensbarrow - St. Agnes Beacon		73 4 13 N E	92877.4	28179.9
Deadman - · · ·	73 14 17 S E	97292.5	30849
Karnbouellis - · ·	3 07 27 S W	7741.7	45379.2
Karnminnis - · · ·	61 13 58 S W	74168.1	40719
Bodmin } Lamalloy } - Hensbarrow {	37 30 45 N E	121703.2	65825.8
	75 29 51 S E	152046.3	12733.5
St. Burian - Karnborellis	67 80 59 S W	91831.5	83807.3
Pertinney - · Karnminnis	39 25 32 S W	100465.1	72704.4
Sennen - · Pertinney	40 50 18 S W	113674.4	879868

ART. XXVI. *Latitudes and Longitudes of the Stations in the Series*
of 1795 and 1796.

Meridian of Black Down.

Names of Stations.	Latitude.	Longitude from Black Down.	Longitude west of Greenwich.	
			In degrees.	In time.
	° ′ ″	° ′ ″	° ′ ″	m. s.
Bull Barrow - - -	50 50 59,5	0 13 53,2 E	2 18 29,2	9 14
Mintern - - -	50 50 52,8	0 8 50,8 R	2 29 31,6	9 98,1
Pilsden - - -	50 48 26,9	0 17 0,7 W	2 49 23,1	11 17,5
Charton - - -	50 43 6,1	0 26 30,5 W	2 58 52,9	11 55,6
Dumpdon - - -	50 49 47,2	0 37 12,1 W	3 39 34,5	14 38,3
Rippin Tor - - -	50 33 59,1	1 13 3,8 W	3 45 26,2	15 1,7
Meridian of Butterton Hill.		From merid of Butterton.		
Furland - - -	50 22 7,8	0 23 13,2 E	3 32 34,3	14 10,3
Little Haldon - - -	50 34 3,0	0 21 45,6 E	3 31 1,9	14 4,1
Cawsand Beacon -	50 48 30,14	0 2 14,3 W	3 55 1,8	15 40,1
Bolt Head - -	50 13 15,2	0 4 44,5 E	3 48 3,1	15 12,6
Maker - - -	50 20 36,56	0 18 18,2 W	4 11 8,7	16 44,3
Kit Hill - -	50 31 9,4	0 23 55,7 W	4 16 43,2	17 6,9
Carraton Hill - -	50 30 41,6	0 32 29,5 W	4 25 17,0	17 41,1
Windown - -	50 23 32,9	0 31 53,5 W	4 24 41,0	17 38,7
Hensbarrow - -	50 23 3,3	0 55 20,8 W	4 48 7,7	19 12,5
Meridian of St. Agnes.		From merid. of St. Agnes.		
Lanxallou - - -	50 20 25,7	0 39 10,5 E	4 33 45,7	18 11,0
Bodmin Down - -	50 29 11,6	0 31 15,9 E	4 40 30,8	18 43,8
Deadman - - -	50 13 20,0	0 24 31,3 E	4 47 4,4	19 8,3
Karnbrellis - -	50 10 39,4	0 0 42,0 W	5 12 37,7	20 50,5
Karnminis - - -	50 11 43,8	0 16 56,2 W	5 30 51,9	22 3,5
St. Burian - -	50 4 37,9	0 24 9,2 W	5 36 4,9	22 24,3
Pertinney - - -	50 6 27,0	0 35 36,2 W	5 37 31,9	22 30,1
Senven - - -	50 3 55,6	0 28 56,7 W	5 40 52,4	22 43,5

Art. xxvii. *Bearings of the intersected Objects, from the Stations in the Series of* 1795 *and* 1796, *from the Parallels to the Meridians of Black Down, Butterton Hill, and St. Agnes Beacon; and likewise their Distances from these Meridians.*

Meridian of Black Down.

Bearings from the Parallels to the Meridian.		Distances from merid.	Distances from perp.
At Hull Barrow.		Feet.	Feet.
Portland Light House -	19 47 16 S E	21581	59985
Nail Windmill - -	10 12 56 N E	72842	166029
Nail Steeple - - -	21 53 29 N E	86610	141534
Holy Trinity, - Shaftsbury	25 41 52 N E	81081	116506
St. Rumbold's Steeple, Ditto	28 12 51 N E	80486	109522
Maypowder Steeple - -	45 17 11 N W	29526	61479
Stourbrad House - - -	0 27 46 N W	52881	153800
Mr. Frampton's Obelisk -	10 3 4 S E	63585	3384
Mere Steeple - - -	6 40 55 N E	63893	146984
Mrs. Thornhill's Obelisk -	22 18 51 N W	40391	91778
Odcomb Spire - - -	70 25 0 N W	35474	91194
Milborne Port - - -	38 21 20 N W	20110	101865
At Black Down.			
Pinclaoll Flagstaff -	89 9 57 N W	25612	373
Lambert's Castle - -	65 17 36 N W	67269	30950
Lyme Cobb - - -	82 21 29 N W	89547	22015
At Pilsden.			
Golden Cups - - -	4 44 3 S W	68239	14109
Glastonbury Tor - -	14 19 23 N E	34314	167176
Bridport Beacon - -	8 19 55 S W	72199	91
Lord Rolle's Barn, near Sidmouth	64 34 38 S W	101743	26859
At Dumpdon.			
Naval Flagstaff, Whitlands -	32 45 10 S E	116249	9920
Catherstone Lodge - -	2 29 45 N E	140940	117631
Lord Lisburne's Obelisk -	46 47 34 S W	225502	34159
Sir J. de la Pole's Flagstaff -	52 3 42 S E	86622	8137
Honiton Steeple - -	12 24 9 S W	146681	39339
St. Mary Ottery Steeple -	42 21 56 S W	179904	13028
Sir Robert Palk's Tower -	38 56 2 S W	242012	6526

P

Meridian of Butterton.

Bearings from the Parallels to the Meridian.		Distances from merid.	Distances from perp.
At Little Holdon.		Feet.	Feet.
North Bovey	71 44 23 N W	43315	70889
Eastern Karn	56 27 52 N W	41145	85459
Western Karn	53 12 10 N W	40730	89472
West Down Beacon	63 59 14 N E	126152	76968
Woodley's Summer House	85 39 47 S W	29448	50555
Berry Head Flagstaff	10 22 16 S E	95740	4350
Brixen Steeple	2 29 4 S E	87435	9338
Ipplepen Steeple	22 15 0 S W	63413	17180
Three Barrow Tor	68 43 3 S W	8567	27209
Brent Beacon	56 11 17 S W	15460	10390
At Butterton.			
Chudleigh Steeple	44 4 44 N E	67683	69920
Froward Flagstaff	75 0 28 S E	84348	22587
Start Point Flagstaff	39 22 33 S E	56544	68897
Marlborough Steeple	16 42 32 S E	18439	61393
Bolt Head Flagstaff	14 57 7 S E	18739	70173
Mewstone, highest point	52 35 23 S W	49325	38108
Cupola, Hospital, Plymouth	76 47 30 S W	66891	11699
St. John's Steeple	79 34 44 S W	83991	15447
Saltash Steeple	89 37 12 S W	73727	489
Penlee Beacon	64 59 49 S W	69758	32532
Plymstock Steeple	73 46 15 S W	49117	14326
Statton Barn	64 43 53 S W	53870	25145
Mound Button	70 50 52 S W	38651	20370
Flagstaff, Plymouth Garrison	72 51 17 S W	37031	17591
New Church, Plymouth	75 25 49 S W	56511	14591
Old Church, Plymouth	75 1 56 S W	57505	13374
West Chimney, Governor's House	75 42 15 S W	64497	18455
Flagstaff on Mawal Wise	75 40 55 S W	65181	16652
Chapel, Plymouth Dock	77 33 24 S W	67040	14790
Obelisk, Crimhill Passage, Plymouth	74 7 9 S W	66728	18984
Mount Edgecumbe House	73 18 23 S W	65827	21001
Flagstaff, Maker Tower	70 53 41 S W	68214	23632
Naval Signal Staff, Maker Tower	70 54 3 S W	68332	23686
Eddystone Light House	46 1 27 S W	87190	84147
At Butterton.			
Stonehouse Steeple	65 32 37 S W	53078	24140
Penlinch Obelisk	45 17 40 S W	27480	27223
Flagstaff, Rame Head	65 3 44 S W	70933	33774
At Rippin Tor.			
Great Haldon	52 27 0 N E	72023	89479

Bearings from the Parallels to the Meridian.		Distance from merid.	Distance from perp.
At Maker.		*Feet.*	*Feet.*
Hemmerdon Ball	62 10 37 N E	27722	60277
Brent Tor	5 27 45 N E	62385	69820
Blackhouse Flagstaff	27 51 36 N E	64005	11045
Rame Steeple	20 20 12 S W	74588	33045
Chapel, Dockyard	23 6 30 N E	67042	14795
Flagstaff, Stakes Battery	88 9 5 S E	54178	25719
Windmill, Plymouth Dock	29 47 35 N E	65053	15549
At Kit Hill.			
St. Stephen's Steeple	19 29 31 S E	78182	1079
St. Ive Steeple	56 20 4 S W	11421	23047
Callington Steeple	43 0 14 S W	92219	33613
Linkinhorn Steeple	69 8 31 N W	111417	46105
St. Dominic Steeple	27 19 41 N E	89521	46050
South Petherwin Steeple	34 6 18 N W	115216	71807
South Hill	74 57 40 N W	108044	63142
St. Cleer Steeple	74 42 9 S W	133492	27795
At Carralan Hill.			
Cheese Rings	44 0 29 N W	131198	43540
Liskeard Steeple	13 19 39 S W	131133	15526
Landrake Steeple	46 1 2 S E	94263	3750
Duloe Steeple	15 23 3 S W	137913	5336
Menheniot Steeple	11 59 44 S E	131941	15479
Polperrow Flagstaff	20 8 3 6 W	138871	8521
Lord Camelford's Obelisk	48 33 15 S W	161992	5324
Botconnock Steeple	44 34 58 S W	158753	3692
Roach Steeple	66 30 33 S W	218318	3434
Roach Rock	63 58 15 S W	217204	3969

Meridian of St. Agnes.

At Lanlivery.			
Lanlivery Steeple	56 48 14 N W	119848	34388
Helmen Tor	53 55 17 N W	113618	41845
Mr. Treuaine's Summer House	67 21 40 S W	96548	10787
Gorran Steeple	58 55 59 6 W	95877	21647
Flagstaff, Dradman	51 46 44 S W	97059	31178
Gwineas Rocks	53 9 0 S W	106551	22037
At Hensbarrow.			
Fenddillon Steeple	2 26 59 N W	80918	97463
Stone, St. Braeg's Down	17 31 11 N W	81868	63145
St. Dennis Steeple	83 6 25 N W	77630	30114
Luxulian Steeple	73 43 28 S E	149787	11656
Gerrans Steeple	26 33 53 S W	55357	46773
St. Michael Carhayes Steeple	9 39 51 6 W	84768	19353

P 2

Bearings from the Parallels to the Meridian.	Distances from merid.	Distances from perp.
	° ′ ″	Feet.	Feet.
St. Kivern Steeple - -	17 6 7 S W	30611	93398
Flagstaff, Blackhead - -	34 50 36 S W	31214	104917
Windmill, near Fowey - -	67 2 44 S E	134747	10777
Menabilly House - -	60 16 48 S E	123516	10899
Old Tower at Polruan - -	64 44 37 S E	35892	7978
Flagstaff, St. Anthony's Head (D.*)	16 35 45 S W	48664	60038
At the Deadman.			
St. Veep's Steeple - -	39 4 29 N E	140246	21930
At St. Agnes.			
St. Columb Minor Steeple -	44 7 57 N E	40698	41950
Peranzabulo - -	41 54 34 N E	19354	21563
St. Eval Steeple - -	37 52 39 N E	50875	64632
Cubert Steeple - - -	42 26 53 N E	13773	15991
Flagstaff, Pendennis Castle -	34 19 23 S E	39999	58586
Windmill, St. Mawe's -	45 52 9 S E	48079	46642
Karnbre Castle - -	11 53 47 S W	6480	30760
Illugan Steeple - -	30 1 2 S W	11865	20537
St. Paul's Steeple - -	20 21 16 S W	58457	103660
Lord Dunstanville's House -	40 33 25 S W	19726	23050
Gwinear Steeple - -	39 33 34 S W	39578	47911
Cow and Calf - -	23 7 32 N E	37171	87014
Cumborn Steeple - -	30 16 51 S W	19881	34048
St. Erme Steeple - -	48 42 22 N E	44657	1009
St. Allen Steeple - -	85 13 35 N E	36688	3064
Ludguan Steeple - -	47 39 58 S W	64737	58976
At Karnboallis.			
Lizard Windmill - -	1 47 24 S E	573	114785
Grade Steeple - -	6 41 17 S E	5710	117451
Ruan Major Steeple - -	5 46 21 S E	1486	109496
St. Hilary Steeple - -	66 19 31 S W	49000	65664
Mr. Rogers's Tower, near St. Ives -	83 43 6 S W	18396	47103
Madern Steeple - -	76 53 40 S W	81542	63725
Parklough Flagstaff - -	6 55 11 S W	10735	111840
At Karunkauis.			
St. Buryan Steeple - -	25 45 25 S W	95205	84320
At St. Buryan.			
Chapel Karnbury - -	3 25 16 N W	95472	73098
Flagstaff, St. Leven's Point -	77 29 40 S W	114449	88158
Sennen Steeple - -	83 44 37 S W	122302	85712
At Pertinney.			
Stone, Land's End - -	48 5 30 S W	116882	86847

* The letter D is added (as in the former accounts) to those places respecting which any doubts are entertained.

ART. XXVIII. *Latitudes and Longitudes of such intersected Objects, in the Series of 1795 and 1796, as have been referred to the Meridians of Black Down, Butterton Hill, and St. Agnes.*

Names of Objects	Latitude	Longitude from Black Down	Longitude west of Greenwich. In degrees.	In time.
	° ′ ″	° ′ ″	° ′ ″	m. s.
Portland Light House -	50 31 22,2	0 5 32,9 E	2 16 49,5	9 47,3
Noil Windmill - -	51 8 29,3	0 18 58,7 E	2 13 23,7	8 53,6
Noil Steeple - -	51 4 17,6	0 22 31,8 E	2 19 50,6	9 19,3
Holy Trinity, - Shaftsbury	51 0 20,7	0 21 3,6 E	2 11 18.8	8 45,3
St. Rumbold's Steeple, Ditto	50 59 11,8	0 20 53,9 E	2 11 28,5	8 45,8
Maypowder Steeple -	50 51 19,7	0 7 18,6 E	2 24 43,8	9 38,9
Stourhead House - -	51 6 29,5	0 13 46,0 E	2 18 36,1	9 14,4
Mr. Frampton's Obelisk -	50 41 46,0	0 16 24,5 E	2 15 57,9	9 3,8
Mere Steeple - -	51 5 21,7	0 16 37,6 E	2 15 44,8	9 2,9
Mrs. Thornhill's Obelisk -	50 56 17,5	0 10 28,6 E	2 21 53,8	9 27,6
Odcomb Spire - -	50 56 12,6	0 9 11,1 W	2 41 34,1	10 46,3
Milborne Port - -	50 57 58,0	0 5 13,1 E	2 27 9,3	9 48,6
Pucknoll Flagstaff -	50 41 17,3	0 6 36,4 W	2 38 58,8	10 35,9
Lambert's Castle - -	50 46 17,7	0 17 23,1 W	2 49 45,5	11 19 .
Lyme Cobb - -	50 43 10,0	0 23 7, W	2 55 29,4	11 41,9
Golden Cape - -	50 43 38,5	0 17 37,2 W	2 49 59,6	11 20
Glastonbury Tor -	51 8 47,7	0 8 56,4 W	2 41 18,8	10 45,8
Bridport Beacon -	50 41 13,8	0 18 37,6 W	2 50 59,9	11 24
Ld. Rolle's Barn. near Sidmouth	50 45 35,6	0 26 17,1 W	2 58 39,6	11 54,6
Naval Flagstaff, Whitlands	50 43 47,7	0 30 0,4 W	3 2 22,8	12 9,5
Catherstone Lodge -	51 0 23,0	0 36 36,6 W	3 8 59,0	11 35,9
Lord Lisburne's Obelisk -	50 37 1,3	0 58 5,6 W	3 30 28,1	14 1,9
Sir J. de la Pole's Flagstaff -	50 43 31,9	0 11 21,4 W	2 54 43,8	11 38,9
Honiton Steeple - -	50 47 35,5	0 37 55,7 W	3 10 18,1	12 41,2
St. Mary Ottery Steeple -	50 43 18,9	0 46 26,8 W	3 18 49,2	13 15,3
Sir Robert Palk's Tower -	50 29 52,5	1 2 24,6 W	3 34 47,	14 19,1

Meridian of Butterton Hill.

Names of Objects	Latitude.	Longitude from Butterton Hill.	Longitude west of Greenwich.	
			In degrees.	In time.
	° ′ ″	° ′ ″	° ′ ″	m. s.
North Bovey Steeple (n.) -	50 36 18.7	0 11 9.3 E	3 41 38.1	14 46.5
Eastern Karn - -	50 38 48.4	0 10 36.3 E	3 42 11.8	14 48.7
Western Karn - -	50 39 87.9	0 10 30.1 E	3 42 17.6	14 49.1
West Thorn Beacon -	52 37 80.5	0 12 30.0 E	3 20 17 5	13 21.1
Woodley's Summer House	50 33 4.5	0 7 34.5 E	3 45 13	15 0.9
Flagstaff, Berry Head, Torbay	50 24 0.7	0 24 33.1 E	3 28 14.4	13 52.9
Brixen Steeple - -	50 23 12	0 22 24.8 E	3 30 22.7	14 1.5
Ipplepen Steeple - -	50 27 14.2	0 17 33.8 E	3 35 13.7	14 20.9
Three Barrow Tor - -	50 29 13.5	0 2 13.1 E	3 50 34	13 22.3
Brent Beacon, near Ashburton	50 26 28.6	0 3 58.1 E	3 48 49.4	15 11.3
Chudleigh Steeple -	50 36 14.1	0 17 25.9 E	3 35 22.6	14 81.4
Froward Flagstaff -	50 21 1.4	0 21 36.3 E	3 31 11.2	14 4.7
Flagstaff, Start Point -	50 13 25.9	0 14 20.7 E	3 38 20.4	14 33.6
Marlborough Steeple -	50 14 40.7	0 4 42.5 E	3 48 5.0	15 11.3
Flagstaff, Bolt Head -	50 13 14.1	0 4 47.2 E	3 48 0.3	15 12
Newstone, highest point -	50 18 27.7	0 12 45.1 W	4 5 38.6	16 21.1
Cupola of Plymouth Hospital	50 22 10.1	0 17 8.5 W	4 9 56.1	16 39.7
St John's Steeple (n.) -	50 22 11.8	0 21 31.4 W	4 14 18.9	16 57.2
Saltash Steeple - -	50 24 39.8	0 18 14.3 W	4 11 41.8	16 47.8
Penlee Beacon - -	50 19 24	0 17 52.6 W	4 10 40.1	16 42.7
Plymstock Steeple - -	50 22 84.2	0 12 36.8 W	4 5 24.3	16 21.6
Statton Barn - -	50 20 37.4	0 11 38.6 W	4 6 26.1	16 15.7
Mount Batten - -	50 31 24.3	0 15 1.6 W	4 7 49.1	16 31.1
Flagstaff, Plymouth Garrison	50 21 21.8	0 14 36.5 W	4 7 24.0	16 29.6
New Church, Plymouth -	50 22 20.4	0 14 29.0 W	4 7 16.5	16 29.1
Old Church, Plymouth -	50 22 13.6	0 14 44.1 W	4 7 31.6	16 30.1
Eddystone Light House -	50 10 54.5	0 22 15.4 W	4 15 2.9	17 0.3
West Chimney, Governor's House, Plymouth Dock -	50 22 2.9	0 16 31.6 W	4 9 19.1	16 37.2
Flagstaff, Mount Wise -	50 22 0.7	0 16 43.7 W	4 9 31.8	16 38.1
Chapel, Plymouth Dock -	50 22 19	0 17 10.8 W	4 9 58.3	16 39.9
Obelisk, Crimhill Passage	50 21 37.7	0 17 5.8 W	4 9 53.3	16 39.5
Mount Edgecumbe House	50 21 17.9	0 16 51.8 W	4 9 39.3	16 38.6
Flagstaff, Maker Tower -	50 20 51.8	0 17 28.5 W	4 10 16.0	16 41.1
Naval Flags, near Maker Tower	50 20 51.9	0 17 28.6 W	4 10 16.1	16 41.1
Stonehouse Steeple -	50 20 47.4	0 13 35.7 W	4 6 23.2	16 25.5
Purlinch Obelisk -	50 20 17.5	0 7 2.6 W	3 59 50.1	15 59.3
Rame Head - -	50 18 52.7	0 19 41.5 W	4 12 29.0	16 49.9
Great Holdon - -	50 39 27	0 28 34.2 W	3 34 13.3	14 16.9
Hemmerdon Ball -	50 21 21.2	0 7 6.9 W	3 59 53.6	15 59.5
Brent Tor - -	50 36 13.4	0 16 33.9 W	4 9 21.4	16 37.4
Flagstaff, Blockhouse, Plymouth	50 22 56.4	0 16 24.4 W	4 9 11.8	16 36.8

Name of Objects.	Latitude.	Longitude from Butterton Hill.	Longitude west of Greenwich. In degrees.	In time.
	° ′ ″	° ′ ″	° ′ ″	m. s.
Rame Steeple - -	50 19 16.7	0 37 59.8 W	4 30 47.3	18 3.1
Flagstaff, Statton Battery	50 20 31.8	0 13 54.2 W	4 6 41.0	16 26.9
Windmill, Ply mouth Dock	50 22 11.6	0 12 54.2 W	4 9 41.7	16 38.6
St. Stephen's Steeple -	50 24 15.1	0 20 3.0 W	4 12 50.5	16 51.3
St. Ive Steeple - -	50 28 49	0 29 20.2 W	4 22 7.7	17 28.5
Linkinghorn Steeple -	50 31 17.3	0 28 39.2 W	4 21 26.7	17 25.9
St. Dominic Steeple (o.)	50 32 17.8	0 23 1.2 W	4 15 48.7	17 3.2
South Petherwin Steeple -	50 36 3.4	0 29 40.4 W	4 22 27.5	17 29.8
South Hill Steeple -	50 31 43.3	0 27 46.9 W	4 20 31.4	17 22.1
St. Cleer Steeple - -	50 29 15	0 34 33.1 W	4 27 20.6	17 49.4
Callington Steeple -	50 30 14.9	0 25 14.4 W	4 18 1.9	17 12.1
Cheese Rings - -	50 31 50.5	0 34 14.9 W	4 27 2.4	17 48.1
Liskeard Steeple - -	50 27 14.4	0 33 55.5 W	4 26 43.0	17 45.9
Landrake Steeple -	50 25 20.7	0 23 41.3 W	4 16 30.8	17 6
Duloe Steeple -	50 23 48.0	0 35 31.9 W	4 28 9.4	17 52.6
Menheniot Steeple -	50 27 14.5	0 31 18.3 W	4 24 5.8	17 36.4
Polperrow Flagstaff -	50 25 5.5	0 35 37.4 W	4 28 24.9	17 53.6
Lord Camelford's Obelisk	50 23 11.1	0 42 4.0 W	4 34 51.7	18 19.4
Bocconnoch Steeple -	50 25 15.3	0 40 43.7 W	4 33 31.1	18 14.1
Roach Rock - -	50 23 53.4	0 55 41.8 W	4 48 29.4	19 13.9
Roach Steeple - -	50 23 58.7	0 55 59.1 W	4 48 40.6	19 15.1

Meridian of St. Agnes.

Names of Objects.	Latitude.	Longitude from St. Agnes Beacon.	Longitude west of Greenwich. In degrees.	In time.
	° ′ ″	° ′ ″	° ′ ″	m. s.
Lanlivery Steeple -	50 24 1.9	0 30 44.0 E	4 41 11.7	18 44.8
Helston Tor -	50 25 9.9	0 29 11.9 E	4 42 43.8	18 50.9
Mr. Tremaine's Summer House	50 16 37.8	0 24 41.6 E	4 47 14.1	19 8.9
Gorran Steeple - -	50 14 50.8	0 24 30.4 E	4 47 25.3	19 9.6
Flagstaff, Deadman -	50 13 15.8	0 24 47.7 E	4 47 8.0	19 8.5
Gwineas Rocks - -	50 14 46.3	0 27 14.1 E	4 44 41.6	18 58.6
Hendellian Steeple -	50 34 25.6	0 23 8.5 E	4 48 47.2	19 15.1
Stoke, St. Brag's Down -	50 28 47.6	0 43 1.7 E	4 50 54.0	19 23.6
St. Dennis Steeple -	50 23 22.1	0 19 54.2 E	4 52 2.6	19 28.1
St. Michael Cathayes Steeple	50 25 14.0	0 21 40.5 E	4 50 15.5	19 21
St. K veen Steeple -	50 3 5.8	0 7 47.5 E	5 4 8.2	20 16.5
Flagstaff, Brackhead -	50 1 12.1	0 7 56.4 E	5 3 59.3	20 15.9
Windmill, near Fowry -	50 20 7.2	0 34 24.2 E	4 37 31.5	18 30.1
Menabilly House -	5 20 9.9	0 30 37.8 E	4 40 17.9	18 4.11
Old Tower of Folruan -	50 1 40.1	0 34 47.7 E	4 37 8.0	18 26.5
Flagstaff, St. Anthony's Head	50 8 34.1	0 12 24.7 E	4 59 31.0	19 58.1
St. Veep's Steeple -	50 21 67.5	0 33 54.7 E	4 36 1.0	18 24.1
St. Columb Minor Steeple	50 25 20.1	0 10 26.4 E	5 1 29.3	20 5.9
Perranzabulo - -	50 21 59.1	0 4 57.6 B	5 6 56.2	20 27.9

114   *The Account of a*

Names of Objects	Latitude.	Longitude from St. Agnes Beacon.	Longitude west of Greenwich. In degrees.	In time.
St. Eval Steeple -	50 29 3,5	0 12 54,9 E	4 59 0,8	19 56
Cubert Steeple - -	50 22 43,0	0 6 3,6 E	5 5 50,1	20 23,3
Flagstaff, Pendennis Castle	50 8 48,7	0 10 12,1 E	5 1 43,6	20 6,9
Windmill, St. Mawes -	50 10 46,3	0 12 16,3 E	4 59 39,4	19 58,6
Karnbre Castle - -	50 13 23,6	0 1 39,3 W	5 13 35,0	20 54,3
Illugan Steeple -	50 15 4,4	0 3 1,9 W	5 14 57,6	20 59,8
St. Paul's Steeple -	50 1 24,3	0 9 47,0 W	5 21 42,7	21 26,8
Lord Dunstanville's House	50 14 39,4	0 5 3,5 W	5 16 58,1	21 7,8
Lansallos Steeple -	50 20 15,3	0 38 16,2 E	4 33 39,5	18 14,6
Gerrans Steeple -	50 10 44,8	0 14 7,7 E	4 57 48,0	19 51,2
Gwinear Steeple - -	50 10 34,	0 10 6,0 W	5 22 1,7	21 28,1
Cow and Calf - -	50 32 44,9	0 9 33,7 E	5 2 22,0	20 9,5
Camborn Steeple -	50 12 51,0	0 5 4,7 W	5 17 0,4	21 8
St. Erme Steeple -	50 18 36,3	0 11 25,7 E	5 0 30,0	20 2
St. Allen Steeple - -	50 18 56,8	0 9 23,6 E	5 2 32,1	20 10,1
Ludguan Steeple -	50 8 44,1	0 18 30,7 W	5 28 26,4	21 53,8
Windmill, Lizard -	49 59 35,1	0 0 8,7 E	5 12 4,4	20 48,3
Grade Steeple - -	49 59 8,8	0 1 27,1 E	5 10 22,6	20 41,9
Ruan Major Steeple -	50 0 27,2	0 0 22,6 E	5 11 29,1	20 45,9
St. Hilary Steeple -	50 7 38,7	0 12 29,7 W	5 24 25,4	21 37,7
Mr. Rogers's Tower -	50 10 42,4	0 4 41,7 W	5 16 37,4	21 6,5
Madern Steeple - -	50 7 56,6	0 20 47,5 W	5 32 43,2	22 10,9
Park Lough Flagstaff	50 0 9,9	0 2 43,8 W	5 14 39,5	20 58,6
Inard Flagstaff -	49 57 55,8	0 0 38,1 E	5 11 17,7	20 45,2
St. Buryan Steeple -	50 4 32,8	0 24 14,8 W	5 36 10,5	22 24,7
Karnbury Chapel -	50 6 23,5	0 24 19,9 W	5 36 15,5	22 15
St Leven's Point, Flagstaff	50 3 53,8	0 29 8,5 W	5 41 4,3	22 44,3
Sennen Steeple - -	50 4 18,0	0 28 36,6 W	5 40 29,9	22 41,9
Stone, Land's End -	50 4 6,6	0 29 35,8 W	5 41 31,5	22 46,1

Notwithstanding almost the whole of the above latitudes and longitudes belong to objects near the sea coast, yet I have distinguished those which are actually upon it, from those more remotely situated, by *Italics.*

ART. XXIX. *Bearings of the Stations in the Series of 1797 and 1798, from the Parallels to the Meridians of Black Down, Butterton Hill, and St. Agnes Beacon ; and likewise their Distances from those Meridians*

Meridian of Black Down.

Names of the Stations.		Bearings.	Distances from merid.	Distances from perp.
		° ′ ″	Fath.	Fath.
Pilsden -	} Moor Lynch -	2 33 59 NW	71070	162067
Ash Beacon -		59 52 59 NW		
Mintern -	} Ash Beacon -	5 17 18 NW	5544	117624
Moor Lynch -		59 53 1 SE		
Bull Barrow -	} Long Knoll -	1 2 34 NE	55557	164653
Ash Beacon -		46 45 33 NE		
Pilsden -	} Danton -	12 40 33 NE	41564	145377
Moor Lynch -		53 17 35 SE		
Moor Lynch -	} Mendip -	66 3 36 NE	1621	194072
Ash Beacon -		3 23 1 NW		
Long Knoll -	} Beacon Hill -	82 28 4 NE	189665	182386
Wingreen -		50 16 41 NW		
Long Knoll -	} Westbury -	39 44 34 NE	91715	209344
Mendip -		80 32 31 NE		
Westbury -	} Farley Down -	35 44 37 NW	57751	157920
Dundry -		88 51 23 SE		
Mendip -	} Dundry -	18 59 1 NW	81488	259303
Farley Down -		88 51 22 NW		
Mendip -	} Lamsdown -	22 4 57 NE	32440	271514
Dundry -		77 26 41 NE		

Meridian of Butterton Hill.

Names of the Stations.		Bearings.	Distances from merid.	Distances from perp.
Carraton Hill -	} St. Stephen's -	45 55 47 NE	111457	87635
Kit Hill -		21 40 9 NW		
Carraton Hill -	} Black Down -	64 12 55 NE	31797	72551
St. Stephen's -		76 2 28 SE		

Meridian of St. Agnes Beacon.

Names of the Stations.		Bearings.	Distances from merid.	Distances from perp.
St. Agnes Beacon	} Trevose Head -	45 56 12 NE	41858	88250
Henabarrow -		39 49 34 NW		
Trevose Head -	} Cadon Barrow -	63 14 41 NE	119364	126702
Bodmin Down -		3 11 51 NW		
Bodmin Down -	} Brown Willy -	28 46 20 NE	142745	104165
Cadon Barrow -		46 1 41 SE		

Q

ART. XXX. *Bearings of the Stations in the Series of* 1799, *from the Parallels to the Meridians of Dunnose and Greenwich; and likewise their Distances from those Meridians.*

Meridian of Dunnose.

Names of the Stations.		Bearings	Distance from merid.	Distance from perp.
		° ′ ″	Feet.	Feet.
Highclere	Bagshot Heath	81 40 54 NE	108275	274173
	Nuffield	35 30 40 NE	36747	351450
	White Horse Hill	27 47 37 NW	83796	349533
	Stow on the Wold	14 19 27 NW	114915	409942
	Brill	50 16 17 NE	11955	443235
White Horse Hill	Shotover Hill	53 30 7 NE	3063	413801
	Scutchamfly	84 15 51 SE	32776	344558
	Whitcham Hill	36 30 13 NE	32054	410801
Stow on the Wold	Broadway	33 3 55 NW	143396	513693
Shotover Hill	Epwell	39 34 55 NE	64617	530781
Epwell	Cumner Hill	76 36 3 SW	25416	407209
	Corley Hill	6 39 56 NW	81312	673637
	Arbury Hill	48 5 23 NE	8776	5M288
Brill	Crouch Hill	39 20 49 NW	36102	521584
	Quainton	61 40 13 NE	64963	462648

Meridian of Greenwich.

Nuffield	} Wendover	{ 44 48 19 NB	} 174338	109986
Brill		{ 65 49 3 SE		
Brill	} Bow Brickhill	{ 56 46 9 NE	} 151413	190493
Arbury Hill		{ 54 50 52 SE		
Brill	} Kinsworth	{ 85 8 30 NE	} 130910	141562
Bow Brickhill		{ 31 55 51 SB		
Bow Brickhill	} Lillyhoe	{ 74 6 27 SB	} 84215	171367
Kinsworth		{ 50 54 40 NE		
Bow Brickhill	} Lidlington	{ 67 24 37 NE	} 131834	201802
Lillyhoe		{ 50 6 55 NW		
Bow Brickhill	} Trusler Hill	{ 89 1 15 SE	} 131378	190151
Lillyhoe		{ 68 14 72 NW		

ART. XXXI. *Latitudes and Longitudes of the Stations in the Series of 1797 and 1798, referred to the Meridians of Black Down, Butterton Hill, and St. Agnes Beacon.*

Meridian of Black Down.

Names of the Stations.	Latitude.	Longitude from Black Down.	Longitude west of Greenwich. In degrees.	In time.
	° ′ ″	° ′ ″	° ′ ″	m. t.
Moor Lynch	51 7 50,2	0 18 30,6 W	3 50 53	11 23,5
Ash Beacon	51 0 33,5	0 1 26,4 E	3 30 56	10 3,7
Long Knoll	51 8 10,2	0 14 68,3 E	2 17 54,1	9 11,6
Dundon	51 3 6,4	0 11 10,7 W	2 43 33,1	10 54,2
Mendip	51 13 7,2	0 0 15,9 E	2 32 6,5	10 8,4
Beacon Hill	51 11 1,6	0 49 80,6 E	1 43 1,8	6 52,2
Westbury	51 15 35,3	0 84 13 E	3 8 9,4	8 32,6
Farley Down	51 13 35,7	0 13 7,6 E	3 17 14,8	9 8,9
Dundry	51 23 38,2	0 5 17,7 W	3 38 0,1	10 32,0
Lansdown	51 17 50,4	0 8 30,6 E	2 83 51,8	9 35,9

Meridian of Butterton Hill.

Names of the Stations.	Latitude.	Longitude from Butterton Hill.	Longitude west of Greenwich. In degrees.	In time.
	° ′ ″	° ′ ″	° ′ ″	m. t.
St. Stephen's	50 32 6,7	0 28 59,6 W	4 81 47,1	17 27,1
Black Down	50 36 40,9	0 13 20,5 W	4 6 8,0	16 24,5

Meridian of St. Agnes Beacon.

Names of the Stations.	Latitude.	Longitude from St. Agnes Beacon.	Longitude west of Greenwich. In degrees.	In time.
	° ′ ″	° ′ ″	° ′ ″	m. t.
Trevose Head	50 32 56,5	0 11 1,5 E	5 0 54,2	20 3,6
Cudon Barrow	50 30 18,1	0 30 46,5 E	4 41 9,2	18 44,6
Brown Willy	50 35 27,9	0 36 15,3 E	4 35 10,4	18 20,6

ART. XXXII. *Latitudes and Longitudes of the Stations in the Series of* 1799, *referred to the Meridians of Dunnose and Greenwich.*

Meridian of Dunnose.

Names of the Stations.	Latitude.	Longitude from Dunnose.	Longitude west of Greenwich. In degrees.	In time.
	° ′ ″	° ′ ″	° ′ ″	m. s.
Nuffield	51 34 52.2	0 9 39.9 E	1 1 56.1	4 7.7
White Horse Hill	51 34 31.6	0 22 1.7 W	1 33 37.7	6 14.5
Stow on the Wold	51 54 16.3	0 30 26.7 W	1 42 2.4	6 48.1
Broadway	52 1 25.2	0 38 5.3 W	1 49 41.3	7 18.7
Brill	51 49 56.6	0 7 39.4 E	1 3 56.6	4 15.7
Southampfly	52 33 44.1	0 8 37 W	1 40 13.0	5 20.6
Shotover Hill	51 45 6.7	0 0 48.5 E	1 10 47.5	4 43.1
Whittsham Hill	51 46 15.4	0 8 28.1 W	1 19 48.1	5 19.2
Cumner Hill	51 44 1.5	0 6 41.4 W	1 18 18.4	5 13.2
Epwell	52 4 19.8	0 17 10.8 W	1 28 46.8	5 55.1
Corley Hill	52 30 28.3	0 9 39.9 W	1 21 15.9	5 25.0
Arbury Hill	52 13 26.6	0 0 44.4 W	1 12 20.4	4 49.1
Crouch Hill	52 2 58.7	0 9 35.6 W	1 21 11.6	5 24.7
Quainton	51 53 7.2	0 17 12.1 E	0 54 23.9	3 37.6

Meridian of Greenwich.

Names of the Stations.	Latitude.	Longitude west of Greenwich. In degrees.	In time.
	° ′ ″	° ′ ″	m. s.
Wendover	51 45 6.0	0 46 1.4	3 4.1
Bow Brickhill	51 59 50.5	0 40 1.8	2 44.1
Kinsworth	51 52 50.6	0 31 59.9	2 7.9
Lillyhoe	51 56 46.5	0 22 19.5	1 29.3
Lidlington	52 1 54.0	0 32 21.7	2 9.4
Trusler Hill	51 59 48.0	0 34 50.5	2 19.3

ART. XXXIII. *Bearings of intersected Objects, from the Stations in the Series of 1797 and 1798, from the Parallels to the Meridians of Black Down, Butterton Hill, and St. Agnes Beacon ; and likewise their Distances from those Meridians.*

Meridian of Black Down.

Bearings from the Parallels to the Meridian.		Distances from merid.	Distances from perp.
At Moor Lynch.		Feet.	Feet.
Walton Windmill	75 12 31 S E	51340	150858
Westonzoyland Steeple	63 42 36 S W	46028	154135
Middlezoy Steeple	31 48 21 S W	79339	148733
Chedzoy Steeple	85 18 45 N W	90459	103058
Higham Windmill	49 57 17 S E	58858	140880
Higham Steeple	22 51 39 S E	62691	142196
Bridgewater Spire	48 39 25 N W	104717	101080
Somerton Steeple	47 4 54 S E	41197	134898
Burton Pynsent Obelisk	10 35 4 S W	78428	122688
At Dundry.			
Puckle Steeple	55 19 25 N E	26010	298363
Westleigh Steeple	46 49 43 N E	23610	301818
Bristol Cathedral	26 7 30 N E	11836	279164
Redcliff Steeple	33 8 32 N E	9407	276007
Long Ashton	0 51 38 N W	21696	273385
Clifden Windmill	9 52 50 N E	19181	272472
Ware Castle	1 49 16 N E	20268	297874
Penpole Park Obelisk	11 43 37 N W	28680	296155
Duke of Beaufort's House, Stoke	3 31 31 N E	651	294818
Durham Steeple	63 28 33 N E	38049	289219
Knowle Steeple	13 41 30 N E	8112	314410
Mangotsfield Steeple	47 44 31 N E	13921	291077
Winterbown Steeple	31 14 10 N E	7050	300:69
Harfield Steeple	20 11 9 N E	93478	292:46
Laigh on Mendip	33 59 55 S E	21483	295:94
Dundry Steeple	71 23 20 S W	22831	259498
At Long Knoll.			
Douling Spire	48 59 51 N W	9544	182322
Frome Steeple	5 20 25 N W	58415	198272
At Farley Down.			
Devizes Steeple	79 51 10 S E	129342	245113
Cold Aston Steeple	33 43 21 N W	44362	277983

Meridian of Butterton Hill.

Bearings from the Parallels to the Meridian.		Distances from merid.	Distances from perp.
At Farland.	° ′ ″	Feet.	Feet.
Hope's Nose - -	23 7 55 N E	93759	18745
At St. Stephen's.			
Werrington Steeple - -	89 37 83 N E.	109839	9841
Boyton Steeple - -	0 55 35 N W	112787	106733
St. Stephen's Steeple - -	45 55 4 S E	110738	85968
North Petherwin Steeple -	49 15 49 N W	125044	98473
At Carraton Hill,			
Stoke Climsland Steeple -	65 56 1 N P.	96381	49988
Launceston Steeple - -	81 26 54 N E	108285	82689
Launceston Chapel - -	81 14 13 N E	108513	82561

Meridian of St. Agnes Beacon.

At Bodmin.			
St. Minvern Steeple - -	58 18 36 N W	79549	91845
St. Minvern Windmill - -	61 51 46 N W	90966	82260
At Trevose Head.			
St. Iury Steeple - -	61 8 12 S E	68456	74081
St. Merian Steeple - -	57 59 38 S E	58096	82476

ART. XXXIV. *Bearings of intersected Objects, from the Stations in the Series of 1799, from the Parallels to the Meridians of Dunnose and Greenwich; and likewise their Distances from those Meridians.*

Meridian of Dunnose.

At Epwell.			
Warwick Steeple - -	16 25 48 N W	87242	607508
St. Martin's, Coventry	8 3 42 N W	69028	653327
Soleyhul Spire - ,	31 8 35 N W	118816	656971
At Arbury Hill.			
Dunchurch Windmill -	13 55 48 N W	10724	626734
Breadon Hill, Summer House -	7 37 31 N W	16700	765031

Bearings from the Parallels to the Meridian.					Distances from merid.	Distances from perp.
	°	′	″		Ten.	Fret.
Mashfield Windmill	5	20	7	N W	18608	755819
Newnham Windmill	59	36	1	N E.	2761	589344
At Corley Hill.						
Gazebo, Brezdon Hill	35	45	58	S W	188086	585408
At Croath Hill.						
Deddington Steeple	18	6	0	S E	18646	499771
Hoxham Spire	16	15	11	S W	39519	511110
Aynoe Steeple	49	16	1	S E	11944	501902
Adderbury Spire	37	16	59	S E	26811	509671
Farthingo Steeple	56	16	49	S E	6431	502904
At Arbury Hill.						
Round House, Edge Hills	56	15	5	S W	57501	549714
Windmill, near the Round House	55	39	29	S W	58398	548186
At Brill.						
Wingrove Steeple	81	17	5	N E	103826	454713
Hardwick Steeple	78	6	1	N E	83299	454887
Luggersal Steeple	44	56	1	N E	35106	419401
Granborough Steeple	53	9	30	N E	70781	474574
Bicester Steeple	43	27	16	N W	6854	466560
Marq. Buckingham's House, Wooton	79	17	25	N E	43490	445984
Islip Steeple	24	26	3	S W	8944	439540
Wordstock Steeple	85	25	45	N W	35563	418393
Kidlington Spire	88	29	39	S W	14401	441989
Witchwood Beacon	29	11	34	S W	76971	444786
At Whitehorse Hill.						
Abingdon Spire	62	38	18	N E	19054	383037
Wallingford Steeple	84	54	39	N E	17497	358560
Great Coxwell Windmill	43	41	11	N W	96959	376819
Drayton Steeple	67	18	0	N E	14691	374055
Highworth Steeple	57	49	58	N W	110543	370009
Witney Spire	14	14	57	N E	64757	414386
Hampton Steeple	4	36	29	N h	79056	408334
Radley Steeple	61	25	12	N E	12112	388576
Buckland Steeple	20	8	12	N E	69616	388204
At Stow.						
Stow on the Wold Steeple	20	55	15	N W	118442	479166
At Broadway.						
Sanden Chapel	52	29	8	S E	86195	469777
Bourton Chapel	14	36	35	S E	125636	501076
Walford Spire	82	36	42	S E	94704	507924

Meridian of Greenwich.

Bearings from the Parallels to the Meridian.	Distance from merid.	Distance from perp.
At Wendover.	*Feet.*	*Feet.*
Pitchcot Windmill 19 11 59 N W	191077	149055
Ivinghoe Spire 45 44 37 N E	143187	131397
Quainton Steeple 34 47 15 N W	205750	146203
Leighton Buzzard Spire 11 41 12 N E	150016	160665
At Quainton.		
Southern Obelisk, Stow Park 12 1 36 N W	127554	204673
Northern Obelisk, ditto 11 50 48 N W	118505	207531
At Kinsworth.		
Aylesbury Spire 77 56 58 S W	190234	126765
Maulden Steeple 16 30 28 N E	105968	801124
Harlington Steeple 16 12 37 N E	110395	177730
Millbrook Steeple 3 1 41 N E	117732	201645
Streeley Steeple 35 83 47 N E	99961	171044
Sauldon Windmill 60 20 46 N W	178043	174433
At Bow Brickhill.		
Hanslope Spire 38 58 48 N W	185668	232843
North Crawley Steeple 9 41 15 N E	145589	224961
Pavenham Spire 22 15 49 N E	122215	261812
St. Paul's Spire, Bedford 43 9 11 N E	104408	240651
Sharnbrook Spire 19 81 54 N E	123533	260816
Woburn Market-House 73 52 37 S E	139255	180978
Ridgemont Station 72 28 11 N E	130927	196964
Wootton Spire 41 33 7 N E	120265	225035
Cranfield Spire 30 44 21 N E	136184	215933
Husborne Crawley Steeple 65 44 51 N E	136827	197004
Woburn Steeple 75 33 58 S E	139373	187394
Soeldroge Spirt 16 32 49 N E	124801	179861
Windmill near Tharfield 86 6 12 N E	22577	199950
Tottenhoe Station 27 42 7 S E	130412	154496
Chalgrave Spire 53 51 5 S E	116215	164780
Keysoe Spire 31 17 59 N E	95682	282155
Moulshoe Steeple 1 19 30 N W	154432	215608
Renhold Spire 44 56 16 N E	91651	250385
Lidlington Windmill 62 30 6 N E	115895	201797
At Lillyhoe.		
Knotting Green Elm Tree 16 17 56 N W	117482	284339
Ravensden Steeple 7 25 2 N W	95142	255304
Bow Brickhill Steeple 73 20 18 N W	151490	191301

Bearings from the Parallels to the Meridian.		Distances from merid.	Distances from perp.
		Feet.	Feet.
Colmworth Spire	0 18 51 N W	84580	258984
Sundun Windmill	75 0 6 S W	109052	164718
Silsoe Steeple	28 9 25 N W	95502	194145
Flitton Steeple	38 20 31 N W	102852	194903
Shillington Steeple	7 49 43 N E	81919	188066
Westoning Steeple	64 42 19 N W	113366	185143
Wrest-Garden Obelisk	26 26 8 N W	94797	192652
Flitwick Steeple	57 11 27 N W	114694	191016
Ampthill Steeple	39 6 3 N W	109957	203041
St. Neot's Steeple	13 31 16 N E	59630	273475
Pullox Hill Steeple	47 5 30 N W	102236	188118

ART. XXXV. *Latitudes and Longitudes of such Places, in the Series of 1797 and 1798, as have been referred to the Meridians of Black Down, Butterton Hill, and St. Agnes Beacon.*

Meridian of Black Down.

Names of the Objects.	Latitude	Longitude from Black Down.	Longitude west of Greenwich. In degrees.	In time.
	o , "	o , "	o , "	m. s.
Walton Windmill	51 6 59.5	0 13 42.4 W	2 45 44.5	11 2.9
Westonzoyland Steeple	51 6 33.8	0 12 12.9 W	2 44 35.3	10 58.3
Middezoy Steeple	51 5 38.3	0 29 38.5 W	2 53 5.2	11 32.3
Chedasy Steeple	51 8 5.1	0 23 31.7 W	2 55 56.8	11 43.7
Higham Windmill	51 4 21.8	0 15 18.6 W	2 47 42.0	11 10.7
Higham Steeple	51 4 34.6	0 16 18.5 W	2 48 40.9	11 14.7
Bridgewater Spire	51 7 42.7	0 27 86.3 W	2 59 38.7	11 58.6
Somerton Steeple	51 3 27.3	0 10 42.7 W	2 43 5.1	10 52.3
Burton Pynsent Obelisk	51 1 21.6	0 10 22.7 W	2 50 85.1	11 31
Westleigh Steeple	51 30 42.4	0 6 12.0 E	2 20 1.04	9 11.7
Bristol Cathedral	51 27 6.3	0 3 6.1 W	2 35 28.6	10 41.9
Redcliff Steeple	51 26 54.8	0 3 28.0 W	2 34 58.4	10 39.3
Long Ashton	51 26 9.1	0 5 41.3 W	2 38 5.7	10 32.2
Clifton Windmill	51 25 57.2	0 5 3.7 W	2 37 25.7	10 29.7
Blaze Castle	51 30 10.4	0 5 19.3 W	2 37 41.7	10 30.8
Penpole Gazebo	51 29 31.7	0 7 31.7 W	2 39 54.1	10 39.6
Duke of Beaufort's House, Stoke	51 29 34.5	0 0 19.6 E	2 32 32.2	10 8.8
Durham Steeple	51 28 44.5	0 9 59.0 E	2 22 13.4	9 49.5
Knowle Steeple	51 32 53.7	0 2 7.9 W	2 34 30.3	10 18
Margotsfield Steeple	51 29 9.5	0 3 39.2 E	2 28 42.3	9 54.8
Winterbown Steeple	51 31 3.4	0 1 51.2 E	2 30 31.2	10 2.1
Harfield Steeple	51 29 15.3	0 24 32.2 W	2 56 54.6	11 47.6
Leigh Steeple on Mendip	51 13 24.	0 5 36.3 E	2 26 46.1	9 47.1
Dundry Steeple	51 23 47.7	0 5 58.8 W	2 38 21.3	10 33.4

R

Names of the Objects.	Latitude.	Longitude from Black Down.	Longitude west of Greenwich. In degrees.	In time.
				m. s.
Doulting Spire - -	51 11 11,4	0 2 29,3 E	2 29 53,1	9 59,5
Devizes Steeple -	51 21 85,5	0 33 51,2 E	2 58 31,2	11 54,1
Frome Steeple - -	51 13 47,9	0 13 40,8 E	2 18 41,6	9 16,7
Cold Aston - -	51 26 53,9	0 11 38,0 E	2 20 44,4	9 24,9
Puckle Steeple -	51 29 16,8	0 6 49,6 E	2 15 32,8	9 42,2

Meridian of Butterton Hill.

Names of Objects.	Latitude.	Longitude from Butterton Hill.	Longitude west of Greenwich. In degrees.	In time.
				m. s.
Hope's Nose, Torbay -	50 27 48,5	0 16 44 E	3 26 43,1	13 46,9
Wartington Steeple -	50 39 52,2	0 28 19,4 W	4 21 8,9	17 24,4
Boyton Steeple - -	50 41 14,9	0 19 6,1 W	4 21 53,6	17 27,5
North Petherwin -	50 40 52,5	0 32 15,3 W	4 25 2,8	17 40,2
St. Stephen's Steeple -	50 38 50,5	0 28 32,6 W	4 21 20,1	17 15,3
Stokeclimsland Steeple -	50 32 55,8	0 24 47,5 W	4 17 35,0	17 10,3
Launceston Steeple -	50 38 18,1	0 27 54,1 W	4 20 41,6	17 22,7
Launceston Castle -	50 38 16,8	0 27 57,9 W	4 20 45,4	17 23

Meridian of St. Agnes Beacon.

Names of Objects.	Latitude.	Longitude from St. Agnes Beacon.	Longitude west of Greenwich. In degrees.	In time.
				m. s.
St. Minvern Steeple -	50 33 30,6	0 10 18,1 E	4 51 27,6	19 25,8
St. Mlavern Windmill -	50 31 55,5	0 03 23,5 E	4 48 32,2	19 14,1
St. Issy Steeple -	50 30 36,0	0 17 36,8 E	4 54 80,1	19 37,3
St. Merlan Steeple -	50 31 59,5	0 13 23,8 E	4 58 31,9	19 54,1

ART. XXXVI. *Latitudes and Longitudes of such Places, in the Series of 1799, as have been referred to the Meridians of Dunnose and Greenwich.*

Meridian of Dunnose.

Names of Objects.	Latitude.	Longitude from Dunnose.	Longitude west of Greenwich. In degrees.	In time.
				m. s.
Warwick Steeple -	52 16 53,0	0 43 18,3 W	1 34 54,3	6 19,6
St. Martin's Spire, Coventry	52 24 25,4	0 18 29,5 W	1 30 5,5	6 0,3
Soleyhull Spire - -	52 2 30,4	0 34 13,8 W	1 45 49,3	9 3,3
Dunchurch Windmill -	52 20 4,6	0 5 32,5 W	1 17 8,5	5 8,6

Names of Objects.	Latitude.	Longitude from Dunnose.	Longitude west of Greenwich.	
			In degrees.	In time.
	° ′ ″	° ′ ″	° ′ ″	m. s.
Gazebo, Bardon Hill *	51 42 47.6	0 7 12.2 W	1 18 48.1	5 15.2
Markfield Windmill	51 41 16.8	0 5 1.0 W	1 16 37.0	5 6.5
Breedon Hill Building †	52 3 16.7	0 49 59.7 W	2 1 35.7	8 6.4
Newnham Windmill	52 13 55.7	0 0 36.2 E	1 10 59.8	4 43.9
Deddington Steeple	51 59 13.9	0 7 36.1 W	1 19 12.1	5 16.8
Bloxham Spire	51 1 5.6	0 10 29.7 W	1 22 5.7	5 28.4
Aynoe Steeple	51 59 35.2	0 3 10.2 W	1 14 46.2	4 59.1
Adderbury Spire	52 0 51.6	0 6 3.7 W	1 17 39.7	5 10.6
Farthingo Steeple	51 59 45.1	0 1 48.4 W	1 13 18.4	4 53.2
Round House, Edge Hills	52 7 15.6	0 15 18.4 W	1 20 54.4	5 47.6
Round House Windmill	52 7 11.4	0 15 31.6 W	1 27 8.6	5 48.6
Wingrove Steeple	51 51 46.6	0 17 18.7 E	0 44 7.3	2 56.5
Hardwick Steeple	51 51 47.8	0 22 2.6 E	0 49 33.4	3 18.2
Luggersal Steeple, Bucks	51 50 57.5	0 9 17.2 E	1 1 18.8	4 9.8
Greenborough Steeple	51 55 4.3	0 18 45.2 E	0 52 50.8	3 31.4
Bicester Steeple	51 53 46.8	0 1 48.9 E	1 9 47.1	4 39.1
Abingdon Spire	51 40 3.8	0 5 1.2 W	1 16 37.2	5 6.5
Wallingford Steeple	51 36 2.4	0 4 36.1 E	1 6 59.8	4 27.9
Great Coxwell Windmill	51 38 59.8	0 25 32.4 W	1 37 8.4	6 28.5
Drayton Steeple	51 38 35	0 6 30.1 W	1 18 6.1	5 12.4
Highworth Steeple	51 37 51.4	0 30 38.1 W	1 42 14.1	6 48.9
Witney Spire	51 46 49.9	0 17 6.9 W	1 28 41.9	5 54.8
Brampton Steeple	51 44 11.2	0 20 51.9 W	1 32 27.9	6 9.8
Radley Steeple	51 40 58.5	0 31 57.4 W	1 43 33.4	6 54.2
Buckland Steeple	51 40 53.3	0 18 21.1 W	1 29 57.1	5 59.8
Witchwood Beacon	51 50 9.8	0 20 11.6 W	1 31 57.6	6 7.8
Stow on the Wold	51 55 46.9	0 31 23.6 W	1 43 59.6	6 51.9
Saruden Chapel	51 54 16.4	0 22 49.9 W	1 34 25.9	6 17.7
Bourton Chapel	51 59 22.5	0 33 20.7 W	1 44 56.7	6 59.8
Walford Spire	52 2 31.6	0 26 13.5 W	1 37 48.5	6 31.2
Islip Steeple	51 49 20.7	0 2 11.9 W	1 13 57.9	4 55.2
Woodstock Steeple	51 50 47.4	0 9 24.5 W	1 21 0	5 24
Kidlington Spire	51 49 41.6	0 4 51.9 W	1 16 37.9	5 5.8

Meridian of Greenwich.

Names of Objects.	Latitude.	Longitude west of Greenwich.	
		In degrees.	In time.
	° ′ ″	° ′ ″	m. s.
Pitchcot Windmill	51 52 52.5	0 50 35.3	3 22.3
Iringhot Spire	51 50 9.1	0 57 51.3	3 31.4
Quainton Steeple	51 52 28.7	0 54 28.0	3 37.8
Southern Obelisk, Stow Park	52 2 2.2	1 0 27.1	4 1.8
Northern Obelisk, ditto	50 2 30.2	1 0 42.9	4 2.9

* In page 658, this is, by mistake, called Breedon Hill Summer House.
† In page 659, this building is called Gazebo.

R 2

Names of Objects.	Latitude.	Longitude west of Greenwich, in degrees	in time.
	° ′ ″	° ′ ″	m. s.
Leighton Buzzard Spire	51 54 56.5	0 39 54.4	2 39.6
Aylesbury Spire	51 49 18.9	0 50 18	3 21.2
Hanslope Spire	52 6 45.2	0 49 17.8	3 17.2
North Crawley Spire	52 5 31.1	0 38 38.4	2 34.5
Parenham Spire	52 11 36.3	0 32 27.0	2 9.8
St. Paul's Spire, Bedford	52 8 8.8	0 27 43.3	1 50.9
Sharnbrook Spire	52 12 55.1	0 32 48.0	2 11.2
Woburn Market-House	51 59 17.4	0 36 58.5	2 27.9
Woburn Steeple	51 59 21.8	0 37 0.3	2 28
Ridgemont Station	52 0 36.4	0 34 45.7	2 19
Wootton Steeple	52 5 39.2	0 31 55.7	2 7.7
Cranfield Spire	52 4 3.1	0 36 11.1	2 24.7
Husborne Crawley Steeple	52 0 57.0	0 36 19.8	2 25.3
Souldrope Spire	52 14 38.6	0 33 9.1	2 12.6
Windmill near Tharfield	52 1 30.9	0 3 20.4	0 13.3
Tottenhoe Station	51 53 18.9	0 34 37.5	2 18.5
Chalgrave Steeple	51 55 40.8	0 30 51.4	2 3.4
Keysoe Spire	52 14 58.5	0 25 24.3	1 41.6
Moslahoe Steeple	52 2 59.0	0 40 39.6	2 42.6
Renhold Spire	52 9 41.5	0 24 20.1	1 37.3
Lidlington Windmill	52 2 4.2	0 33 25.0	2 13.7
Maulden Steeple	52 1 52.8	0 27 20.2	1 49.3
Harlington Steeple	51 57 48.4	0 29 18.6	1 57.2
Millbrook Steeple	52 1 43.6	0 31 25.5	2 5
Streatley Steeple	51 56 42.8	0 16 12.4	1 44.8
Sauldon Windmill	51 57 9.7	0 47 20.9	3 9.8
Knotting-Green Elm Tree	52 15 26.6	0 31 11.5	2 4.7
Ravensden Station	52 10 33.9	0 25 15.7	1 41
Bow Brickhill Steeple	52 0 1.1	0 40 13.4	2 40.9
Colmworth Spire	52 12 49.3	0 12 27.0	1 28.5
Sundon Windmill	51 57 52.8	0 28 57.0	1 55.8
Silsoe Steeple	52 0 33.0	0 25 81.4	1 41.4
Flitton Steeple	52 0 42.1	0 27 14.4	1 48.9
Shillington Steeple	51 59 51.7	0 21 45.0	1 27
Westoning Steeple	51 59 2.7	0 30 5.9	2 0.4
Wrest-Garden Obelisk	52 0 16.8	0 15 10.7	1 40.7
Flitwick Steeple	51 59 58.6	0 30 27.1	2 1.8
Ampthill Steeple	52 1 27.8	0 29 11.7	1 56.7
St. Neot's Steeple	52 13 34.7	0 15 49.9	1 3.3
Pollux Hill Steeple	51 59 32.8	0 27 9.7	1 48.6

ART. XXXVII. *Latitudes and Longitudes of some remarkable Places, not contained in the preceding Tables.*

St. Nicholas's or Drake's Island, in Plymouth Sound.

The bearing of Kit Hill, from the meridian of Butterton, is 67° 19′ 12″, and the angle between it and the flagstaff on Drake's Island, 41° 40′ 8″; therefore, the bearing of the latter from the meridian is 71° 7′ 40″; consequently, its distance from the meridian is 60531 feet, and from the perpendicular 20692 feet, which respectively subtend 9′ 53″,6, and 3′ 24″,5. These, with the latitude and longitude of Butterton, 50° 24′ 46″,9 and 3° 52′ 47″,5, give 50° 21′ 21″,1 for the latitude, and 4° 8′ 17″,9 for the longitude, of the flagstaff on Drake's Island.

The latitude and longitude of this spot was determined by Mr. BAYLEY, in the year 1792. The observations for the former were as follows:

$$50° 21′ 20″ \quad ⊙ \text{'s LL.}$$
$$50 \; 21 \; 30,5 \quad \text{ditto.}$$
$$50 \; 21 \; 31 \quad \text{ditto.}$$
$$50 \; 21 \; 29 \quad α \text{ Aquilæ.}$$
$$50 \; 21 \; 26,5 \; α \text{ Ophiuchi.}$$
$$50 \; 21 \; 55 \quad ⊙ \text{'s LL.} \quad \text{The mean of these is } 50° 21′ 28″,5.$$

The place chosen by Mr. BAYLEY, as I have been lately informed, was a few feet northward of the staff; therefore, 7″,4 may be taken for the true difference between our determinations.

The longitude of Mr. BAYLEY's station, found by the *moon's transit*, was 4° 18′ 52″; but the longitude deduced from the recent operations, is 4° 8′ 17″,9; there is, therefore, a difference of 10′ 34″,1 between the two determinations.

St. Andrew's or the Old Church, at Plymouth.

The angle at Butterton, between the Old Church tower and Kit Hill, is 37° 45′ 5″,2 ; its bearing, therefore, south-west from the meridian, is 75° 1′ 56″ ; consequently, its distance from the meridian is 57505 feet, and from the perpendicular 15374 feet. These respectively subtend 9′ 24″, and 2′ 32″,1 : hence, its latitude becomes 50° 22′ 13″,6, and longitude 4° 7′ 31″,6 = 16ᵐ 30′,1 in time, west of Greenwich.

As it is of very great importance that the truths of the conclusions given in this Work should receive support, wherever I can find it, I think it right to mention the result of his Excellency the Count de Bruhl's endeavours to ascertain the longitude of Plymouth, by means of chronometers. The following is a copy of his communication, made in the year 1795.

Journey from Plymouth to London.

Green Timekeeper.

June 8th, 1783. 14th.	Mr. Muder's clock* at Plymouth, fast for mean time	0ᵐ	32′,15
	Timekeeper faster than Mr. Muder's clock	0	25,6
	Timekeeper slower than London clock	14	29,4
	London clock slow for mean time	0	46,5
	Difference of longitude	16	3,65

Blue Timekeeper.

June 8th, 14th.	Mr. Muder's clock at Plymouth, fast for mean time	0ᵐ	32′,15
	Timekeeper faster than Mr. Muder's clock	0	37,4
	Timekeeper slower than London clock	14	17,2
	London clock slow for mean time	0	36,5
	Difference of longitude	16	3,25
	Mean difference	16	3,55

The longitude of St. Paul's, west of Greenwich, is 23′,1 in

---

* It is, perhaps, right to observe, that Mr. T. Muder's transit, at Plymouth, was made by the late Mr. Bird, and properly set up between stone pillars. The clock, the entire work of his own hands, was a most excellent one.

time; and Mr. Dutton's house in Fleet-street is about 2' west of St. Paul's; * wherefore, its longitude west of Greenwich is 25': consequently, $16^m 3',55 + 25' = 16^m 28',55$, is the difference of longitude between Greenwich and Plymouth, as shewn by the timekeepers.

Now the meridian of Mr. Mudoe's transit-room, at Plymouth, passed only 35 feet to the eastward of the centre of St. Andrew's Tower, his northern meridian mark being on the church itself; therefore, the longitude of the church and transit-room may be considered the same. From the survey, we find it to be $16^m 30',1$; and, from Count Bruhl's determination, making a just allowance for the difference of longitude between the late Mr. Dutton's house and Greenwich, $16^m 28',5$.

It is left for the public, and this learned Society in particular, to determine how far the near agreement of these several methods, tends to corroborate the assertion I have advanced, of the dependence which may be placed on the deductions drawn from the observations made at Beachy Head and Dunnose. If there had been only one watch employed on the occasion, the result would not have been so satisfactory as the circumstance of two being used seems to make it. As the occasion calls for the remark, before I dismiss this article, I must observe, that the highest advantages would accrue to geography, were the ideas of the Astronomer Royal carried into execution, (and which I shall endeavour to do at some future period,) respecting the discovery of the difference of longitude between Greenwich and some very remote point on the western side of the island, (St. David's Head for instance,) by means of timekeepers,

* According to Horwood's Map of London, the distance from the centre of St. Paul's to Bolt Court, at the corner of which Mr. Dutton's house is situated, is 31 chains.

carried backwards and forwards in the mail coaches. If this
excellent scheme were executed, and the watches employed
equal to the best now made, it is probable that the true difference of longitude would shortly be determined. The geodetical
situation of St. David's Head will, ere long, be ascertained from
a prosecution of the survey : a knowledge, therefore, of its true
longitude would be attended with eminent advantages.

Lizard Light-Houses.

The light-houses on this head-land were observed from Pertinney and Karnbonellis. At the latter, Pertinney bears 74°
22′ 41″ south-west, from the parallel to the meridian of St.
Agnes ; and, as the angle between the western light-house and
Pertinney is 78° 40′ 5″, it follows, that the bearing of the light-
house from the said parallel is 4° 17′ 24″ south-east. Computing
with this angle and the distance from Karnbonellis to the light-
house, we get 3944 feet, and 126499 feet, for the distances of
that object from the meridian and perpendicular of St. Agnes :
therefore, admitting the length of the degree in the meridian, in
the middle point between St. Agnes and the light-house, to be
60830 fathoms, and 61182 for the length of a degree of a great
circle perpendicular to it, we get 20′ 47″,4, and 32″,8, for the
small arcs which those spaces respectively subtend. These
data, with the latitude and longitude of St. Agnes, 50° 18′
27″, and 5° 11′ 55″,7, give the latitude of the light-house =
49° 57′ 44″, and longitude west of Greenwich 5° 11′ 4″,8, in
time, 20ᵐ 44ˢ,3.

This light-house was also observed from the station on
Karnminnis. The triangle resulting from that observation,
together with the angle at Karnbonellis, is

Kamminnis - 41° 9′ 46″
Karnbonellis - - 98 1 30
Western Light-house 37 48 44: which gives 8134 $\frac{2}{...}$
feet, for the distance between the station Karnbonellis and the
Light-house. This distance is said, in the Philosophical Transactions for 1797, p. 501, to be 8134/8 feet, which differs only
6 feet from the above determination; but it is probable the distance first given is most correct, as the two light-houses appearing nearly in the same line at Karmminnis, was the means of
preventing us from clearly distinguishing the apex of either,
and it was principally on this account that we preferred the observation made at Pertinney. The agreement however proves,
that no inconsistency can be found to obtain with respect to the
data before given, for settling the situation of this important
headland.

In the Philosophical Transactions for 1797, page 502, it is
mentioned, that the distance from the spot where the late Mr.
BRADLEY made his observations, to the place where his meridian
mark was fixed, was 800 feet. But there appears to be some inconsistency in this particular; as Mr. BRADLEY's own words, in
an extract of a letter now before me, are, *it was just 480 feet.*
Adding to this, 24 feet, the distance between the place of the
meridian mark and the line joining the centre of the light-
houses, we get the distance of the point O, or the place of the
Observatory, (see Phil. Trans. 1797, p. 502,) from the line joining the light-houses W, E, = 504 feet; a space corresponding
to 5″ of latitude, nearly; therefore, from the trigonometrical
operations, we get,

and $\begin{array}{l} 49°\ 57′\ 44″ \\ 5\ 11\ 4\ ,8 \end{array}$ for the latitude $\Big\}$ of Mr. BRADLEY's station.

S

Mr. BRADLEY's observations for finding the latitude, were
made with a quadrant of one foot radius, the workmanship of
Mr. BIRD; they were as follows.

Nine meridional altitudes of the sun's limb, the
  extreme results of which were 49° 57′ 27″,5 and
  49° 57′ 44″, gave for the latitude of the Observatory   -   -   -   49° 57′ 35″
Six meridional observations of the Pole Star below the Pole, the extreme results of which were
  49° 57′ 35″ and 49° 57′ 20″,4 gave for the latitude   -   -   -   -   49 57 23 ,2
Thirteen observations of Arcturus, α Coronæ Bo-
  realis, and α Serpentis, the extreme results of
  which were 49° 57′ 54″,7 and 49° 57′ 2″,7, gave
  for the latitude   -   -   -   49 57 29
Fifteen observations of α, β, γ Draconis, the extreme results of which were 49° 57′ 22″,2 and
  49° 57′ 2″7, gave for the latitude   -   49 57 33

          The mean of which is - 49 57 30

According to the trigonometrical operations, the latitude is
49° 57′ 44″; there is, therefore, a difference of 14″ between the
results; a quantity so large as justly to excite surprise, if it were
not generally understood, that much dependance cannot be
placed on observations made with an astronomical quadrant
precisely similar to that made use of by Mr. BRADLEY. The
extreme results in the above, differ so widely as to authorise the
truth of the supposition on this occasion.

The longitude of the Lizard was determined by the transit
of Venus, Sun's eclipse, transit of the Moon, and two emersions

of Jupiter's first satellite, as particularly set forth in the Preface
to the Nautical Ephemeris of 1791. The conclusions were as
follows.

Four transits of the Moon, calculated by Mr. WALES,
    gave for the longitude -   -   20° 30',6
Two emersions of Jupiter's first satellite, calculated
    by ditto -   -   -   -   21 14 ,5

Transit of Venus, calculated by	Doctor MASKELYNE	20	57 ,0
	Mr. WITCHELL -	20	56 ,5
	Mr. WALES -	20	57 ,0
Sun's eclipse, calculated by	Mr. WITCHELL -	20	44 ,5
	Mr. SEJOUR -	20	45 ,1
	Mr. EULER -	20	59 ,0
	Mr. LEXEL -	20	51 ,0

Mean of the whole -   20 52 ,12

From the trigonometrical operations, we find the longitude
in time to be 20° 44',3 ; there is, therefore, a difference of 7',82
between these different determinations: this is, probably, as
near as we could have expected to find it; yet it can scarcely
be supposed, that of this difference, more than 2' can be laid to
the account of the survey.

In the Philosophical Transactions for 1797, p. 500, it is observed, that angles were taken at the Lizard Light-house and
Naval Signal-Staff, to determine the situation of the *Point* itself. This Point, marked P in the diagram, makes an angle
of 2° 23' 16" S W, with the parallel to the meridian of St. Agnes
at the station on Karnbonellis, and is therefore 636,6 feet
from that meridian, and 126394 feet from the perpendicular;
therefore 49' 57' 40",6 is the latitude } of the Lizard Point.
and   5 11 46   the longitude }

Scilly Islands.

To determine the distances of the objects in these islands, from the stations near the Land's End, with sufficient accuracy, proper corrections were made for reducing the horizontal angles to those formed by the chords. On the present occasion, it will be right to use the horizontal, and not the chord angles; the distances from the meridians, and from their perpendiculars, being computed on the supposition of the earth's surface being a plane, which, within the limits of our fixed meridians, may be considered as true.

The angles for finding the distances of these objects are given in the Philosophical Transactions for 1797, p. 503: from whence, and the *data* contained in this Work, we get the bearing of

the *Day-mark* in the Island of St. Martin's from $\left\{\begin{array}{l} \text{St. Buryan} \quad 75^\circ\ 44'\ 52''\ \text{S W} \\ \text{Pertinney} \quad 71\ 14\ 22\ \text{S W} \\ \text{Sennen -} \quad 75\ 30\ 9\ \text{S W} \end{array}\right.$

which, combined with the distances of the stations from the meridian of St. Agnes, give

$\left.\begin{array}{l} 246801 \\ 246804 \\ 246821 \end{array}\right\}$ feet, for the distance of the Day-mark from the meridian of St. Agnes;

and $\left.\begin{array}{l} 122409 \\ 122410 \\ 122414 \end{array}\right\}$ feet, for the distance of it from the perpendicular.

The mean of the first is 246809 feet, and the mean of the last 122411 feet; but the latter becomes 122419, because a line drawn from the Day-mark, perpendicular to the meridian of St. Agnes, cuts that meridian eight feet *below* the parallel. Again, we get the bearing of

the Windmill - - - $\left.\begin{array}{l} \\ \end{array}\right\}$ In the Island of St. the Flagstaff of the Fort $\left.\begin{array}{l} \\ \end{array}\right\}$ Mary, from $\left\{\begin{array}{l} \text{Pertinney} \quad - \quad 65^\circ\ 32'\ 10''\ \text{S W} \\ \text{Pertinney} \quad - \quad 66\ 53\ 5\ \text{S W} \end{array}\right.$

from whence, after a similar correction with that just made, we find the distance of

the Windmill 26304 } feet from the { 143597 } feet from the perpendicular of
the Flagstaff 160152 } meridian, and { 140876 } St. Agnes.

From the same page, and the *data* furnished in this work, we also find the bearing of

St. Agnes Light- ⌠Sennen - 68° 6′ 54″ S W
House from ⌡ St. Buryan 69 3 56 S W; which gives

265865 } feet, for the distance from the meridian, and
265879 }

149121 } feet, for the distance from the perpendicular of St. Agnes.
149128 }

The mean of the first is 265872 feet, and the mean of the last, when corrected, 149133 feet.

With the above data, and also the latitude and longitude of St. Agnes, we get

the latitude of ⌠ Day-mark in St. Martin's - 49° 58′ 2″.9
⎮ Windmill, St. Mary's - 49 54 32.7
⎮ Flagstaff, ditto - 49 54 59.1
⌡ St. Agnes Light-House* - 49 53 36.8

In Time.

and longitude west ⌠ Day-mark 1° 2′ 42″.1 ⌠ from the meri- ⌠ 6° 14′ 38″.8 24ᵐ 58ˢ.6
from St. Agnes. ⎮ Windmill 1 5 3.1 ⎮ dian of Green- ⎮ 6 16 58 .7 25 7 .9
⎮ Flagstaff 1 6 ″.7 ⎮ wich. ⎮ 6 17 57 .4 25 11 .9
⌡ Light House 1 7 27.7 ⌡ - ⌡ 6 19 23 .4 25 21 .5

* In the *Requisite Tables*, published by order of the Board of Longitude, the latitude of the Scilly Lights is said to be 49° 56′ 0″, and longitude 6° 46′ 0′. The latitude, according to the survey, is 49° 53′ 36″.8, and longitude 6° 19′ 43″.4. An error of 2′ 23″ in the latitude, may not perhaps be considered extraordinary; but how, in a maritime country, like our own, where chronometers are in such constant use, so great an error as 26′ 37″ (1ᵐ 46ˢ¾ in time) in the longitude, should have remained undetected, excepting by one person, is surprising. J. Huddart, Esq. visited the Scilly Isles, having with him a watch made by Arnold, and obtained his time at that spot in the island of St. Mary where the body of Sir Clowdisley Shovel is said to have been thrown ashore, by means of equal altitudes of the Sun's limb; he then found, comparing his time with that shewn by the watch, that 0ʰ 25ᵐ 18ˢ was the difference between the meridians of Greenwich and this spot in St. Mary's. Now St. Agnes Light-house is about 2′ of a degree west of the place to which Mr. Huddart alludes; therefore, 25′ 18″ + 8″ = 25′ 26′ is the longitude of St. Agnes, through these means; which differs only 4ˢ.5 in time from that found by the survey.

The Observatory of his Grace the Duke of MARLBOROUGH, *at Blenheim.*

The staff erected over the quadrant, was observed from White Horse Hill and Whiteham Hill. At the former station, the latter makes an angle of 36° 30′ 13″,5, with the parallel to the meridian of *Dunnose.* The staff, therefore, bears from the parallel 25° 59′ 29″,75 N E.; consequently, its distance from the meridian of Dunnose is 36540 feet, and from the perpendicular 416458 feet. These respectively subtend 5′ 58″,3, and 1° 13′ 21″,4; therefore, the latitude of the Observatory is 51° 50′ 28″,3, and its longitude 9′ 39″,9 from Dunnose: but 1° 11′ 36″ is the longitude of that station; therefore, 1° 21′ 15″,9, or 5′ 25″,9 in time, is the longitude of the Observatory west from Greenwich.

As the meridian of Dunnose passes at no great distance from that of Blenheim, I have deduced the latitude and longitude from the former, to avoid the errors which creep in, when computations are carried on from remote meridians. It may be worth while, however, to show that the extent of those errors would not be great, were the meridian of Dunnose neglected, and the Observatory at Blenheim referred to the meridian of Greenwich.

The distance of White Horse Hill from the meridian of Greenwich is found to be 356050 feet, and from its perpendicular 39425 feet; the bearing of Nuffield, from the parallel at that station, being 89° 59′ 27″ S E. Blenheim will, therefore, be found to bear 26° 55′ 25″ N E from the parallel at White Horse Hill; consequently, its distance from the meridian of Greenwich is 507224 feet, and from its perpendicular 135569 feet. These give the arcs 50′ 12″,4, and 22′ 16″,1; from whence we get 51° 50′ 28″,1 for the latitude, and 1° 21′ 16″ for the longitude,

of the Observatory west of Greenwich. Either of these determinations may be taken for the true result, but I shall prefer
the first.

Being favoured by his Grace with the latitude and longitude
derived from astronomical observations, we have the following
comparisons:

		Degrees.	Time.
Latitude { observed	51° 50′ 24″.9	Longitude west { 1° 21′ 6″.0	5ᵐ 24′.4
computed	51 50 28 .1	from Greenwich. { 1 21 15 .9	5 25 .1

Observatory at Oxford.

The angle at the station on Shotover, between the Atlas on
the top of the Observatory and the parallel to the meridian of
Dunnose, is 79° 50′ 51″.75 N W: therefore, its distance from
the meridian is 14719 feet, and from the perpendicular 416985
feet. The figure representing Atlas is 33½ feet *due east* of the
Quadrant Room; consequently, no correction will be required
in the computed latitude. The space 14719 feet subtends an arc
= 2′ 24″.3, and 416985 feet an arc of 1° 8′ 30″.8. These *data*,
with the latitude and longitude of Dunnose, give 51° 45′ 38″
for the latitude, and 1° 15′ 29″.2 for the longitude, of the Observatory. As in the former case, with respect to Blenheim, so in
the present instance, it is immaterial whether the calculations
be carried on from the meridian of Greenwich or that of Dunnose, as differences of only 0″.1 in both the latitude and longitude
are found in the results.

The latitude and longitude of this Observatory are given in
the *Requisite Tables;* the first is 51° 45′ 38″, and the last
1° 15′ 30″, or 5ᵐ 2ˢ in time. Doctor HORNSBY, however, has
furnished me with what he conceives to be more accurate

determinations; from which, and the above, we have the following comparisons:

				Degrees.	Time.
Latitude	{ observed	51° 45′ 39″.5	Longitude west {	1° 15′ 22″.5	5ᵐ 1ˢ.5
	{ computed	51 45 38 .0	from Greenwich. {	1 15 29 .2	5 1 .9

I conclude this article with expressing an opinion, that the
coincidence between the computed and, no doubt, accurately
observed longitude of this Observatory, affords strong reason
for supposing, that the operations at Beachy Head and Dunnose,
in 1794, for finding the length of a degree of a great circle
perpendicular to the meridian on the earth's surface, were made
with the required accuracy.

SECTION THIRD.

*Trigonometrical Surveys of the Northern and Western Parts of
Kent, the County of Essex, and Parts of the adjoining Counties,
Suffolk and Hertford, executed in the Years 1798 and 1799.
(See Plate XXXII.)*

It will be convenient to treat of the operations carried on in
the north of Kent and Essex, before we speak of those executed
in the western parts of the former county.

In a former article I have observed, that from the old station
at Wrotham, (General Roy's,) the view towards the north is obstructed, and also that it became necessary to select a new one:
this station was found to be 205,5 feet from the other; the distance was accurately measured, and afterwards the angle taken
at the *old* station, between the staff on Severndroog Tower,

Shooters Hill, and the one newly chosen; this angle subtended 94° 19′ 0″.5.

The distance from Severndroog Tower to the old station at Wrotham, is 79960 feet. But, it must be observed, this distance is not precisely the same as that given by General Roy, because an allowance is made for the error in the reduction of the bases, in the surveys of 1787 and 1788.

With the distances 79960 feet and 205.5 feet, and the included angle, 94° 19′ 0″.5, we find the distance of the Flag-staff on Severndroog Tower, from the new station = 79944 feet; with this distance, a part of the following triangles have their sides computed.

Art. xxxviii. *Principal Triangles.*

Names of stations.	Observed angles.	Distances of the stations.	
Wrotham Gravesend Severndroog Tower	62 34 38 82 39 41	} Gravesend	Feet. 45578 71261
Gravesend Langdon Hill Severndroog Tower	95 53 52 33 47 125	} Langdon Hill	44886 88470
Gravesend Hadleigh Steeple Langdon Hill	54 31 53 43 15 51	} Hadleigh Steeple	64076 37171
Gravesend Hadleigh Halstow	30 24 19—21 41 46 32—53 107 49 5— 6 179 59 57	} Halstow Steeple	44839 34064
Gravesend Halstow Gadshill	31 38 21 24 78 21	} Gadshill	22277 28390
Halstow Hadleigh Steeple Sheppey Isle	59 18 6 —5 49 15 33½—1¾ 31 26 24 —23 180 0 3 .5	} Sheppey	49452 64587

T

The distances of Gadshill from Halstow, and from Halstow to the Isle of Sheppy, in the following triangle, viz.

 Halstow 108 34 18
 Sheppey 18 18 3
 Gadshill   give the distances between Gadshill and the station in the Isle of Sheppey 70687 and 70685 feet: the mean, 70686 feet, may be taken for the true distance.

Names of stations.	Observed angles.	Distances.	
Hadleigh - -	36 43 19	Southend - - -	{ 27596
Southend - -	119 10 3		{ 46104
Sheppey			

To find the distance between Langdon Hill and the spindle of the weather-cock on Rayleigh Steeple, we have the following quadrilateral.

 Langdon Hill 112° 2' 46"
 Gravesend • 64 56 14
 Halstow - 111 20 14
 Rayleigh . 61 40 46

   360 0 0, which gives the distance from the centre of Rayleigh Steeple to the staff on Langdon Hill = 44131 feet; but the point on the top of Rayleigh Tower, over which the instrument was placed, was just 7 feet farther from Langdon Hill than the spindle; therefore, 44131 + 7 = 44138 feet, is the distance between Langdon Hill and the station on the steeple.—The angles in the following triangles,

 Hadleigh - 136° 11' 55"
 Sheppey - 16 16 30
 Langdon Hill

 Langdon Hill 49 8 3
 Sheppey - 17 4 46
 Rayleigh   give the distance of

the *Spindle* on Rayleigh Tower from { Langdon Hill = 44131 } Feet.
           { Hadleigh = 15554 }

From the preceding quadrilateral, the distance between the spindle on Rayleigh Tower and the station on Langdon Hill, was found = 44131 feet, which is the same as the other determination.

Names of stations.	Observed angles.	Distances.	
	° ′ ″		Feet.
Halstow - - -	95 46 57	} Spindle - -	{ 49413
Sheppey - - -	42 6 39		73313
Rayleigh Tower Spindle			
Halstow - - -	35 1 8	} Prittlewell - -	{ 46800
Hadleigh - - -	99 3 3		17206
Prittlewell Steeple			
Halstow - - -	64 16 58	} Prittlewell - -	{ 46803
Sheppey -	55 24 34		51843
Prittlewell			
Halstow -	73 45 42	} Canewdon - -	{ 71311
Sheppey - - -	66 39 49		74461
Canewdon Steeple - -			
Rayleigh - - -	53 5 0	} Canewdon - -	{ 31438
Prittlewell - - -	73 41 30		26189
Canewdon			
Hadleigh - - -	58 52 14	} Flagstaff - -	{ 51846
Halstow - - -	86 10 13		34060
Flagstaff of the Garrison,			
Sheerness			
Severndroog Tower - -	17 48 23	} Purfleet Cliff - -	{ 40423
Gravesend - -	20 21 40		35498
Purfleet Cliff - - -	141 48 57		
	180 0 0		
Rayleigh - -	97 7 47	} Danbury - -	{ 37514
Langdon Hill - -	43 18 8		64740
Danbury Spire			
Severndroog Tower - -	26 44 33	} Frierning - -	{ 103659
Langdon Hill - - -	95 25 0		46312
Frierning Steeple			
Langdon Hill - -	88 14 19	} Frierning - -	{ 46314
Frierning - - -	44 13 19		63270
Rayleigh			

Mean distance from Langdon Hill to Frierning Steeple 46313 feet.

Names of Stations.	Observed angles.	Distances.	
Frierning Langdon Hill *Danbury Steeple*	98 15 6 45 20 17	} Danbury	Feet. { 49080 82748
Langdon Hill Rayleigh *Signal Staff, Sherbury-ness*	14 27 33 132 51 23	} Signal Staff	{ 83902 47408
Triptree, old station Rayleigh *Frierning*	47 8 50 73 45 24	Triptree, old station, from { Rayleigh Tower Frierning	74053 82800
Triptree Danbury *Rayleigh*	31 59 21 124 20 48	Danbury Spire from Triptree Heath	56000
Triptree, old station Tillingham Steeple *Danbury Spire*	100 28 19 30 14 40	Tillingham from { Triptree Danbury	54172 70281
Tillingham Peldon *Danbury*	84 51 34 62 39 36	} Peldon	{ 48460 78803
Tillingham Peldon *Flagstaff on St. Osyth Priory*	48 18 50 83 40 46	} Flagstaff	{ 57433 43595
Peldon Thorp *Flagstaff, St. Osyth Priory*	80 49 10 32 47 18	} Thorp	{ 64802 28612
Peldon Thorp *Stoke Steeple*	74 46 5 51 6 31	} Stoke	{ 61951 78171
Peldon Great Tey *Danbury*	71 48 20 75 51 33	} Great Tey	{ 43475 77304

Names of the Stations.	Observed angles.	Distances.	
Peldon Great Tey Stoke	46 14 2 90 50 9	} Stoke	Feet. 63941* 40181

From a former triangle, the distance between Peldon and Stoke Steeple was found to be 63931 feet; wherefore, 63936 feet, the mean, may be taken for the true distance.

Thorp Little Bentley *Dover Court*	98 51 10 53 1 30	} Little Bentley	20481 40981
Thorp Little Bentley *Peldon*	41 12 51 183 30 18	} Little Bentley	20481 51205
Tillingham Danbury Spire *West Mersea*	96 57 10 61 46 57	} West Mersea	{ 18914 79173
Rayleigh West Mersea *Danbury*	54 17 44 29 13 0	} West Mersea	{ 96701 79170
Great Tey Stoke Staircase, St. Mary's Steeple, Colchester	58 11 44 45 11 57		
	St. Mary's Steeple from Stoke - - -		36796
Little Bromley Stoke St. Mary's, Colchester	54 11 28 47 58 16	} Little Bromley	{ 44356 33706
Dover Court Stoke Tattingstone	18 58 19 14 53 50	} Tattingstone	{ 38446 49850
Thorp Stoke Tattingstone	37 52 49 39 12 4	} Tattingstone	{ 50690 49845
Dover Court Rushmere Falkenham Steeple	50 26 54 38 25 20	} Falkenham	{ 31851 39270

The distance from Dover Court Steeple to Stoke Steeple is 84425 feet, and from Rushmere Steeple to Stoke Steeple 75955 feet; the included angle at Dover Court Steeple is 61° 38 20'. These give the distance of Dover Court Steeple from Rushmere, 50921 feet.

Names of Stations.	Observed angles.		Distances.	
Dover Court Rushmere Tattingstone	43 40 51 49 46 9	} Tattingstone	{	Per. 38946 35838
Dover Court Rushmere Woodbridge Steeple	25 55 13 96 25 30 57 39 17	} Woodbridge	{	59894 86345
	180 0 0			
Falkenham Rushmere Woodbridge	41 25 50 58 0 10	} Woodbridge	{	35761 86345
Falkenham Woodbridge Butley Steeple	48 42 0 83 10 0	} Butley	{	45013 34058
Falkenham Butley Orford Light House	21 58 1 116 14 19	} Orford Light House	{	60589 85207
Rushmere Woodbridge Otley Steeple	61 45 1-0 63 30 1-0 53 45 0	} Otley	{	29138 29044
	180 0 1			
Rushmere Otley Henley Steeple	40 25 30 46 25 0 93 9 30	} Henley	{	21111 18988
	180 0 0			
Dover Court Rushmere Obelisk, Woolverstone Park	12 43 40 13 21 10	} Obelisk	{	26766 25503
Rushmere Copdock Steeple Obelisk	61 35 38 53 5 10	} Copdock	{	28984 28057
Rushmere Copdock Henley	85 25 0 37 46 0 56 49 0	} Henley	{	21109 14580
	180 0 0			

Names of Stations.	Observed angles.	Distances.	
	° ′ ″		Feet.
Henley - - -	58 31 42—40	} Naughton - - {	15518
Copduck - - -	74 30 11—10		40894
Naughton Steeple - -	46 57 11—10		
Naughton - - -	74 24 2	} Lavenham - {	25867
Stoke - - -	45 58 58		48039
Lavenham Steeple -	59 37 0		
Lavenham - - -	67 48 30	} Bulmer - {	36837
Stoke - - -	44 59 10		48246
Bulmer Steeple - -	67 18 80		
Lavenham - - -	47 34 25	} Glemsford - {	25746
Bulmer - - -	44 18 40		27046
Glemsford Steeple			
Lavenham - -	18 02 0	} Topplesfield - {	67362
Bulmer - - -	141 15 80		34983
Topplesfield			
Lavenham - -	51 36 40	} Twinstead - {	43369
Stoke - - -	58 8 10		40006*
Twinstead Steeple			
Stoke - - -	50 4 48	} Twinstead - {	40006*
Great Tey - -	56 15 56		36895
Twinstead			
Friesling - -	156 48 10	} Southwald - {	30138
Danbury - - -	8 50 0		77622
Southwald Steeple			
Danbury - - -	151 18 36	} Gallywood - {	16097
Triptree, old Station - -	18 0 34		68211
Gallywood Common			
Triptree, old Station -	37 41 44	} Pleshley - {	63213
Gallywood - -	75 13 56		39973
Pleshley Steeple			
Danbury - - -	55 31 11	} Pleshley - {	48455
Gallywood - -	91 54 46		39904
Pleshley			
Gallywood - -	15 45 30	} High Easter - - {	47767
Pleshley - - -	134 49 0		14293
High Easter Steeple			

Names of stations.	Observed angles.	Distances.	
	° ′ ″		Feet.
Danbury	12 4 30	} Hatfield Broad Oak - {	85096
Pleshley	152 53 10		39058
Hatfield Broad Oak Steeple			
Danbury	25 45 6	} Thaxted - - {	101330
High Easter	29 43 54		53489
Thaxted Spire			
Hatfield Broad Oak	54 20 51	} Beauchamp Roding - {	24853
Pleshley	39 25 0		31806
Beauchamp Roding Spire			

The angle observed from the station on Danbury Steeple, between Hatfield Broad Oak and Thaxted, was 30° 35′ 40″; this, with the including sides, 85094 and 101330 feet, gives the following triangle:

Danbury　　　-　　30° 35′ 40″
Hatfield Broad Oak　91 24 0
Thaxted　　　-　　57 2 20, which gives the distance between Thaxted and Hatfield Broad Oak = 51566 feet.

Danbury	- - -	27 24 19	} Stoke - - {	122630
Petdian		118 2 28		63952
Stoke				

Again, the angle observed at Danbury, between Thaxted and Stoke was 66° 45′ 8″; this, with the sides which form it, Danbury and Thaxted, Danbury and Stoke, gives the following triangle:

Danbury　　　-　　66° 45′ 8″
Stoke　　　-　-　48 25 16
Thaxted　　　-　　64 51 36, from which we find 124450 feet, for the distance from Thaxted to Stoke.

The angle at Lavenham Steeple, between Stoke and Thaxted, was likewise observed, and found to be 89° 10′ 30″, which, with the distances of these latter stations from Lavenham, 48039 and 124450 feet, gives

Lavenham　　-　　89° 10′ 30″
Stoke　　　-　-　68 7 0
Thaxted　　　-　　22 42 30, from which we find 115480 feet to be the distance from Thaxted Spire to Lavenham Steeple.

The angle at Danbury, between Southweald and Hatfield Broad Oak, was found to be 54° 44′ 30′. The distances from Danbury to Southweald and Hatfield Broad Oak have been already found, the former being 77688 feet, and the latter 85096 feet; from these we get the triangle,

Danbury - 54° 44′ 30″
Southweald - 67 41 5
Hatfield Broad Oak 57 33 25, which gives 75104 feet, for the distance between Hatfield Broad Oak and Southweald Steeples.

In order to connect the preceding triangles with those carried on for the survey of the south-western part of Essex, and of Hertfordshire, stations were selected on Hampstead Heath, and on Highbeech in Epping Forest, to which the great theodolite was taken, as related in the article detailing the particulars of the operations in 1799. The triangles making this connection are the following. The first, namely,

Severndroog Tower 18° 58′ 10″
Southweald - 94 49 5
Langdon Hill - 56 12 45. It had from the included angle at Severndroog Tower, 18° 58′ 10″, and the sides Severndroog Tower and Langdon Hill; the first is 73787 feet, and the second 88470 feet. From these data, we obtain the distance between the station on Langdon Hill and that on Southweald Steeple = 43001 feet.

Names of Stations.	Observed angles.	Distances.	
Severndroog Tower - Langdon Hill - Brentwood Steeple	14 24 35 62 26 39	} Brentwood -	{ Feet. 78553° 36610
Severndroog Tower - Southweald - Brentwood	4 33 29 125 53 12	} Brentwood -	{ 78553° 1788

Foot of the cross on the dome of St. Paul's from the station on Severndroog Tower 39962°, Phil. Trans. for 1787, p. 250.

| Severndroog Tower - St. Paul's - Highbeech | 33 53 4
51 24 12 | } Highbeech - | { 71534
61919 |
| Severndroog Tower - Highbeech - Southweald | 44 34 28
69 53 13 | } Southweald | { 73795°
55156 |

U

From the last triangle, we find the distance from Severndroog Tower to the station on Southweald Steeple to be 73795 feet: this, it will be perceived, is deduced from the distance between the cross on the dome of St. Paul's and Severndroog Tower; but 73791 feet has been found by the triangle, which is derived from the distance between the latter station and Wrotham. A difference of 4 feet on such a distance, all things considered, is not a large quantity.

Names of Stations.	Observed Angles.	Distances.	Feet.
Severndroog Tower ·	49 6 1	} Brentwood ·	78558°
Highbeech · ·	71 16 44		63727
Brentwood Spire			
Severndroog Tower ·	51 24 12	} Hampstead Heath ·	64855
Highbeech · ·	58 29 19		59155
Hampstead Heath			
Highbeech · ·	24 36 5	} St. Paul's · ·	61919
Hampstead · ·	83 1 11		25966
St. Paul's			

As it became necessary to ascertain the situation of a high building near Berkhamstead, which, for distinction sake, I shall style the Gazebo, the instrument was removed from the station on Highbeech, to another farther west of it, as some trees obstructed the view of this object from the former. To get the distance from St. Paul's to this new station, the distance between it and the old one was measured, and found = 156 feet. The angles in the following triangle were also observed.

       Highbeech, old station   66° 31′ 47″
       Highbeech, new station   113 3 46
         St. Paul's   which gives the distance from
St. Paul's to the new station 61738 feet.

Highbeech, new station ·	105 21 46	} Gazebo · ·	49631
Berkhamstead Gazebo ·	41 55 23		88872
St. Paul's ·			
Southweald · ·	16 46 15	} Epping Windmill ·	46717
Highbeech, old station ·	51 16 51		17042°
Stand of Epping Windmill			
Severndroog Tower ·	10 8 44	} Epping Windmill ·	81891
Highbeech · ·	132 10 41		17043°
Stand of Epping Windmill			

Names of Stations.	Observed Angles.	Distances.	
Highbeech, old station - Berkhamstead Gazebo - *Stand of Epping Windmill*	99 19 16 17 41 25	} Epping Windmill -	*Feet.* { 17049 55567

At the new station on Highbeech, the angle between the staff on the Gazebo at Berkhamstead and the old station was observed, and found to be 141° 45′ 50″. This angle, with the measured distance between the stations, and also the distance from the Gazebo to the new station, which are respectively 460 and 49628 feet, gives 49987 feet, for the distance between the new station on Highbeech and Berkhamstead Gazebo.

Names of Stations.	Observed Angles.	Distances.	
Hatfield Broad Oak Steeple - Berkhamstead Gazebo - *Epping Windmill* -	59 1 0 43 12 50	} Hatfield Broad Oak -	{ 87140 60219
Berkhamstead Gazebo - Hatfield Broad Oak - *Nasing Steeple*	14 9 55 17 19 38	} Nasing - -	{ 39573 53844
Hatfield Broad Oak - Berkhamstead Gazebo - *Henham on the Mount Steeple*	107 39 57 20 41 30	} Henham on the Mount	{ 39265 105890
Hatfield Broad Oak - Henham on the Mount - *Thorley Steeple*	71 28 54 36 6 30	} Thorley - -	{ 24275 39058
Henham on the Mount - Thorley Steeple - *Atterbury Steeple*	15 24 0 69 33 0	} Attebury - -	{ 37882 23430
Henham on the Mount - Thorley - - - *Rickling Steeple*	87 20 0 24 57 50	} Rickling - -	{ 17816 43169
Henham on the Mount - Rickling - - *Elmdon Steeple*	20 54 0 146 35 0	} Elmdon -	{ 45275 29327

The angle between Albury and Elmdon Steeples was observed, at Henham on the Mount, and found to be 72° 47′ 38″. The distances from the former stations to the latter are 57882 and 45875 feet, which give the following triangle:

         Henham   -   72° 47′ 38″
         Albury   -   60 28 27
         Elmdon   -   46 43 35, from whence we get the distance
between Albury and Elmdon = 49702 feet.

Names of Stations.	Observed angles.	Distances.	
Henham on the Mount - Elmdon • • • *Thaxted Steeple*	106 30 50 23 2 40	} Thaxted - -	{ Feet. 22088 56302
Elmdon • • • Thaxted • • *Balsham Steeple*	71 54 10 53 18 44	} Balsham -	{ 55262 65504
Elmdon • • • Balsham • • *Babraham Mount Station*	23 38 46 48 40 38	} Babraham Mount -	{ 43659 23251
Elmdon • • • Babraham Mount - - *Triplow Steeple*	29 46 30 32 56 30	} Triplow • •	{ 24806 29185

The angle at Henham on the Mount, between Hatfield Broad Oak and Thaxted Steeples, is 109° 10′ 44″; and the distances of the latter stations from the former are 39266 and 22988 feet; from these *data* we have the triangle.

         Henham   -   109° 10′ 44″
         Thaxted   -   45 56 29
         Hatfield Broad Oak   -   24 52 47, which gives 51608 feet for
the distance of Thaxted from Hatfield Broad Oak.

Hatfield Broad Oak - • Beauchamp Roding • *High Easter Steeple*	51 9 50 84 26 10	} High Easter •	{ 24858 21460
Severndroog Tower - • Langdon Hill • - *Hornchurch Steeple*	21 6 9 24 10 20	} Hornchurch - -	{ 50989 44832°
Langdon Hill • • • Gravesend • • • *Hornchurch Steeple*	77 57 33 50 39 0	} Hornchurch •	{ 44837° 56438

Names of Stations.	Observed angles.	Distances.	
Gravesend - - - Hornchurch - - - *Purfleet Cliff Station*	24 33 30 31 26 62	} Purfleet Cliff -	{ Feet. 35517 22282
Severndroog Tower - - Hornchurch - - - *Staircase of Barking Steeple*	39 43 2 27 10 44	} Barking - -	{ 25383 35404
Severndroog Tower - - St. Paul's - - - *Westham Steeple*	39 41 6 44 15 27	} Westham - =	{ 28046 25602

ART. XXXIX. *Secondary Triangles.*

St. Paul's from Severndroog Tower 39962 feet.

Severndroog Tower - - St. Paul's - - - *Limehouse Steeple*	13 1 7 22 36 13	} Limehouse	{ 26371 15456
Severndroog Tower - - Highbeech - - - *Chigwell Steeple*	9 15 30 32 36 30	} Chigwell -	{ 57757 17242
Severndroog Tower - - Frierning - - - *Billericay Chapel*	11 57 6 74 34 30	} Billericay - -	{ 100110 21506
Westham Steeple - Staircase of Barking Steeple - *Station on Bank of the Thames*	45 58 0 68 35 0	} Station - -	{ 15640 12077
Station on Bank of the Thames Westham Steeple - - *Perry's Mast House*	41 21 0 56 15 0	} Perry's Mast House	{ 13120 10424
Hornchurch - - - Staircase of Barking Steeple *Chimney of Public House at Barking Creek*	16 31 20 68 52 0	} Chimney -	{ 31236 9005
Purfleet Cliff - - - Hornchurch - - *Guzzard Station*	54 57 0 46 40 6	} Guzzard - -	{ 21002 23638

Names of Stations.	Observed angles.	Distances.	
Purfleet Cliff - - - Hornchurch - - - *Rainham Steeple*	34 11 30 32 1 0	} Rainham - •	{ Feet. 16387 17370
Purfleet Cliff - - - Hornchurch - - - *Lord Eardley's, Belvidere*	81 9 0 31 50 50	} Belvidere - •	{ 16211 30169
Purfleet Cliff - - - Rainham - - - *Station at Cold Harbour*	42 18 30 41 45 0	} Cold Harbour -	{ 10971 11090
Guzzard - - - Hornchurch - - - *Aveley Mill*	56 8 10 56 43 20	} Aveley Mill - •	{ 21436 21301
Purfleet Cliff - - - Hornchurch - - - *Valence Tree*	34 2 40 95 3 40	} Valence Tree - •	{ 36305 20404
Gravesend - - - Severndroog Tower - - *Chadwell Steeple*	79 19 30 13 41 10	} Chadwell •	{ 17008 70717
Gravesend - - - Chadwell Steeple - - *Greys Steeple*	35 59 0 79 31 30	} Greys - - •	{ 28479 10953
Gravesend - - - Chadwell Steeple - - u *Flagstaff on Mr. Button's House*	37 46 0 94 24 0	} Flagstaff - -	{ 22880 14054
Gravesend - - - Chadwell Steeple - - *West Thurrock Steeple*	51 43 0 80 2 30	} West Thurrock -	{ 22457 17897
Gravesend - - - Hornchurch - - - *Horndon Spire*	49 8 30 36 7 5	} Horndon - •	{ 31382 42833
Gravesend - - - Chadwell - - - *West Tilbury Steeple*	18 52 0 59 16 30	} West Tilbury -	{ 5617 14956
Gravesend - - - Chadwell - - - *Northfleet Steeple*	69 31 27 30 27 42	} Northfleet •	{ 8755 16179

Names of Stations.	Observed angles.	Distances.	
Gravesend - - - Chadwell - - - East Tilbury Flagstaff	57 16 0 59 13 10	} East Tilbury - - {	Feet 16148 15947
Chadwell - - - Mr. Button's Flagstaff - Station near Ockendon -	51 23 0 93 22 30	} Station - - {	25526 20031
Mr. Button's Flagstaff - Station near Ockendon - Orset Steeple	54 20 30 54 54 30	} Orset - - - {	17360 17840
Gravesend - - - Halstow - - - Fobbing Steeple	45 9 13 62 0 10	} Fobbing - - {	41433 33270
Hadleigh Station - Halstow - - - Fobbing Steeple	65 31 12 45 48 50	} Fobbing - - {	26221 33279
Halstow - - - Gravesend - - - Thundersley Steeple	101 39 57 37 16 40	} Thundersley - - {	41342
Halstow - - - Hadleigh - - - Hadleigh Spire - -	7 53 10 117 13 23	} Hadleigh - - {	5713 37028
Hadleigh - - - Halstow - - - - Leigh Steeple Staircase -	89 20 40 24 54 37	} Leigh - - {	11735 37357
Halstow - - - - Sheppey Station - Leigh Steeple Staircase	74 23 61 42 26 8	} Leigh - -	37359 53545
Halstow - - - Sheppey - - - Sheerness Fort Flagstaff	13 17 45 46 5 47	} Sheerness - {	41434 13063
Hadleigh - - - Sheppey - - - South Church Steeple	38 43 29 21 56 26	} South Church - {	71233 74461
Hadleigh - - - Sheppey Station - Prittlewell Steeple	11 6 2 80 16 46	} Prittlewell - {	27208 5311

Names of Stations.	Observed angles.	Distances.	Feet.
Canewden Steeple Prittlewell *Little Wakering Steeple*	15 50 0 60 46 30	} Little Wakering	{ 23850 19603
Canewden Prittlewell *Bank Flagstaff*	64 17 0 67 46 30	} Bank	{ 38739 31908
Prittlewell Station on Bank *Shoebury ness*	33 10 0 39 20 30	} Shoebury-ness	{ 21208 18302
Canewden Bank Flagstaff *Foul-ness Chapel*	38 51 30 81 20 0	} Foul-ness	{ 35481 19473
Rayleigh Peldon *Foul-ness Signal Staff*	47 18 6 43 45 33	} Signal Staff	{ 71822 76311
Tillingham Steeple Peldon *Signal Staff, Tillingham Grange*	139 21 10 9 44 89	} Signal Staff	{ 13990 53860
Tillingham Peldon *Signal Staff, Bradwell Point*	43 27 58 24 10 18	} Signal Staff	{ 18808 31591
Tillingham Peldon *Brightlingsea Steeple*	11 3 10 100 50 20	} Brightlingsea	{ 56094 29603
Tillingham West Mersey Steeple *Tolesbury Steeple*	39 48 40 57 33 13	} Tolesbury	{ 24611 18673
Tillingham Tiptree, old Station *Althorn Church*	63 55 6 35 34 3	} Althorn	{ 31946 49330
Tillingham Althorn *Burnham Steeple*	26 32 10 55 49 0	} Burnham	{ 26664 14400
Tillingham Peldon *Toleshunt Major Steeple*	47 33 35 56 33 25	} Toleshunt	{ 36561 32317

Names of stations.	Observed angles.	Distance.	
	° ′ ″		Feet.
Prittlewell Steeple -	33 10 0	} Signal Staff - - {	81308
Bank Flagstaff - -	39 40 30		16302
Signal Staff, Shoebury-ness			
Triptree, new Station -	38 5 18	} Maldon - - {	19425
Danoury - - -	30 11 27		23819
Maldon Spire			
Triptree, new Station -	36 43 30	} Purleigh - - {	36118
Danbury - - -	72 9 0		22734
Purleigh Steeple			
Danbury - - -	17 47 32	} Steeple - - {	49647
Purleigh Steeple -	148 16 30		28850
Steeple Steeple			
Danbury - - -	26 17 40	} Hockley - - {	41401
Canewden - -	51 8 0		23553
Hockley Steeple			
Danbury - - -	27 41 50	} Hockley - - {	41400
Rettenden - - -	109 28 0		20170
Hockley Steeple			
Danbury - - -	53 39 40	} Rettenden - - {	30079
Canewden - -	35 25 0		41810
Rettenden Steeple			
Rettenden - -	34 41 0	} Stow, St. Mary's - {	13571
Canewden - -	30 53 0		26131
Stow, St Mary's Steeple			
Rayleigh - -	71 51 18	} Rettenden - - {	20760
Langdon Station - -	27 38 45		43316
Rettenden Steeple			
Rayleigh - - -	51 8 10	} Runwell - - {	81107
Langdon - -	18 10 40		34975
Runwell Steeple			
Danbury - - -	48 57 11	} Burghstead - - {	53254
Rayleigh - - -	72 39 17		42079
Great Burghstead Steeple			
Danbury - - -	59 11 7	} Hanningfield - {	17666
Gallywood Station -	41 40 10		22832
East Hanningfield Steeple			

X

Names of stations.	Observed angles.	Distances.	Feet.
Frierning Steeple Danbury Stock Steeple	36 7 48 15 38 36	Stock	16826 36793
Triptree, old Station Tillingham Steeple Southminster Steeple	18 39 11 83 33 14	Southminster	55075 17711
Peldon Steeple Tillingham Layer Marney Steeple	97 35 51 43 54 4	Layer Marney	10180 49369
Peldon Tillingham Signal Staff, St. Osyth Point	80 20 6 61 39 14	Signal Staff	60701 67990
Thorp Steeple Little Bentley Great Clackton Signal Staff	143 7 36 18 54 19	Signal Staff	81517 39844
Thorp Peldon Great Clackton Steeple	71 35 55 16 58 13	Great Clackton	18920 61508
Dover Court Steeple Thorp Finton Steeple	24 36 48 92 26 41	Finton	38998 16857
Dover Court Thorp Finton Signal Staff	39 16 34 70 11 16	Signal Staff	34686 23340
Dover Court Thorp Walton Tower or Sea-mark	53 15 16 47 58 11	Walton	26075 22389
Dover Court Thorp Cupola, Landguard Fort	133 57 30 13 29 57	Cupola	15085 46517
Thorp Peldon Ardleigh Steeple	46 16 17 47 1 36	Ardleigh	47494 46901
Peldon Great Tey Steeple Frating Steeple	106 10 16 32 32 11	Frating	35433 63274

Names of Stations.	Observed angles.	Distances.	Feet.
Thorp - - - Little Berniey Steeple - Thorrington Steeple	30 17 55 90 41 13	} Thorrington - {	23890 12053
Dover Court - - Thorp - - - Kirby Steeple	23 10 12 59 41 37	} Kirby - - {	30343 13847
Dover Court - - Kirby Steeple - - Little Oakley Steeple	33 8 12 18 33 0	} Little Oakley - {	12216 21193
Tillingham - - - Layer de la Hay Steeple - Tolesbunt Major Steeple	38 45 0 45 18 0	} Tolesbunt Major - {	36541 32082
Dover Court - - Tattingstone Steeple - Branthum Steeple	16 48 13 98 16 0	} Brantham - - {	42590 12447
Dover Court - - Rushmere Steeple - Hardstead Steeple	30 52 58 16 51 2	} Harkstead - {	19946 35319
Dover Court - - Tattingstone - - Arwarton Steeple	33 17 30 14 20 0	} Arwarton - - {	13053 18941
Tattingstone - - Arwarton Steeple - Bradfield Steeple	66 10 0 43 18 0	} Bradfield - - {	20998 18059
Dover Court - - Rushmere - - Harwich Spire	78 48 50 9 58 0	} Harwich - - {	8381 45036
Dover Court - - Rushmere - - Holleslcy Steeple	56 48 10 67 58 30	} Holleslcy - - {	57475 51881
Dover Court - - Rushmere - - Shottisham Steeple	47 7 40 68 4 20	} Shottisham - {	58205 41334
Dover Court - - Rushmere - - Bawdsey Steeple	65 59 15 51 42 10	} Bawdsey - - {	46177 53024

X 2

Names of Stations.	Observed angles.	Distances.	
	° ′ ″		Feet
Dover Court	52 48 11	} Felixstow — — {	28926
Woodbridge Steeple	28 31 0		48162
Felixstow Signal Staff			
Dover Court	43 12 55	} Bawdzey {	41265
Woodbridge	44 53 0		44510
Bawdzey Signal Staff			
Rushmere	45 41 10	} Orford — — {	75267
Falkenham Steeple	103 52 0		55472
Orford Steeple			
Woodbridge	28 28 0	} Rendlesham + {	21686
Butely Steeple	34 37 0		18204
Rendlesham Steeple			
Butely	153 23 0	} Orford + {	15762
Rendlesham	11 20 0		33057
Orford Steeple			
Dover Court	8 1 6	} Kesgrave — — {	7371
Rushmere	66 54 0		48505
Kesgrave Steeple			
Dover Court	34 14 16	} Waldringfield — {	43460
Rushmere	62 15 50		28841
Waldringfield Steeple			
Dover Court	30 58 10	} Wherstead — — {	40331
Kesgrave Steeple	56 8 30		24593
Wherstead Steeple			
Falkenham	30 59 0	} Nacton — {	15098
Rushmere	36 2 50		21959
Nacton Steeple			
Dover Court	13 29 58	} Capel — — {	55110
Stoke	22 45 20		33325
Capel Steeple			
Stoke	14 14 18	} Hintlesham — {	40790
Capel Steeple	103 0 34		17186
Hintlesham Steeple			
Stoke — —	39 43 10	} Bildeston {	42238
Lavenham Steeple —	63 31 40		23821
Bildestone Steeple			

Names of Stations.	Observed angles.	Distances.	Feet.
Stoke - - - Bildestone Steeple - - *Aldham Steeple*	33 53 40 48 50 10	} Aldham - -	{ 32055 23740
Lavenham - - - Naughton - - *Hadleigh Spire*	29 39 50 93 17 20	} Hadleigh - -	{ 42673 21154
Lavenham - - - Naughton Steeple - *Lindsey Steeple*	31 40 10 42 22 50	} Lindsey - -	{ 25138 19587
Stoke - - - Lavenham - - *Newton Steeple*	21 7 30 24 48 40	} Newton - .	{ 27153 25413
Stoke - - - Newton - *Groton Steeple*	27 1 0 41 49 0	} Groton - -	{ 19660 13140
Bulmer Steeple - - Glemsford Steeple - - *Waldingfield Steeple*	67 27 40 53 37 50	} Waldingfield -	{ 25637 29407
Lavenham - - - Glemsford - - *Acton Steeple*	56 59 0 33 6 50	} Acton - -	{ 14065 21097
Lavenham - - - Bulmer - - *Beauchamp Church, St. Paul's*	26 13 10 91 21 20	} Beauchamp -	{ 42546 18360
Lavenham - - - Toppesfield Steeple - - *High western part of Hedingham Castle*	12 31 50 52 7 20	} Hedingham Castle	{ 52159 16316
Lavenham - - - Bulmer - - *Ridgewell Steeple*	26 57 0 123 32 0	} Ridgewell - .	{ 61325 33886
Stoke Steeple - Naughton Steeple - *Langham Steeple*	101 57 15 20 32 45	} Langham - .	{ 17904 49907
Stoke Steeple - Great Tey Steeple - *Great Horkesley Steeple*	21 17 20 8 23 40	} Great Horksley -	{ 23615 33859

Names of Stations.	Observed angles.	Distance.	
	° ′ ″		Feet.
Stoke	71 21 0	} Great Horksley — {	13615
Twinstead Steeple	19 53 0		37819
Great Horksley Steeple			
Stoke	41 84 0	} Mount Bures — {	19360
Great Horksley	109 43 0		81821
Mount Bures Steeple			
Stoke	63 30 40	} Earles Colne — {	47756
St. Mary's, Colchester	70 48 0		44804
Earles Colne Steeple			
Great Tey	14 47 20	} West Bergholt — {	11557
St. Mary's Colchester	33 14 0		16139
West Bergholt Steeple			
Danbury	6 6 0	} Braxted — {	41558
Great Tey	6 56 40		36349
Braxted Steeple			
Great Tey	4 37 24	} Kelvedon — {	36349
Braxted Steeple	11 43 36		15407
Kelvedon Steeple			
Great Tey	30 14 50	} Messing — {	22390
Kelvedon	58 32 0		13271
Messing Steeple			
Great Tey	51 43 10	} East Thorp — {	15462
Kelvedon	36 4 0		26016
East Thorp Steeple			
Danbury	50 48 0	} Black Notley — {	31487
Triptree, new station —	85 12 36		46039
Black Notley Steeple			
Danbury	33 51 34	} Witham — {	33850
Triptree, old station	77 29 26		14852
Witham Steeple			
Danbury	47 47 25	} Tarling — {	31874
Triptree, old station	58 17 35		27751
Tarling Spire			
Danbury	51 43 0	} Braintree — {	51928
Triptree, old station —	90 45 56		46152
Braintree Steeple			

Names of Stations.	Observed angles.	Distances.	
	° ′ ″		Feet.
Triptree, new station	56 13 54	} Feltstead	6 574
Gallywood station	64 47 51		5 409
Feltstead Steeple			
Danbury	86 31 30	} Braintree	58 918
Feltstead Steeple	73 49 10		87 392
Braintree Steeple			
Danbury	17 39 30	} Feltstead	60 336
Pleshley Steeple	116 15 43		80 409
Feltstead Steeple			
Triptree, new station	87 23 20	} Hatfield Peverel	80 867
Danbury	87 35 30		80 132
S. Spire of Hatfield Peverel Abbey			
Pleshley	68 3 0	} Great Leigh	24 915
Feltstead	64 81 0		25 635
Great Leigh Steeple			
Danbury	41 29 44	} Great Baddow	16 345
Pleshley	16 39 0		37 796
Great Baddow Steeple			
Danbury	83 59 8	} Chelmsford	24 110
Pleshley	80 81 0		28 186
Chelmsford Spire			
Danbury	38 36 36	} Whittle	33 552
Pies' ley	41 51 80		27 122
Whittle Steeple			
Danbury	19 16 30	} Willingale Spain	60 488
Hatfield Broad Oak	33 29 15		34 390
Willingale Spain Steeple			
Pleshley	36 18 0	} Roxwell	19 937
Gallywood station	86 14 36		26 630
Roxwell Steeple			
Pleshley	103 44 45	} White Roding	33 689
Gallywood station	34 9 50		57 926
White Roding Steeple			
Southweald Steeple	87 51 51	} Doddinghurst	17 880
Fryerning Steeple	30 14 50		16 590
Doddinghurst Steeple			

Names of stations.	Observed angles		Distances.		Feet.
Southweald Epping Windmill *Theydon Mount Steeple*	3 49 0 7 31 0	}	Theydon	{	31098 15814
Southweald Theydon Mount Steeple *Navestock new Windmill*	49 11 0 16 16 0	}	Navestock	{	9656 15846
Southweald Theydon Mount *Theydon Garnon Steeple*	5 19 0 149 43 0	}	Theydon Garnon	{	37107 6797
Theydon Mount Theydon Garnon *Havering Steeple*	111 19 30 53 38 0	}	Havering	{	11090 24397
Severndroog Tower Highbreech Station *Cupola of a house at Woodford*	5 40 10 14 49 4	}	Cupola	{	52160 30197
Southweald Highbreech *Ruins near Ilford*	36 10 10 05 36 10	}	Ruins	{	51340 33405
Highbreech St. Paul's *Cheshunt Station*	101 38 0 16 2 0	}	Cheshunt	{	34708 77151
Berkhamstead Gazebo Naseing Steeple *Hunsdon Steeple*	25 59 0 88 51 14	}	Hunsdon	{	43157 18911
Naseing Hunsdon Steeple *Broxbourn Steeple*	94 35 0 34 41 0	}	Broxbourn	{	13899 24348
Berkhamstead Gazebo Harfield Broad Oak Steeple *Harlow Steeple*	8 33 28 20 11 11	}	Harlow Steeple	{	62518 16964
Harfield Broad Oak Naseing *Sabridgworth Steeple*	19 44 10 11 48 5	}	Sabridgworth	{	81014 34763
Thorley Steeple Albury Steeple *Great Hadham Steeple*	45 17 0 40 19 0	}	Great Hadham	{	15153 16995

Names of stations.	Observed angles.	Distances.	
Henham on the Mount Steeple Albury Steeple *Bishop Stortford Steeple*	31 43 3½ 53 14 0	Bishop Stortford	30524 29993
Henham on the Mount Albury *Stanstead Mountfitchet Steeple*	42 32 34 23 35 3	Stanstead Mountfitchet	16571 28009
Henham on the Mount Stanstead Mountfitchet *Farnham Steeple*	31 3 0 109 2 0	Farnham	14419 13373
Henham on the Mount Albury *Meesdon Windmill*	38 53 0 73 13 10	Meesdon	39054 25421
Henham on the Mount Elmdon Steeple *Chimney on an octagon Lodge*	40 10 40 25 58 10	Octagon Lodge	21677 31938
Balsham Steeple Elmdon *Shady Camps Steeple*	75 15 8 25 0 22	Shady Camps	83740 53410
Balsham Shady Camps *Ashdon Steeple*	35 7 10 99 19 0	Ashdon	30778 16180
Danbury Thaxted Spire *Little Saling Steeple*	9 35 0 16 0 9	Little Saling	76459 28886
Elmdon Rickling Steeple *Newport Steeple*	22 27 0 64 25 0	Newport	26492 11116
Danbury Little Saling Steeple *Stebbing Steeple*	7 55 6 61 18 0	Stebbing	71826 11198

Y

The Account of a

ART. XL. *Principal Triangles for the Survey of the Western Part of Kent.* Plate XXXIII.

Frant Steeple from Botley Hill 90361.4 feet.

Names of stations.	Observed angles.	Distance.	
	o ′ ″		Fær.
Frant Steeple	42 17 10	}Sevenoaks {	58492
Botley Hill	32 52 47		44032
Sevenoaks old Windmill			
Frant	11 17 10	}Chiddingstone {	42875
Sevenoaks Windmill	40 52 50		24858
Chiddingstone Steeple			
Frant	35 2 17	}Mount Sion {	57874
Chiddingstone	97 43 43		33532
Mount Sion Station			
Frant	31 28 30	}East Peckham {	58964
Mount Sion	76 9 30		31707
East Peckham Steeple			
Mount Sion	48 14 0	}Tudely Steeple {	31363
East Peckham	65 11 0		25772
Tudely Steeple			
Botley Hill	11 1 42	}Seal Chart {	59563
Sevenoaks Windmill	141 42 12		18368
Seal Chart Station			
Seal Chart	74 10 0	}Tunbridge {	26851
Sevenoaks Windmill	66 49 0		28101
Tunbridge Steeple			
Seal Chart	78 1 0	}Otford Mount {	10327
Sevenoaks Windmill	54 39 0		84462
Station on Otford Mount			
Sevenoaks Windmill	69 27 0	}Silverden Farm {	28395
Otford Mount	61 24 0		30884
Silverden Farm Station			

Norwood from Severndroog Tower 39155 feet.

Norwood	53 7 40	}Well Hill {	57393
Severndroog Tower	84 8 0		48155
Well Hill Station			

Names of stations.	Observed angles.	Distances.	
	° ′ ″		Feet.
Severndroog Tower	55 4 14	} Crayford	{ 16479
Well Hill	35 0 31		37840
Crayford Steeple			
Well Hill	77 37 40	} Ash	{ 34738
Crayford	48 8 40		45555
Ash Steeple			
Ash	53 7 10	} Northfleet	{ 32837
Crayford	44 32 4		36767
Northfleet Steeple			
Ash	15 30 4	} Gravesend	{ 32664
Northfleet	85 1 8		8762
Gravesend Station			
Ash	47 33 30	} Belvidere	{ 56308
Northfleet	97 53 40		41951
Lord Eardley's, Belvidere			

Gravesend from Halstow 44836 feet.

Gravesend	31 38 20	} Gadshill	{ 22275
Halstow	24 18 20		28388
Gadshill Station			
Halstow	128 34 18		
Sheppey	18 18 3		
Gadshill		Sheppey from Gadshill	70686
Sheppey	28 28 0	} Stockbury	{ 43144
Hernhill Steeple	37 8 0		71603
Stockbury Steeple			
Frinsted Steeple	65 27 18	} Hernhill	{ 57820
Sheppey	64 9 24		58439
Hernhill Steeple			

Art. xli. *Secondary Triangles.*

Frant Steeple	16 37 80	} Bidborough	{ 26066
Botley Hill Station	9 52 49		68071
Bidborough Steeple			
Frant	30 52 0	} Station	{ 27887
Chiddingstone Steeple	29 5 0		29951
Station near Bidborough Church			

Y 2

Names of stations.	Observed angles.	Distances.	Feet.
Frant Botley Hill *Remarkable Tree near Kibben's Cross*	104 24 36 13 40 51	} Remarkable Tree -	24886 99801
Frant Station near Bidborough Church *Cowden Steeple*	46 31 0 93 3 30	} Cowden - -	41943 30485
Station near Bidborough Church Chiddingstone Steeple *Mount Sion Station*	76 2 0 68 42 0	} Mount Sion -	31194 35532
Station near Bidborough Church Mount Sion *Leigh Steeple*	10 37 0 10 21 0	} Leigh - -	11241 82031
Frant Chiddingstone *Ide Hill Station*	10 5 30 149 38 30	} Ide Hill - -	61547 11689
Chiddingstone Ide Hill *Edenbridge Steeple*	67 41 0 49 43 0	} Edenbridge -	18639 21606
Seal Church Steeple Otford Mount *Sevenoaks Steeple*	37 45 0 46 5 0	} Sevenoaks -	15131 17766
Mount Sion Station Peckham Steeple *Hadlow Steeple*	10 36 0 47 56 0	} Hadlow - -	25291 11987
Seal Chart Station Otford Mount *Sundrich Steeple*	50 45 0 86 11 0	} Sundrich - -	19824 23131
Otford Mount Silverden Station *Seal Steeple*	94 17 0 37 20 0	} Seal - -	9705 32484
Well Hill Station Norwood *Windmill, Ketson Common*	17 40 40 14 5 12	} Ketson Common Windmill	16538 33103
Well Hill Beverndroog Tower *Flagstaff on Hayes Common*	56 39 0 37 39 0	} Flagstaff - -	28273 38664

Norwood from Severndroog Tower 31155 feet. Between the triangles

Names of Stations.	Observed angles.	Distances.	Feet.
Norwood Severndroog Tower *Hayes Common*	6 53 30 48 30 0	} Flagstaff	{ 30718 38654"
Norwood Hayes Common *Flagstaff on Addington Common*	34 27 30 39 41 0	} Flagstaff	{ 20391 18068
Well Hill Norwood *Cudham Steeple*	36 11 40 33 44 5	} Cudham	{ 20860 48958

Well Hill from Otford Mount 19206 feet.

Orford Mount Well Hill *Knockholt Beeches, East End*	52 11 0 73 58 0	} Knockholt Beeches	{ 21860 18790
Well Hill Crayford Steeple *Dome of a Race House*	33 33 46 41 17 10	} Race House	{ 27859 16075
Well Hill Norwood *Windmill, Bromley Common*	70 35 40 39 36 24	} Windmill	{ 57560 38945
Well Hill Severndroog Tower *Farnborough Station*	59 1 0 13 58 0	} Farnborough	{ 11650 41381
Well Hill Farnborough *St. Mary's Cray Steeple*	58 51 0 79 32 0	} St. Mary's Cray	{ 17855 15019
Well Hill Norwood *Halstead Steeple*	79 42 26 8 40 4	} Halstead	{ 8653 56492
Norwood Severndroog Tower *Bromley Steeple*	36 36 40 32 52 50	} Bromley	{ 22696 24932
Well Hill Severndroog Tower *Bromley Steeple*	32 29 0 51 13 0	} Bromley	{ 36198 22938

Names of Stations.	Observed Angles.	Distances.	
Well Hill – – – Bromley – – *Hayes Steeple*	14 19 0 53 35 0	} Hayes – –	{ feet. 31009 9805
Bromley – – Severndroog Tower – *Lewisham Steeple*	45 18 0 51 28 0	} Lewisham – –	{ 19640 17846

Severndroog Tower from Chiselhurst Steeple, 16778.

Severndroog Tower – Chiselhurst Steeple – *New Cross Station*	100 42 0 42 22 0	} New Cross –	{ 23129 36309
Severndroog Tower – New Cross – – *Eastcombe Point Station*	38 0 0 49 55 0	} Eastcombe Point –	{ 18014 14496
Severndroog Tower – Eastcombe Point – *Woolwich Steeple*	49 39 0 31 55 0	} Woolwich – –	{ 9688 13879
Severndroog Tower – Crayford – – *Bexley Steeple*	15 1 10 57 48 80	} Bexley – –	{ 23453 7185
Well Hill – – – Crayford – – *Charlton Farm*	61 48 0 36 39 0	} Charlton – –	{ 22835 33714
Crayford – – Charlton Farm – – *Darent Steeple*	23 17 10 28 14 0	} Darent –	{ 20374 17080
Ash Steeple – – Crayford – – *Dartford Brent Mill*	12 56 40 30 32 18	} Dartford Brent –	{ 33636 14830
Crayford – – Stone Steeple – – *Dartford Brent*	16 16 18 31 0 0	} Stone – –	{ 21153 8069
Ash – – Northfleet Steeple – *Hartley Steeple*	15 42 50 4 56 30	} Hartley – –	{ 7869 24730
Northfleet – – Ash – – ∴ *Ridley Steeple*	8 40 40 101 42 0	} Ridley – –	{ 33675 5189

Names of Stations.	Observed angles.	Distances.	Feet.
Northfleet - - Gravesend Station - *Southfleet Steeple*	90 15 30 49 26 6	}Southfleet - - {	10290 13545
Gadshill - - - Sheppey Isle - - *Shottenden Windmill*	28 8 54 121 36 55	}Shottenden Mill - {	119539 60221
Gravesend Station - Gadshill - - *Cliff Steeple*	40 46 7 98 28 1	}Cliff - - {	10590 19907
Gravesend Station - Gadshill - - *Higham Steeple*	35 48 14 70 47 15	}Higham - {	14115 13489
Gravesend Station - Halstow Station - *Gravesend Steeple*	86 16 16 4 18 19	}Gravesend - {	5373 64747
Gravesend - - Halstow - - *Chalk Steeple*	25 8 43 8 11 44	}Chalk - - {	11841 34673
Gravesend - - Gadshill - - Lower Hope Point, Chimney of *the Guard Room*	59 31 43 78 5 57	}Lower Hope Point - {	82287 25577
Gravesend - - Gadshill - - *Flagstaff, Tilbury Fort*	99 28 57 15 26 18	}Tilbury Fort - {	6539 24288
Gadshill - - Sheppey - - - *Rainham Steeple*	28 52 26 26 24 22	}Rainham - - {	38843 41527
Gadshill - - - Halstow - - *Swanscombe Spire*	128 37 56 29 12 53	}Swanscombe - - {	36747 58814
Gadshill - - Halstow - - *Northfleet Steeple*	124 43 26 28 58 11	}Northfleet - {	31014 51658
Halstow - - - Gravesend - - *Southfleet Steeple*	4 37 23 159 53 20	}Southfleet - {	57736 13534

Names of Stations.	Observed angles.	Distances.
Gravesend - - - Halstow - - - Sborn Mill	3ȷ 36 50 15 44 0 } Sborn Mill - -	Feet. { 14947 34435
Sheppey - - Stockbury - - Gillingham Steeple	39 23 14 79 31 3 } Gillingham - -	{ 48453° 31157
Sheppey - - Gillingham - - St. James's Church, Isle of Grain	63 7 51 14 34 17 } St. James's Church -	{ 10164 43117
Halstow - - - Sheppey - - Gillingham Steeple	73 41 28 28 9 15 } Gillingham - -	{ 13822 48453°
Gadshill - - - Sheppey - - Friendsbury Steeple	23 35 24 4 10 33 } Friendsbury -	{ 11049 60731
Halstow - - - Sheppey - - Chimney of the Star Inn	73 39 6 31 45 47 } Star Inn - -	{ 30617 50870
Halstow - - - Sheppey - - High Staff at the Upper Bell Inn	88 11 56 44 45 13 } Bell Inn - -	{ 47500 67456
Sheppey - - Twinstead - - Hove Steeple	75 21 37 50 42 20 } Hove - - -	{ 59215 4732
Gadshill - - - Sheppey - - Upchurch Spire	17 4 23 25 36 26 } Upchurch - -	{ 44466 31395
Gadshill - - - Sheppey - - Bobbing Spire	21 19 45 57 26 29 } Bobbing - -	{ 60739 26811
Sheppey - - Halstow - - - Flagstaff, Sheerness Garrison	46 5 47 13 7 45 } Flagstaff - -	{ 13063 41434
Sheppey - - Painted - - Hucking Spire	17 13 51 93 18 29 } Hucking -	{ 51765 15656

Names of Stations.	Observed Angles.	Distances	
	° ′ ″		Feet.
Sheppey East Church Station *Hernhill Steeple*	29 17 6 136 15 56	} Hernhill	{ 58439 41564
East Church Sheppey *Milton Steeple*	44 20 17 95 42 22	} Milton	{ 52313 22696
Sheppey Milton *Iwade Steeple*	36 56 30 32 24 0	} Iwade	{ 12997 14544
Hernhill Frinstead *Witchling Steeple*	7 28 0 45 6 35	} Witchling	{ 51579 9461
Hernhill Sheppey *Tenham Steeple*	25 1 0 25 51 16	} Tenham	{ 33833 30536
Tenham Sheppey *Bapchild Spire*	75 31 0 24 42 40	} Bapchild	{ 29846 12846
Sheppey Hernhill *Sheldwich Steeple*	21 12 42 75 8 0	} Sheldwich	{ 56869 81581
Sheldwich Sheppey *Queenborough Steeple*	4 41 0 126 20 44	} Queenborough	{ 60719 6158
Hadleigh Sheppey *Minster Steeple*	21 19 45 114 32 31	} Minster	{ 69035 9771
Halstow Hadleigh *St. Mary's Steeple*	70 9 35 11 54 16	} St. Mary's	{ 7095 32352
Hernhill Sheppey *Feversham Spire*	29 11 0 9 39 42	} Feversham	{ 15830 44537
Tenham Hernhill *Harley Steeple*	41 29 0 36 36 0	} Harley	{ 20617 21906

Z

Names of Stations.	Observed Angles.	Distances.		Feet.
Hernhill - - - East Church - - *Sea Salter Steeple*	85 18 0 82 15 10	} Sea Salter - -	{	17031 43580
Tenham - - - - Sheppey - - - - *Whitstable Steeple*	105 8 0 48 28 58	} Whitstable - -	{	50935 65697

SECTION FOURTH.

Determination of the Altitudes of the Stations above the Level of the Sea; and the mean Refractions deduced from observed Angles of elevation and depression.

ART. XLII. *Elevations and Depressions.*

At Trevose Head.

The ground at Cadon Barrow - - -	*elevated*	39 24
Bodmin Down - - - -	*elev.*	10 48
St. Agnes - - -	*depressed*	6 39
Hensbarrow - - -	*elev.*	29 8

At Bodmin Down.

The ground at Carraton Hill - - -	*elev.*	27 49
Trevose Head - - -	*depr.*	22 33
Cadon Barrow - - -	*elev.*	16 0
Brown Willy - - -	*elev.*	54 24

Cadon Barrow.

The ground at Trevose Head - - -	*depr.*	36 49
Brown Willy - - -	*elev.*	36 3
The horizon of the sea in the direction of Trevose Head	*depr.*	30 56
Ditto in the direction north - - -	*depr.*	31 13

St. Stephen's Down.

The ground at Black Down - - -	*elev.*	25 31
Carraton Hill - - -	*elev.*	35 18
Brown Willy - - -	*elev.*	42 9

Black Down, near Lydford.

The ground at Maker Heights - - - depr. 31′ 8″
     Carraton Hill - - - depr. 3 46
     St. Stephen's Down - - - depr. 35 18

Mendip Hills.

The ground at Bradley Knoll - - - - depr. 6 11
     Westbury Down - - - depr. 14 59
     Farley Down - - - - depr. 18 21
     Lansdown - - - depr. 14 4
     Moor Lynch - - - depr. 34 53
     Dundry - - - depr. 15 45
     Dundon Beacon - - - depr. 38 24
     Ash Beacon - - - - depr. 10 45

Dundry.

The ground at Mendip - - - - elea. 5 8
     Farley Down - - - - depr. 10 1
     Lansdown - - - - depr. 3 19

Lansdown.

The ground at Dundry - - - - depr. 5 44
     Mendip - - - - depr. 1 39

Farley Down.

The ground at Westbury - - - - depr. 0 11
     Mendip - - - - elev. 5 51
     Dundry - - - - depr. 1 46

Bradley Knoll.

The ground at Bull Barrow - - - - depr. 8 59
     Ash Beacon - - - - depr. 20 18
     Westbury - - - - depr. 4 36

Westbury Down.

The ground at Beacon Hill, Amesbury - - depr. 10 9
     Bradley Knoll - - - - elev. 7 1
     Mendip - - - - elev. 1 18
     Farley Down - - - - depr. 9 9

Z 2

Dundon Beacon.

The ground at Moor Lynch	- - - -	depr.	0 6 0
Logihorn Corner	- - -	depr.	3 56 13
Mendip	- - - -	elev.	18 18
Pilsden -	- - -	elev.	8 38

Moor Lynch.

The ground at Greylock's Foss-way	- - -	depr.	1 59 14
Logihorn Corner	- - -	depr.	30 45
Dundon Beacon	- - -	elev.	0 9
Mendip	- - - -	elev.	13 22
Pilsden -	- - - -	elev.	9 2
Ash Beacon	- - -	elev.	6 57

Greylock's Foss-way.

The ground at Moor Lynch	- - -	elev.	2 53 56
Dundon Beacon	- - -	elev.	34 48
Top of the staff (20 feet high) at Greylock's Foss-way	-	elev.	0 34

Logihorn Corner.

The ground at Moor Lynch	- - - -	elev.	27 21
Dundon Beacon	- - -	elev.	1 20 58
Top of the staff (20 feet high) at the west end of the base	depr.	1 9

Beacon Hill, Amesbury.

The ground at Westbury	- - -	depr.	4 36
Inkpin	- - -	elev.	6 22

Inkpin Hill.

The ground at White Horse Hill	- - -	depr.	10 54
Highclere	- - -	depr.	15 0
Beacon Hill, Amesbury	- -		18 24

White Horse Hill.

The ground at Highclere	- - - -	depr.	7 39
Nuffield	- - -	depr.	12 6
Shotover Hill -	- - -	depr.	17 6

Scutchamfly Barrow.

The ground at Wendover · · · · depr. 5' 36"
Whiteham Hill · · · · depr. 11 20

At Shotover Hill.

The ground at Scutchamfly Barrow · · elev. 0 20
Nuffield · · · · elev. 1 17
Wendover · · · · elev. 3 58
White Horse Hill · · · elev. 1 36

Brill on the Hill.

The ground at Nuffield · · · · depr. 4 48
Wendover · · · elev. 3 55
Bow Brickhill · · · depr. 10 44
Epwell · · · · depr. 6 57
Stow · · · · depr. 7 6
White Horse Hill · · · depr. 5 45

Nuffield.

The ground at White Horse Hill · : · depr. 4 45
Top of the Staff at Brill on the Hill. Staff 13½ feet high depr. 6 2
Bagshot · · · depr. 6 43
Highclere · · · depr. 4 18
N. B. The half stage belonging to the Royal Society was used at this station.

Wendover.

The ground at Brill on the Hill · · · depr. 14 59
Shotover Hill : · · · depr. 17 21
Bow Brickhill · · ; depr. 17 28
Stanmore · · · depr. 19 57

Stow on the Wold.

The ground at Shotover · · · · depr. 13 46
White Horse Hill · · depr. 7 30
Broadway Beacon · · · elev. 11 29
Brill on the Hill · · · depr. 14 45
Epwell · · · · depr. 8 0

Broadway Beacon.

The ground at Stow · · · · depr. 19 0
Epwell · · · · depr. 17 25

Epwell.

The ground at Stow		*depr.* 3 55
Arbury Hill -		*depr.* 6 39
Brill on the Hill		*depr.* 11 51
Corley -		*depr.* 20 8
Broadway Beacon		*elev.* 8 31

Arbury Hill.

The ground at Epwell		*depr.* 14 25

Bow Brickhill.

The ground at Wendover		*elev.* 3 59
Kinsworth -		*elev.* 5 35
Brill on the Hill		*depr.* 5 18

Kinsworth.

The ground at Brill on the Hill		*depr.* 18 37
Bow Brickhill		*depr.* 17 25
Arbury Hill		*depr.* 13 44
Stanmore		*depr.* 17 4
Lillyhoe -		*depr.* 23 44

Bagshot Heath.

The ground at Nuffield		*elev.* 1 19
Stanmore		*depr.* 7 18

Stanmore.

The ground at Bagshot Heath		*depr.* 9 34

ART. XLIII. *Heights of the Stations.*

Stations.	Ground above low water mark. Feet.
Trevose Head -	874
St. Agnes Beacon	621
Heasburrow	1034
Bodmin Down	645
Black Down	1160
St. Stephen's Down	605
Bradley Knoll	973

Stations.	Ground above low water mark. Feet.
Mendip	979
Westbury Down	775
Dundry	790
Lansdown	813
Parley Down	700
Moor Lynch	330
Dundon Beacon	360
Lugshorn Corner	49
Greylock's Foss-way	48
Ash Beacon	655
Cadon Barrow	1011
Brown Willy	1368
Inkpin	1011
Nuffield	757
White Horse Hill	893
Shotover Hill	599
Muzzle Hill, (Drill station)	744
Whiteham Hill	576
Wendover, ground above	905
Bow Brickhill	683
Kimworth	904
Lillybne	664
Stow on the Wold	813
Epwell Hill	836
Broadway Beacon	1086
Arbury Hill	804

ART. XLIV. *Mean Terrestrial Refractions.*

Between	Mean Refractions.
Bodmin Down and Cadon Barrow	1/7
Bradley Knoll and Westbury Down	1/8
Maker Heights and Black Down	1/8
Highclere and Inkpin	1/7
St. Agnes Beacon and Trevose Head	1/8
Moor Lynch and Lugshorn Corner	1/14
Hensbarrow and Trevose Head	1/14

Wingreen and Bradley Knoll	$\frac{1}{11}$
Bodmin Down and Trevose Head	$\frac{1}{11}$
Carraton Hill and Black Down	$\frac{1}{11}$
Westbury Down and Mendip	$\frac{1}{11}$
Carraton Hill and St. Stephen's Down	$\frac{1}{11}$
Farley Down and Mendip	$\frac{1}{12}$
Beacon Hill and Westbury Down	$\frac{1}{12}$
Dundry and Farley Down	$\frac{1}{13}$
Dundon Beacon and Mendip	$\frac{1}{11}$
Bradley Knoll and Mendip	$\frac{1}{13}$
Lansdown and Mendip	$\frac{1}{11}$
Moor Lynch and Dundon Beacon	$\frac{1}{14}$
Dundry and Mendip	$\frac{1}{14}$
Westbury Down and Farley Down	$\frac{1}{13}$
St. Stephen's Down and Black Down	$\frac{1}{14}$
Moor Lynch and Dundon Beacon	$\frac{1}{13}$
Dundon and Lugshorn Corner	$\frac{1}{2}$
Moor Lynch and Greylock's Foss-way	$\frac{1}{2}$
Lugshorn Corner and Greylock's Foss-way	o
Cadon Barrow and horizon of the sea in the direction of Trevose Head	$\frac{1}{11}$
Ditto in a northern direction	$\frac{1}{11}$
Brill and Nuffield	$\frac{1}{2}$
Broadway and Stow	$\frac{1}{14}$
Epwell and Broadway	$\frac{1}{11}$
Highclere and White Horse Hill	$\frac{1}{11}$
Nuffield and White Horse Hill	$\frac{1}{12}$
Nuffield and Hagshot	$\frac{1}{11}$
Epwell and Stow	$\frac{1}{11}$
Brill and Stow on the Wold	$\frac{1}{11}$
Wendover and Bow Brickhill	$\frac{1}{11}$
Kinsworth and Bow Brickhill	$\frac{1}{11}$
Shotover and White Horse Hill	$\frac{1}{11}$
Epwell and Brill	$\frac{1}{11}$
Bow Brickhill and Brill	$\frac{1}{11}$

ART. XLV. *Particulars respecting the Altitudes of the Stations.*

The height of the station on Trevose Head, above the surface of the sea at low water, was determined in 1797, by levelling. The transit instrument was used for the purpose; and there is reason to believe the result, $274\frac{1}{18}$ feet, is within a very few inches of the truth.

In the Philosophical Transactions for 1797, p. 471, the height of the station on Maker Heights is said to be 401 feet; this was also found by levelling. The altitude of St. Agnes Beacon, determined from that station, is 599 feet; (see the same volume and page;) but, if the calculation be made from the base of altitude at Trevose Head, the height of that station, above the level of the sea, will be 621 feet, which gives a difference of 22 feet. It must be recollected, however, that in the first result, the computation was carried through two intermediate stations, which gave three arcs, and as many mean refractions; and, considering the extreme variableness to which refractions are liable, we are assuredly not to consider 22 feet deviation from the truth as a large quantity.

Besides St. Agnes Beacon, the altitudes of Cadon Barrow, Brown Willy, Hensbarrow, and Bodmin Down, have been determined from that of Trevose Head. Of the remaining stations, some are derived from Maker Heights, others from Dunnose: most of them are mean results, that is, each station has generally been found two ways; and, as it will serve to shew what errors proceed from irregularity of refraction, and imperfection of observation, I shall exhibit a few particulars in relation to them.

A a

Height of	deduced from		Feet.	Mean.
Black Down	Maker Heights	-	1169	1160
	Carraton Hill	- -	1152	
St. Stephen's Down	Black Down	-	609	605
	Carraton Hill	-	600	
Westbury Down	Bradley Knoll	-	779	775
	Beacon Hill	- -	771	
Farley Down	Mendip Hills	-	703	700
	Westbury Down	-	696	
Moor Lynch	Mendip Hills	- -	335	330
	Ash Beacon	-	325	
Lugshorn Corner	Dundon Beacon	-	46	49
	Greylock's Foss-way		52	
Inkpin Beacon	Highclere	- -	1014	1011
	Beacon Hill	-	1009	
Ash Beacon	Bull Barrow	- -	653	655
	Bradley Knoll	-	657	

The above will sufficiently shew, what dependence is to be
placed on the heights deduced from observed angles of elevation or depression; the results are, indeed, often less consistent,
and frequently unsatisfactory; but, generally, they run on a
parallel with these. The *data* from which all the heights
have been computed, accompany this article.

The measurement of the base on Sedgemoor, shewed a fall of
about 7 feet, from Lugshorn Corner to Greylock's Foss-way:

therefore, supposing that fall to be gradual and constant, all the way from the latter station to the surface of the sea at Bridgewater Bay, we shall get 24 feet, for the height of Lugshorn Corner from the surface of the sea. The altitude of this station, deduced from that of Trevose Head, is 49 feet; and, subtracting 3 feet from it, (the height of the bank on which the instrument stood above the moor,) we get 46 feet for the height of the moor at Lugshorn Corner, above the level of the sea at Bridgewater Bay. But this height, *supposing the fall regular*, is proved to be 24 feet. There is, therefore, a difference of 22 feet, granting the whole of this to be an error on the side of the survey: but, as the general surface of the moor at Bridgewater Bay is several feet above the surface of the sea, we may take a moiety of 24 feet, for the error of the computed height of the station at Lugshorn Corner.

ART. XLVI. *Matters relating to Refraction.*

The refractions contained in this account, like those in our former Papers, tend to prove, that when rays of light pass horizontally, and considerably distant from the surface of the earth, they are less bent or refracted from their rectilinear courses, than theory and opinion have laid down as fact. It is very certain, however, that objection lies against particular conclusions drawn from such *data* as we possess; because the angles of elevation and depression of corresponding stations are observed *at different times*, and almost always, therefore, under different circumstances; but, with the experience and continual practice of thus obtaining means of computing these refractions, although we may not be able to determine the refracting power of the air under given circumstances, yet, as the causes which render it variable, are as likely to predominate when the angles of depression or elevation are observed from low stations as when observed from high ones, we may be enabled to make some general deductions.*

When the instrument formerly made use of by General Roy was intrusted to my care, I possessed the means of determining, in a more accurate manner than had yet been done, the refractive power of the air near the horizon. To devote much time to it, has not, as yet, been in my power; because a more rapid extension of the survey was an object of greater

---

* As many instances of strong atmospherical refraction have been related, and ingeniously accounted for, in some of the late publications of the Royal Society, I think it right to mention, by way of note, a very extraordinary instance of its variability.

In the month of June, 1795, when the instrument and party were stationed at Plisden Hill, in Dorsetshire, on a particular day, at about the hour of four, I employed myself in observing the angles of depression or elevation of the surrounding hills. After I had done all that was necessary in this matter, I turned the telescope to *Glastonbury Tor*, and observed the depression of it. The air was so unusually clear, that, desirous of proving to a gentleman then with me in the observatory tent, the excellence of the telescope, I desired him to apply his eye to it; this he did, and, agreeably to a desire he expressed, I again took the depression of the upper part of the old building, which I was enabled to do with great accuracy, and found it 2° different; the first being 30',0", and the last 30',2". The unusual distinctness of this object, led me to keep my eye a long time at the telescope; and, whilst my attention was engaged, I perceived the top of the building *gradually rise* above the micrometer wire, and to continue to do, till it was elevated 10',45" above its first apparent situation; it then remained stationary, and as night drew on, the object became indistinct. The following evening, I observed the depression again, and found it 29',30". To what cause this extraordinary change in the refraction could be owing, I am at a loss to conjecture. The former part of the day had been warm, with little wind, and cloudy. The thermometer, at the time of observation, was 65°, and continued stationary for a considerable time. The sky was cloudy, but yet, as I have before observed, the air was remarkably clear. The top of Glastonbury Tor, I suppose, is about 300 feet from the surface of Sedgemoor, over a considerable tract of which, the line joining Plisden with that object passes. The gentleman of whom I speak, as being with me in the tent, was Captain Darcy, of the Royal Engineers, who, no doubt, well remembers the circumstance.

importance. I did not, however, lose any opportunity which the subsequent season offered; the first was, when the instruments were at White Horse Hill and Whiteham Hill; the second, when one was stationed at Brill and the other at Arbury Hill; and the third opportunity offered itself, when one party was stationed at the latter place and the other at Wendover.

On these occasions, the instructions which I communicated to Mr. WOOLCOT, and by which I governed myself, were to observe the elevation or depression of the corresponding station at the expiration of every hour, beginning at six A. M. and to have the watch well regulated from observed altitudes of the sun's limb. I requested him also to be very minute in entering on his book the state of the weather; to keep the instrument properly sheltered from the wind; to be always cautious to adjust his level; and also to insert the state of the air, as to temperature and density, by noting the thermometer and barometer.

During the time we were at the two first stations, White Horse and Whiteham Hills, there was only one day when the air was sufficiently clear for the purpose; this was the 6th of June. On that day, the following observations were made *at the same time as shewn by signal.*

Whiteham Hill. June 6th, 1799.

Hours.	Wh. Horse H. Elevated.	Barometer.	Thermometer.	Remarks.
3	6 4	In. pts 29,730	Degrees 60.9	Light air at SW. Sun not shining; remarkably clear.
4	6 14	29,724	62,5	Ditto. Ditto ditto.
5	6 14	29,728	58,7	Ditto. Ditto ditto.
6	6 10	29,738	58,5	Ditto. Ditto ditto.
7	6 11	29,728	57,5	Ditto. Ditto ditto.
8	6 21	29,732	57	Very calm, and cloudy, but clear.
9	5 37	29,736	55,7	Ditto. Lamp at Shotover very bright. Dew falling.
10	5 39	29,740	55,5	Ditto. Ditto.

White Horse Hill. *June 6th.*

Hours.	Whitehorse H. Depressed.	Barometer.	Thermometer.	Remarks.
	' "	In. pts.	Degrees	
3	18 31	29.411	57,7	Light airs at SW. Sun not shining; very clear.
4	18 16	29.408	59.5	Ditto. Ditto ditto.
5	18 14	29.410	57,6	Ditto. Sun shining a little; not so clear.
6	18 10	29.413	55,5	More wind. Sun not shining, and darker.
7	18 15	29.413	55,5	Calm and cloudy.
8	18 15	29.438	54,3	Quite calm, and a little dew falling.
* 9	18 10	29.438	53,4	Ditto. Fine night. Lamp at Whitehorse very distinct.
*10	18 75	29.638	53,3	Ditto, but lamp rather indistinct.

Similar observations were also made when the instruments were at Brill and Arbury Hill: they were as follows.

Arbury Hill. *July 11th, 1799.* Watch regulated.

Hours.	Brill Depressed.	Barometer.	Thermometer.	Remarks.
	' "	In. pts.	Degrees	
9 A.M.	11 15	29.180	65 ,5	Light airs at SW. Cloudy, but sun shining now and then.
10	11 15	29.200	70 ,0	Ditto. Cloudy.
11	11 15	29.100	70 ,7	Ditto. Ditto.
12	11 6	29.199	70 ,2	Ditto. Ditto.
3 P.M.	11 6	29.161	68 ,0	Ditto. Ditto. Very clear.
4	10 5	29.168	71 ,5	Ditto. Sun shining a little, yet free from any tremor.
* 9	10 30	29.131	65 ,0	Ditto. Lamp at Brill perfectly distinct.

Brill on the Hill. *July 11th, 1799.* Watch regulated.

Hours.	Arbury H. Depressed.	Barometer.	Thermometer.	Remarks.
	' "	In. pts.	Degrees	
9 A.M.	8 40	29.10c	63 ,0	Light airs at SW. Appearances of rain from SW. Cloudy.
10	8 36	29.11c	63 ,5	Ditto. Clearer, but cloudy. Arbury Hill very distinct.
11	8 36	29.110	67 ,5	Ditto. More cloudy and equally clear. (round.
12	8 36	29,11c	65 ,0	The air remarkably clear and free from tremor. Cloudy all
3 P.M.	8 36	29,11c	71 ,0	Ditto ditto. More cloudy.
4	8 46	29,15c	71 ,5	Ditto ditto. Not so cloudy.
* 9	8 48	29,20c	63,75	The lamp at Arbury H. very bright. A very fine quiet night.

The next opportunity which offered, was at the former station and Wendover: the observations were as follows.

Arbury Hill. July 27th, 1799. Watch regulated.

Hours.	Wendover Depressed.	Barometer.	Thermometer.	Remarks.
12	12 1	28,728	62 ,0	Fresh wind from SW. Rather dark weather, sun shining here [and there.
1	12 3	28,734	64 ,2	Ditto. Air tremulous, ditto.
2	12 11	28,740	64 ,0	Ditto. Ditto, ditto.
3	12 10	28,738	63 ,5	Ditto. Air more steady, ditto. Clearer.
4	12 12	28,740	64 ,0	Ditto. Very steady. Sun shining a little.
5	11 50	28,740	64 ,2	Ditto. Ditto. Ditto.
6	12 17	28,740	61 ,0	Less wind, and the air very clear. Wendover perfectly distinct.

Wendover. July 27th, 1799. Watch regulated.

Hours.	Arbury H. Depressed.	Barometer.	Thermometer.	Remarks.
5 A.M.	16 12	29,030	53 ,2	Wind at SW, rather fresh; sun shining, and air very clear.
6	16 12	29,030	53 ,0	Ditto. ditto.
7	15 16	29,030	54 ,5	Less wind, and the air very steady. Arbury Hill very distinct.
8	14 44	29,100	54 ,0	Little wind. Dew falling very fast. Ditto.

Another opportunity for making contemporary observations occurred, when the parties were on Broadway Beacon and Epwell: I place them last, because I think them inferior to the others.

Epwell. June 26th, 1799. Watch regulated.

Hours.	Broadway B. Elevated.	Barometer.	Thermometer.	Remarks.
12	6 6	29,100	60,5	Wind SW. Cloudy. Much rain preceding night.
1 P.M.	6 2	29,100	63,2	Ditto, but calmer; sun not shining at Broadway.
2	6 12	29,208	60,7	Very calm, and cloudy all round.
3	6 10	29,100	59,0	Ditto. Appearances of rain in SW quarter.
4	6 31	29,100	57,5	Foggy, but easily perceive the tent at Broadway Beacon.

Broadway Beacon. June 26th, 1799. Watch regulated.

Hours.	Epwell Depressed.	Thermometer.	Remarks.
2	19 0	57,5	Light airs from SW. Inclinable to rain.
3	19 2	57,5	Ditto. Still more so.
4	19 3	57,5	Ditto, but calmy. Barometer tube broken.

To determine the refractions on the first arc, White Horse and Whiteham Hills, we have the distance between those stations = 88662,2 feet, which subtends an arc of 14′ 32″ nearly.

To determine those on the second, we have the distance between Brill and Arbury Hill = 146530 feet, subtending an arc of 24′ 8″,9: those on the third, Wendover and Arbury Hill, 210628 feet = 34′ 35″: and, for finding the refractions from the two last tables, we have the distance from Broadway Beacon to Epwell = 80611,4 feet, which subtends an arc of 13′ 11″ nearly.

The depressions and elevations were all taken to the ground, excepting those which are marked with asterisks. At White Horse Hill and Whiteham Hill, lamps were used at the hours of 9 and 10: they were also made use of at Arbury Hill and Brill at 9 o'clock. In the first instances, the lamps were placed (the centres of them) $1\frac{1}{2}$ feet from the bottoms of the respective instruments; and in the last $2\frac{1}{2}$ feet.

The height of the transit telescope above the ground was always $5\frac{1}{2}$ feet; therefore, an allowance must be made, at each station, for the angle which that space subtends at its corresponding one; this premised, the refraction will be found from one of the two following rules, *viz.* if A be the contained arc, and D *d* the observed depressions, the quantity answering to the refraction, R, will be expressed by $\frac{A - D - d}{2}$; or, if one of the angles should be an elevation, *e*, then $R = \frac{A + e - d}{2}$: these rules give the refractions in the following table.

Refractions found from the preceding Angles of Elevation and Depression.

1. Arc. White Horse Hill & Whiteham Hill.				2. Arc. Brill and Arbury Hill.				3. Arc. Arbury Hill and Wendover.				4. Arc. Brudeny Beacon and Epwell.			
Hours	Refraction per mil. arc.	Barom.	Therm.	Hours	Refraction per cont. arc.	Barom.	Therm.	Hours	Refraction per cont. arc.	Barom.	Therm.	Hours	Refraction per cont. arc.	Barom.	Therm.
		in. pts	°			in. pts	°			in. pts	°			in. pts	°
3 P.M.	$-\frac{1}{38}$	29.5	58.0	9 A.M.	$-\frac{1}{38}$	29.1	69.2	5	$-\frac{1}{38}$	28.8	54.6	9	$-\frac{1}{38}$	99.2	54.1
4	$-\frac{34}{38}$	29.5	61.0		$-\frac{1}{38}$	29.2	68.7	6	$-\frac{1}{38}$	28.8	61.5	3	$-\frac{1}{38}$	57.5	58.2
5	$-\frac{3}{38}$	29.5	58.1		$-\frac{1}{38}$	29.2	68.1					4	$-\frac{1}{38}$	99.1	57.5
6	$-\frac{3}{38}$	29.5	57.0		$-\frac{1}{38}$	29.2	67.6								
7	$-\frac{3}{38}$	29.5	57.0	3 P.M.	$-\frac{3}{38}$	29.2	72.5								
8	$-\frac{3}{38}$	29.6	55.6	4	$-\frac{1}{38}$	29.2	72.0								
9	$-\frac{3}{38}$	29.6	54.3	9	$-\frac{3}{38}$	29.2	62.3								
10	$-\frac{1}{38}$	29.5	54.3												

B b

On examining the refractions obtained on the first arc, we perceive them to have been tolerably regular from 9 o'clock till 8; the mean being $\frac{1}{18,7}$ part of the contained arc. The height of Whiteham Hill is 576 feet, and that of White Horse Hill 899 feet, above the level of the sea: the ray passes, therefore, through a tract of air considerably elevated, as the country between the stations is, for the most part, flat and low.

The air is not often clear enough, or sufficiently free from tremulous motions, for these delicate observations. On the present occasion, however, the state of it was highly fit for the purpose; and, as care was taken, I am of opinion an error of more than 3″, taking that of the arch of altitude into the account, cannot have obtained in any of the angles. The refractions at 9 and 10 o'clock are less than at the preceding hours; but this does not appear to have been owing to any change in the refractive power of the air throughout the whole extent of the ray, because the depression of Whitcham Hill, from the other station, varied little at those hours. These changes in the observed angles of elevation at Whiteham, (44″ and 42″ being the differences,) *without* corresponding ones at White Horse Hill, prove that some *partial* alteration, from floating strata, had taken place in the refraction near the former station. Whoever considers the matter, must perceive a case may be constructed in which this will take place, causing a great variation in one of the angles, whilst the other *apparently* remains the same: and this suggested the idea, that to afford any accurate conclusions in this way, a long series of observations would be necessary. It furthermore appears, that dew could not have caused these differences at Whiteham Hill, since the same cause would equally operate to vary the observed angles at White Horse Hill; but those remained nearly the same.

The refractions on the second and third arcs, I consider as most accurate, on account of the great distance between the stations; and also as more to be depended on, from the circumstance of the ray generally passing 300 feet above the ground. The fourth arc affords another instance of the refraction varying at one station, and remaining constant at the other. This, no doubt, was owing to the intervention of some partial stratum of air, nearer to Epwell than Broadway Beacon. The refractions, deduced from these contemporary observations are certainly inconclusive. The mean refractions, (neglecting the fourth arc) brought under one point of view, will be as follows.

Arc.	Mean height of ray above the sea.	Refraction. Propl. pt.	Barom.	Therm.
	Feet.		in. pts.	
1. White Horse Hill and Whiteham	734	$\frac{1}{10.0}$	29.5	57.8
2. Arbury H. and Brill, 5 first refracs.	774	$\frac{1}{10.5}$	29.9	67.8
3. Arbury Hill and Wendover -	854	$\frac{1}{13.8}$	28.8	58.1

If the air had been in a quiescent state, previous to and also at the times when these observations were made, it might be expected that the differences of altitudes in the stations would be obtained, tolerably near the truth, *barometrically.* The remarks in the tables appertaining to the first and second arcs, shew that such opportunities offered; but those which belong to the third, prove the wind to have been fresh; and, as the space between the stations which constitute the extremities of that arc is 34 miles, nearly, it is not to be expected that a true result should be obtained. The differences of altitudes of the stations constituting the extremities of the two first arcs, obtained by means of the observed angles of elevation and depression, as well as from the heights of the mercury in the barometer, will be as follows.

Arcs.	Obs. Ang.	Barom.	Diff.
1	317	262	55
2	60	15	45

The little done on this subject, points out the necessity of doing more; it therefore remains with me to observe, that I shall lose no opportunity of employing the apparatus committed to my charge in the best and most diligent manner, both as relating to matters of refraction, and to all others connected with the Trigonometrical Survey.

In the Introduction, page 2, it is stated that this Account would be comprised in three sections, but it was afterwards thought more convenient to divide it into four.

In Page 45, line penult. *dele* and Prittlewell.
——— 137, —— 14, *for* 1792, *read* 1772.

Printed by W. Bulmer and Co.
Cleveland-row, St. James's.

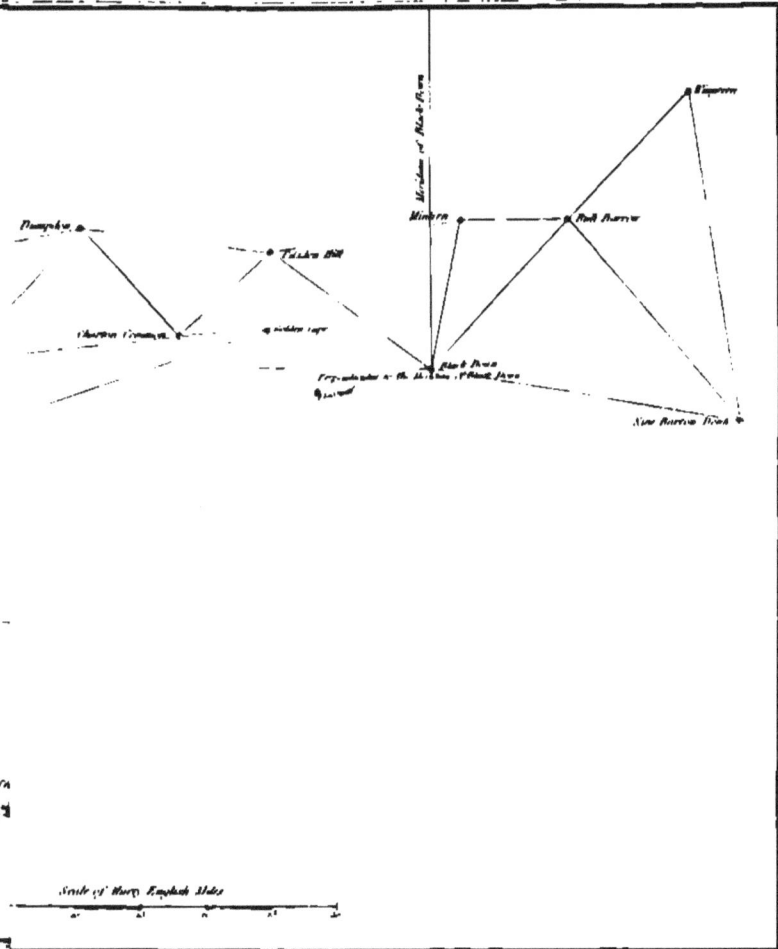

Scale of thirty English Miles

measured thereon .

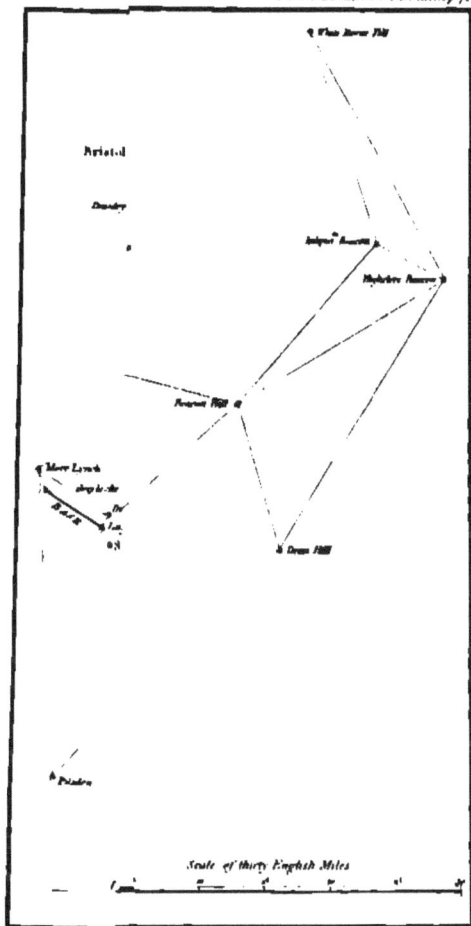

TRIGONOMETRICAL SURVEY, 1798.

Philos. Trans. MDCCC. Tab. XXIX p. 70

Bristol

Dundry

Inglesombe Beacon

Hinton Beacon

Black Dewn Hill

Bream Down Hill

White Sheet Hill

Scale of thirty English Miles

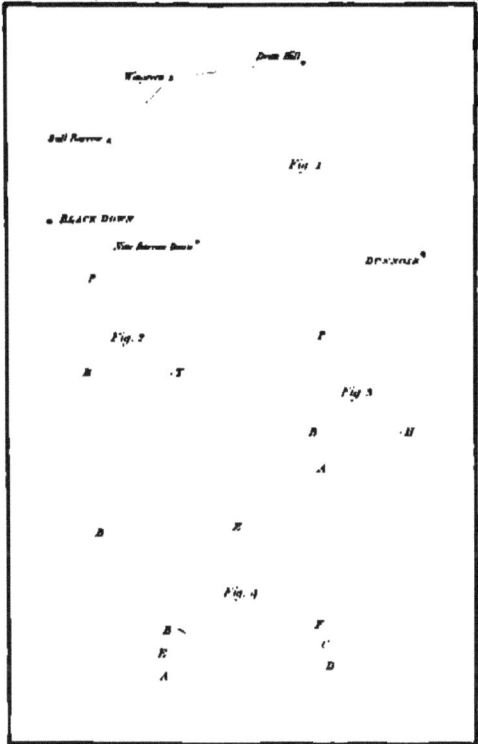

Windover s

Drew Hill

Bull Barrow s

Fig. 1

BLACK DOWN

New Barrow Down

DUNNOSE

P

Fig. 2

B · T

P

Fig. 3

B · M

A

B E

Fig. 4

B F
E C
A D

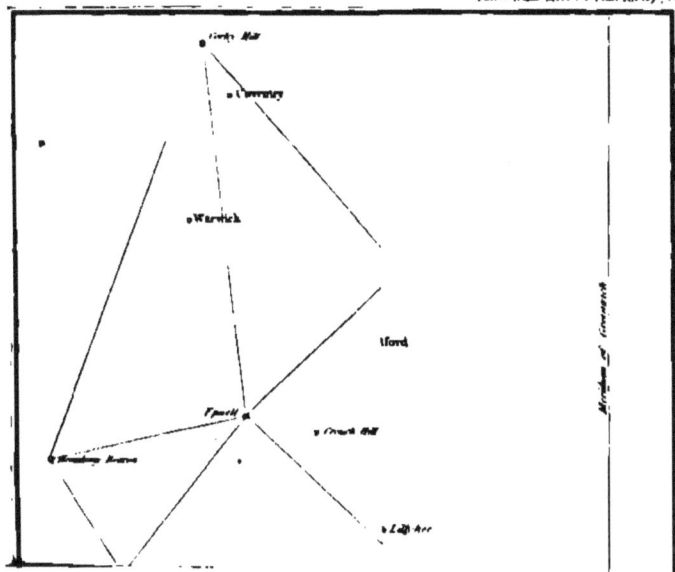

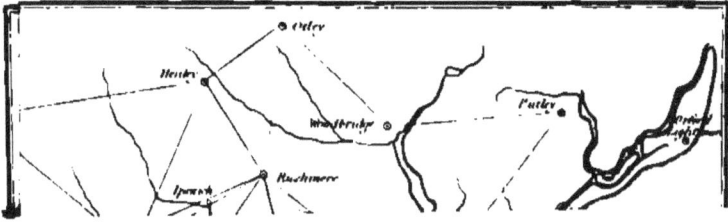

NTIES. 1797. 1798. 1799.

Publ. Trans. MDCCC Plate XXXII p.721

AN

ACCOUNT OF THE MEASUREMENT

OF AN

ARC OF THE MERIDIAN,

EXTENDING FROM

DUNNOSE IN THE ISLE OF WIGHT, TO CLIFTON IN YORKSHIRE,

IN COURSE OF THE OPERATIONS CARRIED ON FOR

THE TRIGONOMETRICAL SURVEY OF ENGLAND,

IN THE YEARS 1800, 1801, AND 1802.

BY MAJOR WILLIAM MUDGE,

OF THE ROYAL ARTILLERY, F. R. S.

INTENDED AS A SECOND PART TO VOLUME II.

ILLUSTRATED WITH EIGHT COPPER-PLATES.

FROM THE

PHILOSOPHICAL TRANSACTIONS.

LONDON:

PRINTED BY W. BULMER AND CO. CLEVELAND-ROW, ST. JAMES'S,
FOR W. FADEN, GEOGRAPHER TO HIS MAJESTY,
AND TO HIS ROYAL HIGHNESS THE PRINCE OF WALES,
CHARING CROSS.

1804.

CONTENTS.

MEASUREMENT OF THE BASE ON HOUNSLOW HEATH, IN 1784.

b 2

TRIGONOMETRICAL SURVEY, 1795, 1796.

PLATES.

Hz

AN

A C C O U N T

OF THE

MEASUREMENT OF THE BASE ON HOUNSLOW HEATH,

IN THE YEAR 1784:

AND ALSO OF THE

TRIGONOMETRICAL OPERATIONS

CARRIED ON IN THE

YEARS 1787, AND 1788,

FOR THE PURPOSE OF

DETERMINING THE DISTANCE BETWEEN THE MERIDIANS OF

GREENWICH AND PARIS.

BY THE LATE

MAJOR GENERAL ROY, F.R.S. AND A.S.

O

AN ACCOUNT, &c.

By William Roy.

INTRODUCTION.

Accurate surveys of a country are universally admitted to be works of great public utility, as affording the surest foundation for almost every kind of internal improvement in time of peace, and the best means of forming judicious plans of defence against the invasions of an enemy in time of war; in which last circumstances their importance usually becomes the most apparent. Hence it happens, that if a country has not actually been surveyed, or is but little known, a state of warfare generally produces the first improvements in its geography: for in the various movements of armies in the field, especially if the theatre of war be extensive, each individual officer has repeated opportunities of contributing, according to his situation, more or less towards its perfection; and these observations being ultimately collected, a map is sent forth into the world, considerably improved indeed, but which, being still defective, points out the necessity of something more accurate being undertaken, when times and circumstances may favour the design.

The rise and progress of the rebellion which broke out in the Highlands of Scotland in 1745, and which was finally suppressed, by his Royal Highness the late Duke of Cumberland, at the battle

B

of Culloden in the following year, convinced Government of what infinite Importance it would be to the State, that a country, so very inaccessible by nature, should be thoroughly explored and laid open, by establishing military posts in its inmost recesses, and carrying roads of communication to its remotest parts. With a view to the commencement of arrangements of this sort, a body of infantry was encamped at Fort Augustus in 1747, under the command of the late Lord Blakeney, at that time a Major-General ; at which camp my much respected friend, the late Lieutenant-General Watson, then Deputy Quarter-Master-General in North Britain, was officially employed. This officer, being himself an engineer, active and indefatigable, a zealous promoter of every useful undertaking, and the warm and steady friend of the industrious, first conceived the idea of making a map of the Highlands. As assistant Quarter-Master, it fell to my lot to begin, and afterwards to have a considerable share in the execution of that map ; which being undertaken under the auspices of the Duke of Cumberland, and meant at first to be confined to the Highlands only, was nevertheless at last extended to the Lowlands ; and thus made general in what related to the mainland of Scotland, the islands (excepting some lesser ones near the coast) not having been surveyed.

Although this work, which is still in manuscript, and in an unfinished state, possesses considerable merit, and perfectly answered the purpose for which it was originally intended ; yet, having been carried on with instruments of the common, or even inferior kind, and the sum annually allowed for it being inadequate to the execution of so great a design in the best manner, it is rather to be considered as a magnificent military sketch, than a very accurate map of a country. It would, however, have been completed, and many of its imperfections no doubt remedied ; but the breaking out of the war of 1755 prevented both, by furnishing service of other kinds for those who had been employed upon it.

On the conclusion of the peace of 1763, it came for the first time under the consideration of Government, to make a general Survey of the whole Island at the public cost. Towards the execution of this work, whereof the direction was to have been committed to my charge, the map of Scotland was to have been made subservient, by extending the great triangles quite to the northern extremity of the Island, and filling them in from the original map. Thus that imperfect work would have been effectually completed, and the nation would have reaped the benefit, of what had been already done, at a very moderate extra-expence.

It will not be expected, that I should here attempt to assign causes for the long delay that has taken place in carrying a work of so laudable a nature into execution : suffice it to say, that a period of twelve years having elapsed, since the scheme had been first proposed, as a work that could be best executed in time of profound peace, without any thing being done in it, previous to the nation's being unfortunately involved in the American war ; it was sufficiently obvious, that peace must be once more restored, before any new effort could be made for that purpose. In the mean while, as I still entertained hopes that a work which seemed to merit the attention of the public, would, at some future period, be begun, and, by gradual perseverance, ultimately brought to perfection ; therefore, in the course of my ordinary military employments, wherein the very best opportunities have offered of acquiring a thorough knowledge of the country, I have not failed to observe, at least in a general way, such situations as seemed to be the best adapted for the measurement of the bases that would be necessary for the formation of the great triangles, and connecting the different series of them together.

The peace of 1783 being concluded, and official business having detained me in or near town during the whole of that summer, I embraced the opportunity for my own private amusement, to

measure a base of 7744.3 feet, across the fields between the Jews-
Harp, near Marybone, and Black-Lane, near Pancras; as a foundation for a series of triangles, carried on at the same time, for
determining the relative situations of the most remarkable steeples,
and other places, in and about the Capital, with regard to each
other, and the Royal Observatory at Greenwich. The principal
object I had here in view (besides that it might possibly serve as
a hint to the public, for the revival of the now almost forgotten
scheme of 1769) was, to facilitate the comparison of the observations, made by the lovers of astronomy, within the limits of the
projected survey; namely, Richmond and Harrow, on the west;
and Shooter's Hill and Wansted, on the east: and thinking, that
a Paper, containing the result of these trigonometrical operations,
might not prove unacceptable to the Royal Society, I was engaged
in making the computations for that purpose, when, very unexpectedly, I found that an operation of the same nature, but much
more important in its object, was really in agitation. This I saw
would supersede, at least for the present, my own private observations, and perhaps render them wholly useless, unless it were as a
matter of mere curiosity hereafter, to see how far such as depended
on a short base, and a small instrument (a quadrant of a foot radius)
would agree with those founded on a much longer base, and angles
determined by a large circular instrument, being that proposed,
as the best that could be made use of in the operation now to be
mentioned.

In the beginning of October, 1783, Comte d'Adhemar, the
French Ambassador, transmitted to Mr. Fox, then one of his Majesty's principal Secretaries of State, a Memoir of M. Cassini de
Thury, in which he sets forth the great advantage that would
accrue to astronomy, by carrying a series of triangles from the
neighbourhood of London to Dover, there to be connected with
those already executed in France, by which combined operations

the relative situations of the two most famous observatories in
Europe, Greenwich and Paris, would be more accurately ascertained than they are at present."

This Memoir the Secretary of State, by his Majesty's command,
transmitted to Sir Joseph Banks, the very respectable and worthy
President of the Royal Society; who, about the middle of November, was pleased to communicate it to me, proposing at the
same time, that I should, on the part of the Society, charge myself
with the execution of the operation. To this proposition I readily
assented, on being soon afterwards assured, through the proper
official channels, that my undertaking it met with his Majesty's
most gracious approbation.

A generous and beneficent Monarch, whose knowledge and love
of the sciences are sufficiently evinced by the protection which he
constantly affords them, and under whose auspices they are seen
daily to flourish, soon supplied the funds that were judged necessary.
What his Majesty has been pleased to give so liberally, it is our
duty to manage with proper and becoming frugality, consistent
with the best possible execution of the business to be done, so as
to make it redound to the credit of the Nation in general, and of
this Society in particular.

The operation, whereof we are now to give some account, being
the first of the kind, on any extensive scale, ever undertaken in
this country, naturally enough subdivides itself into two parts.
First, the choice and measurement of the base, with every possible
care and attention, as the foundation of the work; secondly, the
disposition of the triangles, whereby the base is to be connected
with such parts of the coast of this island as are nearest to the coast
of France, and the determination of their angles, by means of the

* M. Cassini's Memoir, with the Astronomer Royal's remarks on what is therein
alleged, concerning the uncertainty of the relative situations of the two Observatories,
will be given in the sequel.

best instrument that can be obtained for the purpose, from which
the result or conclusion will be drawn. It is the first part only, as
a subject of itself sufficiently distinct, that we are now to lay before the Society; it having been judged more advisable, to shew
that no time has been lost in making reasonable progress, than to
defer the account till the whole operation should be ultimately
completed.

Choice of the Base. Pl. I.

1. Hounslow Heath having always appeared to be one of the
most eligible situations, for any general purpose of the sort now
under consideration, because of its vicinity to the Capital and
Royal Observatory at Greenwich, its great extent, and the extraordinary levelness of its surface, without any local obstructions
whatever to render the measurement difficult; being likewise
commodiously situated for any future operations of a similar nature, which his Majesty may please to order to be extended from
thence, in different directions, to the more remote parts of the
island, it was proposed to Sir Joseph Banks, that the local circumstances should be actually examined; so far, at least, as to enable us to form some judgment, of the best position of the line to
be measured.

The 16th day of April, 1784, being accordingly fixed on for the
purpose, and Mr. Cavendish and Dr. Blagden accompanying the
President on this occasion, we began our observations at a place
called King's Arbour, at the north-west extremity of the Heath,
between Cranford Bridge and Longford; and having proceeded
from thence through the narrow gorge, formed by Hanworth Park
and Hanworth Farm, we finished at Hampton Poorhouse, near the
side of Bushy Park, at the south-east extremity; the total distance,
from the survey of Middlesex, being upwards of five miles.

On this inspection it was immediately perceived, that the first part of the operation, in order to facilitate the measurement, would be, the clearing from furze bushes and ant hills, a narrow tract along the heath, as soon as the ground should be sufficiently dry to permit the base to be accurately traced out thereon.

First tracing of the Base, and clearing of the Ground. Pl. I.

8. Chiefly with a view to the more effectual execution of the work, it was judged to be a right measure to obtain and employ soldiers, instead of country labourers, in tracing the base, clearing the ground, and assisting in the subsequent operations. For, at the same time that this was obviously the most frugal method, it was evident, that soldiers would be more attentive to orders than country labourers; and by encamping on the spot would furnish the necessary centinels, particularly during the night, for guarding such parts of the apparatus, as it was foreseen must remain carefully untouched, in the frequent interims of discontinuing and resuming the work. Accordingly, a party of the 12th regiment of foot, consisting of a serjeant, corporal, and 10 men, were ordered to march from Windsor to Hounslow Heath, where they encamped on the 26th of May, close by Hanworth Summerhouse, to which spot the necessary tents, camp equipage, and entrenching tools, &c. had been previously sent.

Whatever might have been the particular direction given to the base, considered by its extremities, from consulting the plan it will easily appear, that it must always necessarily lead through the narrow gorge of the Heath formed by Hanworth Park and Hanworth Farm. The first point therefore to be attended to, in tracing it out, was, that it might lead through this pass, without interfering with certain ponds, or gravel-pits full of water, which are in it. These were easily avoided by carrying the line pretty near to Hanworth Summerhouse; and in directing the telescope from

thence towards the south-east, it was accidentally found, that by
leaving Hampton Poorhouse a very little to the westward, or
right, the line would coincide with a remarkable high spire, seen
at the distance of eleven or twelve miles, and known afterwards to
be Bansted Church. As there could not be a better situated, or
more conspicuous object than this, therefore the first or south-east
section of the base, comprehended between the Summerhouse and
the angle of the small field adjoining to Hampton Poorhouse, was
immediately directed upon it; and the soldiers were the same day
set to work to clear the tract, which, at a medium, was made from
two to three yards in breadth. This operation continued eight or
ten days, owing to the lower part of the Heath, between Wolsey
River and the Poorhouse, being encumbered with brushwood.

When the clearing of the first section was completed, the second,
comprehended between the Summerhouse and the great road leading from Staines to London, was traced out in the following manner. One of the pyramidal bell-tents (whereof two had been provided, one of twenty-five, and the other of fifteen feet in height)
being placed at the station near the Summerhouse, camp colours
were then arranged from distance to distance, so as to be in a line
with the bell-tent and Bansted Spire. In like manner, the third
section, comprehended between the Staines Road and King's Arbour, was traced out.

This first tracing of the base was done by means of a common
telescope held in the hand only, that no time might be lost in employing the soldiers to smooth the tract which was to be measured;
because the transit instrument (my own property, for which a
portable stand had been for some time preparing) was not yet
ready to be applied, as it afterwards was, in tracing out the base
more accurately.

The camp still remained, where it was originally pitched, at the
angle of Hanworth Park, this being a very convenient position,

with regard to the first and second sections; but being too remote
from the third, that time might not be lost, and the men unneces-
sarily fatigued in marching backwards and forwards; therefore,
one half of the party, under the command of the corporal, was detached to the northward, and quartered in the neighbouring vil-
lages, to clear the third section, while the serjeant, with the remainder, were occupied in smoothing the second. Owing to the
extraordinary wetness of the season, this operation required more
time than had been at first imagined, not having been entirely
finished before the first week of July. We shall therefore leave it
going on, and in the mean time proceed to describe the instruments that were subsequently made use of in the first and second
measurements.

Steel Chain. Pl. II.

3. One of the first instruments, which that able artist Mr.
Ramsden had orders to prepare, was a steel chain, one hundred
feet in length, the best that he could make. Not that it was intended, nor could it be supposed, that we should absolutely abide
by the result that this chain should furnish us with, for the length
of the base; but it was hoped, that an instrument of this sort
might be made, which would measure distances much more accurately than any thing of that kind had ever done before: and it
was considered as an object of some consequence, to endeavour to
simplify, and render as easy as possible, the measurement of bases
in future: an operation which, hitherto, has always been found
to be tedious and troublesome, to which we may now further add,
uncertain likewise, when done with rods of deal, as will appear
from the account hereafter to be given.

The construction of the chain, which is on the principles of that
of a watch, will be understood from the representation of some of
its chief parts, to the full size, In Pl. II. where the first, or zero-

C

end link, is shewn both in plan and elevation, in the state in which
it was originally applied to measurement on the surface of the
ground. Each link consists of three principal parts; namely, a
long plate; two short ones, half the thickness of the former, with
circular holes near the extremities of each; and two cast-steel
pins, or axes, suited to the diameters of the holes, which serve to
connect the adjoining links together. The holes in the short plates
are made rough, or jagged with a file; so that when they have
embraced the ends of two adjoining long ones, and the pins have
passed through all the holes, in rivetting their extremities, they
are made perfectly fast, and as it were united to the short plates;
while the embraced ends of the long ones turn freely round on the
middle part of the pins.

At every tenth link the joint, just now described, has a position
at right angles to the former; that is to say, the short plates lie
here horizontally, and the pins passing through them stand vertically. Thus, there being in the whole chain two hundred cast-steel
pins, one hundred and eighty lie horizontally; and twenty, including the two by which the handles are attached, stand vertically.
These cross joints, which were chiefly intended that the chain
might fold up in a smaller compass, by returning upon itself at
every tenth link, are likewise useful in presenting a horizontal
surface, to which small circular pieces of brass are screwed, with
figures 1, 2, 3, &c. to 9, engraved on them, denoting the decimal
parts of the length. Thus the middle cross joint, or that which
separates the 50th from the 51st link, is shewn in the Plate with
the figure 5 upon it.

The chain, in its first construction (for we are now to point out
some alterations that were afterwards made in it), was one hundred feet in length, including the two brass handles; in the extremity of each of which there was a semicircular hole, of the
same diameter with the steel arrows successively fixed in the

ground, and serving to keep the account of the number of chains, when applied to common measurement. In this its first mode of application, it was soon discovered, as we shall have occasion to mention hereafter, how admirably the chain performed ; and that, with some farther precautions, a still greater degree of exactness might be attained, by supporting it on stands, or even on planks, laid on, or but little removed from, the common surface of the earth. For this purpose, the two end links were altered, each being now made equal to one foot, exclusive of the handles. By referring to Pl. II. the nature of this alteration will be easily conceived. It consisted in screwing to the under side of the handles, very near the joints, two feather-edged pieces of brass; * the one denoting zero, and the other 100 feet. Over the dart at the first, a plummet with a fine silver wire being suspended, that wire, by a very simple apparatus, hereafter to be described, may be brought accurately to coincide with any point whatever of commencement : and at the second, a fine line with a knife, or other sharp instrument, being drawn on a piece of card placed there for the purpose, and changed as often as needful ; or, as was likewise practised, and found to answer better, a line on a moveable slide of brass, attached to the top of the staud or plank, being brought to coincide with the feather-edge, and then fastened underneath ; the extremity of the 100 feet is readily ascertained : and thus the measurement may be continued on with great accuracy to any distance at pleasure.

That the chain, in this its altered state, may still be advantageously applied to ordinary measurement on the surface of the earth, the pieces above described, having steady pins, and being fastened with screws, can be easily removed, and others, exactly of the same length, substituted in their stead, with semicircular holes (as re-

* They were originally of brass, but are now of steel, that the edges by being harder might run less risk of being damaged.

presented in the Plate by dotted lines near the joint of the handle)
to receive the steel arrows, then to be made use of in the manner
already mentioned.

This most excellent chain seems not to have suffered any perceptible extension from the use that has hitherto been made of it.
It is so accurately constructed, that when stretched out on the
ground, as in common use, all the long plates lying vertically or
edge-wise, if a person, laying hold of either end with both hands,
gives it a flip or jerk, the motion is, in a few seconds, communicated to the other end, in a beautiful vertical serpentine line ;
when the person, holding that handle, receives a sudden shock, by
the weight of the chain pulling him forcibly. The chain weighs
about eighteen pounds, and when folded up is easily contained in
a deal box, about fourteen inches long, eight inches broad, and the
same in depth.

Deal Rods. Pl. III.

4. The bases which have hitherto been measured in different
countries, with the greatest appearance of care and exactness, have
all, or for the most part, been done with deal rods of one kind or
other, whose lengths being originally ascertained by means of
some metal standard, were, in the subsequent applications of them,
corrected by the same standard. Having thus had so many pre-
cedents, serving as examples to guide us in our choice, it was natural enough that we should pursue the same method in the measurement to be executed on Hounslow Heath ; taking, however,
all imaginable care, that our rods should be made of the very best
materials that could be procured ; with this farther precaution,
that by trussing them, they should be rendered perfectly inflexible,
a circumstance not before attended to.

As some difficulty had been found in procuring well seasoned
pine wood of sufficient length, and perfectly free from knots, for

the intended purpose; therefore Sir Joseph Banks had early applied to the Admiralty for assistance in this respect; and forthwith obtained an order to be furnished with what we might have occasion for, from his Majesty's yard at Deptford, where an old New England mast, and also one of Riga wood, were speedily cut up for our use.

New England white pine is lighter, less liable to warp, and less affected by moisture, than Riga red wood. But the New England mast, when it came to be very minutely examined, was found to be too much wounded by shot-holes in some parts, or too much decayed or knotty in others, to afford us a sufficiency. This being the case, we had recourse to the Riga wood, which was indeed extremely smooth and beautiful; and so perfectly straight grained, that a fibre of it, when lifted up, might be drawn, like a thread, almost from one end to the other.

It had been in contemplation to make the rods of twenty-five or thirty feet in length; and one of the former dimensions was actually constructed: but this being found to be rather too unwieldy, it was judged best to content ourselves with those of about twenty feet.

Different opinions have been entertained with regard to the best mode of applying rods in measurement; some contending that contacts, or that of butting the end of one rod against the end of the other, is the best; while others (with more probability of being right) are of opinion, that the adjustment by the coincidences of lines should have the preference. The first is undoubtedly the most expeditious method; but seems at the same time to be liable to this very objectionable circumstance, that the probable errors fall all one way : whereas, in the second method, although by far the most tedious, the errors of coincidence falling sometimes on one side, and sometimes on the other, they compensate for, or destroy each other; and therefore no error is committed.

With the view of satisfying both parties, and in order to put
the matter, if possible, out of doubt, it was judged proper to construct the rods in such a manner as to admit of both methods being tried, that we might adhere to that which should be found by
experience to be the best.

Three measuring rods were accordingly ordered to made, and
also a standard rod, with which the former were from time to
time to be compared. Their general construction will be better
conceived from the plan and elevation, and other representations of their principal parts, in Pl. III. than by any description,
however particular, conveyed in words. It will be sufficient to say,
that the stems of the three measuring rods are each twenty feet
three inches in length, reckoning from the extremities of the bell-
metal tippings; very near two inches deep; and about 1¼ inch
broad. Being trussed laterally and vertically, they are thereby rendered perfectly, or at least as to sense, inflexible. The standard
rod could only be trussed laterally ; and it is justly represented by
the plan of the other rods, excepting that its stem is something
stronger, and that it has two or three inches at each end of extra-
length, the reasons for which differences will appear hereafter.

By referring to the Plate it will be observed, that two narrow
pieces of ivory, each fastened with two small screws, are inlaid
into the upper surface of the rods, within one inch and a half of
the extremities of the tippings. These ivory pieces received the
fine black lines cut into them when the lengths of the rods were
laid off, in the manner hereafter to be mentioned, and accurately
determined the intermediate distance of 20 feet, or 240 inches, the
measure to be used in the application by coincidences : whereas,
in that by contacts, the space comprehended between the extremities of the projecting lips of the tippings, is 243 inches.

Immediately behind each ivory piece, a cavity is formed underneath, in the middle of the stem. This receives a brass wheel,

about eight-tenths of an inch in diameter, whose axis turns in the fork of a brass spring, five inches long, fastened by a screw to the under surface just before the cross feet. These springs are only of such strength as to permit the wheels to be forced up into the cavities by the weight of the rod, which, in its adjusted state, always rests entirely on the surfaces of the two stands that support its extremities. But when the rod is to be raised from the stands, then the milled-headed screws, projecting above the upper surface, and standing over the middle of the springs, being brought to act, the wheels are thereby pressed downwards, and receive the full weight of the rod, which is then easily moved backwards or forwards to its true position, either of contact or coincidence.

The cross feet, placed about $5\frac{1}{2}$ inches from the ends of the rods, and $1\frac{3}{4}$ inch from the insertion of the trussings, are each about nine inches long, $1\frac{1}{2}$ broad, and nearly an inch in depth, having their lower surfaces level with that of the stem. By means of these, the rods are not only kept more steady on the stands, against the common action of the wind upon the trussings; but they likewise serve as holds for the vertical and horizontal brass clamps, whereby the rods are made fast to the stands on one side or other, and in both modes of application, contacts and coincidences; as will be more fully explained hereafter, in describing the tops of the stands.

Brass Standard Scale, and Method of laying off the Lengths of the Deal Rods.

5. At the sale of the instruments of the late ingenious optician Mr. James Short, I purchased a finely divided brass scale, of the length of 42 inches, with a Vernier's division of 100 at one end, and one of 50 at the other, whereby the 1000th part of an inch is

very perceptible. It was originally the property of the late Mr.
Graham, the celebrated watchmaker; has the name of Jonathan
Sisson engraved upon it; but is known to have been divided by
the late Mr. Bird, who then worked with Sisson.

It is sufficiently well known to this Society, that their brass
standard scale, about 42 inches long, which contains on it the
length of the standard yard from the Tower, that from the Exchequer, and also the French half-toise, together with the dupli-
cate of the said scale, sent to Paris for the use of the Royal Academy of Sciences, were both made by Mr. Jonathan Sisson, under
Mr. Graham's immediate direction. Now, although there seemed to
be every reason to suppose, that the scale at present in my possession, originally Mr. Graham's property, would correspond with
those above mentioned, which he had been directed by the Royal
Society, with so much care and pains, to provide; yet, that nothing of this sort might remain doubtful, it was judged right, in
settling the absolute length, of the base, which I measured near
London in 1789, as has been mentioned in the Introduction to
this paper, that the two scales should be actually compared. Having accordingly obtained an order from the President, for admission into the Society's apartments, I went there in the afternoon
of the 13th of August, and laid both scales, taken out of their
cases, on the table of the meeting-room, with thermometers alongside of them, that they might acquire the same temperature. On
the forenoon of the 15th of August the comparison was made, with
the assistance of Mr. Ramsden, who for that purpose carried along
with him his curious beam-compass, whose micrometer-screw
shews very perceptibly a motion of $\frac{1}{1000}$th part of an inch. Thus
the extent of three feet, being carefully taken from the Society's
standard, and applied to my scale, it was found to reach exactly
to 36 inches, the temperature being 65°. In like manner, the
beam-compass being applied to the length of the Exchequer

yard, the extent was now found by the micrometer to over-reach that yard by $\frac{4}{10000}$th, or nearly $\frac{1}{1000}$th parts of an inch.

Having thus shewn that my scale is accurately of the same length with the Society's standard, it remains to point out the use that was made of it, for ascertaining the lengths of the deal rods, intended for the operation on Hounslow Heath. In the first place, Mr. Ramsden prepared a beam-compass, sufficient to take in twenty feet, trussed in all respects like the measuring rods, but something deeper, and fitted as usual with proper points and micrometer. The standard rod being now constructed was laid on the shop-board, strongly framed for the purpose, and nearly level. To one side of it, at the distance of about twenty feet two inches from centre to centre, two strong bell-metal cocks were firmly screwed. These cocks were about $2\frac{1}{4}$ inches in length, three-eighths in thickness, and rose above the stem nearly two inches, so as to be on the same plane with the surface of the measuring rods, when placed upon it.

A large plank, cut from the New England mast, upwards of thirty feet long, nine or ten inches broad, and about three inches thick, being set edgewise in the same room, on part of the stands now ready for the operation, was, in that position, planed perfectly smooth and straight. A silver wire being then stretched very tight, along the middle of the plank, from one end to the other, six spaces of forty inches each were marked off by the side of the wire, at which points seven brass pins, about one-tenth of an inch in diameter, were driven into the wood, and their tops polished with the stone. During the whole of this operation, and that which followed, the thermometer, lying by the side of the brass scale, continued steadily at or very near 63°.

A fine dot being now made on one of the extreme pins, and the silver wire being stretched over the dot, and as near as possible over the middle of the other pins, in which position it was made fast; the extent of forty inches, taken with the utmost care from the brass scale, was then marked off, by placing one point of the beam-compass in the dot, and with the other describing a short faint arc on the surface of the second pin. The beam being then removed, and one point placed in the intersection of the arc and wire, with the other point a dot was made on the third pin, under the middle of the wire. Upon this dot, as a centre, a faint arc was next described on the same pin where the first had been traced. In this manner the six times forty inches were marked off, alternately with dots and arcs; a method found by Mr. Ramsden, in his practice, to be more accurate, than when dots only are made use of.

The exact length of twenty feet, thus obtained, was next taken between the points of the long beam-compass, and transferred to the tops of the bell-metal cocks, placed, as has been already mentioned, on the side of the standard rod, in such manner as to leave more than one inch and a half of the said cocks beyond or without the lines denoting the extent of the twenty feet. This being done, the measuring rods were successively placed on the standard, and their sides applying close to the cocks, the distance of twenty feet was readily transferred from them to the inlaid ivory pieces, on which fine lines were afterwards cut, by marks accurately made for that purpose.

With regard to the adjustment of the lips of the bell-metal tippings, which extend exactly one inch and a half beyond the ivory lines, so as to make the total length of the rod 243 inches, it is to be observed, that they terminate in flat curves of $9\frac{1}{2}$ inches radius, passing through the inch and half points, to which they were cautiously ground down, that at first they might rather exceed than be defective in length. Any two of the rods, lying in the same plane, and also in the same straight line, being brought into contact with each other; if of the true length, the space in that position, comprehended between the two lines on the inlaid ivory pieces, must be exactly three inches. For the purpose of this adjustment, the extent of three inches was therefore taken from the brass scale and cut upon the side of a detached piece of ivory; which being readily applied to the aforesaid intermediate space, the same was gradually reduced, by grinding the lips equally, till it exactly corresponded with that taken from the scale.

The three rods are numbered by a cipher on the surface of the metal at each end, 1.2; 3.4; 5.6; and that being the order in which they were to be applied in actual measurement, so it was likewise the order in which they were adjusted; that is to say, the rod 1.2 was adjusted with 3.4. and with 5.6: and the rod 3.4 was, in like manner, adjusted with 1.2 and 5.6.

One of these deal rods, when finished, was found to weigh twenty-four pounds. They were intended to be contained in two chests, one large and the other smaller. The large chest, which is about 2½ feet deep, may be called a double one, because it has two lids that lift quite off, which, in turning upside down, become alternately top and bottom, having between them, but much nearer to the one than the other, a bottom that is common to both. The shallow side holds the standard rod; and the other, two of the measuring rods; which last is rendered practicable by having one of the side braces of each fixed only with screws, so as to be removed and replaced at pleasure. Thus one of the rods being laid in its place, the other is put over it in an inverted position; and both having the proper fastenings to keep them in their positions, the lid is then put on, and fixed by screws. The chest being now turned upside down, and the other lid removed, the standard is thereby discovered resting on the common bottom, which has bands laid across it for the purpose, a few inches below what has now become the surface of the chest. It was necessary that the standard should rest thus high, both that the light might come freely upon it, and that, being supported by the deep sides of the chest, it might be prevented from twisting, for it will be remembered that it is only trussed laterally. By means of a small brass spring fixed to each end of the standard, a fine silk thread, as being less liable to accident than silver wire, is stretched along its stem, which, by small wedges prepared for the purpose, and slipped in between it and the bands on which it rests, is always brought into the same position. This being done, the silk thread is turned off, so as to permit the measuring rods to be laid on the standard for comparison. With regard to the smaller chest, such a one was actually made, and sent down to the Heath, towards the close of the operation with the deal rods; but from some mistake in its dimensions, it would not admit the third rod.

Stands for the Measuring Rods. Pl. III. and IV.

6. From the extraordinary levelness of Hounslow Heath, the ascent from the south-east towards the north-west being little more than one foot in a thousand in the distance of five miles, it was easily seen, that the computed base line, or that actually forming a curve parallel to the surface of the sea, at that height above it, would fall so little short of the hypothenusal distance, measured on, or parallel to, the surface of the Heath, as scarcely to deserve notice, had it not been thought necessary to shew, how much one end of the base was really higher than the other; and to convince the world, that in an operation of this sort, where so much accuracy was expected, no pains were spared, nor the most trivial circumstances neglected.

From the trouble and uncertainty attending the frequent use of plummets, especially in windy weather, instead of measuring level or base lines, as has hitherto been customary (in which case it would have been necessary to make use of the plummet, or some such contrivance, at every step of ascent or descent) it was judged to be a better method to measure hypothenuses, and, having obtained the relative heights of the stations by the accurate application of the telescopic spirit-level, to compute the base lines. Thus it was proposed, that the length of the base on Hounslow Heath should be obtained by measuring a line through the air, drawn parallel to the common surface from station to station, in equal distances of 200 yards or 600 feet each, and represented in the figure at the top of Pl. III.

For this purpose, two kinds of stands were used; one whose height was fixed, to be placed at the beginning and end of each 200 yards; and the others, whose heights were moveable, that their surfaces might be brought more easily to coincide with the line passing through the air from one fixed stand to the other. The fixed stands in their first state, represented by that towards the left hand in the Plate for the deal rods, were only two feet seven inches in height; but when the glass rods were afterwards used, they had an additional piece of ten inches fastened to the top (as in the left-hand stand of Pl. IV.) which made their total height above the Heath, including the platform on which they stood, three feet and a half. They are tripods of white deal, whose legs extend about three feet from each other; and being braced diagonally, are mortised at top into circles of the same sort of wood. Over this circle, a square table of about 11½ inches is fixed, composed of oak, and mahogany at top; but both taken together do not exceed 1¼ inch in thickness.

The nature of the moveable stands, whereof there were at last no fewer than seventeen provided, will be comprehended from the representations of them towards the right hand in Pl. III. and IV. Their general construction, in what regards the part of them which is fixed, differs not from that of the others, excepting that they were of different he ghts, from two feet to about two feet eight inches, so as better to suit the irregularities of the ground where it might be necessary to place them. In the middle of each of these, an hexagonal wooden pipe descends, from the top to within two or three inches of the bottom, where it is joined by a brace reaching from each leg. This pipe receives the common cheese-press wooden screw (having three sides screwed and three plane), to the top of which the square table is attached. It is embraced by the circular nut, or winch with four handles, whereby the table is elevated or depressed at pleasure ; and being brought to its proper height, is there made perfectly fast by means of the flat-headed iron screw, which passing through one of the legs, presses an iron plate, fixed in the inside of the pipe, against one of the plane sides of the screw.

In describing the deal rods, there has already been occasion to make mention of the vertical and horizontal clamps, whereby the cross feet are fastened to the table on the top of the stand. The nature of these tables will be best understood by consulting the two plans of them towards the right hand in Pl. III. ; whereof one represents the two grooves fitted for the alternate reception of the horizontal clamp, according to the side on which the rod lies that is to be moved on into coincidence ; and the other shews it actually in its place, with the clamp itself detached in elevation alongside of it. Thus from the plan it may be perceived, that the first, or adjusted rod, lies towards the farther side of the table, and is there secured by the vertical clamp. The second, or moveable rod, lies on the hither side, and therefore the horizontal clamp is placed in the farther groove, where it is firmly pinched by the nut underneath. The rod has been brought to coincidence by working with the two milled-headed screws against the opposite sides of the cross foot. This apparatus, although perfectly good in theory, was found to be much too confined in its nature to answer well in practice, requiring the stands to be placed with a degree of precision, which could not be effected in the field without great loss of time ; and this was the real cause, as will be seen hereafter, that the measurement by coincidences with the deal rods was given up, and that by contacts adhered to.

Towards the left hand of Pl. III. the plan of one of the square tables is represented with the ends of the second and third rods upon it in contact. In this operation it will be perceived, that only one cross foot of each rod could now rest on and be clamped to the stand, the tables having been inadvertently cut too small to admit of both ; and although this has the appearance of imperfection, yet no inconveniency whatever was found to result from it in practice, experience having shewn, that the clamping of either end sufficed to keep the rod steady. Alongside of the table, the vertical clamp, being that now solely made use of, is likewise represented in elevation.

On the face or exterior side of each leg of all the stands, fixed as well as moveable, a plate of brass is screwed near the bottom, with two holes in each, over a groove purposely made in the wood underneath. By means of these plates, parallelopiped leaden weights, about fourteen pounds each, having brass pins with heads suited to enter the holes, and fall down in the grooves, into a narrow-pointed part of them, are readily slipped on or off each leg. Thus every stand, exclusive of its own weight, which is about thirty-one pounds, being loaded with forty-two pounds of lead, is thereby rendered perfectly firm and steady.

A number of wedges were also prepared, and always ready to be placed under the legs ; by means of which, and a spirit-level laid on the table, its plane is brought to the proper position.

Notwithstanding all these precautions, it having been found, in the measurement with the deal rods, that time was lost in levelling the stands, particularly in situations where the surface happened to be more than usually uneven, or where it was of a loose or spongy nature ; therefore Mr. Smeaton advised (and no man's advice is more deserving of attention), that deal platforms, standing on pickets driven into the ground, and properly levelled, should be used to receive the legs of the stands. Accordingly, for the operation with the glass rods (Pl. IV.) twenty such triangular platforms made of inch deal, whose sides were each three feet two inches in length, and void in the middle, were provided ; as also a number of beech pickets, about an inch and a half square, and of different lengths, from seven to twelve or fourteen inches. Three of these pickets, short or long as the situation required, being driven into the ground, till their heads (by the carpenter's level) were brought to the proper height, the platform was laid upon them ; and on that the stand itself being placed, its position was ultimately corrected by the spirit-level laid on the top of the table. Each of the beech pickets had a hole bored through its top, fit to receive a piece of strong tent-line, by which, and the help of one of the camp mallets, the pickets were easily pulled up again, when the platform was to be removed to a new situation.

Boning Telescope and Rods. Pl. III.

7. In order to trace the line of 100 yards or 600 feet through the air, from one fixed stand to the other, it was usual, in the first place, to stretch a cord extremely tight along the ground, and to divide the space into rod lengths, by small wooden pins placed close by the cord, which remained there, and accordingly marked, very nearly, the points over which the centres of the intermediate stands were to come. A piece of wood, about fourteen inches in length, and one and a half in breadth, painted white, with a narrow black line along the middle of it, being prepared for the purpose, was laid on the surface of the farther stand. The boning telescope, fourteen inches long, and one and a half in diameter, with a small

magnifying power, and moveable object-glass, so as to fit it for very
short distances, was then laid on the surface of the nearest stand ;
which, by means of wedges placed under the legs, had that side
towards the farther stand so elevated or depressed, as to bring the
cross wires to coincide with the black line on the painted board.
Twenty-four boning rods had been originally provided ; but it
rarely happened, that more than eight or ten of that number were
used in any one station. They are of clean deal, upwards of five
feet in length, one inch square, and pointed with plate iron at the
bottom, so as to be easily fixed into the ground. Each rod carries
a cross vane, six or seven inches in length, and three-quarters of
an inch in breadth. This cross vane, being moved upwards or downwards along the rod, till its upper surface coincided with the cross
wires of the telescope and black line on the painted board, its under
surface then marked the height to which the surface of the stand
was to be brought at that particular place. In this manner, a
certain number of points, in the line passing through the air from
one fixed stand to the other, being accurately obtained, it was very
easy, at all the intermediate places, by the application of the eye
alone to the surface of any one stand or rod, to bring the surfaces
of the other stands near it, into the same plane.

*Cup and Tripod for preserving the Point upon the Ground, where the
Measurement was discontinued at night, and resumed next morning.
Pl. III.*

8. It has been already mentioned, and, in giving the account
of the rough measurement with the chain, there will be farther
occasion to remark, that the base was divided into hypothenuses
of 200 yards or 600 feet each, where square pickets were driven
into the ground, and regularly numbered, so as to be easily referred
to on any occasion. In the measurement with the rods, it was

customary to finish the day's work at or near one of these stations. When the rods of twenty feet were used, the termination of a rod was, of course, always found to be within a few inches of the picket corresponding with the hypothenuse, as determined by the chain. But with the rods of twenty feet three inches, the day's work was always ended with a fractional rod, by suspending a plummet from some convenient part of the stem, marked for the purpose, and which consequently became the point of commencement next morning.

The brass cup, made use of on these occasions, is of the figure of an inverted truncated cone, whose mean diameter is four inches, and its depth about five, with a very small inclination in the sides. It was placed in a hole dug for it in the earth, immediately under the point of suspension of the plummet, serving only to hold the water in which it vibrated.

The nature of the tripod will be best conceived from the plan and elevation of it in Pl. III. It consists of two strong pieces of beech wood, mortised into each other, so as to resemble a half cross, or the letter T inverted, having three strong iron prongs, about twelve inches in length, which pass through the ends of the wood, and are fastened to it by square nuts at top. On the surface of the tripod lies a similar half cross of mahogany, moveable by means of grooves in the direction of the longest side, and fixable by its proper screws, when brought to the desired position. This mahogany half-cross carries on its surface a brass ruler, moveable at right angles to the former direction, fixable also by means of its own screws, and on whose end is cut a very fine intersection. Thus any day's operation having been finished, the tripod was placed near the cup, with its longest side parallel to the line of measurement, and its prongs driven into the ground, so as to be rendered perfectly immoveable without great violence. The plummet being then suspended by a fine gilt wire, at any part of the

stem of the deal rods indifferently, but always at the fixed * or
hindermost end of the glass rods, the brass ruler was advanced
so near as almost to touch the wire, and there made fast. This
being done, the mahogany half-cross was lastly moved backwards
or forwards, in the direction of the line of measurement, until the
Intersection, as seen by a person lying down on the ground for
the purpose, accurately coincided with the gilt wire, where it was
likewise fastened by its proper screws. A tent was then pitched
very near the apparatus, for the soldiers who furnished the centinel
for its security, till the measurement was resumed : and particularly to guard it from being disturbed by cattle during the night.

*Wheels for terminating, in a permanent manner, the Extremities of
the Base.* Pl. III.

9. Before any accurate measurement could ultimately be made
of the base by means of rods, in order that we might with certainty
refer to the same point, on any occasion that might arise of correction or repetition of the work, it had all along been foreseen, that
it would be absolutely necessary to sink deep into the ground
wooden pipes, or such like things, at the extremities of the base,
which could not be removed, or even disturbed, by idle or ignorant
people, without very considerable labour. Mr. Mylne, F. R. S.
was accordingly requested to order two such pipes to be provided,
about six feet in length each, and one foot in diameter, with a
bore of four inches in the uppermost end, for the depth of two feet,
and cross arms near the lowermost end, in the style of the common
warping posts. As an improvement on this idea, Mr. Mylne very

* That this might be conveniently done, a moveable stand was placed, under the
glass rod, about four feet from the fixed end, and its table elevated till, by bearing
against the lower part of the case, it received its weight. This permitted the stand
under the fixed end to be lowered and removed, to make room for the apparatus.

judiciously proposed that, instead of the cross arms, the lower ends of the pipes should pass through the nave of an old coach-wheel, and then be secured by a bolt underneath. This alteration was approved of; and the machines, thus executed, were sent soon after by water to Hampton.

The plan and section of one of these wheels, with the dished side downwards, are represented towards the left hand in Pl. III. where it will be perceived, that by means of four knee-pieces, made of crooked oak, the pipe is firmly bolted to the wheel, and thereby kept at right angles to its plane. The top of the pipe is also secured exteriorly by an iron hoop, and has a cast-iron box driven into it, whose inner diameter is four inches, answering to that of the bore. Four oak piles for each wheel were prepared to be driven into the bottoms of the pits dug for their reception, which were six feet in diameter, and the same in depth. The soil near Hampton Poor-house being of a loose sandy nature, there the piles were easily driven into the bottom, until their tops were on the same level. The flat of the fellies of the wheel being then laid on the piles, the earth was filled in and well rammed around the pipe, quite up to the surface, with which its mouth is even. But the soil at King's Arbour, being a hard-bound gravel, the piles could not be driven into the bottom of that pit; wherefore, the flat of the wheel rests there on the gravel only.

The brass cup, formerly described, was from the first intended to be placed in the pipes, for which purpose it has two lids; one a semicircle, with the central point marked by a line cut on its diameter, brought into the direction of the base; with which line the gilt wire, suspended at the extremity of the first rod, was made to coincide on the commencement of the measurement. The other lid has a very small hole made in its centre, through which the plummet wire is to pass, when suspended from the centre of the instrument, hereafter to be made use of for the determination of the angles at the base, or in nny other station whatever, where it may be necessary to bring it very accurately over a point on the surface of the ground underneath.

Rough Measurement of the Base with the Chain, and Determination of the relative Heights of the Stations by means of the Telescopic Spirit-Level. Pl. I. and II.

10. Having in the preceding description of the various instruments, originally provided for the measurement of the base, fully explained their constructions, uses, and modes of application : and having thereby anticipated, in a great degree, what must otherwise have been said to make them understood in any account, blended with that of the execution ; little more now remains to be given than the journal of our proceedings from day to day, and the ultimate result of the operation.

Mr. Ramsden having produced his hundred-feet chain, with the portable transit instrument ; and having lent us an excellent telescopic spirit-level, for determining the relative heights ; two sections of the base being likewise cleared by the soldiers, and some progress made in the third, we found ourselves, on the 16th of June, in readiness to begin the rough measurement.

Lieut. Colonel Calderwood, of his Majesty's Horse-Guards, F. R. S. had, from the beginning, been so good as to promise his assistance in the operation. Lieut. Colonel Pringle too, of the Corps of Engineers, obligingly became a volunteer on the occasion ; as did also Mr. Lloyd, F. R. S. a few days afterwards ; while Ensign Reynolds, of the 94th regiment, who had for some time past been employed in surveying the environs of the Heath, continued that work with such spare hands as could be afforded him for that purpose ; and it is to the Plan (Pl. I.) done by that officer, that it will be necessary to refer in any thing regarding locality, in what has hitherto been said, as well as in the subsequent relation.

The lower end of the base had for some time past been distinguished by a St. George's flag fixed to the top of a fir spar, thirty-five feet in height; and one of the signal bell-tents still remained at the station near the Summerhouse. A rope of 200 yards being made very fast by a strong iron picket, driven into the ground at the bottom of the flag-staff, the other end was carried on along the base, and placed at the bottom of a camp colour, in a line with the bell-tent. The rope being wound around a strong iron reel, prepared for the purpose, was thereby stretched extremely tight, a person occasionally lifting it up in the middle, or at other places, and letting it drop again, so as to bring the whole into the same straight line. Five persons were necessary for the proper management of the chain; two at each end for its adjustment there, and one towards the middle, to lay it close to the rope, or to bear it up in any particular place, where the circumstances of the ground rendered such precautions useful. The zero or rear end of the chain being strained back, so as to coincide with the point of commencement, a steel arrow was placed as erect as possible in the semicircular cavity of the brass handle at the other end. The chain being then drawn on, till the cavity in the rear handle could be applied to the first arrow, a second was then placed in that of the front handle, and so on, until six chain lengths were thus measured off; which terminating the first hypothenuse, a beech picket, something more than an inch square, and about seven in length, with No. 1. cut upon it, was driven into the ground, till its head was nearly level with the surface. It is however to be remarked, that the sixth arrow of each hypothenuse was constantly left in the ground till the first of the succeeding one was placed, to avoid the error that would have otherwise arisen in applying the rear end of the chain to the picket instead of the arrow.

In this manner we proceeded on the 16th of June, and in the space of about three hours and a half, completed the first measurement of the south-east section of the base, comprehending the thirteen hypothenuses between the flag-staff and station near Hanworth Summerhouse, the distance being 78 chains, or 7800 feet, making 2600 yards; and the mean temperature of the air being 69°.

On the subsequent day this section was re-measured with equal care, when the total extent fell short of the thirteenth picket only five inches. And here it is to be observed, that a considerable part of this difference probably arose from the stretching of the chain across Wolsey River, at the same time that the irregularities of the ground are greater in this than in either of the other two sections. The mean heat of this day was 65°.

The operation with the chain was suspended during the 18th and 19th of June, those days having been employed in settling certain matters with Mr. Ramsden relative to the deal rods, as well as to give time for the making of a holdfast for the rear end of the chain, invented by Lieut. Colonel Pringle. This machine, whereof the plan at large is represented by dotted lines at the handle of the chain, as it is in small by the two elevations adjoining in Pl. II. consists of a semicircular iron plate, from the bottom of which projects two double and one single prong. In the middle, between two double prongs, a semicircular cavity is formed, fitted to receive the steel arrow on one side, while that in the brass receives it on the other. In a socket in the middle, a strong wooden handle, resembling that of a spade, is placed. Thus the rear handle of the chain being applied to the arrow, the holdfast embraces with its double prongs the straight part of the brass, and in that position, being forced into the ground by the action of a man at the handle, the rear end of the chain is thereby kept so firm as to be immoveable by the efforts of the two men at the other end, in stretching it to its true position, for the front arrow.

On Monday, the 21st of June, the operations were resumed, by measuring twice with the chain (forwards and again backwards) the thirteen hypothenuses comprehended in the second section of the base, between Hanworth Summerhouse and the north-west bank of the great Road (an old Roman way) leading from Staines to London. This being the smoothest part of the Heath, and the holdfast being now applied, the two measurements differed only one inch and a half in the distance of 7800 feet. This instance of accuracy is alone sufficient to prove the great excellence of the chain, although another will be given hereafter still more surprising.

On the same day that the second section of the base was measured, the levels of that and the first were taken. The operation of levelling is so universally known, as to render any detail of it unnecessary. It will be sufficient to say, that the spirit-level made use of on this occasion was a very good one, about eighteen inches in length, and could at all times be very readily and accurately adjusted, by inversion in its Y's. The tops of the pickets, marking the hypothenusal distances, were the points on which the levelling rods were placed on each side of the level; which being inverted at the intermediate picket, points equidistant from the centre of the earth were thereby obtained at the cross vanes of the levelling rods, and no correction for curvature or refraction necessary. It will be readily understood, that the relative heights of the pickets were found by measuring their distances from the centres of the cross vanes and axis of the telescope respectively.

The six first columns towards the left hand of the first or general table subjoined to this Paper, shew distinctly every thing relating to the levels of the whole base, those of the third section having been determined on the 22d of June. By examining the table it will be seen, that the ascent on the first section is   10.555 feet,

on the second   -   -   8.580

and on the third   -   -   19.130

Total   -   -   -   -   31.265 feet,

between the lower extremity at Hampton Poorhouse, and the higher near King's Arbour.

The computed numbers in the seventh column are the reductions * depending on the aforesaid heights, or the differences between the hypothenusal distances of 600 feet each and the reduced base distances. With regard to the remaining columns of the table, or those towards the right hand, they will be severally spoken to hereafter, in taking into consideration the expansion of metals, as determined with great accuracy by the experiments with the pyrometer.

Hitherto no use had been made of the transit instrument : for, in order that it might be applied to advantage, there was a necessity for laying the wheel into the ground at the lower end of the

---

* The reduction in the seventh column, I have computed by the difference between the square of the hypothenuse, actually measured, and the square of the height found by the level ; and Lieut. Col. Calderwood has done the same thing by a much shorter method. Thus, in the annexed figure, CE being the hypothenuse of 600 feet, DE the perpendicular height obtained by levelling, DB the reduction required, or the difference between the hypothenuse and true base ; then, substituting the chord BE instead of DE, the following analogy is obtained ; AB : BE : : BE : DB ; consequently, $\frac{BE^2}{AB} = DB$: that is, the square of the perpendicular height being divided by double the distance, or 1200 feet, the quotient is equal to DB the reduction, without sensible error. For if DE were four feet, the greatest perpendicular height in the base, BE the chord would only exceed it $\frac{1}{4}$'s part of an inch. The difference between the results, by the two modes of computation, is so trifling as not to deserve notice.

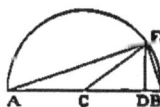

F

base, and so to modify the St. George's flag-staff that, being placed in the pipe, it might be steadily supported by braces in a true vertical position; which we found, from experience, could not be effected by ropes only.

The wheel being accordingly laid in its place, and the other precautions taken for securing the flag-staff, which was likewise painted white, that it might be more distinctly seen from the farther extremity; on the 22d of June, the transit instrument was adjusted over the thirteenth picket at Hanworth Summerhouse, while directed upon the flag-staff. But it being now found, that the vertical plane passing through the flag-staff fell to the eastward of the centre of Bansted Spire, therefore the transit was gradually moved to the eastward, until by repeated trials the three points were perceived to be in the same vertical plane, when the picket was moved, and replaced exactly under the axis of the telescope, a few inches from its first position. The same operation was repeated at the twenty-sixth station, on the farther bank of the Staines Road; and, lastly, at the forty-sixth, forming the north-west extremity of the base; where a pit was immediately dug for the wheel, which was placed therein, without however filling in the earth for the present, that being deferred till near the completion of the measurement with the deal rods. Thus the two extremities, and two intermediate points of the base, being accurately placed, by the help of the transit instrument, in the same vertical plane with Bansted Spire, it was easily seen, that by arranging camp colours in the intervals at any time, all the other points might be brought so nearly to coincide with these first, as not to occasion, by deviation, any sensible error in the measurement afterwards to be made. This application of the transit shewed us, however, that some labour had been lost by not using it sooner: for at the Staines Road, the tract cleared by the soldiers deviated about two feet and a half too much to the westward for the true line; and at King's Arbour it was twice as much : so that we were now obliged to widen the cleared tract, by adding to the eastern side of it.

On the same day that the chief points in the base were fixed by means of the transit, and the levels of the third section taken as before mentioned, the rough measurement of that section with the chain was completed, and found to contain nineteen hypothenusal distances of 600 feet each, and one of 404.55, making in the whole 11804.55 feet, between the twenty-sixth station at the Staines Road and the centre of the pipe near King's Arbour, the mean temperature being 62°½. Here it is to be observed, that this last section was only measured once with the chain, the tract not being yet sufficiently cleared to admit of its being done to the best advantage; and, when completed, it was judged to be better to proceed directly in the operation with the rods, than to lose time in the usual repetition, since the merits of the chain, in this way of applying it, were already sufficiently well established ; and any future tests to which it was to be put were proposed to be of a more rigid nature.

When the length of the chain, in its original state, was ascertained by the dots on the brass pins in the New England plank, it was found, in the then temperature of 74°, to exceed the 100 feet by near one quarter of an inch, or 0.245 inch. Therefore, in the temperature of 63°, being that in which the lengths of the deal rods were laid off, and differing very little from what was likewise the meant heat of the air, when applied upon the Heath, the chain, according to the experiments on the expansion of the very same steel, would exceed the 100 feet by 0.161 inch, or 0.0134 foot. Hence the sum of the three sections of the base, 274 chains, being multiplied by 0.0134 foot, we shall have 3.67 feet for the equation of the chain + 4.55 feet, to be added to its length, which will then become 27408.22 feet from the centre of one pipe to the centre of the other : and this would have been the true length of the base, as given by the rough measurement with the chain, if the surface had

F 2

been one uniform inclined plane throughout its whole extent. But, although the ascent of Hounslow Heath is so small, and so gradual, as to occasion little more than half an inch of reduction, from the 46 hypothenusal to the 46 base distances, into which it is divided, as may be seen by referring to the table ; yet each of these hypo-thenuses containing again many other small irregularities, all of which affect the measurement by the chain, in proportion to their number and height, in every space of 600 feet, their united effects, including the lateral deviations from the true line in measuring, do somewhat more than compensate for the extra-length of the chain, as will be seen hereafter in comparing the length of the base just now obtained with that given by the rods.

The weather, which during the greater part of June had been wet, became still worse towards the end of the month and first week of July; so much so, that even if the deal rods had been ready, they could not have been used with advantage. The soldiers, ne-vertheless, were not idle, being, when the weather would permit, partly employed in clearing the Heath, and partly in assisting Mr. Reynolds in the survey, towards the perfecting of which many chief points were fixed by means of my astronomical quadrant, placed for that purpose at several different stations of the base. At this time too (July 8th) I levelled from the lower end of the base to the surface of the Thames at Hampton, and found the descent to be 96.1 feet.

Measurement of the Base with the Deal Rods. Pl. I. and III.

11. Such extraordinary care and pains had been bestowed in the construction of the deal rods, in order to render them the best which had ever been made, that, although begun early in June, they were not completely finished before the 15th of July. They were brought that afternoon by Mr. Ramsden, together with the

various parts of the apparatus necessary for their application in the field, to the camp, now moved from Hanworth Summerhouse to the intersection of the base with Wolsey River; whence they were transported, early next morning, to the pipe near Hampton Poorhouse, where we were met by Sir Joseph Banks, accompanied by Mess. Blagden, Cavendish, Lloyd, and Smeaton, all ready to lend their assistance in the subsequent mensuration.

Before I proceed farther, I think it here incumbent upon me very gratefully to remark, that the respectable and very worthy President of the Royal Society, ever zealous in the cause of science, and who had repeatedly visited the Heath, to offer aid, if such had been necessary, while the first and rougher part of the operations were going on ; now, that others of a more delicate nature were to commence, and where it was of importance, that those entrusted with the execution should meet with as few, and as short interruptions as possible, not only gave his attendance from morning to night in the field, during the whole progress of the work ; but also, with that liberality of mind which distinguishes all his actions, ordered his tents to be continually pitched near at hand, where his immediate guests, and the numerous visitors whom curiosity drew to the spot, met with the most hospitable supply of every necessary and even elegant refreshment. It will easily be imagined, how greatly this tended to expedite the work, and how much more comfortable and pleasant it rendered the labour to all who obligingly took part in it ; but more especially to him, who, being a volunteer in it at first, considered himself as bound to persevere in his best endeavours to bring it to a successful conclusion.

From the description th.t has been given of the deal rods, it will be remembered, that they are fitted to be applied in measuring, either by the coincidences of lines, inlaid one inch and a half from each extremity, or by the contacts of the spherical lips of the bell-metal with which they are tipped. The first, seeming to be the most accurate, although the most tedious method, was that by which we proposed to set out.

The flag-staff having been previously removed from the pipe, and the brass cup filled with water put in its stead, all the necessary precautions being likewise taken for preserving the line of direction, horizontally, by the rope stretched along the first hypothenuse, and vertically, by means of the boning rods; the first ivory line on the first rod was brought by the plummet to coincide with the centre of the cup, in which position, being clamped, it accurately marked the commencement of the base. The second rod being now applied to the first, and moved up by the apparatus formerly described (Pl. III.) till its line coincided with that on the first; and, in like manner, the third rod being applied on the alternate side of the second, moved up and clamped as the rest; thus the exact distance of sixty feet was ascertained; care being always taken, that the first adjustments were not disturbed, while the subsequent ones were forming. The clamps fastening the first rod to its stands being then detached, it was carried by two men and laid on the alternate side of the third; and so on in succession, until fifteen rod lengths were measured off, being the half of the first hypothenuse.

The time consumed in measuring this short distance of 900 feet was not less than five hours; owing, as has been formerly mentioned, to the confined nature of the apparatus for moving the rods on into coincidence, which required such nicety in placing the stands, as could not be effected until after several repeated unsuccessful trials. All the executive people were therefore of opinion, that it would be proper to discontinue this mode of measurement, at least until a more convenient apparatus could be thought of for the purpose; and that, in the mean time, we should proceed by the method of contacts, as the only alternative we could for the present adopt.*

The rods being accordingly placed in contact with each other, we soon made greater progress, finishing the operations of the day at the middle of the fourth hypothenuse, where the tripod, with its guard, was placed, to preserve the point of commencement for the ensuing morning.

The measuring rods, when put into the chest in London, had been compared and found to agree with the standard. The comparison was not repeated on the 16th; but this being done on the 17th, at 7^h A. M. under the oil-cloth canopy at the camp, they were found at a medium to exceed the standard by one-fiftieth of an inch, the temperature then being $62°$. After the comparison they were carried to the place of the tripod, when the operation was resumed by bringing, with the help of the plummet, the same point of the rod with which we had left off work, to coincide with the intersection on the brass ruler. The measurement of this day was closed at the end of the tenth hypothenuse, when the rods being carried back to camp, were compared, and found accurately to agree with the standard.

A considerable fall in the barometer, between the evening of

* Although I acquiesced in the change thus become necessary, yet it was with much reluctance, because it left undecided the contested point, with regard to coincidences and contacts. If we could have proceeded with the coincident rods till eighty-one lengths were measured off, and then measured back the same space by placing eighty rods in contact, the point would have been clearly settled. For if the termination of the eightieth rod agreed exactly with the point of departure, contacts being the most expeditious would have been judged the best method. On the contrary, if the eightieth rod fell short of reaching the point of departure, there could have been no doubt, that the difference must have arisen from butting one rod against the other, whereby a certain small proportion of each rod came to be lost in the account, by being measured twice over.

the 17th and the morning of the 19th, portended rain. Nevertheless, all parties repaired to the place of rendezvous, which was appointed at the lower end of the base, in order to remeasure the two first hypothenuses, by placing all the rods in contact, which on the 16th had been done partly one way and partly the other. The operation being accordingly repeated with great care, the point of the sixtieth rod, which formerly corresponded to the centre of the second picket, was now found to be pushed forward exactly forty-five inches, answerable to the deficiency on the fifteen coincident rods, with which the mensuration was begun. It now began to rain, therefore the rods were carried back to camp, and being severally compared, they were found to exceed the standard each by one-thirtieth of an inch, occasioned by the extraordinary humidity of the air. A heavy rain ensued; and what made this much more regretted by all, was, that in the forenoon their Majesties graciously condescended to honour the camp with their presence, and continued there some time; but the weather becoming rather worse, it was utterly impossible to shew their Majesties the nature of the operation, by any progress that could at that time be made in the work.

After a continuance of unfavourable weather for several days, the operations were resumed at 9ʰ A.M. of the 23d, when the rods being compared, were found still to exceed the standard by one-thirtieth of an inch, and the temperature now was 61°. Here it is to be observed, that in our progress forward, an accurate register had been all along kept of that point of each rod corresponding to the centre of the hypothenusal pickets, by noting its distance from either end, whereby the error of the chain at each station was readily discovered, at the same time that the revolutions of the three rods served to keep the account of the total measurement. In order, therefore, that this method might be distinctly adhered to, it was judged proper to push on the rod that lay over the

tripod at No. 10. exactly forty-five inches, to make good the deficiency of the first fifteen coincident rods, and that the account might
be kept from the lower end of the base in entire rods of 249, and
complete revolutions of 729 inches each. This being done, the
rest were placed in the ordinary succession ; and we finished the
business of the day at the eighteenth station, where the rods
being compared at 6ʰ P.M. their mean length was found to exceed
that of the standard $\frac{1}{77}$th part of an inch, the temperature then
being 54°.

On Saturday the 24th of July, the rods were three times compared ; at 7ʰ 30′ A.M.; 11ʰ 15′ A.M.; and 5ʰ 45′ P.M. Their mean
excess above the standard was found to be one-thirtieth of an inch,
and the mean heat 64°. In the course of the day, the measurement was continued from the eighteenth to the twenty-seventh
station, or first of the third section of the base, where the tripod
was placed as usual ; and there it remained untouched, on account
of bad weather, till Monday the 2d of August.

Considering how much time and labour had been bestowed in
obtaining what we certainly had every reason to conclude were
the best deal rods that ever were made, it was no small disappointment now to find, that they were so liable to lengthen and shorten,
by the humid and dry states of the atmosphere, as to leave us no
hopes of being able, by their means, to determine the length of
the base to that degree of precision we had all along aimed at. But
since more than one half of it was already measured, it was judged
proper to proceed with them in their present state, and then to
have them carefully painted or varnished, before they should be
farther used.

The unfavourableness of the season, and delays in obtaining the
instruments, had already been the causes of protracting the operations on Hounslow Heath greatly beyond what was at first
expected ; and the failure of the deal rods gave no immediate pro-

G

spect of their being speedily brought to a conclusion. On revolving in my own mind the different alternatives we might ultimately be obliged to have recourse to, metal rods of some kind or other, whose expansion could always be determined by experiment, seemed to promise a result that might be safely relied on. Cast iron was what I had thoughts of proposing, knowing, from an experiment which I had made myself, that it expanded less than steel. The cumbersomeness of its weight appeared indeed objectionable ; but that inconvenience was either to be submitted to, or one of another kind, namely, the reduction of the length, which was always, if possible, to be avoided.

At this time Lieut. Colonel Calderwood could not conveniently lend us his assistance in the field ; but he visited us occasionally, and on one of these visits proposed to me, that glass rods should be made use of instead of deal ; putting me in mind of another experiment * that I had made, which seemed to shew that solid glass rods expanded less than tubes. This proposition the Lieutenant Colonel, before he came to the Heath, had made to Mr. Ramsden, who appeared averse from making the trial, because of the great length of the rods, and the brittleness of the material. Nevertheless, it being sufficiently obvious, that glass rods or tubes of the full length, or something approaching towards it, would be much

* The experiment here alluded to was made with Mr. Cumming's pyrometer, which from its construction did not admit of a very accurate estimation of the heat communicated to the standard bar, the rod, and tube respectively. Either, therefore, the natures of the glass rod and tube, made use of at that time, must have been very different, to cause the difference of expansion ; or some circumstance in the instrument unattended to, had occasioned the fallacious appearance : for it will be found, from the experiments hereafter to be given in detail, that a solid glass pendulum rod expands fully as much as, nay, in this particular instance, even more than a tube ; but different glass, having different specific gravities, will no doubt be susceptible of different degrees of expansibility.

sooner provided than any metal rods whatever, and the saving of time being a point of consequence; Lieut. Colonel Calderwood was accordingly requested to make the trial at the glass-house, as soon as possible after his return to town. Next day he succeeded in getting a fine tube drawn, eighteen feet long, and about one inch in diameter; and there seemed to be no longer any doubt, that those of the proper length might be obtained. It was found, that solid glass rods of such extraordinary dimensions could not be had, it being impossible to take at once a sufficient quantity of the melted metal on the irons, made use of for drawing them at the glass-house.

The week of rainy weather, which ended the month of July, occasioning, as has been said, a total suspension of the operations on the Heath, was employed in procuring a sufficient number of glass tubes (one whereof was not less than twenty-six feet long) and regulating with Mr. Ramsden every thing concerning their construction into measuring rods. The description of them we shall however defer until the time of their application in the field, after having finished the operation with those of deal.

On Monday the 2d of August, the operations on the Heath were resumed at 8ʰ 30′ A. M. by comparing the rods with the standard, which they were found to exceed by one-fortieth of an inch, the temperature then being 66°. The forward end of the rod now placed over the tripod at No. 27, completing the 800th length, reckoned from the lower end of the base by rods of 243 Inches each; and these being equal to 810 rods of 240 inches; it was judged proper to mark a point upon the ground corresponding to this forward end, that it might be referred to in returning back with the measurement by the glass rods. This was done by sinking two small pickets into the ground, about a foot asunder, one on each side of the base, and at right angles to it. A silk thread being then stretched over the tops of the pickets, and gently moved on till it touched the silver wire suspended from the end of the rod, fine notches were then made with a pen-knife in the tops of the pickets, whereby the thread could be replaced in the same situation; which being done, the pickets were covered over with earth. In the course of this day nine hypothenuses were measured; and at 7^h P.M. the tripod was placed at the thirty-sixth station. The rods, being now compared, were found to agree with the standard; and the temperature was $67°\frac{1}{2}$.

On Tuesday the 3d of August, the rods were compared at 7^h A.M. and found only to exceed the standard by one-sixtieth of an inch. Being arrived at the middle of the forty-first hypothenuse, a point corresponding to the forward end of the 1215th rod was transferred to the ground, by the double pickets and silk thread, as had been done at the twenty-seventh station. The measurement was then continued to the north-west extremity of the base, which was found in the whole to contain 1353 complete long rods of 243 inches each + 21 inches, where the tripod was placed, in the point which of course corresponded to the 1370th short rod of 240 inches each, equal to 328800 inches, or 27400 feet. To which distance we have yet to add 4.31 feet, being the space intercepted between the intersection on the tripod and the centre of the pipe marking the north-west extremity of the base; whose total length, as given by the deal rods, without regard to expansion, or reduction of the hypothenusal line, becomes 27404.31 feet. And here it is to be observed, that the intersection on the tripod terminating the 27400 feet only overshot the picket answering to the 274th chain by two inches and nine-tenths. But this nice agreement between the result by the deal rods, and that furnished by the rough measurement with the chain, arises from the extra-length of this last, which so nearly compensated for all the irregularities of the surface.

The measurement with the deal rods being finished, they were

[45]

compared at 5^h P.M. and found to agree with the standard, the temperature then being $75°$.

Expansion of the Deal Rods.

19. It has been an opinion generally enough, although, as we have seen, erroneously received, that very straight fibred deal was not at all, or but little, affected longitudinally by the humidity of the air. That we might not be led astray by trusting to fallacies of this sort, the standard rod had been provided; which being always closely shut up in its chest, except during the short interim of comparison, could feel but a small proportion of the effects which the measuring rods suffered; these being constantly exposed to the open air throughout the day, as well as to the moisture of the night, when lying under the oil-cloth canopy. The standard rod, it is true, could not be accurately compared with the brass scale: for although, when constructed, brass pins, forty inches asunder, had been driven into its stem, for the purpose of such comparison, yet these had afterwards been displaced, or at least the points upon them defaced, by the plaining over of the upper surface. This circumstance, which was unattended to when the operations commenced, is now of no consequence; because, from an experiment hereafter to be mentioned, the lengthening of the standard may be pretty nearly ascertained. But since there are some contradictory circumstances, soon to be mentioned, in the operation with the deal rods, which would have made a repetition of it absolutely necessary, if we had not now obtained those of a different kind, so very unexceptionable in their nature and mode of application, as, in the present case, to admit of no competition between the two results, and to render it improper on our part ever to have farther recourse to the first; so there can be little doubt, that deal rods will be universally rejected by other

countries, in any measurements they may have occasion to make
in future.

About the 10th of July, two rods, one of New England and the
other of Riga deal, being measured by the fixed points in the
great plank in Mr. Ramsden's shop, and having each two brass
pins driven into them at the distance of twenty feet, were laid on
the top of the house, where they remained until the 26th, the
weather, for the greater part of the time, having been very wet.
They were then taken down, and being, by means of the long
beam-compass, compared with the measures on the plank, the
New England rod was found to have lengthened 0.031 inch, and
the Riga rod 0.041 inch. By which experiment the fact seems
to be established, that Riga red wood, notwithstanding the quantity of turpentine which it contains, is more susceptible of the
effects of moisture than New England white wood. Mr. Ramsden likewise finds, that the great plank so often mentioned, suffers,
in ordinary summer weather, an alternate expansion and contraction, amounting at a medium to 0.0041 of an inch every day:
that is to say, if the distance between the twenty-feet brass points
be measured from the scale, by means of the beam-compass, in
the evening, it is found to have lengthened next morning 0.0041
of an inch, by the humidity of the intervening night. In the
course of the following day it contracts again to its former length,
and so on. Mr. Ramsden has often observed this alternate change
in the deal plank ; but it was particularly on the 11th and 12th
of August, that the quantity was actually measured. It will
readily be understood, that any difference of temperature which
might have happened in the brass scale, at the times of comparison, was always carefully taken into the account.

Now, from this last experiment, it seems probable, that we shall
not be very wide of the truth in supposing, that the standard deal
rod, which lay closed up in its chest, under the canopy on Houn-

slow Heath, would suffer the same sort of alternate expansion and contraction with the abovementioned plank; that is to say, being of Riga wood, its mean expansion about the middle of the day would be $\frac{1}{16000}$ of an inch. By this quantity then we must augment the actual observed expansion of the measuring rods, in order to obtain within certain probable limits (since we cannot determine it accurately) the equation for the expansion; or that space by which the apparent measurement, given by the 1370 deal rods, should be augmented, in order to obtain the true length of the base; or that which would have been given by unalterable rods, of the same original length with those of deal, as expressed in the following table.

			Table of the Expansion of the Deal Rods.					
Days.	Nᵒ of rods mean.	Mean of temperature.	Temp. of the mt.	Observ. of re- pansion.	Decimal mean.	Equation for the turn. rods.	Equation for the standard.	Total expan- sion.
		h. '	°	In.		In.	In.	In.
July 16	105	5 0 A.M 8 0 P.M	48 62	¹⁄₄ th 0	0.010	1.050	0.1615	1.3125
17	195	7 0 A.M 6 0 P.M	62 —	¹⁄₄ th 0	0.010	1.950	0.4375	2.4375
23	240	9 0 A.M 6 0 P.M	61 54	¹⁄₈ ⁴⁄₈	0.021	5.040	0.6000	5.6400
24	270	7 30 A M 11 15 A.M	63 66	¹⁄₈ ¹¹⁄₁₆	0.033	8.910	0.6650	9.5750
Aug. 2	170	3 45 P.M 8 30 A M 7 0 P M	64 66 67½	¹⁄₁₆ ¹⁄₈	0.0115	3.375	0.6650	4.0400
3	290	7 0 A M 5 0 P.M	56 75	¹⁄₈ 0	0.017	0.493	0.7250	1.2180
Total	1370	—	—	—	—	—	20.818	3.405	24.223

N. B. Although the rods were not compared with the standard on the 16th of July, yet the expansion probably was, and therefore has been estimated, at the same rate as it was found on the following day.

By examining the preceding table, it will appear, that the total expansion of the 1970 deal rods, including the small equation for the lengthening of the standard, amounts to 24.223 inches, or 2.02 feet; which being added to the apparent length of the base 27404.91 feet, formerly obtained, we shall have, for the hypothenusal length, 27406.93 feet: and from this deducting 0.07 foot, the excess of the hypothenusal above the base line, or the reduction contained in the seventh column of the general table of the base, there will remain 27406.86 for the distance given, by the deal rods, between the centres of the pipes terminating the base, reduced to the level of the lowest, or that at Hampton Poorhouse, in the temperature of 63°, being that of the brass scale when the lengths of the deal rods were laid off. All this, however, supposes three things to be absolutely certain : first, that the expansion of the rods has been accurately estimated ; secondly, that no error has arisen from the butting of the rods against each other, in order to bring them into contact ; and, thirdly, that no mistake of any kind has been committed in the execution. When we come to give the true length of the base, as ultimately ascertained by means of the glass rods, it will appear, that one or more of these three have actually taken place ; although it is most probable, that only the two first sources of error have contributed their share of the total difference between the two results. But the discussion of this point must be deferred for the present ; and I shall now finish the subject of the expansion of the deal rods, by mentioning two other comparisons of them, which serve to shew still more obviously, how improper they are for very accurate measurement !

It has already been remarked, that the last week of July was so wet as to occasion a total suspension of the operations on Hounslow Heath. On the 26th of that month, at 8ʰ A. M. the temperature being then 63°, the rods were compared with the standard, and found to exceed it, at a medium, one-fifteenth part of an inch. Now, if we suppose the whole base to have been measured with the rods in that state, the difference would have amounted to more than $7\frac{1}{2}$ feet, exclusive of what the standard itself might have altered from its original length.

The other comparison was made at Spring Grove, in the beginning of September, after our operations on the Heath had been finished, and the deal rods with their apparatus deposited under the roof of Sir Joseph Banks's barn. The object here in view was the measurement of such a space as the garden would conveniently admit of, when the rods were in their dry or contracted state ; and to re-measure the same space next morning, when the rods, being left out for the purpose, had imbibed all the humidity they could from the moisture of the intervening night. Accordingly, the fourth being a fine dry day, the sun shining bright, and the thermometer about 68°, seventeen stands were arranged in the long walk, with so much nicety in the same inclined plane as to appear but like one. The first or lowermost stand had a brass cock screwed to its top. The two uppermost, that is to say, the sixteenth and seventeenth, were of the fixed kind, each with a brass slide, and placed only forty-five inches asunder. The first deal rod was made to butt against the brass cock, and the rest successively against each other, until fifteen rod lengths were measured off, and a fine line drawn on the slide marking the extremity of the fifteenth. That rod being removed, forty-five inches, taken from the brass scale, were then laid off backwards from the line on the slide of the seventeenth to the slide of the sixteenth stand, where another fine line was drawn. Thus the space comprehended between this last line and the cock on the first stand, was just 900 feet, or fifteen coincident rods. During the night of the 4th, which was very fine, the rods lay on the smooth grass. About sun-rising of the 5th there came on a thick fog, which

H

entirely dispelled about 8 o'clock. At 7ʰ A. M. the rods being lifted
from the grass, it was perceived, that the under sides were perfectly dry, while all the rest was quite wet with the dew that had
fallen. The fourteen stands, comprehended between the first and
sixteenth, having their distances gradually reduced from twenty
feet three inches to twenty feet, the operation of re-measurement
was then begun, by placing the rods in coincidence with each
other (which was now found to be easily and accurately effected
by a few repeated strokes with a wooden wedge only) until the
fifteen rod lengths were measured off, and a fine line, corresponding with the ivory on the fifteenth, was drawn on the brass slide.
This line was found to be 0.$\frac{498}{1000}$, or near half an inch beyond that
which terminated the 300 feet the preceding evening. Hence it
is evident, that the dew imbibed only in one night, or a space of
time not exceeding fourteen hours, occasioned such an expansion
in the deal rods, as in the whole base would have amounted to
45.484 inches.

It is sufficiently obvious, that this last mentioned experiment
was more accurate, in the proportion of about fifteen to one, than
any comparison we could at that time have made with the standard. But since immediately after it was finished, the sun shone
out very bright, it is by no means certain, how soon the rods
would again have contracted to their former length, or near it,
had they been exposed to his rays. Repeated comparisons for ascertaining facts of this sort, at very short interims, are absolutely
incompatible with the nature of such tedious and troublesome
operations as the measurement of long bases: and here, indeed,
lies the great objection to the use of deal rods, that at no time
can we be certain how soon, after a comparison has been made,
they may alter their length in a proportion, and sometimes too
even in a sense, different from what was expected.

*Description of the Glass Rods, ultimately made use of to determine
the Length of the Base.* Pl. IV.

19. It has been already mentioned, that the week of rainy
weather in the end of July was employed in providing the glass
tubes, and in concerting matters with Mr. Ramsden, relative to
their construction as measuring rods. Notwithstanding their great
length, they were found to be so straight that, when laid on a
table, the eye, placed at one end looking through them, could see
any small object in the axis of the bore at the other end.

The nature and construction of the glass rods, whereof three
were finished for the operation, will be best conceived by considering, with care and attention, the plans and elevations of them,
in whole or in part, to different scales in Pl. IV. where likewise
may be seen, plans and sections of the ends of the tubes, in their
real dimensions, for the better understanding the several parts of
the apparatus placed therein.

The case containing the tube, and which serves to keep it from
bending in its original straight position, is every where of the
depth of eight inches, of the same width in the middle, and tapers
from thence, in a curvilinear manner, towards each end, where it
is only two inches and a quarter broad. It is made of clean white
deal, the two sides being half an inch, and the top and bottom
three-eighths in thickness. These last are placed in grooves fitted to receive them, about half an inch from the upper and lower
edges of the sides, which bending easily, and applying closely,
are then firmly fastened by two rows of wood screws on each
side, to the top and bottom respectively. Thus, the depth of the
sides in one sense, and the spring which they have by bending in
the other, act as trusses, prevent the case from warping, and render it sufficiently strong, although at the same time, considering
its great length, very light.

H 2

The plan of the middle rod represents the case with the top off, that the tube may be seen placed therein : the right and left-hand rods have the tops on, whereby may be seen the oval opening in the middle of each, shut by a mahogany lid ; and also the positions of the two thermometers, with tubes bent at right angles, so as to place the ball about two inches downwards within the case, for the better ascertaining the temperature of the glass, as will easily be conceived, by considering the representation of the tube and ball in the section across the middle of the rod.

It is to be observed, that the middle of the tube is made fast to the middle of the case in the following manner. First, around the middle of the tube, a quantity of packthread, immersed in liquid glue, was wound by several returns on itself, for the space of about two inches in length ; and upon this mass of packthread, while the glue was warm, a strong mahogany collar was forced ; whereby the three substances became so perfectly united to each other, that they might be considered as one only. Across the bottom of the case in the inside, three mahogany braces or girders, one in the middle, and one half way between it and each end, are fastened, by means of screws, to the bottom and sides. These rise about $1\frac{1}{2}$ inch above the bottom, so as to place the axis of the tube, when in use, about $2\frac{1}{4}$ inches above the surface of the stands on which it rests. The end-pieces of the case are likewise of mahogany, about $1\frac{1}{4}$ inch thick. Each consists of two parts, a lower and an upper. In the lower parts, as well as in the cross braces, there are semicircular cavities lined with broad cloth, fitted to receive the diameter of the tube, which rests in them, and is consequently supported at five different points. The upper end-pieces, having likewise semicircular cavities fitted to embrace the upper part of the tube, slip down upon it, when it has been, by repeated trials, brought to its true position ; that is to say, the axis of the bore into the same straight line, the case

being all the while supported by its extremities on two stands
only, in the manner in which the rods are applied in actual measurement. The braces within the case have also their upper
pieces, which, in like manner, apply closely to the tube, and are
fixed to the lower ones by means of screws. The whole together
serve only as stays to keep the tube in its true place from
shaking; but without binding it, however, too closely. Lastly,
the mahogany collar glued to the packthread on the middle of
the tube, being strongly fixed by four screws to the middle brace,
as may be seen in the section, is that by which the tube is kept
perfectly immoveable with respect to the middle of the case;
while it is unconfined longitudinally in the cavities lined with
broad cloth every where else.

Both ends of the tube are ground perfectly smooth, and truly at
right angles to the axis of the bore. That end, which in measuring usually lies towards the left hand (since most people will
work the screw with the right) projects about seven-tenths of an
inch without the case, and is called the fixed end, because the apparatus belonging to it is fixed. The other end towards the
right hand projects about nine-tenths of an inch, and, having a
moveable apparatus, is called the moveable end.

The fixed apparatus consists of a cork about three inches in
length, made of the very best material, and so nicely fitted to the
bore, as just to admit of being forced into without bursting it. In
the middle of the cork a cylindrical brass tube is placed, whose
sides are thin, the inward end thick, and the outward end open.
It receives a steel pin, whose inward end being formed into a
screw, is thereby fixed into the thick metal of the tube. The
steel pin carries outwardly a button and neck of bell-metal. The
neck fits so very closely the open end of the brass tube as to
prevent any shake there; at the same time that the inside
of the button applies very justly to the ground end of the glass

tube, to which the outward surface (being a true plane) is exactly parallel.

The moveable apparatus consists, like the other, of a cork and brass tube of the same length. Before the insertion of this cork, an oblong piece seven-tenths of an inch long, and two-tenths broad, was cut from it, in that part of its cylinder answering to the upper part of the outward end of the glass tube, on the inward surface of which, about half an inch from the end, a fine line had been previously cut by a diamond point. The brass tube in this cork contains within it a loose steel worm, or helical spring, something less than the interior diameter of the tube. Along the cavity formed by the spiral, there passes a steel pin, like that in the fixed end; but it is longer, and has no screw at the inward end, that being nicely ground, so as to fit a circular hole in the inward end of the brass tube, while a triangular bell-metal neck fits one of that figure in the outward end. Thus the pin moves freely backwards or forwards without any shake, and presses upon the steel spring, by means of a circular brass collar, placed for the purpose, at the inward end of the neck; while the outward end is attached to a bell-metal button. The outward surface of this moveable button is spherical, described on a radius of about two inches; while the inward surface, like that at the fixed end, would apply closely to the ground end of the glass tube, but should not be pushed so far forward as to touch it. A circle and narrow slide, cut from a solid cylinder of ivory, fitted originally to enter easily the glass tube, is attached to the inside of the button by small screws, and permits the neck to pass through a hole made on purpose in the circle. The slide is about eight-tenths of an inch long, and has a fine intersection cut upon it near the inward end, made black to render it more conspicuous. Thus, two rods being brought into contact, and the fixed button of one being pressed against the moveable button of the other, the inter-

section is thereby pushed forwards until it coincides with the
diamond line on the interior surface of the tube; whose length
is so adjusted, as that, when the coincidence is perfect, the distance between the plane surface of one button, and the spherical
surface of the other, is exactly twenty feet. The left-hand side of
the plate represents the relative positions of the extremities of the
first and second rods, when the ivory is in coincidence with the
diamond line. And the right-hand side shews the relative situations of the extremities of the second and third rods, before the
ivory is brought to coincidence with the diamond line, the slide
being then pushed out by the action of the spiral spring within
the cork.

Every rod has four wheels, two at each end. They are two
inches in diameter, and connected by a common steel axis, which
rises and falls in a vacuity prepared for its admission in the mahogany end-pieces, the under part of which vacuity is afterwards
filled up.

A brass strap or bridle, about eight-tenths of an inch broad,
passes over the top of the case, and descending down each side,
bends outwards, so as to form a projection for the reception of
the wheels, whose pivots turn in, but near to the lower end of the
bridle, which is kept in its place by means of the two side screws
working in grooves, and the milled-headed screw at top. This
last serves likewise to raise or depress the wheels at pleasure.

Each rod has two cross feet, placed immediately behind their
respective pair of wheels, extending outwards about 4¾ inches
from the centre on each side. Under their outward extremities,
small pieces of hardened steel, formed into the teeth of a file, are
fixed by means of screws. When the first rod has been laid in
its true place, by unscrewing the milled heads, the wheels are suffered to rise; whereby the whole weight is removed from them, and
thrown upon the teeth of the files, which then indent themselves

into the surface of the stand, and become as it were united to it.
But when the fixed button of the second rod is brought to press
against the moveable button of the first, the weight being then
thrown upon the wheels by screwing the milled heads at top, the
rod is easily moved on by the following apparatus.

The three rods are numbered, as were those of deal, 1.2 ; 3.4 ;
5.6. On the first or odd end of each rod 1. 3. and 5. there stands
a brass fork, about two inches high, fixed by four screws and an
oblong plate to the top of the case. On the second, or even end
of each, 2. 4. and 6. there stands a brass pillar, of the same height
with the fork, likewise fixed to the top of the case by four screws
and a circular plate. Two steel rods or hooks were indifferently
used for bringing up the moveable rod (the weight then lying on
the wheels) into its true place. They are both represented in the
plate, and only differ from each other in the shape of the brass
milled-headed nuts that work upon the screw, of about 2¼ inches
in length, into which the right-hand end of each hook is formed.
Thus, while the nut enters very freely into, and rests upon, the
fork, the left-hand end of the hook has a circular hole in it, whereby it slips easily off and on the brass pillar. By referring to
the plate, it will appear sufficiently obvious, from the nature of
the nut on the left-hand hook, that it could only move the rod on
to coincidence, and could not bring it back again, if the business
happened at any time to be overdone ; in which case it was
necessary to move the rod a little backwards by the hand, and
then to work anew with the nut, until the coincidence was accurate : whereas the nut on the right-hand hook, having two shoulders, could either push or pull the rod forwards or backwards :
and although this appeared to be an advantage, yet it was found
from experience, that it rather bound the hook too much, and
occasioned a kind of spring in the parts, which sometimes disturbed the coincidence on the removal of the hook ; wherefore it

was often applied, like the other, by placing the screw itself in the fork, and working with both shoulders of the nut behind it.

The positions of the thermometers, and mahogany oval lid on the top of the case, have already been mentioned. This last being unlocked and removed, permits the case to be looked into, or the hand to be admitted, in order to be certain that the fastenings remain safe and entire in the inside. Brass caps, with the respective number of the rods engraved on them, are likewise screwed on the male-screws in the ends of the case, through which the extremities of the tubes project, to preserve them from accidents when not in use. And, lastly, to strengthen the cases, but more particularly to prevent them from being rent, when long exposed to the sun's rays in the field, the sides are covered with brown linen laid on very smoothly, and carefully glued with thin glue, used as a stronger kind of paste, to which it may yet be necessary to add a coat of oil paint.

Each of the glass rods, completed in the manner abovementioned, weighs about sixty-one pounds. Their lengths were ascertained by means of new brass points placed in the great plank, the space of forty inches being laid off, with the utmost care, from the brass scale, when the temperature of all had remained for the greater part of two days (August 15th and 16th) at or very near 68°. For this purpose, two brass rectangular cocks, whose alternate surfaces had been previously ground together, were placed upon the plank, so as to bisect the extreme dots; in which situation they presented to each other surfaces that were truly parallel. The rods being then severally placed between the cocks* (or, as was found to be a better method, between the point

* The first of these cocks, or that to which the fixed button was applied, had a hole in it exactly of the height of the centre of the button, and large enough to permit the point of the micrometer screw to pass through it, the said screw being fixed

I

of a micrometer screw, supplying the place of the first cock, and the second) the ivory intersection was at first necessarily carried beyond the diamond line, so as to make the intermediate space less than it should be, until by the gradual grinding down of the moveable bell-metal button, it was enlarged to twenty feet, as then shewn by the accurate coincidence of the intersection with the diamond line.

It was by these distances in the great plank, prolonged to twenty-five feet, that the new length of the steel chain was now settled, so as to obtain the full one hundred feet at four measurements. At this time too, brass points were introduced into the chain at every twenty-five feet, whereby its extent may be compared on any future occasion; but the temperature had now fallen to $66°\frac{1}{4}$.

on the farther side, or beyond the cock. Thus, while the temperature continued accurately at 68°, the fixed button, or any other plane surface, being brought up to the hole in the cock, and the micrometer point screwed so far as just to touch it, the coincidence continuing in the interim perfect, the exact distance of twenty feet was obtained between the point of the screw and the second cock; at which time the division answering to the index on the head of the micrometer was carefully noted. This being done, the cock with the hole was removed from the plank, and the rods were severally adjusted by being placed between the point of the screw and the second cock. This substitution of the micrometer point, instead of the first cock, was found necessary; because, during the operation of adjustment, the temperature would sometimes change a degree, generally in excess, from handling the instruments. One degree of alteration, producing a difference of about $\frac{1}{710}$th part of an inch in the twenty feet, was very easily and accurately allowed for by such a micrometer as this, which shewed the coincidence of the ivory intersection with the diamond line to be more or less perfect, when the head of the screw was moved two divisions, that is to say, $\frac{1}{2000}$ths or $\frac{1}{1000}$th part of an inch.

Disposition of the Stands for the Double Measurement with the Chain and Glass Rods ; Description of the Apparatus then applied to the Ends of the Chain ; and ultimate continuation of the Measurement with the Glass Rods alone. Pl. II. and IV.

14. From the various circumstances already mentioned, in the course of this tedious, yet necessary recital, it had been for a considerable space of time foreseen, that the result given by the measurement with the deal rods must be entirely rejected, and that by the glass rods adhered to, as every way deserving of the preference ; because of the obvious impropriety there would be, in taking a mean between one indisputably good and another less perfect, however small or trifling in reality the difference of the two might ultimately be found, on a minute and scrupulous comparison.

In order, therefore, to avoid any repetition of the operation with the glass rods, and at the same time to give something like a fair trial to the chain, it was proposed, that a double measurement should be carried on with both at once ; that is to say, that the number of stands, and several other parts of the apparatus, should be so far augmented, as to admit the chain to be placed twice in advance, and then the rods to follow in succession on the same stands. Accordingly, the various articles having been sent to the north-west end of the base on the evening of the 17th of August, the operation of the double measurement commenced next morning, the 18th.

By referring to Pl. II. it will be seen, that seventeen stands were necessary for supporting the chain, the apparatus attached to each end of it, and ten coffers, whereof every five made about ninety-eight feet, in order that, one length of the chain being measured off in the first five, it might be drawn forward into the last five, and so on. These seventeen stands were disposed of in three groups of three each, and four intermediate, between the central and extreme groups. The middle or slide stand of each group (so distinguished because some of them had brass slides on their tops) supported the handle of the chain, and of course received the traces made at the feather-edged pieces of brass, terminating the beginning and ending of the hundred feet. Thus, there were in all six stands, intermediate to those in the centre of each group that supported the ninety-eight feet of coffering, which was kept so much short of the hundred feet, that its extreme parts might not rest upon, or even touch, the central stands. To that on the left of the centre was attached the apparatus for the first or zero end of the chain; and to that on the right of the centre was attached the apparatus for the last end of the chain. When the second chain length had been measured off, the first and sixth of the coffer stands of the first chain were moved forward to prepare for the third chain; and the four remaining coffer stands were raised, until their surfaces came into the same plane with the slide stands, for the reception of the glass rods. The space by which these stands were raised was about three inches; for so much higher was the surface of the intersole or flooring of the coffers than the stands which supported them.

The apparatus attached to the first end of the chain, or that which served to pull it back to the point of commencement, while a weight continued suspended at the farther end, consists of two parts, as may be seen by referring to the left-hand side of Pl. II. First, a small wooden frame, fitted to slip on to the top of any one of the ordinary stands, placed immediately to the left of that which supports the handle. Secondly, a flat steel rod, about two feet in length, wherein a number of holes are pierced, about an inch asunder, for the reception of a steel pin placed in one of the holes, as best suits the distance of the stand from the handle. That end of the steel rod nearest to the end of the chain is formed into a screw about four inches in length, and it receives upon it a forked hook, fitted to lay hold of the straight part of the handle of the chain. Within the forked hook there works a strong mill-headed brass nut, which acting upon the bottom of the fork, the chain is thereby pulled back, until the wire suspending the plummet from the dart on the feather-edge coincides with the point of commencement on the ground underneath; for which purpose there is a hole in the top of the stand through which the wire passes. The apparatus stand, thus serving to pull back the chain, was commonly loaded with double weights, placed on the two hindermost legs.

The apparatus for the last end of the chain consists, like the former, of a small wooden frame, that can be readily slipped upon any of the common stands, as may be seen by referring to the right-hand side of Pl. II. This frame carries a pulley, over which a rope passes, having fourteen pounds weight suspended at one end of it, while a forked iron hook at the other end lays hold of the straight part of the brass handle. By means of these two apparatuses the chain is always kept to the same degree of tension in its coffers, in each of which a thermometer was placed to indicate the temperature; the whole being covered up from the direct rays of the sun by a narrow piece of linen cloth, stretched along it from one end to the other.

Each coffer consisted of three boards about half an inch thick. The sides were about five inches deep, nailed at the middle to an intersole bottom of four inches, in such manner as to be represented in section by the letter H. They were ill made, being by their parallelogram shape apt to warp, which might have been prevented by giving them the figure of the cases of the glass rods, that is to say, making them wide in the middle, and narrow at each end.

We are now to proceed to give some account of the double measurement with the chain and glass rods; wherein it must be remembered, as also in continuing the operation with the glass rods alone, that in referring to the map for the daily progress in the work, we are going from the forty-sixth towards the first station; and in having recourse to the general table of the base, for altitude, temperature, or correction for expansion, we are ascending from the bottom towards the top, contrarily to the order in which the operation with the deal rods was conducted.

On the morning of the 18th of August, the stands with the various parts of the apparatus being placed in the manner just now described, the operation was begun by bringing the first end of the chain to coincide with the intersection on the tripod, answering to the end of the 1370th deal rod, and 4.91 feet distant from the centre of the pipe terminating the north-west extremity of the base. The chain being stretched along its five coffers by the fourteen pounds weight suspended over the pulley at the farther end, and the temperatures of the five thermometers being registered in a book kept for that purpose, a fine trace was made on a piece of card, fastened under the feather-edge at the farther handle, denoting the end of the first hundred feet. The chain being then moved on into the next five coffers, those that had been thus vacated were carried forward, to prepare for the third chain length, and thereby permit the first set of stands to be elevated for the reception of the glass rods; and so in succession with the others.

In this manner we proceeded, and in the course of the day were only able to measure the length of ten chains, or 1000 feet, being the forty-sixth and forty-fifth hypothenuses of the base, the first of 400 and the last of 600 feet. Being arrived at this point, it was found, that the fine line on the brass slide, marking the extremity of the tenth chain, fell short of another fine line on the same slide, denoting the end of the fiftieth glass rod, just two-tenths of an inch. Now it will appear hereafter, when we come to shew, by the experiments with the pyrometer, what the real contractions of the chain and glass rods were, for the degrees of difference of temperature* below that in which their respective lengths were laid off, that this small apparent difference of two-tenths of an inch, between the two modes of measuring the thousand feet, should have been 0.17938 in. to have made the two results exactly agree, which is a real difference of only 0.02062 of an inch. Supposing then every thousand feet of the base to have been measured by the chain with the same attention, and consequently with the same, or nearly the same success (and there surely cannot be any reason to doubt of the practicability), we shall have 27.404 x 0.02062 in. = 0.565 in. or a defect of something more than half an inch on the whole length of the base.

* When the length of the chain was laid off, the heat was 66°¼, and that of the glass rods 68°. They will, therefore, only agree with each other accurately in these respective temperatures. The mean of twenty thermometers for the four chain lengths of the forty-sixth hypothenuse gave a heat of 61°.6; and for the six chain lengths of the forty-fifth, the mean of thirty thermometers gave 59°.75. The temperature of the 400 feet of glass, by the mean of forty thermometers, was 65°.3; and of the 600 feet, by the mean of sixty thermometers, it was 60°.8. Now, from these data, and the expansions of steel and glass, as determined by the pyrometer, the computation will stand as follows:

$$\text{Steel}\begin{cases}400 & 66.5-61.6 = +9 \times 0.03052 = 0.14955\\600 & 66.5-59.75 = 6.75 \times 0.04578 = 0.30901\end{cases} = 0.45856\begin{cases}\text{contract. of 1000}\\ \text{feet.}\end{cases}$$

$$\text{Glass}\begin{cases}400 & 68.0-65.3 = 1.7 \times 0.02068 = 0.05584\\600 & 68.0-60.8 = 7.2 \times 0.01102 = 0.13334\end{cases} = 0.17918\begin{cases}\text{contract. of 1000}\\ \text{feet.}\end{cases}$$

The 1000 feet of steel should have been contracted more than the 1000 feet of glass, $\Big\} = 0.17918$

But the difference was found to be = 0.20 00

Therefore the error of the chain in defect was — 0.02062 x 27.404 = 0.565 in. or little more than half an inch on the whole base.

So nice an agreement between two results, with instruments so very different, could not fail to be considered as astonishing ; and as it rarely happens, that the graduation of thermometers will so nearly correspond with each other, as not to occasion a much greater error, all were very desirous that it could have been further confirmed by continuing the operation in the same way through a more considerable proportion of the whole length. But besides the tedious nature of the double measurement, owing to the multiplicity of stands, platforms, coffers, and other articles, that were now successively to be moved forward, and for which purpose it had been found necessary to reinforce the party of soldiers with six additional men; the operation had already trained out to a much more considerable length than had been expected ; the summer was now far advanced, and the continuance of good weather uncertain ; the coffers likewise for the chain, having been constructed in a hurry, were found to be defective : in short, all these reasons contributed to induce us to give up, for the present, any farther experiment with the chain, and to proceed with the glass rods alone in the completion of the measurement.

Accordingly, on Thursday the 19th of August, the operation with the glass rods was continued for the five hypothenuses, from the forty-fourth to the fortieth inclusive. It will be remembered, that in proceeding with the deal rods, double pickets had been placed in the ground, at the middle of the forty-first hypothenuse, or that point which terminated the 1215th rod, reckoning from the south-east, or the 155th from the north-west end of the base. Now, in returning to this point with the glass rods, the extremity of the 155th fell short of the silk thread stretched from picket to picket, just one-tenth of an inch. The expansion of the brass standard scale, and that of glass being taken into the account, it

appears, that the small expansion * of the deal rods from the humidity of the air, must, at this point, have exceeded what it was
estimated at in the general table by 0.931 of an inch, supposing
no error of any kind whatever to have arisen in the execution,
from bringing the rods into contact, or otherwise.

On Saturday the 21st of August, the measurement was resumed
at the thirty-ninth station, and continued for five hypothenuses
to the thirty-fifth inclusive.

This day, about noon, his Majesty deigned to honour the operation by his presence, for the space of two hours, entering very
minutely into the mode of conducting it, which met with his
gracious approbation.

On Monday the 23d, the mensuration was farther continued
for five hypothenuses, that is, to the thirtieth inclusive.

On Tuesday the 24th, we proceeded with the measurement for
the space of seven hypothenuses, finishing the business of the day
at the twenty-second station.

It will be remembered, that in carrying on the operation with
the deal rods, double pickets were left in the ground at the twenty-
seventh station, answering to the extremity of the 810th rod
from the first, or the 560th from the last end of the base. Now,
on arrival at this point, the 560th glass rod overshot the silk thread,

In.

* 155 deal rods
= 3100 feet
{ +0.383 for 1° excess of temperature of the brass scale from 62°
to 63°.
+0.651 proportionable part of the estimated expansion from humidity.

+1.034 equation of the deal rods on 3100 feet.

155 glass rods
= 3100 feet
{ +2.301 for 6° excess of the heat of the brass scale from 62° to 68°.
−0.436 observed contraction of the glass from the 11th and 12th
columns of the table.
+0.100 by which the 155th rod fell short of the thread.

+1.965 equation of the glass rods on 3100 feet.

0.931 { Difference of the two equations, under-rated in the expansion of the deal rods.

K

stretched from one picket to the other, 9.595 Inches. Here again we find, that the lengthening * of the deal rods, from the moisture of the atmosphere, differs but little from what it has been estimated at by comparison with the standard, being over-rated only two-tenths of an inch on the 560 rods. In this day's operation, in passing the bridge laid over the old river, the measurement, instead of being made in the hypothenusal, was carried on in the level line, for the space of twenty rods, namely, fifteen rods of the twenty-seventh, and five of the twenty-sixth hypothenuse; which occasions the alteration in the reduction of these two spaces, marked with asterisks in the general table.

As some trouble had been found to attend the crossing of the great road, in the first measurement, owing to the number of carriages that were continually passing, the depth of the ditches, and height of the banks of the old Roman way; therefore tressels, suited for the purpose, had been now prepared: and lest any accident might have happened in conducting this part of the operation, so as to oblige us to a repetition, double pickets were placed in the usual manner in the ground, two rod lengths from the twenty-sixth station, to which we could have referred, without going back as far as the tripod left at the twenty-ninth station, the point from which we had departed in the morning.

Bad weather prevented any progress being made on the 25th;

In.
* 560 deal rods = { + 1.390 for 1° excess of heat of the brass scale from 62° to 63°.
11200 feet   { + 5.258 estimated expansion from moisture.

+6.648 equation of the 560 deal rods.

560 glass rods = { +8.343 for 6° excess of heat of the brass scale from 62° to 68°.
11200 feet   { +1.821 observed expansion of glass } from columns 11th
          { −1.191 observed contraction of ditto } and 12th.
          { −2.525 over-shot the silk-thread.

+6.448 equation of 560 glass rods.

0.200 difference over-rated in the expansion of the 560 deal rods.

and, on the 26th, all that could be done was to measure the twenty-second and twenty-first hypothenuses.

On Friday the 27th, the work went on more expeditiously, having in the course of that day measured six hypothenuses, and placed the tripod at the fourteenth station.

On Saturday the 28th, eight hypothenuses were measured, and the tripod was placed at the sixth station. In this day's operation, being arrived near the bridge laid over Wolsey River, double pickets were placed in the ground in the point answering to the extremity of the 117ad rod, reckoning from the north-west, or the 198th rod from the south-east end of the base, that we might recur to them in case of accident; and the eighteen rod lengths, between this point and the sixth station, were measured on the level, instead of the hypothenusal line, which required the alteration of the reduction, as distinguished by the asterisk in the general table.

On Monday the 30th of August, the measurement with the glass rods was completed; * when the extremity of the 1970th rod overshot the centre of the pipe terminating the base towards the south-east by 17.875 inches, or 1.49 foot. Hence, when the several equations for expansions are respectively taken into the account, we find, that the alteration of the deal rods from the humidity of the air, which, by comparison with the standard, was apparently most considerable in the first and second sections of the base, has now wholly vanished; that is to say, the total amount

* The gentlemen who were present at, and assisting in, the last day's operation, were Captain Bisset, Mr. Greville, Sir William Hamilton, Mr. Lloyd, and Dr. Usher, Professor of Astronomy in the College of Dublin. This last gentleman was so obliging as to observe, with the most scrupulous attention, throughout the whole operation with the glass rods, that the coincidence of the second with the first remained undisturbed, while that of the third with the second was completing.

of it has been over-rated by 0.964 inches; * and this is the contradictory circumstance that has been formerly alluded to.

I have already suggested what appear to me to have been the only three possible causes of this difference, found between the estimated and real expansion of the deal rods; and as we are to abandon that measurement entirely, it is of little or no importance now to endeavour to discover, were it possible, whence it may have arisen. If any error was actually committed, which is the least of all probable, it could only have happened at the place of the tripod, by bringing a wrong point of the stem over it when the operation was resumed. But it is well known, how much care and pains were taken to prevent any thing of that sort. Indeed the hypothenusal distances, as given by the chain, agreed so nearly among themselves, that even a foot or ten inches would have made so remarkable a difference in the situation of the next picket, as could not have passed unobserved. Besides, in returning with the glass rods, after passing the Staines Road, the measurement was gradually found (without any leap whatever) to overshoot the pickets, and at last over-reached the south-east pipe by 17.875 inches. I am therefore inclined to believe, that the difference arises partly from what may have been lost by constantly butting one rod against the other, whereby the end of the 1970th did not reach so near to the north-west pipe as it ought

---

* 1370 deal rods $=$ 27400 ft. $\left.\begin{array}{l}\\ \\ \end{array}\right\}$

In.
$+$ 3.389 for $1°$ of the brass scale from $61°$ to $63°$.
$+$ 24.223 estimated expansion from humidity.

$+$ 27.612 equation of the 1370 deal rods.

1370 glass rods $=$ 27400 ft. $\left.\begin{array}{l}\\ \\ \\ \end{array}\right\{$
$+$ 20.336 for $6°$ of the brass scale from $62°$ to $68°$.
$+$ 5.989 observed expansion of glass $\left.\begin{array}{l}\\ \end{array}\right\}$ from columns 11th and
$-$ 1.802 observed contraction of ditto $\left.\begin{array}{l}\end{array}\right.$ 12th.
$-$ 17.875 space by which the 1370th rod overshot the pipe.

$+$ 6.648 equation of the 1370 glass rods.

20.964 over-rated in the total expansion of the deal rods.

to, and would have done, if the rods had been applied to each other by coincident lines. It must, however, be confessed, that the near agreement between the glass and deal rods in the upper part of the Heath seems not perfectly reconcileable to this supposition. Nevertheless, the descent being quickest, and the irregularities of the surface much more considerable in the lower than the upper part, might produce some effect in one, which did not take place in the other. But the chief part of the difference I take to have proceeded from over-rated expansion ; that is to say, the rods, when brought into use, contracted sooner than we imagined, and thereby gave a shorter measure than what was assignable to them from the mean of any two or more comparisons.

The last day of August was employed in discharging the party, and removing the various parts of the apparatus to Spring Grove House.

Description of the Microscopic Pyrometer, made use of for determining, by experiment, the Expansion of the Metals concerned in the Measurement of the Base. Pl. V.

15. Having, in the preceding part of this Account, given a very minute detail of the actual operations in the field, that the public, being thus informed of every circumstance, might be the better enabled to judge of the accuracy of the result, it remains yet to point out, in what manner the equations for the expansions of the standard scale, steel chain, and glass rods, applied to the apparent measurement of the base, in several of the preceding notes, have been obtained by means of experiments with the pyrometer.

It is sufficiently well known, that many years ago, a very ingenious and valuable Member of the Royal Society did publish in the Philosophical Transactions (Vol. XLVIII. 1754. No. 79.) an account of experiments made with a pyrometer of his invention.

No doubt was entertained of the accuracy of the experiments here
alluded to; on the contrary, they will be confirmed by the account
now to be given of these recently made, with which they very
nearly agree. But as different pieces of metal of the same kind
are certainly susceptible of different degrees of expansion, it was
judged best, on the present occasion, to put rods to the test of
those very metals that had been made use of in the actual measurement of the base. For, supposing both sets of experiments to
have been made with instruments equally perfect, and to have
been in other respects equally well conducted, this must always
be considered as the most unexceptionable method. Besides, the
expansion of rods of the length of five feet being ascertained, the
unavoidable error of observations of this delicate nature, becomes
lessened in proportion to the excess of their length above shorter
rods. In these new experiments too, another sort of pyrometer,
invented by Mr. Ramsden, has been applied, of such accurate construction, that it seems not easy to improve it.

The microscopic pyrometer, so named, because by means of
two microscopes attached to it, the expansion is measured, consists
of a strong deal frame, five feet in length, nearly twenty-eight
inches broad, and about forty-two inches in height. The elevation of the eye-piece side, or that which presents itself to the observer, and also of the micrometer end, or that which is towards
his right-hand, as well as the general plan of the top, are represented by a scale of one inch to a foot, or one-twelfth part of the
real dimensions, in Pl. V. where likewise may be seen the angular
view of the fixed end, together with plans, sections, and elevations,
of several of the principal parts, done to larger scales. From
these, it is hoped, the construction of the machine will be easily
understood, without entering into a minute description of the
almost numberless smaller parts whereof it is composed.

On the top of the frame, two deal troughs, upwards of five feet in length, are firmly screwed. That towards the observer over-hangs the frame something more than an inch: that on the far-ther side is even with the back part. Each of these troughs, which are about three inches square in the inside, contains a cast iron standard prism, whose sides are $1\frac{1}{4}$ inch. The manner in which the prisms are fastened to the bottoms of their respective troughs, and the nature of the apparatuses they carry on their extremities, will be readily conceived, by referring to the parti-cular plans and elevations of them, comprehended in the group of eight small figures towards the right hand of the general plan. Four of these appertain to the left-hand or fixed microscope; and the other four to the right-hand or micrometer microscope, so dis-tinguished, because it has a micrometer attached to it. By means of the brass collars which embrace the prisms, their left-hand or fixed ends are screwed down extremely fast to the brass pieces whereon they rest, so as to be perfectly immoveable there with regard to their troughs; whereas their right-hand ends are kept easy, yet without shake, in their collars, that they may contract or lengthen freely as the temperature may require, without occa-sioning any strain upon the parts. The prism in the nearest trough may be called the eye-piece prism, because it carries the eye-pieces of the microscopes; and that in the farther trough, the mark prism, because it carries the marks or cross wires at which the microscopes respectively point. The troughs are covered with pitch in the inside, to make them hold water; and each has a cock in the left-hand end for discharging it.

Between the two deal troughs, one of copper, as a boiler, is placed, somewhat shorter than the former, but still upwards of five feet in length. It is about $2\frac{1}{4}$ inches broad, and $3\frac{1}{2}$ in depth. The centre of the boiler, or rather the centre of the object lens which stands in it, as we shall have occasion soon to point out, is distant from the cross wires of the mark 5.81 inches; and

from the wires of the micrometer attached to the corresponding
eye-piece 20.33 inches. The boiler rests on five small rollers,
one being fixed to each end of the frame, and the other three to
the braces which run across it. This copper trough has likewise
a cock in the left-hand end; and in the general plan a cast iron
prism is represented in it; but this last carries no apparatus, as
those in the wooden troughs do, being exactly of the length of
five feet, and only placed there as one of the rods whose expansion
was tried, and to shew that the machine was capable of receiving a rod of that weight and magnitude.

By referring to the general plan it will be seen, that twelve
lamps are made use of to bring the water in the copper to boil.
They stand on four shelves, three in each compartment formed by
the cross braces of the frame. They can readily be pushed forwards or drawn backwards, and when actually in use, their
handles are only seen, projecting from under the copper. It
was found, by burning oil in the lamps, the heat of the water
could not be raised above 209° or 210°; but with spirits of wine
it was brought into violent ebullition. The plan of the frame
likewise shews, that the tubes of the microscopes are subdivided
into several distinct parts; and that one of these parts is attached
by a collar to a mahogany prism, which reaches from one end to
the other. But the use of these contrivances it will be best to
defer speaking of, till after having described the apparatuses that
are placed within the copper boiler.

At the bottom of the plate the boiler is represented, both in
plan and longitudinal section, to a scale of one-fourth part of its
real dimensions. It contains within it two brass slides, the one
long and the other short; which, from the braces that bind the
cheeks together, very much resemble the form of a ladder. The
long slide, whose cheeks are 1½ inch deep, reaches almost the whole
length of the copper, although every where unconnected with it,

except at the points A and B. At the first of these, two strong pieces of brass, fixed to the cheeks, and notched underneath, embrace the ends of a brass cylindrical bar fastened to the bottom. At the last, the cheeks of the slide rest on a roller. Whence it follows, that the copper and slide remain immoveable with regard to each other at A; but from thence, towards either end, they have full liberty to change place; that is to say, to expand by heat, or contract by cold, in any proportion their different natures may require. The left-hand end of the slide is shut up by a strong perpendicular piece of brass, connected with the two side rings which support the object lens of the fixed microscope, whose centre corresponds accurately with its inward face. This piece being firmly screwed to the cheeks of the slide, and counter-arched outwardly, forms a strong butt for the fixed end of the expanding rod (supposed here to be the steel bar) to act against. Within the right-hand end of the long slide, rests a short one of about 14½ inches in length, whose cheeks are 1½ inch deep. Its outward end, at C, rests on the cylindrical surface of the last brace of the long slide, fitted purposely to receive it; while a narrow longitudinal bar fixed in its inward end, at DE in the section, moves freely in the notch of a bridge F, framed for it in the long slide. The outward end of this short slide is shut up in a similar manner with the opposite end of the long one.

This end piece is also connected with the two side rings which support the tube containing the object lens of the micrometer microscope, whose centre is perpendicularly over its inward face, and being fortified outwardly by an edge bar, it forms a butt for the expanding end of the rod, that is in experiment, to push against. By attending to the plate it will be perceived, that to this end of the boiler a brass tube (R) is fixed, which contains within it a brass rod, surrounded by a helical steel spring; which acting upon

L

a broad shoulder of the rod prepared for the purpose, thereby presses its inward end, which enters the boiler, against the perpendicular surface of the end piece of the short slide. Thus, the farther end of the rod in experiment, supposed now to be in its contracted state, is constantly made to bear against the surface that is under the fixed microscope. But on the application of heat, the irresistible force of expansion in the rod obliges the spring to give way ; the short slide changes its place, and with it the object lens of the micrometer microscope moves on a space proportionable to the degree of heat that is applied ; and it is this distance, measured by means of the micrometer, as hereafter will be shewn, that determines the quantity of expansion, or the space by which the rod has lengthened. From the plate it will be further observed, that the rod in experiment rests on the surfaces of three rollers, about an inch in diameter ; and by means of three pair of milled-headed nuts, 1¼ inch in diameter, which move on axes that are formed into screws, until they almost touch the sides of the rod, this is kept in its true centrical position, whatever may be its form or lateral dimensions.

The microscope towards the left hand has been denominated fixed, because it corresponds with the first or fixed end of the rod in experiment, and never changes its place while these are of the length of five feet. But it appearing to be of consequence, that the expansion of the standard brass scale, which is not quite forty-three inches long, should be determined, the pyrometer has therefore been adapted for the reception of any rods less than five feet, whereby it is made more universally useful. For this purpose it becomes necessary to move the marks and eye-pieces of the fixed microscope, along their respective prisms, to the proper position for the rod that is to be tried. Nevertheless, the object lens remains in its original place ; and in its stead another lens, of the same focal distance, is fixed on a similar end piece, that can be firmly clamped to any corresponding place whatever of the cheeks of the long slide. Hence will appear the reason for breaking the screening tubes of the microscopes into several parts, and the use of the mahogany prism, along which the thick part of the tube moves from one end to the other.

The pyrometer, since it was first made and tried, has undergone several small alterations, by way of improvements, which it is now unnecessary to describe particularly. One of these was the application of cross levels to the parts of the tube (SS in the general plan) connected with the object glasses. The manner in which they are fixed on will appear from the representations of them in the lowermost left-hand angle of the plate. And the section at the right-hand angle shews the appearance of the double brass hook, universal joint, and milled-headed nut, applied across the middle of the boiler (at TU), whereby the levels are brought to be consistent, when the water is boiling, with the position they had been adjusted to when the temperature was at freezing ; that is to say, they are kept parallel to themselves in both states. This was thought necessary, because the application of the boiling water sunk the middle of the slide a small matter, and thereby made the levels run outwards.

The micrometer so often mentioned, being a very essential part of the machine, is represented, both in elevation and horizontal section, to the full size. Its chief parts consist of a micrometer steel screw, which works in the square nut of a brass slide, while the plane part of it enters into a long brass socket, nicely ground to receive it, and thereby preventing all shake. To the square nut, one end of a watch chain is attached ; the other end having passed around is fixed to a barrel, which contains a watch spring, coiled up in the usual manner. By this contrivance, any loss of time in the motion of the moveable wire, fixed to the square slide, is effectually prevented, whether the screw be turned backwards or forwards. The fixed wire, so called because it is only made use of occasionally, appears in the elevation to the left hand of the former, and is farther removed from the observer, being attached to the oval slide which bounds the field of the micrometer. This wire is moved by the insertion of a milled-headed key (although not represented in the plate) fitted to slip upon the square end of its proper screw, which may be seen, in the elevation, projecting above the micrometer head. It has but little motion, being only intended for the measurement of small differences of expansion, or any small space, by leaving it there, while the other wire is repeatedly brought to coincide with, and again depart from it. For particular purposes this wire may be useful ; nevertheless, the instrument would have performed very well without it.

The construction of the microscopes will be readily understood, by referring to the figures under that head on the right-hand side of the plate; where the relative situations of the different eye-glasses, with regard to the wires or place of the magnified image, as well as to the eye, are truly represented in their real dimensions ; but the distances from these to the object lenses and marks respectively, are contracted or broken off, from want of sufficient room to delineate them otherwise. To increase the angle of vision in microscopes, it is always necessary that they should have at least two eye-glasses, and the fixed microscope in the plate shews them in their usual position, the image from the object lens there being formed between the two, that the dispersion of rays in the first may be corrected by that of the second. But although this construction serves perfectly well every purpose of the fixed microscope, yet it could not answer in the moveable one, to which the micrometer is attached, where equal parts of an image, or their motion, are to be measured by the equable motion of the object

lens, as shewn by the micrometer: for in that case, the interpo-
sition of an eye-glass before the image was formed, would not
only have diminished its size, and thereby rendered the measure
less accurate ; but likewise, by refracting the oblique pencils more
than those nearer the centre, it would have destroyed the equality of the scale, and made equal parts of the object itself to have
been represented unequally in the magnified image, and consequently erroneously measured by unequal parts of the micrometer. It was to remedy a defect of this sort that Mr. Ramsden
proposed this new system of eye-glasses, described in the Philosophical Transactions, Vol. LXXIII. 1783, No. 5. And he has here
applied that system in the construction of the micrometer microscope ; where it will be perceived, that both glasses stand between
the eye and the image, whereby the greater magnitude of this last
is obviously preserved, as well as the just similarity of all its parts
to those of the object itself.

With regard to the scale of the pyrometer, it is, in the first place,
to be observed, that the head of the micrometer screw, which is
nine-tenths of an inch in diameter, is divided into fifty equal
parts, each of which being reckoned two, it is therefore numbered to 100. Fifty-five revolutions of the head, being equal
to 0.77175 of an inch, as measured with great accuracy by
Mr. Ramsden's straight-line engine, it follows, that there are
71.97 threads of the screw in an inch ; that seven revolutions
and nearly $\frac{1}{100}$th parts move the wire of the micrometer one-
tenth of an inch ; and that $\frac{1}{100}$th part of a revolution, or half a
division, answers to a motion of something more than 0.00014 of
an inch.

Having thus obtained the number of revolutions and parts of
the micrometer (7.19) corresponding to one-tenth of an inch at
the wires, it is sufficiently obvious, that the number answering to

one-tenth LM at the mark being likewise obtained, and added to the former, their sum will give the measure of one-tenth at the object lens, or the space by which the expanding rod has lengthened, as shewn by the motion of the lens from o to p. This measure of one-tenth of an inch at the mark, was ascertained in two different ways, and the results exactly agreed with each other. In the first place, a very thin ivory slide, whereon several twentieths of an inch were nicely divided by exceeding fine lines, was prepared, and made to move in the mark where the brass slide now exists. A candle being then placed behind it at night, while the pyrometer stood within doors, and the micrometer wire being repeatedly moved by the screw, its coincidence with the lines was distinctly seen through the ivory; whereby two of the spaces were found to be measured by 24.93 revolutions of the head. The second method was, by means of two exceeding fine wires placed parallel to each other on the brass slide, where they now remain, at the distance of one-twentieth of an inch on each side of the intersection wires, as may be seen by observing the real mark, or rather its magnified image, as shewn in the oval field of the micrometer, in the central figure of construction. The revolutions of the micrometer answering to the distance between these parallel wires was, as before, found to be 24.93; which being added to 7.13. we have 32.06 for the number of revolutions measuring a motion of one-tenth at the object lens, or the expansion of one-tenth. In this manner Mr. Ramsden obtains the scale of his pyrometer, in the easiest and most simple way imaginable, without any necessity for knowing the absolute distances of the object lens from the wires of the mark on one hand, and those of the micrometer on the other; distances not easily ascertained by actual measurement, on account of the position of that glass in its cell, which cannot conveniently be come at. Thus, in Pl. V. as well as in the annexed figure, LM being the object at the distance of the mark, equal to one-tenth of an inch; then ml will be its magnified image, in proportion to the former as mo is to oM. And if, through the point p, the place to which the object lens o has been carried by the motion of the expanding rod, a line Mq be drawn parallel to Ll, we shall have $ml = 24.99 + lq = 7.13 = mq = 32.06$, the number of revolutions of the micrometer measuring op, the expansion. Having thus obtained the total number of revolutions corresponding to mq; and having likewise measured the total distance $mM = 26.144$ inches, a space easily ascertained between the wires of the micrometer and those of the mark, the partial distances mo and oM may then be readily found by computation: for $mq : ml :: mM : mo = 20.33$ inches; and $mq : mM :: op : oM = 5.814$ inches.

In order to finish the description of the pyrometer, it is only necessary to observe farther, that the circular scale, seen in the elevation of the micrometer, whose zero appears to coincide with the dart on the plane part of the brass, is that which serves by its motion to register the turns of the head. A forked key, fitted to enter the holes near the circumference of the circle, is made use of for the adjustment of this zero. The circle should never be turned backwards, or towards the left, lest the watch chain should thereby be thrown off the barrel, but always forwards, or towards the right, even if it should be necessary to move it almost an entire revolution. The zero of the head is that which should be first brought to correspond with its proper dart. They may be seen to coincide in the horizontal section of the micrometer; and the departure of zero from this dart, indicates, by the number of divisions that are intercepted, the value of any fractional part of a revolution.

Account of the Experiments with the Pyrometer.

16. Although the instrument which I have here endeavoured to describe was begun early in the winter of 1784, yet it was not finished till the beginning of last April; at which time it was brought to Argyll-street, and being placed truly level on the stone pavement of the yard, was covered with an oil-cloth canopy, that the experiments might not be interrupted by rainy weather.

To fill the three troughs completely, it required from twenty-five to thirty pounds of pounded ice, which was always put in with great care, so as to apply as compactly as possible to the standard prisms and rod respectively, with but little common water * at first added; it having been found in these experiments, that ice water only, such as drains from the ice itself, is that which should properly be made use of to mix with the pounded ice, in order to bring the whole mass to the true freezing temperature. Being at the commencement uncertain what time might be necessary for the rods, especially when of so large a size as the standard prisms, to acquire the just temperature of freezing: at first the ice was put into the troughs over-night, to prepare for the continuation of the experiment next morning. But after many repeated trials, this precaution was found to be needless; a quarter of an hour being more than sufficient to give to all the freezing temperature, as well as to render the lens on

* When common water was used, although not in any very considerable proportion, the thermometer kept always half, and sometimes three quarters of a degree above 32°.

the expanding rod stationary, after the water supplying the place of the Ice had been brought fairly to boil.

The instrument, in its first state, having in some cases made the expansion appear to be progressive, and not equable ; therefore its rate was attempted to be ascertained, by noting the progression answering to 60°, 120°, and 180° above freezing. But when the instrument was rendered perfect, and that no sensible difference was found between the expansion at the lower and that at the upper part of the scale, a fair mean being taken between its ascending and descending rates, and allowing for the difficulty of keeping the water, for any length of time, precisely to the same intermediate heat : then this tedious mode of conducting the experiments was given up, and the expansion for 180° was at once determined by bringing the water to boil around that rod, which but a little before had been lying in melting ice, and which the standard prisms still continued to do throughout each experiment, care being taken to have a supply of pounded ice always ready, to keep these two troughs quite full.

Two observers are necessary for the effectual application of the pyrometer. He who observes with the fixed microscope, takes care that its object lens is kept in its true place ; that is to say, that the wire in the eye-piece accurately bisects the intersection wires of the mark. This he is enabled to do by means of the apparatus attached to the fixed end of the boiler, as will be best conceived by observing the plan (at WX) along with the elevation of that end placed near it. The apparatus consists of two milled-headed screws, working in brass plates fastened to the end of the frame, and acting against a small cock which projects from the lower part of the boiler, whereby this last receives such longitudinal motion to and fro on its rollers, as is sufficient for the adjustment of the lens. He who observes with the micrometer microscope, having brought the zero of the micrometer head to its

M

dart, as shewn in the horizontal section, and also the revolution zero to its dart, as represented in the elevation, takes care, when the rod has acquired the freezing temperature, that the micrometer wire bisects the intersection wires of its proper mark. This he effects by working with the milled-headed screw, represented in the plan and elevation of that mark, whereby the mark itself is moved until the bisection is accurate; and during the whole of this time, the first observer must be extremely attentive to keep his lens adjusted.

One assistant at least is necessary, who takes his station on the opposite side of the pyrometer, to observe the levels, and keep them adjusted, by means of the double hook applied near the middle of the boiler, and represented in the section on the line TU, at the lowermost right-hand angle of the plate.

The pyrometer having been adjusted in the manner here described, by giving sufficient time for the standard prisms and rod to contract to the true freezing temperature, as was easily known by the wires becoming perfectly fixed and stationary, with regard to the marks; the ice was then removed from the copper trough: and the same being filled with water nearly on the boil, the ebullition was completed, and kept up, by means of the lamps now lighted for the purpose, and slipped in underneath.

The expansion, answering to the 180° between freezing and boiling, was now measured by working with the micrometer screw until the bisection* of its wire with those of the mark was again complete; the observer at the fixed microscope taking also especial care all the while to keep his bisection perfectly accurate.

* This bisection of the wires may always be made to a great degree of precision, by one with a tolerably good eye, and accustomed to observations of this sort. I have myself repeatedly adjusted the wires eight or ten times running, allowing another person to read off and unadjust each time, without the mean difference exceeding one-fourth of a division of the head, which is only ₁/₁₀₀₀th part of an inch.

The number of revolutions, registered by the number of entire
divisions that the zero of the circular scale had departed from its
dart or index, and also the value of any fractional revolution, registered by the divisions on the head intercepted between zero
and its proper dart, were then noted, as expressed in the first
column of the subjoined table of experiments ; which requires no
other explanation than what is therein inserted, and which has
been extended purposely to shew at one view, from inspection
only, how much the length of our base would have been affected,
if measured by these metals respectively, in temperatures between
32° and 62°.

All the experiments were repeated at least twice, and some of
them three times, except the standard scale and glass pendulum
rod, whose expansions were only tried once.   The difference of a
few divisions between the mean and extremes on the heat of 180°,
being, in things of this sort, of no importance, it was judged
wholly unnecessary to aim at a greater degree of precision in repeating them oftener.   By referring to the table, particularly
that column containing the expansions on one foot by 180°, it will
be perceived, that they are uniformly a small matter less than
what has been assigned to the same metals respectively, in the
experiments formerly alluded to.

Ultimate Determination of the Length of the Base on Hounslow Heath.

17. In the former part of this Account, we have had occasion to
speak of the seven first columns of the General Table of the base ;
and the titles at the tops of the others respectively serve sufficiently to explain those towards the right hand ; the expansion
of glass above, and its contraction below 62° contained in the

M 2

eleventh and twelfth columns, being deduced from the recent experiments with the pyrometer.

Feet.

The hypothenusal length of the base, as measured
by 1369.923501 glass rods of twenty feet each +
4.31 feet, being the distance between the last rod
and the centre of the north-west pipe, is found
to be - - - - 27402.8204
The reduction contained in the seventh column of
the general table to be deducted is - - 0.0714
Hence the apparent length of the base, reduced to
the level of the south-east extremity, becomes 27402.7490
The apparent length is to be augmented by the
excess of the expansion above the contraction of the
glass rods, contained in the thirteenth column of the
general table=4.1867 inches, reduced to the heat of
62°, as has been usually done in former operations of
this nature - - - - 0.3489
The apparent length is farther to be augmented
by the equation for 6° difference of temperature of the
standard brass scale and the glass rods, between 62°
and 68°, this last being the heat in which the lengths
of the glass rods were laid off =11,8368 inches, * as
deduced from the experiments with the pyrometer - 0.9864
Hence we have the correct length of the base in the
temperature of 62° reduced to the level of the lowermost extremity near Hampton Poorhouse, - 27404.0843

In.   In.
* Expansion for 6° on the whole { brass standard=3.38938 × 6=20.33628
base   { glass rods   =1.41058 × 6=8.49948
                                                    feet.
                                          diff. 11.8368=0,9864.

Feet.

This last length requires yet a small reduction for
the height of this lowermost end above the mean level of the sea, supposed to be fifty-four feet, or nine
fathoms,   -   -   -   -   0.0706

Hence the true or ultimate length of the base, reduced to the level of the sea, and making a portion of
the mean circumference of the earth, becomes   -   27404.0137

As some small degree of uncertainty remains with regard to
this last reduction, it may not be improper to say yet a few words
on the principles that have been adhered to in making the computation. It will be remembered, that the measurement was made
$3\frac{1}{2}$ feet above the surface of the Heath, that being the height of the
stands whereon the rods were placed ; and that the telescopic
spirit level gave a descent of 96.1 feet from the lowermost pipe to
the surface of summer water in the Thames at Hampton. The
accurate section of the river lately published, gives a fall of 19.33
feet from Hampton to the level of low-water spring tides at Isleworth. Now these three being added together, we have nearly
fifty-three feet for the height of the base above Isleworth. Having
had no immediate means of determining what real difference there
may be between Isleworth and low-water spring tides at the mouth
of the Thames (for instance at the Hope or the Nore), I have supposed that fall to be about seven feet, so as to make the total descent sixty feet. Now, supposing the spring tides at the Nore to
rise eighteen feet, if, according to M. De la Lande's method, we
deduct one-third of eighteen, viz. six feet from sixty, we shall
have fifty-four feet, or nine fathoms, that the mean surface of
the sea is below the measured base. Whether this conclusion be
perfectly accurate or not is of no moment, since a whole fathom
of difference (and I apprehend we are not farther from the truth)

does not vary the reduction quite one-tenth of an inch. The reduced base has therefore been found by the following analogy : as the mean semi-diameter of the earth (supposed here to be 3492915 fathoms) augmented by nine fathoms, is to the mean semidiameter, so is the measured base 27404.0843 to the reduced base 27404.0137 at the level of the sea.

It will doubtless be allowed, that infinite pains have been taken in the field and otherwise throughout the whole of this operation, to obtain a just conclusion.

30	- -	0.165	19.715	- 6	0.0
31	0.14	- -	19.855	+ 7	0.0
32	- -	0.18	19.735	- -	0.0
33	- -	0.14	19.595	+ 6	0.0
34	1.21	- -	20.805	- 6	0.0
35	1.405	- 6	22.21	- 7	0.0
36	2.34	- -	24.55	+ 7	0.0
37	+	1.085	23.465	- 7	0.0
38	0.47	- ...	23.935	- 6	0.0
39	0.525	- -	24.46	+ 7	0.0
40	1.285	- -	25.745	- 6	0.0
41	1.13	- -	26.905	- 6	0.0
42	-	0.19	26.715	6 -	0.0
43	1.563	- -	28.28	- -	0.0
44	1.485	- -	29.765	+ 6	0.0
45	0.24	- -	30.005	- -	0.0
46	1.26	- -	31.265	12.130	0.0
400 ft.					
	20.44	9.175	31.265	31.265	0.0

Hypothenusal length of the base containing 1369.9255
Reduction contained in the seventh column to be subt...

Total apparent length of the base reduced to the level...
Add to the apparent length the difference between t...
62°, contained in the thirteenth column = + 1867...
Add further to the apparent length, the equation for...
glass rods, between 62° and 68°, the heat in which...

Correct length of the base in the temperature of 62°, ...
Reduction for the height of the lower end of the base...
y fathoms -

True length of the base reduced to the mean level of...

Description of	expansion in			Bases of 27400 feet of these metals would expand.			
	on feet.	600 feet.	1000 ft.	By 1°.	By 10°.	By 20°.	By 30°.
	In.	In.	In.	In.	In.	In.	In.
Standard brass scale.	Supp 42.187 thickne expansi the mic have be	.04948	0.07421	0.1137	3.38931	33.8931	67.7876	101.6814
English plate brass, in form of a rod.	Leng 0.15 in. its thin	.05048	0.07573	0.1161	3.45781	34.5781	69.1576	103.7364
English plate brass, in form of a trough.	Leng loch; straight	1.05051	0.07578	0.1163	3.46061	34.6061	69.1114	103.8168
Steel rod.	Leng 0.3 inc very sar	.05051	0.04578	0.0763	1.09061	10.9061	41.8114	61.7186
Cast-iron prism.	Leng weight the stra	.02960	0.04440	0.0740	1.02760	10.2760	40.5520	60.8180
Glass tube.	Leng 1 lb. 13. with the	.02068	0.03101	0.0517	1.41651	14.1651	28.3316	42.4974
Solid glass rod.	Leng meter th It had its expa of the would h	.02156	0.03234	0.0539	1.47686	14.7686	29.5372	44.3058

○

An Account of the Trigonometrical Operation, whereby the Distance between the Meridians of the Royal Observatories of Greenwich and Paris has been determined. By Major-General William Roy, F. R. S. and A. S.

Introduction.

18. THE trigonometrical operation which becomes the subject of this work, had its commencement, as will be remembered, in the measurement of a base on Hounslow Heath in 1784, an account of which was given to the Royal Society in the following year.

In the spring of 1787, Sir Joseph Banks opened (through the official intercourse of his Majesty's secretary of state, the Marquis of Carmarthen, with the ambassador at the court of France) a correspondence with the Academy of Sciences, regarding the co-operation expected on their part, for connecting the triangles which we were now preparing to extend along the English coast, with those formerly executed on the coast of France, opposite to Dover. And Dr. Blagden had engaged to assist in the business, on the appointment of the Royal Society, whenever we should be enabled to assign any probable time, for the different parties to repair to their respective coasts, for the aforesaid co-operation.

About the same time likewise, a paper was laid before the Royal Society, intended as a sketch of the mode proposed to be followed in carrying the scheme into execution; for which purpose it was accompanied with a general map, shewing nearly the disposition of the triangles.

For several months of the spring and summer of 1787, Mr. Ramsden had been seriously at work, in endeavouring to finish the instrument intended for the measurement of the angles. Not having employed a sufficient number of workmen upon it at the outset, it was now evident, that he had even deceived himself, by leaving too much to be done at the latter end. At length, however, the instrument was produced, and placed, on the 31st of July, at the station near Hampton Poorhouse.

By commencing an operation of this nature, at so advanced a season of the year, it was sufficiently obvious, that only very faint hopes could be entertained of bringing it to a conclusion before the bad weather would set in. But it being of much importance to get the triangles, which extend across the Channel, at all events executed, it was therefore proposed to Comte de Cassini, who by this time had been appointed by the Academy of Sciences, to superintend their part of the business, that he should fix the time that might suit him best for our meeting on the coast; that we would then discontinue the operation to the westward, and, having in concert executed the coast triangles, we would resume the inland parts of our own series at some more convenient opportunity.

This proposition being readily acceded to by Comte de Cassini, the 20th of September was appointed for our repairing to the coasts of Dover and Calais respectively.

In the mean time our operation was continued, with all imaginable care and assiduity, through the first ten stations of the series of triangles, from Hampton Poorhouse to that at Wrotham Hill inclusively.

The instrument, and the various parts of the apparatus, were then removed to Dover, at which place Mess. de Cassini, Mechain, and Le Gendre, three distinguished members of the Academy of Sciences, arrived on the 23d of September.

In the course of two days that these gentlemen honoured us with their company at Dover, every thing was settled in the most amicable manner possible, with regard to the times of reciprocal observation.

A great number of white lights, fitted for long distances, and several reverberatory lamps had been previously provided. Having been supplied with such a proportion of the lights as seemed necessary for their side of the Channel, and one of the lamps, the French gentlemen departed for Calais on the 25th, accompanied by Dr. Blagden, who attended them during the time of the co-operation, until it was finally closed on the 17th of October.

For the greater part of the time, the weather was extremely bad; nevertheless, on the particular nights when the most important observations on our side were made, namely, those at Dover and Fairlight Down, the nights happened very fortunately to be favourable, so as to enable us to intersect, with great accuracy, the two distant points on the French coast of *Blancnez* and *Montlambert*,* and thereby to establish for ever, the triangular connection between the two countries.

The Duke of Richmond, Master General of his Majesty's Ordnance, had, in the most liberal manner possible, given every assistance to the operation (from that great department over which he presides with so much honour to himself and advantage to the public) by furnishing an officer and a detachment of artillery-men for the work; ordering the laboratory at Woolwich † to supply whatever fire-works might be wanted for signals; and temporary scaffolds to be erected at Greenwich Observatory, Shooter's Hill, and Dover Castle, for the reception of the instrument. But what was still of more importance than any of these, his Grace had permitted Lieut. Fiddes (one of the engineers, on the survey then under my direction) to be employed, in the summers of 1786 and 1787, in making a very accurate plan of that part of Romney Marsh where the base of verification was to be measured. In a country so much

* The name of this hill is vulgarly pronounced *Boulemberg*, and it is even written in the same manner in the book, *La Méridienne vérifiée*.

† Major Congreve, of the Royal Artillery, had the management of the lights at Shooter's Hill; and his assistance was found to be most essentially useful.

N

intersected by ditches, and where there were so many ponds of
water to be avoided, without such a plan raised beforehand ; an
operation of so delicate and difficult a nature could not have been
effected.

The apparatus for the measurement of the base with the steel
chain, notwithstanding the urgency of the case, was not sent to its
destination until the end of the first week of October. To Lieut.
Fiddes the engineer, was then joined Lieut. Bryce of the Royal Artillery ; and It was not before the beginning of December, that
these two gentlemen, with the most unremitting labour and perseverance, were able to accomplish the measurement, as will be
seen hereafter in the detailed account of that operation.

In finishing the co-operation with the French Commissioners,
at Lydd on the 17th of October, our instrument had now passed
through sixteen stations out of twenty-three. There of course remained yet seven stations where it was to be placed, and observations to be made. Eagerly wishing to bring the business to a
conclusion, we struggled on through five of the seven. But the
weather at length became so tempestuous, that it was utterly impossible to continue it, with any hopes of being able to make satisfactory observations. Perched on the tops of high steeples, such
as Lydd and Tenterden, or on heights, such as Hollingborn Hill,
we sufficiently experienced, that operations of this sort, where
the most important observations could only be made at night, by
means of the white lights, should never be undertaken in the latter
season.

On the second of November, the instrument was accordingly
removed from the top of Hollingborn Hill, and sent to town, leaving the stations on Goudhurst and Frant Churches, both likewise
situated on eminences, unoccupied until the ensuing season.

The winter months were employed in calculating the observations that had been made ; and from these we were very well
enabled to judge to what a degree of accuracy we had arrived in

[93]

determining the sides and angles: for Frant and Goudhurst, having been intersected from Botley Hill, Wrotham Hill, and Hollingborn Hill; Goudhurst having been observed from Tenterden, and Frant having (contrary to our expectation) been seen and observed from Fairlight Down, we had thereby the certain means of determining very nearly what difference there would be between the measured and computed length of either base as given by the other, although observations had not been made at the two intermediate stations of Goudhurst and Frant. This difference, it was seen, would be but trifling. In as far, therefore, as the results of the plane triangles were concerned, we might have proceeded with the computations, and drawn the consequent conclusions, without hesitation, or any risk of sensible error.

But, besides that it might still have been said that the instrument had not been placed at these two stations, there were reasons of a different kind, which rendered it in some degree necessary to place the instrument not only at Goudhurst and Frant, but also at Botley Hill and Folkstone Turnpike, where it had formerly stood.

We made observations of the pole-star at Dover Castle, but that station, though about 466 feet above the sea, is nevertheless surrounded on the land side with eminences, at the distance of six, or seven miles, still higher than itself. From that circumstance, we found it impossible to connect it with the triangles to the westward, otherwise than by a short side: and consequently the observations of the star became useless. Botley Hill, Goudhurst, and Folkstone Turnpike, therefore, presented themselves as eligible stations for observing the directions of the meridian.

In 1787, when at the station on St. Ann's Hill, in a very high wind, the box containing the axis-level was blown from the scaffold, and unluckily broken. Another sort of clamp: also an eye-piece, with a diagonal prism, for more conveniently observing the pole-star (or other high object), were necessary improvements. Those,

N 2

however, with a new axis-level, were not ready till the beginning
of August, 1788.

The observations at Goudhurst, Frant, Botley Hill, and Folkstone Turnpike, having been finished early in September, the instrument was brought back to town, in the neighbourhood of which
it was employed for three days for the following purpose.

In 1787, when at the stations of Hundred Acres, Norwood, Greenwich, and Shooter's Hill, we had only been able to determine, in
a satisfactory manner, two points within the limits of the Capital,
namely, St. Paul's Church and Argyll-street, the last by means of
the white lights. Bearings of some others, it is true, were obtained ;
but, in order that these might be intersected in the best manner,
it became necessary to place the instrument at one or more stations
to the northward of the town.

With the view, therefore, of laying the foundation hereafter
for a much more accurate plan of London than could possibly be
obtained in any other way, the instrument was placed, first, at
Hornsey Hill, to the eastward of Highgate ; and secondly, on
Primrose Hill, between London and Hampstead.

Although the weather was rather unfavourable at the time of
making the observations from these two new stations; and that
the smoke constantly hanging over the town in the latter season
impeded us greatly : nevertheless, the former bearings were intersected, and the situations of a considerable number of remarkable
steeples within London and its environs, were accurately determined, as will more fully appear in treating of the secondary triangles.

Having thus briefly shewn the order, with regard to time, in which
the recent operation, through its various steps, was progressively
carried on and completed, it is proper that I should mention, that
Mr. Dalby, who had been recommended as an assistant, has ac-
quitted himself throughout the whole perfectly to my satisfaction.

Description of the Apparatus made use of in the Measurement of the
Base of Verification in Romney Marsh, with the hundred-feet steel
chain, in the autumn of 1787, with the result of that operation.
Reference to be had to Plates VI. and VII.

Preamble.

19. In the account of the measurement of the base on Hounslow
Heath in 1784, we had occasion to show, how very accurately distances might be determined by the steel chain, when applied in
the ordinary way on the natural surface of the ground, if that surface happened to be tolerably smooth, which was the case in the
instance alluded to. By the comparison of the measurement of a
length of one thousand feet with the glass rods, and with the chain
when used with an apparatus adapted to the purpose, it further
appeared, that the difference between the results was so very small
as scarcely to be discernible, since it would not have exceeded half
an inch on the whole length of that base of 27404 feet.

Having always considered the experiment on Hounslow Heath,
just now mentioned, as positive proof of the excellency of the
chain, it had been resolved on to apply it to the mensuration of
the base of verification in Romney Marsh, even if no other reasons had existed to make that choice eligible. But besides the
danger of having the glass rods broken, in transporting to so great
a distance from London, and, on such an event happening, the
impossibility of getting them replaced with others, at the advanced
season of the year in which we were unfortunately thrown with
the operation, it was obvious, that in a plain of the breadth of
six miles, so much intersected with ditches full of water as Romney Marsh in reality is, the laying of bridges for the tripod stands,

which must have been used with the glass rods, would alone have been a very troublesome and tedious operation.

Beech Posts.

20. In the first place, about thirty posts made of beech wood, three inches in diameter, and of different lengths, from two feet three inches to three feet six, and a few of them still longer, were provided. They were shod with iron, and each of them carried on its top a cast-iron ferrule, with two dovetails projecting from it; care being taken in driving them into the ground, that the dovetails should stand in or nearly in the direction of the base, as represented by the plan and section of a single post in the middle part of Plate VI. The arrangement of twenty-four of these posts may be seen at the top of the said plate, for the measurement of a portion of the base equal to one hundred yards, or the length of three chains. Sixteen of the posts, reckoning from that which stands in the centre of the first group, to that which stands in the centre of the second, and so on from right to left, were placed at the distance of twenty feet from each other. The first is supposed to coincide with the mouth of the pipe sunk into the earth, at the eastern extremity of the base, at a place called High Nook near Dymchurch; and every fifth post from that towards the left, marks the end of a chain. The other eight posts in the arrangement, that is to say, the right and left posts of each of the four groups, are supposed to stand twelve or fifteen inches from those in the centre. By referring to the elevation near the top, and the plans and section in the middle part of Plate VI. it will be perceived, that these posts, together with certain other iron parts of the apparatus fixed to them, hereafter to be described, support the ends of the coffering for each chain, free and independently of the central posts, to which last the brass scales alone are attached.

Deal Coffers.

21. Fifteen deal coffers, numbered from one to fifteen, were necessary for the length of three chains, being five to each. Six of them, that is to say, the first and fifth, the sixth and tenth, the eleventh and fifteenth, being the first and last of each chain, were only nineteen feet four or five inches in length. The other nine, being the three in the middle of each chain, were of the complete length of twenty feet. These coffers perfectly resembled in shape, and nearly in dimensions, the cases of the glass rods, being ten inches broad in the middle, and uniformly of that depth throughout their whole length. But from the middle they became gradually narrower, in a curvilinear manner, towards each end, where they were only two inches wide. The two cheeks or sides were about half an inch thick, and the bottom, which entered Into a shallow groove in the middle of the cheeks, was an inch in thickness. Thus the cheeks being thin, bent and applied easily to the bottom, to which they were firmly nailed, and the whole was fortified by small blocks of wood fastened at intervals in the inside, sometimes above and sometimes below the bottom. From the elevation it will be perceived, that nine or ten inches of the under extremities of the cheeks were cut off, so as to permit the bottom itself to rest on the irons. This construction of the coffers was found to answer very well, that is to say, they were, considering their length, not so heavy as to be unmanageable, at the same time that by their general figure, and particularly the depth of the cheeks, they were entirely prevented from warping.

In addition to the fifteen coffers, just now described, a sixteenth, not represented in the plate, was afterwards prepared at Hythe, by Lieut. Fiddes, to be used occasionally, when the end of one chain, and commencement of another, coincided with a deep ditch or one of the sewers full of water, and where of course it would have been

extremely difficult, if not impossible, to have fixed steadily the
group of three posts in the usual manner. In this coffer there
was a double or false bottom, with grooves adapted for the purpose ; and the brass scale, pulley, &c. were removed from the
irons, and placed on this bottom.

Apparatus of cast iron, &c. for the Ends of the Chain.

22. By referring to the plate, where the several parts of the
apparatus for the extremities of the chain are represented in plan
and section, by a scale equal to one-fourth of their real dimensions, it will appear that the cast-iron pieces were of two different
forms, one long, and the other short; but both applied in the
same manner, on the ferrules binding the tops of the posts, as has
been already mentioned. Of the long kind there were in all
fifteen or sixteen, that is to say, one for each post in a length of
three chains. Each iron had two clamps on its under side, which
being slackened, it was placed on its ferrule at right angles to the
line of measurement ; and being turned round 90°, the dovetails
of the ferrule, standing originally in the direction of the base,
came within the clamps, which were then tightened by four
screws, turned with square keys adapted to the purpose.

It is sufficiently obvious, that so many irons, with such a number of screws to each, could not fail of rendering this operation
tedious ! The business would have been greatly expedited if there
had been only two such screws, one on each end, in a middle
situation ; and, instead of the four screws, there should have
been four steady pins, entering easily into holes prepared for them
in the under side. A short groove, of two or three inches in
length, in each extremity of the bottom, would, on this supposition, have been necessary to suffer the square heads of the screws
to pass ; and it will be readily conceived, that the thickness of the

bottom would have effectually secured the chain from touching
them, prevented the mutilation of its handles, and saved much
loss of time. Indeed the same purpose might have been effected,
but not so advantageously, by laying the original four screws
lower in the iron, which its thickness easily admitted of. Finally,
in order to avoid such like Inconveniences in future, there is still
one imperfection more, which it is incumbent on me to remark,
namely, that cast-iron ferrules will not answer ; for the force that
was found to be necessary to drive the posts into the ground, burst
almost the whole of them, so that before the operation was completed, they were obliged to be replaced with others made of
hammered iron, forged for the purpose.

Of the short irons, only three were necessary, one for each end
of the chain, and a spare one in case of accident. They were
placed, turned, and clamped on the ferrules, in all respects similarly with those of the long kind. By inspection of the plate it
will be seen, that each of them carried on its surface a brass scale
of six inches in length, divided into inches and quarters, and
moveable in a slide, either backwards or forwards, by a finger-
screw adapted to the right-hand end.

The right-hand post of each group is called the *drawing-post*,
because the iron fixed on its top carries a small apparatus of brass,
which being connected with the flat iron rod and hooks formerly
used at Hounslow Heath, for a like purpose, lays hold of the rear
handle of the chain, and draws it back until zero coincides with
the point of commencement. The left-hand post in each group
is called the *weight-post*, because it carried a brass pulley, over
which a weight of 28 *lbs.* was hung by a small rope attached to
the hooks that laid hold of the front handle of the chain. This
weight acting against the force of the screw at the other end, the
chain was thereby kept perfectly straight in the coffers, and constantly in the same degree of tension, until some certain division

O

(the nearest for instance) of the scale could be brought, by means of the screw, accurately to coincide with 100 feet at the front end. That division, whatever it might be, was of course registered in the field book of the operation, together with the true temperature of the chain, as shewn by five thermometers, one being laid for that purpose in each coffer, and secured with white cloth from the sun's rays, as occasion might require.

Fifteen coffers were always arranged on the ground at the same time, comprehending a space of the base equal to the length of three chains, or 100 yards. The extremities of the first chain having been accurately transferred, in the manner above mentioned, to the brass scales on the tops of the central posts, and these remaining firm and motionless, as being wholly unconnected with any other parts of the apparatus, the chain was then moved forward into the second set of coffers, where the thermometers were also placed. In the mean time, the first set of coffers, now vacated, with their posts, &c. were carried on and arranged in the front, for the measurement of the second 100 feet: and so on continually with the others in succession.

Of the Survey of Romney Marsh previously to the Measurement of the Base.

23. In the introduction to this Account, it has been mentioned that the Duke of Richmond had permitted Lieutenant Fiddes, of the Royal Engineers, to be employed in 1786 and 1787 in raising a plan of that part of the Marsh where, on examination, it should be found, that the base of verification might be the best executed. In justice to that Officer, I consider it as incumbent on me to say, that it was impossible for any person to fulfil the duties entrusted to him better than he did, either in the course of the survey, or subsequent measurement of the base, whereof he also had the

direction. The general instructions given to him were, that after
having, by a base of his own, determined certain triangles in the
neighbourhood of Dymchurch, Ruckinge, and Romney, by way
of foundation for his work, he should preserve Ruckinge as the
point whereon the *alignement* of the great base was to be directed,
and vary the position of that end next the sea-wall in such a
manner as to meet with the fewest local obstructions to the measurement between the two extremities. By inspection of the
plan, Plate VII. which comprehends a tract of country of two miles
in breadth, one on each side of the base line, it will be perceived,
that besides the numberless ditches with which this singular plain
is intersected, and which it was impossible to avoid crossing, there
is almost in every field a watering pond for the cattle, many of
them of considerable depth. Nevertheless, so very attentive had
Mr. Fiddes been to the accuracy of his survey, that he was enabled,
after several trials of other directions, to run a line from High
Nook on Dymchurch Sea-wall, upon the small spire of Ruckinge
Church, of the length of nearly six miles, without interfering with
any one of the watering ponds, or meeting with any other local
obstruction of consequence. So very minute was he in his remarks, and so accurate in the situation of particular trees, that in
tracing his line with the telescope, he managed so as to avoid
them all, a few insignificant bushes excepted ; which I believe to
be an instance of exactness scarcely to be equalled.

Pipes sunk in the Ground.

24. Permission having previously been obtained from the pro-
prietors of the soil, pipes were sunk into the ground at the two
extremities of the base, and also one on Allington Knoll, which
last point with Lydd Church* form that side of one of the great

* Mr. Cobb, of Lydd, an ingenious gentleman, well acquainted with Romney
Marsh, was so obliging as to present me with a manuscript map of that singular

triangles depending on the base on Hounslow Heath, to be first
verified by the measurement of this new base. Every field is
surrounded with a ditch, in cleaning of which the earth and mud
are continually thrown out on each side, whereby flat dikes are
gradually formed on either side. That the measurement might
be carried on as nearly as possible in the same plane, that is to
say, about fifteen or eighteen inches above the common surface,
therefore narrow grooves were cut in these flat dikes, which the
different farmers readily consented to without murmuring. Here
it is to be observed, that there was no occasion for levelling the line,
Romney Marsh having been formerly covered by the sea, and a
considerable part of it, particularly towards the bottom of the
range of hills that separate it from the Wealds of Kent, being
still lower than the sea at high water, would again be overflowed
by it, if much care and expence were not annually bestowed in
securing and repairing the dikes, whereby it is protected. Thus
the line of the base may be considered as an inclined plane, descending gradually about five feet from the mouth of High Nook
pipe to within 246 yards of the Ruckinge end, where the ground
in that direction seems to be the lowest. Thence it rises com-
paratively suddenly, about fifteen feet, to the mouth of the pipe
situated in a small field immediately adjoining to Ruckinge Churchyard.

Result of the Measurement.

25. Lieutenant Fiddes, in the course of his trigonometrical survey, and of the different measurements he had actually made of
the line with a common iron chain, which from time to time was

plain, compiled by himself from actual surveys, where the names and boundaries of
the *waterings*, and many other curious particulars, are very distinctly expressed.—
Our plan of the base has therefore derived advantage by adhering to such respectable
authority.

compared with standard rods of deal, had determined the total length of the base within a few feet of the truth, before the ultimate operation began. He had likewise driven into the ground, at the end of every thousand feet, a strong picket, which were numbered 1, 2, 3, &c. from the pipe at High Nook to the 28th near Ruckinge. In all this preparatory part of the business he had no other assistants than the artillery-men of his surveying party. But for the ultimate determination, the aid of some person in whom he could confide for the management of the operation in general, and particularly for the adjustment of the scale at one end of the chain, while he himself was adjusting that at the other was absolutely necessary; therefore Lieutenant Bryce, of the Royal Artillery (now of the corps of Royal Engineers), an attentive officer, and mathematician, was left with him for those essential purposes. These two gentlemen began the operation on the 15th of October, and after experiencing many difficulties, arising from the badness of the weather in that late season of the year, and the defectiveness of the apparatus, it was only by dint of great labour, and the utmost perseverance, that they were enabled to accomplish the measurement on the 4th of December following.

The annexed table of the base, which contains three columns, shews the progress that was made in the work from day to day. The first column contains the date; the second, the spaces measured each day, reckoned by hundreds of yards, and denoted in the general plan by strong dots; and the third shews the temperature of the chain deduced from the mean of fifteen thermometers, or five for each chain.

Table of the Measurement of the Base of Verification on Romney Marsh, executed in the Autumn of 1787.

Days	Spaces measured Yards	Mean temp. by thermo.	Days	Spaces measured Yards	Mean temp. by thermo.	Days	Spaces measured Yards	Mean temp. by thermo.
Oct.			Nov.			Nov.		
15	100	54.7	2	3100	50.9		6100	42.1
16	200	62.7		3200	49.1		6200	39.3
	300	61.3		3300	50.4	21	6300	43.3
17	400	57.0		3400	48.5		6400	46.5
	500	52.2		3500	42.6		6500	45.6
	600	53.6	5	3600	52.3	22	6600	42.6
20	700	46.8		3700	53.0		6700	42.2
	800	58.9		3800	52.4		6800	41.2
23	900	53.9		3900	47.3	23	6900	39.8
	1000	55.3	7	4000	55.6		7000	39.0
24	1100	55.7		4100	55.2		7100	37.7
	1200	50.0	10	4200	55.3	24	7200	36.2
	1300	55.2		4300	53.6		7300	42.1
26	1400	59.1		4400	49.0		7400	40.5
	1500	60.0	12	4500	50.1	26	7500	35.2
27	1600	59.1		4600	47.9		7600	39.8
	1700	63.1	13	4700	44.7		7700	38.5
	1800	68.1		4800	44.8	27	7800	33.0
	1900	57.9		4900	4'.0		7900	38.9
29	2000	60.8	14	5000	41.8	28	8000	32.7
	2100	65.0		5100	42.9		8100	36.8
	2200	64.1	15	5200	45.3		8200	39.2
	2300	56.7		5300	44.1		8300	39.5
30	2400	58.7		5400	40.4	29	8400	34.8
	2500	59.5	16	5500	41.5		8500	42.5
31	2600	57.3		5600	44.8		8600	42.3
	2700	54.6		5700	44.6	30	8700	30.5
Nov.	2800	53.9	17	5800	40.6		8800	44.3
1	2900	49.0		5900	39.4	Dec.	8900	46.0
	3000	54.0		6000	41.3	1	9000	43.0
							9100	45.6
							9200	46.7
						3	9300	41.1
							9400	46.9
						4	9512.2454	48.4
								4552.7

By the table, it appears that the total apparent length of the base, as given directly by the chain, was 9512.2454 yards, or 285.96736 chains = 28536 feet, 8.835 inches.

But when the new points, at the distance of 25 feet from each other, were laid off on the chain in Mr. Ramsden's shop, from the original points on the great plank of New England deal, the temperature was 55°. *The original points here alluded to* (by General Roy), *must be those mentioned in the account of the Hounslow Heath base (5), which were fixed in the plank, from the brass standard, in the temperature of 63°.* [*] Therefore, as the chain in the temperature of 55° was equal to 100 feet of the brass standard in that of 63°, it follows from the table of expansions (p. 88.) that its length in 59°$\frac{7}{10}$ was equal to 100 feet of the brass standard in 62°; and consequently 59°$\frac{7}{10}$ is the temperature to which the measurement by the chain must be reduced. Now the sum of all the degrees, shewn by the thermometers being 4552.7 × 15 = 68290.5; and the apparent length = 285.96736 chains, we have 285.96736 × 53$\frac{7}{10}$ − $\frac{68290.5}{5}$ × .00769 inch. = 12.8 inches, the contraction below 59°$\frac{7}{10}$. This correction to be *subtracted* from the apparent length.

Previous to the measurement, the length of the chain was laid off, in the temperature of 55°$\frac{1}{4}$ on St. James's churchyard wall, two brass pins being fixed in the coping for that purpose. After the measurement on Romney Marsh was finished, the chain, in the temperature of 39°, being stretched out on the wall, it fell short of the original points in the brass pins by $\frac{121}{1000}$ of an inch. Now 55°$\frac{1}{4}$ − 39° = 16°$\frac{1}{4}$, and 16$\frac{1}{4}$ × .00769 = 0.126 inch. Hence 0.126 − $\frac{121}{1000}$ = 0.023 inch, is what the chain had lengthened during the measurement : half of this, or 0.0115 multiplied by 285.97

---

[*] The chain was tried against the new ones when the base on Hounslow Heath was re-measured in 1791: from whence h appeared that 63° must have been the temperature ; nearly.

(chains) gives 9.282 inches. This correction to be *added* to the apparent length.

	Feet.	In.
Apparent length, - -	28536	8.835
Correction for contraction of the chain, - *sub.*	1	0.8
Correction for the wear of the chain, - *add.*	0	9.282
Correction for two hypothenusal distances; the Ruckinge end of the base being suddenly elevated 15 feet above the lowest part, - *sub.*	0	9.083
Correction for height of the base above the mean level of the sea, supposed to be about 15¼ feet, *sub.*	0	0.166
Length of the base in the temperature of 62° of Fahrenheit's thermometer, or the length, supposing it had been measured with the brass standard in that temperature, - -	28535	8.128

As a proof that the expansion of the chain was accurately determined, I shall close this article with a remark repeatedly made by the two gentlemen entrusted with the execution of this last measurement. At the close of each day's work, the two scales marking the extremities of the last chain (after registering the divisions of coincidence) were left upon their respective posts until the next morning. They were secured during the night, from being disturbed by cattle, with a certain number of the spare posts driven into the ground around them. A tent was also pitched between the two, where some men of the party constantly lay, by way of a guard for the whole apparatus. On the recommencement of the operation the subsequent morning, the chain being applied anew to the brass scales : if the temperature continued the same, the coincidences were found to be equally accurate as on the preceding night ; but if it had changed one or two degrees, the chain never failed unequivocally to shew it, by falling short of the divisions on the scales, if the cold had increased, or by over-reaching them, if it had diminished.

Finally, with respect to the subject of these bases, it is here to be remarked, that the base of verification in Romney Marsh makes with the meridian of the pipe at High Nook an angle of 54° 28′ 66″ north-westward; and that on Hounslow Heath makes with the meridian of the pipe at Hampton Poorhouse an angle of 44° 41′ 49″, also north-westward. But those bearings are determined by computation, and therefore cannot be considered as very correct.

General Description of the great Instrument with which the Angles, in the recent Trigonometrical Operation, were observed; shewing also its various adjustments for practice. Reference to be had to Plate VIII. a general View of the entire Machine; Plate IX. a Plan and two Sections; Plate X. various Parts represented to large scales; and Plate XI. the Microscopes and Eye-pieces.

Preamble.

26. In endeavouring to describe the curious instrument made use of for observing the angles in the recent trigonometrical operation, it has been judged best to confine ourselves to the principal parts, without entering into any detail of the *minutiæ*; for even to have mentioned these, with the almost infinite number of little screws that serve to unite them into one entire machine, which could only have been done by references to a multitude of great and small Roman and Greek characters, would have been a disgusting labour. By the help of the four plates which this description refers to, and which have been executed with great care, that fewer words might suffice, it is hoped, that the instrument may be understood by two classes of people for whom it is chiefly intended; first, by those who being possessed of such a machine,

P

would wish to make themselves masters of its use ; and, secondly,
by such ingenious artists as would attempt to construct such another ; for these last, in particular, the parts that are of brass, of
bell-metal, or of steel, are distinguished from each other. And
here it is necessary to observe, that the plates must not only be
frequently consulted, but also attentively considered, and repeatedly compared with each other, in the course of this description.

General View of the Instrument.

27. It is a brass circle, three feet in diameter, and may be called
a great Theodolite, rendered extremely perfect ; having this advantage in particular, which common theodolites have not, that its
transit telescope can be nicely adjusted by inversion on its supports ; that is to say, it can be turned upside down, in the same
manner that transit-instruments are, in fixed observatories.

The circle is attached by ten conical tubes, as so many *radii*, to
a large vertical, conical hollow axis, of twenty-four inches in
height, which may be called the exterior axis. Within the base
of this hollow axis, a collar of cast steel is strongly driven ; and on
its top there is inserted a thick bell-metal plate, with sloping
cheeks, which, by means of five screws, can be raised or depressed
a little.

The instrument rests on three feet, which are firmly united to
each other at the place where they branch off, by a strong circular
plate of bell-metal, upon which rises another vertical hollow cone,
of less size than the former, being included within it, and is therefore called the Interior axis. On its top is inserted a cast-steel
pivot, with sloping cheeks, passing through the bell-metal plate
on the top of the exterior axis, the cheeks of the one being nicely
ground to fit the cheeks of the other. The bell-metal base of this
interior axis is in like manner ground to fit the cast-steel collar in
the base of that which is without it. Thus the circle being lifted

up by two men laying hold of its *radii*, and the exterior being
placed upon the interior axis, the cheeks at the top being at the
same time adjusted to their proper bearing, it turns round very
smoothly, and is perfectly, or at least as to sense, free from any
central shake. This mode of centering is one of the chief excel-
lencies of the instrument. From the use that has been made of
it both years, it seems not to have suffered in the least; and it is
perhaps the only construction that could have answered for a
machine of such magnitude, undergoing so many quick transitions
from place to place, and so often raised to high situations without
any risk of being thereby hurt.

Mahogany Planes under the Instrument.

28. By inspection of the plates, but more particularly the VIIIth,
and the section towards the right hand in the Xth, it will be seen,
that there are three planes of mahogany under the metal parts of
the instrument; namely, that which forms the top of the stand,
which, although a square of about three feet four inches at bottom,
becomes, by the separation of the legs, an octagon at top. In the
centre there is a circular opening of nine inches diameter, the use
of which will appear hereafter. Over the top of the stand lies
another plane of mahogany, likewise an octagon, of somewhat
greater dimensions than the former, with a circular curb running
around it, about half an inch within the planes of its sides. This
octagon hath in its centre an open conical socket of brass, three
inches in diameter; and on four of its opposite sides there are
fixed four strong brass screws, one on each side, which acting
against pieces of brass, inlaid into the opposite sides of the top of
the stand, the octagon plane, with every thing that rests on it,
may thereby be moved in four opposite directions, until the plummet suspended from the centre of the instrument above, is accu-

rately brought to coincide with the point marking the station underneath. The third or uppermost plane of mahogany is in fact a part of the instrument itself, being at all times by screws or otherwise united to it, and carrying the handles whereby it is lifted out for use, or in again into its case, to be transported from place to place. In the middle of this plane or bottom to the instrument, there is another conical brass socket, of three inches and a quarter in diameter, fitted to slip over and turn easily on that in the centre of the octagon underneath. In the brass cover of this socket, there is a very small hole concentric with the instrument, to suffer the thread or wire to pass, which suspends the plummet; and in the view, Pl. VIII. may be seen another small box that contains the thread, with a winch-handle for raising or lowering the plummet, according as the height of the instrument above the station on the ground, or edifice where it stands, may require.

Feet Screws for levelling the Instrument.

29. By attending to the group representing the front elevation of the feet screws, with its side nuts, in the right-hand upward angle of Pl. X. it will appear, that they are slackened, which is always the case before the instrument is levelled, to give room for that operation by the action of the screws. This being done, the side nuts are brought to press gently on the horizontal plate that embraces the whole group, and thereby keeps the instrument as it were united to the mahogany until some fresh adjustment becomes necessary. When the instrument is to be put into its case, then the feet are let down, and by the side nuts the horizontal plate is brought to press strongly on the whole group, whereby it is kept perfectly fast and secure from motion, in carrying from one situation to another.

Blocks of Box Wood and conical Rollers under the Feet Screws.

30. By referring also to Pl. X. It will appear, that directly below each foot there is fixed to the lower surface of the mahogany
a small block of box wood, curvilinear in the direction of its motion. On these three blocks rests the whole weight of the instrument, which nevertheless can be moved circularly on them alone.
But to render the motion perfectly easy, three conical brass rollers,
placed somewhat nearer to the centre, are, by means of their respective springs and regulating screws, brought to act and receive
such a proportion of the weight as it may be necessary to lay upon
them. The head of one of these screws, which give more or less
action to the rollers, may be seen at D in the principal view of the
instrument Pl. VIII. as well as in the plan and section Pl. X.

Screws giving Motion to the whole Instrument.

31. By examining attentively the general view of the instrument, may be seen, in two positions, the great screw with the flat
ivory head, whereby the entire machine received a circular motion.
In one, it is attached to the curbs, as when in use in 1787; in the
other, it is laid upon the mahogany bottom, as was the case the
same year every time it was carried to a new situation. But this
ivory-headed screw having been found to act by jerks in moving
so great a weight, and consequently to be troublesome in adjusting the instrument to the fixed point, or that of commencement
in measuring angles; it was therefore laid aside in 1788, and another apparatus or clamp was adapted for the same purpose. This
last may be seen attached to the curbs, as represented towards the
right hand of Pl. X. It consists of a brass cock, fixed to, and projecting outwards from, the curb of the instrument; which cock is

acted upon by two screws working on the opposite sides against
it, and which are clamped to the curb of the octagon.

Mahogany Balustrade and Cover.

32. The curb, whereon the three feet of the instrument rest,
carries a balustrade of mahogany fitted to receive, on the top thereof, a mahogany cover, no where represented except in the two
sections in Pl. IX. In this cover there are only four small openings (besides that which allows the great vertical axis to pass),
viz. one for each vertical microscope, one for the clamp of the
circle, and one for the socket of the Hook's-joint. The two last
are less than the former. At the same time that this cover effectually secures the circle with its cones from dirt and from accidents, it serves conveniently for laying the Hook's-joint upon, or
any thing that may be constantly wanted near at hand; but more
particularly for placing the lanterns used at night, for reading off
the divisions on the limb of the instrument that come immediately
under the vertical microscopes.

Achromatic Telescopes.

33. Two achromatic telescopes, each of thirty-six inches focal
length, with double object-glasses of two inches and a half aperture, belong to the instrument. They are excellent of their kind,
and are furnished with eye-pieces of different magnifying powers,
for erect as well as inverted vision. The lower telescope lies exactly under the centre of the instrument, and is directed through
one of the openings of the balustrade. Being only used for terrestrial objects, it requires but a small elevation or depression, and
therefore is only supplied with a short axis of seventeen inches in
length, supported by braces attached to the feet. The eye end of

this telescope is purposely made heavier than the object end ; and
resting on an horizontal arm, that is raised or depressed by rack-
work, it is thereby readily brought to bear, and remain very steadily, upon its object. The rack-work may be seen in the view of
the instrument, and also on the left side of the right-hand section
in Pl. IX. But there is a small horizontal motion that can be given
to the right-hand end of the axis of this telescope, which is effected
by means of a handle inserted through the vacancy of the balus-
trades, and placed on a dovetail at E, which could not be shewn
in the plate. Thus the instrument being nicely levelled, the upper
telescope at zero, and likewise on its object, the lower telescope,
by the help of this adjustment, is brought accurately to the same
object, supposed to be the point of commencement, or that from
which angles are measured.

By referring to Pl. VIII. and IX. and likewise to the section
on the left side of Pl. X. It will be seen, that a horizontal bar extends across the top of the vertical axis, supported by two side
braces that spring from the cone, about one-third of its height
above the plane of the instrument. The horizontal bar carries the
Ys or supports, in which the pivots of the upper telescope move.
They are of such height as to permit a semicircle of six inches
radius, attached to the axis of the transit, to pass freely, and consequently the telescope to be directed to the sun or stars in high
elevations, but not to be brought to the zenith. The arc of excess
of the semicircle likewise admits of several degrees of depression
being measured thereon.

Spirit-Levels.

34. The Instrument has two very good spirit-levels, that are
fitted with the several means of adjustment, as is usual in such
cases, the detail of which it is unnecessary here to enter into.

The first, or axis level, because it is only applied on the axis of the telescope, is that whereby it is set horizontal, as in the ordinary transit instrument; and it is likewise used for placing the conical axis truly vertical, so that the instrument may turn round without sensible alteration of the level, previously to observations of the pole-star, or of other heavenly bodies.

The second, or elevation level, is that whereby the telescope is brought to be truly horizontal, when angles of elevation or depression are to be taken. At such times it is suspended on a rod attached to the outside of the telescope, to whose axis of vision the rod, by adjustment, can be made parallel, as will readily be conceived, by observing the representation of these parts in the right-hand section of Pl. IX.

When the angles of elevation or depression to be determined are very small, they are measured by the motion of an horizontal wire in the focus of the eye-glass of the telescope; but, when great, their quantity is measured by the arc of motion of the semicircle, as shewn by its proper horizontal microscope.

The elevation level is likewise made use of for levelling the instrument when horizontal angles only are to be taken, for which purpose it is suspended on two pins, which are seen projecting from the horizontal bar in the plan, and one of them in each of the sections in Pl. IX. This was the ordinary position of the elevation level when the angles of the triangles were observed, and thereby it was easily seen in the course of the operation, whether the instrument had suffered any change to render a re-adjustment necessary.

Lanterns for illuminating the Wires.

35. The axis of the transit telescope is hollow, and in the middle there is placed, at an angle of 45° with the axis of vision, a perfo-

rated elliptical illuminator for throwing light on the wires in night observations. The light is communicated from a small lantern attached to the horizontal bar at its junction with the brace, directly opposite to the end of the axis, which has a bit of thin glass placed before it to prevent dust from entering. There is another such lantern for the lower telescope, not however represented in the plate. As the light given by these lanterns was found to be rather too weak, especially that for the upper telescope, therefore it was customary in practice to illuminate the wires, by holding up frontwise one of those seen in the section in Pl. IX. against the end of the axis of the upper telescope, when directed to the polestar. The same method was used by presenting it obliquely to the object-glass of the lower telescope, when it became necessary to examine whether the intersection of the wires continued without sensible variation on a reverberatory lamp, commonly placed twelve or fifteen miles off, and sometimes even at the great distance of twenty or twenty-four miles.

Lanterns for throwing Light on the Divisions of the Instrument.

96. Besides the two small lanterns for illuminating the wires of the telescopes in night observations, two larger ones may be seen, as already mentioned, standing on the mahogany cover in the section in Pl. IX. used for reading off the divisions of the instrument under the vertical microscopes. The front of one of these is shewn, and the back, or that to which the handle is fixed, of the other. Their narrow sides are presented towards the microscopes, there being in each a silvered reflector of copper at F F ; and opposite to it, at GG, a screen of talc or transparent oiled paper. The light from a wax candle being thrown on the reflectors, and thence back again through the screens, on the divisions of the instrument under the microscopes, these could be very distinctly read off and registered : for the light communi-

Q

cated in this way was very strong, at the same time that the
glare of it, which otherwise would have been disagreeable to the
sight, was removed by passing through the screen.

*Arms projecting from the bell-metal Plate under the Plane of the
Instrument.*

37. By referring to Plates VIII. and IX. but more particularly
the latter, it will be perceived, that there are three flat arms,
strongly fixed by screws to the edge of the circular bell-metal
plate, forming, as has been already mentioned, the basis of the interior vertical axis. These arms, which are also firmly braced to
the feet of the instrument, rise gradually as they project outwards
towards the circumference of the circle, whose radius they exceed
about an inch and a quarter, and their extremities are about an
inch lower than its upper surface. One arm, lying directly over
one of the feet, is that to which are attached the wheels and screw
moved by the Hook's-joint, and also the clamp of the circle, as represented in Pl. X. The other two arms, whereof one lies also over
a foot, and the other directly opposite to it, become thereby a diameter to the circle, having their extremities terminated in a kind
of blunted triangular figure, forming the bases of pedestals whereon stand the vertical microscopes hereafter to be described. The
arms, together with the horizontal bar and braces carrying the
transit telescope, are every where pierced, in order to lessen the
weight, without diminishing the strength of the parts.

Vertical Microscopes.

38. Two vertical microscopes, distinguished A and B, are used
for reading off the divisions on the opposite sides of the circle immediately under them. They are exactly of the same construction, and the chief parts of that marked A are represented in their

real dimensions towards the left hand of Pl. XI.; where, beside
the general, may be seen particular plans of the slides, and also
that of the pedestal, containing within it the gold tongue, with its
axis and screws for adjustment. Next to these plans stand the
elevation and optical lines, shewing the position of the glasses,
with the magnified scale at the bottom.

Each microscope contains two slides, one lying immediately
over the other, their contiguous surfaces being in the focus of the
eye-glasses. The uppermost, or that nearest the eye, is a very
thin plate of brass, to the lower surface of which is attached the
fixed wire, having no other motion than what is necessary for adjustment, by the left-hand screw to its proper dot, as hereafter to
be explained.

The steel slide immediately under the former is made of one
entire piece, of sufficient thickness to permit the micrometer screw,
of about 72 threads in an inch, to be formed of it. To its upper
surface is fixed the moveable wire, which changes its place by the
motion of the micrometer head, seen in the plan and elevation
towards the right hand. The head is divided into 60 equal parts,
each of which represents one second of angular motion of the telescope. By examining the particular plan of this steel slide, it
will be seen, that it is attached by a chain to the spring of a
watch, coiled up in the usual manner, within a small barrel adjacent to it in the frame. By this provision no time whatever is
lost; the smallest motion of the head being instantly shewn, by a
proportionable motion of the wire, to one hand or the other, in
the field of the microscope.

It is necessary to remark, that the whole microscope between
its pillars can be raised or depressed a little more or less, with regard to the plane of the circle, by the help of two steel levers,
seen one on each side of the elevation, which for that purpose are
applied in the holes represented above and below the projecting

plate that unites the tops of the pillars. By means of this motion, distinctness is obtained at the wires; and by the motion of the proper screw of the object lens, which necessarily follows that given to the whole microscope, the scale is so adjusted as that fifteen revolutions of the head shall move the wire over fifteen minutes, or one grand division, on the limb, equal to nine hundred seconds, each degree on the circle being only divided into four parts. This operation being delicate, requires great patience and many repetitions, before the purpose can be exactly, or even nearly, effected: for at the same time that the fixed wire must bisect the dot on the gold tongue, the moveable wire must also bisect the dot at 180° on the limb, as well as the first notch in the magnified scale at the bottom of the plate, where the minutes in the field of the microscope are represented in the proportion of between fifteen and sixteen to one, as painted on the eye of the observer. In this adjustment there is yet another circumstance to be attended to, which is, that sixty on the micrometer head should stand nearly vertical, so as to be conveniently seen. A few seconds of inclination to one side or the other are of no moment, because the dart or index being brought to that position, whatever it may be, must at all times remain there without alteration, unless some derangement that may have happened to the instrument, in transporting from one place to another, should have rendered a fresh adjustment necessary. But if, when the wires coincide with their respective dots and the first notch, sixty on the micrometer head should happen to be underneath, or so far over from the vertex on either side as to be seen with difficulty, then the gold tongue must be moved a little by means of the capstan-headed screws, which act against each other on the opposite extremities of its axis. Thus, by repeated trials, the wished-for object will at length be effected, that is to say, sixty, to which the dart is to be set, will stand in a place easily seen. But it is not to be expected, that each microscope will give just nine hundred seconds for the run of fifteen minutes. Without great loss of time this cannot be done; besides that two observers, of different sights, will adjust the microscopes differently. Accordingly, in 1787, after many trials of the runs in measuring fifteen minutes on the different parts of the limb, microscope A was found to give only 896″, while B gave at a medium 901″. But in 1788, microscope A gave 900″, while B gave no more than 894″. These differences were of course registered and allowed for in the estimation of the angles for computation, whereby any difference between them almost wholly disappeared.

The gold tongue, which is extremely thin, applies very closely to the surface of the circle. In the plan it is supposed to be seen through a thin plate of brass, covering the whole pedestal, and also through a small square plate lying over the former, and fastened to it by three screws. In the under side of this last, there is a cavity for the projecting part of the tongue. This contrivance of the tongue with its dot was to guard against any error that might arise from accidental motion given to the instrument between one observation and another, which from this precaution could never happen, without being immediately discovered; for the wires being adjusted to their dots under the microscopes respectively, if the instrument be then turned round 180°, the wires will reciprocally bisect the dots that were originally opposite to them, and thereby shew, that they are accurately in the diameter of the circle; and so on with regard to any other dots whatever. Hence this becomes the most severe mode of trying the justness of the divisions of the instrument.

Manner of reading off Angles with the Microscopes.

39. By attending to the magnified scale at the bottom of the plate, it will appear, that the dot on the gold tongue, which is

here inverted, is about one minute to the left of zero, and also of the first notch, with which the moveable wire alone coincides. Now it will easily be conceived, from what has been said in this description, how readily, as well as accurately, any observation of an angle can be read off with such an instrument; for the degrees and quarters, that is to say, the 15′, 30′, or 45′, being seen with the naked eye, and registered, the value of the fractional space between zero and the last past grand division, seen in the field of the microscope, is obtained by turning the micrometer head until the moveable wire bisects the dot at that grand division. The number of notches towards the right hand passed over, on the scale, equal to so many revolutions of the head, are the number of minutes, always less than 15′, to be added. If there be no odd seconds, the dart will then stand at 60 on the head; but, if any number of seconds are to be added, the dart will shew, by its position with regard to 60, what that number is. Thus, by adding the parts together, the measure of the total angle is obtained.

The construction, adjustment, and application of these vertical microscopes have been given more fully, because they form a most essential part of the Instrument: for the fixed wire constantly remaining on its dot, the fractional space may be repeatedly measured many times over, if necessary, and a mean result may then be taken. But it rarely happens that two observers, reading off with the opposite microscopes, differ more than half a second from each other at the very first reading. If time therefore permits, and the circumstances of the weather should also be favourable for repeating the observation with the telescope, it is sufficiently obvious to what a wonderful degree of accuracy the measure of angles may in this way be obtained.

Horizontal Microscopes.

40. Besides the two vertical microscopes, applied in the manner that has been described to the measurement of the fractional space in horizontal angles, there is yet another to be mentioned, which is placed horizontally on the bar that carries the transit telescope, and is directed to the divisions on the semicircle attached to its axis, for the measurement of angles of elevation or depression, as has already been taken notice of. This microscope, which is of the same construction with the others, but larger, being upwards of nine inches in length, is represented in its full dimension in Pl. XI. It has, like the others, a slide made of steel, of such thickness as to permit the micrometer screw to be formed of it; and it carries a vertical wire placed in the focus of the eye-glasses, in which position it is moved parallel to itself from left to right, by turning the micrometer head. This slide is also attached to a watch spring, which acts in a contrary direction to the head, as in other microscopes of this sort.

Each degree of the semicircle being divided into two parts, or 30′, and one revolution of the micrometer head moving the wire in the field of the microscope 3′; therefore in 10 revolutions it changes its place half a degree, or 30′, which are shewn by a scale of 10 notches in the upper part of the field of the microscope, and also represented towards the top of the Plate. Each notch corresponds to 3 minutes or 180 seconds, and the head being divided into 3 minutes, and each minute into twelve equal parts, therefore each part is of the value of five seconds.

Concerning the Semicircle.

41. With regard to the semicircle, which has been repeatedly mentioned in the course of this description, it is yet necessary to make some remarks; and particularly to shew how, by its means,

the axis of vision of the telescope, when adjusted, is brought and
kept truly horizontal, which is effected in the following manner.

On the opposite sides of the horizontal bar that carries the telescope there are fixed four small, but finely polished bell-metal
planes, two on each side, on the right and left of the top of the
vertical axis, in such a manner as that the surfaces of the two on
either side are directed to, or in the same plane with, the centre of
the axis of the telescope. These planes will be best conceived by
observing attentively the top of the vertical axis in the section towards the right hand of Plate IX. On the edge of the semicircle
may likewise be seen a moveable clamp, easily made to slip, with
the hand only, around its circumference, and it carries with it a
very fine steel screw. When the semicircle is towards the left
hand of the telescope, which is its ordinary position, the point of
the steel screw rests, or may be made to rest, perpendicularly on
the surface of the plane that is on the left of the vertical axis. But
when the telescope is inverted in its Ys, or turned upside down, as
is the case in adjusting the line of collimation, the semicircle being
then on the right of the telescope, and the clamp necessarily
brought down, the point of the steel screw accordingly rests perpendicularly on the surface of the plane to the right of the vertical
axis. Thus it will be readily conceived, that in adjusting the
telescope by the level for elevations, which is then constantly suspended on its proper rod, parallel to the axis of vision, the action
of the steel screw on the bell-metal plane serves not only for the
adjustment of the telescope in a truly horizontal position, for angles
of elevation or depression, by the motion of a wire in the focus of
its eye-glass, in the manner hereafter to be described, but also to
keep it in that position, by the superior weight of the eye end,
rendered so on purpose. By the same means the telescope remains
steadily on any object that it may be directed to for intersection,
whether above or below the plane of the horizon.

Eye-glasses of the Telescopes, and Mechanism of the Wires in their Foci.

49. It has been already mentioned, that the telescopes of the instrument are furnished with eye-glasses of different magnifying powers for erect and inverted vision, six for each telescope, as follows, *viz.*

	Erect vision.		Inverted vision.	
	No.	Power.	No.	Power.
For the lower telescope,	1.	58.	1.	43.
	2.	88.	2.	59.
	3.	117.	3.	87.
For the upper telescope,	1.	54.	1.	40.
	2.	81.	2.	55.
	3.	108.	3.	80.

With regard to these eye-glasses, it is only necessary here to mention, that those of the least magnifying powers were found both in day and night observations to answer the best.

In the focus of the eye-glass of the lower telescope there are only two wires crossing each other in acute angles, which are vertical, instead of being placed at right angles, horizontally and vertically, as was the ancient method. Since the lower telescope never moves through more than a few degrees of a vertical arc, the wires require little or no adjustment. Nevertheless this was provided for, by allowing room for a small circular motion of the end-piece, which, when adjusted, is then fastened by its proper screws, and never afterwards needs any alteration.

By referring to the middle part of Plate XI. two representations of the eye end of the upper telescope will be seen, with the eye-piece removed. Five wires are shewn in this end, namely, two that intersect each other in acute angles, similarly to those

R

in the lower telescope ; and three that lie horizontally or parallel
to each other. Four of these, *viz.* the two that form the acute
angles, and the two extreme horizontal wires, are fixed in the
focus of the eye-glasses to the farther surface of a thin brass slide,
supposed to be seen through the outward brass, and therefore
shaded more dark than the rest. This slide, as will be conceived,
lies nearest the eye, and is moveable from right to left, and, *vice
versâ*, horizontally, for the adjustment of the line of collimation,
by the insertion of a small mill-head key, on a square pin fitted to
receive it, and secured by a socket on the right-hand side. The
fifth or middlemost horizontal wire is attached to the nearest surface of a steel slide, that lies contiguously to, but beyond the
former. It is made of one entire thick piece, like those of the
microscopes, to permit the micrometer screw to be formed of it ;
and it is represented in the uppermost figure attached to a watch
spring coiled up in the usual manner.

By the motion of the micrometer head, the slide, and with it
the wire, moves upwards or downwards in the field of the telescope, a space equal to half the distance of the extreme wires from
each other. This motion above or below the central point, which
was made to correspond with the acute intersection of the wires
placed in the axis of vision of the telescope, is performed in ten
revolutions of the head, as denoted by the motion of the dart, ten
divisions upwards or downwards, in the narrow groove seen at
the top of the figure.

Now, by the means of this piece of mechanism in the eye-end
of the telescope, it will appear sufficiently obvious, that small
angles of elevation or depression may be determined with great
accuracy, when the value of a certain number of revolutions and
parts (the circumference of the head being divided into 100) have
been once ascertained by repeated observations of the altitude of
any well-defined object taken by the semicircle. Thus it was

found, by experiment, that $7\frac{11}{100}$ revolutions of the micrometer
head were equal to an angle of elevation or depression of 10′ 59″
or 659″, on the semicircle. Whence it follows, that one revolution raises or depresses the wire above or below the central point
1′ 24″.8134, or a little more than 84″81. And hence a motion of
one division on the head raises or depresses the wire nearly $\frac{11}{100}$
of a second.

In this manner were determined the reciprocal elevations or
depressions of the several stations of the series of triangles with
regard to each other.

By observing attentively the four screws represented in the outward end of the telescope, a dotted groove will be seen under the
head of each. And in the uppermost figure there appears a flat
brass ring, soldered to the inside of the tube about half an inch
from the outward end, which carries on its surface four studs to
receive the lower extremities of the four screws. Thus the grooves
allow room for a small circular motion to be given to the end-
piece for the vertical adjustment of the fork of the wires, those
that are horizontal being by construction at right angles with it.
This being done, the screws are made very fast in the studs below,
and thereby the whole machinery of the end-piece is rendered
perfectly firm and secure.

There remains yet one piece more to be barely mentioned. It
is the prism eye-tube, represented by dotted lines towards the
right-hand side of Plate XI. as attached to the eye end of the
transit telescope, instead of the common eye-piece with two con-
vex glasses. In leaning over our instrument to observe the pole-
star, highly elevated in these latitudes, the body is necessarily
thrown into an inconvenient fatiguing posture, whereby some risk
is run of deranging the instrument, and consequently of making
the observations less accurately than when the observer can look
directly forward, without bending the body so much. For this

purpose, Mr. Ramsden promised to supply the prism tube in 1787; but it was not obtained till 1788, by which time Mr. Dalby had accustomed himself to observe very well without it, so that it was never used.

By employing this piece, light is no doubt lost ; because the image passes through more glasses before it reaches the eye, than when the common eye-piece is used. But for observations of stars nearer the zenith than the pole-star is in our latitudes, it would be indispensably necessary. It would likewise be advantageously used in looking at the meridian sun in summer, for which purpose it is furnished with dark glasses, placed in a slide moved by rack-work, as may be seen from inspection of the plate. They consist of three prisms, laid close to each other, so as to form, when thus assembled, a parallelopiped. Here the green prism stands nearest to the eye, a dark one farthest from it, and between the two, one of white flint glass, for correction of the refraction which would otherwise take place. It will easily be conceived, from the disposition of the prisms, that the darkest medium is here towards the left ; and that it becomes gradually lighter towards the right hand, where a void part in the frame is brought into the field when the stars are observed ; or when, from the circumstances of the weather, it may be unnecessary to screen the eye from the sun's rays.

General Management of the Instrument for Observation.

43. When the instrument is used on the ground, it is covered from the weather, under a circular tent, eight feet in diameter. Four short piles, hooped and shod with iron, are driven into the earth, and their heads levelled, by laying across from one to the other a mahogany straight ruler, having a spirit level attached to one side of it. The feet of the stand being then placed on piles,

are firmly fastened to them by means of long square-headed screws, only one of which may be seen in the view of the instrument, belonging to that foot which stands nearest the eye. By working with the four screws fixed in the octagonal mahogany plane, the plummet suspended from the centre of the instrument is brought accurately over the point on the ground that marks the station. The screws of the feet, with the side nuts appertaining to them, are then slackened, to give sufficient room for the adjustment of the instrument, which by them is brought to be level.

Adjustment of the Axis Level.

44. The axis of the upper or transit telescope being brought over any one of the feet, and the circle being clamped, hang the axis level on the pivots or *ansæ* of the telescope, and bring the bubble to the two indexes; then reverse the level, that is, turn it end for end, and note the difference. Bisect this difference, one half by the level's proper adjusting screw, and the other half by that foot-screw only which is in a line with the axis. This operation being repeated until the difference wholly vanishes, the level will be truly adjusted; that is to say, the bubble will rest between the same points in both positions.

Adjustment of the Elevation Level.

45. This level being suspended on the rod attached to the outside of the transit telescope, screw the erect eye-tube on, to make that end preponderate. Adjust the bubble to the indexes by the steel finger-screw at the tail of the semicircle's clamp. Reverse the level, and note the difference. Then bisect that difference, and correct one half by the finger screw, and the other half by the proper adjusting screw under the level, and so on repeatedly until

the difference wholly vanishes. The level may then be hung on the two pins that project from the horizontal bar which carries the telescope, where, being parallel to the axis level, it will shew when that is removed (as is commonly the case when terrestrial objects only are observed) whether the plane of the instrument suffers any alteration. If this should have happened, the level on the horizontal bar is at all times sufficient to correct it.

To set the vertical Axis perpendicular.

46. This may be done by either level, but best with the axis level, which being suspended on its pivots, must be brought parallel with two of the feet of the instrument; and by the screws of these two feet, the bubble is to be brought between its indexes. The circle being then turned round 180°, if the bubble changes its place, half the difference is to be corrected by one of the feet-screws, and the other half by two capstan-headed screws, that act against each other, under and belonging to one of the Ys or supports, in which the pivots rest. When the bubble is found to be just in these two positions, turn the circle 90°, which will necessarily bring the axis over the third foot of the instrument. Then correct any error there may be by that foot screw. In this manner the circle will be made to revolve again and again, without any alteration whatever of the bubble, which shews that the vertical axis is then truly perpendicular to the horizon.

To make the Line of Collimation in the Telescope at right Angles with the transverse Axis.

47. The pivots resting in their Ys, direct the telescope to some distant well-defined object, and let the circle be clamped. Then reverse the axis, that is, turn the telescope upside down. If the

intersection of the wires does not coincide with the object in both
positions, half the difference must be corrected by the motion of
the circle with the Hook's-joint, and the other half by the motion
of the brass slide in the eye end of the telescope, by applying the
milled-head key in the small socket, seen on the right-hand side
in Plate XI.; and so repeatedly until the difference wholly dis-
appears.

*To set the Rod on which the Elevation Level hangs parallel to the Line
of Collimation.*

48. The vertical axis being supposed to be nearly vertical, hang
the level on its rod, and rectify the bubble by the finger screw of
the clamp. Set the horizontal wire on the steel slide, to intersect
the centre of the oblique wires, and place the dart or index at zero
on the micrometer head. Then observe some distant distinct object covered by the horizontal wire. Take off the level, and turn
the telescope upside down ; and bring the wire upon, or nearly
upon, the same object : then hang the level on again. Now, if
the level be not right, rectify it by the finger screw at the tail of
the clamp. If the telescope does not now accurately cover the
same object as in the former position, bisect the difference by the
finger screw of the clamp, and then rectify the bubble by the
capstan-nuts under one end of the rod. Repeat this operation
until the level is right, when the telescope shews the same objects
in both positions, and thereby the rod will be brought parallel in
altitude to the line of collimation or axis of vision.

The adjustments of the microscopes having been already sufficiently explained, in giving the description of the essential parts
of the instrument, it is unnecessary here to repeat them.

Of the Weight of the Instrument, and Mode of transporting it from Place to Place.

49. The instrument, whose description and uses we have here attempted to give in a general way, without reference to its minute parts, by a multitude of different characters, weighed in the whole about 800lbs. It is contained in two deal boxes; one of a circular form for the body of the instrument; and the other of an oblong-square figure, for the transit telescope. Within this last box there is one of mahogany, that holds all the smaller parts of the apparatus. The stand, steps, stools, pullies, ropes, tent, and canopy for the scaffold, &c. &c. weighed at least as much more. The whole attirail was transported from place to place, in a four-wheeled spring carriage, drawn by two, and sometimes by four horses. The carriage part, originally that of a crane-necked phaeton, was presented, with his usual liberality, by Sir Joseph Banks; and upon it was built a kind of caravan, covered with painted oil-cloth, whereby every thing within was kept dry and secure.

Description of various Articles of Machinery made Use of in the Tri-gonometrical Operation referred to in Plate XII.

Portable Scaffold.

50. In the account of the measurement of the base on Houn-slow Heath, we have shewn that the surface of that remarkable plain is not elevated more than fifty or sixty feet above the mean level of the sea. From this small elevation, and the circumstance of its being surrounded, almost on every side, with lofty trees, it was from the beginning sufficiently obvious, that, in order to be

[131]

enabled to make the observations of the collateral stations from the extremities of the base, it would be absolutely necessary to raise the instrument, by some means or other, to a considerable height above the ground. For this purpose the portable scaffold, whose plan and elevation are represented on the left-hand side of Plate XII. was constructed. It consisted, as may be seen, of an inward scaffold for supporting the instrument, and an outward one for the observers, wholly free and independent of each other, the platforms of both being framed about thirty-two feet above the lower ends of the scantlings which rest on the ground. These being made of squared deal, and the several parts being bolted and screwed together with many iron screws secured by nuts, the whole could be readily taken to pieces, carried in a waggon (for which it made a complete load), and replaced again in any new situation. This scaffold answered very well the purpose for which it was intended; for the step-ladders, or stairs leading to the platform, being attached to the outward frame, the inward one that carried the instrument remained undisturbed by the motion of those who went up and down, or walked around the top. The silk thread, that suspended the plummet, was secured from the effects of the wind by a sort of funnel or trunk, composed of three deals (one side being left open), and so contrived as to be easily turned round to any quarter of the heavens, whereby the open side was always presented to leeward. The instrument was covered from the weather by a canvas canopy, about seven feet square, to which side walls could be hooked, for screening it from the wind, as occasion might require. By referring to the elevation it will be seen, that the scaffolds, both outward and inward, might be divided horizontally into two parts, so as to permit the uppermost half alone to be used, when it became unnecessary to raise the instrument to a greater height than fifteen or sixteen feet above the ground. The whole together was never made use

S

of, except at the two extremities of the Hounslow Heath base.
The uppermost half was applied at three of the stations only,
namely, St. Ann's Hill, Botley Hill, and Padlesworth near Dover.

Tripod Ladder.

51. Next to the scaffold the Plate represents, in plan and section, a tripod ladder, about thirty-five feet in height. It carries
on its top a globe lamp, of about one foot in diameter, in which
was used a simple Argand's burner, of a large size, made for that
purpose. The lamp being removed, a socket for a white light
might occasionally be substituted in its place; or (as was the case
when we observed the station at King's Arbour from St. Ann's
Hill) a flag-staff might be added at the top, which was secured in
a truly vertical position, by braces fixed to the legs of the ladder
underneath. It will be readily conceived, that by a contrivance
of this sort a white light could be raised to a considerable height
above the ground, if the circumstances at any time had rendered
such elevation necessary; and that it could, by the help of a
heavy plummet, be always placed in a truly vertical position over
the point on the ground marking the station. The globe lamp
was found to answer very well for short distances, of six or eight
miles, when the weather was favourable; but it could not be depended upon in observations of distances that were considerably .
greater.

Common Flag-staff.

52. After the tripod ladder, comes in the Plate the plan and
elevation of a common flag-staff with its braces, carrying likewise
two reverberatory lamps. These two were attached to the same
iron bar, at the distance of three feet from each other. They

had concave copper reflectors, nine inches in diameter, extremely
well polished and silvered. They were intended at first for experiments near London, and were very well seen at the distance
of fifteen or sixteen miles. To secure us from any uncertainty
that might have arisen, by mistaking other lights for our own,
one lamp was placed over the other. But when we came afterwards to be better acquainted with the appearance of these lamps,
that precaution was found to be entirely unnecessary; wherefore
single reverberatories were provided, with *specula* of ten inches
diameter, and they were supplied with still larger burners, which
could be seen at the distance of twenty or twenty-four miles. But
here it is proper to remark, that these lamps must be carefully
watched, especially in exposed windy situations; for if the cotton
be drawn out a little too far, they are apt to smoke, whereby the
front glass becomes obscure, and therefore must be wiped frequently. They are easily turned on the posts that support them;
and were, by the help of a telescope laid on one side, parallel to
the axis of the rays (for which a contrivance was provided in the
tin work) accurately presented towards the station occupied by
the instrument at the time from whence they were to be observed.
There was constantly one of these lamps, and sometimes two, at
two different stations, burning each night, when we were making
observations of the pole-star, or white lights, of short duration,
placed at other distant stations.

Tripod for White Lights.

59. Next after the flag-staff (whereon a socket for white lights
could likewise be placed, when the flag itself was removed) is represented a small tripod intended for white lights only. The
same socket that fitted the top of the flag-staff, or lamp-post,
could be applied to the tripod, by the help of three small sockets

S s

soldered for that particular purpose to the sides of the principal
one. Deal rods, of five or six feet in height, or hazels cut from the
nearest hedge, served as the legs of this stand. The sockets themselves were made of copper, because those of iron would have been
dissolved by the sulphur ; and the upper part, which was only an
inch, or an inch and an half, in height, was square or round, according to the figure of the boxes containing the composition, sometimes of one kind, and sometimes of the other. These white-light
tripods, being readily placed, by the help of a plummet, over the
point marking the station, were found to be very convenient on
the top of an open hill, or on the leads of a church steeple, as the
person attending them could easily light the box with the portfire, without the aid of a ladder.

Portable Crane.

54. On the right-hand side of the plate is represented, in plan
and section, and by a larger scale than the others, a portable crane
for weighing up the instrument to the tops of such towers, church
steeples, or other buildings, as became stations In the series of
triangles It was constructed in the Tower of London, and answered very well the purpose for which it was intended, although
it might still be improved. Before we were supplied with this
crane, we made shift, by the help of a long beam, and a moveable
trestle by way of fulcrum for it to rest upon, to get the instrument
up to the top of its own proper scaffold, and one that was still
higher, erected over the transit-room of the Royal Observatory
at Greenwich.

Distinction of the Stations.

55. In the course of the trigonometrical operation, the centre of
the instrument has constantly been brought, even almost to mathe-

matical exactness, over the precise point marking the station, whereby reductions to the centre, on account of eccentricity, have been avoided ; and the stations have been distinguished, as far as possible, by permanent marks, in such a manner, that, while these remain, the centre of this or any other instrument may be again brought into the same vertical line. By these means our recent observations may be repeated on any future occasion, and connected with others, which it is to be hoped will be made hereafter : for this operation, the first of its kind in Britain, should only be considered as the foundation or commencement of a series of others, which by degrees will be carried to the remotest parts of the Island.

The stations may be distinguished into two sets. First, those which are permanently marked by pipes sunk in the earth; and, secondly, those where the instrument was elevated to the top of some tower, church steeple, or other building. The plans of the platforms of this last set are given in Plate XIII. along with such dimensions as are necessary to shew, with regard to the side walls, the precise spot over which the centre of the instrument was placed. As often as was possible, these situations were further defined, by means of concentric circles described on the leads.

The stations of the first set, marked with pipes, are fourteen in number, viz.

Hampton Poorhouse, King's Arbour,	} the extremities of Hounslow Heath base.
St. Ann's Hill, -	about the middle on the east edge.
Hundred Acres, -	near the west end of the garden. *
Norwood, - -	towards the Croydon end of the heights.
Botley Hill, - -	{ in a field belonging to Limpsfield Lodge Farm.

* This spot has since been inclosed, and the pipe is entirely gone.

Wrotham Hill, - in a field belonging to Mr. Johnston.

Hollingborn Hill, - in a field belonging to Mr. Duppa.

Fairlight Down, - { 947 feet southward from the Windmill, which makes with Fairlight Church, an angle of 105° 59′ 20″.

Ruckinge, - -
High Nook, - - } the extremities of the base of verification.

Allington Knoll, - { an artificial mount belonging to Sir John Honeywood.

Padlesworth, { eastward from the Church, in the Broom-field belonging to Mr. Brockman.

Folkstone Turnpike - westward from the Public-house

The stations of the second set, where the instrument was elevated on buildings, are nine in number, viz.

Hanger-hill Tower.

Transit-room of Greenwich Royal Observatory.

North-west turret of Severndroog Castle, on Shooter's Hill.

Swingfield Church Steeple.

North turret of the Keep of Dover Castle.

Lydd Steeple.

Tenterden Steeple.

Goudhurst Steeple.

Frant Steeple.

Excess of the Angles of Spherical above those of Plane Triangles.

56. Since the sum of the three angles of a spherical triangle is greater than' two right angles, it follows, that the sum of the three observed angles of each of the following triangles ought to exceed 180°. The fourth column contains the computed excess, or what should have been given by observation, and the fifth, the error in the observed sum.

It had been at first proposed to multiply the observations as much

---

as possible, and particularly by successively changing the zero of the instrument to new points, to measure the same angles on different parts of the circle, so as to subdivide any errors that might arise from inaccuracy of division, or shake at the centre. This principle, perfectly good in theory, and which was adhered to as far as the circumstances would permit, was nevertheless found, on many occasions, to be impossible in practice, without sacrificing much more time than we could afford, consistently with the engagements entered into with the French Gentlemen, for the co-operation on the Coast. At particular times, especially in hot weather, there was such a tremulous motion or boiling in the air, that it was only during a very short space, chiefly in the mornings and evenings, that the objects were sufficiently distinct to be observed with accuracy. So difficult it is to do any thing perfectly good in this way, that a whole day has frequently been spent, after watching with anxious care, in obtaining a single one that was perfectly satisfactory! At such times as these it would have been absurd to have attempted to change the zero, which always rendered it necessary to re-adjust the instrument by its levels.

In very favourable circumstances of the weather a good observation by day is preferable to one by the white lights at night; because, in the first case, the observer has time at his leisure nicely to bisect a fine flag-staff, and repeatedly to read off the angle; whereas, in the short duration of the burning of the light, he is somewhat hurried, from the fear of losing some of the lights at other distant stations, if two of them happened to come together, which now and then they did, from the irregularity of the rates of the watches of the artillery-men attending at the different stations. It was, however, by the assistance of the white lights only, that the most distant stations could be rendered visible; and there cannot be a doubt that, in great trigonometrical operations of this sort, they will be universally adopted hereafter.

Sometimes an observation has been entirely lost, or at least that which had been obtained was not thought a very good one. In such cases, a blank has been left in the column of observed angles, and also in that expressing the error. But no bad consequence has arisen on that account, there being always such other checks from the collateral stations, as to leave nothing doubtful.

The quantity by which the sum of the three observed angles of spherical triangles should have exceeded 180° was found as follows.

Because the excess of the three angles of a spherical triangle above 180° × earth's radius = its area, therefore $\frac{\text{Area}}{\text{earth's rad.}}$ = excess above 180° in seconds, if the area and radius are taken in seconds. Now, 60859.1 fathoms being = 1° nearly, supposing the earth to be a sphere, we get the log. of the feet in a second = 2.0061743, and twice this, or 4.0123486 is the log. of the square feet in a square second. Therefore log. area in feet — 4.0123486 = log. area in seconds; and the log. of the earth's radius in seconds being 5.3144251, we have log. area in feet — 4.0123486 — 5.3144251 = log. area in feet — 9.3267737 = log. excess in seconds; that is to say, *from the logarithm of the area of the triangle taken as a plane one, in feet, subtract the constant logarithm 9.3267737, and the remainder is the logarithm of the excess above 180° in seconds nearly.*

Calculation of the Triangles, Plate XIV.

37. Base on Hounslow Heath measured with glass rods (17), - - - - -   27404.01 Feet.

By the re-measurement, in 1791, with a steel chain,   27404.32

Mean length -   27404.2

No. of triangles.	Names of the stations.	Observed Angles.	Spheri-cal excess.	Diff. of error.	Angles corrected for calculation.	Distances.
I.	Hanger Hill Tower	41 2 32			41 2 34	Fet.
	Hampton Poorhouse	67 55 39			67 55 39	
	King's Arbour	70 1 48			70 1 47	
		179 59 59	0.29	−1 29		
	The Base between Hampton Poorhouse and King's Arbour				— — —	27404.8
	Hanger Hill Tower from { Hampton Poorhouse				— — —	3*460.4
	{ King's Arbour				— — —	37011.9
II.	St. Ann's Hill	44 18 51.5			44 18 51.5	
	Hampton Poorhouse	61 26 33.1			61 26 33 5	
	King's Arbour	74 14 35			74 14 35	
		179 59 59.6	0.21	−0.61		
	St. Ann's Hill from { Hampton Poorhouse				— — —	37753.6
	{ King's Arbour				— — —	34455.8

Hence, in the quadrilateral formed by *Hampton Poorhouse*, *King's Arbour*, *Hanger Hill Tower*, and *St. Ann's Hill*, making use of the two obtuse angles, as contained within their respective known sides, we have for the mean distance of the points of the acute angles at Hanger Hill Tower and St. Ann's Hill, expressed by a dotted line in the plan of the triangles, 68895.8 feet.

III.	Wardrobe Tower of Windsor Castle	— — —			58 9 58.5	
	King's Arbour	62 40 27.5			62 40 27 5	
	St. Ann's Hill	59 9 14			59 9 14	
			0.25			
	Windsor Castle from { King's Arbour				— — —	34819
	{ St. Ann's Hill				— — —	36032
IV.	Hundred Acres	53 58 35.75			53 58 36.5	
	Hanger-hill Tower	68 24 44			68 24 44	
	St. Ann's Hill	57 36 39.5			57 36 39.5	
		179 59 59.25	1.08	−1.83		
	Hundred Acres from { Hanger Hill Tower				— — —	71932 8
	{ St. Ann's Hill				— — —	79400.7

T

No. of triangles.	Names of the stations.	Observed angles.	Spheri-cal excess.	Diff. or error.	Angles corrected for calculation.	Distances.
V.	Severndroog Castle, Shooter's Hill	53 31 10	«	"	53 31 9.75	Feet.
	Hanger Hill Tower	55 53 44.3			55 53 44	
	Hundred Acres	70 35 6.75			70 35 6.25	
		180 0 1.05	1.18	—0.13		
	Severndroog Castle from { Hanger Hill Tower				— — —	84375
	Hundred Acres				— — —	74076.2
VI.	Norwood	107 53 37			107 53 35.75	
	Hanger Hill Tower	26 12 22.5			26 12 23	
	Severndroog Castle	45 54 1.5			45 54 1.25	
		180 0 1	0.44	+0.56		
	Norwood from { Hanger Hill Tower				— — —	63672.1
	Severndroog Castle				— — —	39154.4
VII.	Norwood	88 5 58			88 5 58.07	
	Hanger Hill Tower	29 41 10.75			29 41 11	
	Hundred Acres	— — —			62 12 40.93	
			0.53			
	Norwood from Hundred Acres				— — —	35642.5
VIII.	Transit Room, Greenwich Observatory	111 56 50			111 56 50	
	Severndroog Castle	47 48 14			47 48 13	
	Norwood	20 14 58			20 14 57	
		180 0 2	0.1	+1.9		
	Greenwich Observatory from { Severndroog Castle				— — —	146103
	Norwood				— — —	31273.9
IX.	Botley Hill	74 37 12.5			74 37 18	
	Hundred Acres	66 0 56.2			66 0 56	
	Severndroog Castle	39 21 46.25			39 21 46	
		179 59 59.95	0.78	—0.83		
	Botley Hill from { Hundred Acres				— — —	48725.8
	Severndroog Castle				— — —	70193.4
X.	Wrotham Hill	54 25 1			54 25 1.25	
	Botley Hill	67 53 22			67 53 10.25	
	Severndroog Castle	57 41 49			57 41 48.5	
		180 0 1	1.12	—01.2		
	Wrotham Hill from { Botley Hill				— — —	74951.7
	Severndroog Castle				— — —	29060.6

No. of triangles.	Names of the stations.	Observed angles.	Spherical excess.	Diff. or error.	Angles corrected for calculation.	Distances.
XI.	Frant - - - Botley Hill - - Wrotham Hill -	50 19 19 57 15 11.25 72 25 31.2			50 19 18 57 15 11 72 25 31	Feet,
		180 0 1.45	1.5	+0 15		
	Frant from { Botley Hill Wrotham Hill				— — — — — —	90362.4 79722
XII.	Hollingborn Hill - Wrotham Hill - Frant - - -	— — — 84 12 24.5 48 28 37.5			47 18 59 84 12 23.5 48 28 37.5	
			1.52			
	Hollingborn Hill from { Wrotham Hill Frant				— — — — — —	81195 107835.7
XIII.	Fairlight Down - Frant - - - Hollingborn Hill -	48 25 55.5 79 23 3 — — —			48 25 55 70 23 2 52 11 3	
			2.85			
	Fairlight Down from { Frant Hollingborn Hill				— — — — — —	113926 141744.4

Thus far the computations have been made from the base on Hounslow Heath (27404.2 feet). We shall now proceed to the base of verification on Romney Marsh, by the fewest triangles which present themselves; but it may be necessary to premise what follows respecting the *data*.

As that part of the earth's surface to which the operation is confined, has been considered as a plane, it is evident that the mode of correcting the angles for computation must, in some degree, have been arbitrary; and therefore it follows, that in reducing the observed angles to those of plane triangles, each angle may be varied to certain limits; and consequently the opposite sides may be varied to certain limits also; but it is evident, that the means of the extreme results, obtained in this manner, must be very near

T 2

the truth, and perhaps will be considered more accurate than the distances deduced from a single correction of the same angles. Accordingly, if we vary the angles (in reducing them to 180°), from Hounslow Heath, to the XIII. triangle, so as to produce the greatest and least lengths of the opposite sides, we shall have 141746 feet, nearly, for the mean distance of Hollingborn Hill from Fairlight Down; which, however, is only about 1½ feet more than the distance in the XIII. triangle.

The computation may be carried on to the base of verification by means of the three following triangles; and the XXIII. and XXIV.

	Angles observed.	For computation.
Hollingborn Hill	48 56 31¼	48 56 31
Allington Knoll	88 25 43	88 25 42
Fairlight Down	- -	42 37 47
Allington Knoll	32 59 22½	32 59 22½
Lydd -	225 42 0¼	125 42 0
Fairlight Down	- -	21 18 37½
Ruckinge	- -	103 18 8
Allington Knoll	- -	57 38 33.4
Lydd -	- -	19 3 18.6

derived from the XXIII and XXIV.

Those triangles, with 141746 feet (Hollingborn from Fairlight), give 41534.4, for the distance of Lydd from Ruckinge; hence, from the XXIII. triangle, the base of verification is found to be 28533.9 feet: which is about 28 inches short of the measurement.

For the distance of Hollingborn Hill from Fairlight Down, deduced from the measured base on Romney Marsh.—As 28533.9 : 28535.66 (the measured base) : : 141746 : 141758 feet, the distance required: the mean of this, and 141746 is 141752 feet.

From this mean distance, all the sides of the remaining triangles
in the principal series are derived. And it has not been thought
necessary to alter any of the angles, as originally corrected for
computation, because of the trifling variations which would consequently arise in the distances on that account.

We should have computed the distances in the vicinity, and to
the eastward of Romney Marsh, from the base of verification
only, but there are reasons to suppose that it was not measured so
accurately as the other on Hounslow Heath.

No of triangls.	Names of the stations.	Observed angles.	Spheri-cal excess.	Diff. or error.	Angles corrected for calculation.	Distances.
XIV.	Goudhurst - - Botley Hill - - Wrotham Hill -	35 16 31.5 40 4 45 104 28 46	´	´	35 16 34.5 40 4 48 104 38 43.5	Feet.
		179 59 58.5	1.35	—1.85		
	Goudhurst from { Botley Hill Wrotham Hill				— — — — — —	121813 5 81000.2
XV.	Goudhurst - - Frant - Wrotham Hill -	78 23 31.5 75 33 16 31 3 11.8			78 23 33.87 75 33 13.63 31 3 12.5	
		180 0 1.3	0.81	+0.49		
	Goudhurst from Frant -				— — —	44391.2
XVI.	Hollingborn Hill - Wrotham Hill - - Goudhurst -	63 46 44 52 9 11.5 64 4 35			63 46 47 52 9 11 64 4 1	
		179 59 59	1.22	—1.22		
	Hollingborn Hill from Goudhurst -				— — —	71898.5
XVII.	Tenterden - Goudhurst - - Hollingborn Hill -	67 7 55 68 13 81 — — —			67 7 56.46 68 13 19.5 44 38 44.04	
			0.85			
	Tenterden from { Goudhurst - Hollingborn Hill				— — — — — —	54376.5 71887.5

No. of triangles.	Names of the stations.	Observed angles.	Spherical excess.	Diff. of error.	Angles corrected for calculation.	Distances.
XVIII.	Fairlight Down				35 10 58.42	Feet.
	Goudhurst	49 39 34			49 39 35.77	
	Tenterden	94 59 26			94 59 25.81	
			0.91			
	Fairlight Down from { Goudhurst				— — —	93629.1
	Tenterden				— — —	71637.2
XIX.	Allington Knoll	48 24 32			48 24 39	
	Hollingborn Hill				40 0 58.96	
	Tenterden	91 34 23			91 34 22.04	
			10.5			
	Allington Knoll from { Hollingborn Hill				— — —	96039.8
	Tenterden				— — —	81777.5
XX.	Lydd	— — —			63 14 9.82	
	Allington Knoll	73 0 27.5			73 0 27	
	Tenterden	43 45 22			43 45 23.18	
			0.67			
	Lydd from { Allington Knoll				— — —	47850.9
	Tenterden				— — —	66169.1
XXI.	Fairlight Down	54 59 18.5			54 59 17.31	
	Lydd				62 27 50.18	
	Tenterden	62 32 53			62 32 52.51	
			0.99			
	Fairlight Down from Lydd				... ...	71893.2
XXII.	Allington Knoll	32 59 22.5			32 59 43	
	Lydd	125 42 0.25			125 42 0	
	Fairlight Down	— — —			21 18 37	
			0.33			
	Allington Knoll from Fairlight Down				— — —	106916.1
XXIII.	Lydd	43 20 48.25			43 20 48.5	
	Ruckinge	48 58 49.75			48 58 44.5	
	High Nook near Dymchurch	87 40 21.75			87 40 22	
		179 59 59.75	0.21	—0.26		
	Lydd from { Ruckinge				— — —	41535.3
	High Nook				— — —	31363.7

No. of triangles.	Names of the stations.	Observed Angles.	Spherical excess.	Diff. or error.	Angles corrected for calculation.	Distances.
XXIV.	Allington Knoll -	91 27 30			91 27 19.5	Feet.
	Ruckinge -	54 19 17			54 19 18.5	
	High Nook -	34 13 21			34 13 22	
		179 59 56	0.09	—1.09		
	Allington Knoll from { High Nook / Ruckinge				— — — / — — —	23185.7 / 16053
XXV.	Folkstone Turnpike -	24 17 6.25			24 17 6.25	
	Allington Knoll -	76 1 54			76 1 53.25	
	High Nook - -	79 41 0.75			79 41 0.5	
		180 0 1	0.29	+0.71		
	Folkstone Turnpike from { Allington Knoll / High Nook -				— — —	55463.6 / 14708
XXVI.	Folkstone Turnpike -	— — —			31 6 56.89	
	Allington Knoll -	109 50 40			109 50 39.35	
	Lydd - -	38 2 14			38 2 23.76	
			0.59			
	Folkstone Turnpike from Lydd				— — —	64662.8
XXVII.	Padlesworth -	108 9 34.5			108 9 34.5	
	High Nook -	— — —			14 48 25.5	
	Folkstone Turnpike -	57 2 0			57 2 0	
			0.16			
	Padlesworth from { High Nook - / Folkstone Turnpike				— — —	48305.2 / 14714.3
XXVIII.	Padlesworth -	105 29 40.5			105 29 40	
	Lydd - -	9 38 19			9 38 19 36	
	Folkstone Turnpike -	— — —			64 51 50.04	
			0.27			
	Padlesworth from { Lydd - / Folkstone Turnpike				— — —	79536.2 / 14714.3
XXIX.	Padlesworth -	12 16 3			12 16 2.65	
	Lydd - -	154 5 54.75			154 5 54.4	
	Fairlight Down -	— — —			13 38 2.95	
			0.59			
	Padlesworth from Fairlight Down				— — —	247392

No. of triangles.	Names of the stations.	Observed angles.	Spherical excess.	Diff. or error.	Angles corrected for calculation.	Distances.
XXX.	Swingfield	48 38 15			48 38 15	Feet.
	Padlesworth	70 54 5.5			70 54 5.5	
	Folkstone Turnpike	60 27 39.5			60 27 39.5	
		180 0 0	0.06	-0.06		
	Swingfield from { Padlesworth				— — —	17056.6
	{ Folkstone Turnpike				— — —	18525.8
XXXI.	Dover Castle, North Turret	34 39 26.5			34 39 26.5	
	Swingfield	75 36 40			75 36 40	
	Folkstone	69 43 53.5			69 43 53.5	
		180 0 0	0.13	-0.13		
	Dover Castle from { Swingfield				— — —	30560.4
	{ Folkstone Turnpike				— — —	31555.7

The two last triangles give 48562.7 feet for the distance of Dover Castle from Padlesworth. The angle at Dover Castle, between Folkstone Turnpike and Padlesworth, was 15° 18′ 44″½ by observation; and that at Padlesworth, between Dover Castle and Folkstone Turnpike, 34° 29′ 42″½.

XXXII.	Dover Castle	— — —			21 37 55.42	
	Padlesworth	152 15 25.5			152 15 25.15	
	Fairlight Down	— — —			6 6 39.43	
			0.69			
	Dover Castle from Fairlight Down				— — —	186119
XXXIII.	Dover Castle	— — —			87 30 29.58	
	Fairlight Down	— — —			43 19 58.50	
	Montlambert	— — —			49 9 31.9	
			7.4			
	Montlambert from { Dover Castle				— — —	168827
	{ Fairlight Down				— — —	245786
XXXIV.	Fairlight Down	— — —			25 33 55.08	
	Dover Castle	— — —			110 55 29.83	
	Blancnez	— — —			43 30 35.15	
			4 7.8			
	Blancnez from { Fairlight Down				— — ∟	252505.6
	{ Dover Castle				— — —	116660

No. of triangles.	Names of the stations.	Observed angles.	Spherical excess.	Diff. or error.	Angles corrected for calculation.	Distances.
XXXV.	Dover Castle —	23 25 0.25	'	"	23 25 0.25	Feet.
	Montlambert —	— — —			36 53 18.11	
	Blancnez —	— — —			119 41 41.64	
			1.84			
	Blancnez from Montlambert				— — —	77137.7
XXXVI.	Dover Castle —	12 46 33½	— —	— —	12 46 42	
	N. D. Calais — —	— — —			47 27 6	
	Blancnez sig. —	— — —			119 46 12	
	Norre-Dame at Calais from Dover				— — —	137455
XXXVII.	Calais from Dunkirk 123727 feet.					
	N. D. Calais — —			—	139 17 30	
	Dover Castle }		computed {		19 14 12	
	Dunkirk }				21 28 18	
	Dover Castle from the Tower of Dunkirk	—			— — —	144916

The acute angles in the xxxii. triang. result from the other angle and the including sides.

The angles in the xxxiii. and xxxiv. triangles were obtained in the following manner:

At Dover Castle, the angle between the white lights at Mountlambert, and the lamp at Padlesworth, was observed   —   —   —   109 8 25.5

For computation   —   109 8 25

At Fairlight Down, the angle between the white lights at Montlambert, and Blancnez, was observed,   17 46 5

For computation   —   17 46 3.5

At Fairlight Down, between the lamp at Lydd and white lights at Blancnez   —   —   11 2 31

For computation   —   18 2 31¼

Angles at Fairlight { in the xxix. triang.   —   13 38 2 95

{ in the xxxii.   —   sub. 6 6 39.43

Angle at Fairlight, between Dover and Lydd   7 31 23.52

U

	°	′	″
	7	31	29.52

Angle at Fairlight, between Lydd and Montlambert (17° 46′ 3″½ + 18° 2′ 31″½) - add, 35 48 35

Angle at Fairlight in the xxxiii. triangle - 43 19 58.52

Angle at Dover, between Padlesworth and Montlambert - - - - 109 8 25

Angle at Dover, in the xxxii. triang. sub. 21 37 55.42

Angle at Dover in the xxxiii. - - 87 30 29.58

The third angle, or 49° 9′ 31″.9 at Montlambert, is the supplemental one.

If from the angle at Fairlight, in this triangle, we take 17°46′ 3″.5
we have 25′ 33′ 55″.02, the angle at Fairlight in the xxxiv.
triangle : and if to 87° 30′ 29″.58 we add 23° 25′ 0″.25 (the ang.
at Dover in the xxxv. triang.), it gives 110° 55′ 29″.83, the angle
at Dover : that at Blancnez is the supplemental one.

The angle at Dover, in the xxxvi. was obtained thus : a
mean of the several observations between the lamp at Blancnez and white lights fired on the gallery of the church of Notre-
Dame at Calais, gave 12° 46′ 33″½. Dr. Blagden very carefully determined the position of the point on the gallery, with
respect to the axis of the church spire ; this corresponded to an
angle of 9″, which added to 12° 46′ 33″½, gives 12° 46′ 42″½.
The other angles of this triangle are reduced from those in a
plan of the French triangles, communicated by M. Cassini. And
the angle at Calais, with the distance of Calais from the Tower of
Dunkirk in the xxxvii. triang. are taken from the same paper.

The angles at Montlambert and Blancnez in the xxxv. triang.
result from our distances by computation. The French gentlemen, however, very carefully found them by observation, to be

36° 53′ 29″ and 119° 41′ 29″, the common difference is about 12″ which agreement, perhaps, is as near as can be expected, when it is considered, that a variation of six or seven feet, in either of our computed distances of Dover from Blancnez and Montlambert, will produce that difference.

The situation of the station at Montlambert, as determined by the observations made on this side of the Channel, has not however, totally depended on those made at Fairlight and Dover: another observation at Padlesworth has been used by way of check, or verification; this was made in a very favourable state of the air, when the angle between the flagstaff at the station on Dover Castle, and the mast at Montlambert, was 58° 27′ 11″¼, being 1″¼ more than that found by computation.

Dover Castle was the only station on our side to which the French academicians made observations. We therefore shall close this article with the following comparison. The distances on their part, being taken from " *Exposé des Opérations faites en France en* 1787, *pour la jonction des Observatories de Paris et Greenwich; par* M M. Cassini, Méchain, *et* Legendre."

			By the Eng. triang.	By the French triang.	Diff.
Dover from	Montlambert	feet	168827	168806	21
	Blancnez		116660	116648	12
	Calais		137455	137442	13
	Montlambert from Blancnez		77238	77228	10

But if our distances are determined from the base on Hounslow Heath *only*, the differences will be 14, 7, 7, 6, feet, respectively.

Operations at Greenwich Observatory.

58. By means of a scaffold, perfectly similar in principle to that formerly described, but more slight, as being made for the tem-

porary purpose only, the stand of the instrument was raised to the
height of thirty-eight feet above the floor of the transit-room of
the Observatory. At this elevation all the surrounding objects
which we wished to observe (St. Paul's excepted, which is hidden
by the camera turret of the great room) could be distinctly seen,
and the angles between them and the south meridian mark accurately measured. As that mark is but at a short distance, namely,
about 1600 feet from the transit, and consequently $\frac{1}{75}$th of an
inch, corresponding to about a second of an angle on the mark;
it was therefore very necessary that the centre of the instrument
should be brought with great precision over the centre of the axis
of the transit-telescope underneath. In this operation, and indeed
in every other while at Greenwich, the Astronomer Royal gave
us his best assistance. In the first place, the central point of the
axis was determined by the intersection of diagonal lines drawn
across the square part in the middle. On this square part, when
the telescope was in its horizontal position, a bason of quicksilver
was placed, having a small cross made of two thin bits of wood
fitted to the inside of the bason, and lying very near the surface of
the quicksilver, in such a manner as to make the centre of the
cross coincide with the intersection on the brass underneath.
A small perspective glass being then fixed in a moveable board
under the centre of the instrument, this was made to slide at right
angles to itself in the direction of the meridian, and that of the
axis of the transit, until the centre of the cross coincided with
the axis of vision in looking downwards. The board being there
fastened, and the perspective removed, the intersection of silk
threads stretched across the board, marked very accurately the
point corresponding with the centre of the transit, over which the
centre of our instrument was brought by the help of the plummet.
The second method was still more direct. Dr. Maskelyne had an
object glass prepared for his transit telescope, of a focus suited to

the vertical height of the stand of our instrument above it. This glass being applied to the transit, and the aperture contracted by a piece of pasteboard with a circular hole in the middle, a very small pin-hole being likewise made in the board at top, the same was gradually moved by directions from the observer below, looking through the telescope in its vertical position, until the pin-hole nicely coincided with the axis of vision. The instrument was then brought as before, by the help of the plummet, exactly over the pin-hole. In this manner, which was that adhered to, no doubt remained of more than about $\frac{1}{105}$th part of an inch, with respect to the centre of the instrument being in the intersection of two vertical planes passing through the axis of vision, and that of motion of the transit underneath. After having remained a week, the coincidence of the pin-hole with the axis of vision of the telescope was tried, and found to have suffered no alteration.

Bearings and Distances of the Stations.

59. Let (fig. 2. Pl. XV.) G be Greenwich Observatory; MM its meridian; PP, the perpendicular to the meridian; S, Severndroog Castle; W, Wrotham Hill. Draw SB parallel to the meridian MM; and SA, WM parallel to PP the perpendicular.

From the angles in the v. triangle to the x. inclusive, (see the plan of the triangles) we get the

angle - - - GSW = 152 28 56

The angle GSB = 16° 10′ 26″ (the complement of AGS) + 90° - - - sub. 106 10 26

There remains the angle BSW, or the bearing of Wrotham Hill from the parallel SB, south-eastward } 46 18 30

The distance GS = 14610.3
(triang.viii.) with AGS = 73° 49′ 34″ } AS = 14032   AG = 4070
and its complement, give   -

And the distance SW = 79960.6
(triang. x.) with BSW = 46° 18′ 90″ } BW = 57817   BS = 55233
and its complement, give   -

Wrotham Hill from Greenwich } MW = 71849 MG = 59305
merid. and its perpendicular

In like manner, by drawing parallels through the several stations, all the bearings and distances have been obtained. Those on the western side of the meridian, of course, are derived from the bearing of Norwood.

The direct bearings and distances from Greenwich, are computed with the distances from the meridian and its perpendicular. Thus MW = 71849, and MG = 59305, with the right angle at M, give 50° 27′ 48″, for the bearing; and 93163 feet, the distance of Wrotham Hill.

Table, containing the Bearings of the Stations from the Parallels to the Meridian of Greenwich: also their Distances from the Meridian and its Perpendicular.

Stations.	Bearings.		Distances from	
			Meridian.	Perpend.
At Greenwich.	° ′ ″		Feet.	Feet.
Severndroog Castle observed {	73 49 34	SE	14032	4070
Norwood	98 7 16	SW	19306	24603
At Norwood.				
Hundred Acres - -	42 22 39	SW	43333	50937
Hanger Hill - -	49 31 29	NW	67739	16729
At Hanger Hill.				
Hampton Poorhouse -	23 30 53	SW	89085	18537

Stations.	Bearings.	Distances from Meridian. Feet.	Perpend. Feet.
St. Ann's Hill - -	48 34 42 SW	119402	28852
King's Arbour - -	65 33 27 SW	102269	1098
At Severndroog Castle.			
Botley Hill - -	11 23 18 SW	172	72881
Wrotham Hill - -	46 18 30 SE	71849	59305
At Wrotham Hill.			
Frant - - -	6 50 58 SW	62341	138458
Goudhurst - -	25 12 15 SE	106945	132596
Hollingborn Hill - -	77 21 26 SE	151082	77079
At Goudburst.			
Tenterden - -	72 54 53 SE	158321	148571
Fairlight Down - -	23 15 17 SE	143312	218618
At Tenterden.			
Lydd - - -	50 27 12 SE	209345	190701
Allington Knoll - -	85 47 25 NE	219933	144036
At Allington Knoll.			
Ruckinge - -	70 25 32 SW	204807	149414
High Nook - -	21 1 48 SE	228253	165678
Folkstone Turnpike -	82 56 19 NE	274976	137216
At Folkstone Turnpike.			
Padlesworth - -	64 18 47 NW	261715	190839
Swingfield - -	3 51 8 NE	273730	118731
Dover Castle - -	65 52 46 NE	303773	124322
At Dover Castle.			
Montlambert - -	27 56 55 SE	382910	273458
Blancnez Signal - -	51 21 55 SE	394904	197159
Calais Spire - -	64 8 37 SE	427470	184268
Tower of Dunkirk -	83 22 49 SE	547058	152556

Dunkirk is 1420 toises = 9080 feet from the meridian of Paris *(Exposé des Opérations, &c. en* 1787, p. 66.), which taken from 547058, its distance from that of Greenwich, there remains 537978 feet, the distance of the meridians of Paris and Greenwich on the parallel (to the perpendicular) passing through Dunkirk, being only five feet short of the distance when the inclination of the meridian of Paris to that parallel, is brought into the computation.

Table containing the Bearings and direct Distances of the Stations from Greenwich Observatory.

Stations.	Bearings.	Distances.	Stations.	Bearings.	Distances.
	South-west-ward.	Feet.		South east-ward.	Feet.
Norwood -	38 7 16	31274	Goudh. Steeple	38 43 49	169974
Hundred Acres	40 23 18	66876	Hollingb. Hill	62 58 13	169608
Hanger Hill			Tenterd. Steepl	46 49 11	217115
Tower -	76 7 39	69774	Fairlight Down	33 14 47	261404
Hampt. Poorh.	77 25 22	85128	Lydd Steeple	47 40 6	289182
St. Ann's Hill	76 24 56	122836	Allington Knoll	56 46 44	262901
King's Arbour	89 25 6	102268	Ruckinge	53 53 16	253517
	South-east ward.		High Nook	54 1 33	282044
			Folkst. Turn-pike "	63 28 49	307811
Severndr. Cast.	78 49 34	14610	Padleaworth	64 26 17	292598
Botley Hill -	0 8 7	72881	Swingfield Stee.	66 33 2	298372
Wrotham Hill	50 27 48	98163	Dover Castle	67 44 34	328931
Frant Steeple	24 14 28	151846			

Of the horizontal Angles on a Spheroid.

60. Let C (fig. I. Pl. XV.) be the centre, CP, CE the polar and equatorial semi-axes; PF, PE two given meridians; B, O two points on the meridians having given latitudes. Draw the verti-

cals BR, OS, or perpendiculars to the meridians, to meet the axis in R and S; from which points draw RH, SK parallel to SO, RB respectively. Let C be the centre of a sphere on which the points *b, o*, have the same latitudes and difference of longitude as the points B, O, on the spheroid: draw the radii C*b*, C*o*, and arc *bo*. Then because C*b* is parallel to RB and SK, and C*o* is parallel to SO and RH, the planes C*bo*, RBH, SKO are parallel to each other; and therefore each of the angles BRH, KSO is equal to the angle *bCo*, or arc *bo* on the sphere. And since the planes SKO, RBH, C*bo*, are equally inclined to the meridians, the angle KOP on the spheroid will be equal to *bop* on the sphere; and the angle HBP equal to *obp* (supposing those angles to denote the true inclinations of the planes). Hence, the horizontal angle OBP on the spheroid, will exceed *obp* on the sphere, by the angle OBH : and for the like reason, the angle BOP on the spheroid will be less than *bop* on the sphere by the angle BOK. And because the planes BRH, KSO are parallel to each other, a third plane (BRO) intersecting them, will make the alternate angles equal to each other; therefore the excess on one side, is equal to the defect on the other, or the angle OBH equal to BOK; and consequently the sum of the angles PBO, POB on the spheroid, equal to the sum of the angles *pbo, pob* on the sphere, supposing those angles to represent the inclinations of the planes.

From B and O draw the tangents BG, BD, OQ to the arcs BH, BO, OK, meeting RH, SO, SK produced ; draw GD, which will be in the plane of the horizon of the point B, and also in that of the meridian EP. In like manner, a line from Q meeting a tangent to the arc OB drawn from O, would be in the planes of the horizon of the point O, and the meridian FP ; but this line, with some others, are omitted in the figure to prevent confusion.

Since in the present position of the planes, the horizontal angle HBP, or GBP is equal to the angle *obp* ; and KOP or QOP is equal

X

to *bop*, if we conceive the planes GBR, QOS to revolve equably about the verticals BR, OS, it is evident, that in every contemporary position, the sum of the horizontal angles at B and O will be the same, and therefore there are an indefinite number of points in the verticals SD, RB (supposing the latter to be produced upwards) through which the planes may be drawn to make the sum of the horizontal angles on the spheroid *accurately*, the same as the sum of the spherical angles at *b* and *o*. Conceive the plane GBR to move round the vertical RB, till it cuts the vertical SD in D, then the horizontal angle (OBP) on the spheroid will exceed *obp* on the sphere by the angle GBD included between the tangents BG, BD. Now, suppose it to cut the vertical in O at the surface; through O draw RI to meet the plane of the horizon of the point B in I, then the difference of the horizontal angles in that case, will be the angle GBI (supposing BI to be joined), being greater than the horizontal angle GBD by the angle DBI. Hence, if we suppose an instrument at B which measures angles in the plane of the horizon, and BD its telescope which may be moved in a vertical plane, it is evident that the horizontal angle PBD is diminished as the point (D) in the vertical (OD) to which the observation is made, is elevated: and for the like reason, the horizontal angle (POB) will be augmented when the instrument is at O on the other meridian. This supposes the latitude of the place O to be greater than that of B; for when the latitudes are the same, the planes of the verticals will coincide, and the horizontal angles will become equal, and the same as on a sphere.

61. To find a point in the vertical RB (produced if necessary) through which the vertical plane at O must pass, to make the difference of the horizontal angles at the point O, the same as a given difference in the horizontal angles at B. Let the angle GBD be the given difference at B; then if an equal angle be made at O in the plane of that horizon, OQ being one of the containing sides, the

other side will meet the plane of the meridian K P (continued to the horizon of O) in some point, from which if a line be drawn to S, it will cut the vertical RB in the point required : this will be evident by conceiving lines to be drawn in the plane of the meridian BP similar to those in the plane of the other meridian. From hence it will appear, that if the horizontal angles (OBP, BOP) on the spheroid, are taken in the planes of the respective horizons, or the tangents are in horizontal positions, and directed to the verticals, their sum (OBP + BOP) will be *less* than the sum (*obp + bop*) on the sphere. If the angles are taken to the verticals at the points O, B, on the surfaces, their sum will be *greater* : but if OD be bisected, and also the like part of the other vertical between B and the plane of the horizon of the point O, and the horizontal angles are taken to those points of bisection, their sum will be equal to the sum of *obp* and *bop*. In the two former cases, however, it will be difficult to determine the difference by computation, because of the minute angles subtended by DI, and the similar line in the plane of the other horizon, except the spheroid be very oblate.

6s. From what has been said, it follows, that if the latitudes of two points B, O, and the horizontal angles PBO, POB are given on a spheroid, the third angle BPO cannot be found by spherical computation in the usual manner. But because their sum (PBO + POB) may be considered as equal to the sum (*pbo + pob*) on a sphere, the corresponding spherical angles may be found as follows :

Having two sides, and the sum of the opposite angles of a spherical triangle, to find those angles :

As the tangent of half the sum of the sides,
Is to the tangent of half their difference ;
So is the tangent of half the sum of the angles,
To the tangent of half their difference.

Or thus. Let *s* and *c* represent the *sine* and *cosine* of the sum of the angles; *m* the *sine* of the greater side, *n* that of the less ; then

X 2

$\frac{\not{L}}{\pi \pm \not{M}}$ will be the *tangent* of the less angle. The negative sign taking place when the sum of the angles is above 90°.

The angles (HBP, KOP) for computation being thus found, the angle at P, or the difference of longitude will from thence be determined ; and consequently the value of the arc BO on the spheroid.

63. *Method of computing the horizontal angles.* Let the figure be an ellipsoid whose semi-axes CE, CP are 3496740, and 3477810 fathoms : and suppose the latitudes of the places B, O, are 49° 40', and 50° respectively ; and their difference of longitude 30'.

The two co-latitudes and the included angle 30' will give the spherical angles *pbo, pob,* 43° 51' 48".3 and 135° 45' 16".9 respectively; and the arc *bo*, or angle *b*Co = 27'49".7. Now because the verticals BR, OS are respectively parallel to the radii *b*C, *o*C ; and the tangents BG, OQ parallel to the tangents of the arc *bo* at *b* and *o*, therefore the planes of the horizons of B and O will intersect the verticals RB, SO (produced), and their parallels RG, SQ, in the same angles as the planes of the horizons of *b* and *o* on the sphere would cut the radii C*b*, C*o* produced : these angles may be determined with the *co-tangents*, and *co-secants* of the latitudes, and the *secant* of the arc *bo* to any radius. And hence we get the angle DGB = 44° 14' 40".3 and the angle DGR = 89° 40' 4" ; GD being the intersection of the plane of the horizon of B and the plane of the meridian EP. And the angles at Q in the plane of the other meridian, will be 43° 51' 44".7, and 89° 59' 56".

Let *a* denote the *sine* of an arc whose *tang.* is $\frac{CE}{CP}$ x *co-tang.* 49° 40' (the *lat.* of B), then $\frac{a \times CE}{\text{co-sin. } 49° 40'}$ = 3508110 fath. the vertical BR. In like manner, the vertical OS = 3508295 fath. Hence, from the nature of the ellipse, we get RS the distance of the verticals in the axis = 148 fath. Draw RW parallel to GD, then we have the angle SWR = 90° 19' 56" the supplement of DGR ; and the angle WSR being 40° (the *co-lat.* of the point O), we get RW, or GD = 95.13 fath. In the same manner, if RL be drawn parallel to the intersection of the planes of the other meridian and horizon, its length will be 95.79 fath. Now the angles BRG, OSQ being each 27′ 49″.7 (the angle *b*Co), the tangents BG, OQ to the radii BR, OS, will be BG = 28398.5, and OQ = 28399.5. Hence BG, and GD with 44° 14′ 40″.3, the included angle at G, will give the angle GBD = 8′ 3″¼, the difference of the horizontal angles on the sphere and spheroid at B. And the angle at O (with OQ and RL, and 43° 51′ 44″.7 the included angle at Q), will be found the same, or 8′ 3″¼. Therefore the horizontal angles on the spheroid will be PBO = 43° 51′ 48″.9 + 8′ 3″¼ ; and POB = 135° 45′ 16″.2 − 8′ 3″¼. Those angles are computed on a supposition that the tangents BG, OQ are horizontal ; but no sensible variation would arise if they were directed to the verticals at the surfaces O and B, for the vertical SO, and the distance SR with the included angle at S = 40°, will give the angle SOR (DOI) not more than 5 or 6″ ; and therefore, was the point D a mile above the surface, the length of DI which subtends the variation in the horizontal angle at B, would be less than 3 inches.

64. The application is only the reverse of what is given above. For suppose the latitudes of two places B,O on a spheroid are 49° 40′ and 50°, and the observed horizontal angles OBP, POB to be 43° 59′ 51″.55 and 135° 37′ 12″.95 ; to find the difference of longitude;

The sum of the observed angles being 179° 37′ 4″.5, we get (62.) 45° 56′ 45′ for half the difference of the spherical angles ; therefore KOP = 135° 45′ 17″¼, and HBP = 43° 51′ 47″¼ are the angles for computation : hence the angle OPB, or difference of longitude = 30′, and the opposite side BO = 27′ 49″.7.

65. If we determine the side OP, with the observed angle OBP, and the two including sides, it will be found = 40° 0′ 5″.6, which exceeds the truth by 5″.6 ; but it will fall short when that angle is greater than BOP : this excess (or defect) is the arc HO which subtends the difference in the horizontal angles on the sphere and

spheroid, which arc, in the present case, is 5".6 (the difference in
the horizontal angles being 8′ 4″.9). Therefore as the angles at
B and O approach to equality, the computed results with the observed angles become nearer the truth : and hence it follows, that
when the observed angle OBP is a right one, and the arc BO is not
of great extent, the spherical computations will give the latitude
and longitude of the point O without sensible error.

66. But when the latitude of the place (B) is given, together
with the observed angle (OBP) between the meridian (BP) and a
given arc (BO), proceed thus for the latitude of the place O, and
the difference of longitude. Suppose PSD (fig. 3. Pl. XV.) to be
the observed angle, SP the co-latitude, and SD the given arc on
a spheroid. With the two sides and included angle as a spherical
triangle, compute the angle PDS, which will always be nearly the
same as would be found by observation ; then make the angle
SDA (which will fall on the lower side of SD, if PD is greater
than PS), equal to half the difference of the angles PSD, PDS :
now, if we consider the triangle SDA as a plane one, the angles
PAD, PDA will be equal, and SA will be the difference of latitude of the points S, D, which being found with the given length
of SD (allowing for the curvature of the sides), we have the
latitude of the point D : then with the three given sides of the triangle PSD, find the angle SPD by spherical computation, which
will be the difference of longitude.

Distance of the Parallels of Latitude of Paris and Greenwich.

67. Suppose (fig. 3. Pl. XV.) PS, PD to be the meridians of
Greenwich and Dunkirk; G Greenwich Observatory; D the Tower
of Dunkirk ; GE the perpendicular to the meridian at Greenwich ;
RD, RG the distances of Dunkirk from the meridian of Greenwich,
and its perpendicular, or 547058, and 152556 feet (59) ; DS the
vertical or great circle passing through D, and making the angle
at S a right one.

The perpendicular DS to the meridian at S, will fall below R about 5½ feet. It is found thus: assume DR, or DS = 1° 29′ 25″, which will be its value nearly (for great accuracy is not necessary in this case): then, as *cosin*. DS : *rad*. : : RG (152556 feet,) : 152608 feet, or 25435 fath. = GS.

Now in the right angled triangle PSD, it follows (65.) that the side PD, computed spherically with the other two sides, will always fall short of the truth by a quantity determinable from the nature of the spheroid; which in the present case (supposing the earth an ellipsoid, and the degrees on the meridian, and perpendicular at S, to be 60869, and 61184 fath.) will be 0″.9 nearly: therefore, if the latitude of the point D be given, and that of S is to be computed from DP and the other *data*, it will be necessary to diminish DP by that quantity (0″.9). According to the latest observations, the latitude of the Tower of Dunkirk is 51° 2′ 11″.4 (*Conn. des Tems*, 1797-98, p. 372), therefore PD = 38° 57′ 48″.6, from which take 0″.9, and we have 38° 57′ 48″.9 for computation. Hence, as *cosin*. 1° 29′ 25″ (SD): *rad*. : : *cosin*. 38° 57′ 48″.3 : *cosin*. 38° 56′ 22″ = SP; consequently, GS = 38° 56′ 22″ − 38° 31′ 20″ = 25′ 2″. And if DA be the parallel of latitude of Dunkirk, DP − SP = 38° 57′ 48″.6 − 38° 56′ 22″ = 1′ 26″.6. Now, GS being 25435 fath. (answering to an arc of 25′ 2″) we have 25′ 2″ : 25435 : : 1′ 26″.6 : 1466¼ fath. = SA, which added to SG gives 26901¼ fath. the length of the arc of latitude between Greenwich and Dunkirk. In pag. 69, "*Exposé des Opérations, &c. en* 1787", we have 125505.92 toises * = 133757.9 fath. the distance of the parallels of lat. of Paris and Dunkirk; the sum of this, and 26901¼, is 160659 fath. the distance of the parallels of Latitude of Paris and Greenwich. Now, if the latitude of the Observatory at Paris is 46° 50′ 14″, the

---

* The length of the French toise, is to that of the English fathom, as 4263 to 4000. *Philos. Trans. Vol. LVIII. p. 326.*

difference of latitude between Paris and Greenwich will be 2° 38′ 26″, hence 2° 38′ 26″ : 160659 : : 1° : 60843 fath. the length of the degree on the meridian in latitude 50° 10′ (the middle latitude nearly, between Paris and Greenwich), which differs but little from M. Bouguer's hypothesis (Philos. Trans. 1787); and exceeds M. Lalande's on the ellipsoid about 7 fathoms (*Astron. Art.* 2711.) But if the lat. of Paris be 48° 50′ 15″ (*Conn. des Tems*, 1797-98, p 373.) we get the degree = 60849 fath.

There is, however, an inconsistency in the foregoing results, not easily accounted for without supposing the latitude of Greenwich, or that of Dunkirk, or Paris, to be erroneous. The distance of the parallels of latitude of Greenwich and Dunkirk is 269011⁄2 fath. answering to 26′ 28″.6, the difference of latitude ; whence we get 60962 fath. for the degree in lat. 51° 151⁄4 (the middle lat. between Greenwich and Dunkirk, nearly). And the length of the meridional arc between Paris and Dunkirk is, 133758 fath. corresponding to the difference of lat. 2° 11′ 56″.4, these give but 60827 fath. for the degree in lat. 49° 57′ : the difference is 135 fath. which is about 100 fath. greater than the increase from lat. 49° 57′ to 51° 151⁄4 on any of the spheroids hitherto assumed for the figure of the earth. Some small errors may have arisen from our method of reducing the observed angles to those for computation ; but the final results could only be varied a few feet on that account. But even supposing an error of 4 fath. or 24 feet, on our part, in the distance of Dunkirk from the perpendicular, it will not amount to 0″1⁄4 of latitude.

Nor is the length of the meridional arc materially affected by any probable value of the perpendicular DS; or a small variation in the latitude of Dunkirk. For suppose its latitude to be 51° 2′ 9″.3 (as determined by M. La Caille). and the arc DS = 1° 29′ 35″: then proceeding as above, we get SA = 1470.7 fath. which exceeds the former length about 41⁄2 fath. But the degree in latitude 51°

15'½ is 60892 fath. And (taking the lat. of Paris 48° 50' 15") that in 49° 57' will be 60849 ; therefore in this case, the difference in the degrees is but 49 fath. instead of 135.

But the difference in the two values of the arc of latitude GS will evidently be the same (very nearly), as the difference in the latitudes of the point D : for let DP be 98° 57' 48".3 and 98° 57' 50".4 and the arc SD = 1° 29' 25" as before ; then PS = 98° 56' 22" and 98° 56' 24".1, the difference being 2".1 (the same as that in the latitudes of D) ; and the two values of the arc GS are 25' 2" and 25' 4".1 ; therefore the length of the arc GS being 25435 fath. we have 60963, and 60878 fath. for the meridional degrees in lat 51° 16'.

From hence it appears, that if the latitudes of Paris, Dunkirk, and Greenwich, are 48° 50' 15", 51° 2' 11".4, and 51° 28' 40" respectively, the difference in the meridional degrees in latitudes 49° 57' and 51° 16' is about 135 fath. ; which will not accord with any of the received hypotheses.

The latitude of the tower of Dunkirk was deduced by M. Delambre from that of the place where he made his observations. He took the altitudes of the pole-star with the *circle of repetition* * (about 1 foot in diameter), and determined his latitude from 900 observations, differing, as we are told, somewhat less than 1"½ of a degree. This instrument is now in general use with the French astronomers. But though their method of determining the meridional altitude of a star is extremely ingenious, yet those cele-brated mathematicians may rely too much on the instrument itself, in an operation which requires the greatest nicety. For it is the opinion of the first artist in England, who has examined its con-struction, as far as it can be done from the description and engraving, that it is wholly a matter of chance if the plane of the circle be

* For the description see *Conn. des Tems*, 1797-98.

Y

vertical when it is adjusted for observation ; and therefore, if
the same mode of adjustment is constantly adhered to, the results may be consistent, but finally erroneous. The same ingenious artist, however, intends to publish his remarks on the
construction of this instrument, with the description of another
of his own invention for the same purpose, but less liable to
objection.

*Directions of the Meridians at Goudburst and Botley Hill. And
Length of a Degree perpendicular to the Meridian.*

68. A small table had been previously computed of the times
when the pole-star was at its greatest apparent elongations from
the meridian. On these occasions the Board of Longitude's *pre-
mium watch*, by the late Mr. Harrison, was made use of. Its rate
of going all the time that it was in the field in 1787, was very uniformly 9½ seconds a day faster than mean time. But in the winter
months the watch gradually changed its rate from *plus* to *minus;*
and when it was carried into the field in 1788, and, during the
five weeks that it continued there, it regularly lost on mean time
from 3½ to 4 seconds each day ; having in that short interim been
twice compared, with an excellent clock made by
Cumming, with an improved Ellicott's pendulum.

Let B (fig. 4. Pl. XV.) be Botley Hill ; PBR its meridian, O
Greenwich Observatory (which is nearly on the meridian of Botley
Hill) ; G Goudhurst ; W Wrotham Hill ; T Tenterden ; GR an
arc of a great circle, making the angle at R a right one; also let
* * represent the circle of the pole-star's apparent declination ;
and B*, G* be two azimuth circles touching that circle.

Aug. 14. 1788, at Goudhurst, the angle * GT, or that between
the pole-star when at its greatest apparent distance from the

meridian on the east side, and the lamp at Tenterden was observed.

		°	′	″
den was observed. - - - -		104	32	19½

The angle BGT between the lamps at Botley Hill and Tenterden was repeatedly observed - - 167 43 56

Angle ✳ GB - - - - - diff. 63 11 36½

Aug. 29, 1788, at Botley Hill, the angle ✳ BW, or that between the pole-star at its greatest apparent elongation, and the lamp at Wrotham Hill, was observed † - - - - - - - - 76 21 37

The angle WBG by repeated observations was 40 4 42

Angle ✳ BG - - - - - sum 116 26 19

To obtain the star's azimuths at B and G it will not be necessary to have the latitudes very correct. We therefore may take the values of the meridional arcs from M. Bouguer's hypothesis, which agrees nearly with the measurement in these latitudes. And as Botley Hill is but 172 feet from the meridian of Greenwich, OB will be 72881 feet (59.), the distance from the perpendicular, without sensible error.

The latitude of the middle point between B and O (Botley Hill and Greenwich) is about 51° 29′ : the degree in this latitude is

---

· † The observations of the pole-star at Goudhurst and Botley Hill, were repeated for several nights at each place, but those here given are the most exact. At Goudhurst the angle which the star made with the lamp being noted, the telescope removed, and the plane of the instrument being turned 180°, or half round ; the telescope replaced and directed again to the star, the difference on the circle was found to be only 1″]. And at Botley Hill the difference between the readings was no more than 1″½.

At Folkstone Turnpike by means of the star's double azimuth, we obtained the direction of the meridian with High Nook 120° 24′ 57″.87. And with Fairlight Down 120° 47′ 45″.87. But nothing conclusive was deduced from those angles for want of reciprocal observations.

= 60844 fath. (Bouguer, *Fig. de la Terre*, p. 305. or Philos. Trans.
1787); hence the arc OB = 72881 feet, will be 11′ 59″, which
added to OP, the co-lat. of Greenwich, gives 38° 43′ 19″ = BP :
now in the right angled spherical triangle P * B we have PB =
38° 43′ 19″, and P * = 1° 49′ 22″.8, the star's apparent polar distance nearly on Aug. 23 ; hence the angle PB *, or azimuth, =
2° 54′ 51″.1, which added to the angle * BG gives 119° 21′ 13″.1,
the angle PBG.

In the right angled triangle BRG, we have BG = 1218134 feet
(triang. xiv.) and the angle RBG = 60° 38′ 47″ the supplement
of PBG, whence RG = 106174, and RB = 59719 feet : the value
of the latter on the meridian will be 9′ 48″.7 nearly ; and that of
RG (from a few trials) is about 17′ 20″. Hence 38° 43′ 19″ + 9′
48″.7 = 38° 53′ 7″.7 = RP, which, with 17′ 20″ (RG), and the
included right angle, will give GP = 38° 53′ 11″. The star's apparent distance from the pole on Aug. 14, was 1° 49′ 25″.9 nearly †;
hence the star's azimuth, or angle PG * = 2° 54′ 20″.7 which taken
from the angle BG *, there remains 60° 17′ 15″.8 = BGP.

It is evident that a considerable variation in the value of the arc
RG produces but a small one in that of the latitude of the point G,
which, in the present case, principally depends on the value of the
arc RB, or of RO ; we therefore will suppose GP = 38° 53′ 11″,
as found by the computation above. Then in the spheroidical triangle BPG we have the sides PB, PG, with the angles at B, G ;
whence (62.) we get 60° 7′ 38″ and 119° 30′ 50″.9, the angles for
computation at G and B (the difference of the horizontal angles
on the sphere and spheroid, in this case, being 9′ 37″.8): from these
angles and their opposite sides, the difference of longitude BPG
will be found 27′ 36″.74 ; and the arc BG 19′ 55″.13. Therefore

† In 1786, the Astronomer Royal very accurately determined the declination of the
pole-star, whence the mean polar distance at the beginning of that year was 1° 50′
8″.35. The mean annual precession in declination being 19′.55.

as 19′ 55″.13 : 191813½ feet (BG) : : 1°: 61155 fath. the length of
a degree on the spheroid in the direction BG, and in lat. 51° 11′½,
the lat. of the middle point between B and G. And as *rad.* : *sin.*
PG : : *sin.* RPG : *sin.* 17′ 20″.06 = RG the perpendicular arc =
106174 feet ; whence the degree in the latitude of the point R =
61251 fath. nearly.

In the foregoing computations the values of the meridional arcs
are nearly the same as the values, which may be inferred from the
measured arc between Greenwich and Paris, supposing the latitude
of the latter to be 48° 50′ 14″. Small errors, however, in the values
of the arcs OB, BR, are of little consequence, because that of the
oblique arc BG, and also of the perpendicular one RG principally
depend on the horizontal angles at B and G, for a small variation
in either angle will make a considerable one in the degrees derived from those arcs when, as in the present instance, they are
small. For that reason, in the following table, we have adopted
the perpendicular degree, as determined by the operation in 1793,
on a distance of 64 miles, which therefore is probably much more
correct than the above.

Table of the meridional and perpendicular Degrees from Lat.
50° to 52°.

Lat.	Deg. on Merid.	Deg. perp. Merl.
° ′	fath.	fath.
50 0	60839	61177
10	60843	61178
20	60846	61180
30	60850	61181
40	60853	61182
50	60856	61183
51 0	60860	61184
10	60863	61186
20	60867	61187
30	60871	61188
40	60874	61189
50	60877	61190
52 0	60881	61191

This table is computed on an ellipsoid derived from 60843 fath.
the meridional degree in lat. 50° 10′ (67.), and 61182 fath. the
perpendicular degree in lat. 50° 40′.

Of the Longitudes of Dunkirk and Paris from Greenwich.

69. Let (fig. 3. Pl XV.) PS, PD be the meridians of Greenwich
and Dunkirk; G Greenwich Observatory, D the Tower of Dunkirk;
and DS the perpendicular to the meridian at S, as in Art. 67.
Then GS = 25435 fath. and SD = 91176 fath.

From the table in the last Article we get the arc GS = 25′ 4″.4;
therefore PS = 98° 56′ 24″.4; then from the same table, the perpendicular degree in the lat. of S is = 61185 fath.; consequently
the arc SD = 1° 29′ 24″.6 nearly; or 1° 29′ 24″.7, allowing for the
variation in the curvature. Now those sides, with the included right

angle at S, give 2° 22′ 13″, the angle at P, or difference of longitude ; and 38° 57′ 50″.7 = DP, or 51° 2′ 9″.3, the computed latitude of Dunkirk. This latitude is in excess (65.), the correction,
however, may be found as directed in Art. 66. ; but the more exact
method is to determine what would subtend the difference In the
horizontal angles on the sphere and spheroid at the points S and D
(63.), which will be about 34 feet, answering to 0″.3 nearly (67.):
this taken from 51° 2′ 9″.3 leaves 51° 2′ 9″, the latitude of D.

The longitude of the Tower of Dunkirk being 2′ 22″ east of
Paris *(Mém. de l'Acad.* 1788), we have 2° 19′ 51″, or 9ᵐ 19′.4, the
difference of meridians of Greenwich and Paris.

Was the earth an ellipsoid, whose axes are as 230 to 229, the
longitude of Paris, from the above measurements, would be 9ᵐ 20′
nearly (Philos. Trans. 1791): but M. Lalande, in a Memoir on
the difference of meridians of Greenwich and Paris *(Conn. des
Tems,* 1797-98) objects to this, and contends that the longitude is
9ᵐ 21′. First, because it agrees nearly with a supposition made by
the late Gen. Roy (Philos. Trans. 1787, p. 194). Secondly, because among 61 longitudes, deduced from the eclipses of Jupiter's
first satellite, some are found to differ but a few seconds from 9ᵐ 21′.
Thirdly, M. Legendre finds 9ᵐ 21′ by computation on a spheroid
(Mém. de l'Acad. 1788).

Gen. Roy's words are, " the difference of longitude between the
" two Observatories, as far as can be judged from the map of
" Kent, corrected for the error in the direction of its meridian,
" amounts to about 2° 20′ 20″:" this authority is evidently too
vague to merit attention. And with respect to the results from
Jupiter's satellite (Philos. Trans. 1787), they vary from 9ᵐ to 10ᵐ,
and therefore afford nothing conclusive. M. Lalande, however,
should have stated the deductions of MM. Sejour and Mechain,
from the solar eclipse in 1769, and the occultations in 1786, where

the limits are 9ᵐ 18ˢ and 9ᵐ 20ˢ (see Dr. Maskelyne's Paper, Philos. Trans. 1787); and he might have added that of Professor Piazzi, who found 9ᵐ 19ˢ.3 from the sun's eclipse in June, 1788, (Philos. Trans. 1789.)

Taking the longitude of Paris 9ᵐ 20' 15", according to M. Legendre, the angle SPD is 8° 28' 37", whence the arc SD = 1° 29' 40", which gives 61011 fath. for the perpendicular degree in lat. 51° 4', agreeing nearly with M. Lalande, who has given a table of the degrees of latitude and longitude on a spheroid whose axes are as 900 to 899; Astron. edit. 3, Art. 2711. Therefore the length of the perpendicular degree, according to those gentlemen's hypothesis, is about 170 fath. shorter than that deduced from our measurement.

M. Lalande says, " it is now known that the earth is not an " homogeneous spheroid :" this perhaps will not be disputed ; but it is also as well known, that the experiments with pendulums, like the different measurements, have not been consistent, nor accurate enough, to afford satisfactory conclusions respecting the ratio of the earth's axes, notwithstanding the computations have lately been made by the first mathematicians, on a supposition that the earth is an heterogeneous ellipsoid. But if the earth be not homogeneous, it may, or it may not be an ellipsoid. The different measurements, however, seem to prove that it cannot be an ellipsoid of any kind.

Nor do we infer from the table (68.) that the earth is an ellipsoid, but some figure upon which the lengths of the degrees on the meridian, and at right angles to it in lat. 50° 40', are 60853 and 61182 fath. nearly : this granted, the values of the other degrees in the table, though computed on an ellipsoid, cannot be wide of the truth.

In M. Lalande's table the meridional degrees in latitudes

39° 12' and 23° 28', exceed the measurements * by 92 and 118 fath. respectively. At the polar circle, however, his hypothesis falls 207 fath. short. But in his memoir we find an article respecting that celebrated operation, in substance as follows: " They write " me from Sweden, that M. Mallet, professor of mathematics at " Upsal, having been at Pello in 1769, to observe the transit of " Venus, examined the stations which had served for the mea- " surement of a degree, and found that country full of high moun- " tains, the attraction of which might influence the direction of " gravity, and consequently affect the length of the degree. His " discussion on the different measured degrees is to be found in " the first volume of the Physical Description of the World, pub- " lished at Upsal in 1772.

" We may add, that the angles of the triangles have not the " precision which we might have hoped for; there is 29".4 of " difference upon the three angles of the first triangle; (Mauper- " tuis, *Fig. de la Terre*, p. 88.): those angles are altered in the ap- " plication differently from what is warranted by the observations.

" CTK, p. 80,   -   24° 22' 58".8 and p. 90, 24° 22' 54".3
" HAC, p. 82,   -   112 21 48.6   -   112 21 32.9
" KHN, p. 81 and 82, 143 6 19   -   143 6 3.2"

It has also been conjectured, that the degree in Peru is consi- derably too long, in consequence of the lateral attraction of the high lands where the measurement was performed (Philos. Trans. 1768). But the results at the polar circle and equator are of very little consequence in settling the point in question; because the distance between the meridians of Greenwich and Paris, and also the perpendicular degree, having been measured in nearly the

---

* The former by Mess. Mason and Dixon in America, and the latter by Mr. Bur- row in Bengal. See a short account of Mr. Burrow's operation, sold by Elmsly and Bremner, Strand, London.

Z

same latitude, the longitude cannot be said to depend on any hypothesis; for a considerable variation in the length of the meridional degree will but little affect that of the perpendicular one. And therefore the difference of meridians obtained from the measurement is a proof that the deductions of Mess. Sejour, Mechain, and Piazzi are true to a second in time; and that 9^m 21^s resulting from an hypothesis, is more than that quantity too great.

70. *Table containing the Latitude of the Stations ; and their Longitudes from Greenwich.*

	Lat.	Long.	In time.
	° ′ ′	West. ° ′ ′	m. s.
Greenwich Ob. -	51 28 40		
Norwood - -	51 24 37½	0 5 3	0 20.2
Hundred Acres - -	51 20 17½	0 11 20	0 45.3
Hanger Hill Tower -	51 31 25½	0 17 48	1 11.2
Hampton Poorhouse -	51 25 35½	0 21 47	1 27.1
King's Arbour - -	51 28 47½	0 26 50	1 47.3
St. Ann's Hill - -	51 23 51½	0 31 17	2 5.1
		East.	
Botley Hill - -	51 16 41½	0 0 3	0 0.2
Severndr. Castle on Shooter's Hill	51 28 0	0 9 41	0 14.7
Frant Steeple - -	51 5 54	0 16 13	1 4.9
Wrotham Hill - -	51 18 54	0 18 47	1 15.1
Goudhurst Steeple -	51 6 49½	0 27 40	1 50.7
Fairlight Down -	51 52 39	0 37 7	2 28.5
Hollingborn Hill - -	51 15 53½	0 39 28	2 37.9
Tenterden Steeple - -	51 4 8	0 41 11	2 44.8
Ruckinge - -	51 3 55	0 53 16	2 33.1
Lydd Steeple - -	50 57 7½	0 54 19	3 37.3
Allington Knoll -	51 4 46	0 57 13	3 48.9
High Nook, near Dymchurch	51 1 11½	0 59 18	3 57.2
Padlesworth - -	51 6 50½	1 8 8	4 32.5

	Lat.		Long.			In time.
	° ' "		° ' " East.			m. s.
Swingfield Steeple - -	51	8 48	1 11 18			4 45.2
Folkstone Turnpike -	51	5 45½	1 11 33			4 46.2
Dover Cast. N. turret of the Keep	51	7 47½	1 19 7			5 16.5
On the Coast of France.						
Montlambert near Boulogne	50	43 2	1 38 51			6 35.9
Blancnez - - -	50	55 31½	1 42 24			6 49.6
N. D. at Calais - -	50	57 80½	1 50 56			7 23.7

The method of computation given in Art. 69. is sufficient to show how all the latitudes and longitudes have been obtained: only it has not been thought necessary to apply any corrections, as in that example, three or four of the most distant places excepted. The latitudes are to the nearest ¼ second; and the longitudes to the nearest second.

Relative Heights, and terrestrial Refractions.

71. Before we proceed to give any account of the observed angles of elevation or depression, at the stations reciprocally, for trying the quantity of terrestrial refraction, it may be proper to call to remembrance, that, in the measurement of the base on Hounslow Heath, the mouth of the pipe at Hampton Poorhouse was shewn to be elevated about 60 feet above low-water spring-tides at the sea, as far as could then be determined, by referring it to the surface of high water at Isleworth; and that the extremity of the base near King's Arbour, was found, by levelling, to be higher than the former end by 31¼ feet.

The mouth of the pipe at the south-east end of the base of verification at High Nook near Dymchurch, in Romney Marsh,

Z 2

Lieut. Fiddes found, by levelling, to be above low-water mark, at spring tides, 22.1 feet.

The top of the parapet of the north turret of the Keep of Dover Castle was found by Lieut. Hay, of the Royal Engineers (by levelling from the top of the cliff, at Queen Elizabeth's gun, downwards, and adding to that the height of the ground and Castle above the said gun), to be 465.8 feet above low-water at spring tides. Having also measured a base for the purpose, he determined the height of the cliff geometrically, which agreed within less than a foot of the result by levelling.

In 1779, the height of the floor of the upper story of the Bull Inn at Shooter's Hill, was found, by levelling, to be 444 feet above the Gun Wharf in Woolwich Warren. Since that time the top of the parapet of Severndroog Castle, has been found to be 13½ feet higher than the floor at the Inn. And allowing 22 feet for the height of the Wharf at Woolwich, above low-water at the Nore, the top of Severndroog Castle will be 479½ feet above low-water spring tides.

Lastly, the altitudes of all the intermediate stations have been established by the reciprocal angles of elevation or depression,* gradually carried on from station to station, throughout the whole series of triangles; and no greater uncertainty has been found at Hampton Poorhouse than a few feet, occasioned, no doubt, by the

---

* Dr. Maskelyne remarks, that it would be of use to have a person to note the thermometer at the object, as well as at the station of the observer, whereby the refraction might be more accurately computed by the application of a new correction. Thus, calling $r = \frac{d}{10} = \frac{1}{10}$th of the arc of distance; $b =$ the height of the uniform atmosphere; $t =$ the difference of the thermometers at the two stations; $x =$ the difference of altitude of the two stations above a common level; the correction would then be $= \frac{rtk}{400x}$; and the true or whole refraction would be $= r \mp \frac{rtk}{400x}$, according as the thermometer stood lower or higher at the upper station.

uncertainty of terrestrial refraction: for it is to be remarked, that, to the westward of Greenwich, no double, but only single, observations were obtained; wherefore the relative heights of these stations have been determined by taking $\frac{1}{13}$ of the arc of distance for the effect of terrestrial refraction.

7⁰. Suppose C (fig. 5. Pl. XV.) to be the centre of the earth; A and B two stations above the surface SS; AD, BO the horizontal lines at right angles to OC, DC; also, suppose A and B to be the *true* places of the points reciprocally observed, and *a* and *b* their *apparent* ones:

In the quadrilateral AEBC, the angles at A and B are right ones, therefore the sum of the angles EAB, EBA, is equal to the angle at C, or the arc SS contained between the stations: in other words, the sum of the reciprocal depressions (DAB + OBA) below the horizontal lines AD, BO, would be equal to the contained arc, if there was no refraction. But *a* and *b* being the apparent places of the objects at A and B, the angles of depression will be DA*b*, OB*a*; therefore their sum taken from the angle C, or the contained arc, will leave the sum of the angles *b*AB, *a*BA, or the sum of the two refractions; hence, if we suppose half that sum to be the mean refraction, we have the following rule, when the objects are reciprocally depressed: *subtract the sum of the two depressions from the contained arc, and half the remainder is the mean refraction.*

If one of the objects (B) instead of being depressed, is elevated, suppose to the point G, the angle of elevation being GAD; then the sum of the angles *e*AB + *e*BA will be greater than the sum EAB + EBA (the angle C, or contained arc SS) by the angle of elevation *e*AD; but if from *e*AB + *e*BA we take the depression OB*a* there will remain *e*AB + *a*BA the sum of the two refractions: therefore, the rule for the mean refraction in this case is:

subtract the depression from the sum of the contained arc and eleva-
tion, and half the remainder is the mean refraction.

Previously, however, each observation must be reduced to the place of the axis of the instrument, as in the two following examples.

1. At Allington Knoll, the top of the staff on Tenterden Steeple was depressed 3′ 51″ by observation; and the top of the staff was 3.1 feet higher than the axis of the instrument when it was at that station: now the distance of the stations being 61777 feet, we shall find that 3.1 feet will, at that distance, subtend an angle of 10″.4, which added to 3′ 51″, gives 4′ 1″.4 for what the place of the axis at Tenterden would have been depressed, had it been observed instead of the top of the staff.

On Tenterden Steeple the ground at Allington Knoll was depressed 3′ 35″: but the axis of the instrument, when at Allington Knoll, was 5¼ feet above the ground, which will subtend an angle of 18″.4, this taken from 3′ 35″, leaves 3′ 16″.6 for what the place of the axis at Allington Knoll would have been depressed.

Contained arc (61777 feet)	-	-	10′ 6″ nearly.
Sum of depressions 4′ 1″.4 + 3′ 16″.6		sub.	7 18
			2 48
Mean refraction	-	-	1 24

or about ⅐ of the contained arc.

For the relative heights. The mean refraction added to the depression of the axis at Allington Knoll is 1′ 24″ + 3′ 16″.6 = 4′ 40″.6, being 22″.4 less than half the contained arc, and therefore the place of the axis at Allington Knoll is higher than its place when on Tenterden Steeple, by what that difference, or the angle 22″.4 subtends, which will be found = 6.7 feet; this taken from 329 feet, the vertical height of the axis at Allington Knoll, leaves 322.3 feet, its height when on Tenterden Steeple.

2. At Allington Knoll the ground at High Nook was depressed - - - - - 46' 43"

At High Nook the ground at Allington Knoll was elevated - - - - - - - 48 34

The height of the axis above the ground at each of those stations was 5½ feet, which, with 29186 feet, the distance between the stations, will give 49" nearly, the angle subtended by the height of the axis above the ground.

Ground at High Nook - -	depr.	46 43
	sub.	0 49
Place of the axis - -	depr.	45 54
Ground at Allington Knoll -	elev.	48 34
	add,	0 49
Place of the axis - -	elev.	49 29
Contained arc (29186 feet) -	-	3 48.4 nearly.
Sum of contained arc and elevation	-	47 11.4
Depression - - -	sub.	45 54
	diff.	1 17.4
Mean refraction - -	half	0 38.7

or ¼ of the contained arc.

Subtract the mean refraction from 49' 29" and there remains 49' 44".9 for the elevation of the place of the axis at Allington Knoll corrected for refraction, which, with the distance of the stations, give 301.7 feet, for the height of Allington Knoll above High Nook: this being added to 27.6 feet, the height of the axis at High Nook above low-water, and we have 929 feet, the height of the axis at Allington Knoll.

Refraction between Dover Castle and Calais Church.

73. Let C (fig. 6. Pl. XV.) be the earth's centre, SS the surface; D the station on Dover Castle; B the top of the great balustrade of Calais Steeple; DO the horizontal line; also let $Sd = SD$; then the angle $ODd = $ half the angle C, or arc SS.

Calais from Dover is 197455 feet, which answers to 22° 29' nearly, the angle C, or contained arc, therefore $ODd = 11'\ 14''\frac{1}{2}$.

	Feet.
The height of D above low-water spring tides -	469
The height of B (communicated by the French Gentlemen) - - - -	140$\frac{1}{4}$
Bd =	928$\frac{1}{4}$

The distance 197455 with 928$\frac{1}{4}$ give the angle dDB =	8' 14''
angle ODd =	11 14$\frac{1}{2}$
The depression, supposing no refraction, - ODB =	19 28$\frac{1}{2}$
But the depression, by observation, was	17 59
Refraction - - - diff.	1 29$\frac{1}{2}$

or $\frac{1}{13}$ of the contained arc. Which may be considered as the actual refraction at that time, because the relative heights are given.

Refraction between Padlesworth and the Horizon of the Sea.

74. Oct. 7, 1787, at the station near Padlesworth, the depression of the horizon of the sea, in a S W direction nearly, was

[179]

observed 26° 27'. A degree of a great circle in that direction is about 61000 fathoms, and therefore 61000 × 6 × 57.2957795 = 20970255 feet, will be the radius of curvature nearly. The height of the station above low-water spring tides (as determined by alternate observations at this place and Dover Castle) is 642 feet; hence $\frac{20970255}{20970255+642}$ = .9999693861 the natural cosine of 26° 54' the *dip*; therefore 26° 54" —26° 27" = 27', is what the horizon was elevated by refraction. The state of the tide, however, is not taken into consideration, but the time was about noon. The weather was calm and cloudy, and the horizon clear. Barom. 29.6. Thermom. 70°, at one P. M.

This refraction coming out so small, might almost induce one to suspect that some error had crept into the observation, though it was made with much care and attention.

75. *Table of the Refractions, and vertical Heights.*

Mean Refr.			Instrum. above low-water.
$\frac{1}{2}$	of the contained arc between	Allington Knoll —	329 feet.
		and Ruckinge — —	37
$\frac{1}{6}$	— —	High Nook — —	28
		and Lydd — —	130
$\frac{1}{6}$	— —	Allington Knoll	
		and High Nook	
$\frac{1}{7}$	— —	Allington Knoll	
		and Tenterden —	322
$\frac{1}{8}$	— —	Paddlesworth — —	642
		and Lydd	
$\frac{1}{8}$	— —	Frant — — —	659
		and Botley Hill —	880
$\frac{1}{10}$	— —	Dover Castle — —	469
		and Padlesworth	

A 2

Mean Refr.		Heights above low water.
$\frac{1}{15}$ of the contained arc between	{ Fairlight Down and Tenterden	599 feet.
$\frac{1}{11}$ — —	{ Goudhurst and Frant	497
$\frac{1}{13}$ — —	{ Tenterden and Lydd	
$\frac{1}{13}$ — —	{ Fairlight Down and Lydd	
$\frac{1}{16}$ — —	{ Goudhurst and Tenterden	
$\frac{1}{33}$ — —	{ Allington Knoll and Lydd	
$\frac{1}{34}$ — —	{ Dover Castle and Folkstone Turnpike	575
$\frac{1}{7}$ — —	Folkst. Turnpike and Calais	
$\frac{1}{15}$ — , —	Dover Castle and Calais	
$\frac{1}{17}$ — —	Folkstone Turnpike and Montlambert	
	Greenwich Observatory	214
	Severndroog Castle	482
	Norwood	389
	Hundred Acres	443
	Hanger Hill Tower	251
	Hampton Poorhouse	101
	King's Arbour	132
	St. Ann's Hill	342
	Swingfield	530
	Hollingborn Hill	616

Remarks.

The refractions on the distances across the Channel, depend upon the heights on the opposite coast communicated by the

French Gentlemen: that at Calais was determined by actual measurement.

There is reason to suppose that the height of St. Ann's Hill,
in the above table, is considerably too great: it was found from
that of Hampton Poorhouse, by taking $\frac{1}{15}$ of the contained arc for
the effect of refraction. In 1787, at Hampton Poorhouse, the
ground at St. Ann's Hill was elevated 17' 39", but in 1792, at the
same station, the elevation was no more than 8' 11". By the
barometer, the height of St. Ann's Hill was found to be 200
feet above the Thames at Shepperton, to which, adding 33 feet,
for the fall to low-water at the sea, and 21 feet for the height of
the telescope above the ground at St. Ann's Hill, the sum is 254
feet; which probably is within 30 feet of the truth.

N. B. When the instrument stood on the ground, the height of
the telescope was about 5½ feet. On the half scaffold it was 21
feet. And on the whole scaffold 37½ feet from the ground.

*Secondary Triangles, subdivided into two Sets, for the Improvement
of the Maps of the Country, and the Plan of the City of London
and its Environs.* Plate XVI.

76. In the series of great triangles, the extreme smallness of
the error on the sum of the three angles of each triangle sufficiently proves that the general result would not have differed
greatly, if only two of the angles had actually been observed.
But in an operation of so much importance, this could not have
been depended upon; nothing was to be left doubtful; and therefore, in the execution of the various parts, the most minute attention was paid to every circumstance whereby the accuracy might
be affected, and particularly to the placing of the lights and in-

strument reciprocally over the same point marking the station, that no possible error might arise from parallax or eccentricity.

From this mode of conducting the operation, it will readily be seen, that, if time had permitted, the situation of a multitude of other points in the country might have been very accurately determined, besides those actually marking the points of the triangles, whereby the ordinary maps would have been greatly improved by such as chose at any time hereafter to make use of these as so many given distances. But the circumstances not having permitted us to multiply those points to the extent that might have been wished, and that would have been easily practicable, if the operation had commenced at an earlier season of the year: we have therefore been obliged to limit the number to a few of the most conspicuous and best defined objects.

These secondary triangles are subdivided into two sets. The first set consists of thirty-three, whereby the relative distances of so many points have been determined from certain stations of the principal series, beginning with those objects that have been intersected from the most westerly stations, and so on, proceeding gradually with the others towards the east. Two angles only of each of those triangles being observed, the third is that at the intersected object, or the supplement to 180°. Although the distances thus obtained cannot be quite so accurate as the sides of the principal series; yet there is no reason to apprehend, that they will be found to differ widely from the truth, when they come to be proved in the course of any subsequent operation, by which alone they can be put to the test.

1

Computation of the first Set of Secondary Triangles.

Triangles.	Angles.	Distances of the stations from the intersected object in feet.	
King's Arbour - St. Ann's Hill - *Stanwell Church*	8 52 57 4 4 44 167 2 19	} from Stanwell {	10927 93720
King's Arbour - Hanger Hill Tower *Harrow on the Hill* -	28 35 34 89 23 52 62 0 34	from Harrow on the Hill {	42943 20553
King's Arbour - Hanger Hill Tower *Banstead Church* -	70 1 47 82 19 25 27 98 48	from Banstead Church {	80992 76811
Hampton Poorhouse King's Arbour - *Kew Pagoda* -	88 58 23 40 14 25 50 47 12	from Kew Pagoda - {	22819 35364
Harrow on the Hill St. Paul's Church - Spring Grove House, Sir Jo. Banks * -	69 49 8 35 58 9 74 18 43	} from Spring Grove House -	35850 57253
Hanger Hill Tower Spring Grove House * *Richmond Royal Observatory* - -	19 33 4 82 46 16 77 40 40	from Richmond Royal Obsery. { Hanger Hill from Spring Grove	20164 6802 19857
Hundred Acres - St. Paul's * - *Battersea Church* -	14 13 27 34 3 49 131 42 44	from Battersea Church - {	50664 22226
Hundred Acres - Fulham Church * *Stretham Church* -	27 51 56 46 12 54 105 55 10	from Stretham Church {	35957 23279
Hundred Acres - Severndroog Castle Clapham Common, Mr. Cavendish -	36 59 96 33 98 20 109 32 4	from Clapham Common {	43351 47295

Triangles.	Angles.	Distances of the stations from the intersected object in feet.	
Norwood - - -	76 19 15	} from Argyll Street {	40082
Severndroog Castle	52 41 37	Observatory	48963
Argyll Street Observatory, Major Gen. Roy	50 59 8		
Norwood - - -	62 30 24	} from St. Paul's {	37840
Severndroog Castle	57 8 8	Church -	39964
St. Paul's Church -	60 21 28		

N. B. By combining the results of these two last triangles
a third is formed, which gives for the distance of Argyll
Street from St. Paul's - - - - - 9632

And from this triangle and the viii, the angle at Greenwich in the next triangle is obtained.

Norwood - - -	42 15 27		
Greenwich Observatory	82 41 1	from St. Paul's	25655
St. Paul's - -	55 3 32		
Norwood - - -	36 36 32	} from Bromley {	22695
Severndroog Castle	32 52 48	Church -	24990
Bromley Church -	110 30 40		
Norwood - - -	31 53 3	} from Chislehurst {	26777
Severndroog Castle	67 48 12	Church -	20981
Chislehurst Church -	80 18 45		
Greenwich Royal Observatory -	92 38 14	} from Wanstead {	34412
Severndroog Castle	64 46 33	House -	37999
West Pediment of Wanstead House -	22 35 13		
Greenwich Royal Observatory -	131 45 43	} from Loampit {	6352
Severndroog Castle	14 7 0	Hill -	19428
Loampit Hill -	34 7 17		

Triangles.	Angles.	Distances of the stations from the intersected object in feet.	
Greenwich Royal Observatory -	22 41 33	from Eltham Church	15531
Severndroog Castle	87 18 31		5998
Eltham Church -	69 59 56		
Severndroog Castle	21 56 44	from Knockholt Beeches -	58932
Botley Hill -	54 48 27		26950
Knockholt Beeches -	103 14 49		
Severndroog Castle	31 40 29	from Leith Hill Tower -	144758
Botley Hill -	124 53 14		92666
Leith Hill Tower -	23 26 17		
Botley Hill -	39 17 16	from Firedean Tower	44780
Frant Church -	26 58 39		62506
Firedean Tower -	113 44 5		
Botley Hill -	19 51 20	from Crowborough Beacon	88975
Frant Church -	77 32 33		80949
Crowborough Beacon -	82 36 7		
Botley Hill -	24 22 7	from Sevenoaks Windmill	44032
Wrotham Hill -	28 57 42		87519
Sevenoaks Windmill -	126 40 11		
Frant Church -	46 5 9	from Wadhurst Church	20675
Goudhurst Church	26 21 46		33540
Wadhurst Church -	107 33 5		
Goudhurst Church	42 6 25	from Brightling Windmill	58618
Fairlight Down -	38 5 33		63710
Brightling Windmill	99 48 2		
Fairlight Down -	22 40 17	from Rye Church	37599
Lydd Church -	21 23 25		39735
Rye Church -	135 56 18		
Fairlight Down -	19 34 30	from Dengeness Light House	81086
Dover Castle, north turret -	13 54 25		113094
Dengeness Light House	146 31 5		
Fairlight Down -	60 29 28	from Ore Church	7606
Goudhurst Church	4 12 42		90126
Ore Church -	115 17 50		

Triangles.	Angles.	Distances of the stations from the intersected object in feet	
Fairlight Down -	23 32 23	from Fairlight	5385
Lydd Church -	1 50 43	Church -	66790
Fairlight Church -	154 36 54		
Tenterden Church -	30 42 37	from Ashford	51716
Allington Knoll -	56 45 7	Church -	31581
Ashford Church - -	92 32 16		
Lydd Church -	43 34 51	from Ruckinge	41684
High Nook near Dym-		Church -	28759
church - -	87 40 22		
Ruckinge Church -	48 44 47		
High Nook -	42 44 45	from LymneCastle	20692
Allington Knoll -	60 21 48		16158
Lymne Castle -	76 53 27		
Lydd Church -	2 10 29	from Folkstone	78950
Folkstone Turnpike -	27 26 22	Church -	6502
Folkstone Church -	150 23 9		
Folkstone Turnpike	24 35 59	from Beachbo-	99376
Padlesworth	123 46 35	rough Summer H.	11682
Beachborough Summer			
House - -	31 37 26		

Remarks.

The Royal Observatory in Richmond lower Park could not be seen from any of the stations of the great series of triangles, except Hanger Hill Tower, from whence the bearing of it was taken. In order to intersect this bearing, the assistance of certain operations made with the astronomical quadrant in 1789, at Spring Grove House, has been called in, by the help of which, the situations of the Observatory and of Spring Grove House have been determined. In like manner, the bearings of Battersea and Stretham, taken from the Hundred Acres, have been intersected with the quadrant from

St. Paul's and Fulham. The stations where the quadrant was used
are distinguished with asterisks.

Observed angles.

At Hanger Hill; between Richmond Ob. and the		12° 26′ 42″
Pagoda - - - - - - -		
At Spring Grove in 1783; between	Richmond Ob. and the Pagoda	13 10 13
	The Pagoda and St. Paul's -	23 17 15
	St. Paul's and Harrow Spire -	74 18 43
On Fulham Ch.; between - -	Stretham Ch. and St. Paul's -	70 24 52
	St. Paul's and Hampstead Ch.	44 50 46
	Hampstead Ch. and Hanger Hill Tower - - -	57 27 43
At the Hundred Acres; between	Hanger Hill and Battersea Ch.	23 59 44
	Hanger Hill and Stretham Ch.	42 3 57
On St. Paul's; between Battersea Ch. and the SW. Pinnacle of Westminster Abbey - -		} 0 9 46

The results from the observations made on Fulham Church,
however, cannot be considered as very exact, because Hanger Hill
Tower itself was the object, instead of the flag-staff placed on it
in 1787.

Second Set of Secondary Triangles.

77. In the Philos. Trans. 1787, sufficient reasons have been
given for avoiding St. Paul's as a station in the series of great
triangles. Indeed, if no other objection had existed, the smoke of
the capital alone would have been found extremely inconvenient.
This was experienced at Shooter's Hill, where we were detained
a whole week, before the white lights, notwithstanding their extraordinary brilliancy, could be seen at Hanger Hill Tower, or even
at Argyll Street, the north-east wind, which then prevailed, having
brought the impenetrable mass of smoke between the station of the
instrument and the points to be observed ; and at last we were
obliged to watch all night, till towards the morning, the fires of

London being extinguished, the white lights could then be intersected.

It is not therefore surprising, that from the stations of Norwood,
Greenwich, and Shooter's Hill, we should only be able to fix, in
a satisfactory manner, two points in London, namely, St. Paul's
and Argyll Street. Bearings, it is true, of others were taken ; but
that these might be intersected by angles not too acute, it became
necessary to make use of observations that had been formerly obtained at Argyll Street, and at St. Paul's, with the astronomical
quadrant. Moreover, by way of finishing the operation, and furnishing such part of the inhabitants of the metropolis as may be
curious in matters of this sort with a set of distances that cannot
fail to be useful to them, two new stations were chosen for the
great instrument to the northward of London, one on *Hornsey
Hill*, and the other on *Primrose Hill*. Thus, from the combined
operations at these several places, we have been able to determine the situation of thirty conspicuous points, consisting chiefly
of the most remarkable steeples in and near the capital.

By referring to Plate XVI. which is in fact the skeleton, but on a
very small scale, for an improved plan of London and its environs,
the relative situations of these points, with regard to St. Paul's and
the four nearest stations of the great series, will be seen. Some of
the principal of these secondary triangles have been represented by
dotted lines in the plan. To have expressed more of them in that
way, would only have occasioned confusion. Here it is to be remarked, that the distance of Argyll Street from St. Paul's, 9632
feet, (p. 184.) becomes a base in the quadrilateral formed by *St. Paul's,
Argyll Street, Hornsey Hill*, and *Primrose Hill*. Hence, by the
observed angles at these two last stations, and the assumed length
of one of the unknown sides, all the angles of the quadrilateral are
computed ; by which means, and the true length of one side given,
the true lengths of all the others are readily obtained.

Computation of the second Set of Secondary Triangles.

Situations determined with the great instrument from Hornsey Hill and Primrose Hill.

Triangles.	Angles.	Distances of the stations from the Intersected object in feet.	
Hornsey Hill -	46 42 41	}from St. Paul's {	23297
Primrose Hill -	89 21 27.5	} Church - {	17072.5
St. Paul's -	49 55 51.5	Hornsey Hill from	
		Primrose Hill	17949
Hornsey Hill -	29 8 34	} Argyll Street {	23803
Primrose Hill -	112 49 57	} Observatory {	10150.5
Argyll Str. Observ.	44 1 29		
Hornsey Hill -	23 33 59	}from Hampstead {	17972
Primrose Hill -	78 29 43	} Church - {	7335
Hampstead Church	78 2 18		
Hornsey Hill -	29 11 4	}from Mr. Duve- {	7198
Primrose Hill -	16 44 50	} luz's Cupola - {	12181
Mr. Duvelux's Cupo-			
la, Hornsey Lane,			
Highgate -	134 4 6		
Hornsey Hill -	47 30 42	}from Islington {	14272
Primrose Hill -	51 42 39	} Church - {	13409
Islington Church -	80 46 39		
Hornsey Hill -	55 23 32	}from Highbury {	8868
Primrose Hill -	29 28 52	} House - {	14845
Highbury House,			
Mr. Aubert -	95 2 36		
Hornsey House	50 52 33	}from St. Luke's {	19393
Primrose Hill -	68 59 37	} Church - {	16057
St. Luke's Church,			
Old Street -	60 7 50		
Hornsey Hill -	62 9 30	} from St. Leo- {	19816
Primrose Hill -	69 36 33	} nard's Church {	19560
St. Leonard's Ch.			
Shoreditch -	54 13 57		

	Triangles.	Angles.	Distances of the station from the intersected object in feet.	
With the great Instrument from Hornsey Hill and Primrose Hill.	Hornsey Hill - Primrose Hill - Christ Church, Spitalfields -	61 19 6 70 33 39 48 7 13	}from Christ Ch. } Spitalfields -	22733 21149
	Hornsey Hill - Primrose Hill - Bow Ch. Cheapside	49 20 39 81 21 4 49 18 17	}from Bow Ch.	23404 17959
	Hornsey Hill - Primrose Hill - St. Bride's Church, Fleet Street -	42 33 43 86 44 24 50 41 53	}from St. Bride's } Church -	29158 15689
	Hornsey Hill - Primrose Hill - St. George's Church, Bloomsbury -	31 16 11 94 11 25 54 32 24	}from S. George's } Church -	21977 11438
	Hornsey Hill - Primrose Hill - St. Giles's Church	29 32 9 100 13 30 50 14 21	}from St. Giles's } Church -	22978 11510
	Hornsey Hill - Primrose Hill - St. Ann's, Soho -	28 2 38 106 40 20 45 17 2	}from St. Ann's } Church -	24197 11875
One angle taken with the great instrument, and the other with that in Argyll Street Observatory.	Hornsey Hill - Argyll Street Observatory - Highgate Chapel -	59 52 55 22 37 48 97 29 17	}from Highgate } Chapel -	9298 20766
	Primrose Hill - Argyll Str. Observ. St. Clement's Ch.	20 43 50 123 0 9 36 16 1	}from St. Clement's Church	14391 6074
	Primrose Hill - Argyll Street Ob. St. Mary's Church in the Strand -	17 52 31 127 21 15 34 46 14	}from St. Mary's } Church -	14148 5463
	Primrose Hill - Argyll Street Ob. St. Martin's Church in the Fields -	7 32 8 152 0 27 20 27 25	}from St. Martin's Church	13631 3809

	Triangles.	Angles.	Distances of the stations from the intersected object in feet.	
One angle with the ... inst. and the ... with that in Argyll Street Ob.	Primrose Hill - Argyll Street Observatory - Pantheon -	3 13 0 102 32 39 74 14 21	from the Pantheon -	10295 592
A small Hadley's sextant used in Argyll Street.	Primrose Hill - Argyll Street Ob. St. George's Church, Hanover Square	5 35 34 120 13 56 54 10 30	from S. George's Church -	10816 1220
	Primrose Hill - Argyll Street Ob. South Audley Chapel	16 7 10 103 34 59 60 17 51	from South Audley Chapel	11359 3244
A small Hadley's sextant used at St. Paul's.	Hornsey Hill - St. Paul's Church Newington Church	38 14 6 16 35 7 125 10 47	from Newington Church -	8196 17640
	Hornsey Hill - St. Paul's Church St. Matthew's Ch. Bethnal Green	20 29 59 66 7 5 92 22 56	from St. Matthew's Church	21321 8166
The astronomical quadrant were at St. Paul's in 1783.	Hornsey Hill - St. Paul's Church St.George's, Ratcliff	18 29 9 105 32 24 56 5 27	from S.George's Church, Ratcliff	27045 8846
	Primrose Hill - St. Paul's Church St. James's Church	30 44 17 45 39 31 103 36 12	from St. James's Church -	12562 8978
	Primrose Hill - St. Paul's - Limehouse Church	14 33 10 149 20 0 16 6 50	from Limehouse Church -	31374 15456
	Argyll Street Ob. St. Paul's Church SW. pinnacle of the S. tower of St. Peter's Ch. Westm.	61 47 27 39 42 24 78 30 9	from St. Peter's Church, Westm.	6279 8662
Circle used ... and Argyll Street instrument.	Norwood - Argyll Street Ob. The Monument	18 5 5 64 9 56 97 44 59	from the Monument -	36409 19557

Both with the astronomical quadrant. — One angle with the Argyll Street instrument, and the other with the astronomical quadrant. — Both angles observed with the astronomical quadrant in 1783.

Triangles.	Angles.			Distances of the stations from the intersected objects in feet.	
Jew's Harp station	52	52	55	from St. Paul's Church -	13582
Black Lane station	92	12	30		10790
St. Paul's Church	34	54	37	from Jew's Harp to Black Lane, the base of 1783 -	7744
Jew's Harp station	89	56	56	from Argyll Street	5657
Black Lane station	36	9	50		9586
Argyll Street Observatory -	53	53	14		
Argyll Street Ob.	95	30	56	from the British Museum	5488
Jew's Harp station	30	5	26		6995
Wind Vane of the British Museum	54	23	38		
Argyll Street Ob.	74	26	17	from Charlotte Street Chapel	1848
Jew's Harp station	19	1	56		5459
Charlotte Street Chapel -	86	31	47		
Jew's Harp station	85	27	45	from Portland Chapel -	4098
Black Lane station	28	53	30		8474
Portland Chapel	65	38	45		
Jew's Harp station	60	43	55	from Fitzroy Chapel -	4015
Black Lane station	31	12	45		6759
Fitzroy Chapel -	88	3	20		
Jew's Harp station	63	25	50	from the Tabernacle -	4781
Black Lane station	37	14	40		7048
Tabernacle -	79	19	30		
Jew's Harp station	19	45	45	from the Small-Pox Hospital	6670
Black Lane station	56	57	45		2690
Small-Pox Hospital	103	16	30		
Jew's Harp station	4	41	45	from St. Pancras Church -	5728
Black Lane station	12	58	25		2089
St. Pancras Church	162	19	50		

78. That these secondary triangles may be more generally useful to the inhabitants of London and its environs, the angles, which the 59 points comprehended in Plate XVI. respectively form with each other at the centre of the dome of St. Paul's, are collected in the annexed table, together with their several distances from that central point. The objects are arranged into two classes, according as they are situated to the eastward or westward of the meridian of St. Paul's. Those of the first class commence at the north meridian, and proceed by the east to 180°. These of the second commence at the south meridian, and proceed, in like manner, by the west to 180°. From this table the total angle between any two objects being had by simple subtraction, and the distances from St. Paul's given, the distances of the objects from each other are readily obtained. Whoever, therefore, should be desirous of knowing accurately his own situation in this great metropolis, may easily satisfy himself, by taking two angles from the top of his house with a good Hadley's sextant or theodolite, between any known objects near to him and the best disposed for the purpose. By the help of these *data*, and a very simple trigonometrical computation, he will obtain what he wants; and he may even satisfy another curiosity which will probably occur, namely, that of putting to the test our original operation, by trying how nearly different triangles bring out the same result. It will readily be conceived that, for trials of this sort, the points whose situations have been determined by the great instrument should be chosen preferably to the others; and next to these, the objects that have been fixed by one angle, taken with the Argyll Street instrument, as more to be relied upon than those observed with the astronomical quadrant or sextant. Thus an excellent foundation is laid for the improvement of the plan of London and its environs, which may by these triangles be rendered more accurate than would have been possible by any other mode.

Table, shewing the Bearings and Distances of Objects situated in and near London, from the Centre of the Dome of St. Paul's.

Objects.	Bearings from the north meridian eastward.	Distances in feet.
Eastward from the Meridian of St. Paul's.		
Newington Church - -	9 59 39	17641
St. Luke's Church, Old Street -	12 37 37	4263
St. Leonard's Church, Shoreditch -	44 54 59	6743
The West Pediment of Wanstead House -	55 53 46	36308
St. Matthew's Church, Bethnal Green -	59 31 37	8166
Christ Church, Spitalfields - -	70 38 37	5878
Bow Church, Cheapside - -	87 48 4	1078
Limehouse Church - - -	92 58 41	15456
St. George's Church, Ratcliff Highway	98 56 56	8846
The Monument - - -	115 15 46	3114
Severndroog Castle, Shooter's Hill -	115 25 50	39965
Transit-room of Greenwich Royal Observat.	120 43 46	25655
Eltham Church - - -	129 46 4	41090
Loampit Hill - - - -	134 40 10	23430
Station at Norwood - -	175 47 18	57840
South Meridian of St. Paul's	180 0 0	
Westward from the Meridian of St. Paul's.		
Stretham Church - - -	13 57 8	31739
Clapham Common, Mr. Cavendish -	26 29 52	24565
Battersea Church - - -	52 22 28	22226
St. Peter's Church, Westminster, SW. pinnacle of the S. Tower - -	52 32 13	8662
Fulham Church - - -	57 39 45	30746
Kew Pagoda - - -	71 2 36	47577
Richmond Royal Observatory -	71 42 0	51940
St. Martin's Church, in the Strand -	74 28 59	6748
Spring Grove House, Sir Jos. Banks, Bart.	76 9 49	57259
St. James's Church - - -	77 49 10	8978

Objects.	Bearings from the south merid. westward.			Distances in feet.
South Audley Chapel - -	81	49	43	12211
St. Mary's, New Church in the Strand	81	57	28	4291
St. Clement's Church - - -	85	57	37	3592
St. Ann's Church, Soho - -	86	9	59	7754
St. George's Church, Hanover Square	86	23	13	10304
St. Bride's Church, Fleet Street -	90	12	43	1687
Argyll Street Observatory, Maj. Gen. Roy	92	14	38	9632
The Pantheon - - - -	93	19	17	9067
Hanger-hill Tower - -	94	25	0	45844
St. Giles's Church - - -	94	36	28	6917
Portland Chapel - - -	100	34	39	10301
Charlotte Street Chapel - -	101	30	24	8500
St. George's Church, Bloomsbury Square	103	15	50	6221
Wind Vane of the British Museum -	105	45	46	6701
The Tabernacle, Tottenham Court Road	107	19	47	8776
Fitzroy Chapel - -	109	41	10	9560
Harrow on the Hill Church - -	112	7	58	58763
Jew's Harp station of 1783 - -	112	58	31	13522
Primrose Hill station of 1788 -	123	28	41	17072
Hampstead Church -	128	56	12	24148
St. Pancras Church - - -	136	43	26	10600
The Small-Pox Hospital - -	137	38	38	8732
Black Lane station of 1788 -	147	53	8	10790
Highgate Chapel - - -	130	59	18	24062
Mr. Duveluz's Cupola, Highgate -	155	27	13	22646
Hornsey Hill station of 1788 -	173	24	32	23297
Islington Church -	174	40	21	9028
Highbury House, Mr. Aubert -	178	43	15	14595
Ditto, the Transit-room of his Observatory	179	1	57	14561
North meridian of St. Paul's	180	0	0	- -

The bearing of Greenwich from the meridian of St. Paul's, on which the other bearings in the above table depend, was found as follows:

St. Paul's bears from Greenwich 59° 11′ 43″ NW; distant from the meridian 22035 feet; and 13138 feet from the perpendicular; answering to 3′ 35″.9, and 2′ 9″¼ respectively; the latter taken from 38° 31′ 20″ the co-lat. of Greenwich, leaves 38° 29′ 10″½; which, with 3′ 35″.9 as the legs of a spherical triangle, give 89° 55′ 29″ for the angle at St. Paul's, between its meridian and the perpendicular to that of Greenwich, which added to 30° 48′ 17″, (the complement of 59° 11′ 43″) makes 120° 49′ 46″, as in the table.

79. *Table, containing the Bearings of Thirty-two of the interior Objects from the Parallels to the Meridian of Greenwich; also their Distances from that Meridian and its Perpendicular.*

Objects.	Bearings.				Distances from Meridian.	Perpend.
	°	′	″		Feet.	Feet.
At Greenwich Ob.						
Wanstead House -	13	32	13	NE	8035	33456
Eltham Steeple -	51	8	1	SE	12093	9746
St. Paul's - -	59	11	43	NW	22035	13138
At Norwood.						
Argyll Street -	17	57	1	NW	31662	13528
At the Hundred Acres.						
Clapham Common	13	45	28	NE	33029	8830
At King's Arbour.						
Harrow Spire -	36	57	53	NE	76441	35350
Kew Pagoda - -	84	39	11	SE	67053	2257
Banstead Spire -	44	24	46	SE	45582	56817
At St. Ann's Hill.						
Windsor Castle -	29	19	25	NW	137048	2569
Stanwell Spire -	25	45	5	NE	109094	7488

Objects.	Bearings.		Distances from Meridian.	Perpend.
At St. Paul's.	° ′ ″		*Feet.*	*Feet.*
Spring Grove House	76 14 20	SW	77645	481
Richmond Observatory	71 46 31	SW	71370	3106
Battersea Steeple	52 26 59	SW	39656	407
Stretham Steeple	14 1 39	SW	29728	17654
Highbury Transit R.	0 53 32	NW	2226½	27697
St. James's Church	77 53 41	SW	30813	11255
At Severndroog Castle.				
Bromley Church -	25 29 25	SW	3303	26572
Chiselhurst Steeple	9 26 0	SE	17471	24767
Leith Hill Tower -	43 3 47	SW	84809	109831
At Botley Hill.				
Sevenoaks Windmill	76 21 24	SE	42962	83267
At Frant.				
Wadhurst Steeple	51 30 40	SE	78523	151325
Fairden Tower -	70 26 59	NW	3439	117541
At Goudhurst.				
Brightling Windmill	18 51 8	SW	87404	188069
Ore Church - -	19 2 35	SE	135751	217790
At Fairlight Down.				
Rye Steeple - -	44 24 41	NE	169624	191760
Dengeness Light House	79 8 4	NE	222044	203333
Fairlight Church -	89 22 39	SE	148697	218676
At Tenterden.				
Ashford Steeple -	55 4 28	NE	200723	118963
At Lydd.				
Ruckinge Church -	6 30 22	NW	204622	149285
Folkstone Church -	52 59 51	NE	272395	143185
At Padlesworth.				
Beechborough Sum. H.	59 27 48	SW	251653	136775
At High Noak.				
Lymne Castle -	21 42 56	NE	235909	146454

The bearings and distances in the foregoing table, have been obtained In a similar manner to those in the table, Art. 59 ; thus, taking Windsor Castle for an example :

If a line be drawn through St. Ann's Hill parallel to the meridian of Greenwich, (see the Plan of the triangles) then the bearing of King's Arbour from that line will be   29° 49′ 49″ NE.

The angle at St. Ann's Hill between King's Arbour and Windsor Castle (triang. III. Art. 57.)   59   9   14

Bearing of Windsor Castle from the parallel
to the meridian of Greenwich   -   diff. 29 19 25 NW.

The sine and co-sine of 29° 19′ 25″, with 36032 feet, the distance of Windsor from St. Ann's, as radius, give 17646 feet for what Windsor is westward, and 31415 feet, what it is northward from St. Ann's.

	Feet.
St. Ann's Hill from the meridian of Greenwich (59)	119402
add	17646
Windsor Castle from the meridian of Greenwich	137048
St. Ann's Hill from the perpendicular (southward)	28852
	31415
Windsor Castle from the perpendicular (northward) diff.	2563

80. *Computed Latitudes and Longitudes of the interior Objects in the foregoing Table.*

Objects.	Lat.	Long. from Greenwich.	In time.
		West.	m. s.
St. Paul's - -	51 30 49	0 5 47	0 23.1
Highbury House Trans. R.	51 33 19	0 5 51	0 23.4
Stretham Steeple -	51 25 46	0 7 48	0 31.2
St. James's Church -	51 30 31	0 8 5	0 32.3
Argyll Street Ob. -	51 30 53	0 8 19	0 33.3
Clapham Common	51 27 13	0 8 40	0 34.7
Battersea Steeple -	51 28 36	0 10 24	0 41.6
Banstead Steeple -	51 19 19	0 11 55	0 47.7
Kew Pagoda - -	51 28 16	0 17 56	1 10.4
Royal Ob. Richmond	51 28 8	0 18 43	1 14.9
Harrow Steeple -	51 34 27	0 20 6	1 20.4
Spring Grove House	51 28 34	0 20 22	1 21.5
Leith Hill Tower -	51 10 35	0 22 7	1 28.5
Stanwell Steeple -	51 27 23	0 28 37	1 54.5
Windsor Castle -	51 29 0	0 35 28	2 21.9
		East.	
Bromley Church -	51 24 18	0 0 52	0 3.5
Fairden Tower - -	51 9 21	0 0 54	0 3.6
Wanstead House -	51 34 10	0 2 7	0 8.5
Eltham Spire - -	51 27 4	0 4 30	0 18
Chiselhurst Steeple	51 24 36	0 4 35	0 18.3
Sevenoaks Windmill	51 14 29	0 11 13	0 44.9
Wadhurst Steeple -	51 3 46	0 20 25	1 21.7
Brightling Windmill	50 57 44	0 22 41	1 30.7
Ore Church - -	50 52 48	0 35 10	2 20.7
Fairlight Church -	50 52 38	0 38 31	2 34
Rye Steeple - -	50 57 1	0 44 0	2 56
Ashford Steeple -	51 8 56	0 52 18	3 29.2
Ruckinge Church -	51 3 56	0 59 13	3 32.9
Dengeness Light House	50 55 1	0 57 48	3 51.2
Lymne Castle - -	51 4 20	1 1 22	4 5.5
Beechborough Summer H.	51 5 53	1 5 30	4 22
Folkstone Church -	51 4 47	1 10 52	4 49.5

⊙

AN

ACCOUNT

OF THE

TRIGONOMETRICAL SURVEY

CARRIED ON IN THE

YEARS 1791, 1792, 1793, AND 1794,

BY ORDER OF THE DUKE OF RICHMOND,

THEN MASTER GENERAL OF THE ORDNANCE.

BY

LIEUT. COL. EDWARD WILLIAMS,

AND

CAPT. WILLIAM MUDGE,

OF THE ROYAL ARTILLERY;

AND

MR. ISAAC DALBY.

ACCOUNT, &c.

INTRODUCTION.

81. A ɢᴇɴᴇʀᴀʟ Survey of the Island of Great Britain, at the public expence, was (as we learn from the Introduction to the account of the measurement on Hounslow Heath) under the contemplation of Government as early as the year 1763, the execution of which was to have been committed to the late Major General Roy, whose public situation and talents well qualified him for such an undertaking. Various causes procrastinated this event till the year 1783, when the late M. Cassini de Thury transmitted a memoir to the French ambassador at London, which paved the way to a beginning of this important work. Calculated for the advancement of science, this memoir was presented to the King, and readily met with the approbation of a monarch, so eminently distinguished, from the æra of his reign, for his liberal patronage of the arts and sciences. By his Majesty's command, the memoir was put into the hands of Sir Joseph Banks, P. R. S. accompanied with such marks of royal munificence, as speedily obtained all the valuable instruments and apparatus necessary for carrying the design into immediate execution.

General Roy, to whose care the conduct of this important business was committed, lived to go through the several operations

D d

pointed out in the memoir, the particulars of which have been detailed in the two foregoing Accounts. The further prosecution of the Survey of the Island, to which the operations hitherto performed might be deemed only as subservient or introductory, seemed to expire with the General.

The liberal assistance which his Grace the Duke of Richmond had on all occasions given to this undertaking; and particularly the essential services performed by Captain Fiddes, and Lieutenant Bryce, of the corps of royal engineers, in the survey and measurement of the base of verification on Romney Marsh, are acknowledged by General Roy in the strongest terms. A considerable time had elapsed since the General's decease without any apparent intention of renewing the business, when a casual opportunity presented itself to the Duke of Richmond of purchasing a very fine instrument, the workmanship of Mr. Ramsden, of similar construction to that which was used by General Roy, but with some improvements; as also two new steel chains of one hundred feet each, made by the same incomparable artist. Circumstances thus concurring to promote the further execution of a design of such great utility, as well as honour, to the nation, his Grace, with his Majesty's approbation, immediately gave directions to prepare all the necessary apparatus for the purpose, which was accordingly provided in the most ample manner.

*An Account of the Measurement of a Base on Hounslow Heath,
with an hundred Feet Steel Chain, in the Summer of the year* 1791.

Preamble.

8a. Previous to entering upon the ensuing account, it may not,
perhaps, be improper to enumerate some preliminary matters
relative to the subject. The first mode of mensuration adopted
by General Roy was that with deal rods, which had also been
used and approved of in other countries. In the course of the
measurement, however, it appeared, that the sudden and irregular
changes which these rods were liable to, from dryness, humidity,
or other causes, rendered them totally unfit for ascertaining the
length of the base with that degree of precision, of which it was at
first thought they were capable. On this account they were laid
aside, and glass rods substituted in their stead. These rods were
contrived with great ingenuity to answer the purpose, as fully appears by the account given of them in Art. 4. But this mode of
mensuration being the first of the kind, seemed to require some
proof of its accuracy, which consideration induced General Roy
to make a comparison between the glass rods and the steel chain,
which Mr. Ramsden had made for the Royal Society. For this
purpose a distance of one thousand feet was carefully measured
with the rods and the chain. The result of these measurements
appeared to be such as would have produced a difference of little
more than half an inch upon the whole base, had it been measured with each of them respectively. But notwithstanding the
apparent degree of accuracy which this, or any other mode of
measuring may be supposed capable of, yet it seems necessary
that every base, intended to become the groundwork of such nice

D d e

operations, ought always (when circumstances will permit) to be
measured twice at least.

The manner in which the glass rods were applied in the measurement, is supposed to have rendered the operation liable to some
small errors, which lying different ways, might possibly have
counterbalanced each other, and produced a true result : but this
supposition ought never to be admitted in experimental inquiries,
unless such errors can be nearly estimated. The principal cause of
error is supposed to arise from the ends of the two adjacent rods
being made to rest on the same trestle ; because when the first rod
is taken off, the face of the first trestle, being then pressed by the
end of one rod only, will acquire a tendency to incline a little forward. The error arising from this cause will evidently tend to
shorten the apparent base.

Another source of error is supposed to arise from the casual
deviation of the rods from a right line, in the direction of the base,
tending to increase its apparent length. And a third error is supposed to result from the method which was used of supporting the
ends of the rods on two trestles only, by which they become liable
to bend in the middle. This concave form of the rods would also
tend to lengthen the base. The first of these causes of error was
submitted to experimental Inquiry in the garden of Richmond
house, Whitehall, in the presence of his Grace the Duke of Richmond, Sir Joseph Banks, Mr. Ramsden, and Mr. Dalby ; when it
appeared evidently, that the glass rod had a small motion when the
other rod, which had counterbalanced it, was taken from the trestles.

These considerations, therefore, rendered it necessary to compare the measurement with the glass rods, with that performed by
some other method ; not on account of any doubt being entertained of the care with which General Roy's operation had been
performed, but solely with a view to bring this new mode of measuring to some proper test. No method of comparison could,

perhaps, be better than measuring the same base with the steel chain. General Roy himself, in his remarks on the comparative accuracy of the two bases, that of Hounslow Heath and Romney Marsh, evidently gives the preference to the chain; which, every circumstance considered, it is certainly right to do. These reasons induced his Grace the Duke of Richmond to direct the base on Hounslow Heath to be remeasured with the steel chain; and although the result does not differ from the glass rods by so small a quantity as General Roy's experiment assigned, yet it does not amount to more than three inches on a base exceeding five miles.

Of the Apparatus provided for the Measurement of the Base.

89. The apparatus, provided for the measurement, consisted of the following articles, viz..

1. A transit instrument.

2. A boning telescope..

3. Two steel chains, 100 feet each, with the apparatus for the drawing-post and weight-post.

4. Three sets of deal coffers, each coffer being nearly 20 feet long, for receiving the chain when extended in a right line.

5. Thirty-six strong oaken pickets of $3\frac{1}{2}$ and $4\frac{1}{2}$ feet long; shod, and hooped with iron.

6. Four brass register heads, carrying graduated sliders moved by finger-screws, for adjusting the ends of the chain. One of these registers has a micrometer-screw attached to it, proper for measuring small quantities expanded or contracted by the chain.

7. Thirty-six cast iron heads, to fix on the pickets.

As many of these articles have been described very circumstantially by General Roy in the two preceding Accounts, it will only be necessary here to give a description of the transit instrument, boning telescope, and the two new chains.

[208]

The Transit Instrument. Pl. XVII.

84. This instrument, made by Mr. Ramsden, may be considered as a transit combined with a telescopic level, which makes it
serve two purposes; one for determining points in the same vertical plane; the other to show how much a measured line deviates
from the level. It consists of a telescope about eighteen inches
long, with an achromatic object-glass of about 1$\frac{4}{5}$ inches diameter. The telescope passes through an axis in the manner of a
transit, and as it must be used for viewing objects at very different
distances, the images from the object-glass will vary in the same
proportion; it therefore becomes necessary to vary the distance
of the wires, so that they may be exactly in the same place with
the image. For this purpose there is a pinion, moveable by turning a milled head at A, whereby the small tube, with the wires
which are contained in the box B, are made to approach, or recede
from the object-glass.

The two pivots, or extremities of the axis, are made with great
accuracy to the same diameter; and they turn in angles in the
uprights C and D. Each of the angles is fixed in a slider; one at
D, to move horizontally, by turning a finger-screw E; the other
vertically, by turning the finger-screw F.

The level G is here represented as suspended by its hooks on the
transverse axis. Its use is to show when that axis is horizontal;
and it is furnished with an adjusting screw H, by which the two
hooks may be made exactly of the same length, so that the axis on
which it is suspended may become parallel to a tangent to the
middle of the glass tube. This level also serves to set the line of
collimation in the telescope horizontal; for which purpose there
are two pins, K and L, attached to the side of the telescope, parallel to the axis thereof: one of these pins is furnished with an

adjusting-screw M, by which the line of the hooks is made parallel to the line of collimation in this direction, with the greatest precision. The level may be suspended on these pins in the same manner as on the horizontal axis.

The cross wires at N, in the common focus of the object and eye-glasses, are fixed at right angles to each other ; but instead of being placed horizontally and vertically, as in the common way, they make each an angle of 45° with the plane of the horizon. This mode of fixing wires is of the greatest advantage in making nice observations, as it remedies the inconvenience and error arising from their thickness. To bring the line of collimation in the telescope at right angles to the horizontal or transverse axis, there are two nuts for the purpose, one on each side of the box at N, which serve to move the intersection of these wires towards the right or left.

In the eye end of the telescope is a micrometer, which serves to measure small angles of elevation or depression. It consists of a moveable horizontal wire, placed as close as possible to the cross wires already mentioned. By turning the micrometer-screw O, this wire is moved across the field of the telescope, and the space which it moves through is shown in revolutions of the micrometer-screw, by means of an index, moveable in a slit, and the divisions on the stem Q. The parts of a revolution are shown in 100ths by an index P, on the micrometer head.

In tracing out a base by intermediate stations, the instrument must be frequently shifted to the right or left, till the telescope shows that the middle of its axis and the extremities of the base are in the same vertical plane. To expedite this operation, there are slits cut through the top of the mahogany board, for receiving the screws which fasten the supports of the telescope ; by which means the telescope, with its supports, can be moved a little to the right or left, whilst the stand remains fixed. Over another slit in the top, and directly under the centre of the axis of the telescope at R, is a small hole for a wire or thread to pass through, suspending a plummet for marking a point on the ground, when the telescope is brought into the desired vertical plane.

The method of levelling the axis, adjusting the line of collimation, &c. are similar to those for the upper telescope of the great theodolite, as described in Art. 44, &c.

Boning Telescope.

85. This telescope is in every respect the same as that which was made use of by General Roy, therefore it will only be necessary to explain the application of it, for fixing the pickets in the direction of the base, with the tops of those belonging to the same hypothenuse in the same right line.

A rope being stretched along the ground, in the direction of the base, distances of 100 feet were marked upon it by means of a twenty-feet deal rod. After a sufficient number of these distances were set off, the telescope was laid on a narrow piece of board, truly planed, and fixed to the top of the picket at the beginning of the hypothenuse; and another picket was driven into the ground at a convenient height at the other end. To the top of this last, a thin deal spar was fixed, and the telescope directed to it, whilst the intermediate pickets were driven to their proper height. To determine this height more accurately, another spar, whose thickness was equal to the height of the axis of the telescope above the top of the picket, which supported it, was repeatedly laid on the top of each picket at the time of driving it, till its upper edge and the fixed spar appeared in a right line. Whilst the pickets were driving, they were moved a little to the right or left, as directed by signals from the observer at the telescope, till their tops appeared in the same right line.

The Chains.

86. These chains were made by Mr. Ramsden, and are of similar construction in the joints to that which he made for the Royal Society, described in Art. 9.; but they differ from that in other respects. Instead of one hundred links, each of these new chains contains forty, of 2½ feet long. The link is in form of a parallelopipedon, of half an inch square, which renders it considerably stronger than that of the Royal Society; and the chain having fewer links, becomes less liable to apply itself to any irregularities which the coffers may be subject to. The handles are made of brass, and being perfectly flat on the under side, they move freely upon the brass register-heads, by which means the coincidence between the arrows at the extremities of the chain, and the divisions on the scales, are readily and accurately obtained. The two chains will hereafter be distinguished by the letters A and B.

On Saturday July the 23d, all the foregoing articles were conveyed from the Tower to the end of the base near King's Arbour, where tents were pitched for a party of the royal regiment of artillery, consisting of one serjeant and ten gunners, who were employed in the laborious part of the operation.

Experiments made to ascertain the relative Lengths of the Chains, before and after they were used; and also to determine the Expansion of one Chain; or one hundred Feet of blistered Steel, by one Degree of Fahrenheit's Thermometer.

87. For this purpose, two strong oaken pickets were driven two feet into very firm ground, and the drawing-post was made fast to them. Five coffers were arranged in a right line, and supported

E e

upon courses of bricks. The chain was then placed in the coffers, and stretched with a weight of fifty-six pounds. Notwithstanding the great resistance which it was thought these pickets were capable of, yet it was found insufficient to counteract the friction between the coffers and the chain, when the expansion or contraction took place. Three pickets, therefore, of forty-four inches long, were driven into the ground, within six inches of their tops, and the drawing-post was fastened to them by several folds of strong rope. The pickets and rope were also covered with earth, to prevent their being warped by the sun.

The micrometer-screw, attached to the brass register-head, by means of which the expansion or contraction was measured, contains 56 threads in an inch. The circular head is divided into 10 equal parts, and consequently each division will measure $\frac{1}{560}$th part of an inch. But as the eye readily subdivides each of the divisions into 4 parts, the micrometer will measure the $\frac{1}{1640}$th of an inch tolerably exact.

For finding the relative Lengths of the Chains.

88. In order to accomplish these experiments in the most unexceptionable manner, after the chain was properly stretched in the coffers, and the thermometers placed by it, the whole remained till all the thermometers stood steadily at the same height. The ends of the chain being then in perfect coincidence with particular divisions on the brass register-heads, the chain was quickly taken out and replaced by the other, which being properly stretched in a right line, and a coincidence made at the drawing-post end of the chain, the variation of the other end from the division on its register-head showed the difference of the lengths of the chains, which was measured with the micrometer. As it required weather particularly steady to succeed in these experiments, we were

obliged to catch the most favourable opportunities that presented
themselves, which happened on the 29th and 30th of July; on
those days the chains were compared with each other, and the
results were as follow.

July 29th. *Thermometers remaining steadily at* 75° *during and
after the operation.*

The chain B was found to be $6\frac{1}{2}$ divisions of the micrometer
head shorter than the chain A; and on being shifted, A was found
to exceed B $6\frac{1}{4}$ divisions. ·

Same day. Thermometers steady at 67°$\frac{1}{2}$.

The chain B 6 divisions shorter than A; and being shifted, the
chain A was 6 divisions longer than B. The mean from these experiments is, A $6\frac{1}{4}$ divisions longer than B.

In the table containing the particulars of the operation it will
be found, that the chain B was laid aside after measuring 38
chains, on account of one of the links appearing to be a little
bent. Before it was sent to Mr. Ramsden it was compared with
the chain A (at first intended to be kept as the standard chain),
when it was found to be only $4\frac{1}{4}$ divisions longer; which being
$1\frac{3}{4}$ divisions less than the mean $6\frac{1}{4}$ as found above, shows, that the
chain B had lengthened $1\frac{3}{4}$ divisions in measuring 38 chains; for
when Mr. Ramsden afterwards straightened the link, he could
not perceive any difference in its length.

The remainder of the base was measured with the chain A (the
chain B being kept as a standard), and when that was completed,
a comparison was again made between A and B, when it appeared
that A exceeded B by $14\frac{7}{10}$ divisions of the micrometer head;
therefore the wear of A, by lengthening of the joints, in measuring
256 chains, was 14.2 — 4.5 divisions = 9.7 divisions of the micrometer.

For finding the Rate of Expansion.

89. The chain being placed in a right line, along the horizon-tal bottoms of the coffers, and kept in a state of tension by a weight of fifty-six pounds, five thermometers were placed close by the chain; one in the middle of each coffer; and the whole was co-vered with a white linen cloth, when the sun shone out. After remaining a few minutes, till the thermometers were nearly of the same temperature, a perfect coincidence was made on the register heads, at each end of the chain, and the thermometers noted. Every thing remained in this state till the coincidence at the weight end of the chain was observed to be altered, and the thermometers nearly the same; at which instant, they were again read off, and the alteration of coincidence measured with the micrometer.

August 5th, cloudy.

Thermometer.					Mean.	Micr. Divisions.	Total contr. Inches.	Contr. on 1° Inches.
1	2	3	4	5				
75.75	75.5	76	76.25	76	75.9	25¼	.096642	.0074
62.5	62.75	63	63	63	62.85			

Here the contraction of the chain is 25¼ divisions of the micrometer $= 25\frac{1}{4} \times \frac{1}{310}$ inches $= .096642$ inch. and the corresponding va-riation of the thermometers, taking the difference of the means, is 13°.05; consequently the contraction on 1° $= \frac{.096642}{11.05} = .0074$ inch.

Aug. 6th, cloudy.

89.5	89.75	90	90	90.5	89.95	38.5	.148077	.00719
69.5	69.5	69.25	69	69.5	69.35			

Aug. 7. Coffers covered with the linen cloth.

| Thermometers. | | | | | | | Total contr. | Contr. |
1	2	3	4	5	Mean.	Micr. Divisions.	Inches.	on 1°. Inches.
102.5	10.25	102.75	102	102	102.35	29.5	.113462	.00749
87	86	87	88	88	87.2	8	.030769	.00779
89	89.75	93	92	92	91.15	16.25	.062500	.00781
98	95	102	99.75	101	99.15	9.33	.035885	.00748
93	92	96	95	95.75	94.35			

Aug, 7th, in the evening. Coffers covered with the linen cloth.

90	91	89	91	92	90.6	19	.073077	.00746
80	80	81.5	81.5	81	80.8	23.5	.090985	.00735
67	68	69.5	69	69	68.5	13	.050000	.00746
60.75	62.75	62	62	62	61.8			

The mean result from these nine experiments is 0,007492, or 0.0075 inch to 1° of Fahrenheit, on 100 feet of blistered steel; which differs only $\frac{1}{10000}$th parts of an inch from General Roy's conclusion with the pyrometer; but the number .0075 is preferred in these measurements, as being deduced from experiments made with the chain itself.

Particulars relative to the Commencement of the Operation, &c.

90. After the chains were compared, and the rate of expansion determined, as related in the preceding article, several trials were made of arranging the pickets and coffers in such a manner as might be supposed proper for the reception of the chain. It was soon found, however, that this method of measuring would be neither so expeditious or accurate, as if the coffers were placed

upon trestles, such as were made use of by General Roy in his measurement with the glass rods. An application was therefore made to Sir Joseph Banks, who very obligingly complied with the request, and lent the trestles belonging to the Royal Society. A description of them is given in Art. 6.

As the upper part of the pipe at the north-west end of the base was found to be exceedingly rotten, it became necessary to saw off 13 inches of it, which left enough of the cylinder remaining to fix the brass cup in, as it had been originally bored to the depth of two feet. This cup, which was also lent by the Royal Society, being inserted in the pipe, fitted it exactly.

On the 15th of August, having previously traced out the line of the base, by means of the transit instrument, the operation commenced, in the presence of Sir Joseph Banks, Dr. Maskelyne, and several other members of the Royal Society. The following table, which contains the particulars of it, will explain the order of time in which the different parts of the measurement were performed. As it would swell this table to a great extent, were the degrees shewn by the thermometers inserted therein, it has been considered as proper to give only their sum, which is sufficient for finding the correction to be applied in the reduction of the base, on account of the lengthening or contracting of the chain by variation of temperature. It may, however, be remarked, that the five thermometers were laid close by the chain, and suffered to remain till they had nearly the same temperature, when they were read off, and registered in a field book, whilst an observer at each end of the chain preserved a perfect coincidence between the arrow and a particular division on the brass scale. When the sun shone out, the chain was covered with a white linen cloth, the ends of which were put over the openings of the first and last coffers, to exclude the circulation of air. The thermometers usually remained in the coffers from 7 to 15

minutes, according to circumstances; when the sky was much
overcast, a shorter time generally was found to be sufficient.

91. *Table, containing the Particulars of the Measurement: the first Column shewing the
Day of the Month when each Hypothenuse was finished; the Second, the Number of
Hypothenuses; the Third, the Number of Chains in each Hypothenuse; the Fourth,
the Perpendicular belonging to each Hypothenuse, or the datum for reducing it to the
Plane of the Horizon; the Fifth, the computed Reduction; the Sixth, the new Points
of Commencement above or below the Head of the last Picket when a new Direction was
taken; the Seventh, the total Descent of the Extremity of each Hypothenuse; and the
Eighth, Remarks, or general Occurrences.*
*N. B. The Numbers in the 4th and 6th Columns connected according to their signs + and
—, give the total descent in the 7th Column.*

1791. Month.	No. of hypoth.	No. of the in hypoth.	Perpendicular.	Reduction of hypothen.	New point of descent.	Total descent.	Remarks.
			Inches.	Inches.	Inches.	Inches.	
Aug. 15	1	1	+ 5.8	0.00467	+ 14.0	19.8	The 1st chain commenced 14
16	2	3	0.0	0.00000	+ 1.8	21.6	inches above the head of Ge-
22	3	12	— 57.	0.04233		35.4	neral Roy's pipe before it was cut off smooth.
23	4	14	+ 80.15	0.02803		62.65	Began measuring with chain A
25	5	10	+ 11.1	0.00010	— 4.9	68.85	at 4th hyp. one of the links on
29	6	19	0.0	0.00000	— 7.9	60.95	the chain B appearing to be a
Sept. 2	7	34	+ 28.8	0.00101 7		89.75	little bent. [8th hypot.
4	8	1	— 3.8	0.00000		85.95	Crossed the river Cuda at the
6	9	13	+ 69.25	0.13321		155.20	Crossed the Staines road at the
8	10	17	+ 15.3	0.00574	— 4.25	166.25	9th hypothenuse.
9	11	8	+ 33.5	0.00032		199.75	
11	12	13	+ 1.9	0.00002		201.65	
12	13	7	+ 54.5	0.19680	— 8.25	247.90	
13	14	6	0.0	0.00000		247.90	
14	15	5	+ 7.5	0.00049	— 5.25	250.15	
14	16	9	0.0	0.00000		250.15	
16	17	8	+ 5.3	0.00146	9.8	245.95	
17	18	10	+ 2.9	0.00035		248.85	
20	19	3	+ 4.8	0.00192		253.65	
20	20	4	+ 8.1	0.00685		261.75	
21	21	8	— 1.3	0.00012		260.25	
22	22	6	+ 35.4	0.08703		295.65	
22	23	1	+ 6.4	0.01907		302.05	Crossed the Wolsey river at the
23	24	10	+ 14.5	0.00876		316.55	23d hypothenuse.
25	25	12	+ 54.4	0.10875		370.95	
25	26	3	— 24.5	0.01201		346.45	
25	27	5	— 1.0	0.00001		345.45	
26	28	6	+ 11.3	0.01064		356.75	The head of the last picket
26	29	1	+ 9.0	0.03375		365.75	was 2½ feet above the head of
26	30	5	+ 6.9	0.00397		372.65	the pipe before it was cut off smooth.
		Total reduction =	1.02867	= 0.08:72 feet.			

Sum of all the degrees shewn by the thermometers = 96795.25.

Remarks.

92. It having been our wish, that some scientific persons should be present at the completion of the measurement, his Grace the the Duke of Richmond was pleased to desire Dr. Maskelyne, astronomer royal, and Dr. Hutton, professor of mathematics in the royal military academy at Woolwich, to attend upon this occasion ; to whom Mr. Ramsden was necessarily joined, as his standard brass scale, and beam compasses, were requisite to conclude the business with the wished for accuracy. Accordingly, on Wednesday the 28th of September the remaining three chains were measured in their presence ; and the horizontal distance from the end of the last chain to the axis of the pipe was found to be 21,055 inches, as determined by Mr. Ramsden ; and consequently the apparent length of the base was 274 chains, and 21,055 inches.

The height of the last picket above the pipe was 35 inches, from which deducting the 5 inches of the rotten part, which was cut off, there remains 30 inches, or $2\frac{1}{2}$ feet, for the height of the last picket, above General Roy's pipe; which makes the whole descent 33.55 feet ; or about $2\frac{1}{4}$ feet more than was determined by the former measurement.

Reduction of the Base to the Temperature of 62°.

93. Apparent length, namely, 274 chains + 1.755 Feet.
feet - - - - - - 27401.755

The correction for the excess of the chains lengths * above 100 feet, and half their wear, is $\frac{256 \times .0056 + 18 \times .05189}{11}$; and this add - - - 2.0539

The sum of all the degrees shewn by the thermometers was 96795.25; therefore $\overline{\frac{96795.25}{5} - 54°}$ $\times 274 \times \frac{.0075}{11}$ is the correction for the mean heat in which the base was measured, above 54°, the temperature to which the chains were reduced; and this also add - - - - - 2.8519

Hence these corrections, added to the apparent length, give - - - - 27406.6608

Again, for the reduction of the base to the temperature of 62° we have $\frac{8°}{11} \times 3.38938$; and this subtract 2.9596

By the table, the sum of all the corrections for reducing the several hypothenuses to the plane of the horizon is 1.02867 inches = 0.08572 feet; and this subtract - - - - - 0.0857

Hence these corrections taken from the above length leaves that of the base in the temperature of 62° 27404.9155

Being about 2¼ inches greater than the measurement with the glass rods (17.); therefore 27404.2 feet, the mean of the two results, may be taken as the true length of the base.

* For the lengths of the chains A and B see the next Article.

F f

Mr. Ramsden's Method of ascertaining the actual Lengths of the Chains A and B. Pl. XVIII.

94. These chains were originally compared with the brass points inserted in the stone coping of the wall of St. James's churchyard; but the temperature at the time of that comparison was afterwards forgotten by Mr. Ramsden. After the mensuration on Hounslow Heath was finished, the chains were again compared with those points; but the result did not prove to be satisfactory, as there were reasons for supposing that some alteration had taken place in the length of the coping; but, independent of this, the great irregularities between the joints of the stones, some of which projected half an inch above others, rendered it at best a very rude and inaccurate operation. Mr. Ramsden had points remaining on his great plank, which had been transferred from the brass standard, but as the plank itself was found to be subject to a daily expansion and contraction, he turned his thoughts to the invention of some other method of measuring the lengths of the chains, in a more unexceptionable manner.

On considering that the expansion of cast iron is nearly the same as that of the steel chain, he procured a prismatic bar of that metal, of 21 feet long, judging it to be the most proper material for the present occasion, as well as for establishing a permanent standard for future comparisons of the same kind. The manner in which the bar was fitted up for the purpose will be readily understood by attending to Pl. XVIII.

The great plank was cut to the length of about 22 feet, and on one of its narrow edges 21 brackets were fixed; each of which had a triangular notch to receive and support the bar, with one of its angles downwards, so that the upper surface became one of the faces of the prism. Before the brass points were inserted in this bar, Mr. Ramsden compared his brass standard with that belonging to the Royal Society, for which purpose, on Nov. 22d, 1791, it was sent to their apartments in Somerset house, where, after the two standards had remained together about 24 hours, they were found to be precisely of the same length. Brass points were then inserted in the upper surface of the bar, from Mr. Ramsden's standard, at the distance of forty inches from each other, the whole length of 20 feet being laid off on those points in the temperature of 54°.

The chains were measured in the Duke of Marlborough's riding-house, where the light was very convenient for the purpose, and the whole apparatus was sheltered from the wind and sun. The plank and bar were supported on five of the trestles, or tripods, belonging to the Royal Society, and the upper surface of the bar was brought into an horizontal plane by means of screws and a spirit level. The brass points on the upper surface of the bar were brought into a right line, by stretching a silver wire along the top, and pressing the bar laterally with wedges, till all the points fell under the wire. Part of the chain was then placed on rollers, which rested on narrow slips of wood fixed on the side of the plank, about five inches below, and exactly parallel to the bar; and whilst it was fastened to an adjusting-screw near one end of the plank, it was kept straight on the rollers by a weight of fifty-six pounds.

From the extremities of the 20 feet on the edge of the bar, two fine wires with plummets were suspended, which were immersed in vessels of water, the wires hanging so as nearly to touch the chain. One end of the chain being then brought under its wire, by means of the adjusting-screw, a fine point was made on the chain coinciding with the other wire. This part of the chain was then shifted, and another 20 feet measured in the same manner; and the operation continued till the length of each chain was thus obtained at five successive measurements. The result was, that In the temperature of $51°\frac{1}{2}$, in which the operation was preformed, the chain A was found to exceed 100 feet by 0.114 inch. and the chain B, by 0.058 inch. Now, according to the table page 88, the expansion due to 1° Fahrenheit on 100 feet of cast iron is 0.0074 inch. and that of the chain being 0.0075, their difference is 0.0001, and therefore for $2°\frac{1}{2}$ it will be 0.00025; consequently, as the points were put on the bar in the temperature of $54°$, and the chains measured in $51°\frac{1}{2}$ or $2°\frac{1}{2}$ less, their lengths In the temperature of $54°$, agreeing with the points on the bar, will be.

Feet. In.

$A = 100 + 0.11425$

$B = 100 + 0.05825$

The comparison of the chains with each other, as related in Art. 88, together with this determination of their lengths, furnish the *data* necessary for the reduction of the base on Hounslow Heath.

The wear of B, in measuring 38 chains, appeared (*vid.* Art. 88,) to be $1\frac{3}{4}$ divisions of the micrometer head $= \frac{1.75}{260} = 0.00673$ inch.: and the wear of A was 9.7 divisions $= \frac{9.7}{260} = 0.0373$ inch.

	In.	In.
Then, from the excess of A above 100 feet, namely,	0.11425, and of B	0.05825
subtract half the wear	0.01865	0.00336
	0.0956	0.05489

And we get the lengths of the chains in the temperature of 54 deg. before they were used in the measurement, namely,

$\left\{ \begin{array}{l} \text{Ft.} \quad \text{In.} \\ A = 100 + .0956, \text{ and} \\ B = 100 + .05489, \text{the} \\ \text{lengths used in the re-} \\ \text{duction of the base.} \end{array} \right.$

Method of fixing the Iron Cannon at the Extremities of the Base on Hounslow Heath, 1791.

95. As the pipes were found in a very decayed state, and it became certain, were they suffered to remain as the *termini*, that in a few years the points marking the extremities of the base would be lost, it became necessary to re-establish them in a more permanent manner. Amongst the various means which were proposed for this purpose, that of heavy iron cannon was adopted, having been previously sanctioned with the approbation of Mr. Ramsden, and other competent judges. Two guns were therefore selected at Woolwich by order of the Master-general, from among those which had been condemned as unfit for the public service, and sent to Hampton by water.

The placing of these guns accurately being an operation of a delicate nature, and attended with some difficulty, on account of their great weight, the mode of performing it was very deliberately considered; and every precaution afterwards taken to render the operation unexceptionable. The method was as follows.

Four oaken circular pickets, of 9 inches diameter, were driven into the ground, at the distance of 10 feet each from the centre of the pipe, two of them being in the direction of the base, and the others at right angles to it. Melted lead was then run into a hollow made in the head of each picket, and afterwards filed off perfectly smooth. On the brass cup, belonging to the Royal Society, being adjusted in the pipe, silver wires were stretched from the heads of the opposite pickets, and moved till their intersection coincided with the centre of the cup; and in this position a fine line was drawn on the lead of each picket, exactly under and in the direction of the wire. This operation being performed, and the truth of it re-examined, the pipes were taken out of the ground,

in doing which it became necessary to make an excavation of about
four feet, in order to clear the circumference of the wheel. It had
been at first intended to have inserted the gun so far in the ground
as that its muzzle should be even with the surface of the original
pipe : but upon considering that this was a matter not absolutely
essential to the ascertaining of the actual length of the base by any
future measurement, provided the axes of the guns were made to
coincide with those of the pipes, it was determined to fix the cannon, without digging the pit to a greater depth than that of ten
feet. In this position, however, it was evident, that the muzzle of
the gun would rise higher than the surface of the pickets, which
had been put into the ground for finding the centre ; which rendered it necessary to drive in and adjust four outer pickets, of a
proper height, to determine the centre of the bore of the gun, by
the intersection of another set of wires. The tops of the first set of
pickets were therefore cleared, and the silver wires extended along
the fine lines which had been made on the lead. A plummet was
then suspended from above, and moved till it fell on the intersection of the wires. Being fixed in this position, another set of
wires was stretched across the tops of the four outer pickets, till
their intersection also coincided with the vertical wire of the plummet, in which position, fine lines were drawn under the wires on
the top of each of the outer pickets. The truth of the operation
now depending on these last pickets, they were carefully guarded
by another set which surrounded each of them, and these last were
again bound round with ropes, to preserve the centre pickets from
any possible accident. These precautions being taken, and the
pit cleared, a large stone of $2\frac{1}{2}$ feet square, and 15 inches deep,
containing a circular cavity in its upper surface to receive the
cascabel of the gun, was placed in the bottom of it, the centre of
the hole being nearly under the intersection of the wires, as determined by a plummet. The gun was then let into the pit, and

brought, while resting upon the stone, into a position nearly vertical, at which time a quantity of earth and stones were thrown into the pit sufficient to steady the gun. This being done, the cross wires were stretched over the outer pickets, and a pointed plummet suspended from above, having its line coinciding with the intersection of the wires, was let fall into the cylinder, in which a cross of wood that exactly fitted it was placed, whose centre corresponded with that of the bore. The gun was then moved till a dot, marking the centre of the cross, came directly under the point of the plummet; when earth and stones were rammed round the gun; care being taken to force it by that operation into its proper position, as shown by the plummet and cross. In this manner the guns were fixed at the extremities of the base; and it remains only to be observed, that to prevent the unequal settling of the earth, rammed within the pit, from moving them out of their proper positions, four beams of wood were placed in an horizontal direction, having their ends resting against the sides of the pit and the gun. It may also be added, that iron caps were screwed over the muzzles to preserve the cylinders from rain.

Particulars relative to the Commencement of the Trigonometrical Operation.

96. Having, by the re-measurement of the base on Hounslow Heath, sufficiently determined its accuracy, it became necessary, upon the approach of the following spring, to form some plan which might enable us to commence the Survey with the most advantage.

Of those which were suggested, that of proceeding immediately southward with a series of triangles seemed the most eligible, not only because, in the first instance, the execution of it would forward one great design of the business, in an early determination of some principal points upon the sea-coast, but also because a junction of the eastern part of the series with that of the western of General Roy, would afford an early proof of what degree of accuracy had attended both operations.

To ascertain the truth of the General's work, by verifying some principal distance or distances, was an object which presented itself, not only as interesting and curious, but as highly necessary, in order to determine whether, by the result, the triangles might stand good, and become a part of the general series.

In addition to this reason, there was another which offered itself, and that was, the prospect of being able to obtain the length of a degree of longitude in an early stage of the Survey; for it had been suggested, and upon inquiry was found to be true, that Dunnose in the Isle of Wight was visible, in particular moments of fine weather, from Beachy Head on the coast of Sussex: but at the same time it was resolved, whatever preference might in future be given to those on the coast for this important operation, that at all events such observations should be made, which might determine the distance between Shooter's Hill and Nettlebed, as situations eligible for observing the directions of the meridians.

Having therefore formed an outline for the operation of the year 1792, upon the approach of spring, we explored the country, over which it was intended to carry the triangles, and visited such stations in the series of General Roy as were judged to be proper for the above purpose.

In the choice of those stations which were about to be selected, instructions had been given by his Grace the Duke of Richmond to avoid towers and high buildings, as getting an instrument on them had, by the experience which the former operation afforded, been found difficult and dangerous; such of them therefore as were thus circumstanced were avoided, and near the most proper ones, stations were chosen on the ground. From these directions the points of junction were necessarily confined to Saint Ann's Hill, Botley Hill, and Fairlight Down, because the pipe sunk near Hundred Acre House was found to be destroyed; but this was considered immaterial in its consequence, as it would have been improper to have chosen it for a principal station, because the high ground near Warren Farm took off the view of Leith Hill.

A disadvantage however, which seemed to result from this resolution of avoiding high buildings for stations, occurred in the difficulty which offered itself of proceeding from Hanger Hill and St. Ann's Hill, with a mean distance of that side as given by General Roy; for the station chosen at the former place being on the ground, there was scarcely a possibility of erecting a staff at King's Arbour, sufficiently high to afford a view of its top from Hanger Hill: a quadrilateral therefore, similarly posited, could not be fixed on; but as a proper substitute, a station was chosen upon the elevated ground near Banstead, which was visible from St. Ann's Hill, King's Arbour, and Hanger Hill: and this, together with St. Ann's Hill and Hanger Hill, formed two triangles, which would give the distance between St. Ann's Hill and Banstead, independent of each other.

Upon our return from this expedition, in which we had selected many of the principal stations, and, by examining the face of the country, had formed some judgment of the future disposition of the triangles, preparations were made for taking the field; and the party which had been engaged in the measurement of the base, were ordered to be attached to the trigonometrical operation.

Little difficulty was found in determining upon the choice of the necessary apparatus. Lamps were constructed by Mr. Howard of Old-street, which were afterwards found to equal every thing which could be expected from them. Instead of the reflector

G g

being exposed to the wind, these lamps were inclosed in strong tin cases, having plates of ground glass in their fronts, which effectually prevented the bad effects of an unequal and unsteady light. In the centre of the back of each case, there were straps and semicylinders of tin, which, moving upon joints, clasped the staff to which in their use they were braced. Two of the lamps were of twelve inches diameter, and a third of twenty-two; and the last of these, prior to the use of it in the ensuing season, was lighted on Shooter's Hill, and clearly distinguished at the distance of thirty miles. Copper nozles of different sizes were likewise provided for holding the white lights.

During the measurement of the base, an observatory for the reception of the instrument was making at the Tower, as likewise two carriages, to be used in conveying them from station to station. One was made with springs for the greater safety of the instrument, which resting upon a cushion in the carriage, was sufficiently secured from any jolting upon the road.

As it was easily foreseen that upon eminences, on which it was certain the instrument would be placed, it would be hazardous to trust it in a receptacle of slight construction, great pains had been taken to make the observatory strong. It consisted of two parts, the interior one of which, or the observatory itself, was eight feet in diameter, and its floor of a circular form, and from the sides of it eight iron pillars rose to the height of seven feet, which were connected at the extremities by oaken braces. The roof was formed of eight rafters which united at the top, having their ends fastened into the heads of the iron stancheons, and were otherwise sufficiently clamped. The sides and roof were each composed of four-and-twenty frames, covered with painted canvas, any of which could be removed at pleasure; and the whole was covered with a tent formed of strong materials.

Having thus detailed, in as short a manner as possible, the heads

of such particulars as it may be necessary the public should be
acquainted with, It remains only to give some account of the improvements in our great theodolite, before we narrate the progress
made in the Survey in the summer of the year 1791.

Account of the Improvements in the great Theodolite.

97. Mr. Ramsden has considerably improved this instrument,
which, in other respects, is of the same dimensions and construction as that made use of by General Roy, which has already been
described. The construction of the microscopes render them very
superior to those of that instrument; as the means by which the
image is proportioned to the required number of revolutions of the
micrometer-screw, and also the mode of adjusting the wires to that
image, are much facilitated : (Art. 98.)   For the first, there are
three prongs proceeding from the cell which holds the object-
glass; these, after passing through slits in the small tube which
constitutes the lower part of the microscope, are confined between
two nuts which turn on this small tube, so that by turning the nuts
the object-lens is moved towards, or from, the divisions on the
circle, as occasion may require. To adjust the wires In the micrometer to the image ; in the upper part of the body of the microscope are two nuts, one sliding within the other. To the upper
end of the interior one the micrometer is fixed ; and near the
lower end are three prongs similar to those above mentioned, but
something longer. These prongs pass through slits In the exterior
tube, and are confined between nuts, in the same manner as the
object-lens. This construction has many advantages over that
described in Art. 38.

To obviate the necessity of the gold tongue (p. 119), besides
the moveable wire in the field of the microscope, there is a second
one, which may be considered as fixed, having only a small motion

for its adjustment. When the instrument is adjusted, and the index belonging to the micrometer-screw stands at the *zero* on its circle (the moveable wire cutting one of the dots on the limb of the instrument), this fixed wire must be made to bisect the next dot; as by this means it may be perceived at any time, whether the relative position of the wire has varied.

By graduating the limb of the instrument to every ten minutes instead of fifteen, we are enabled to measure with the micrometer-screw, not only the excess of the measured angle above any of the ten minutes, but also its complement to the next division on the circle, and thereby to correct any small inequality which may happen between the divisions.

Particulars relating to the Operations of the Year 1792.

98. Although it might have been reasonably supposed, that the angles of the triangle King's Arbour, Hampton Poorhouse, and St. Ann's Hill, had been observed with sufficient accuracy in 1787, yet that this operation might not rest on *data* afforded by any former one, it was considered as proper to determine them with our own instrument.

By a reference to Art. 50, it will be found, that General Roy was obliged to elevate the instrument at the extremities of the base; for which purpose a stage of thirty-two feet high had been constructed. The same necessity existing with us, an application was made to the Royal Society for it; and in the autumn of 1791, that part of it which had been left at Dover, was brought to the Tower.

The first station to which the instrument was taken this year was Hanger Hill, because it was found upon examination, that the part of the stage which had been left at Shepperton was much damaged, and stood in need of considerable repair. It was, how-

ever, soon fitted for use, and a new tent for the top having been
provided, the half stage was erected over the pipe at St. Ann's
Hill, to which from Hanger Hill the instrument was conveyed.
Here, as well as at the other stations where the stage was used, a
plumb-line was let fall from the axis of the instrument over the
point marking the station, being sheltered from the wind by a
wooden trough. In the use of the half stage, the instrument was
sufficiently steady when the wind blew moderately; but from the
crazy state of the lower part, it was only by watching for moments
particularly calm, that satisfactory observations could be made
when the whole of it was used.

The following observations will sufficiently explain the detail
of this year's operations, which are given in the order of time in
which they were made. By an examination of them it will be perceived, that most of the angles have been observed more than
once: indeed, it was a position which we laid down upon our
commencing this business, and which, as far as circumstances
would admit, has since been adhered to, namely, that of observing
the angles upon different arcs. When staffs were erected, which
was generally the case when the stations were not more remote
than fifteen miles, the angles were repeated till their truth became
certain, and the same was also done, when angles were determined
by the lamps: but it sometimes happened, that only one of the
two white lights, which were burned at the distant stations, was
seen; in which case, if the observation appeared to be made without any error, but that which an inequality in the division of the
instrument might be supposed to produce, it was considered as
sufficient; otherwise fresh lights were sent to the station and observed.

In the use of the white lights, it is conceived that sufficient
precautions were taken, as the firing of them was always committed to particular soldiers of the party, selected from the rest

on account of their capacity and steadiness, who had instructions to place the copper nozle immediately over the point marking the station, by means of a plumb-line let fall from the bottom. In observing them with the instrument, the angle was not taken till the light was going out. But the men commonly guarded against the flame being blown greatly on one side, by erecting something to windward of the light.

In the use of the lamps also, care was taken to give them their proper direction; for when the ground about the station would not admit of the lamp being placed immediately upon it, slender staffs were erected supported by braces, and made upright, by being plumbed In directions at right angles to each other. Precautions were also used to put those staffs precisely over the points, by centering the holes in the cross-boards.

To such a part of the staff as was judged to be the most convenient, the lamp was buckled, and its direction obtained by bringing a mark in the middle of it to correspond with another on the staff, which was determined to be opposite the station, by directing a ruler to it from each side of the staff, and marking the places touched. The distance between those marks was then bisected, which gave the situation for the middle of the lamp.

In a very early stage of the business it was found, that the effects of heat and cold on the limb of the instrument were likely to produce the greatest errors; for if the canvas partitions, forming the sides of the observatory, were open to windward, streams of air passing unequally over the surface of it, would cause such sudden effects, that little dependence could be placed on any observations made with the instrument in such a state. To avoid this; it was the constant practice when the wind blew with any degree of violence, to prevent the admission of it as much as possible, by keeping up the walls of the external tent, leaving only a sufficient opening for the discovery of the lamp or light; and at other times when the wind blew moderately, and a greater difference appeared in the readings of the opposite microscopes, than an error in division might be supposed to produce, the walls of the external tent were entirely thrown down, and the instrument kept in an equal temperature by the admission of air on all sides.

In taking the angles, it was a general rule for some person to keep his eye at one of the microscopes, and bisect the dot, as the observer moved the limb with the finger-screw of the clamp. This precaution is very necessary when white lights are used, for should there be a mistake in reading off an angle, when several are taken from the same lamp as the permanent object, it sometimes may prove troublesome to rectify the error, without sending other white lights to the stations. We found that to be the case at Ditchling Beacon, when only one person happened to be at the instrument, and a reading was set down 10″ wrong. A similar circumstance occurred at Brightling. For these reasons, lamps are greatly preferable to white lights, when the distances are not too great.

As the instrument was sometimes found to sink on the axis, which was partly owing to wear by the constant use of it, and the screws of the centre work loosening a little by the shaking of the carriage; whenever it came to a new station, the opposite points were examined; and if it was found that the circle had fallen, which would be shewn by the runs of the micrometers, it was raised a little, and the microscopes re-adjusted.

At the different stations, after the observations had been made, large stones, from a foot and a half to two feet square, were sunk in the ground, generally two feet under the surface, having a hole of an inch square made in each of them, whose centre was the precise point of the station.

Angles taken in the Year 1792.

99. At Hanger Hill.

Between		°	′	″	Mean.
Shooter's Hill and Banstead	-	62	18	49.5 49.75 51.5	″ 50.25
St. Ann's Hill and Banstead	-	62	40	34.75 34.75 35.75	35
St. Ann's Hill and Hampton Poorhouse		24	39	16.5 16.5 17.75	17

At St. Ann's Hill.

		°	′	″	
King's Arbour and Hampton Poorhouse		44	18	51.5 52 52.25	52.25
Hind Head and Banstead	-	90	43	33	
Banstead and Hanger Hill	-	63	56	46.5 47 47.5	47
Leith Hill and Banstead	-	44	3	3	
Leith Hill and Hind Head	-	46	40	30.5	
Bagshot Heath and Banstead		144	39	26	
Hanger Hill and Hampton Poorhouse		25	17	40.5 41	40.75
Banstead and Hampton Poorhouse	-	38	39	6 6.25	6
Shooter's Hill and Hanger Hill	-	30	28	17 17	17

At King's Arbour.

Between	°	'	"	Mean.
St. Ann's Hill and Hampton Poorhouse	74	14	35 / 35.75	} 35.25
St. Ann's Hill and Banstead -	71	46	23 / 23.5	} 23.25

At Hampton Poorhouse.

	°	'	"	Mean.
St. Ann's Hill and King's Arbour	61	26	33.5 / 33.5	} 34.5
St. Ann's Hill and Hanger Hill -	130	9	3 / 3.5	} 3.25

At Banstead.

	°	'	"	Mean.
Shooter's Hill and Botley Hill -	57	11	36 / 36.25	} 36
St. Ann's Hill and Hanger Hill -	53	22	39.5 / 40	} 39.75
Botley Hill and Leith Hill -	108	50	47.5 / 48.25 / 51.5	} 49
Leith Hill and St. Ann's Hill -	77	37	33.75 / 37.25	} 35.5
King's Arbour and St. Ann's Hill -	25	15	42 / 42.5 / 42.5	} 42.25
Shooter's Hill and Hanger Hill -	62	57	20 / 24	} 22
Leith Hill and Shooter's Hill -	166	2	23.5 / 23.5	} 23.5

At Leith Hill.

	°	'	"	Mean.
Banstead and Botley Hill -	31	21	8 / 12	} 10
Banstead and Hind Head -	140	28	18.5 / 18.75	} 18.5

H h

Between	°	'	"	Mean. "
Hind Head and Chanctonbury Ring	79	56	49.5 / 51.25	} 50.25
Ditchling Beacon and Chanctonbury Ring	32	43	56.25 / 58.5	} 57.5
St. Ann's Hill and Hind Head	82	8	51	
Hind Head and Crowborough Beacon	143	57	47.5 / 47.75	} 47.5
Hind Head and Bagshot Heath	56	37	29.5	
Shooter's Hill and Nettlebed	86	23	24 / 27.5	} 25.75
Hind Head and Shooter's Hill	148	28	30 / 32.5 / 33.25 / 33.25 / 33.75	} 32.5

At Shooter's Hill.

	°	'	"	
Botley Hill and Banstead	37	8	25.75'	
Banstead and Blackheath	42	52	48.5	
Hanger Hill and Blackheath	11	51	1.25	
Leith Hill and Blackheath	48	50	6 / 7.5	} 6.75
Nettlebed and Blackheath	7	58	25.5	
Nettlebed and Leith Hill	56	48	30 / 32	} 31
St. Ann's Hill and Blackheath	12	41	15.75 / 17.25	} 16.5

At Bagshot Heath.

	°	'	"	
St. Ann's Hill and Hind Head	101	49	23.75	
St. Ann's Hill and Leith Hill	53	52	13.5	
Leith Hill and Hind Head	47	57	7 / 7	} 7

Between	°	′	″	Mean.
Nettlebed and Leith Hill - -	168	59	12 13 16	} 13.75
Nettlebed and Highclere - -	60	10	26 22	} 24
Nettlebed and Penn Beacon -	42	50	13.25 13.75	} 18.5
Leith Hill and Highclere - -	131	17	22.5	

At Hind Head.

	°	′	″	Mean
Nettlebed and Leith Hill - -	94	9	57.5 57.75	} 57.5
Nettlebed and Bagshot Heath -	18	44	31.25 33.25	} 32.25
Leith Hill and St. Ann's Hill -	51	10	38 41.5	} 39.75
Leith Hill and Rook's Hill -	111	57	2 4.5	} 3.25
Leith Hill and Butser Hill -	156	25	10.75 8.25	} 9.5
Leith Hill and Chanctonbury Ring	61	52	25.5	
Chanctonbury Ring and Rook's Hill	50	4	37	
Nettlebed and Highclere - -	43	8 9	58.5 0.5	} 59.5

At Rook's Hill.

	°	′	″	Mean
Chanctonbury Ring and Butser Hill -	147	49	26.5	
Chanctonbury Ring and Hind Head -	82	42	45 46.5	} 45.75
Chanctonbury Ring and Dunnose -	137	16	48.5	
Chanctonbury Ring and Beachy Head	14	17	34	
Chanctonbury Ring and Motteston Down	153	1	1	

H h 2

At Butser Hill.

Between	°	′	″	Mean.
Rook's Hill and Hind Head -	70	25	15 / 14.5	} 15.75
Rook's Hill and Dunnose - -	80	21	58	
Rook's Hill and Motteston Down -	101	7	7 / 9	} 8
Rook's Hill and Highclere - -	154	56	56 / 58.5	} 57.25
Rook's Hill and Dean Hill - -	156	34	14 *dubious.*	

At Chanctonbury Ring.

	°	′	″	Mean.
Rook's Hill and Leith Hill - -	92	23	25 / 25.25	} 25
Rook's Hill and Hind Head -	47	12	37 / 39.25	} 38
Hind Head and Leith Hill - -	45	10	46	
Rook's Hill and Ditchling Beacon -	179	8	4 / 8	} 6

Further Particulars respecting the Operations of the Year 1792.

100. Excepting the stations Nine Barrow Down, Black Down, Wingreen, Long Knoll near Maiden Bradley, Beacon Hill, Inkpin Beacon, with those about the base of verification, all the stations which constitute the series hereafter given, were selected this year.

From an opinion which we entertain, that triangles, whose sides are from 12 to about 18 miles in length, are preferable for the general purposes of a survey, to those of greater dimensions, we have endeavoured to select such stations as might constitute a series of that description. In those which were chosen to the eastward of Bagshot Heath, Hind Head, and Butser Hill, we have in

some degree succeeded ; but, from local circumstances, we have
not been equally fortunate with those to the westward. Instead of
Dean Hill, it was hoped that the ground upon which *Farley Monument* stands, might have suited our purpose ; but the wood to the
west of the hill was found to be so high, that even with the whole
stage, the instrument would not be sufficiently elevated. There remained, therefore, no other expedient but fixing upon Dean Hill,
which is the highest spot near Farley Monument. It must be also
observed, that Highclere is the only situation which affords the
means of carrying on the triangles from the side Bagshot Heath
and Hind Head, without forming a quadrilateral.

When the Instrument was at Shooter's Hill, a staff was erected
on Blackheath, for the purpose of enabling us to determine the direction of the meridian with respect to Nettlebed. This, however
was not done, the weather proving too unfavourable ; but as
some of the stations were referred to this staff, it may be proper
to observe, that on account of its being so near Shooter's Hill, a
small portfire was placed in a groove cut in it, which afforded the
means of taking an angle very exactly, as the light had the appearance of a bright point.

The interior stations which were selected for the use of the
small instrument, were Bow Hill, near Rook's Hill ; Portsdown
Common, on the road to Portsmouth ; and Sleep Down, near
Steyning. To the first and last of these the instrument was taken,
for the purpose of fixing such objects as could not be intersected
from the principal station. The points on the coast were particularly wanted, for the construction of some maps which were
making for the use of the Board of Ordnance. Those places
so fixed will be given hereafter ; but it must be observed, that few
opportunities were lost of searching for church towers, and other
objects whose situations were to be determined. That the bearings
of those might be taken with precision, the observations were

made either in the morning or evening, when the air was free from vapour, and without that quivering motion, which, in summer, it generally has in the middle of the day.

Improvement in the Axis of the great Theodolite ; and the Progress of the Survey in the Year 1793.

101. Towards the conclusion of the last year's operation, it was found that the axis of the instrument, by the frequent use of it, was considerably worn, and which was, perhaps, increased by the motion of the carriage, as the arch could not be clamped with tightness sufficient to prevent the circle from moving within the limits of the bell-metal arms, and the upright part of the travelling case. The consequence was, that it sometimes became necessary to let the circle lower by means of the screws , and as it was found to be exceedingly difficult to turn them equally, and by a quantity which was just sufficient, an application was made to Mr. Ramsden to apply something to the axis, which might enable us to adjust the circle with greater ease and accuracy. Accordingly, upon the party arriving in town, the instrument was taken to his house, and left there for the winter, during which he made the desired alteration.

The progress made in the Survey during the last season, determined the extent of the business for this year : and it was then imagined, that with good weather, we might be enabled to join the triangles to the eastward with those of General Roy, and likewise observe the remaining angles in the series, having first made the necessary observations at Dunnose and Beachy Head for obtaining the directions of the meridians. It had also been foreseen, that it would soon become necessary to select some spot for the measurement of a new base, not only to verify the triangles remote from Hounslow Heath, but likewise to determine the sides of those which might be hereafter projected for the survey of the West of England. The situation which we had looked forward to, as being the only one which would afford a base line of sufficient extent, was Sedgemoor in Somersetshire, not having then imagined that any place could be found fit for the purpose to the eastward of that situation.

After maturely deliberating upon the steps to be taken for this necessary business, we were of opinion, that Sedgemoor, was rather too far westward for a base, which was intended to be applied as a test to the sides of the great triangles now constituted. Inquiry was therefore made after a spot which might be less exceptionable; and as information was obtained that Longham Common, near Poole in Dorsetshire, was likely to afford such a base, we examined it in the January of this year; but not finding it fit for the purpose, we proceeded to Salisbury Plain, where we found that a base line of nearly seven miles might be measured without much difficulty, between Beacon Hill, near Amesbury, and the Castle of Old Sarum. With respect to the nature of the ground, as any observations concerning it will be introduced with more advantage when we treat of the particulars of the measurement, it will be only necessary to observe, that prior to determining upon the possibility of measuring it with the necessary accuracy, we considered of the errors which would be likely to creep in from the many hypothenuses which the base would consist of, and from other circumstances which the ground from its inequality might be supposed to produce.

As the principal object of this year's business was, to determine the directions of the meridians, the party left London for the Isle of Wight early in the month of March, that it might arrive at Dunnose in proper time for making the required observations. The instrument, however, was first taken to Motteston Down, for the purpose of intersecting many places whose bearings had been

last year taken when the instrument was at Rook's Hill, and which
were now wanted by the surveyors of the Ordnance. This station
had been selected for that purpose, and was never intended to become a principal one in the series; but when the instrument was
on the spot, it was considered as proper that some observations
should be made to the stations which were at that time chosen.
For this reason, when the time for observing the star approached,
and most of the lights had been fired without our having seen them,
it was not considered of consequence to remain there any longer,
and the instrument was therefore taken to Dunnose.

A small staff, of about three inches diameter, was erected on
Brading Down, which is about six miles from the station, for the
purpose of referring the star to it; a small lamp of six inches diameter, constructed upon the same plan as the large ones, being
when made use of, buckled to the bottom of the staff.

As the best method of obtaining the direction of the meridian,
is by observing the star upon each side of the pole, whence the
double azimuth is nearly obtained without any correction for the
star's apparent motions, every opportunity was watched, of observing it at the times of its greatest apparent eastern and western
elongations. But in the unsettled season of the month of April,
when almost every wind brought a fog over the station, many
days elapsed without our seeing either the star or staff; and it
was on that account we continued so long at Dunnose.

As the truth of the deductions must entirely depend on the
accurate determination of the directions of the meridians, the
greatest care was taken in making the observations. An hour,
and generally more, before the star came to its greatest elongation,
the observers repaired to the tent for the purpose of getting the
instrument ready. The method of adjusting it, was first by levelling it in the common way with the spirit level which hangs on
the brass pins; and afterwards, by that which applies to the axis

of the transit. The criterion which determined the instrument
to be properly adjusted, was the bubble of the latter level remaining immoveable between its indexes, while the circle was turned
round the axis.

As the star, four minutes either before or after its greatest elongation, moves only about a second in azimuth, the time was shown
sufficiently near, by a good pocket watch, which was regulated as
often as opportunities offered. When the star was supposed to be
at its greatest elongation, the observer, if at night, brought it upon
the cross wires, and bisected it, leaving equal portions of light on
each side of the cross: but if it was in the day, when the star
appeared like a point, the telescope was moved in the vertical till
it came near the vanishing point of the cross. At either of these
times, when the observer was satisfied of the star being properly
bisected, or brought into the vanishing point formed by the wires,
another person who had kept his eye at the microscope, bisected
the dot. The transit was then taken off, and the instrument being
turned half round, and the telescope replaced, the star was observed again. This precaution was taken to obviate the errors
which might arise, from the arms of the instrument being out of
the parallel with the plane of the circle, owing to any imperfections in the positions of the Ys, on which the transit rested. It
was, however, seldom found, that a greater difference subsisted
between the readings of the opposite microscopes, than what
might be supposed to be the consequence of a shake in the centre,
or errors in division. A mean of the readings was always taken.
It must be also mentioned, that out of twenty, three and four inch
white lights, which were fired at Beachy Head, only three of them
were seen: but the angle between that place and the staff on
Brading Down was considered, from the near agreement in the
observations, to be determined with the necessary accuracy.

After the business was finished at Dunnose, the instrument was taken to Chanctonbury Ring, and Ditchling Beacon; and from the latter place to Beachy Head, in order to observe the direction of the meridian; but after placing a staff upon the high ground above Jevington, we were obliged to defer the attempt, as it was found, that owing to the effects of heat, the air was not sufficiently steady for the staff to be seen distinctly, when the star came to its greatest elongation in the day time, if the sun shone out. We therefore left Beachy Head, and proceeded to the following stations, *viz.* Fairlight Down, Brightling, Crowborough Beacon, and Botley Hill; from which latter place we returned in June to Beachy Head, and observed the direction of the meridian.

From this station, the party went to Dean Hill, and thence to Salisbury Plain, for the purpose of fixing on the extremities of the new base. This being done, the instrument was taken to Old Sarum, Four Mile Stone, Beacon Hill, Thorney Down, and High-clere, where the operations of this year terminated. But it must be observed, that owing to a strain which the clamp of the instrument sustained when at Thorney Down, no dependance could be placed on the observations which were made at Highclere. Upon this being discovered, and the season too far advanced to permit of any business being done after the instrument might be repaired, the party returned to London.

Angles taken in the Year 1793.

102. At Motteston Down.

Between					Mean.
		°	′	″	″
Nine Barrow Down and Dunnose	-	159	51	2.5 / 5	} 3.75
Butser Hill and Dunnose	-	-	64	41	2
Rook's Hill and Dunnose	-	-	44	57	46 *dubious.*

At Dunnose.

Between	°	′	″	Mean,
Dean Hill and Brading staff -	55	58	38.5 38.75	} 38.5
Motteston Down and Brading staff -	94	49	19	
Nine Barrow Down and Brading staff	109	11	3.5 8	} 5.75
Butser Hill and Brading staff -	0	15	31.5	
Rook's Hill and Brading staff -	24	28	42.5 45.5	} 44
Chanctonbury Ring and Brading staff	40	11	44	
Beachy Head and Brading staff -	60	42	40 42 42.25	} 41.5
Pole star and Brading staff, Apr. 21, aftern.	24	4	21.25	
22, aftern.	24	4	22	
28, aftern.	24	4	23	
29, morn.	18	24	0	
May 5, aftern.	24	4	27.25	
12, aftern.	24	4	29.5	
13, morn.	18	29	53.25	

At Chanctonbury Ring.

	°	′	″	
Beachy Head and Shoreham staff -	32	49	48.5 49	}
Dunnose and Shoreham staff -	98	9	48.75 49.75	} 49.25
Rook's Hill and Shoreham staff -	125	10	2.25	

At Ditchling Beacon.

	°	′	″	
Beachy Head and Lewes staff -	20	52	0.75	
Crowborough Beacon and Lewes staff	57	8	36	
Leith Hill and Lewes staff -	135	27	1.75 4	} 3

I i 2

Between				Mrns.
	°	′	″	

Between
Brightling and Lewes staff   -   25 40 18.25
Chanctonbury Ring and Lewes staff   164 1 31

$$\left.\begin{array}{l}32.5 \\ 33.5\end{array}\right\} 32.25$$

At Fairlight Down.

Bightling and Beachy Head   -   59 33 $\left.\begin{array}{l}1.5 \\ 2\end{array}\right\} 1.75$

At Brightling.

Fairlight Down and Beachy Head   -   80 44 $\left.\begin{array}{l}17.5 \\ 21\end{array}\right\} 19.25$

Crowborough Beacon and Beachy Head   102 58 $\left.\begin{array}{l}14 \\ 17\end{array}\right\} 15.5$

Ditchling and Beachy Head   -   -   59 29 $\left.\begin{array}{l}13.5 \\ 14.5\end{array}\right\} 14$

At Crowborough Beacon.

Brightling and Leith Hill   -   -   168 27 $\left.\begin{array}{l}20.5 \\ 22\end{array}\right\} 21.25$

Brightling and Ditchling Beacon   -   105 2 $\left.\begin{array}{l}43 \\ 44.75\end{array}\right\} 44$

Brightling and Botley Hill   -   145 20 27

At Botley Hill.

Banstead and Wrotham Hill   -   152 57 $\left.\begin{array}{l}2.5 \\ 6\end{array}\right\} 4.25$

Banstead and Shooter's Hill   -   85 39 58.5
Banstead and Crowborough Beacon   129 23 3.5
Crowborough Beacon and Leith Hill   89 35 1

At Beachy Head.

Brightling and Jevington staff   -   46 59 $\left.\begin{array}{l}33.25 \\ 34.75\end{array}\right\} 34$

Between	°	'	"	Mean.
Fairlight Down and Jevington staff -	86	42	12 14	} 13
Rook's Hill and Jevington staff -	48	39	59	
Chanctonbury Ring and Jevington staff	40	57	21 23	} 22
Dunnose and Jevington staff - -	69	26	51.25 52 52 53.25	} 52
Ditchling Beacon and Brightling -	73	38	25 28	} 26.5
Pole star and Jevington staff, Jul. 15 at night	30	19	54.5	
16 night	30	19	57.5	
26 morn.	24	38	19	
30 night	30	19	50.5	
Aug. 1 morn.	24	38	20.25	
1 night	30	19	49.5	
2 night	30	19	50.25	
3 morn.	24	38	23.5	
* 11 night	30	19	47.25	

At Dean Hill.

	°	'	"	Mean.
Beacon Hill and Highclere -	50	18	47.5 47.5	} 47.5
Beacon Hill and Wingreen - -	82	56	47 50	} 48.5
Beacon Hill and Dunnose - -	160	46	8.5	
Beacon Hill and Nine Barrow Down	134	23	32.25 32.75	} 32.5
Beacon Hill and Motteston Down	174	34	56.5 58.5	} 57.5

* Many observations of the star at this station, and also at Dunnose, are rejected on account of their being made under unfavourable circumstances.

[248]

Between	°	'	"	Mean.
Beacon Hill and Four Mile Stone	39	29	1.5 / 5	} 3.25
Beacon Hill and Butser Hill	118	41	36 / 36.5 / 38	} 36.75

At Old Sarum.

	°	'	"	Mean.
Beacon Hill and Four Mile Stone	85	58	21.5 / 21.75 / 22.25 / 23.75	22.5
Beacon Hill and Thorney Down	48	26	3 / 4.25 / 6.5	} 4.5

At Four Mile Stone.

	°	'	"	Mean.
Beacon Hill and Old Sarum	70	1	45.75 / 47.25 / 48.25 / 49	47.5
Beacon Hill and Dean Hill	72	4	46.5 / 49.25	} 48

At Beacon Hill.

	°	'	"	Mean.
Old Sarum and Four Mile Stone	23	39	50.25 / 52.25	} 51.75
Old Sarum and Thorney Down	33	33	23.75 / 24 / 26	} 24.5
Dean Hill and Four Mile Stone	68	26	8.5 / 10.25 / 11	} 10
Dean Hill and Highclere	102	45	23.5	
Thorney Down and Highclere	113	38	13.75 / 16.75	} 15.25

At Thorney Down.

Between		° ′ ″	Mean.
Beacon Hill and Highclere	-	53 22 28.5 } 30	29.25
Beacon Hill and Old Sarum	-	98 0 29.25 } 32.5	31

At Highclere.

Dean Hill and Beacon Hill	-	26 55 53 } 54	53.5

Particulars relating to the Operations of the Year 1794.

103. The party this year took the field the fourth of March, and proceeded from London to the Isle of Purbeck, taking Butser Hill in its way. In the observations of the year 1792, the angle at that station, between Rook's Hill and Dean Hill, is noted to be dubious. The reason which induced us to be of that opinion was, that the telescope, by some accident, was thought to have been moved after the observation of the light, and just at the time when the angle was about to be read off. As the season was then far advanced, and four lights had been fired, without our having seen more than one of them, it was determined to leave the final observation of that angle till this year. Accordingly upon our arrival at Butser Hill this second time, a lamp was sent to each of the stations, and the angle repeatedly taken, as given in the following article. The party from thence proceeded to Nine Barrow Down in the Island of Purbeck.

The reason of the business commencing so early in the season, arose from the necessity of beginning the measurement of the base on Salisbury Plain, towards the latter end of June, that it might be finished before the year should be far advanced, when the cultivated ground a mile to the northward of Old Sarum would be ploughed. It was also necessary that the angles at Wingreen and Highclere should be observed.

On account of the magnitude of the 24th and 27th triangles, the instrument was kept at the station in the Island of Purbeck till the angles between Dean Hill and the stations in the Isle of Wight were determined very accurately. It was, therefore, not till a month after the two first lights were fired, that as many observations were made as we deemed to be sufficient.

As it will answer our purpose better, to give an account of the stations which were chosen this year, for the further prosecution of the Survey, in another part of this work; it remains only to be observed, that from Nine Barrow Down the instrument was taken to Black Down near Dorchester, and thence to Wingreen, Highclere, and Beacon Hill; the observations which were made this year being concluded at the latter place in the beginning of June. It may, however, be mentioned, that in addition to the interior stations chosen in the year 1793, for the future use of the small instrument, three others were selected in this and the preceding season, namely, *Ramsden Hill*, near Christchurch; *Thorness* in the Isle of Wight; and *Stockbridge Hill*.

Angles taken in the Year 1794.

104. At Butser Hill.

Between	°	′	″	Mean.
Rook's Hill and Dean Hill -	156	34	19.75 20.5 19.75	} ″ 20

At Nine Barrow Down.

	°	′	″	
Dean Hill and Wingreen - -	39	34	27.75 30.25 28.5	} 28.75
Dean Hill and Motteston Down -	56	9	55 55.5	} 55.25

Between				Mean.
Dean Hill and Dunnose	-	61 57	20.75 20 19	} 20
Lulworth and Bull Barrow	-	52 47	34.25 32	} 33
Dean Hill and Bull Barrow	- -	71 31	55.5 56.5 53 52	} 54.25
Black Down and Bull Barrow	-	38 58	19 19.5	} 19.25

At Black Down.

Charton Common and Bull Barrow	-	125 32	33.25 33.25	} 33.25
Bull Barrow and Nine Barrow Down		56 30	18.25 19.5 18 19.75	} 18.75
Bull Barrow and Lulworth-	-	65 35	40.5 41 42.5 45.5	} 42.5
Lulworth and station above } Chesil, in Portland - }	-	43 3	16.25 19.75 19.75 21.75 21	} 19.75
Lulworth and station near } Portland Light House }	-	52 43	49.25 51.25 53.25 53.25	} 51.75
Pilsden Hill and Mintern	- -	66 51	19.25 21 24.75	} 21.75

K k

Between				Mea.
Mintern and Bull Barrow	-	-	31 25 56.75 57 59	} 57.5

At Wingreen.

Beacon Hill and Dean Hill	-	-	30 13 29.75 28 29.5	} 29
Dean Hill and Nine Barrow Down		88 58 45.25 47.75	} 46.5
Dean Hill and Bull Barrow	-	143 28 21 22 23.75 25.25	} 23
Bull Barrow and Bradley Knoll	-	96 20 39.25 36.5 39.25 38.25 37.25	} 37
Bradley Knoll and Beacon Hill	-	89 57 40.25 37.75 37.75 37.25 35	} 37.75

At Highclere.

Butser Hill and Dean Hill	-	-	69 8 33.5 36.75 35	} 35
Dean Hill and Beacon Hill	-	-	26 55 50.5 52.25	} 51.5
Thorney Down and Beacon Hill	-	12 59 10.5 9.25	} 10
Beacon Hill and Inkpin Beacon	-	-	56 0 29 30.25 30	} 29.75

Between	°	′	″	Mean.
Beacon Hill and White Horse Hill (near Wantage) - - -	90	28	20 21	} 20.5 ″
Nuffield and Bagshot Heath -	46	10	17.5 19.5	} 18.5
Bagshot Heath and Hind Head -	34	46	14.75 15.75 16.75	} 15.75
Butser Hill and Hind Head - -	29	12	22 22.25	} 22

At Beacon Hill.

	°	′	″	
Dean Hill and Wingreen - -	66	49	52.25 51.75	} 52
Wingreen and Bradley Knoll -	32	11	44.75 44.25 43.5 40.75	} 43.25
Inkpin Beacon and Dean Hill -	120	28	2.25 1.25 3	} 2
Wingreen and St. Ann's Hill (near Devizes) - - -	106	27	9 8 7	} 8

Situations of the Stations.

105. *Hanger Hill.* The station on this Hill is in the field to the eastward of the Tower, and within 13 feet of the eastern hedge. The Tower bears due west of the station.

Shooter's Hill. The station is in the north-west corner of the field, opposite to the Bull Tavern.

Banstead. The station is in a field belonging to Warren Farm, near the road leading to Ryegate. It is 14 feet north of the hedge, and may be easily found, as Leith Hill and an opening between two rows of trees on Banstead Common, are in a line with the station.

Leith Hill in Surrey. The station is 32 feet from the north-east corner of the Tower, and in that direction from it.

Crowborough Beacon, Sussex. The station is about 600 feet due south of the spot on which the beacon was formerly erected.

Brightling, Sussex. The station is about 70 feet south-west of the gate belonging to the field in which stands Brightling Windmill.

Beachy Head. Twelve yards south-west of the Signal-house. The muzzle of the gun is above the surface of the ground.

Ditchling Beacon, Sussex. The station is in the middle of a small rising, which has the appearance of having once been a Barrow.

Chanctonbury Ring, Sussex. This place is near Steyning; and the station is situated 50 feet from the ditch on the west side of the Ring.

Rook's Hill, near Goodwood, Sussex. The station is east of the Trundle, and near it.

Butser Hill, Hampshire. There is no precise way of pointing out the spot on which the instrument was placed: the general situation of it, however, may be known: it is on the middle of the hill, which is itself near, and to the northward of the Fifty-four Mile-stone on the Portsmouth road.

Dunnose, Isle of Wight. The station is 87 feet northward of Shanklin Deacon Pole: the muzzle of the gun is above the surface of the ground.

Molleston Down, Isle of Wight. The station is on the west Barrow.

Nine Barrow Down, Isle of Purbeck. The station is on the highest of the *Nine Barrows*.

Black Down in Dorsetshire. The station is 23 feet west of the North Barrow. Black Down is six miles from Dorchester, and near the village of Winterbourn.

Bull Barrow Hill, near Milton Abbey in Dorsetshire. The station is on the Barrow.

Wingreen, Dorsetshire. The hill so named, is four miles east of Shaftesbury, and the station is about 80 feet south-west of the Ring, or clump of trees.

Beacon Hill, about two miles from Amesbury, near the Andover road, Wiltshire. The muzzle of the gun is 8 or 9 inches above the ground.

Old Sarum. The station is south-east of the Two Mile-stone, and near it. The muzzle of the gun is 7 or 8 inches above the ground.

Four Mile-stone, Wiltshire. The station is in the field west of the Four Mile-stone on the Devizes road, leading from Salisbury. It is on the rising which is in the middle of the field.

Thorney Down, Wiltshire. The Down is near Winterbourn, and the station to the north of the wood.

Dean Hill, Hampshire. This place is near the village of Dean, and about 6 miles east of Salisbury: the station is in the north-west corner of a field belonging to Mr. Haliday.

Inkpin Beacon, Wiltshire. This place is above the village of Inkpin, and the station is in the centre of the small field circumscribed by a ditch and parapet of an ancient fortification.

Highclere, Wiltshire. The station is in the centre of the Ring on Beacon Hill, about half a mile south-east of Highclere.

Bagshot Heath. The station is on the brow of an eminence two miles north of the Golden Farmer, and directly west of the north corner of Bagshot Park.

Hind Head, Surrey. The station is near the Gibbet, being about 22 feet north-west of it.

The situations of those stations which are common to this operation and that of General Roy, are not described, the same being done in Art. 55.

As it is probable that some individual will avail himself of the particulars given in this performance, by forming more correct maps of the counties over which the triangles have been carried, and who consequently may wish to visit certain of the stations, it is proper to observe, that small stakes are placed over the stones sunk in the ground, having their tops projecting a little above it. For some years there will be little difficulty in finding the stations, as the spots are well known to the neighbouring inhabitants.

Measurement of the Base of Verification on Salisbury Plain with an Hundred Feet Steel Chain, in the Summer of the Year 1794

Apparatus provided for the Measurement, and the Method of using particular Articles of it.

106. The apparatus with which this base was measured arrived at Deacon Hill the 25th of June, and consisted of the two steel chains, the trestles belonging to the Royal Society, and the coffers which were used on Hounslow Heath, together with the pickets, iron-heads, and a few other articles, which in the beginning of this year had been made at the Tower. As it was foreseen that the truth of this measurement would, in a great degree, depend on the accurate reduction of the several hypothenuses to the plane of the horizon, an application was made to Mr. Ramsden in the foregoing winter, to consider of some means by which their inclinations might be obtained. He therefore applied an arch S to the side of the transit telescope, as exhibited in Pl. XVII. which he divided into half degrees; and opposite to this he placed a

microscope T, with a moveable wire in its focus, by means of which, and the micrometer of the telescope, an angle could be taken.

On the first convenient opportunity after the arrival of the apparatus, we determined the value of any number of revolutions of the micrometer-screw in parts of a degree, by the following method.

At the distance of an hundred feet from the transit, a picket was set up, on which a dot was made with chalk, and the instrument being adjusted, was moved by the finger-screw till the edge of the micrometer-wire touched some prominent part of that mark. The wire in the focus of the microscope was then made to bisect a dot upon the arch, and the telescope moved in the vertical till the next dot was bisected, by which the instrument had described half a degree upon its axis, and the micrometer-wire was afterwards moved till it touched the same part of the chalk mark, the revolutions being counted, which were consequently equal to thirty minutes. This operation was repeatedly tried, with a picket placed from one to six hundred feet successively from the telescope, the runs of the micrometer-screw being in each case nearly the same, as indeed they ought to be according to theory.

The number of revolutions equal to 30′ was found, from a mean of those trials, to be $12\frac{40}{100}$.

Having determined this, the chains A and B were compared with each other, when they were found to have the same difference of lengths as when measured by Mr. Ramsden.

For the purpose of tracing out the line of the base, as Beacon Hill had a commanding view of almost the whole of it, the instrument was kept in the tent after the observations were finished: and at different times, when the air was sufficiently steady for the purpose, many points in the true direction were found by bisecting the staff erected at Old Sarum, and moving the transit in the vertical, whilst a person placed a camp-colour in the proper situation

on the ground, by means of signals which were made at Beacon
Hill.

As it appeared, when this spot was first selected for the measurement, that in the course of it there would be frequent necessity for
changing the directions of the hypothenuses, a brass bar, of a
prismatic form, had been provided, by means of which, and a
plumb-line, a new direction was easily taken. The method of
using them was as follows.

A picket was driven into the ground close to the handle of the
chain, having its top eight or ten inches above the place where the
preceding hypothenuse was to terminate, one of the register-
heads, with the bar, being screwed on it: the chain was then
stretched, and the silver wire, or plumb-line, made to pass through
the handle, whilst the slider was moved till the wire came upon
the dart, marking by this means, the termination of the hypothenuse. In order, however, to give a more perfect idea of this
matter, a figure is given in Pl. XIX. where B is the bar, with the
wire falling through the handle of the chain, one half of it being
left out, for the purpose of showing its coincidence with the arrow
on the handle.

The experience which we had obtained in the measurement of
the base on Hounslow Heath, led us to discover, that some of the
methods we made use of to execute particular parts of it, might
have been improved. One of them was, the means by which the
heads of the pickets were placed in the plane of the base, which
frequently was the cause of the planes of the register-heads being
out of the direction of the hypothenuses. In this operation, however, the bottoms, as well as the tops of them, were placed in the
true vertical by means of the transit-instrument, and therefore it
was not difficult to bring the planes of their tops into the required
position.

For the purpose of using the transit as a boning telescope, as well as an instrument for taking the angles of elevation or depression, Mr. Ramsden provided two mahogany boards, one of which was fastened to the register-head, and the other (furnished with levelling screws) rested upon it, the transit-instrument being placed on the latter.

The level belonging to the transit was then hung on the arms; and if the axis proved to be horizontal, which it would be if the brass heads were rightly placed, the instrument required no farther adjustment; but if that did not prove to be the case, the axis was made parallel to the horizon by the screws of the levelling-board, which were turned in contrary directions, having in the first instance been worked till within half the limits of their adjustment. By this means the axis was kept at a constant height from the brass heads.

A board with a cross piece, whose upper edge from the bottom of it was equal to the distance of the axis of the instrument from the head of the picket, was placed on another picket which had been driven till its head was at a convenient height in the plane of the base, and the transit moved in the vertical till the edge of the wire in the centre of the glass, coincided with that of the cross piece. The rest of the pickets in that hypothenuse were then driven into the ground, till their tops were in the same right line, as discovered by the application of this board to their heads.

The method of determining the angles which the measured lines made with the plane of the horizon was as follows.

After the hypothenuse was measured, the transit-instrument with its boards were placed on the picket, and the levelling-screws moved as before described, if the axis did not happen to be horizontal. The cross board, upon which a black line was drawn, whose breadth was about twice the apparent thickness of the micrometer-wire, and its distance from the bottom of it equal to that of the axis of the instrument from the register-head, was placed

on another picket in the hypothenuse, having the brass head which
had been before fixed on it still remaining. The telescope was
then made horizontal, the index of the micrometer being placed to
the *zero* on its circle, and the wire of the microscope set to bisect
that dot on the arch which was nearest to the centre of the field.
After this, the telescope was moved in the vertical by the finger-
screw, till another dot was bisected, at the same time that the line
upon the cross board appeared in the glass, by which the angle
that the instrument had described on its axis, was measured in half
degrees. The remaining part of the angle, or rather the fractional
part of an half degree, was measured with the micrometer, the wire
of which was brought from the centre of the glass to bisect the
black line, and was either added to, or subtracted from, the former
quantity, as the angle described by the telescope fell short of, or
exceeded, that formed by the hypothenuse and the plane of the
horizon.

By this method, all the angles of elevation and depression were
taken. And we consider it as probable that they are within a
quarter of a minute of the truth; since the instrument was capable
of being used with great accuracy, the arch having been divided
by one of Mr. Ramsden's best workmen, and the value of one, or
any number of revolutions of the micrometer-screw, had been
accurately obtained. If, therefore, any considerable errors have
taken place in this part of the operation, they must have arisen
from the axis of the transit-instrument and the line on the cross
board not being of the same height from the brass heads on which
they were placed : but we think there is almost a certainty that
this difference was confined to such limits as will not introduce
any errors of consequence ; for even supposing the register-heads
were placed on the pickets so unskilfully that it became necessary
to turn the screws on the levelling-board as much as they were
capable of, whilst the third remained unmoved, in order to adjust

the transit, the error introduced on that account would be only
half a minute, even though the hypothenuse should consist of but
one chain, and be inclined to the horizon eight degrees. We
therefore think ourselves justified in the opinion which we entertain of these angles being determined with sufficient accuracy ;
since, if an error of one minute had taken place in the inclination
of each hypothenuse, and those errors lay all one way, the length of
the base, as hereafter given, would only be varied three inches by
that circumstance.

It may, perhaps, be imagined that some small errors have arisen
from the handle of the chain not lying flat upon the brass heads
when the new directions have been commenced. To obviate this,
precautions were always taken to drive the pickets at the termination of the hypothenuses in such a manner, that the arrow on
the handle could be made to coincide with one of the divisions near
the end of the brass scale, by which any error arising from their
not being exactly in the same vertical plane, was rendered so
trifling as not to be worth notice.

Having now related, with as much conciseness as the subject
will admit, the methods which were adopted for the execution of
the most essential parts of this operation, there remain only a few
other particulars to be related before we give the reduction of the
base.

After as many points as were judged necessary had been fixed
in the true direction, by the means heretofore described, and the
chains compared with each other, the mensuration was begun, and
continued without much interruption for seven weeks, when it was
finished with that part of the 566th chain which terminated its
apparent length.

The method taken to mark this last mentioned chain, was by
cutting a small hole in the bottom of the coffer, through which a
plumb-line was made to pass, the point of the plummet being

brought over the end of the base, and the chain moved till it touched the wire ; a slight scratch was then made with a file at the point of contact.

On the first favourable opportunity, subsequent to this conclusion of the measurement, the chains A and B were compared with each other, when it was found that the wear of the former, by the constant use of it, was only one division of the micrometer head, or $\frac{1}{310}$ th of an inch. The smallness of this quantity in the measurement of a base of such great length, was doubtless owing to the pivots, and pivot holes of the joints being smoothed, and as it were polished, in the operation on Hounslow Heath ; and it may also be adduced as some proof, that the joints had not rusted while the chains remained in the Tower ; but to prevent this, care had been taken to deposite them in a dry place, being afterwards frequently examined and oiled.

Thus concluded the measurement of this base, in which it is certain that great pains were taken to produce an accurate result ; and we are not without hopes, that the many obstacles which offered themselves have been surmounted with success ; but this is left to the decision of the candid and intelligent reader.

The following table contains the particulars of this operation. The first column showing the number of hypothenuses : the second, that of the chains in each hypothenuse ; the third, the observed angles of elevation or depression given to the nearest 10″; the fourth and fifth, the perpendiculars answering to the elevations and depressions ; the sixth, the reduction of the hypothenuses to the horizontal lines, or the versed sines of the elevations and depressions to the hypothenuses as *radii ;* the seventh and eighth, the perpendicular distance between the termination and beginning of any two hypothenuses when a new direction was commenced above or below.

107. *Table of the Measurement of the Base of Verification.*

Hypotheses No.	Obs.	Angles of Elev. or Deps.	Perpendiculars. Elevation.	Depression.	Reduction.	Below.	Above.
		° ′ ″	Feet.	Feet.	Feet.	Inches.	Inches.
1	1	7 32 30		13.7012	0.9431		
2	1	11 31 40		19.9843	2.0172		
3	1	10 5 0		17.5080	1.5446		
4	1	7 25 20		12.9180	0.8379		
5	1	5 41 50		9.9072	0.4940		
6	7	4 49 30		52.8788	1.4806		
7	6	4 18 40		45.1033	1.6977		
8	3	3 48 30		19.9257	0.6625	31.5	
9	3	3 13 0		16.8336	0.4787	22.5	
10	1	0 9 0		0.8018	0.0003		
11	1	2 27 30	4.2893		0.0920		
12	1	0 58 30	1.7016		0.0145		
13	3	0 5 0	0.4363		0.0003		
14	6	0 34 10		5.9631	0.0791	11.5	
15	1	3 9 10	5.4959		0.1514		
16	2	1 25 20	4.9040		0.0610		
17	2	0 24 10	1.4059		0.0049		
18	5	0 8 10		1.1078	0.0014		
19	4	0 49 10	5.7106		0.0409		
20	4	0 10 30	1.2605		0.0020		
21	3	1 19 20		6.9225	0.0799	7.0	
22	7	1 38 20		10.0201	0.1804		
23	6	1 33 40		13.6216	0.1856	5.5	
24	8	1 18 20		13.6706	0.1558	11.3	
25	1	1 34 30		2.7185	0.0378		
26	9	1 15 0		19.6534	0.2141		
27	6	1 6 50		10.6169	0.0939		
28	2	0 5 40	0.3297		0.0003		
29	3	0 49 50	4.3486		0.0325		
30	5	0 75 10	2.2059		0.0049		
31	3	0 18 20		1.5999	0.0043	28.5	
32	5	0 8 50	1.2849		0.0017		
33	3	0 53 30	4.6686		0.0361		
34	8	0 8 50	2.0556		0.0026		
35	10	0 45 10	13.1381		0.0863		
36	4	0 14 0		1.6290	0.0033		
37	5	0 52 0		7.5618	0.0572		
38	2	1 40 10		5.8266	0.0849		
39	7	0 35 30		7.2284	0.0375		
40	4	1 3 10		7.3494	0.0675		
41	3	0 33 50		2.9525	0.0145	19.25	
42	2	0 54 80	1.5756		0.0124		
43	2	1 37 0	5.6425		0.0796		
44	3	0 8 40		0.7563	0.0009		
45	3	0 50 10		4.3777	0.0319		
46	4	0 55 50		6.4951	0.0519	20.0	
47	12	0 31 40		10.1385	0.0457		

Hypobrusate. No.	Cha.	Angles of Elev. or Depr.			Perpendiculars. Elevation.	Depression.	Reduction.	Below.	Above.
		°	′	″	Feet.	Feet.	Feet.	Inches.	Inches.
48	3	0	45	30		3.9705	0.0163		
49	3	1	18	40		6.8644	0.0783		
50	2	2	58	50		6.9121	0.1195		
51	2	3	49	30		13.3418	0.4455		
52	2	3	14	20		11.8806	0.3532	29.25	
53	2	3	10	50	11.6774		0.3413		
54	2	2	31	10	8.7917		0.1913		
55	2	1	7	0	3.8476		0.0580		24.5
56	7	0	25	40		5.2262	0.0195		
57	5	0	55	40		8.0960	0.0656		
58	8	3	2	50		10.6318	0.2828		
59	2	5	34	10		19.4104	0.9441		
60	1	2	4	50		3.6305	0.0659		
61	4	0	34	10	3.9754		0.0198	8.5	
62	2	0	51	40		3.0057	0.0285		
63	3	1	21	40		7.1261	0.0847	33.00	
64	9	3	4	30	48.2788		1.2958		29.0
65	4	2	16	10	15.8396		0.3137		28.75
66	6	0	14	20	2.5016		0.0052		
67	6	1	19	10		13.8160	0.1591		
68	3	1	56	30		10.1646	0.1722		
69	3	0	25	10	8.1962		0.0080		
70	2	0	51	10	2.9766		0.0282		
71	5	0	48	20		7.0296	0.494		
72	4	0	35	40	4.1499		0.0215		
73	4	1	30	0	10.4708		0.1373		
74	4	1	5	10	7.6014		0.0722		1″.5
75	4	0	38	50		4.5184	0.0255		6.0
76	5	1	56	30		10.9410	0.2871	42.0	
77	12	0	34	50		12.1579	0.0616		
78	7	1	3	50		14.0150	0.1403		
79	9	1	37	40		15.5656	0.3632	13.0	
80	3	1	49	40		9.5686	0.1526		
81	4	2	1	0		.1163			
82	7	1	25	0		17.3002	0.2140		
83	4	1	46	40		13.4092	0.1925		
84	7	0	41	50		8.5180	0.0518		
85	3	0	46	20	6.7387		0.0454		
86	3	0	10	40	2.8035		0.0054		12.0
87	3	1	34	10		8.2311	0.11 9		
88	3	3	7	10	16.3253		0.44 5		
89	5	1	2	10	9.0655		0.0820		
90	6	0	4	20		0.7565	0.0005		
91	3	1	34	50		8.8747	0.1141	4.0	
92	3	0	23	30	1.8762		0.0059		
					118.6937	634.8202	20.9158	278.0	117.85

Reduction of the Base measured on Salisbury Plain, to the Temperature of 62°.

108. The overplus of the 566th chain was measured by Mr. Ramsden, and found to be 9.939 feet; therefore the apparent length of the base was   **Feet.** 36590.061

By the measurement in the Duke of Marlborough's riding-house, the chain A was found to exceed 100 feet in the temperature of 54°, by 0.11425 inches; to which adding half the wear, namely, $\frac{1}{576}$ inch, we get $\frac{0.11617}{12}$ feet for the excess of the chain's length above 100 feet; therefore $\frac{0.11617}{12} \times 365.9$ (chains) $= 3.542$ feet, is the correction for excess and wear; which add $+3.542$

The sum of all the degrees shown by the thermometers, was 146051; wherefore $\overline{\frac{146051}{5} - 54°} \times 365.9$ $\times \frac{0.0075}{12} = 5.232$ feet, is the correction for the mean heat in which the base was measured above 54°, the temperature to which the chains were reduced; and this add   -   -   -   - $+5.232$

Hence these corrections, added to the apparent length, give   -   -   -   -   36598.835

Again, for the reduction to the temperature of 62°, viz. for 8° on the brass scale, we have $\frac{0.01117 \times 365.9 \times 80}{12}$ $= 3.017$ feet; which subtract   -   - -3.017

By the tables, the sum of the versed sines of the hypothenuses, or the corrections for reducing them to the plane of the horizon, is 20.916 feet; and this subtract   -   -   - -20.916

36574.902

The sum of the corrections, for the reduction of the several horizontal lines from the height of the different hypothenuses above the centre of the earth, to the height of Beacon Hill above ditto, is 0.581 feet; this add - - - - + 0.501

Therefore the apparent length of the base, as reduced ———
to the level of Beacon Hill, is - - feet 36575.401

But it will be hereafter shown, that the height of Beacon Hill above the sea is 690 feet nearly, and that of King's Arbour 118, and of Hampton Poorhouse 86 feet; therefore the height of Beacon Hill above the mean point between King's Arbour and Hampton Poorhouse, is 588 feet, or 98 fathoms.

Now as the base thus reduced, may be supposed to have been measured 98 fathoms farther from the centre of the earth, than that on Hounslow Heath, it must be reduced to the same level. Therefore if we take 3481794 fathoms from the mean semi-diameter, and add 98 fathoms to it, we shall get the length by this proportion, viz. 3481892 : 3481794 :: 36575.4 : 36574.4 the length of the base nearly.

With respect to that step by which the base is reduced to the level of Beacon Hill, or the correction 0.501 foot is obtained, it will be proper to show on what principle it is founded.

In the adjoining figure, let D a, a e, e c, and e O be the several hypothenuses, or measured lines; then will the sum of the corrections for their reduction to the plane of the horizon, as given in the table, exhibit that of the differences between the horizontal lines, b a, d e, f c, b O, and their corresponding hypothenuses.

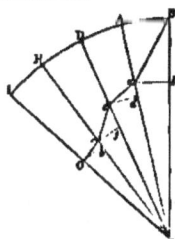

Again, with the radius C B, C being the centre of the earth,

describe the arc B I, or that subtended by the base, and through
the terminations of the several hypothenuses, draw the lines C A,
C D, C H, and C I ; then will the lines B A, A D, D H and H I be
those to which the horizontal ones *b a, d e, f c,* and *b* O are to be
reduced, and which may therefore be done by the proportions of
the lines, C *a,* C *e,* C *c,* and C O, to the constant radius C B.
Upon this principle, the correction o.501 foot has been obtained,
and which is the sum of the differences between the lines *b a, d e,*
f c, and *b* O, and their corresponding ones in the arc D I.

Height of Beacon Hill above the Southern Extremity of the Base.

	Feet.
109. The sum of the perpendiculars or elevations in the fourth column, is	218.6937
And of the depressions in the fifth column	634.8222
Therefore the depressions exceed the elevations	416.1285
The difference of the sums in the seventh and eighth columns, add	13.35
Hence the sum is the height of the beginning of the first chain above the end of the last, namely	429.48
But the handle of the chain at Beacon Hill was 6.7 feet above the stone, and at the other end it was 1.3 feet; therefore their difference is 5.4 feet, which subtract	5.4
Hence the surface of the stone at Beacon Hill is higher than the surface of the stone at Old Sarum	424.08

110. When this situation was first examined, and selected for the
measurement, it was imagined that one of the extremities of the
base would be fixed on somewhere near the southmost clump of fir
trees, not far from the Amesbury road, because from that spot
Highclere can be seen. Those trees are near the 52d hypothenuse,
and therefore about a mile from Beacon Hill; consequently, if

that situation had been fixed on, the base would have been no more than six miles, and the correction for the reduction of the hypothenuses to the plane of the horizon only about 16 feet.

Now, although we think that the fixing on Beacon Hill as the northern extremity, is justified from the circumstance of a mile being added to the base, which is conceived to be more than a counterbalance for any errors which may arise from measuring down the side of a hill; there were other reasons which made it proper; a principal one is, that by selecting that spot, the base can be applied as a test to the triangles, without making the connection by means of several small ones; and another is, that if a place near the trees had been fixed on, a station must afterwards have been chosen on Beacon Hill, in order to have a view of Long Knoll, near Maiden Bradley, and Inkpin Beacon towards Hungerford.

We shall now close the account of the base by observing, that this measurement has been almost without an alternative, since Sedgemoor, the only spot west of Salisbury proper for an operation of this kind, is about to be inclosed. Therefore had we not adopted this expedient, the triangles which may hereafter be carried on to the remote parts of the West of England, would probably have depended on the Hounslow Heath base. But we are led to believe, that this base has been measured with nearly the same accuracy which would have attended the operation, had the ground been nearly level; since there is a certainty of the angles formed by the hypothenuses and the plane of the horizon, being determined within a minute of the truth. Now if an error of a minute in those inclinations, supposing them all to lie the same way, produce only that of three inches in the whole base, it may be concluded that 36574+ is very nearly its true length.

Calculation of the Sides of the great Triangles. Pl. XX.

111. *Of the Division of the Series into different Branches.*

In order to methodize the process of computation, it has been considered as proper to divide the series into different branches, as the triangles of which they are composed seem naturally to resolve themselves into distinct classes.

The first branch, is that which immediately connects the base of departure on Hounslow Heath, with that of verification on Salisbury Plain, and is bounded by the sides connecting the stations, Hanger Hill, St. Ann's Hill, Bagshot Heath, Highclere, Beacon Hill, and Four Mile-stone on the north, and on the south side by Four Mile-stone, Dean Hill, Butser Hill, Hind Head, Leith Hill, and Banstead.

The second branch, is that which proceeds from the side Hind Head and Leith Hill, to the coast of Sussex and the Isle of Wight, and principally affords the sides which will be hereafter used in finding the distance between Beachy Head and Dunnose. This branch also proceeds westward for the survey of the coast, and is bounded by the sides connecting the stations Leith Hill, Hind Head, Butser Hill, Dean Hill, and Wingreen on the north, and on the south by those connecting the stations Nine Barrow Down, Molteston Down, Dunnose, Rook's Hill, Chanctonbury Ring, and Ditchling Beacon.

The third branch, is that which proceeds from the side Hanger Hill and Banstead, to Botley Hill and Leith Hill, and from thence towards Beachy Head and Brightling, joining the series formerly projected at Botley Hill and Fairlight Down; the branch being bounded to the westward by the sides connecting the stations Hanger Hill, Banstead, Leith Hill, Ditchling Beacon, and Beachy Head.

M m 2

[470]

The fourth branch, or remaining class of triangles, is that by which the distance between Beachy Head and Dunnose is obtained, and is formed by the sides connecting the stations Beachy Head, Ditchling Beacon, Chanctonbury Ring, Rook's Hill, and Dunnose.

Of the Selection of the Angles constituting the principal Triangles, and the Manner of reducing them for Computation.

112. The angles of the several triangles, constituting the general series, are, with a very few exceptions, those arising from using the means of the several observations given in the foregoing part of this work; for although the rejecting of such as might apparently suit the purpose, would give the sums of the three angles of many of the triangles, nearer to 180 degrees *plus* the computed excess; yet as all the observations have been made with equal care, and are for the most part to be considered as of equal accuracy, it has been thought proper to select those means, as being the fairest mode of proceeding.

If the observations had been made on a sphere of known magnitude, and the angles accurately taken, the most natural method of computing the sides of the triangles from the measured bases, would be by spherical trigonometry; but if the magnitude was such, that the length of a degree of a great circle was equal to a degree of the meridian in these latitudes nearly, in order to obtain the sides true to a foot from such computation, with any facility, a table of the logarithmic sines of small arcs computed to every $\frac{1}{100}$ of a second of a degree, would be necessary, because the length of a second of a degree on the meridian is about 100 feet. As the lengths of small arcs and their chords are nearly the same (the difference in these between Beachy Head and Dunnose being less than 4 feet) it is evident this business might be performed sufficiently near the truth in any extent of a series of triangles, by plane trigonometry, if the angles formed by the chords could be determined pretty exact. We have endeavoured to adopt this method in computing the sides of the principal triangles, in order to avoid an arbitrary correction of the observed angles, as well as that of reducing the whole extent of the triangles to a flat, which evidently would introduce erroneous results, and these in proportion as the series of triangles extended.

In the *Connaissance des Temps* for 1793, M. Delambre has given three tables, by which the angles of a spherical triangle may readily be reduced to those formed by the chords. But the Astronomer Royal has favoured us 'with the following investigation, which is extended so as to render the tables unnecessary for this purpose.

Demonstration of M. Delambre's Formula for reducing a Distance on the Sphere to any great Circle near it, or the contrary. By Nevil Maskelyne, D. D. F. R. S. and Astronomer Royal.

119. Put $A =$ angle subtended by two terrestrial objects; $a =$ the same reduced to the horizon; H, b the two apparent altitudes: if either is a depression, it must be taken negative.

By spherics, c, $A = c$, $a \cdot c$, $H \cdot c$, $b + s$, $H \cdot s$, b.

Put $A = a + d a$, where $d a$ signifies $A - a$, and not their differential.

By trigonometry, c, $A = c$, $a \cdot c$, $d a - s$, $a \cdot s$, $d a = c$, a

$\times \overline{1 - vs}$, $d a - s$, $a \cdot s$, $d a = c$, $a - c$, $a \times 2 s^2$, $\frac{1}{2} d a - s$, $a \cdot s$, $d a$

(by theorem above) $= c$, $a \cdot c$, $H \cdot c$, $b + s$, $H \cdot s$, $b \cdot s$, $d a + 2 s^2$, $\frac{1}{2} d a \cdot 't$, $a = 't$, $a - 't$, $a \cdot c$, $H \cdot c$, $b - s$, $H \cdot s$, $b \times \mathrm{cosec.}\ a = t'$, a

$- 't$, $a \times \frac{1}{2} c$, $H - b + \frac{1}{2} c$, $\overline{H + b} - \mathrm{cosec.}\ a \times \frac{1}{2} c$, $H - b - \frac{1}{2} c$,

$\overline{H + b}$ (because t', $a = \frac{1}{2}'t$, $\frac{1}{2} a - \frac{1}{2} t, \frac{1}{2} a$; and cosec. $a = \frac{1}{2}'t \frac{1}{2} a$

$+ \frac{1}{2} l, \frac{1}{2} a) = \overline{\frac{1}{2} l', \frac{1}{2} a} - \frac{1}{2} l, \frac{1}{2} a \times \overline{1 - \frac{1}{2} c, H - b} - \frac{1}{2} c, \overline{H + b}$

$- \frac{1}{2} 'l, \frac{1}{2} a + \frac{1}{2} l, \frac{1}{2} a \times \frac{1}{2} c, \overline{H - b} - \frac{1}{2} c, \overline{H + b} = \frac{1}{2} 'l, \frac{1}{2} a$

$\times \overline{1 - c, H - b} - \frac{1}{2} l, \frac{1}{2} a \times \overline{1 - c, H + b} = \frac{1}{2} 'l, \frac{1}{2} a \times vs, \overline{H - b}$

$- \frac{1}{2} l, \frac{1}{2} a \times vs, \overline{H + b} = 'l, \frac{1}{2} a . s', \frac{1}{2} \overline{H - b} - l, \frac{1}{2} a . s', \frac{1}{2} \overline{H + b}.$

Put $n = 'l, \frac{1}{2} a . s', \frac{1}{2} (H - b) - l, \frac{1}{2} a . s', \frac{1}{2} (H + b),$

We shall have

$s, d a + 2 s', \frac{1}{2} d a . 'l, a = n;$

and $s, d a = n - 2 s', \frac{1}{2} d a . 'l, a.$

But $s, d a = 2 s, \frac{1}{2} d a . c, \frac{1}{2} d a$

$\therefore s, \frac{1}{2} d a = \frac{s, d a}{2 c, \frac{1}{2} d a} = \frac{n - 2 s', \frac{1}{2} d a . 'l, a}{2 c, \frac{1}{2} d a},$

and $s, d a = n - 2 s', \frac{1}{2} d a . 'l, a = n - 2 l', a \left(\frac{n - 2 s', \frac{1}{2} d a . 'l, a}{2 c, \frac{1}{2} d a} \right)',$

because $\overline{\left(\frac{n - 2 s', \frac{1}{2} d a . 'l a}{2 c, \frac{1}{2} d a} \right)}' = \frac{n - 4 n . s', \frac{1}{2} d a . 'l, a + 4 s'', \frac{1}{2} d a . 'l', a}{4 \times 1 - s'', \frac{1}{2} d a}$

$= \frac{n^2}{4} + \frac{n^2 l', \frac{1}{2} d a.}{4} - (n . s', \frac{1}{2} d a . 'l, a - n . s', \frac{1}{2} d a . 'l, a$

$+ s'', \frac{1}{2} d a . 'l', a) = n - \frac{1}{2} n^2 . 'l, a - \frac{1}{2} n^2 . 'l, a . s', \frac{1}{2} d a$

$+ 2 n . 'l', a . s', \frac{1}{2} d a + 2 n 'l', a . s', \frac{1}{2} d a - 2 'l', a . s' + \frac{1}{2} d a,$

by substituting for $s, \frac{1}{2} d a$ its near value $n,$

$= n - \frac{1}{2} n^2 l', a - \frac{n^2 l', a}{2} + \frac{1}{2} n^2 l', a + \frac{1}{2} n'' 'l', a - \frac{1}{2} n^2 'l', a,$

where the last term but one containing the 5th power of n may
be rejected, as it has been omitted by M. Delambre.

As $d a$ is always very small, the arc $d a$ in parts of the radius,
unity, $= s, d a$ in parts of the same radius, therefore

$s, 1'' : 1'' : : s, d a$ (in parts of radius unity) $: \frac{1}{s, 1''} \times s, d a = d a$ in
seconds,

$= \frac{1''}{s, 1''} \times n - 2 s', \frac{1}{2} d a . 'l, a = \frac{1''}{s, 1''} \times \overline{n - d a . s, \frac{1}{2} d a . 'l, a} = \frac{1'' \times n}{s, 1''}$

$- \frac{1'' \times d a . s, \frac{1}{2} d a . 'l, a}{s, 1''} \therefore$ if we put $n = \frac{1''}{s, 1''} \times l', \frac{1}{2} a . s, \frac{1}{2} (H - b)$

$- l, \frac{1}{2} a . s', \frac{1}{2} (H + b),$ and $d a = a$ number of seconds, we shall have, $d a = n - d a . s, \frac{1}{2} d a .'t, a$; and, for the most part, without any sensible error, $d a = n - n . s, \frac{1}{2} n .'t, a$.

Table I. contains $\frac{s' \times t. \frac{1}{2}a}{10000}$, and $\frac{s' \times 't. \frac{1}{2}a}{10000}$; Table II. contains 10000 × s', $\frac{1}{2}$ (H ∓ b). Table III. contains the term $- n . s, \frac{1}{2} n .'t, a$. The argument on the side is a, and that on the top is n or the result found by the help of the two first tables. If this correction should be considerable, with the value of da, found after this correction has been applied, enter Table III. again at the top, and with a on the side as before; the number now found subtracted from n will give the correct value of da.

By the investigation,

$d a = \frac{1}{2} 't, \; \frac{1}{2} a . v s \overline{H \asymp b} - \frac{1}{2} t, \; \frac{1}{2} a . v s, \; \overline{H \pm b} - v s, \; d a .'t a,$

where the upper or lower signs are to be used, according as the objects are on the same, or on contrary sides of the great circle to which they are referred; the third term will be negative or positive, according as a is less or more than 90°.* If da should come out negative, A will be less than a, or a greater than A. In the case of reducing a spheric angle to the angle between the chords, the spheric angle will be represented by a, and the angle between the chords by $A = a \mid d a \mid$ and $d a - \frac{1}{2} 't, \; \frac{1}{2} a . v s,$ $\overline{H \sim b} - \frac{1}{2} t, \frac{1}{2} a . v s, \overline{H + b} - v s, d a .'t, a$ (if D, d represent the arcs to the chords) $= \frac{1}{2} 't, \frac{1}{2} a . v s, \frac{1}{2} (D \sim d) - \frac{1}{2} t, \frac{1}{2} a . v s, \frac{1}{2} (D + d)$ $- v s, d a .'t, a$;

$A = a - (\frac{1}{2} t, \frac{1}{2} a . v s, \frac{1}{2} \overline{D + d} - \frac{1}{2} 't, \frac{1}{2} a . v s \frac{1}{2} D \sim d) - v s, d a .'t, a;$ where the last term will change its sign to affirmative, if a is greater than 90°. If the answer is required in seconds, the correction must be multiplied by 206265, the number of seconds in

---

* Compute the two, which will give the approximate value of da, and make use of them in computing the third term ; and join the three terms together according to their signs, which will give da still nearer ; and, if this should prove considerable, compute the third term a second time with the new value of da.

an arc = radius. The calculation will be easily made by logarithms.

Practical Rule.

The practical rule deduced from the above conclusions is the following, and given in the words of the Astronomer Royal.

" To the constant logarithm 5.0134 add L . *t*, ½ *a* and L . *vs*
" $\overline{D + d}$; the sum diminished by 10 in the index is the logarithm
" of the first part of the value of *d a* in seconds, which is always
" negative. To the constant logarithm 5.0134 add L . *t'*, ½ *a*, and
" L . *vs*, ½ $\overline{D \smile d}$, t e sum diminished by 10 in the index, is the
" logarithm of the second part in seconds, which is always affir-
" mative. These two joined together, according to their proper
" signs, will give the approximate value of *d a*. To its logarithmic
" versed sine, add L . *t'*, *a* and constant logarithm 5.3144, the
" sum, diminished by 10 in the index, will be the logarithm of
" the third part in seconds, which will be negative or affirmative,
" according as *a* is less or more than 90°. This applied according
" to its sign, to the approximate value of *d a*, will give the correct
" value of *d a*. If the third part comes out considerable, it should
" be computed anew with the last value of *d a*. The value of *d a*,
" finally corrected, applied to *a*, will give A, the angle between
" the chords."

In the application of the above rule, to the computation of such corrections as may be applied to the angles of any triangle in this Survey, it is manifest that the last step may be entirely neglected on account of the smallness of the *approximate* value of *d a*, whose versed sine is one of the arguments. Being, therefore, confined to the use of the two first steps, the operation is very short. An example is here given in the computation of the correction for reducing the angle at Chanctonbury Ring in the xxxixth triangle, to that formed by the chords.

EXAMPLE.

Constant logarithm - - 5.0134 - - - - - - 5.0134
Log. tang. { a = 78° 56' - 10.7118   Log. co. tang. { a - - - 9.2887
Log. vr. { . $\overline{H+b}$ = 19' 53".5   5.8837   Log. vr. { $\overline{H-b}$ = 5' 53".5   +1669

           0.9483 + 8".88   — 1.4690 + 0".03

       1st correction — 8.88
       2d correction + 0.03

         — 8.85 the correction required.

114. When the three angles of any triangle appear to have been observed correctly, by their sum being equal to 180 degrees *plus* the computed excess, the corrections for the chord angles have been added to, or taken from them, as that correction has been negative or affirmative, and the triangle rendered fit for computation. Also, if in any triangle, where the sum has either fallen short of, or exceeded 180 degrees *plus* the computed excess, one or two of the observed angles have appeared to have been determined with sufficient accuracy, as shown by the agreement of the angles obtained upon different parts of the arch : the corrections for the chord angles have been added to, or taken from them, and the remaining angle or angles considered as erroneous. In the case of one angle being supposed right, and the other two wrong, the errors have been considered equal between the latter, unless the sum of the angles round the horizon at one of the stations, has indicated, that either the whole, or the greatest part of the excess or defect, was due to a particular angle. Likewise, when any triangle has been found in excess or defect, and all the angles have appeared to be determined with equal accuracy, the corrections for the reduction to the angles formed by the chords have been first applied, and then the errors considered equal.

What is called the spherical excess in the fifth column, is computed according to the rule, page 138. These excesses above 180° would, of course, be exactly the same as the respective sums of the

N n

differences between the spherical angles and those formed by the chords, in the fourth column, if both were not obtained from approximating rules.

It is almost unnecessary to remark, that no computations have been attempted with the chords of the sides of the lesser triangles in the principal series.

116. BRANCH I. *Consisting of the Triangles which connect the Base of Departure on Hounslow Heath with that of Verification on Salisbury Plain.*

Distance from King's Arbour to Hampton Poorhouse, 27404.2 Feet.

No. of triangles	Names of the stations	Observed angles	Diff.	Spherical excess	Error	Angles corrected for computation	Distances
I.	St. Ann's Hill	44 11 42 25				44 11 41 75	Feet
	Hampt. Poorhouse	61 16 34 5				61 16 33 75	
	King's Arbour	74 31 43 25				74 31 34 5	
		180 0 0		0.21	+0.79		
	St. Ann's Hill from { Hampton Poorhouse / King's Arbour					— — —	37753.5 / 34455.2
II.	Banstead	55 15 41 25				55 15 41	
	King's Arbour	51 46 57 25				51 46 58	
	St. Ann's Hill	81 57 58 25				81 57 57	
		180 0 3.75		0.61	+3.18		
	Banstead { King's Arbour / St. Ann's Hill					— — —	80131.6 / 76607.7
III.	Hanger Hill	44 39 16 5				44 39 16 5	
	Hampt. Poorhouse	130 3 3.25				130 3 3	
	St. Ann's Hill	25 17 40.75				25 17 40 5	
		180 0 0.5		0.26	+0.24		
	Hanger Hill { Hampton Poorhouse / St. Ann's Hill					— — —	38670 / 69078.1
IV.	Banstead	55 22 39.75	—0.25			55 22 39 5	
	Hanger hill	61 46 34.75	—0.19			61 46 34 25	
	St. Ann's Hill	63 50 46.75	—0.39			63 50 46 25	
		180 0 1.25		1.1	+0.15		
	Banstead { Hanger Hill / St. Ann's Hill					— — —	77347.4 / 76671.4

By these triangles, the distance from St. Ann's Hill to Banstead are 76687.7 feet, and 76688.4 feet; the mean of which is 76688 feet; and with this distance the sides marked with asterisks have been determined by working back.

Banstead from St. Ann's Hill, 76688 feet.

No. of triangles.	Names of the stations.	Observed angles.	Diff.	Spheri- cal excess.	Error.	Angles corrected for calculation.	Distances.
							Feet.
V.	Leith Hill	58 19 22.5	—0.35			58 19 22.25	
	Banstead	77 37 35.5	—0.44			77 37 35	
	St. Ann's Hill	44 3 3	—0.33			44 3 2.75	
		180 0 1		1.1	—0.1		
	Leith Hill { Banstead					—— ——	62655.2
	St. Ann's Hill					—— ——	88019.8

Quadrilateral, formed by the Sides, St. Ann's Hill and Bagshot Heath, Bagshot Heath and Hind Head, Hind Head and Leith Hill, Leith Hill and St. Ann's Hill.

St. Ann's Hill from Leith Hill 88019.8 Feet.

VI.	Hind Head	51 10 39.75	—0.5			51 10 39.25	
	St. Ann's Hill	46 40 30.5	—0.47			46 40 30.25	
	Leith Hill	82 8 51	—0.7			82 8 50.5	
		180 0 1.25		1.7	—0.45		
	Hind Head { St. Ann's Hill					—— ——	111917.4*
	Leith Hill					—— ——	82187.8*
VII.	Bagshot Heath	47 57 7	—0.53			47 57 6.5	
	Leith Hill	56 37 29.5	—0.53			56 37 29	
	Hind Head	75 25 25.15	—0.63			75 25 24.5	
		180 0 1.75		1.7	+0.05		
	Bagshot Heath { Leith Hill					—— ——	107115.9*
	Hind Head					—— ——	92421.9*
VIII.	Bagshot Heath	53 52 14.25	—0.16			53 52 14.25	
	Leith Hill	25 31 22.5	—0.2			25 31 22	
	St. Ann's Hill	100 36 23.5	—0.6			100 36 23.75	
		179 59 59.25		0.96	—1.71		
	Bagshot Heath from St. Ann's Hill					—— ——	46955.3*
IX.	Bagshot Heath	101 49 22.25	—0.02			101 49 21.75	
	Hind Head	24 14 45.5	—0.21			24 14 45.25	
	St. Ann's Hill	53 55 53	—0.17			53 55 53	
		180 0 0.75		1.0	—0.25		
	Bagshot Heath from St. Ann's Hill					—— ——	46955.4*

Bagshot Heath from Hird Head 92,113.9 Feet.

No. of triangles.	Names of the stations.	Observed angles.	Diff.	Spherical excess.	Error.	Angles corrected for calculation.	Distances.
X.	Highclere	34 56 15.75	—0.81			34 46 15	Feet.
	Bagshot Heath	83 30 14 25	—1.36			83 30 14	
	Hind Head	34 46 15 75	—0 88			61 53 31	
		180 0 1 75		3 09	—1 34		
	Highclere { Bagshot Heath		—		— — —	149537 6 b	
	{ Hind Head		—		— — —	160971 2 a	
XI.	Butser Hill	84 31 45.5	—1.2			84 31 44 5	
	Hind Head	66 15 56.5	—0.83			65 15 54.25	
	Highclere	29 12 22	—0 72			29 12 22.25	
		180 0 2		2.7	—0.7		
	Butser Hill { Hind Head		—		— — —	78905 7 b	
	{ Highclere		—		— — —	148031 6 a	
XII.	Dean Hill	62 12 48 75	—1.37			62 12 47	
	Butser Hill	48 28 41.5	—1.23			48 28 40	
	Highclere	69 8 35	—1.5			69 8 33	
		180 0 5.25		4 07	+1.18		
	Dean Hill { Butser Hill		—		— — —	156132 1 a	
	{ Highclere		—		— — —	125082 9 b	
XIII.	Beacon Hill	102 45 23.5	—0.9			102 45 22	
	Highclere	26 55 51.5	—0.26			26 55 50.75	
	Dean Hill	50 18 47.5	—0.15			50 18 47.25	
		180 0 2.5		1.3	+1.2		
	Beacon Hill { Highclere		—		— — —	98604 4	
	{ Dean Hill		—		— — —		

Triangles which connect the Base of Verification with the Sides Beacon Hill and Highclere, and Beacon Hill and Dean Hill.

No. of triangles.	Names of the stations.	Observed angles.	Diff.	Spherical excess.	Error.	Angles corrected for calculation.	Distances.
XIV.	Thorney Down	53 22 30				53 22 31 25	
	Highclere	12 59 10				12 59 10.75	
	Beacon Hill	113 38 16.75				113 38 18	
		179 59 56 75		0.6	—3.85		
	Thorney Down { Highclere		—		— — —	116696	
	{ Beacon Hill		—		— — —	27634 4	

No. of triangles.	Names of the stations.	Observed angles.	Diff.	Spherical excess.	Error.	Angles corrected for calculation.	Distances.
XV.	Old Sarum	4¹ 16 4.5	° ′ ″	′	″	4¹ 16 4.5	Feet.
	Thorney Down	9¹ 0 31				9¹ 0 30.75	
	Beacon H.ll	33 33 24.75				33 33 24.75	
		180 0 0.15		0.13	+0.12	— — —	80416.1
	Old Sarum from Thorney Down -						
XVI.	Four Mile-stone	7¹ 4 46				7¹ 4 47.5	
	Dean Hill	19 19 3 15				19 19 3	
	Beacon Hill	68 16 10				68 16 9.5	
		180 0 1.15		0.5	+0.75	— — —	56775
	Four Mile-stone { Dean Hill	Beacon Hill	•	-	-	— — —	38016.2
XVII.	Old Sarum	85 58 22.5				85 58 21.75	
	Four Mile-stone	70 1 47.5				70 1 47	
	Beacon Hill	23 59 51.75				23 59 51.25	
		180 0 1.75		0.14	+1.61	— — —	15026.4
	Old Sarum from Four Mile-stone -						

The Length of the Base of Verification deduced from that on Hounslow Heath, and the foregoing Triangles.

116. The base on Hounslow Heath is 27404.2 feet, which, with the four first triangles, give 76688 feet for the mean distance of St. Ann's Hill and Banstead.

That mean distance, with the v. vi. vii. x. xi. xii. xiii. xvi. xvii. triangles, will give 36574.7 feet for the base of *verification*.

If the computation be made with the viii. and ix. triangles also, and the mean distance taken between Hind Head and Bagshot, the base will be 36574.9.

And those mean distances of St. Ann's Hill and Banstead, and Hind Head and Bagshot, with the xiv. and xv. triangles (excluding the xvi. and xvii.), will produce 36574.6 and 36574.9 respectively.

Lastly ;—if the computations are carried directly from one base to the other, independent of the mean distances and the xiv. and xv. triangles, the greatest and least results will be 36574.8, and 36573.8, the mean being 36574.3, feet, or about an inch short of the measurement.

Of the several ways by which the base of verification, or distance between Beacon Hill and Old Sarum is deduced, the first seems to have the preference, because the angles of the vi. and vii. triangles appear to have been observed very correctly. The results from the xiv. and xv. triangles cannot be considered as very conclusive, because the angle at Highclere is so acute that a trifling error in it will vary the distance from Beacon Hill to Thorney Down very considerably ; and we had some reasons for being dissatisfied with this angle, and also that in the same triangle at Thorney Down, on account of the strain in the clamp. (Art. 101.)

Although the result of this comparison might afford some reason for supposing, that the sides of the triangles in this branch would be sufficiently near the truth, were all of them computed from the base on Hounslow Heath, yet, to approach more nearly to their correct distances, those which are marked with asterisks, have been computed with each base, and a mean of the results taken. The remaining sides have been determined by the bases in their vicinity,

117. BRANCH II. *Consisting of the Triangles which proceed from Hind Head and Leith Hill to the Coast of Sussex, Isle of Wight, &c.*

Hind Head from Leith Hill 89187.9 Feet, mean Distance.

No. of triangles.	Names of the stations.	Observed angles.	Diff.	Spherical excess.	Error.	Angles corrected for calculation.	Distances.
		° ′ ″	′ ″	″	″	° ′ ″	Feet.
XVIII.	Chanctonbury Ring	45 10 46.5	—0.44			45 10 46	
	Leith Hill -	72 56 50.85	—0.7			72 56 49.85	
	Hind Head -	61 52 25.5	—0.62			61 52 24.75	
		180 0 2.85		1.8	+0.45		
	Chanctonbury Ring { Leith Hill - / Hind Head					— — —	102185.7 / 110774.4
XIX.	Chanctonbury Ring	86 44 41	—0.62			86 44 39 75	
	Leith Hill -	32 43 57.5	—0.39			32 43 56.5	
	Ditchling Beacon	60 31 24.75	—0.38			60 31 23.75	
		180 0 3 25		2 5	+1.75		
	Chanctonbury Ring from Ditchling Beacon -					— — —	63469 1
XX.	Rook's Hill -	82 42 45.75	—0.7			82 42 45.85	
	Chanctonbury Ring	47 12 38	—0.45			47 12 38	
	Hind Head -	50 4 37	—0.46			50 4 36.75	
		180 0 0.75		1.6	—0.85		
	Rook's Hill from Chanctonbury Ring -					— — —	85645.4
	Butser Hill from Hind Head (Triang. 21) 78005 7 Feet.						
XXI.	Butser Hill -	70 25 13	——99			70 25 13	
	Hind Head -	44 28 6.85	—0.3			44 28 6.85	
	Rook's Hill -	65 6 40.75	—0.36			65 6 40.75	
		180 0 0		1.1	—1.1		
	Rook's Hill { Hind Head - / Butser Hill -					— — —	81954.4 / 60933.8
XXII.	Dunnose -	24 44 15.5	—0.58			24 44 16	
	Butser Hill -	80 21 58	—0.81			80 21 58.5	
	Rook's Hill -	74 53 45	—0.65			74 53 45.5	
		179 59 58.5		1.96	—3.46		
	Dunnose from Rook's Hill -					— — —	143558.9
XXIII.	Dunnose -	55 43 7	—1.53			55 43 6 75	
	Butser Hill -	76 12 22	—1.99			76 12 21.5	
	Dean Hill -	48 4 38.05	—1.54			48 4 31.75	
		180 0 1.85		5.0	—3.75		
	Dunnose { Butser Hill - / Dean Hill -					— — —	140580.1 / 185496.1

No. of triangles.	Names of the stations.	Observed angles.	Diff.	Spherical excess.	Error.	Angles corrected for calculation.	Distances.
		° ′ ″		° ′ ″		° ′ ″	Feet.
XXIV.	Dunnose -	53 12 27.25	−2.05			53 12 25.5	
	Dean Hill -	64 50 19	−2 06			64 50 16.75	
	Nine Barrow Down	61 57 19.75	−2.21			61 57 17.75	
		180 0 6		6.5	−0.5		
	Dunnose from Nine Barrow Down -					— — —	280181.8
	Distance from Beacon Hill to Dean Hill, as got by the Base on Salisbury Plain					— — —	58086.3
XXV.	Wingreen -	30 13 23	−0.35			30 13 22.5	
	Beacon Hill -	66 49 52.25	−0.39			66 49 51.5	
	Dean Hill -	82 56 47	−0.68			82 56 46	
		183 0 2.25		1.43	+0.82		
	Wingreen { Beacon Hill -					— — —	114528.4
	Wingreen { Dean Hill -					— — —	101089
XXVI.	Nine Barrow Down	39 34 18.75	−0.82			39 34 18.25	
	Wingreen -	88 58 47.75	−1.59			88 58 46.75	
	Dean Hill -	51 26 15.5	−0.82			51 26 45	
		180 0 2		3.24	−1.24		
	Nine Barrow Down { Wingreen -					— — —	130524.5
	Nine Barrow Down { Dean Hill -					— — —	166497
XXVII.	Motteston Down	— — —	−1.72			72 48 37.5	
	Nine Barrow Down	56 9 55.25	−1.43			56 9 51.75	
	Dean Hill -	51 1 30	−1.3			51 1 28.75	
				4.41			
	Motteston Down { Nine Barrow Down -					— — —	135489.6
	Motteston Down { Dean Hill -					— — —	144766
XXVIII.	Motteston Down	— — —	−1.61			62 39 30.5	
	Dean Hill -	61 53 20.75	−1.64			61 53 19	
	Butser Hill -	55 27 12	−1.47			55 27 10.5	
				4.7			
	Motteston Down from Butser Hill -					— — —	155023.4
XXIX.	Motteston Down	64 41 2	−0.35			64 41 4	
	Butser Hill -	20 45 10	−0.43			20 45 9.5	
	Dunnose -	94 33 17.5	−1 0			94 33 40.5	
		179 59 29.5		1.8	−2.3		
	Motteston Down from Dunnose -					— — —	55104.5

* This distance is the mean, as derived from the Salisbury Base, and from the side Butser Hill and Dean Hill.

The four sides of the first branch, namely, Beacon Hill and Dean Hill, Dean Hill and Butser Hill, and Butser Hill and Hind Head, have been used in the computation of the sides of this branch, because they are supposed to be nearly true : had, however, these triangles been considered as independent of those in the first branch, and the side Hind Head and Leith Hill been used as derived from the base on Hounslow Heath, nearly the same conclusions would have taken place ; for the distance between Beacon Hill and Old Sarum would in that case be 36574.2 feet, which is only two and an half inches less than the measured base. This may be considered as a proof, that the angles of the triangles forming this branch are sufficiently correct, since the series which joins the two bases by this route, is nearly an hundred and twenty miles in extent. Some little variation in that result might be produced by a different correction of the angles of the xxiv. triangle : but as the angle at Butser Hill must be very nearly true, the other angles cannot, on any reasonable supposition, be so corrected as to make the computed base differ from the measured one more than six inches.

118. BRANCH III. *Proceeding from the Side Hanger Hill and Banstead to Bolley Hill and Leith Hill, and from thence to Brighling and Beachy Head, joining the Triangles with those of the late General Roy at Bolley Hill and Fairlight Down.*

Hanger Hill from Banstead 77547.4 Feet.

No. of triangles.	Names of the stations.	Observed angles.	Diff.	Spherical excess.	Error.	Angles corrected for calculation.	Distances.
XXX.	Shooter's Hill - Hanger Hill - Banstead -	54 43 49.75 61 18 50 62 57 22	°	°	°	54 43 40.25 61 18 49 5 62 57 21.25	Feet.
		180 0 1.75		1.4	+0.35		
	Shooter's Hill {	Hanger Hill - Banstead -				--- --- --- ---	84596.3 85107

O o

No. of triangles.	Names of the stations.	Observed angles.	Diff.	Spherical excess.	Error.	Angles corrected for calculation.	Distances.
		° ′ ″	″	″	″	° ′ ″	Feet.
XXXI.	Botley Hill	85 39 58.5				85 39 58.25	
	Shooter's Hill	37 8 25.75				37 8 25.75	
	Banstead	57 11 30				57 11 30	
		180 0 0.25		0.9	−0.65		
	Botley Hill { Shooter's Hill / Banstead						70894.9 / 60587
XXXII.	Leith Hill	31 51 10	−0.08			31 21 9.75	
	Banstead	108 50 48.25	−0.13			108 50 47.75	
	Botley Hill	39 48 2.5	−0.06			39 48 2.5	
		180 0 0.25		0.7	+0.05		
	Leith Hill from Botley Hill						92631.5

In this triangle, using the side from Leith Hill to Banstead as got by the first branch, we find the distance between Leith Hill and Botley Hill to be 92632.9 feet; hence the mean distance is 92632.2 feet.

XXXIII.	Crowboro' Beacon	46 12 21.75	−0.45			46 12 21.25	
	Botley Hill	89 35 8	−0.98			89 35 0.25	
	Leith Hill	44 12 49	−0.45			44 12 48.5	
		180 0 1.75		1.9	−0.15		
	Crowborough Beacon { Botley Hill / Leith Hill						80492.5 / 118133.9
XXXIV.	Ditchling Beacon	78 48 27	−0.91			78 48 25.5	
	Crowboro' Beacon	63 14 37.25	−0.69			63 14 36.25	
	Leith Hill	38 10 59.75	−0.62			38 10 58.25	
		180 0 4		2.2	+1.8		
	Ditchling Beacon { Leith Hill / Crowborough Beacon						117190.6 / 61192.2
XXXV.	Brightling	43 29 1.5	−0.16			43 29 1	
	Crowboro' Beacon	105 2 44	−0.76			105 2 42	
	Ditchling Beacon	31 28 17.75	−0.22			31 28 17	
		180 0 3.25		1.14	+2.11		
	Brightling { Crowborough Beacon / Ditchling Beacon						61597.6 / 113962.3
XXXVI.	Beachy Head	73 58 26.5	−0.77			73 58 26.5	
	Ditchling Beacon	46 32 19	−0.56			46 32 19.5	
	Brightling	59 29 14	−0.64			59 29 14	
		179 59 59.5		2.0	−2.5		
	Beachy Head { Ditchling / Brightling						102132.4 / 86048

No. of triangles.	Names of the stations.	Observed angles.	Diff.	Spheroidal excess.	Error.	Angles corrected for calculation.	Distances.
		o ′ ″	″	″	″	o ′ ″	Feet.
XXXVII.	Fairlight Down	59 33 1.75	—0.39			59 33 1.75	
	Brightling	80 44 19.25	—0.51			80 44 19.25	
	Beachy Head	39 42 39	—0.36			39 42 39	
		180 0 0		1.28	— 1.28		
	Fairlight Down {	Brightling		—		— — —	63773.1
		Beachy Head		—		— — —	98513.7

Comparison of the Distances from Botley Hill to St. Ann's Hill, and Fairlight Down, deduced from the recent Observations, and those made in 1787, 1788.

119. The stations on St. Ann's Hill, Botley Hill, and Fairlight Down, connect our triangles with those of General Roy; and therefore the two distances from the middle station, Botley Hill, which are common to both series of triangles, afford the readiest, and indeed almost the only means of comparing independent deductions from both operations; the triangle St. Ann's Hill, King's Arbour, Hampton Poorhouse, excepted.

The distances from the station at the Hundred Acres to St. Ann's Hill and Botley Hill, (see the IV. and IX. triangles in Art. 57.) are 79209.7 and 48795.8 feet; and from the IV. V. and IX. triangles it appears, that the included angle at that station is 169° 25′ 21″.25; these give 127421.3 feet for the distance of St. Ann's Hill from Botley Hill.

According to our observations, the distances of St. Ann's Hill and Botley Hill from Leith Hill are 88019.3 and 92632.2 feet respectively, and the included angle for computation at Leith Hill 89° 40′ 32″; hence, from the recent triangles, the distance of the stations will be 127420 feet; which is about 1¼ feet less than the result from General Roy's triangles.

O o 2

To compute the distance of Fairlight Down from Botley Hill
by means of the triangles in Art. 57, we shall make use of the
mean distance of Hollingborn Hill from Fairlight Down, as deduced from both bases. This distance, 141752 feet (p. 142), with
the XIII. XII. and XI. triangles (p. 141), give 150790 feet, for
the distance of Hollingborn Hill from Botley Hill, and 88° 27′ 0″.½,
the included angle at Hollingborn Hill between Botley Hill and
Fairlight Down: hence the distance of the latter station from
Botley Hill will be 204274 feet.

For determining this line from our triangles, we have 92639.2
and 117190.4 feet, the distances of Botley Hill and Ditchling
Beacon from Leith Hill; also 102132.4 and 98519.7 feet, the distances of Ditchling Beacon and Fairlight Down from Beachy
Head, respectively: these, with the included angles at Leith
Hill and Beachy Head, give Ditchling Beacon from Botley Hill
139567.4, and from Fairlight Down, 167986.5 feet, and the
included angle at Ditchling Beacon 82° 41′ 6″.8; hence the distance from Botley Hill to Fairlight Down will be 204276 feet
nearly; or 2 feet greater than the deduction from the other
triangles.

120. BRANCH IV. *Consisting of the nearest Triangles to the northward of Beachy Head and Dunnose, for finding the Distance
between those Stations.*

No. of triangles.	Names of the stations.	Observed angles.	Diff.	Spheri-cal excess.	Error.	Angles corrected for calculation.
XXXVIII.	Dunnose - -	15 43 0	+0.55	"	"	15 43 0.5
	Rook's Hill - -	137 16 48.5	—3.88			137 16 44.5
	Chanctonbury Ring -	27 0 13	+1.37			27 0 15
		180 0 1.5		1.96	—0.46	

By this triangle, using the distance from Rook's Hill to Chanctonbury Ring as found by the first branch, we get the distance
between Rook's Hill and Dunnose, 143559.3 feet ; but by the same
branch, 143558.9 feet was found to be the distance ; and if the
side Butser Hill and Dean Hill be made the base, we shall get, by
the xxii. and xxiii. triangles, the distance from Rook's Hill to Dunnose 143557.1 feet : hence 143558.4, the mean of these three
distances with the above triangle, give 214498.4 feet, for the distance between Dunnose and Chanctonbury Ring.

No. of triangles.	Names of the stations.	Observed angles.	Diff.	Spheri-cal excess.	Error.	Angles corrected for calculation.
XXXIX.	Beachy Head - - Rook's Hill - - Chanctonbury Ring -	7 42 37 14 17 33.25 157 59 50.75	+2.56 +5.22 —8.85	"	'	7 42 40 14 17 38 157 59 42
		180 0 1		1.19	—0.19	

By this triangle, with the side Chanctonbury Ring and Rook's
Hill, as found by the second branch, we get the distance between
Chanctonbury Ring and Beachy Head, 157592.5 feet ; and by the
following triangle,

XL.	Beachy Head - - Ditchling Beacon - Chanctonbury Ring -	13 58 29.5 143 9 31.5 22 52 3.25	+0.48 —2.35 +0.99			13 58 28 143 9 30 22 52 2
		180 0 4.25		0.9	+3.35	

using the side Chanctonbury Ring and Ditchling Beacon as got
by the second branch, we get another distance between Beachy
Head and Chanctonbury Ring, namely, 157590.8 feet ; wherefore the mean distance is 157591.6 ; and this, with the xxxix.
triangle, give 239160.2 feet for the distance between Rook's Hill

and Beachy Head : hence we have four principal distances, namely,

Dunnose from $\begin{cases} \text{Rook's Hill} & - & 143558.4 \\ \text{Chanctonbury Ring} & 214498.4 \end{cases}$ feet.

Beachy Head from $\begin{cases} \text{Rook's Hill} & - & 299160.2 \\ \text{Chanctonbury Ring} & 157591.6 \end{cases}$ feet.

And these sides used in the two following triangles,

No. of triangles.	Names of the stations.	Observed angles.	Diff.	Spherical excess.	Error.	Angles corrected for calculation.
XLI.	Beachy Head - -	20 46 15	—0.2	"	"	20 46 52.75
	Rook's Hill - -	122 59 14.5	—7.7			122 59 8
	Dunnose - - -	36 13 58	+ 1.17			36 13 59.25
		180 0 55		6 77	—1.27	
XLII.	Dunnose - -	20 30 58	+ 0.86			20 30 58.75
	Chanctonbury Ring -	130 59 57.75	—8.77			130 59 29
	Beachy Head - -	28 29 30	+ 1.92			28 29 32.25
		180 0 5.75		6.01	—0.26	

give the four distances of Beachy Head from Dunnose, as beneath :

$$\begin{rcases} 339394.6 \\ 339395.0 \\ 339399.2 \\ 339401.5 \end{rcases} \text{feet.}$$

Hence 339397.6, the mean, may be considered as very nearly the true distance.

In the correction of the angles of the triangles which compose this branch, we have been a little more particular than with the others of the series, as it is of much consequence that the distance between Beachy Head and Dunnose should not be left doubtful.

In the XLII. triangle, it must be observed, that there is a defect of $\frac{1}{4}''$ nearly in the sum of the observed angles ; in the XXXVIII. about $\frac{1}{2}$ a second ; and in the XLI. a defect of about $1''\frac{1}{4}$: the sum in the XXXIX. is nearly right, but the angles of it are considered as residuary, or remaining angles ; the triangle being too oblique to be admitted as a principal one in the series, though numbered and inserted as such.

Now it is evident, that If all the angles of the four triangles contained in the quadrilateral formed by the stations on Dunnose, Rook's Hill, Chanctonbury Ring, and Beachy Head, were accurately corrected for computation, the distance from Beachy Head to Dunnose would be found the same from each triangle, by making use of the side Rook's Hill and Chanctonbury Ring (which is common to the two most oblique ones) : therefore, having assumed that distance, we found by computation, that if each of the above errors is supposed to be in *one angle* only of the respective triangles, these angles must be the three observed ones, namely, 28° 29′ 30″; 27° 0′ 19″; and 122° 59′ 14″.5 ; these are augmented accordingly, before the angles are finally corrected for computation. The angles of the xxxix. triangle, resulting from those of the other triangles, are

Chanctonbury Ring - 157° 59′ 51″.25
Rook's Hill - - 14 17 32.75
Beachy Head - - 7 42 37.75

before they are reduced to the angles formed by the chords.

121. *Triangles for finding the Distance of Nettlebed from Shooter's Hill.*

Names of the stations.	Observed angles.	Spherical excess.	Angles corrected for calculation.	Distances.
				Feet.
Leith Hill -	23 20 51		23 20 51	
Botley Hill -	125 28 1		125 28 1.25	
Shooter's Hill -	91 11 7.5		91 11 7.75	
	179 59 59.5	1.23		
Leith Hill from Shooter's Hill -				145696.2
Shooter's Hill -	96 8 50.75		96 8 49.5	
St. Ann's Hill -	77 31 38.75		77 31 30.75	
Leith Hill -	66 19 41.5		66 19 39.75	
	180 0 5	2.77		
Shooter's Hill { St. Ann's Hill -				196665.5
Leith Hill - -				145698.6

Hence the mean distance between Shooter's Hill and Leith Hill is 145697.4 feet.

Nettlebed -	- -		23 44 58.75	
Hind Head -	94 9 57.5		94 9 56.25	
Leith Hill - -	62 5 6		62 5 5	
		3.48		
Nettlebed { Hind Head - -				180925.4
Leith Hill - -				203531.5

Then, by using the sides Shooter's Hill and Leith Hill, and Nettlebed and Leith Hill, in the following triangle,

Names of the stations.	Observed angles.	Sphe-rical excess.	Angles corrected for calculation.	Distances.
		′		Feet.
Shooter's Hill -	56 48 51		56 48 59	
Leith Hill -	86 23 25.75		86 23 23.25	
Nettlebed -	- -		96 48 7 75	
		6.97	- -	

we get 242730 and 242732 feet for the distance of Shooter's Hill from Nettlebed, the mean being 242731 feet.

Of the Directions of the Meridians at Dunnose and Beachy Head; and the Length of a Degree of a great Circle, perpendicular to the Meridian, in Latitude 50° 41′.

Of the Direction of the Meridian at Dunnose with respect to Brading Staff.

122. On April 28th in the afternoon, the angle between the pole star, when at its greatest apparent elongation from the meridian, and the staff, was observed   -   -   -   -   -   24 4 23
And on April 29th in the morning   -   18 24 0
Wherefore half their sum is the angle between the meridian and Brading Staff, namely   -   21 14 11.5
On May 12th, in the afternoon, the angle between the star and staff was observed   -   24 4 29.5
And on May 13th, in the morning   -   18 23 53.25
Wherefore half their sum is the angle between the meridian and Brading Staff, namely   -   21 14 11.4
Hence 21° 14′ 11″.5 may be taken for the angle between the

P p

meridian and Brading staff, as determined by the double azimuths.

The apparent polar distances of the star, on these days which do not refer to corresponding observations on the opposite side of the meridian, are as follow :

Azim.

April 21st	1 47 57.2	which, with the lat. of	2 50 11.2
April 22d	1 47 57.4	Dunnose, *viz.* 50° 37′ 8″	2 50 11.5
May 5th	1 48 0.7	nearly, give the azi-muths for those days	2 50 16.8

And these subtracted from the observed angles (102.) give - - - -
{ 21 14 10.05
21 14 10.5
21 14 10.45

The mean of which is 21° 14′ 10″.9 for the angle between the meridian and the staff, which is a little more than 1″ different from that obtained by the double azimuths ; we shall, however, take 21° 14′ 11″.5 for the true angle.

Of the Direction of the Meridian at Beachy Head with respect to Jevington Staff.

129. On August 1st, in the morning, the angle
between the pole star and the staff was observed   24 38 20.25
And at night - - - -   30 19 49.5
Therefore half their sum is the angle between
the meridian and Jevington staff, namely -   27 29 5
On August 2d, at night, the angle between the
star and staff was observed - -   30 19 50.25
And on August 3d, in the morning -   24 38 23.5
Therefore half their sum is the angle between
meridian and Jevington staff, namely -   27 29 7
Hence 27° 29′ 6″, the mean by the double azimuths, may be taken as the angle between the meridian and the staff.

The apparent polar distances of the star, on those days which do not refer to corresponding observations on the opposite side of the meridian, are as follow :

Azim.

$$
\text{July} \begin{cases} \text{15th} & 1 \; 48 \; 4.6 \\ \text{16th} & 1 \; 48 \; 4.4 \\ \text{26th} & 1 \; 48 \; 2.9 \\ \text{30th} & 1 \; 48 \; 2 \end{cases}
$$ which, with the latitude of Beachy Head, viz. 50° 44′ 25″ nearly, give the azimuths for those days $$\begin{bmatrix} 2 \; 50 \; 49.4 \\ 2 \; 50 \; 49.1 \\ 2 \; 50 \; 46.7 \\ 2 \; 50 \; 45.3 \\ 2 \; 50 \; 41 \end{bmatrix}$$

Aug. 11th 1 47 59.3

And these applied to the observed angles give $$- \begin{cases} 27 \; 29 \; 5.1 \\ 27 \; 29 \; 8.4 \\ 27 \; 29 \; 5.7 \\ 27 \; 29 \; 5.2 \\ 27 \; 29 \; 6.25 \end{cases}$$

The mean of which is 27° 29′ 6″.1, for the angle between the meridian and Jevington staff, being the same as that obtained from a mean of the double azimuths.

Determination of the Length of a Degree of a great Circle, perpendicular to the Meridian, in Latitude 50° 41′.

104. In Pl. XIX. fig. 1. let D and B be Dunnose and Beachy Head, and P the pole, forming the spheroidical triangle DPB ; and let C and A be the staffs at Jevington and Brading Down, respectively.

Now the angle at Dunnose, between the meridian and the staff, or PDA, was found by the double azimuths to be   - - - -   21 14 11.5

And the angle between the staff and the station on Beachy Head, or ADB   - - -   60 42 41.5

Therefore their sum is the angle between the meridian and the station on Beachy Head, or PDB ; which is   - - -   81 56 53

Again ; at Beachy Head the angle between the
meridian and the staff, or PBC, was found by the
double azimuths to be   - - -   27 29 6

And the angle between the staff and the station
on Dunnose, or CBD   - - -   69 26 52

Therefore their sum is the angle between the ————
meridian and the station on Dunnose, namely   -   96 55 58

Hence, in the spheroidical triangle DPB, we have the angles
PDB and P BD gic.

Again, (Pl. XIX. fig. 2.) let PGM be the meridian of Greenwich ; then if MB be the parallel to the perpendicular at G,
Greenwich, we have (Art. 131.) MB $=$ 58848 feet, and GM $=$
269328 feet ; therefore, taking 60851* fathoms for the length of
the degree on the meridian, as derived from the difference of latitude between Greenwich and Paris, applied to the measured arc,
(supposing the lat. of Paris 48° 50′ 14″), we get GM $=$ 44′ 15″.26 ;
consequently the latitude of the point M, (that of Greenwich
being 51° 28′ 40″), is 50° 44′ 24″.74 ; and the co-lat. PM $=$
39° 15′ 35″.26.

With respect to the value of the arc M B, for the present purpose, it is not of consequence on what hypothesis it be obtained ;
but if 61179 fathoms be assumed for the length of a degree of a
great circle perpendicular to the meridian at M, then M B $=$
9′ 37″.19, and the latitude of B, or Beachy Head, will be found $=$
50° 44′ 23″.71.

---

* In the original account of the operation in 1787, 1788, the degree in lat.
50° 10′ is 60842 fath. whence this in 50° 41′ was inferred; and is about 2 fath. less than
that in the table, p. 168, which was obtained from *data* somewhat different. But there
still remains an uncertainty respecting the length of this meridional degree ; for if
the latitude of Paris observatory is 48° 50′ 15′, the result will be about 7 fath.
greater : see Art. 67. These variations however, in the value of a degree, are too
trifling to be of any consequence in deducing the latitudes of the stations, &c.

Again, (fig. 3.) let W B be the arc of a great circle perpendicular to the meridian of Beachy Head at B, meeting that of Dunnose in W ; and let D R be another arc of a great circle perpendicular to the meridian of Dunnose in D, meeting that of Beachy Head in R ; then we shall have two small spheroidical triangles W D D and R D B, having in each two angles given, namely, W D B = 81° 56′ 53″, and W B D = 6° 55′ 58″ in the triangle W B D ; and D B R = 83° 4′ 2″, with B D R = 8° 3′ 7″ in the triangle D B R ; and these reduced to the angles formed by the chords, give the following triangles for computation, namely,

$$\text{In the triangle W B D} \begin{cases} \text{W B D} = & \dot{6} \ \dot{5}5 \ \dot{5}7.2 \\ \text{W D B} = & 81 \ 56 \ 52.4 \\ \text{D W B} = & 91 \ \ 7 \ 10.4 \end{cases}$$

$$\text{And in the triangle B D R} \begin{cases} \text{B D R} = & 8 \ \ 3 \ \ 6 \\ \text{D B R} = & 83 \ \ 4 \ \ 1 \\ \text{D R B} = & 88 \ 52 \ 53 \end{cases}$$

In which it must be noted, that the reduced angles are given to the nearest $\frac{1}{4}$″.

Now the chord of the arc B D, or the distance between Beachy Head and Dunnose, is 339397.6 feet (120.) which used in the

Triangle W B D { B W = 316115.6 feet } and the triangle { D R = 336980 feet.
          - { D W = 40973.4 feet }   B D R   - { B R = 37547.1 feet.

Again ; let B L and D E be the parallels of latitude of Beachy Head and Dunnose, meeting the meridians in L and E : then, to find L W and E R we have two small triangles which may be considered as plane ones, namely, L B W and E D R, in which the angles at W and R are given, nearly.

Now the excess of the three angles above 180° in the triangle D B W, considered as a spherical one, is 3″ nearly ; therefore the angle D W B will be 91° 7′ 12″ nearly ; hence B W L = 88° 52′ 48″: consequently the angle B L W = 90° 33′ 36″, and L B W = 0° 33′ 36″. Therefore with the chord of the arc W B = 336115.6 feet, we get W L = 3285.2 feet, which added to W D, as found above, gives 44258.6 feet, for the distance between the parallels of Beachy Head and Dunnose.

Again, in the triangle D D R, considered as a spherical one, the excess is about 3"¼: hence, from the two observed angles at D and B, namely, 8° 3' 7", and 85° 4' 2", we get the third angle B R D = 88° 52' 54".5 : and taking the triangle E R D as a plane one, the other angles will be 0°39'32".73 (EDR), and 90° 33' 32".75 (DER); therefore, with the chord of the arc D R = 356980 feet, we get R E = 3288.2 feet, which taken from B R, as found above, leaves 44258.9 feet for the meridional arc, or the distance between the parallels of Beachy Head and Dunnose ; which is nearly the same as before.

This method of determining the distance between the parallels is sufficiently correct ; but the same conclusion may be deduced from a different principle, thus :

Let the difference of longitude, or the angle at P, be found, on any hypothesis of the earth's figure, and likewise the latitudes of Beachy Head and Dunnose ; with these compute the latitudes of the points R and W; then it will be found that the arc RE is $\frac{1}{160}$" greater than L W ; and since $\frac{1}{160}$ of a second on the meridian is nearly a foot, RE is 5 feet more than LW ; hence $\frac{47547.1-5+40975.4}{2}$ = 44257.8 feet is the distance between the parallels, which is very nearly the same as found by the other method.

It seems therefore, that whatever be the value of the arch between those parallels in parts of a degree, the distance between them is obtained sufficiently near the truth ; therefore, taking 6:851 fathoms for the length of a degree on the meridian, we get the arch subtended by 44258.7 feet = 7' 16".4, which subtracted from the latitude of Beachy Head, namely, 50° 44' 23".71, leaves 50° 37' 7".31 for the latitude of Dunnose.

We have therefore, for finding the length of the degree of a great circle perpendicular to the meridian at Beachy Head, or Dunnose, the latitudes of the two stations, and the angles which those stations make with each other and the pole.

125. Since the sum of horizontal angles P D B + P B D (Pl. XIX. fig. 1.) is nearly the same as the sum which would be found on a sphere (62.), we shall find the angles for spherical computation as follows:

The co-latitudes of D and B, or the arches D P and B P, are 39° 22′ 52″.69, and 39° 15′ 36″.29, therefore half their sum is 39° 19′ 14″.49, and half their difference 3′ 38″.2.

Half the sum of the angles P D B and P B D is 89° 26′ 25″.5 ; therefore, (p. 157) as *tang.* 39° 19′ 14″.49 : *tang.* 3′ 38″.2 : : *tang.* 89° 26′ 25″.5 : *tang.* 7° 31′ 57″.71, or half the difference of the angles : hence the angles for computation are 81° 54′ 27″.79, and 96° 58′ 23″.21, which, with the co-latitudes of D and B, give the difference of longitude between Beachy Head and Dunnose, or the angle D P B = 1° 26′ 47″.99.

We have now two right angled triangles (fig. 9.), which may be considered spherical, namely, PBW, and PDR, in which the angle at the pole P is given, and likewise the sides PB and PD; therefore, using these *data*, we find the arc B W = 54′ 56″.21, and the arc D R = 55′ 4″.74.

The chords of the two perpendicular arcs are about 3¼ feet less than the arcs themselves ; therefore B W = 336119.1 feet, and D R = 336983.5 feet ; and by proportioning these arcs to their respective values in fathoms, we get the length of the degree of the great circle perpendicular to the meridian in the middle point between W and B = 61189.8 fathoms, and in the middle point between R and D = 61181.8 fathoms. Therefore 61189.3 fathoms is the length of a degree of the great circle perpendicular to the meridian, in latitude 50° 41′, which is nearly that of the middle point between Beachy Head and Dunnose.

If the horizontal angles, or the directions of the meridians, have been obtained correctly, the difference of longitude between Beachy Head and Dunnose, as thus found, must be very nearly true; since the difference between the sums of the angles which would be observed on a spheroid and those on a sphere, having the latitudes and the difference of longitude the same on both figures as those places, is so small as scarcely to be computed: and it is easy to perceive, that the distance between the parallels is obtained sufficiently correct, since an error of 15 or 20 feet in that meridional arc, will vary the length of the degree of the great circle but a very small quantity.

196. It may possibly be imagined, that because the vertical planes at Dunnose and Beachy Head do not coincide, but intersect each other in the right line joining these stations, neither of the two included arcs is the proper distance between them, and that the nearest distance on the surface must fall between these arcs; but it is easy to show, that in the present case, the difference must be almost insensible.

In Pl. XIX. fig. 4, let B be Beachy Head, and E B P its meridian, and N and M, the points where the verticals from Beachy Head and Dunnose respectively meet the axis P P.

Now it is known, that if the planes of two circles cut each other, the angle of inclination is that formed by their diameters drawn through the middle of the chord, which is the line of intersection. Therefore, if we draw B M, and also conceive D to be Dunnose, and E P its meridian, and join D N; it is evident, that either of the angles N B M, N D M will be the inclination of the planes very nearly, because of the short distance between the stations, and their small difference in latitude. In the ellipsoid we have adopted, the distance M N is about 62 fathoms, and hence the angle N B M, or N D M, will be found between 2 and 3″. The value of the arc between the stations is about 55′ 30″, and its length 339401 feet;

hence the versed sine of half the arc will be 685 feet nearly; now, suppose the versed sines to form an angle of 5″, the greatest distance of the vertical planes on the earth's surface between the stations, will be but about $\frac{1}{10}$ of an inch.

It may also be remarked, that the inclination here determined, is the angle in which the vertical plane at one station cuts the vertical at the other; and therefore no sensible variation can arise in the horizontal angles, on account of the different heights of the stations.

127. If the figure of the earth be that of an ellipsoid, (fig. 5.) then B R, which is perpendicular to the surface at the point B, is the radius of curvature of the great circle, perpendicular to the meridian at that point; therefore the length of a degree of longitude is obtained by the proportion of the radius to the cosine of the latitude. Thus at Beachy Head, where the length of the degree of a great circle is 61183 fathoms nearly, we have this proportion; *rad.* : *cosine* 50° 44′ 24″ : : 61183 : 38718 fathoms, for the length of the degree of longitude. And at Dunnose, as *rad* : *cosine* 50° 37′ 7″ : : 61182 : 38818 fathoms for the length of the degree of longitude, being about 100 different from the former. But nearly the same conclusions may be otherwise deduced; for the chords of the parallels may be found from the small triangles BWL and DER, (fig. 3.) and these, when augmented by the differences between them and the arcs, give the length of the degree of longitude at Beachy Head 38719 fathoms, and Dunnose 38819 fathoms.

128. *Problem.* Having the meridional degree, and also the degree perpendicular to the meridian, in a given latitude; to find the earth's axes, supposing it an ellipsoid.

Suppose (Pl. XIX. fig. 5.) APAP to be the elliptical meridian passing through the point B whose latitude is given; CA, CP the equatorial, and polar semi-axes. Let B F be the ordinate to the point B, and draw B R perpendicular to the curve at B, which will be the radius of curvature of the perpendicular degree at that point ; also draw B D parallel to A C. Put c, and t, for the *cosine*, and *tangent* of the given latitude ; p, and m, for the lengths of the perpendicular and meridional degrees, respectively ; and $d = 57°.29$ &c. the degrees in the circular arc which is equal to the radius.

Then, from the properties of the ellipse, we get F C, or B D $= \frac{CA^2}{\sqrt{CA^2 + t^2 CP^2}}$; $BR = \frac{CA^2}{c\sqrt{CA^2 + t^2 CP^2}} = d\,p$, the radius of curvature of the perpendicular degree ; and $\frac{CA^2 . CP^2}{c\sqrt{CA^2 + t^2 CP^2}^3} = d\,m$ the radius of curvature of the meridional degree : but the two latter expressions are as 1 to $\frac{CP^2}{c^2 CA^2 + c^2 t^2 CP^2}$; therefore 1 : $\frac{CP^2}{c^2 CA^2 + c^2 t^2 CP^2}$ $:: p : m$; hence, (putting $\frac{1}{t^2+1}$ for c^2, and $r = p - m$), we get CP^2 : $CA^2 :: m : p + r\,t^2$, or $CP : CA :: 1 : \sqrt{\frac{p+r\,t^2}{m}}$, the ratio of the axes. Let $\sqrt{\frac{p+r\,t^2}{m}} = a$; then $CA^2 = a^2 CP^2$ which substituted for CA^2, and we have $\frac{a^2 CP}{c\sqrt{a^2+c^2}} = d\,p$, whence $CP = \frac{d\,p\,c}{a^2}\sqrt{a^2+t^2}$; and consequently $CA = \frac{d\,p\,c}{a}\sqrt{a^2+t^2}$.

Corol. 1. If $l =$ the length of a *degree of longitude* at the point B, then B D will be its radius of curvature ; therefore, $rad. : c :: BR :$ $BD :: p : l$, hence $p = \frac{l}{c}$, which substituted in the above expressions, we get $\sqrt{\frac{l+c r t^2}{c m}} = a$; and $CP = \frac{d\,l}{a^2}\sqrt{a^2+t^2}$; and CA $= \frac{d\,l}{a}\sqrt{a^2+t^2}$, the semidiameters in this case.

Corol. 2. Because $\frac{CA^2}{c\sqrt{CA^2+t^2 CP^2}} = BR = d\,p$; if b and T represent the *cosine* and *tangent* of some other latitude, and P the *perpendicular degree* in that latitude ; then $\frac{CA^2}{b\sqrt{CA^2+T^2 CP^2}} = d\,P$ the radius of curvature of P. Hence $\dfrac{CA'}{P\,b\sqrt{CA'+P'CP'}} = d$: and the former equation gives $\dfrac{CA'}{p\,c\sqrt{CA'+t'CP'}} = d$; these being equated, we get $\overline{P'b'}.\overline{CA'+T'CP'} = p'c'.\overline{CA'+t'CP'}$. Let s, and S, be the *sines* to the *cosines* c, and b; and put $\dfrac{s}{c}$ and $\dfrac{S}{b}$ for t' and T'; and we shall have $CA : CP :: \sqrt{p'\,t' \sim P'S'} : \sqrt{P'\,b' \sim p'\,c'}$, for the ratio of the axes; which being expounded by $1 : n$, we have $CA' = n'CP'$, this substituted for CA' in the equation $\dfrac{CA'}{p\,c\sqrt{CA'+t'CP'}} = d$, gives $CP = \dfrac{d\,p\,c}{n'}\sqrt{n'+t'}$; whence $CA = \dfrac{d\,p\,c}{n}\sqrt{n'+t'}$. But the same values for the semi-axes will be obtained by substituting in the other equation.

Hence, if l and L be the *degrees* of *longitude* in the given latitudes, we have $p = \dfrac{l}{c}$, and $P = \dfrac{L}{c}$, which substituted for p, and P, and we shall get the expressions for the semi-axes in that case.

189. *Table, containing a Comparison between the Degrees upon the Meridian, which have been measured in different Latitudes, with those computed on three Ellipsoids.*

Deg. on meridian in lat. 50° 41'			1st. Ellipsoid. 60851 faith. 61182		2d. Ellipsoid. 60870 61182		3d. Ellipsoid. 60851 61191	
Deg. perp. to meridian								
	Lat.	Measured Ïnh.	Computed.	Diff.	Computed.	Diff.	Computed.	Diff.
	° '							
Bouguer, &c.	0 0	60452	60182	—360	60183	—199	60103	—379
Mason and Dixon	39 12	60628	60607	—21	60640	+12	60600	—28
Boscovich, &c.	43 0	60725	60687	—38	60716	—9	60683	—42
Cassini	45 0	60778	60730	—48	60756	—22	60727	—51
Leizganig	48 43	60839	60806	—33	60831	—8	60808	—31
Between Greenwich and Paris	50 41	60851	60851	0	60870	+19	60851	0
Maupertuis, &c.	66 20	61194	61148	—46	61150	—44	61156	—38

The contents of the above table are computed from the *data* expressed in the different columns at top. In the third column,

[302]

60851 fathoms is nearly the length of the degree upon the meridian, as derived by the application of the measured arc between Greenwich and Paris to the difference of latitude. (124.) The fifth, contains the degrees on an ellipsoid, computed from a different length of a degree upon the meridian in lat. 50° 41', in order to show how far the varying the length of that degree, will affect the comparison between the measured and computed degrees on the first ellipsoid: and those in the seventh are determined by using 60851 fathoms for the degree upon the meridian, and 61191 fathoms for that of the great circle perpendicular to it; which last degree is obtained by taking the angle at Dunnose, equal to 81° 56' 53".5, instead of 81° 56' 53".

Now this comparison between the measured and computed degrees, seems to prove that the earth is not an ellipsoid, since the differences are, excepting two instances, constantly *minus;* this, however, presupposes that the degree of the great circle perpendicular to the meridian in lat. 50° 41', as we have found it, and likewise the degree upon the meridian arising from the measured arc between Greenwich and Paris, and their difference in latitude, are nearly right. Also, were it of Mr. Bouguer's figure, the degree of a great circle in lat. 50° 41' would be 61266 fathoms, which is 84 fathoms greater than we have derived it; we may therefore safely infer, that his hypothesis is more ingenious than true; since it cannot be supposed that the degree, resulting from these observations, is 84 fathoms in defect; but whether the earth be a figure formed by the revolution of a meridian round its axis, upon which the length of the degrees increase according to any law, or one whose meridians are formed by the combination of many different curves, it appears to be certain, that we may consider 61182 fathoms as nearly the length of the perpendicular degree, in latitude 50° 41', by which we are enabled to settle the longitudes of those places whose situations have been determined in this operation.

The length of the degree in latitude 50° 41', obtained from the directions of the meridians at Botley Hill and Goudhurst, is 61948 fathoms nearly, which is 66 fathoms different from this result : but this is not to be considered as extraordinary, since the distance between those places is not more than 23 miles, and the direction very oblique to the meridian. The stations chosen for this purpose should be nearly east and west ; because if both places were on the same parallel of latitude, the horizontal angles would give the difference of longitude, without adverting to the principle of the sums of the angles on a sphere and a spheroid being nearly equal, when the places on each have corresponding latitudes, and the same difference of longitude.

Was a degree of a great circle perpendicular to the meridian measured in some place remote from the latitude of 50° 41', the diameters of the earth, supposing it an ellipsoid, might be determined from the perpendicular degrees only; (*Corol*. 2. Art. 128.) It is therefore, much to be wished, that such measurements were made in the northern part of Russia, and in the south of France, where the methods we have taken to measure this degree would also be applicable.

Having given the length of a degree of what may be considered a great circle upon the earth's surface, as deduced from the observations which have been made at Beachy Head and Dunnose, and likewise drawn such conclusions as appear to arise from it ; we have to add, that as the preserving of the points marking these stations has been considered of great consequence, his Grace the Duke of Richmond ordered an iron gun to be inserted in the ground at each of those places, which was done in the autumn of 1794. By these points being rendered permanent, the truth of this part of the operation can be examined, by re-observing the directions of the meridians; and that this may be done with the least trouble, we have preserved the points, where the staffs were erected on

Brading Down and the hill above Jevington, by inserting large
stones in the ground, having a small hole in each of them, for the
purpose of denoting the exact points over which the centres of the
staffs were placed; therefore the angles which we have given,
as being the directions of the meridians with respect to those points,
can be examined without the trouble of firing lights at Beachy
Head and Dunnose. There is, however, another method of determining whether 61182 fathoms be nearly the length of a degree of
a great circle perpendicular to the meridian; this may be done by
observing the directions of the meridians at Shooter's Hill and Nettlebed, whose distance is already determined, being 242731 feet
nearly. The points marking these stations are not likely to be soon
removed, and can be found without difficulty.

*Of the Distances of the Stations from the Meridians of Greenwich,
Beachy Head, and Dunnose; and also from the Perpendiculars
to those Meridians.*

130. In operations of this kind, the usual method of obtaining
the distances of the stations from a first meridian, and from a perpendicular to that meridian, is by drawing parallels to those lines
through the several stations, and then proceeding in a manner
similar to that of working a traverse, after the bearings of the stations, with respect to these parallels, have been deduced from the
angles of the triangles. This mode of computation might be considered as accurate, if the surface of the earth to the whole extent
of the triangles was reduced to a flat: and it will not produce very
erroneous results, if the series of triangles are in a north and south,
or an east and west direction nearly, provided they are on, or near
the meridian, or its perpendicular; but if the triangles are considerably extended, and in all directions, the bearings of the same
stations (if they may be so termed) must evidently differ, and that

sometimes considerably, when obtained from different triangles.
To avoid, in a great measure, the errors which might affect the
conclusions derived from the present triangles, if all those distances
were determined from the meridian of Greenwich only, we have
considered the meridians of Beachy Head and Dunnose as first
meridians also, and, with two or three exceptions, calculated the
distance of each station from its nearest meridian. Bagshot Heath,
Leith Hill, Ditchling Beacon, and Beachy Head, with those to the
eastward, are from the meridian of Greenwich and its perpendicular; Chanctonbury Ring from the meridian of Beachy Head; and
the others to the westward, from that of Dunnose.

The advantages in this mode of proceeding are very obvious; for
if the directions of meridians are taken at about 80 miles distance
from each other, near the southern coast, the operation may be extended to the Land's End with sufficient accuracy, without making
astronomical observations for determining any intermediate latitude, as a new point of departure.

In ded cing the bearings of the several stations from the meridians and their perpendiculars, we have taken the observed angles,
instead of those formed by the chords, which were used in computing the sides of the principal triangles; because the latter angles
at each station may be considered as constituting the vertex of a py-
ramid, and consequently their sum is less than 360°; but the operation of determining the distances from the meridians, and their perpendiculars from those reduced, or pyramidical angles and the chords
or sides of the triangles, independent of other *data*, would be very
tedious. Great accuracy however, in these cases seems not absolutely necessary; because, if the latitudes and longitudes obtained
from those distances can be depended upon to $\frac{1}{4}$ of a second (the
latitude of Greenwich, from which the other latitudes are derived,
being supposed exact), the conclusions will certainly be considered
as sufficiently near the truth: 25 feet answers to about $\frac{1}{4}$ of a

second on the meridian ; and it is not difficult to show, that no uncertainty of more than about 10 feet has been introduced, even in the longest distances, in consequence of using the observed angles.

As Botley Hill is nearly south of the Observatory at Greenwich, and it may be supposed, that the distance of it from the meridian, as well as perpendicular, must be nearly true, as given in p. 159, it has not been considered as expedient to make this part of the operation entirely independent of General Roy's, by selecting Greenwich for a station, and observing the direction of the meridian at that place with respect to Banstead, or Shooter's Hill.

In order, therefore, to obtain the necessary *data*, when the instrument was at Botley Hill, the angle between Banstead and the station on Wrotham Hill was observed, and found to be 152° 57' 4" (102.); from which subtracting 79° 16' 29" (6° 50' 58"+72° 25' 31", or the bearing of Frant from Wrotham Hill, p. 159, added to the angle at Wrotham in the 11. triangle, p. 141) the angle which Wrotham Hill makes with the parallel to the meridian of Greenwich, we get 73° 40' 35" for the inclination of Banstead to that parallel ; this, with 50927 feet, the distance of Banstead from Botley Hill, give 48871, and 14314 feet ; therefore 48874 — 172 = 48702 feet, is the distance of Banstead from the meridian of Greenwich ; and 72881 — 14314 = 58567 feet, the distance from the perpendicular.

121. *Table containing the Bearings of the Stations from the Parallels to the different Meridians; and likewise their Distances from those Meridians and their Perpendiculars.*

Names of the stations.		Bearings.		Distances from the	
				Meridian.	Perpendicular.
	Meridian of Greenwich.	° ′ ″		Feet.	Feet.
	Botley Hill - -	—	—	171	7881
Botley Hill -	Shooter's Hill -	11 59 33	NE	14899	3533
	Banstead - -	73 40 35	NW	48705	51567
	Leith Hill - -	66 31 33	SW	86791	109784
Hanger Hill -	Crowborough Beacon	13 3 39	SE	35827	155222
	Hampton Poorhouse	74 11 47	SW	83084	18540
Banstead - -	Hanger Hill -	13 49 33	NW	67034	16713
	King's Arbour -	41 56 31	NW	101261	1036
	St. Ann's Hill -	67 11 13	NW	119400	28854
Crowborough Beacon	Ditchling Beacon -	{ 47 19 83	bW	} 24468	110257
Leith Hill - -		{ 30 58 49	SE		
Crowborough Beacon	Brighling -	57 43 18	SE	87304	188119
Brighling - -	Fairlight Down -	61 25 47	SE	143311	218618
Ditchling Beacon -	Beachy Head -	51 39 48	SE	58848	269318
St. Ann's Hill - -	Bagshot Heath -	77 87 16	SW	165834	39055
	Merid. of Beachy Head.				
Beachy Head -	Chanctonbury Ring -	68 26 28	NW	146567	57908
	Meridian of Dunnose.				
	Rook's Hill - -	45 48 55	NE	104770	100236
	Butser Hill - -	10 58 39	NE	50328	131203
Dunnose - -	Dean Hill - -	34 44 37	NW	104568	150786
	Molleston Down -	73 35 8	NW	52858	15572
	Nine Barrow Down -	87 56 55	NW	188001	6736
Butser Hill -	Highclere -	{ 34 20 37	NW	} 33174	153495
Dean Hill -		{ 34 48 11	NE		
Dean Hill -	Beacon Hill - -	15 30 36	NW	180101	206757
	Four Mile-stone -	54 59 39	NW	151073	183355
Beacon Hill -	Thorney Down -	4 57 42	SE	117871	179811
	Old Sarum - -	48 55 42	SW	137793	174746
Dean Hill - -	Wingreen -	{ 81 33 37	SW	} 109505	135184
Nine Barrow Down		{ 9 28 63	NW		
Rook's Hill -	Hind Head -	5 43 81	NE	117941	161781

132. *Latitudes and Longitudes of the Stations referred to the Meridian of Greenwich.*

Names of the stations.	Latitude.	Longitude.	
		In degrees.	In time.
	° ′ ″	° ′ ″	m. s.
Shooter's Hill - -	51 28 5.1	0 3 54.5 E	0 15.6
Crowborough Beacon -	51 3 9.4	0 9 9.5 E	0 36.6
Brightling - -	50 57 43.3	0 22 39.3 E	1 30.6
Fairlight Down - -	50 52 38.8	0 37 7.4 E	2 28.5
Beachy Head - -	50 44 23.7	0 15 11.9 E	1 0.7
Ditchling Beacon -	50 54 7	0 6 20.5 W	0 25.3
Leith Hill - - -	51 10 35.7	0 22 6.9 W	1 28.4
Banstead - -	51 19 2	0 12 44.1 W	0 50.9
Hanger Hill - -	51 31 23.7	0 17 39.6 W	1 10.6
Hampton Poorhouse -	51 25 35.2	0 21 46.6 W	1 27.1
King's Arbour - -	51 28 47.1	0 26 50 W	1 47.3
St. Ann's Hill - -	51 23 51.4	0 31 16.6 W	2 5.1
Bagshot Heath - -	51 22 7.1	0 43 15.4 W	2 53

133. *Latitude and Longitude of Chanctonbury Ring.*

Lat. of Chanctonbury Ring -	50 53 48.5	
Long. of Beachy Head, east of Greenwich - -	0 15 11.9	
Long. of Chanctonbury Ring, west of Beachy Head -	0 37 58.8	
Long. of Chanctonbury Ring, west of Greenwich -	0 22 46.9 — in time	m. s. 1 31.1

134. *Latitude and Longitude of Dunnose.*

Latitude of Beachy Head - 50 44 23.7
Difference of latitude between } 0 7 16.4
  Beachy H. and Dunn. (124). }

50 37 7.3 lat. of Dunnose.

The difference of long. between Beachy Head and
Dunnose (195.)   -   -   1 26 47.9 W
And the long. of Beachy Head,
east of Greenwich   -   0 15 11.9 E
Therefore the long. of Dunnose,   m. s.
west of Greenwich, is   1 11 36 and in time 4 46.4

195. *Latitudes and Longitudes of the Stations referred to the Meridian of Dunnose.*

Names of the stations.	Latitude.	from Dunnose.	Longitude. West of Greenwich. In degrees.	In time.
	° ′ ″	° ′ ″	° ′ ″	m. s.
Rook's Hill -	50 53 32.5	0 26 37.7 E	0 44 58.3	2 59.9
Hind Head -	51 6 56.1	0 28 53 E	0 42 43	2 50.9
Butser Hill -	50 58 40.8	0 13 3.8 E	0 58 32.2	3 54.1
Motteston Down	50 39 40	0 13 37.8 W	1 25 13.8	5 40.9
Highclere -	51 18 46.2	0 8 40.4 W	1 20 16.4	5 21.1
Dean Hill -	51 1 50.9	0 27 10.5 W	1 38 46.5	6 35.1
Beacon Hill -	51 11 4.4	0 31 18.9 W	1 42 54.9	6 51.7
Four Mile-stone	51 7 8.5	0 39 30.8 W	1 50 56.2	7 23.8
Thorney Down	51 6 30.2	0 30 40.8 W	1 42 16.8	6 49.1
Old Sarum -	51 5 44.7	0 35 51.5 W	1 47 27.5	7 9.9
Nine B. Down	50 98 3.5	0 48 27.8 W	2 0 3.8	8 0.3
Wingreen -	50 59 7.6	0 54 22.9 W	2 5 58.9	8 29.9

136. The longitudes and latitudes of the stations have been
computed spherically, in which we have taken the degrees upon
the meridian, and of the great circle perpendicular to it, from the
following table.

	Degrees on the merid. Fath.	perp. Fath.		Fathoms.
Lat. { 50 41	608 51	611 82 }	Semi-transverse of	
{ 51 5	608 59	611 85 }	this ellipsoid -	3491480
{ 51 28 40	608 68	611 88 }	Semi-conjugate -	3468007

Ratio of the axes 1 : 1.006751, or nearly as 291 to 293 7/8.

R r 2

This ellipsoid is determined from the length of the degree obtained from the directions of the meridians at Beachy Head and Dunnose, and that upon the meridian in lat 50° 41', as resulting from the application of the measured arc between Greenwich and Paris, to their difference in latitude. It is not, however, to be understood, that by using it, we consider the earth to be this ellipsoid : we have adopted the hypothesis, because it is obvious some small increase northward must be made to the degree upon the meridian in 50° 41', in order to approximate to a correct scale for the computation of the latitudes. But it is evident, that any of the received hypotheses (supposing the length of the degree upon the meridian in 50° 41' to be 60851 fathoms nearly) would give the degrees sufficiently correct, since the principal stations, together with most of the objects fixed in this operation, are included between the parallels of 50° 37' and 51° 28'.

In obtaining the latitudes of those places which are referred to the meridian of Greenwich, it is easy to perceive, that little error is introduced by spherical computation, since the spheroidical correction for the latitude of Bagshot Heath is only about $\frac{1}{100}$ of a second. Had indeed the latitudes of the stations, which are far to the westward, been computed with distances from the meridian, and the perpendicular at Greenwich, some small errors might have been introduced, from the uncertainty of the earth's figure, and the consequent inability of computing the spheroidical corrections with sufficient accuracy ; but as the distance between the parallels of Beachy Head and Dunnose is obtained very nearly, the latitude of the latter station may be considered as correct as that of the former one, and consequently the places in the vicinity of Dunnose have their latitudes determined with sufficient precision.

137. *Secondary Triangles, in which two Angles only have been observed. The first seven intersected Places were selected for interior Stations, on account of their commanding Situations.*

Triangles.	Angles observed.	Distances of the stations from the point intersected.	
	° ′ ″		Feet.
Beachy Head -	10 19 30	} Firle Beacon - {	47956
Ditchling Beacon -	8 53 23		55621
Firle Beacon			
Chanctonbury Ring from the support of High Down Windmill 29442 feet.			
Chanctonbury Ring -	64 54 52	} Sleep down - {	17637
High Down Windmill			27159
Sleep Down	79 3 33		
Butser Hill -	10 28 4	} Bow Hill - {	46150
Rook's Hill -	28 19 50		17608
Bow Hill			
Butser Hill -	93 25 15	} Portsdown Hill {	52729
Rook's Hill -	39 23 59		82926
Portsdown Hill			
Dunnose - -	30 31 9	} Thorness - {	57470
Motteston Down -	79 6 47		29764
Thorness		*Isle of Wight*	
Motteston Down -	27 57 12	} Ramsden Hill - {	97051
Nine Barrow Down	42 26 2		67423
Ramsden Hill			
Dean Hill -	71 10 48	} Stockbridge Hill {	54366
Beacon Hill -	51 45 47		65515
Stockbridge Hill			

With respect to these triangles, there is nothing to be remarked, except that the angles of the 1st and 3d, from their being very acute, were determined with considerable care : the distances, however, from Firle Beacon to Ditchling Beacon, and Beachy

Head, may be ascertained, when either the great or small instrument are taken to that station, by the intersection of Hurstmonceux Spire.

Triangles formed by the Intersections of Churches, Windmills, and other objects.

Triangles.	Angles observed.	Distances of the stations from the intersected objects.	
			Feet.
Fairlight down - Brighting - *Bexhill Church*	48 18 18 32 6 24	}Bexhill Church { *Sussex*	34 7 48294
Fairlight Down - Brighting - *Westham Church*	46 56 7 73 7 30	}Westham Church {	70511 53832
Fairlight Down - Brighting - *Pevensey Church*	46 46 20 71 21 47	}Pevensey Church {	68586 52694
Fairlight Down - Brighting - *Blackheath Windmill (near Heathfield)*	4 34 18 154 19 13	}Blackheath Wind-{ mill -	70783 14110
Fairlight Down - Brighting - *Ninefield Church*	25 26 1 40 43 54	}Ninefield Church {	45493 29943
Fairlight Down - Brighting - *Mountfield Church*	10 32 37 16 44 22	}Mountfield Church - {	40071 25458
Beachy Head - Ditchling Beacon - *Hurstmonceux Church*	76 6 36 26 40 41	}Hurstmonceux Church - {	47021 101668
Ditchling Beacon - Crowborough Beacon *Chittingly Church* -	41 17 30 58 11 18	}Chittingly Church {	69960 54380

Triangles.	Angles observed.	Distances of the stations from the intersected objects.	
			Feet.
Ditchling Beacon Crowborough Beacon D *Waldron Church*	18 23 46 65 34 35	Waldron Church {	75316 19165
Ditchling Beacon Crowborough Beacon *Firle Church*	67 16 28 36 30 48	Firle Church - {	49748 77110
Ditchling Beacon - Crowborough Beacon *Jevington Windmill*	70 32 0 58 49 56	Jevington Wind- mill " {	89861 99016
Ditchling Beacon - Crowborough Beacon *Plumpton Church*	34 14 48 3 37 4	Plumpton Church {	8347 74441
Ditchling Beacon - Crowborough Beacon D *Little Horstead Church*	23 34 6 28 0 42	Little Horstead Church - {	48670 41436
Ditchling Beacon - Crowborough Beacon *Spittal Windmill* -	66 41 83 14 29 24	Spittal Windmill {	29558 75458
Ditchling Beacon - Crowborough Beacon *Ditchling Church*	61 49 49 4 48 36	Ditchling Church {	7416 77966
Chanctonbury Ring Ditchling Beacon - *Thakeham Church*	115 19 36 18 56 34	Thakeham Church - {	19754 74103
Chanctonbury Ring Ditchling Beacon - *West Grinsted Church*	66 23 40 28 9 20	West Grinsted Church " {	30044 58342
Chanctonbury Ring Ditchling Beacon - *Keymer Church*	6 40 15 55 52 17	Keymer Church {	59208 8309
Chanctonbury Ring Ditchling Beacon - *Bolney Church*	37 47 12 57 3 58	Bolney Church {	53461 39029

Triangles.	Angles observed.	Distances of the stations from the intersected objects.	
Chanctonbury Ring Ditchling Beacon D Slaugham Church -	50 26 25 66 41 45	}Slaugham } Church -	{ 63501 54985
Chanctonbury Ring Ditchling Beacon - Starting House on the Race Ground near Brightbelmstone	23 2 19 86 0 59	}Starting House	{ 66986 26279
Chanctonbury Ring Ditchling Beacon - Cuckfield Spire	33 58 20 72 9 49	}Cuckfield Spire	{ 67789 38508
Chanctonbury Ring Ditchling Beacon - D Wyvelsfield Church	20 34 55 98 0 8	}Wyvelsfield } Church	{ 71575 25409
Chanctonbury Ring Ditchling Beacon - Hurstpierpoint Church	14 32 35 96 29 25	}Hurstpierpoint } Church -	{ 48545 20498
Chanctonbury Ring Ditchling Beacon - D Lindfield Church	29 51 47 100 41 5	}Lindfield Church	{ 82079 41590
Chanctonbury Ring Sleep Down - Goring Church	52 22 45 96 27 23	}Goring Church	{ 33866 26995
Chanctonbury Ring Sleep Down - Southwick Church	22 46 56 140 53 45	}Southwick } Church - } Sussex	{ 39584 24302
Chanctonbury Ring Sleep Down - Shoreham Church	14 28 30 151 0 0	}Shoreham Church	{ 34094 17578
Chanctonbury Ring Sleep Down - Brightbelmst. Church	32 5 47 136 19 20	}Brighthelmstone } Church -	{ 60672 46680
Chanctonbury Ring Sleep Down - Bramber Windmill	48 9 25 83 16 48	}Bramber Wind- } mill - -	{ 21772 14995

Triangles.	Angles observed.	Distances of the stations from the intersected objects.	
			Feet.
Chanctonbury Ring Sleep Down - *Temple in Findon Park*	88 47 22 37 32 41	Temple in Findon Park -	13341 21889
Chanctonbury Ring Rook's Hill - *West Tarring Church*	82 19 10 17 41 21	West Tarring Church -	26426 86189
Chanctonbury Ring Rook's Hill - *Highdown Windmill*	56 47 5 19 30 39	High Down Windmill.	29442 73752
Canctonbury Ring Rook's Hill - D *Angmering Church*	45 44 35 21 55 49	Angmering Church - -	34579 66912
Chanctonbury Ring Rook's Hill - *Sir R. Hotham's Flag- staff, near Bersted*	30 40 1 63 36 53	Sir R. Hotham's Flagstaff -	80807 44268
Chanctonbury Ring Rook's Hill - *Bersted Church*	27 54 15 64 26 6	Bersted Church	77925 40115
Chanctonbury Ring Rook's Hill - - *Felpham Windmill*	31 22 35 60 52 39	Felpham Wind- mill -	74875 14606
Chanctonbury Ring Rook's Hill - D *Clapham Church*	44 29 25 16 3 16	Clapham Church *Sussex.*	27201 68929
Chanctonbury Ring Rook's Hill - *Oving Church*	14½ 12 22 71 6 26	Oving Church	81303 21089
Chanctonbury Ring Rook's Hill - *Pagham Church*	27 31 18 89 41 40	Pagham Church	96306 44502
Butser Hill - Rook's Hill - - *Lantern of the Vessel moored over the Ower Rocks*	26 55 45 134 6 0	Ower Rocks -	134605 84889

Triangles.	Angles observed	Distances of the stations from the intersected objects.	
	° ′ ″		Feet.
Butser Hill - -	27 45 25	Selsea Church - {	95276
Rook's Hill - -	117 47 8		50154
Selsea Church			
Butser Hill - -	34 42 20	Selsea High	99290
Rook's Hill -	110 6 12	House - {	60199
Selsea High House			
Butser Hill - -	34 40 45	Selsea Windmill {	97545
Rook's Hill - -	109 9 31		58786
Selsea Windmill			
Butser Hill - -	43 21 26	Cackham Tower {	77885
Rook's Hill - -	85 21 20		55613
Cackham Tower			
Butser Hill - -	32 2 28	Bosham Church {	61061
Rook's Hill - -	74 11 13		33667
Bosham Church			
Butser Hill - -	43 28 50	Princested Wind- {	52354
Rook's Hill - -	57 30 20	mill - -	42712
Princested Windmill			
Butser Hill - -	25 41 30	Del Key Wind- {	69090
Rook's Hill - -	92 32 2	mill -	29981
Del Key Windmill			
Butser Hill - -	49 30 10	West Thorney {	61110
Rook's Hill -	63 27 03	Church -	43227
West Thorney Church			
Butser Hill -	58 31 52	South Hayling {	66544
Rook's Hill - -	65 13 29	Church -	62510
South Hayling Church			
Butser Hill - -	43 27 20	Bourn Church - {	44509
Rook's Hill - -	46 55 22		44911
Bourn Church			
Butser Hill - -	49 48 19	Flagstaff - {	72681
Rook's Hill - -	78 49 16		57262
Flagstaff at the Watch-house near Chichester Harbour			

Triangles.	Angles observed.	Distances of the stations from intersected objects.	
			Feet.
Butser Hill " "	69 28 9	}Clark's Folly - {	46151
Rook's Hill "	44 0 16		62212
Clark's Folly			
Butser Hill - "	83 38 24	⌐Portsdown Wind-⌐	49356
Rook's Hill -	41 29 17	J mill " " {	74045
Portsdown Windmill			
Butser Hill " -	69 19 25	}Cumberland Fort {	70049
Rook's Hill " -	61 5 43		74863
West Chimney on the Governor's House, Cumberland Fort			
Butser Hill - "	78 14 54	}South Sea Castle {	77098
Rook's Hill "	59 2 32		87958
South Sea Castle			
Butser Hill - "	87 18 4	⌐St. Catherine's	159328
Rook's Hill "	71 26 30	J Light House {	167881
St. Cath. Light House		Isle of Wight	
Butser Hill - "	84 30 52	⌐Sir R. Worsley's ⌐	145861
Rook's Hill - -	72 3 59	J Obelisk - {	152608
Sir R. Worsley's Obelisk		Isle of Wight	
Butser Hill " -	89 29 28	⌐Ashey Down Sea⌐	117188
Rook's Hill " -	67 44 36	J Mark - {	125806
Ashey Down Sea Mark		Isle of Wight	
Butser Hill - "	103 12 19	⌐Flagstaff, Cowes⌐	104463
Rook's Hill " "	50 10 44	J Fort " " {	132415
Flagstaff of Cowes Fort		Isle of Wight	
Butser Hill "	100 21 10	}Summer House {	115573
Rook's Hill - "	54 17 51		140005
Summer House of the Horse-shoe Inn above Cowes			
Butser Hill - "	109 32 45	⌐Needles Light ⌐	178277
Rook's Hill - "	54 19 57	J House - {	206796
Needles Light House		Isle of Wight	

Triangles.	Angles observed.	Distances of the stations from the intersected objects.	
	° ′ ″		Feet.
Butser Hill -	23 25 47	⎱Southampton	102010
Dean Hill -	32 58 47	⎰ Spire - -	74522
Southampton Spire			
Rook's Hill - -	132 28 11	⎱Box Grove Church⎰	15306
Bow Hill - -	21 57 31		30194
Box Grove Church			
Rook's Hill - -	87 10 9	⎱Portfield Windmill⎰	18468
Bow Hill - -	47 44 17		24916
Portfield Windmill			
Rook's Hill - -	116 1 21	⎱Goodwood House⎰	7898
Bow Hill - -	18 38 9		22321
North-west Chimney on Goodwood House			
Rook's Hill - -	75 29 10	⎱Chichester Spire⎰	21345
Bow Hill - -	59 11 56		24057
Chichester Spire			
Rook's Hill - -	57 8 41	⎱Sir H. Fetherston-⎰	98424
Hind Head - -	27 50 34	⎰haugh's Tower	69110
Sir H. Fetherston-haugh's Tower			
Rook's Hill - -	122 22 23	⎱Windmill near⎰	3512
Hind Head -	2 1 34	⎰Rook's Hill -	83887
Windmill near Rook's Hill			
Rook's Hill - -	53 56 49	⎱Harting Wind-⎰	36398
Hind Head - -	25 52 2	⎰mill - -	67319
Harting Windmill			
Chanctonbury Ring	19 43 52	⎱Petworth Spire⎰	62080
Hind Head -	16 16 96		59576
Petworth Spire			
Chanctonbury Ring	12 50 23	⎱Wisborough⎰	58508
Hind Head -	11 28 10	⎰Green Church	59799
D Wisborough Green Church			

Triangles.	Angles observed.	Distances of the stations from the intersected objects.	Feet.
Chanctonbury Ring Hind Head *Kirdford Church*	5 12 39 6 29 12	} Kirdford Church {	61725 49623
Chanctonbury Ring Hind Head *Billinghurst Church*	24 48 50 16 58 51	} Billinghurst Church {	48543 69755
Chanctonbury Ring Hind Head *Rusper Church*	59 43 43 47 42 51	} Rusper Church {	85901 100281

Chanctonbury Ring from Butser Hill 141003 feet.

Triangles.	Angles observed.	Distances of the stations from the intersected objects.	Feet.
Chanctonbury Ring Butser Hill *The Earl of Egremont's Tower, near Petworth*	20 22 27 18 0 51	} The Earl of Egremont's Tower {	70219 79052
Chanctonbury Ring Butser Hill D *Pulborough Church*	25 12 40 8 5 46	} Pulborough Church {	36163 109375
Leith Hill Hind Head *St. Martha's Chapel*	41 32 40 27 9 5	} St. Martha's Chapel near Guildford {	40257 58505
Leith Hill Hind Head *Euhurst Windmill*	11 39 40 3 49 39	} Euhurst Windmill {	20544 62206
Leith Hill Hind Head *Euhurst Church*	12 25 16 3 27 43	} Euhurst Church {	18135 64596
Leith Hill Hind Head *Norris's Obelisk, Bagshot Heath*	51 9 46 77 52 38	} Norris's Obelisk {	103310 82191
Leith Hill Hind Head *Horsham Spire*	86 36 23 28 38 34	} Horsham Spire {	43558 90710

Triangles.	Angles observed.	Distances of the stations from the intersected objects.	
			Feet.
Leith Hill - - Hind Head - *Farnham Castle*	24 34 44 101 49 30	}Farnham Castle {	99948 42474
Leith Hill - - Ditchling Beacon *Beddingham Windmill*	7 38 23 152 37 54	} Beddingham Windmill - {	159594 46153
Leith Hill - - Ditchling Beacon *Firle Windmill*	9 19 46 149 13 1	}Firle Windmill {	163984 51942
Leith Hill - - Crowborough Beacon D *West Hoathly Church*	6 9 46 10 22 53	} West Hoathly Church - {	81212 48382
Crowborough Beacon from Fairlight Down 125303 feet.			
Crowborough Beacon Fairlight Down - *Willington Church*	45 4 32 43 6 42	} Willington Church - {	85678 88764
Crowborough Beacon Brightling - - *Homehurst Church*	12 21 46 70 18 45	} Homehurst Church - {	58474 13297
Crowborough Beacon Brightling - - *Hailsham Church*	37 38 24 85 39 48	}Hailsham Church {	73490 45009
Crowborough Beacon Brightling - - *Dallington Church*	6 25 16 83 32 52	} Dallington Church - {	61208 6889
Crowborough Beacon Botley Hill *East Grinsted Church*	31 6 44 24 17 45	} East Grinsted Church - {	44729 56173
Crowborough Beacon Botley Hill - *Fairden Tower*	17 4 46 18 51 52	}Fairden Tower {	49295 44777
Crowborough Beacon Botley Hill - *Crowborough Chapel*	93 16 22 2 3 11	} Crowborough Chapel - {	3280 89734

Triangles.	Angles observed.	Distances of the stations from the intersected objects.
		Feet.
Crowborough Beacon Botley Hill - *Rotherfield Spire*	121 34 38 7 42 43	}Rotherfield Spire {	15517 98509
Crowborough Beacon Botley Hill - *Mayfield Spire*	137 42 2 9 35 19	}Mayfield Spire {	27585 111453
Crowborough Beacon Botley Hill - *Bestbeech Windmill*	108 47 35 18 39 16	}Bestbeech Wind- mill - - {	36056 106714
Crowborough Beacon Botley Hill - *Tatesfield Church*	5 2 39 90 24 37	}Tatesfield Church {	89897 7904
Botley Hill - Leith Hill - - D *Charlwood Church*	17 5 35 36 33 33	}Charlwood Church - {	68505 39804
Botley Hill - Leith Hill - - D *Evelyn's Obelisk*	54 41 39 33 25 22	}Evelyn's Obelisk {	51051 75696
Butser Hill - - Hind Head - *Petworth Windmill*	96 49 10 89 42 37	}Petworth Wind- mill - {	91054 54899
Portsdown Hill - Butser Hill - - *Southwick Church*	41 34 33 4 31 23	}Southwick Church{ Hants.	5771 48564
Dunnose - - Butser Hill - *Flagstaff of Carisbrook Castle*	67 7 31 14 59 6	}Flagstaff, Caris- brook Castle - {	36697 130769
Dunnose - - Butser Hill - *Lord Halifax's Tower*	15 4 28 49 11 35	}Halifax Tower - {	118122 40586

Portsdown Hill from Dunnose 90007 feet.

Triangles.	Angles observed.	Distances of the stations from the intersected objects.
Portsdown Hill - Dunnose - - Kingston Church, Port-sea Island	33 53 9¼ 9 20 28	Kingston Church { Feet. 21328 / 79274
Portsdown Hill - Dunnose - - D Horndean Church	150 33 55 7 45 58	Horndean Church { 33430 / 120320
Dunnose - - Motteston Down - East Corner of the Roof of the great Boat House at the Back of the Isle of Wight	12 13 22 35 10 30	Great Boat House { 43127 / 15849
Dunnose - - Motteston Down - Brixton Church, Isle of Wight	5 3 4 25 53 6	Brixton Church { 46795 / 9437
Dunnose - - Motteston Down - East Cowes Sea Mark, Isle of Wight	54 23 57 62 29 15	East Cowes Sea Mark - - { 54796 / 50235
Dunnose - - Motteston Down - Luttrell's Folly	50 34 2¼ 82 14 9	Luttrell's Folly { 74424 / 58020
Dunnose - - Motteston Down - Fawley Church	48 58 19 90 32 45	Fawley Church { 84875 / 64032
Dunnose - - Motteston Down - Flagstaff, Calshot Cast.	54 43 0 80 53 17	Flagstaff, Calshot Castle - - { 77771 / 64296
Dunnose - - Motteston Down - Fareham Church	77 13 3 66 57 30	Fareham Church { 86696 / 91814

Triangles.	Angles observed.	Distances of the stations from the intersected objects.	
			Feet.
Dunnose - - Motteston Down - *Porchester Church*	87 30 .58 57 50 55	}Porchester Church -	{ 82086 96863
Dunnose - - Motteston Down - *Hamble Church*	56 5 32 87 4 16	}Hamble Church	{ 91792 76281
Dunnose - - Motteston Down - *Hamble Saltern* -	56 40 50 84 55 59	}Hamble Saltern	{ 88390 74150
Dunnose - - Motteston Down - *Gov. Hornby's House,* *Centre Pediment*	57 49 18 82 52 7	}Gover. Hornby's House -	{ 86909 73621
Dunnose - - Motteston Down - *Warblington Church*	106 36 6 48 57 49	}Warblington Church -	{ 100482 127660
Dunnose - - Motteston Down - *Bursledon Windmill*	58 39 40 89 30 11	}Bursledon Wind- mill -	{ 104462 89225
Dunnose - - Motteston Down - *Porchester Castle*	87 8 20 48 10 27	}Porchester Castle	{ 82468 96952
Dunnose - - Motteston Down - *Havant Church*	104 6 1 50 25 55	}Havant Church	{ 98725 124221
Dean Hill - - Four Mile-stone - *Winterslow Church*	42 54 34 21 6 1	}Winterslow Church -	{ 82739 43004
Dean Hill - - Dunnose - - *Farley Monument*	60 20 37 16 44 23	}Farley Monument	{ 53239 160629
Motteston Down - Nine Barrow Down *Hordle Church*	33 29 46 16 12 59	}Hordle Church	{ 49640 98000

Triangles.	Angles observed.	Distances of the stations from the intersected objects.	
			Feet.
Motteston Down -	36 52 51	Milford Church {	45098
Nine Barrow Down	15 19 46		103035
Milford Church			
Motteston Down -	33 17 31	Hurst Light	33819
Nine Barrow Down	9 49 13	House -	108820
Hurst Light House			
Motteston Down -	33 32 2	Hurst Castle -	33564
Nine Barrow Down -	9 48 47		109049
Hurst Castle			
Motteston Down -	67 18 34	Sir J. Doyley's	46896
Nine Barrow Down -	20 13 51	House -	125118
Cupola of Sir J. Doyley's House			
Motteston Down -	34 4 47	Milton Church	69782
Nine Barrow Down -	23 22 56		90057
Milton Abbey Church			
Motteston Down -	27 1 16	Lord Bute's House {	71885
Nine Barrow Down -	24 13 18		78937
North Chimney on Lord Bute's House			
Motteston Down -	28 48 39	Belvidere House	71813
Nine Barrow Down -	25 29 50		80396
Centre Pediment of Belvidere House			
Dean Hill - -	66 5 5	Summer House	107975
Motteston Down -	44 20 32	Kilminston Down	141217
Summer House on Kilminston Down			
Nine Barrow Down -	89 46 55	Poole Church	89399
Black Down -	13 5 59		130037
Poole Church			
Nine Barrow Down -	7 54 30	Fordington	101661
Black Down - -	28 11 54	Church -	29601
Fordington Church			

Triangles.	Angles observed.	Distances of the stations from the intersected objects.	
			Feet.
Nine Barrow Down Black Down - Dorchester Church	7 54 33 / 30 35 42	Dorchester Church -	103647 / 28022
Nine Barrow Down Black Down - - Wyke Church, near Weymouth	15 28 23 / 54 29 40	Wyke Church	109854 / 36002
Nine Barrow Down Wingreen - - Obelisk near Milbourn St. Andrew's	41 50 35 / 35 56 53	Obelisk near Milbourn -	78218 / 88882
Nine Barrow Down Wingreen - - Mr. Trenchard's Tower near Lytchel	12 9 2 / 9 3 17	Mr. Trenchard's Tower -	56660 / 75778
Nine Barrow Down Wingreen - - Flagstaff, Mr. Pitt's Factory, Isle of Purbeck.	118 10 7 / 5 30 19	Flagstaff, Mr. Pitt's Factory	14246 / 136456
Nine Barrow Down Wingreen - - Centre of the Barrow on Creech Hill, Isle of Purbeck	73 32 14 / 10 88 14	Barrow on Creech Hill -	24163 / 125334
Nine Barrow Down Wingreen - - Vane on the Castle, Branksea Island	40 45 31 / 7 37 13	Branksea Castle	23101 / 113731
Nine Barrow Down Wingreen - - Horton Observatory	18 12 9 / 27 4 38	Horton Observatory -	83424 / 57250
Nine Barrow Down Wingreen - - Staircase of Alfred's Tower, in Stourhead Park	14 51 23 / 198 58 56	Alfred's Tower -	193843 / 75729

Triangles.	Angles observed.	Distances of the stations from the Intersected objects.	
			Feet.
Nine Barrow Down Wingreen - D Ringwood Church	42 27 2¼ 45 8 30	} Ringwood Church {	92391 87983
Nine Barrow Down Wingreen - - D Summer House at Moyle's Court	41 55 41 53 51 18	} Summer House, Moyle's Court {	105698 87461
Nine Barrow Down Wingreen - - Christchurch Tower	60 36 0 29 45 57	} Christchurch -	65052 120256
Nine Barrow Down Wingreen - - Warren Summer House, Christchurch Head	72 43 29 29 13 29	} Warren Summer- House - - {	64989 127104
Wingreen from Blackdown 149140 feet.			
Wingreen - - - Blackdown - Barrow, Swyre Head, Isle of Purbeck	44 36 0 62 1 41	} Swyre Head -	137466 109289
Motteston Down from Wingreen 197090 feet.			
Motteston Down - Wingreen - - D Sopley Church	11 6 40 10 13 47	} Sopley Church -	96189 104070
Dean Hill - - Beacon Hill - Salisbury Spire	53 21 33 35 37 6	} Salisbury Spire -	33834 46615
Beacon Hill - - Four Mile-stone - Altar-piece at Stone Henge	33 20 34 34 52 8	} Altar-piece at Stone Henge	23900 22978
Beacon Hill - - Four Mile-stone - Amesbury Church	20 44 17 11 52 14	} Amesbury Church {	14817 25506

Triangles.	Angles observed.	Distances of the stations from the intersected objects.	
			Feet.
Beacon Hill - - Four Mile-stone - *South Chimney on Old Hartford Hut, Salisbury Plain*	16 26 51 56 13 38	}Old Hartford Hut {	33801 11513
Beacon Hill - - Four Mile-stone - *Everley Church*	132 24 37 23 7 41	}Everley Church {	96822 69215
Beacon Hill - - Four Mile-stone - *Summer House on Martincel's Hill, near Marlborough*	119 35 53 39 11 38	}Summer House on Martincel's Hill {	67794 93285
Beacon Hill - - Four Mile-stone - *North Windmill, Salisbury Plain*	45 4 20 81 52 17	}North Windmill {	48082 34387
Beacon Hill - - Four Mile-stone - *South Windmill, Salisbury Plain*	41 55 52 74 6 59	}South Windmill {	41554 28871
Beacon Hill - - Wingreen - - *Clay Hill Barrow, near Warminster*	42 46 45 70 18 36	}Clay Hill Barrow, or Copt Heap - {	117216 84554

Triangles for finding the distance of Portsmouth Observatory from Dunnose.

Dunnose - - Motteston Down - *Spindle of the Wind Vane on Portsmouth Church Tower*	92 44 48 48 44 27	}Portsmouth Church - {	66524 88393

Triangles.	Angles observed.	Distances of the stations from the intersected objects.	
			Feet.
Dunnose - -	91 35 32	Portsmouth Aca-	69787
Motteston Down -	50 49 36	demy - -	90113
Ball of the Cupola of Portsmouth Academy			

In order to ascertain the situation of the Observatory, Mr. Bayly, Master of the Academy, measured two angles in the following triangle, viz.

Portsmouth Academy   124 9 15
Observatory   -   53 6 15
Portsmouth Church

The included angle at Dunnose between the Ball on the Cupola of the Academy, and the Spindle of the Wind Vane on Portsmouth Church, is 1° 9′ 16″, and the distances of those objects from Dunnose are 66524 and 69787 feet; therefore the distance between the Academy and the Church will be 3540 feet: this distance, used as a base in the above triangle, gives the distance between the Observatory and the Church 3663 feet; now the angle at the Church, comprehended by the Academy and the Observatory, being 2° 44′ 30″, we shall find the angle at Dunnose, between Portsmouth Church and the Observatory, to be 1° 3′ 30″, and the distance of the Observatory from Dunnose 69962 feet.

Remarks.

In an operation of this kind, it naturally follows, when the objects intersected are at considerable distances from the stations, there must be great difficulty in ascertaining their precise situations from the appearance of the country. Under such circumstances their names sometimes cannot be discovered; and it has been found, that the best maps of which we are in possession, were by no means sufficiently correct to be of much service in that particular. It is obvious also, without a very intimate knowledge of the interior parts of the country (of which it is impossible, in the present state of the Survey, we can be altogether possessed), there must be some difficulty to identify them, when their distances exceed twelve or fourteen miles. We have, therefore, when such an uncertainty existed, had recourse to some intelligent person well acquainted with the country, by whom we have been informed of their names. In this respect we have to acknowledge the services of Mr. Gardner, chief Draftsman at the Tower, by whose assistance, from his intimate knowledge of the county of Sussex, we have been able to determine, with certainty, the names of many places, which we might otherwise have considered as doubtful. Of the triangles here given, there is not much reason to believe there has been any misnomer; but, as there is not altogether a certainty that all are rightly named, or the objects actually intersected, we have prefixed a D to those we consider as doubtful.

It may be proper to observe, that in taking the angles, the most defined parts of the objects have been selected, unless they were church towers without spires or pyramidical roofs, when the angles were taken to the middles of the towers. If the objects were windmills, resting (as they sometimes do) on great spindles, the observations have been made to those spindles; but in other cases, when the supports were undefined, the mills themselves were intersected.

Distances of the Objects intersected in the Course of the Survey, from the Meridians of Greenwich, Beachy Head, and Dunnose, respectively; and from the Perpendiculars to those Meridians ; with their Bearings at the several Stations, from the Parallels to the Meridians.

138. Meridian of Greenwich.

Bearings from the Parallels to the Meridian.				Distances from merid.	Distances from perp.
At Brighling.	°	′	″	Feet.	Feet.
Bexhill Church - -	29	19	25 SE	110956	230225
Westham Church -	11	41	43 SW	76992	240839
Pevensey Church - -	9	56	0 SW	78814	240023
Black Heath Windmill -	87	6	54 NW	73212	187407
Ninefield Church -	20	41	53 SE	97887	216129
Mountfield Church -	78	10	9 SE	112221	193398
At Ditchling Beacon.					
Chittingly Church -	88	37	2 NE	45462	208369
Waldron Church -	60	43	18 NE	41227	173423
Firle Beacon Station -	63	33	11 SE	25332	235029
Firle Church - -	65	24	0 SE	20759	230963
Jevington Windmill -	62	8	28 SE	54978	252248
Plumpton Church -	81	54	20 NE	16211	209034
Little Horsted Church -	70	53	38 NE	21491	194226
Spittal Windmill -	65	58	55 SE	5690	218625
Ditchling Church -	14	30	17 NW	26925	203077
Thakeham Church -	77	33	40 NW	96831	194295
West Grinsted Church -	63	20	56 NW	76612	184087
Keymere Church -	35	37	57 NW	29309	203504
Bolney Church - -	34	26	16 NW	46539	178068
Slaugham Church - -	24	48	29 NW	47538	160946
Starting House, Brighton	2	28	47 SW	25605	236511
Cuckfield Church - -	12	20	25 NW	32711	172580
Wyvelsfield Church -	6	29	54 NE	21592	185011
Hurstpierpoint Church -	55	0	49 NW	41262	198504
Lindfield Church -	9	10	51 NE	17832	169199

Bearings from the Parallels to the Meridian.					Distances from merid.	Distances from perp.
	°	′	″		Feet.	Feet.
At Crowborough Beacon.						
Willington Church -	14	31	53	SE	56724	238159
Homehurst Church -	70	4	58	SE	90204	175142
Hailsham Church -	20	4	48	SE	60458	224245
Dallington Church -	51	17	56	SE	82994	193493
At Botley Hill.						
East Grinsted Church -	1	14	6	SW	1039	129041
Rotherfield Church -	30	46	22	SE	50573	157520
Mayfield Church -	32	38	58	SE	60300	166728
Crowborough Chapel -	25	6	50	SE	38257	154132
Bestbeech Windmill -	41	42	55	SE	71183	152539
Fairden Tower -	4	11	47	SE	3448	117538
Tatesfield Church -	66	31	44	NE	7422	69733
Charlwood Church -	49	25	48	SW	51866	117485
Evelyn's Obelisk -	11	49	44	SW	10294	122847
At Leith Hill.						
Firle Windmill -	40	18	35	SE	21292	234831
Beddingham Windmill -	38	37	12	SE	14819	234476
Horsham Church -	11	54	25	SE	75805	152405
Farnham Castle -	80	43	18	NW	183432	93069
Euhurst Windmill -	86	21	38	SW	195395	111088
Euhurst Church -	62	16	42	SW	100845	118215
St. Martha's Chapel -	63	45	21	NW	120899	91983
Norris's Obelisk (Bagshot Heath) -	54	14	15	NW	168692	49407
West Hoathly Church -	63	6	5	SE	12967	146585
Nettlebed -	43	12	55	NW	224159	38548
At Beachy Head.						
Hurstmonceux Church -	21	26	48	NE	76041	215562

139. Meridian of Beachy Head.

At Chanctonbury Ring.						
Sleep Down -	32	8	34	SE	137189	42974
Brighthelmstone Church -	64	14	21	SE	91925	31829

U u

Bearings from the Parallels to the Meridian.					Distances from merid.	Distances from perp.
At Chanctonbury Ring.	°	′	″		Feet.	Feet.
Shoreham Church - -	46	37	4	SE	191788	34490
Southwick Church -	54	55	30	SE	114171	35161
Goring Church -	20	14	11	SW	158281	26132
Bramber Windmill -	75	17	59	SE	195507	52383
Findon Temple - -	56	38	48	SW	157711	50573
110. Meridian of Dunnose.						
At Hind Head.						
Petworth Church -	28	4	40	SE	135688	135394
Kirdford Church -	50	50	28	SE	149419	150447
Wisborough Green Church	55	49	26	SE	160414	148101
Billinghurst Church -	61	20	7	SE	172148	148382
Rusper Church - -	87	55	49	NE	211158	185404
At Butser Hill.						
Pulborough Church -	86	21	25	SE	159482	124313
Earl of Egremont's Tower	83	43	30	NE	128906	139903
Bosham Church -	27	20	55	SE	78979	77027
Selsea Church - -	31	37	53	SE	100896	50141
Prinsted Windmill -	15	54	28	SE	64678	80914
Del Key Windmill -	33	41	48	SE	88659	73781
Horse-shoe Summer House	41	57	52	SW	26952	45397
Southampton Spire -	73	45	14	SW	47618	102722
Selsea Windmill -	24	42	33	SE	91103	42849
Flagstaff, Chichester Harbour - -	9	34	59	SE	62428	59596
Cackham Tower -	16	1	52	SE	71823	56455
Selsea High House -	24	40	58	SE	91791	41045
Bourn Church -	15	55	58	SE	69546	68464
Ower Rocks - -	32	27	33	SE	122570	17687
South Hayling Church -	0	51	26	SE	51324	64727
West Thorney Church -	15	53	8	SE	67055	72486
Bow Hill Station - -	48	55	14	SE	85116	100937
St. Catharine's Light House	27	54	46	SW	24258	9529
Needles Light House -	50	9	27	SW	86554	17045

Bearings from the Parallels to the Meridian.		Distances from merid.	Distances from perp.
	° ′ ″	Feet.	Feet.
At Butser Hill.			
Worseley's Obelisk - -	25 7 34 SW	11607	796
Ashey Down Sea Mark -	24 6 10 SW	2471	24292
Cowes Fort - -	43 49 1 SW	21998	55887
Portsdown Windmill -	24 15 6 SW	30055	86962
Clark's Folly - -	10 4 51 SW	42250	85825
South Sea Castle -	18 51 36 SW	25425	58961
Portsdown Hill Station -	34 2 0 SW	20816	87565
Petworth Windmill -	87 0 38 NE	141258	136012
At Rook's Hill.			
West Tarring Church -	73 52 32 SE	185568	76299
High Down Windmill -	72 3 14 SE	172934	77311
Angmering Church -	69 38 4 SE	164937	77159
Pagham Church - -	1 25 13 SE	104222	55757
Bersted Church - -	27 7 47 SE	121063	64535
Clapham Church - -	75 30 37 SE	169507	82990
Oving Church - -	20 27 27 SE	110141	80477
Felpham Windmill -	30 41 22 SE	125546	61860
Boxgrove Church - -	40 11 21 SE	112617	88543
Goodwood House - -	23 44 31 SE	105966	92970
Portfield Windmill -	5 6 41 SW	101123	81847
Chichester Spire - -	16 47 40 SW	96609	79801
Harting Windmill - -	48 13 28 NW	75678	124438
Sir H. Fetherstonhaugh's Tower - . -	51 25 10 NW	72732	124196
Sir R. Hotham's Flagstaff	22 57 0 SE	120029	59477
At Dunnose.			
Kingston Church - -	22 42 52 NE	28294	67591
Horndean Church -	21 8 22 NE	45392	112223
Porchester Castle - -	13 33 12 NE	19360	80269
Halifax Tower - -	36 3 7 NE	69517	95499
Carisbrook Castle -	46 10 52 NW	26478	25408
Thorness Station -	43 0 59 NW	39207	42020
Luttrell's Folly - -	23 0 44 NW	29094	68502
Great Boat House -	85 48 30 NW	43011	3152

Bearings from the Parallels to the Meridian.					Distances from metrid.	Distances from perp.
	°	′	″		Feet.	Feet.
At Dunnose.						
Brixton Church	78	38	12	NW	45878	9880
Calshot Castle	18	52	8	NW	25151	73592
Fawley Church	24	96	49	NW	35350	77163
East Cowes Sea Mark	19	11	11	NW	18008	51752
Bursledon Windmill	14	55	28	NW	26904	100938
Hamble Church	17	29	36	NW	27592	87546
Hamble Saltern	16	54	18	NW	25702	84570
Governor Hornby's House	15	45	50	NW	23448	89063
Warblington Church	39	0	58	NE	54750	84255
Farley Monument	18	0	4	NW	49640	152765
Portsmouth Church	19	9	40	NE	21835	62899
———— Academy	18	0	24	NE	21573	66369
———— Observatory	18	6	10	NE	21739	66499
Fareham Church	3	37	55	NE	5488	86462
Porchester Church	13	55	50	NE	19762	79672
Havant Church	30	29	53	NE	50104	85066
At Dean Hill.						
Salisbury Spire	68	52	9	NW	136127	168989
Stockbridge Hill Station	55	40	12	NE	59673	181446
Winterslow Church	12	5	5	NW	109399	179011
At Four Mile-stone.						
N.Windmill,Salisbury Plain	21	11	6	NW	161506	210275
S. Windmill,Salisbury Plain	28	56	44	NW	167717	213446
At Molleston Down.						
Ramsden Hill Station	65	47	6	NW	141969	55377
Hordle Church	60	14	32	NW	95952	40810
Milford Church	56	51	27	NW	90619	40298
Milton Church	59	39	31	NW	107904	47792
Hurst Light House	60	26	47	NW	82272	32950
Hurst Castle	60	12	16	NW	81985	32249
Lord Bute's House	66	43	2	NW	118336	43747
Summer House, Kilmiston Down	23	24	52	NE	3259	145161

Bearings from the Parallels to the Meridian.				Distances from merid.	Distances from perp.
	°	'	"	Feet.	Feet.
At Molleston Down.					
Sir J. Doyley's House -	26	25	44 NW	73731	57566
Belvidere House - -	64	55	39 NW	117904	46004
Sopley Church - -	63	44	46 NW	139119	58118
At Nine Barrow Down.					
Wyke Church - -	84	7	0 SW	297337	4594
Horton Observatory -	8	43	26 NE	175408	89196
Branksea Castle - -	31	16	48 NE	176067	26479
Sywre Head - -	65	41	52 SW	208018	2275
Ringwood Church -	32	58	41 NE	137771	84242
Moyle's Court Summer House - -	32	26	58 NE	131348	95932
Christchurch Tower -	57	7	17 NE	139499	42051
Christchurch Head -	69	14	46 NE	130030	35599
Poole Church - -	9	22	18 NE	189274	35743
Pitt's Factory - -	57	21	10 SW	200051	945
Creech Barrow - -	89	0	57 NW	212045	9675
Mr. Trenchard's Tower	21	37	45 NW	208946	59407
Obelisk, near Milbourn	51	19	18 NW	249123	55619
Fordington Church -	72	30	7 NW	285016	37303
Dorchester Church -	72	30	4 NW	286911	37901
Alfred's Tower - -	24	20	6 NW	267938	183357
At Beacon Hill.					
Amesbury Church -	73	39	50 SW	194320	202589
Summer House, Martincel's Hill - -	7	28	54 NW	198928	273974
Everley Church - -	5	20	10 NE	116677	243419
Stone Henge - -	86	16	7 SW	143950	203902
Old Hartford Hut -	69	22	24 SW	151735	194850
Clay Hill, or Copt Heap	85	54	8 NW	237017	215133

The bearings of the objects from the parallels to the meridians at
the different stations, are inserted in the above table, in order that
the numbers in the two last columns may be examined with greater

facility. The method of obtaining them is similar to that in Art. 59.
and 130, thus:

At Beacon Hill, the bearing of Clay Hill is 85° 54' 8" NW; this,
with the distance between Beacon Hill and Clay Hill, give 116916,
and 8376 feet, for the distances of the latter place from the parallels
to the meridian of Dunnose, and its perpendicular. But the distances of Beacon Hill from that meridian, and perpendicular, are
120101 feet, and 206757 feet; therefore 120101 + 116916 = 237017
feet, and 206757 + 8376 = 215133 feet, are the distances of Clay
Hill from the meridian of Dunnose, and its perpendicular.

Latitudes and Longitudes of the intersected Objects.

141. *Latitudes and Longitudes of such Places upon the Sea Coast, and
near it, as have been referred to the Meridian of Greenwich.*

Names of objects.	Latitude.	Longitude from Greenwich.			
		In degrees.			In time.
	° ′ ″	° ′ ″			m. s.
Bexhill Church -	50 50 46.7	0 28 43.3	E		1 54.9
Pevensey Church -	50 49 11.9	0 20 14.1	E		1 20.9
Westham Church -	50 49 4	0 19 45.8	E		1 19
Willingdon Church -	50 49 31.2	0 14 40.6	E		0 58.7
Jevington Windmill -	50 47 12.3	0 14 12.8	E		0 56.9
Firle Beacon Station	50 50 2.7	0 6 33.3	E		0 26.2
Firle Windmill -	50 50 4.8	0 5 30.6	E		0 22
Firle Church - -	50 50 42.9	0 5 22.4	E		0 21.5
Beddingham Windmill	50 50 8.3	0 3 50.1	E		0 15.3
Hailsham Church -	50 51 48.2	0 15 39.3	E		1 2.6
Spittal Windmill -	50 52 44.7	0 1 28.3	W		0 26
Starting House, Brighton	50 49 48.1	0 6 28.5	W		0 25.9

148. *Latitudes and Longitudes of such Places upon the Sea Coast, and near it, as have been referred to the Meridian of Beachy Head.*

Names of objects.	Latitude.	Longitude west of Beachy Head.	Longitude west of Greenwich.	
			In degrees.	In time.
	° ′ ″	° ′ ″	° ′ ″	m. s.
Brighthelmstone Church - -	50 49 32.2	0 27 7.1	0 11 55.2	0 47.7
Southwick Church (Sussex) -	50 50 6 6	0 29 32.8	0 14 20.9	0 57.3
Shoreham Church - -	50 49 59.5	0 31 31	0 16 19.1	1 5.3
Bramber Windmill - -	50 52 55 7	0 32 39.8	0 17 28.9	1 9.3
Steep Down Station - -	50 51 22.1	0 35 51.1	0 20 29.2	1 21.3
Goring Church - - -	50 48 54.2	0 40 56.5	0 25 44.6	1 43
Findon Temple - - -	50 52 55	0 40 50.8	0 25 38.9	1 42.6

143. *Latitudes and Longitudes of such Places upon the Sea Coast, and near it, as have been referred to the Meridian of Dunnose.*

Names of objects.	Latitude.	Longitude from Dunnose.		Longitude west of Greenwich.	
				In degrees.	In time.
	° ′ ″	° ′ ″		° ′ ″	m. s.
West Tarring Church - -	50 49 29.9	0 48 1	E	0 25 35	1 34 3
High Down Windmill - -	50 49 48.9	0 11 15	E	0 26 51	1 47.4
Clapham Church - -	50 50 37.3	0 43 52.6	P.	0 27 43.4	1 50.9
Angmering Church - -	50 49 40.3	0 41 40.8	E	0 28 55.2	1 55.7
Felpham Windmill - -	50 47 12.7	0 32 17.6	E	0 39 0.4	2 36.6
Bersted Church - -	50 47 39 4	0 31 18.2	E	0 40 17.8	2 41.2
Gov. Hornby's House - -	50 50 46.1	0 6 4.2	W	1 17 40.2	5 10.7
Sir R. Hotham's Flagstaff -	50 46 49.6	0 31 1.7	E	0 40 34.3	2 42.3
Oving Church - -	50 50 17.3	0 18 30.4	E	0 43 5.0	2 52.4
Pagham Church - -	50 46 14	0 16 56.1	E	0 44 39.9	2 18.7
Chichester Spire - -	50 50 11.4	0 25 0.1	E	0 36 35 9	3 6.4
Selsea Church - -	50 45 18.8	0 25 54.7	E	0 45 41.3	3 2.7
Selsea High House - -	50 43 49 6	0 23 48.8	E	0 47 53.8	3 11.5
Selsea Windmill - -	50 44 54	0 25 31.6	F.	0 48 4.4	3 12.3
Del Key, or Dalkey Windmill -	50 49 18.5	0 22 56.5	E	0 51 19.1	3 25.3
Bosham Church - -	50 49 45	0 20 16.9	E	0 51 19.1	3 25.3
Cockham Tower - -	50 46 12.4	0 13 33 7	E	0 53 2.3	3 32.2
West Thorney Church - -	50 49 0.7	0 17 20.8	E	0 54 15.2	3 37
Prinsted Windmill - -	50 50 23.9	0 16 44	E	0 54 51.6	3 39.4
Watch House, Chichester Harbour	50 46 33 8	0 16 8.3	E	0 55 27.7	3 41.8
West Bourn Church - -	50 51 38.4	0 16 11.7	E	0 55 24.3	3 41.6
Warblington Church - -	50 50 57.1	0 14 10.4	E	0 57 25.6	3 49.7
South Hayling Church - -	50 47 44.7	0 13 16.1	E	0 58 19.9	3 53.3
Clark's Folly - -	50 51 15	0 10 56.3	E	1 0 39.7	4 2.6

Names of objects.	Latitude.	Longitude from Dunnose.		Longitude west of Greenwich.	
				In degrees.	In time.
	o ′ ″	o ′ ″		o ′ ″	m. s.
Cumberland Fort	50 47 20.8	0 9 53.2	E	1 2 43	4 6.9
Kingston Church	50 48 13.5	0 7 19.1	E	1 4 16.9	4 17.1
Havant Church	50 51 5.4	0 12 58.3	E	0 58 37.7	3 54.5
Portsdown Windmill	50 51 17.0	0 7 46.9	E	1 8 49.1	4 35.3
Portsdown Station	50 51 30.6	0 5 23.4	E	1 6 12.6	4 24.8
Portsmouth Church	50 47 26.8	0 5 18.7	E	1 5 57.3	4 23.8
Portsmouth Academy	50 48 1.6	0 5 34.7	E	1 6 1.3	4 24.1
Portsmouth Observatory	50 48 2.9	0 5 37.3	E	1 5 58.7	4 23.9
South Sea Castle	50 46 42.5	0 6 34.3	E	1 5 1.7	4 20.1
Porchester Church	50 50 12.7	0 5 6.9	E	1 6 29.1	4 25.9
Porchester Castle	50 50 18.6	0 5 0.5	E	1 6 35.5	4 26.3
Fareham Church	50 51 19.8	0 1 25.3	E	1 10 10.7	4 40.7
Hamble Saltern	50 51 0.9	0 6 39.2	W	1 18 15.2	5 13
Humble Church	50 51 30.3	0 7 8.6	W	1 18 44.6	5 15
Calshot Castle	50 43 12.7	0 6 29.6	W	1 18 5.6	5 12.4
Luttrell's Folly	50 48 22.5	0 7 31.5	W	1 19 7.5	5 16.5
Fawley Church	50 49 47.7	0 9 8.4	W	1 20 44.4	5 22.9
Hurst Castle	50 42 23.4	0 21 9.5	W	1 32 45.5	6 11
Hurst Light House	50 42 23.4	0 21 1.4	W	1 32 50	6 11.3
Ashey Down Sea Mark	50 41 6.8	0 0 36.2	E	1 10 57.8	4 43.8
East Cowes Sea Mark	50 45 37.5	0 4 39.2	W	1 16 15.2	5 5
West Cowes Fort	50 46 18.2	0 5 41.1	W	1 17 17.1	5 9.1
St. Catherine's Light House	50 35 33.1	0 6 14.7	W	1 17 50.7	5 11.3
Nerdles Light House	50 39 53.2	0 22 19.2	W	1 33 55.2	6 15.7
Milford Church	50 43 41.7	0 23 73.9	W	1 34 59.9	6 20
Milton Church	50 44 55.2	0 27 52.4	W	1 39 28.4	6 37.9
Hordle Church	50 43 41.2	0 24 46.5	W	1 36 22.5	6 25.5
Lord Bute's House	50 44 14.5	0 30 33.7	W	1 42 9.7	6 48.6
Christchurch Head	50 42 57.3	0 33 34.5	W	1 45 10.5	7 0.7
Christchurch Tower	50 43 56.8	0 34 27.4	W	1 46 3.4	7 4.2
Ramsdown Hill	50 46 7.5	0 36 32	W	1 48 8	7 12.5
Castle, Branksea Island	50 41 19.5	0 45 25.5	W	1 57 1.5	7 48.1
Poole Church	50 42 50	0 47 41 6	W	1 58 54.6	7 55.6
Flag-staff, Mr. Pitt's Factory	50 36 46.5	0 51 31.9	W	2 3 7.9	8 12.3
Creech Barrow	50 38 9.8	0 54 38.9	W	2 6 14.9	8 25
Barrow, Swyre Head	50 36 38.4	0 53 34.8	W	2 5 10.8	8 20.7
Boat House	50 37 37.9	0 21 49	W	1 22 40.9	5 30.7
Wyke Church	50 35 57.5	1 16 34.1	W	2 28 10.1	9 52.7
Brixton Church	50 38 37.6	0 11 49.1	W	1 23 25 1	5 33.7
Horse-shoe Summer House	50 44 34.2	0 6 57.7	W	1 18 33.7	5 14.2
Sir R. Worsley's Obelisk	50 36 59.5	0 2 59.4	W	1 14 35.4	4 58.3
Over Rocks	50 39 57.3	0 31 36.5	E	0 39 59.5	2 40

144. *Latitudes and Longitudes of those Places remote from the Sea Coast, which have been referred to the Meridian of Greenwich.*

Names of objects.	Latitude.	Longitude from Greenwich. In degrees.		In time.	
	° ′ ″	° ′ ″		m. s.	
East Grinsted Church	51 7 27.9	0 0 16.2	E	0 1.1	
Fairden Tower	51 9 21.3	0 0 53.9	E	0 3.6	
Tatesfield Church	51 17 12.6	0 1 50.4	E	0 7.7	
Evelyn's Obelisk, Felbridge Park	51 8 28.9	0 2 40.9	W	8 10.7	
West Hoathly Church	54 4 35.4	0 3 13	W	0 12.9	
Plumpton Church	50 54 19.1	0 4 12.1	W	0 16.8	
Lindfield Church	51 0 52	0 4 58	W	0 18.5	
Wyvelsfield Church	50 58 16	0 5 36.3	W	0 22.4	
Little Horsted Church	50 56 44.1	0 5 35	E	0 22.3	
Ditchling Church	50 55 17.8	0 6 49.5	W	0 27.3	
Keymer Church	50 55 13.6	0 7 35.9	W	0 30.4	
Cuckfield Church	51 0 18.3	0 8 29.8	W	0 34	
Waldron Church	51 0 9.8	0 10 42.5	E	0 42.8	
Crowborough Chapel	51 3 20.1	0 9 56.8	E	0 39.7	
Hurstpierpoint Church	50 56 2.5	0 10 42.1	W	0 42.8	
Chiltingly Church	50 54 23.2	0 11 47	E	0 47.1	
Bolney Church	50 59 23.9	0 12 5	W	0 48.3	
Slaugham Church	51 2 18.7	0 12 22.4	W	0 49.4	
Rotherfield Church	51 2 46.3	0 13 8.8	E	0 53.6	
Charlwood Church	51 9 21.5	0 13 30.1	W	0 54	
Mayfield Church	51 1 13.3	0 15 40	E	0 2.7	
Homehurst Church	50 59 51	0 21 23.3	E	1 33.7	
Brabeech Windmill	51 3 34.8	0 18 30.7	E	1 14	
Blackheath Windmill (near Heathfield)	50 57 50.9	0 19 0	E	1 16	
Horsham Church	51 3 36	0 19 42.7	W	1 18.9	
Hurstmonceux Church	50 51 34.6	0 19 41.7	E	1 18.8	
West Grinsted Church	50 58 23.5	0 19 53.2	W	1 19.5	
Dallington Church	50 56 50.4	0 21 31.8	E	1 26.1	
Nimfield Church	50 53 7.1	0 23 21.6	E	1 41.4	
Thakeham Church	50 56 41.8	0 25 7.1	W	1 40.5	
Euhurst Church	51 9 21.7	0 26 16.6	W	1 45.1	
Euhurst Windmill	51 10 21.7	0 27 26.9	W	1 49.9	
Mountfield Church	50 56 50.4	0 29 6.7	E	1 56.4	
St. Martha's Chapel	51 13 89	0 31 33.1	W	2 6.2	
Norris's Obelisk	51 20 24.8	0 44 7	W	2 56.5	
Farnham Castle	51 13 6.9	0 47 52	W	3 11.5	
Nettlebed Station	51 34 45.1	0 58 57.1	W	3 55.8	

X x

145. Latitudes and Longitudes of those Places remote from the Sea Coast, which have been referred to the Meridian of Dunnose.

Names of objects.	Latitude.	Longitude from Dunnose.		Longitude west of Greenwich.	
				In degrees.	In time.
	° ′ ″	° ′ ″		° ′ ″	m. s.
Rusper Church	51 7 22.4	0 54 59.1	E	0 16 36.9	1 6.5
Billinghurst Church	51 1 10.6	0 44 43.9	E	0 26 52.1	1 47.5
Pulborough Church	50 57 25.5	0 41 22.4	E	0 30 13.6	2 0.9
Kirdford Church	51 1 44.1	0 38 49.9	E	0 32 46.1	2 11.1
Petworth Windmill	50 59 22.5	0 36 40.7	E	0 34 53.3	2 19.6
Petworth Church	50 59 17	0 35 10.1	E	0 36 25.8	2 25.7
Earl of Egremont's Tower	51 0 1.9	0 33 28.7	E	0 38 7.3	2 32.5
Wisborough Green Church	51 1 20.1	0 41 41	E	0 29 55	1 59.7
Boxgrove Church	50 51 36.7	0 29 10.1	E	0 42 81.9	2 49.7
Portfield Windmill	50 50 31.4	0 26 10.5	E	0 45 25.5	3 1.7
Rook's Hill Windmill	50 53 17.2	0 25 48.9	E	0 45 47.1	3 3.1
Halifax Tower	50 52 47.5	0 18 0 4	E	0 53 35.6	3 34.4
Goodwood House	50 52 20.8	0 17 26.7	E	0 44 9.3	3 36.6
Bow Hill Station	50 53 40.4	0 22 3.3	E	0 40 32.7	3 18.1
Harting Windmill	50 57 32.7	0 19 38.1	E	0 51 57.8	3 27.8
Sir H. Fetherstonhaugh's Tower	50 57 30.5	0 18 52.3	E	0 52 43.7	3 30.9
Horndean Church	50 55 33.8	0 11 25.1	E	1 0 20.9	4 1.4
Southwick Church (Hants)	50 52 27	0 5 22.7	E	1 6 24.3	4 25.6
Summer House, Kilminston Down	51 0 58.5	0 0 50.8	E	1 10 45.1	4 43
Carisbrook Castle	50 41 17.5	0 6 49.9	W	1 18 25.9	5 13.7
Bursledon Windmill	50 53 42.3	0 6 52.3	W	1 18 34.3	5 14.3
Thorness Station	50 44 1.1	0 10 7.5	W	1 21 43.5	5 26.9
Farley Monument	51 7 22.8	0 27 54.1	W	1 24 30.1	5 38
Southampton Spire	50 53 59.5	0 12 20.4	W	1 23 50.4	5 35.8
Stockbridge Hill Station	51 6 55.3	0 25 32.2	W	1 37 8.21	5 48.5
Sir J. Doyle's House	50 46 33.3	0 29 3.4	W	1 30 39.4	6 2.6
Winterslow Church	51 5 29.7	0 28 37	W	1 40 3	6 40.2
Belvidere House	50 44 36.9	0 30 3./3	W	1 41 3.3	6 44.2
Everley Church	51 17 3.3	0 30 29.5	W	1 41 4.3	6 44.3
Ringwood Church	50 50 58	0 35 40	W	1 47 16	7 9.1
Summer House, Martinsel's Hill	51 22 3.6	0 33 45	W	1 45 21	7 1.4
Summer House, Moyle's Court	50 52 48.3	0 34 1.5	W	1 45 37.5	7 2.5
Amesbury Church	51 10 18.9	0 35 0.8	W	1 46 36.8	7 6.5
Salisbury Spire	51 3 48.9	0 35 24.2	W	1 47 0.2	7 8
Sopley Church	50 46 34.7	0 35 57.5	W	1 47 33.5	7 10.2
Stonehenge	51 10 44.3	0 37 32.8	W	1 49 7.8	7 16.5
Old Harnford Hut	51 9 3	0 39 34.1	W	1 51 8.1	7 24.5
3. Windmill ⎱ on Salisbury Plain	51 11 33	0 42 7.2	W	1 53 43.2	7 34.9
N. Windmill ⎰	51 12 34	0 43 44.8	W	1 55 20.8	7 41.4
Horton Observatory	50 51 37.9	0 45 28.3	W	1 57 2.3	7 48.1
Mr. Trenchard's Tower	50 46 40.5	0 54 2.5	W	2 5 36.5	8 22.4
Clay Hill, or Cope Heap	51 12 12	1 1 49.8	W	2 13 25.8	8 53.7
Alfred's Tower	51 6 54.4	1 9 45.4	W	2 21 22.4	9 25.4
Milbourn Obelisk	50 45 57.8	1 4 22.8	W	2 15 58.8	9 3.9
Fordington Church	50 42 52.2	1 13 36.5	W	2 25 13.5	9 40.7
Dorchester Church	50 42 57.7	1 14 4.1	W	2 25 40 1	9 42.7

Heights of the Stations ; and Terrestrial Refractions.

146. *Elevations and Depressions.*

At Hanger Hill.

The ground at St. Ann's Hill *depr.* 4 36
    at Banstead   *elev.* 10 39

At St. Ann's Hill.

The ground at Bagshot Heath *elev.* 11 23 ⎫ Instrument on the half scaf-
    at Banstead   *elev.* 10 2 ⎬ fold ; the axis of the tele-
    at Hanger Hill   *depr.* 6 13 ⎭ scope 20½ feet high.
The top of the flagstaff near
Hampton Poorhouse   *depr.* 12 54
    N.B. The flagstaff was about 41 feet high.

Near Hampton Poorhouse.

The ground at St. Ann's Hill *elev.* 8 17 Instrument on the whole
scaffold ; the axis about 36½ feet high.

At Banstead.

The ground at Leith Hill   *elev.* 17 29 ⎫
    at Shooter's Hill *depr.* 11 7 ⎪
    at St. Ann's Hill *depr.* 22 9 ⎬ On the half scaffold ; the
    at Hanger Hill *depr.* 22 35 ⎪ axis 20½ feet high.
The top of the flagstaff at
Botley Hill - - *elev.* 18 0 ⎭ The staff about 29 feet high.

X x 2

At Leith Hill.

		, "	
The top of the flagstaff at Banstead -	*depr.*	25 57	The staff about 27½ feet high.
of the flagst. at Botley Hill	*depr.*	8 46	
The ground at Hind Head	*depr.*	8 28	
at Crowborough Beacon	*depr.*	15 48	
at Ditchling Beacon	*depr.*	12 34	
at Chanctonbury Ring	*depr.*	13 10	
The horizon of the sea through Shoreham Gap, on July 2d, 1792, at 10 in the forenoon. -	*depr.*	30 6	
The top of Severndroog Castle	*depr.*	22 9	

N. B. The axis of the telescope when at Shooter's Hill, was about 29½ feet lower than the top of the Castle.

At Shooter's Hill.

The ground at Leith Hill	*elev.*	2 35	
at Banstead -	*elev.*	0 15	

On Bagshot Heath.

The ground at Hind Head	*elev.*	10 87	
at St. Ann's Hill	*depr.*	12 30	

At Hind Head.

The ground at Leith Hill	*depr.*	2 59	
at Chanctonbury Ring	*depr.*	11 11	
at Rook's Hill -	*depr.*	14 51	
at Butser Hill -	*depr.*	5 54	
at Bagshot Heath	*depr.*	29 12	
at Highclere -	*depr.*	10 42	

On Rook's Hill.

The ground at Hind Head	*elev.*	3	9
at Dunnose	*depr.*	7	31
at Butser Hill	*elev.*	7	23
at Chanctonbury Ring	*depr.*	1	35
at Bow Hill -	*depr.*	1	5
at Portsdown -	*depr.*	16	22
Horizon of the sea, in the Di- rection of Chichester spire, about noon on Sept. 2, 1792,	*depr.*	25	30

At Butser Hill.

The ground at Highclere	*depr.*	9	29
at Hind Head -	*depr.*	4	44
at Motteston Down	*depr.*	15	27
at Dunnose -	*depr.*	12	30
Top of flagstaff at Rook's Hill	*depr.*	15	6	The staff 20 feet high.

At Chanctonbury Ring.

The ground at Rook's Hill	*depr.*	10	46
at Hind Head	*depr.*	4	20
at Leith Hill	*depr.*	1	13
at Beachy Head	*depr.*	16	27	—On the half scaffold: the axis 20] feet high.

At Dunnose.

The ground at Nine Barrow Down - -	*depr.*	15	37
at Dean Hill	*depr.*	17	24
at Rook's Hill	*depr.*	12	8
at Butser Hill	*depr.*	6	4

On Ditchling Beacon.

The ground at Leith Hill   *depr.*   4 36

On Fairlight Down.

The ground at Beachy Head   *depr.*   7 45
    at Brightling Windmill   *depr.*   0 49   The ground at the Wind-
mill is about 4 feet higher than the axis of the telescope when
at Brightling.

On Brightling Down.

The ground at Fairlight Down   *depr.*   7 56
    at Beachy Head   -   *depr.*   8 44
    at Crowborough Beacon   *elev.*   3 54

At Crowborough Beacon.

The ground at Leith Hill   *depr.*   4 8
    at Brightling Windmill   *depr.*   12 21
    at Botley Hill   -   *depr.*   3 5

At Beachy Head.

The ground at Fairlight Down   *depr.*   5 17
    at Brightling Windmill   *depr.*   1 48
    at Chanctonbury Ring   *depr.*   5 6

At Dean Hill.

The ground at Highclere   *elev.*   0 46
    at Beacon Hill   *elev.*   4 47
    at Wingreen   *elev.*   5 5
    at Dunnose   *depr.*   7 56

At Beacon Hill.

The ground at Highclere	depr.	0	15
at Wingreen	depr.	0	34
at Dean Hill	depr.	13	13

At Highclere.

The ground at Hind Head	depr.	10	42
at Butser Hill	depr.	9	26
at Dean Hill	depr.	18	12
at Beacon Hill	depr.	19	15

On Nine Barrow Down.

The ground at Wingreen	depr.	1	20
at Dunnose	depr.	10	8
The sea in a south direction, about noon, April 11, 1794	depr.	24	16

At Wingreen.

The ground at Beacon Hill	depr.	15	30
at Nine Barrow Down	depr.	17	40
at Dean Hill -	depr.	20	19

N. B. The axis of the telescope was always about 5½ feet from the ground, unless the contrary is specified. And it is also to be noted, that 6' must be subtracted from the elevations, and added to the depressions, on account of the error in the parallelism of the line of collimation of the telescope, and the rod attached to its side, upon which the level is hung.

147. *Height of the Station at Dunnose.*

With a view to obtain the heights of the stations nearly, from their elevations or depressions, we determined the height of that

at Dunnose above low water, in May, 1793, by levelling down to
the sea shore near Shanklin, a distance of about a mile. Instead
of a levelling telescope, we made use of the transit instrument,
which, on account of its very accurate spirit level, seems extremely
well adapted for the purpose. Two circular wooden platforms
were provided, broad enough for the feet of the transit stand;
these platforms rested on pegs driven into the ground, and were
always made horizontal at the time of levelling, by means of a
mahogany spar, or straight-edge, furnished with a spirit level.
The graduated rods, of course, were constantly set vertical on the
lowest platform, while the transit stood on the other.

The ground is favourable enough down to Shanklin Chine: this
is a large deep chasm, opening to the sea; but the descent is not
so sudden on the western side, which is by far the steepest, and to
which we levelled, but a person may get up or down with safety.
We found its perpendicular height by means of several rods placed
end ways against the sloping side, and supported in an horizontal
position, and then letting fall a measuring tape from one rod to
another: but this was the most troublesome and difficult part of
the whole operation. The fall from the bottom of this chasm or
opening, to the water's edge, was found in the usual manner.

The whole perpendicular descent thus determined, was 792 feet;
which, we have no reason to suppose, is more than 2 or 3 feet wide
of the truth. We finished at low water on May 10; and therefore
the height of the station above low water at spring tides will, no
doubt, be a very few feet more.

148. *Heights of Rook's Hill and Butser Hill.*

At Dunnose {	the ground at Rook's Hill	-	-	depr.	12 14
	at Butser Hill	-	-	depr.	6 10
At Rook's Hill {	the ground at Dunnose	-	-	depr.	7 37
	at Butser Hill	-	-	elev.	7 17

At Butser ⎰the ground at Dunnose - - *depr.* 12 36
Hill   ⎱top of the flagstaff at Rook's Hill - *depr.* 15 12

Dunnose and Rook's Hill   23 31 ⎱
Dunnose and Butser Hill   23   9 ⎰ contained arcs nearly.
Butser Hill and Rook's Hill   9 59 ⎰

Hence, the mean refraction between Dunnose and Rook's Hill
will be found 1' 58"; between Dunnose and Butser Hill 2' 16"; and
between Butser Hill and Rook's Hill 47"; which are about $\frac{1}{13}$, $\frac{1}{16}$,
$\frac{1}{13}$ of the contained arcs respectively, as in the table.

By the observations across the water, the ground at Rook's Hill
would be 97 feet lower, and that at Butser Hill 132 feet higher,
than Dunnose: the sum is 229 feet for the difference of heights of
Butser Hill and Rook's Hill, obtained in this manner; but from
the reciprocal observations, the ground at Rook's Hill is only 209
feet lower than at Butser Hill, which is less than the former difference by 20 feet; therefore, supposing each of the mean refractions to have produced an equal error in the heights, we have
$792 - 97 + \frac{20}{3} = 702$ feet, for the height of Rook's Hill; and
$792 + 132 - \frac{20}{3} = 917$ for that of Butser Hill. From those two
determinations, the others in the following table have been obtained (the stations to the westward of Dunnose excepted) by
taking a mean of the heights as derived from different routes.
Those distinguished by an asterisk, were found by taking $\frac{1}{13}$ of the
contained arcs for refraction.

149. *Table containing the Heights of the Stations.*

Stations.	Ground above low water. Feet.
Dunnose	792
Rook's Hill	702

Stations.	Ground above low water.
	Feet.
Butser Hill - -	917
Hind Head - - -	923
Chanctonbury Ring -	814
Leith Hill - - -	993
Ditchling Beacon - -	858
Beachy Head - -	564
Fairlight Down - -	599
Brightling Down - -	646
Crowborough Beacon -	804
Botley Hill - - -	890*
Banstead - - -	576
Shooter's Hill - -	446
Hanger Hill - -	230
King's Arbour - -	118
Hampton Poorhouse -	86
St. Ann's Hill - -	240
Bagshot Heath - -	463
Dean Hill - - -	539
Beacon Hill - -	690
Old Sarum - -	266
Nine Barrow Down -	642
Highclere - - -	900
Wingreen - - -	941
Motteston Down - -	698*
Bow Hill - - -	702*
Portsdown Hill - -	447*

150. *Table of the mean Terrestrial Refractions.*

Between	Mean Refraction.
Banstead and Shooter's Hill -	$\frac{1}{7}$ of the contained arc.
St. Ann's Hill and Hampton Poorhouse	$\frac{1}{8}$
Brightling and Beachy Head -	$\frac{1}{8}$
Beachy Head and Fairlight Down -	$\frac{1}{10}$
Dunnose and Butser Hill - -	$\frac{1}{10}$
Highclere and Butser Hill -	$\frac{1}{11}$
Butser Hill and Hind Head -	$\frac{1}{11}$
Beachy Head and Chanctonbury Ring	$\frac{1}{11}$
Highclere and Hind Head -	$\frac{1}{11}$
Rook's Hill and Dunnose - -	$\frac{1}{12}$
Leith Hill and Hind Head -	$\frac{1}{12}$
Bagshot Heath and St. Ann's Hill -	$\frac{1}{12}$
Dean Hill and Beacon Hill -	$\frac{1}{12}$
St. Ann's Hill and Banstead -	$\frac{1}{12}$
Dunnose and Nine Barrow Down -	$\frac{1}{12}$
Leith Hill and Crowborough Beacon	$\frac{1}{12}$
Rook's Hill and Hind Head -	$\frac{1}{13}$
Rook's Hill and Butser Hill -	$\frac{1}{13}$
Dunnose and Dean Hill - -	$\frac{1}{13}$
Dean Hill and Wingreen - -	$\frac{1}{13}$
Brightling and Fairlight Down -	$\frac{1}{13}$
Leith Hill and Chanctonbury Ring	$\frac{1}{13}$
Leith Hill and Shooter's Hill -	$\frac{1}{13}$
Brightling and Crowborough Beacon	$\frac{1}{13}$
Hanger Hill and Banstead -	$\frac{1}{13}$
Hanger Hill and St. Ann's Hill -	$\frac{1}{13}$
Leith Hill and Banstead - -	$\frac{1}{13}$
Beacon Hill and Wingreen -	$\frac{1}{14}$

Between	Mean Refraction.
Rook's Hill and Chanctonbury Ring	$\frac{1}{11}$ of the contained arc.
Nine Barrow Down and Wingreen	$\frac{1}{14}$
Leith Hill and Ditchling Beacon -	$\frac{1}{16}$
Mean of all the above, nearly -	$\frac{1}{14}$
Leith Hill and the Horizon -	$\frac{1}{15}$
Rook's Hill and the Horizon -	$\frac{1}{18}$
Nine Barrow Down and the Horizon	$\frac{1}{15}$

Remarks.

151. The height of the ground at the station on St. Ann's Hill, (149.) is 240 feet; but in the table, p. 180, it is 321 feet: this very great disagreement, however, principally arises from the variableness in the terrestrial refraction. At Hampton Poorhouse, *when the instrument was at the same height above the ground*, the difference in the elevations of the ground at St. Ann's Hill appears to have been no less than 9' 28", (p. 181). General Roy took $\frac{1}{10}$ of the contained arc for the effect of refraction, and considered the height of St. Ann's Hill, when deduced from that of the station near Hampton Poorhouse, as more accurate than could be obtained by way of the station at the Hundred Acres. But, previous to the Survey in 1787, he found by the barometer, that the station on St. Ann's Hill was 200 feet higher than the Thames at Shepperton; and he added 33 feet for the descent to low water at the sea; the sum is 233 feet, agreeing nearly with our determination.

We take the height of Butley Hill (890 feet) a mean of 900,885,885, which the observations at Leith Hill, Banstead, and Crowborough Beacon respectively produce, by making use of $\frac{1}{13}$ of the contained arcs for refraction: this height of the ground exceeds that deduced from the table, p. 179 (880 — 21 = 859) by 31 feet: but we are not certain of its being nearer the truth: only it may be remarked, that between the several stations from High Nook to Botley Hill, in the same table, the mean refractions are very great.

From the reciprocal observations at Leith Hill, Banstead, and Shooter's Hill, the height of the last station is 446 feet, which is the same, in fact, as that obtained in the following manner. General Roy found by levelling, that the floor of the upper story of the Bull Inn at Shooter's Hill was 444 feet above the Gun Wharf at Woolwich; and he allowed 22 feet for the fall to low water at the sea; the sum is 466 feet. In 1794, we levelled from the Inn to the Station, and found the latter 21 feet lower than the floor, which taken from 466, there remains 445 feet for the Station's height.

Notwithstanding this consistency, and also that in the height of St. Ann's Hill, found by different methods, it is evident from the observations at Dunnose, Rook's Hill, and Butser Hill, that relative heights deduced from elevations, or depressions, cannot always be depended upon to less than about 10 feet, even supposing those heights are the means of two or three independent results, except, perhaps, reciprocal observations were made exactly at the same time. The very great difference in the observed elevations of St. Ann's Hill, proves that no dependance can be placed on single observations. But that was not the only instance; for, at the station on Rook's Hill, we found the depression of the ground at Chanctonbury Ring, vary from 1′ 41″ to 2′ 30″. The observations, however, on which the tables are founded, were made in close cloudy days, or toward the evenings, when the tremulous motion in the air is commonly the least.

It has been conjectured, that the variations in terrestrial refraction, depend on the changes in the atmosphere indicated by the barometer and thermometer: this, however, cannot be the case when the rays of light pass near the earth's surface for any considerable distance. M. De la Lande, in his Astronomy (Art. *Terrest.*

Ref.), remarks, that the mountains in Corsica are sometimes seen
from the coasts of Genoa and Provence, but at other hours on the
same days, they totally disappear, or are lost as it were in the sea.
And the late General Roy frequently mentioned an instance of
extraordinary refraction, which himself and Colonel Calderwood
observed on Hounslow Heath, when they were tracing out the base.
Their levelling telescope at King's Arbour was directed towards
Hampton Poorhouse, where a flagstaff was erected at the end of
the base; this for a long time they endeavoured in vain to discover, till at last, very unexpectedly, it suddenly started up into view,
and so high it seemed to be lifted, that the surface of the ground
where it stood became visible. This will appear the more extraordinary, when it is considered, that a right line drawn from the
eye at King's Arbour to the other end of the base, would pass 8 or
9 feet below the surface of the intermediate ground near the Duke
of St. Alban's Park. The following is still more singular. " I ob-
" served," says Mr. Dalby, " what seemed to me a very uncom-
" mon effect of terrestrial refraction, in April, 1793, as I went from
" Freshwater Gate, in the Isle of Wight, towards the Needles.
" Soon after you leave Freshwater Gate, you get on a straight and
" easy ascent, which extends 8 or 9 miles; a mile, or perhaps a
" mile and an half beyond this to the westward, is a rising ground,
" or hill; and it is to be remarked, that its top and the aforesaid
" straight ascent, are nearly in the same plane: now in walking
" towards this hill, I observed that its top (the only part visible)
" seemed to dance up and down in a very extraordinary manner;
" which unusual appearance, however, evidently arose from unequal
" refraction, and the up-and-down motion in walking; but when
" the eye was brought to about a feet from the ground, the top of
" the hill appeared totally detached, or lifted up from the lower
" part, for the sky was seen under it. This phænomenon I re-
" peatedly observed. There was much dew, and the sun rather

" warm for the season, consequently a great evaporation took place
" at that time." Here, and also on Hounslow Heath, the rays of
light passed near the earth's surface a great way before they arrived
at the eye ; and it is more than probable, that moist vapours were
the principal cause of the very unusual refractions : the truth of
which conjecture seems to be verified by the following circumstance. In measuring the base on Hounslow Heath, we had driven
into the ground, at the distance of 100 feet from each other, about
30 pickets, so that their heads appeared through the boning telescope to be in a right line : this was done in the afternoon. The
following morning proved uncommonly dewy, and the sun shone
bright ; when having occasion to replace the telescope, we remarked that the heads of the pickets exhibited a curve, concave
upwards, the farthermost pickets rising the highest ; and we concluded they were not properly driven, till in the afternoon, when
we found that the curve appearance was lost, and the ebullition in
the air had subsided.

The new raised earth about the gun at King's Arbour, prevented
a very accurate measurement of the height of the instrument above
the point of commencement of the base; and therefore two opportunities only presented themselves for determining the actual terrestrial refraction ; namely, at the ends of the base of verification.
From the depression taken at Beacon Hill, the refraction was 98";
but the elevation of Beacon Hill, observed at the lower end, near
Old Sarum, gives 50". These deductions, perhaps, cannot be
deemed very conclusive ; because, as they depend on the difference
in the vertical heights of the ends of the base, every 2 inches of
error in that difference will produce an error of about 1" in the
computed refraction. We shall close this article with the *data*
whence those refractions were obtained.

At Beacon Hill, the top of the flagstaff near Old Sarum was depressed 42' 6".

At the other end of the base, near Old Sarum, the top of the flagstaff at Beacon Hill was elevated 38′ 42″.

The axis of the telescope at Beacon Hill was 15 inches above, and the top of the flagstaff 91 inches above the point where the mensuration began. Near Old Sarum it was 28 inches higher, and the top of that flagstaff 95 inches above where the base terminated. This end (109.) is 429.48 feet lower than the other. Lastly, the value of the base is 6′ of a degree very nearly.

N. B. In the plan of the triangles (Pl. XX.), the line from the station near the Four Mile-stone to Old Sarum, is drawn a little out of its true position, otherwise it would very nearly coincide with that which joins the former station and Dean Hill.

⊙

AN

ACCOUNT

OF THE

TRIGONOMETRICAL SURVEY

CARRIED ON IN THE

YEARS 1795, AND 1796,

BY ORDER OF THE MARQUIS CORNWALLIS,

MASTER GENERAL OF THE ORDNANCE.

BY

COLONEL EDWARD WILLIAMS,

AND

CAPT. WILLIAM MUDGE,

OF THE ROYAL ARTILLERY;

AND

MR. ISAAC DALBY.

Z z

AN

ACCOUNT, &c

Particulars relating to the Operations of the Year 1795.

158. In an early part of this season, from the necessity which existed of completing the Map of Kent for the Board of Ordnance, by order of the Master General, we had conceived that our former intentions, of continuing the Survey towards the west, would for the present be relinquished : as it was not imagined that the telescope of the small circular instrument, then in the hands of Mr. Ramsden, could be applied, with good effect, in observing staffs erected on very distant stations.

From the obvious importance, however, of adhering to the first resolution, it was determined that a trial should be made of the excellence of this instrument, in the construction of which extraordinary pains had been taken, by operating with it in Kent, and using it for those purposes to which, if the object before spoken of had not been in view, the great theodolite would have been necessarily applied.

This smaller theodolite, therefore, as a substitute, was in May taken into Kent by Mr. Dalby, and Mr. Gardner chief draughtsman in the Tower ; the former being acquainted with the stations in the series of 1787.

On a reference to the account of 1794, it will be seen, that a

Z z 2

station was chosen near Lulworth, and observed both from Nine
Barrow Down and Black Down. It was also intended to be observed from Bull Barrow; by which means, instead of the great
triangle formed by the stations Black Down, Nine Barrow Down,
and Bull Barrow, we should have had two smaller ones. This,
however, it was now found could not be done, as a signal house
had been erected near the station at Lulworth, subsequent to the
operations in 1794, which prevented that spot from being afterwards seen at Bull Barrow : but no consequences very injurious can
have arisen from the impracticability of making use of this station
in the manner originally proposed, since the stations formerly
chosen in Portland, with which that of Lulworth was also intended
to connect, have not been visited with the instrument. The stations
in that island were selected with a view of observing from them,
and Charton Common, some point in the vicinity of Torbay, which
might be a proper station in the series intended to be carried along
the coast. Such a situation, however, could not be conveniently
found, as the view of Devonshire from Charton Common is much
intercepted by trees and other obstacles ; and it would have been
highly improper to shorten the side between Pilsden Hill and the
coast, by choosing a station more remote from the latter than
Charton Common.

As from an inspection of the plan of the triangles annexed to
this account, a doubt may be entertained as to the propriety of
carrying on so very extensive a series from the short side connecting the stations on Black Down and Mintern Hill ; it must be
observed that, admitting the necessity of adopting Bull Barrow
for a station, those on Pilsden and Mintern Hills were naturally
chosen ; the first, because it connected with Dumpdon (a station
that could not be dispensed with) ; and the second, because it was
the point most remote from Black Down, being on the brow of
the high land overlooking the general surface of Somersetshire.

To connect with the station formerly chosen near Maiden Brad
ley, two others were selected whilst the party were at Bull Barrow ; one on Ash Beacon near Sherborne, and the other on the
Quantock Hills. Both these have very commanding views, and
will hereafter easily unite with any stations which may be chosen
to the northward.

From Bull Barrow, the instrument was successively taken to the
following stations, before any other new ones were chosen, viz.
Mintern, Pilsden, and Charton Common ; and whilst the party
were at the latter, nearly all the stations were selected in Devonshire. In the choice of these, much difficulty occurred, as the face of
this county is particularly unfavourable for operations of this kind.
Around Honiton and Chard, there are several small ranges of
hills, nearly of an equal height, running in parallel directions.
Near the former are three thus circumstanced ; viz. Hembury
Fort, Combe Raleigh, and Dumpdon. From the first and second
of these, the station on Charton Common is not visible ; and it is
from the last only, that both Pilsden and the Quantock Hills can
be seen. This station, however, has a disadvantage : Combe
Raleigh, which is to the west of it, takes off all view round Tiver-
ton and Silferton ; so that it became indispensibly necessary to
select a spot on the northern extremity of Dartmoor, called Cawsand Beacon.

To those who are acquainted with the interior of Dartmoor, it
will be unnecessary to assign the reason for not having chosen any
station towards its centre. It may be sufficient to observe, that
two spots were found on its circumference, which render the want
of it trifling in its consequences.

Independent of the stations to which, as we have before observed,
the instrument was taken this year, the following were visited, viz.
Dumpdon, Little Haldon, Furland, and Butterton. From the latter, the party returned to London in the month of October.

153. *Angles taken in the Year* 1795.

At Bull Barrow.

Between	°	′	″	Mean.
Mintern Hill and Black Down - -	46	54	33 34.75 34	} 34
Black Down and Nine Barrow Down -	84	31	22.25 24	} 23.25
Nine Barrow Down and Wingreen -	93	33	0.5 32 59.75	} 0.25

At Mintern Hill.

Bull Barrow and Black Down -	101	39	30 31.25	} 30.5
Black Down and Pilsden - -	68	30	45.75 47	} 46.5

On Charton Common.

Little Haldon and Dumpdon - -	68	12	49.75 51.75 52.75	} 51.25
Dumpdon and Pilsden - -	93	54	36.25 37.5 38	} 37.25
Pilsden and Black Down - -	47	39	17.5 19.25	} 18.5

On Pilsden Hill.

Mintern and Black Down - -	44	37	51.5 52.5 53 54.25 55.5	} 53.25
Black Down and Charton Common -	105	5	27.75 26 26	} 26

Between	°	'	"	Mean
Charton Common and Dumpdon -	47	32	0.25 ⎫ 1.25 ⎬ 1.25 2.5 ⎭	

At Dumpdon.

	°	'	"	Mean
Charton Common and Little Haldon	86	39	7 ⎫ 7.25 8.5 ⎬ 8.25 8.75 9.25 ⎭	
Little Haldon and Cawsand Beacon	35	7	6.5 ⎫ 6.75 ⎬ 7.25 8.25 ⎭	
Pilsden and Charton Common -	98	33	22 ⎫ 22.25 22.25 ⎬ 22.75 23 23.5 23.5 ⎭	

At Little Haldon.

	°	'	"	Mean
Furland and Rippin Tor - -	84	58	42 ⎫ 42.5 43 ⎭	
Rippin Tor and Cawsand Beacon -	29	30	9.25 ⎫ 11 ⎬ 10.5 11 ⎭	
Dumpdon and Charton Common -	25	8	0.75 ⎫ 1.25 2 ⎭	
Dumpdon and Furland -	143	52	32.75 ⎫ 33 ⎬ 33.25 34 ⎭	

At Furland.

	°	'	"	Mean
The Bolt Head and Butterton -	53	15	34.25 ⎫ 35 35.75 ⎭	

Between	°	′	″	Mean.
Butterton and Rippin Tor	-	43	98	4 5.25 } 4.5
Rippin Tor and Little Haldon	-	39	24	36.75 37.75 } 37.25

At Butterton.

	°	′	″	Mean.
Rippin Tor and Furland - -	74	21	56 56.5 57.25 58 58.5 } 57.25	
Furland and the Bolt Head -	63	47	50.75 50.75 } 50.75	
The Bolt Head and Kit Hill -	127	37	36.5 36.75 } 36.5	
Maker Heights and Kit Hill -	42	11	38.75 38.75 } 38.75	
Maker Heights and Carraton Hill -	35	30	28 28.75 29.75 } 28.75	

Particulars relating to the Operations of the Year 1796.

154. By referring to Art. 109, it will be perceived that stones were sunk in the ground at the extremities of the base of verification on Salisbury Plain. To render these points permanent, two iron cannon (selected from among the unserviceable ordnance in Woolwich Warren) were, towards the end of February, sent to Salisbury, and in the beginning of March inserted at the ends of the base. The same methods were adopted for the purpose of fixing these cannon in their proper positions, as those made use of when similar *termini* were sunk in the ground on Hounslow Heath. This operation having been completed on the 10th of March, the

instrument was shortly after carried to Kit Hill, in Cornwall; a station, like that on Bindown, chosen rather for the purpose of a secondary, than a principal place of observation.

It would be tedious, and perhaps unnecessary, to enumerate the names of all the stations selected this year, as many of them do not form any part of the series now given to the public. We shall, therefore, confine ourselves to such remarks on the subject as may serve to abridge this article.

We have before stated, that a station was chosen on Cawsand Beacon, the northern extremity of Dartmoor, for the purpose of connecting with Dumpdon. It should have been observed, that to the westward of the former eminence, and near it, there is a hill considerably higher, which, in point of situation, has many advantages, but which cannot be made use of on account of the ruggedness of its surface, which seems to render the carrying of the instrument to its top almost impossible. From this circumstance, and similar impediments, which the high lands remote from the circumference of Dartmoor offer to our operations, it results, that the body of this moor cannot have any great triangles carried over it: such stations were therefore selected this year as may serve, in conjunction with others, to include this tract of country in a polygon of a small number of sides.

To make observations for the purpose of hereafter determining the longitude and latitude of the Lizard, was a principal object in this year's operations; and as this headland seems to offer itself as very convenient for a station, it will be right to assign our reasons for not having chosen one upon it.

As no other spot but Hensbarrow Beacon could be found in that part of Cornwall proper for a station, it became necessary to fix on the Deadman, or Dodman, for another point in the series. From this place no part of the land within four miles of the Lizard can be seen, as the high ground about Black Head, which is to the

3 A

eastward of the latter, is nearly in a line between them, and is also much higher than both. It will be perceived, however, that no evil can result from the want of such a station, as the light-houses and the naval-signal-staff at the Lizard, have been intersected from several stations. The precise spot on which Mr. Bradley made his observations in the year 1769, for ascertaining the longitude and latitude of this headland, was pointed out by the person having the care of the light-houses, who well remembered the common particulars relating to his operations : such measurements were made from the light-houses to this spot, as may enable us, at a future period, to compare the results from the *data* afforded by the trigonometrical operation, with those deduced from the astronomical observations made by the above gentleman. It may be also mentioned, that angles were at the same time taken at the western light-house and signal-staff, for the purpose of finding the situation of the Lizard Point.

We are now to speak of the most important business performed this year ; that of making observations to determine the distance of the Scilly Isles from the Land's End.

To do this as accurately as possible, it became necessary to find stations affording the longest *base*. The hill near *Rosemergy*, called the *Watch*, and the station near St. Buryan, are certainly the most advantageous places, because all the islands can be seen from both ; but we could not avail ourselves of the former, as difficulties almost insuperable would have attended an attempt to get the instrument upon it. Another station was therefore selected on Karnminnis, near *St. Ives*; a spot as well situated as the place spoken of, provided all the islands could be seen : this, however, does not prove to be the case, *St. Martin's Day-Mark* being the only object in the Scilly Islands visible from Karnminnis.

From the stations near the Land's End (Sennen and Pertinney), as well as that above mentioned (St. Buryan), St. Agnes' Light-house, and two objects in St. Mary's, were observed ; and as the means by which all their distances are determined, except those of the Day-Mark, from the shortness of the bases (which were, however, the longest that could be found) are exceptionable, it will be right to mention, that while we were engaged in that part of the operation now spoken of, the air was so unusually clear, that we could sometimes, with the telescope of the great theodolite, discover the soldiers at exercise in St. Mary's Island.

Under this article, it will be convenient to state, that we have endeavoured to find some spot to the westward, on which a base might be measured. Had we been fortunate in this respect, it undoubtedly would be eminently advantageous : as those triangles, now extended to the Land's End, would, in that case, be verified in some part of the new series. In Devonshire and Cornwall, however, no place has been discovered by any means fit for the purpose ; so that our communicating this work, under the circumstances attending it, is a matter of necessity.

In the present and former seasons, such stations were selected and observed, as were judged to be proper for the future use of the small instrument ; and as we had experienced, in the early stage of this Survey, much delay and disappointment from the white lights not being always seen when fired on distant stations, we have since substituted lamps and staffs in their stead. The operations of the present year were continued till October, when the party returned to London.

155. *Angles taken in the Year 1796.*

At Kit Hill.

Between	°	′	″	Mean.
Butterton and Maker Heights -	48	36	45 / 47.75	}46.5″

3 A 2

Between		°	′	″	Mean.
Maker Heights and Bindown	-	53	21	13.75	"
Carraton Hill and Bindown	- -	50	45	31	

On Maker Heights.

Lansallos and Carraton Hill	-	48	39	54.75	} 54.75
				54.75	
Carraton and Butterton	-	112	18	7.75	} 8.75
				9.75	
Butterton and the Bolt Head	-	45	54	35.75	} 37
				38.5	
Bindown and Carraton Hill	-	28	22	50.75	
Bindown and Kit Hill	- -	51	29	20.5	} 22.5
				24.5	
Kit Hill and Butterton	- - -	89	11	33.25	} 34.75
				36	

At the Bolt Head.

Maker Heights and Butterton	-	48	39	24.5	} 24.75
				24.75	
Butterton and Furland	- -	62	56	36.5	

At Rippin Tor.

Cawsand Beacon and Little Haldon		124	59	12.75	} 13
				13.5	
Little Haldon and Furland	-	55	36	39	} 40.5
				41.75	
Furland and Butterton	- -	61	59	59.25	} 59.5
				59.5	

On Cawsand Beacon.

Dumpdon and Little Haldon	- -	43	14	20	} 21.25
				22.5	
Little Haldon and Rippin Tor	- -	25	30	39.5	} 39.75
				40.25	

On Carraton Hill.

Between		°	′	″	Mean.
Maker Heights and Lansallos	-	67	12	20.25 23.5	} 21.75
Lansallos and Bodmin Down	-	56	21	16.75 17	} 17
Lansallos and Hensbarrow Beacon	-	37	28	57.75 58	} 58
Dutterton and Maker Heights	-	32	11	22.5 23.5	} 23
Kit Hill and Bindown	- -	91	45	22.5	
Maker Heights and Bindown	-	38	58	38.5	

On Bindown.

Lansallos and Carraton Hill	-	119	9	36.25
Carraton Hill and Kit Hill	- -	37	29	5.75
Kit Hill and Maker Heights	-	75	9	24.5

At Lansallos, or Polvinton Farm.

Deadman and Hensbarrow Beacon	-	52	34	2 2.5 5	} 3
Hensbarrow Beacon and Bodmin Down	45	1	10.75 12.75	} 11.75	
Bodmin Down and Carraton Hill	-	54	57	43.25 44.75	} 44
Carraton Hill and Bindown	- -	32	36	43.25	
Carraton Hill and Maker Heights	-	64	7	43.5 43.75 45.75	} 44.25

On Bodmin Down.

Carraton Hill and Lansallos	- -	68	40	57.75	
			41	0.75	} 59
			40	58.5	

Between	°	′	″	Mean.
Lansallos and Hensbarrow Beacon -	67	59	27.5 28	} 27.75

On Hensbarrow Beacon.

	°	′	″	
Carraton Hill and Lansallos -	42	32	8.5	
Bodmin Down and Lansallos -	66	59	21.75 25	} 23.25
Lansallos and Deadman - -	71	13	35 35.25 35.5	} 35.25
Deadman and St. Agnes' Beacon -	77	20	28.5 28.75 31.5	} 29.5

On St. Agnes' Beacon.

	°	′	″	
Hensbarrow Beacon and Deadman -	34	31	17 21 23	} 20.25
Deadman and Karnbonellis - -	75	51	53 53.75	} 53.25
Karnbonellis and Karnminnis -	57	46	31 31.5	} 31.25

On Karnminnis.

	°	′	″	
St. Agnes' Beacon and Karnbonellis	32	30	0.25 0.25	} 0.25
Karnbonellis and St. Buryan -	111	53	15.5 16.5	} 16
St. Buryan and Pertinney - -	19	48	16.75 17 20.75	} 18

At St. Buryan.

	°	′	″	
Karnminnis and Karnbonellis -	41	43	45.25 45.5 45	} 45.25

Between		°	′	″	Mean.
Pertinney and Karnminnis	- -	52	31	27.5 27.5	}27.5
Sennen and Pertinney	- - -	75	36	11 11.75 12	}11.5

At Sennen.

Pertinney and St. Buryan	- -	36	39	18.5 19.25	}18.75

On Pertinney.

Karnminnis and St. Buryan	- -	113	40	15.25 16	}15.5
St. Buryan and Sennen	- -	67	44	30.5 31.25	}31

At Karnbonellis.

St. Buryan and Karnminnis	- -	26	22	59.25 59.5	}59.25
Karnminnis and St. Agnes' Beacon	-	89	43	27.25 28.75 31.25	}29
St. Agnes' Beacon and the Deadman		78	16	39.75 40.5 43	}41

On the Deadman, or Dodman Point.

Karnbonellis and St. Agnes' Beacon	-	25	51	24.5 24.75	}24.75
St. Agnes' Beacon and Hensbarrow Beacon	63	8	12.5 13.75	}13
Hensbarrow Beacon and Lansallos	-	56	12	22.5 22.75	}22.75

156. *Situations of the Stations.*

Mintern or *Revel's Hill.* This station is in Dorsetshire, and situated on Revel's Hill, which is not far from Mintern. It is 17 feet N. E. from the corner of the hedge.

Pilsden. This station is also in Dorsetshire, and near Broad-windsor. The point is on the S. E. corner of the old parapet.

Charton Common. The station is in the field adjoining to, and also to the westward of the Common, and is about two miles from Lyme : it is 50 yards from the eastern hedge, and may be easily found, as Black Down is only visible from that spot, being seen between two trees.

Dumpdon ; about three miles N. E. of Honiton. The station is 10 feet northward of the hedge of the plantation, and nearly on the highest part of the hill.

Little Haldon ; near Teignmouth, in Devonshire. The station is 80 yards from the *Direction Post,* and in a line with it and the Obelisk on *Great Haldon.*

Cawsand Beacon ; near South Zeal. The station is about 200 feet north of the Karn, or great heap of stones.

Rippin Tor. This station is also on Dartmoor, and about 5 miles from Ashburton. The point is mid-way between the two heaps of stones.

Furland ; a field near the turnpike-gate between Brixen and Dartmouth. The station is near the stone, erected in the middle of the field.

Butterton. The station is 45 feet S. W. of the Karn on the hill called by this name, and about 1 mile from Ivy Bridge.

The Bolt Head. The station is on the spot called *White Soar,* above the Bolt ; it is 95 feet in the line produced northward from the west side of the signal-house, and about 90 feet from the nearest corner of it.

Maker Heights. This spot is near Cawsand, and the station is 45 feet from the great flag-staff, in the line produced from Statten Battery passing by the side of the staff.

Kit Hill, near Callington. The station is on the S. W. bastion of a work similar to an Indian fortification.

Carraton Hill. This station is about 4 miles north of Liskeard ; and the point 150 yards south of the highest Karn on the top of the hill.

Bindown, near Looe. The station is about 50 yards eastward of the barrow on this hill.

Lansallos. The station is in a field belonging to *Polvinion Farm,* which is near that town. The point is 159 feet from the western bank, and $90\frac{1}{2}$ from the southern one.

On Bodmin Down. The station 120 yards south of the high road, and about a quarter of a mile east of the turnpike gate. The point is in the centre of a remarkable ring.

Hensbarrow Beacon, near St. Roach. The station is on the top of the barrow.

The Deadman, or *Dodman Head.* The station is about 40 feet south of the bank, and nearly 100 yards to the east of the entrance into the inclosure.

St. Agnes' Beacon. The station is on the southern brow of the beacon, and about 80 yards from the tower.

Karnbonellis. The station is 90 yards south of the northern Karn, or heap of stones. The hill called *Karnbonellis* is near *Porcillis.*

Pertinney. The station is in the middle of the ring on its top. This hill is about 2 miles eastward of *St. Just.*

Sennen. This station is in the north-west corner of a field belonging to Mr. Williams. The field may be easily found, as there

3 B

is no other spot near the town of Sennen, from which the Long ship's Light-house, Pertinney, and St. Buryan, can be seen.

Karnminnis, near St. Ives. The station on the top of this hill, may be found from the following measurements:

		Feet	In.		
The station from 3 large	⎰	8	8	from the south	⎱
moor-stones, south of the	⎰	11	0	—— north	⎱ stones.
the hedge.	⎱	14	1	—— west	⎰

St. Buryan. The station is in a field adjoining the town, and by the side of the *Penzance* road. It is 84½ feet from the stile, and 48 feet from a large stone in the northern hedge. This stone is 81 feet from the stile ; the Station, this stone, and Chapel Karnbury, being in a right line.

157. *Calculation of the Sides of the great Triangles, carried on from the Termination of the former Series, along the Coasts of Dorsetshire, Devonshire, and Cornwall, to the Land's End. Pl. XXI.*

Distance from Wingreen to Nine Barrow Down, 130224.4 Feet (Triang. xxvi. Art. 117.)

No. of triangles.	Names of the stations.	Observed angles.	Diff.	Spherical excess.	Error.	Angles corrected for calculation.	Distances.
XLIII.	Wingreen Bull Barrow Nine Barrow Down	54 29 36.5 93 33 0 1 31 57 25.5	—0.4 —0 91 —0 4	″	′	54 29 36 93 33 59 31 57 25	Feet.
		180 0 2.25		1.72	+0.53		
	Bull Barrow from	{ Wingreen Nine Barrow Down				— — — — — —	69058 100213
XLIV.	Black Down Nine Barrow Down Bull Barrow	56 30 18 75 38 58 19 25 84 31 23 25	—0 53 —0 89 —0.57			56 30 18 5 38 58 19 84 31 22.5	
		180 0 1.25		1.99	—0.74		
	Black Down from	{ Nine Barrow Down Bull Barrow				— — — — — —	126782 85103.8

No. of triangles	Names of the stations	Observed angles	Diff.	Spherical excess	Error	Angles corrected for calculation	Distances
XLV.	Mintern	101 59 30.5	−0.36			101 59 30	Feet.
	Bull Barrow	46 54 34	−0.09			46 54 33.5	
	Black Down	31 15 57.5	−0.11			31 15 56.5	
		180 0 2		0.59	+1.41		
	Mintern from { Bull Barrow				•	− − −	42653.4
	{ Black Down				•	− − −	59730
XLVI.	Pilsden	44 37 53.85	−0.29			44 37 53	
	Mintern Hill	68 30 46.5	−0.36			68 30 46	
	Black Down	66 51 21.85	−0.36			66 51 21	
		180 0 1		1	−0.01		
	Pilsden from { Mintern Hill				•	− − −	78177
	{ Black Down				•	− − −	79110.7
XLVII.	Charton Common	47 39 18.5	−0.10			47 39 18.5	
	Black Down	27 15 16	−0.21			27 15 16	
	Pilsden	105 5 16	−0.60			105 5 15.5	
		179 59 50.5		0.88	−1.38		
	Charton Common from { Black Down				•	− − −	103345
	{ Pilsden				•	− − −	49100.3
XLVIII.	Dumpdon	38 33 22.85	−0.13			38 33 22.85	
	Pilsden	47 31 1.25	−0.14			47 31 1	
	Charton Common	93 54 37.25	−0.36			93 54 36.75	
		180 0 1.25		0.66	+0.59		•
	Charton Common from { Dumpdon				•	− − −	49016.3
	{ Pilsden				•	− − −	78459.3
XLIX.	Little Haldon	25 8 1.15	−0.43			25 8 1	
	Charton Common	68 12 51.25	−0.48			68 12 51	
	Dumpdon	86 39 8.5	−0.78			86 39 8	
		180 0 1		0.66	+0.34		•
	Little Haldon from { Charton Common				•	− − −	136353
	{ Dumpdon				•	− − −	126831
L.	Cawsand Beacon	43 14 31.85	−0.57			43 14 30	
	Dumpdon	35 7 7.25	−0.64			35 7 7	
	Little Haldon	101 38 33.75	−1.93			101 38 33	
		180 0 2.25		3.12	−0.87		
	Cawsand Beacon from { Dumpdon				•	− − −	181334
	{ Little Haldon				•	− − −	106508

* This angle (104.) is considered to be nearly 2″ in defect, and has been augmented for calculation accordingly : It was observed under circumstances less favourable, than those which attended the observations made on Pilsden, and Charton Common.

No. of triangle	Names of the stations	Observed angles	Diff.	Spherical excess	Error	Angles corrected for calculation	Diameters
				"	"	° ' "	Feet.
LI.	Rippin Tor	124 59 13	—0.08			124 59 11.75	
	Cawsand Beacon	15 30 39.75	+0.01			15 30 38.75	
	Little Haldon	19 30 10.5	+0.05			19 30 9.5	
		180 0 3.25		0.69	+2.56		
	Rippin Tor from { Cawsand Beacon					— — —	64080.5
	Little Haldon					— — —	55988.7
LII.	Furland	39 24 37.25	—0.36			39 24 17	
	Little Haldon	84 58 43	—0.44			84 58 42.75	
	Rippin Tor	55 36 40.5	—0.15			55 36 40.25	
		180 0 0.75		0.96	—0.21		
	Furland from { Little Haldon					— — —	78776
	Rippin Tor					— — —	87851
LIII.	Furland	43 38 4.5	—0.38			43 38 4	
	Rippin Tor	61 59 59.5	—0.38			61 59 59.25	
	Butterton	74 21 57.25	—0.44			74 21 56.75	
		180 0 1.25		1.15	+0.1		
	Butterton from { Rippin Tor					— — —	61951
	Furland					— — —	80547.8
LIV.	Bolt Head	61 56 36.5	—0.41			61 56 35.25	
	Furland	53 15 35	—0.38			53 15 34.75	
	Butterton	63 47 50.75	—0.43			63 47 50	
		180 0 2.25		1.23	+1.02		
	Bolt Head from { Furland					— — —	81151
	Butterton					— — —	72479.8
LV.	Maker Heights	45 54 37	—0.42			45 54 37.5	
	Bolt Head	48 39 24.5	—0.53			48 39 24.5	
	Butterton	85 25 58	—0.59			85 25 38	
		179 59 59.5		1.29	—1.79		.
	Maker Heights from { Bolt Head					— — —	100591
	Butterton					— — —	78768.8
LVI.	Maker Heights	112 18 6.75	—1.09			112 18 6	
	Butterton	35 30 28.75	—0.17			35 30 29	
	Carraton Hill	32 11 23	—0.10			32 11 23	
		180 0 0.5		1.36	—0.86		
	Carraton Hill from { Butterton					— — —	131676
	Maker Heights					— — —	62000.3

No. of triangles.	Names of the stations.	Observed angles.	Diff.	Spherical excess.	Error.	Angles corrected for calculation.	Distances.
LVII.	Lanvallos	64 7 44.25	—0 44			64 7 44	Feet.
	Maker Heights	48 39 56.75	—0 36			48 39 56.5	
	Carraton Hill	67 12 21.75	—0 43			67 12 21.5	
		180 0 0.75		1.24	—0.49		
	Lanvallos from { Maker Heights					— — —	84631.4
	Carraton Hill					— — —	68929.7

By the latter triangle we get the distance from Lanvallos to Carraton Hill 68929.7 feet; which being obtained from the least number of triangles, we shall make use of in the calculations of the sides farther to the westward. The same conclusion, however, is nearly obtained by making the computations pass through the triangles connected with Kit Hill and the station on Bindown.

LVIII.	Kit Hill	48 36 46.75	—0.26			48 36 46.75	
	Butterton	42 11 38.75	—0.20			42 11 38.75	
	Maker Heights	89 11 34.5	—0.75			89 11 34.5	
		180 0 0		1.21	—1.21		
	Kit Hill from { Butterton					— — —	100969
	Maker Heights					— — —	67822.3
LIX.	Bindown	75 9 24.5	—0 22			75 9 24.25	
	Maker Heights	51 29 22.5	—0.17			51 29 22.25	
	Kit Hill	53 21 13.75	—0 22			53 21 13.5	
		180 0 0.75		0.70	+0.05		
	Bindown from { Maker Heights					— — —	56194.8
	Kit Hill					— — —	54902.7
LX.	Carraton Hill	91 45 22.5				91 45 23	
	Kit Hill	50 45 31				50 45 31	
	Bindown	37 29 5.75				37 29 6	
		179 59 59 25		0.42	—1.17		
	Carraton Hill from { Kit Hill					— — —	33437
	Bindown					— — —	42554.4
LXI.	Lanvallos	32 36 43 25				32 36 42 25	
	Bindown	119 9 36 25				119 9 35 25	
	Carraton Hill	28 13 43.25				28 13 42.5	
		180 0 2.75		0.33	+2.42		
	Lanvallos from Bindown					— — —	37335.3

By the last triangle we get the distance from Lanvallos to Carraton 68932 feet. We shall, however, as before observed, use the distance between those stations as derived from the LVII triangle.

No. of triangles.	Names of the stations.	Observed angles.	Diff.	Spherical excess.	Error.	Angles corrected for calculation.	Distances.
		° ′ ″		″	″	° ′ ″	Feet.
LXII.	Lansallos	54 57 44	—0.16			54 57 44	
	Carraton Hill	56 21 17	—0.27			56 21 17	
	Bodmin Down	68 40 59	—0.30			68 40 59	
		180 0 0		0.82	—0.82		
	Bodmin Down from { Carraton Hill					— — —	60581.7
	Lansallos					— — —	61597.8
LXIII.	Hensbarrow Beacon	66 59 83.25	—0.13			66 59 22.25	
	Bodmin Down	67 59 27.75	—0.21			67 59 26.75	
	Lansallos	45 ı 11.75	—0.19			45 ı 11	
		180 0 2.75		0.63	+ 2.12		
	Hensbarrow Beacon from Bodmin Down					— — —	47357.4

By this last triangle, the distance from Hensbarrow Beacon to Lansallos is found to be 62044.8 feet, and by the following triangle

LXIV.	Hensbarrow Beacon	42 32 8.5	—0.20			42 32 8	
	Carraton Hill	37 28 58	—0.18			37 28 57.5	
	Lansallos	99 58 55.75	—0.19			99 58 54.5	
		180 0 2.25		0.99	+ 1.26		
	Hensbarrow Beacon from Carraton Hill					— — —	100416

We get 62044.7 feet for the same distance.

LXV.	Deadman	56 12 22.75	—0.25			56 12 22.5	
	Lansallos	52 34 3	—0.24			52 34 2.5	
	Hensbarrow Beacon	71 13 35.25	—0.35			71 13 35	
		180 0 1		0.82	+ 0.18		
	Deadman from { Lansallos					— — —	70686.8
	Hensbarrow Beacon					— — —	59284.3
LXVI.	St. Agnes' Beacon	34 31 20.25	—0.31			34 31 19.25	
	Hensbarrow Beacon	77 20 29.5	—0.54			77 20 28.75	
	Deadman	68 8 13	—0.63			68 8 12	
		180 0 2.75		1.32	+ 1 43		
	St. Agnes' Beacon from { Hensbarrow Beacon					— — —	97084.8
	Deadman					— — —	103066
LXVII.	St. Agnes' Beacon	75 51 53 75	—0.40			75 51 53.5	
	Deadman	25 51 24.75	—0.30			25 51 25.25	
	Karnbonellis	78 16 41	—0.40			78 16 41.25	
		179 59 59 5		1.06	—1.56		
	Karnbonellis from { Deadman					— — —	101084
	St. Agnes' Beacon					— — —	45461.5

No. of triangles.	Names of the stations.	Observed angles.	Diff.	Spheri- cal excess.	Error.	Angles corrected for calculation.	Distances.
LXVIII.	Karnminain - St. Agnes' Beacon Karnbonellis -	32 30 0.25 57 46 31.25 89 43 29	—0.23 —0.35 —0.53			32 30 0.25 57 46 31 89 43 28.75	Feet.
		180 0 0.5		0.77	—0.27		
	Karnminnis from { St. Agnes' Beacon Karnbonellis -					— — — — — —	84610.6 71578.3
LXIX.	St. Buryan - Karnbonellis - Karnminnis -	41 43 45.5 26 22 59.25 111 53 16	—0.03 —0.00 —0.65			41 43 45.25 26 22 59.25 111 53 15.5	
		180 0 0.75		0.75	0.0		
	St. Buryan from { Karnbonellis - Karnminnis -					— — — — — —	99786 47786.7
LXX.	Pertinney - Karnminnis - St. Buryan -	113 40 15.5 13 48 18 52 31 27.5				113 40 15 13 48 18 52 31 27	
		180 0 1		0.16	+0.84		
	Pertinney from { Karnminnis - St. Buryan -					— — — — — —	41497.7 12450.8
LXXI.	Sennen - St. Buryan - Pertinney -	36 39 18.75 75 36 11.5 67 44 31				36 39 18.25 75 36 11 67 44 30.75	
		180 0 1.25		0.08	+1.17		
	Sennen from { St. Buryan - Pertinney -					— — — — — —	19300 8 10199.9

Terrestrial Refractions, and Heights of the Stations.

158. Elevations and Depressions.

At Wingreen.

				′	″
The ground at Bull Barrow	-	-	depressed	6	9

At Nine Barrow Down.

The ground at Black Down	-	-	depr.	3	29
at Bull Barrow	-	-	-	elevated	1	25

At Black Down.

The ground at Nine Barrow Down	-	*depr.*	13 26
at Charton Common	- -	*depr.*	15 11
at Mintern Hill	- - -		0 0
at Bull Barrow	- - - -	*depr.*	1 16
at Pilsden ⁚	- - -	*depr.*	0 50

At Pilsden Hill.

The ground at Black Down	- - -	*depr.*	11 0
at Charton Common	- -	*depr.*	28 39
The horizon of the sea on the 6th of June, at 6 P. M. in a S. E. direction, nearly,		*depr.*	29 23

At Bull Barrow.

The ground at Wingreen	- -	*depr.*	4 53
at Mintern	- - -	*depr.*	6 5
at Black Down	- -	*depr.*	10 39

On Charton Common.

The ground at Black Down	- -,		0 0
at Pilsden	- - - -	*elev.*	20 37
at Haldon	- ⁚ -	*depr.*	3 33

At Dumpdon.

The ground at Pilsden	- - -	*depr.*	9 45
at Charton	- - - -	*depr.*	22 19
The bottom of the Karn, or heap of stones, (nearly on a level with the axis of the telescope) on Caw-sand Beacon - - -		*elev.*	4 42

At Haldon.

The ground at Charton	-	-	-	depr. 15 59
at Cawsand Beacon		-	-	elev. 24 3
at Rippin Tor		-	-	elev. 40 49
at Furland		-	-	depr. 16 6

The horizon of the sea on the 27th of July,
at 6 P. M. In a S. W. direction, nearly, depr. 27 24

On Cawsand Beacon.

The ground at Rippin Tor		-	-	depr. 17 42
at Haldon	-	-	-	depr. 98 57
The lamp at Dumpdon	-	-	-	depr. 29 56

N. B. The lamp was about 5½ feet from the ground.

On Rippin Tor.

The ground at Butterton	-	-	-	depr. 28 38
at Cawsand Beacon	-	-	-	elev. 8 3
at Haldon	-	-	-	depr. 49 31

At Furland.

The ground at Haldon	-	-	-	elev. 5 27
at Butterton	-	-	-	elev. 20 15

At Butterton.

The ground at Kit Hill	-	-	-	depr. 10 49
at Carraton	-	-	-	depr. 9 0
at Maker Heights	-	-	depr. 41 48
at the Bolt Head	-	-	-	depr. 41 48
at Furland	-	-	-	depr. 32 18
at Rippin Tor	-	-	-	elev. 13 54

3 C

On Maker Heights.

The ground at Lansallos	-	-	-	depr.	1 27
at Bindown	-	-	-	elev.	11 32
at Carraton Hill	-	-	-	elev.	27 36
at Kit Hill	-	-	-	elev.	29 45
at Butterton	-	-	-	elev.	30 35
at the Bolt Head	-	-	-	depr.	5 47

At the Bolt Head.

The ground at Maker	-	-	-	depr.	7 48
at Butterton	-	-	-	elev.	31 6

At Kit Hill.

The ground at Butterton	-	-	-	depr.	1 42
at Maker Heights	-	-	-	depr.	37 38
at Bindown	-	-	-	depr.	31 0
at Carraton Hill	-	-	-	elev.	9 38

On Carraton Hill.

The ground at Lansallos	-	-	-	depr.	41 18
at Hensbarrow	-	-	-	depr.	13 27
at Maker Heights	-	-	-	depr.	39 30
at Bindown	-	-	-	depr.	47 48
at Butterton	-	-	-	depr.	9 48
at Kit Hill	-	-	-	depr.	15 19

On Bindown.

The ground at Maker Heights	-	-	-	depr.	19 41
at Carraton Hill	-	-	-	elev.	41 20

The ground at Lansallos   - - - -   *depr.* 16 24
       at Hensbarrow   -   -   *elev.* 7 10
       at Kit Hill   - -   -   *elev.* 22 51

At Lansallos.

The ground at Carraton Hill   - - -   *elev.* 30 18
       at Bindown   - - -   *elev.* 10 46
       at Kit Hill   - - - -   *elev.* 15 27
       at Bodmin Down   - -   *elev.* 2 56
       at Hensbarrow   - - -   *elev.* 23 57
       at the Deadman   - -   *depr.* 11 39
       at Maker Heights   - -   *depr.* 10 30

On Bodmin Down.

The ground at Hensbarrow   - -   *elev.* 24 3
       at Lansallos   - - -   *depr.* 12 9

On Hensbarrow Beacon.

The ground at Carraton   - - - -   *depr.* 0 36
       at Lansallos   - - -   *depr.* 33 23
       at the Deadman   - -   *depr.* 42 8
       at St. Agnes' Beacon   - -   *depr.* 21 53
       at Bodmin Down   - - -   *depr.* 31 21

At the Deadman.

The ground at Karnbonellis   - - -   *elev.* 7 51
       at St. Agnes' Beacon   - -   *elev.* 0 19
       at Hensbarrow   - - -   *elev.* 33 30
       at Lansallos   - - - -   *elev.* 1 30

At St. Agnes' Beacon.

The ground at Karnminnis	-	-	-	*elev.* 2 11
at Karnbonellis	-	-	-	*elev.* 12 45
at Hensbarrow	-	-	*elev.* 8 8
at the Deadman	-	-	*depr.* 14 15

On Karnbonellis.

The ground at St. Agnes' Beacon	-	-	*depr.* 19 51
at Kamminnis	-	-	*depr.* 5 51
at St. Buryan	-	-	-	-	*depr.* 20 56
at the Deadman	-	-	-	*depr.* 22 18

On Karnminnis.

The ground at St. Buryan	-	-	-	*depr.* 32 9
at Karnbonellis	-	-	*depr.* 4 30
at St. Agnes' Beacon	-	-	*depr.* 14 12
at Pertinney Hill	-	-	*depr.* 9 14

At St. Buryan.

The ground at Karnminnis	-	-	*elev.* 24 32
at Karnbonellis	-	-	-	*elev.* 6 50

N. B. The axis of the telescope was about 5½ feet from the
ground at all the above stations. Also, 6″ must be applied as is
directed in Art. 146.

159. *Terrestrial Refractions.*

Between	Mean Refraction.
Maker and Kit Hill - · -	1/7 of the contained arc.
Butterton and Kit Hill -	1/2

Between	Mean Refraction.
Bindown and Lansallos	$\frac{1}{7}$ of the contained arc.
Nine Barrow Down and Black Down	$\frac{1}{10}$
Maker and Lansallos	$\frac{1}{10}$
Maker and the Bolt Head	$\frac{1}{10}$
Carraton Hill and Bindown	$\frac{1}{11}$
Karnbonellis and St. Buryan	$\frac{1}{11}$
Maker and Bindown	$\frac{1}{11}$
Hensbarrow and the Deadman	$\frac{1}{11}$
St. Agnes' Beacon and the Deadman	$\frac{1}{11}$
St. Agnes' Beacon and Karnminnis	$\frac{1}{11}$
Dumpdon and Cawsand Beacon	$\frac{1}{11}$
Haldon and Cawsand Beacon	$\frac{1}{11}$
Kit Hill and Bindown	$\frac{1}{11}$
Carraton Hill and Hensbarrow	$\frac{1}{11}$
Lansallos and the Deadman	$\frac{1}{11}$
Hensbarrow and St. Agnes' Beacon	$\frac{1}{11}$
Karnbonellis and Karnminnis	$\frac{1}{12}$
Furland and Haldon	$\frac{1}{12}$
Butterton and Maker	$\frac{1}{12}$
Butterton and Carraton Hill	$\frac{1}{12}$
Maker and Carraton Hill	$\frac{1}{12}$
Karnbonellis and the Deadman	$\frac{1}{12}$
Karnbonellis and St. Agnes' Beacon	$\frac{1}{12}$
Karnminnis and St. Buryan	$\frac{1}{12}$
Hensbarrow and Bodmin Down	$\frac{1}{12}$
Lansallos and Bodmin	$\frac{1}{12}$
Butterton and the Bolt Head	$\frac{1}{12}$
Haldon and Charton Common	$\frac{1}{12}$
Rippin Tor and Cawsand Beacon	$\frac{1}{13}$
Black Down and Bull Barrow	$\frac{1}{16}$
Black Down and Pilsden Hill	$\frac{1}{18}$

Between	Mean Refraction.
Black Down and Charton Common	$\frac{1}{14}$ of the contained arc.
Lansallos and Hensbarrow	$\frac{1}{12}$
Rippin Tor and Haldon	$\frac{1}{13}$
Dutterton and Furland	$\frac{1}{12}$
Dutterton and Rippin Tor	$\frac{1}{21}$
Kit Hill and Carraton	$\frac{1}{36}$
Pilsden Hill and Charton Common	$\frac{1}{18}$
Wingreen and Bull Barrow	$\frac{1}{11}$
Lansallos and Carraton Hill	$\frac{1}{14}$

Haldon and the Horizon of the Sea	$\frac{1}{11}$
Pilsden Hill and the Horizon of the Sea	$\frac{1}{11}$

160. *Table containing the Heights of the Stations.*

Stations.	Heights.
Black Down	817 feet.
Charton Common	582
Little Haldon	818
Rippin Tor	1549
Furland	589
Butterton	1203
Maker Heights	402
Bull Barrow	927
Mintern Hill	891
Pilsden Hill	934
Dumpdon	879
Cawsand Beacon	1792
Bolt Head	430
Kit Hill	1067
Bindown	658

Stations.			Heights.
Carraton Hill	-	-	1208 feet.
Lansallos	-	-	514
Bodmin Down	-	-	649
Hensbarrow Beacon	-	1026
The Deadman	-	-	379
St. Agnes' Beacon	-	599
Karnbonellis	-	-	822
Karnminnis	-	-	805
St. Buryan	-	-	415

Remarks, &c. on the foregoing Table.

161. The height of the ground at the station on Maker Heights 402 feet, was determined by levelling down to low-water mark, near the passage-house, below Mount Edgcumbe, on April 15, 1796. This, however, had been done several years before, by some officers of the Royal Engineers, who found it to be 401 feet. The height of the station near Dunnose, in the Isle of Wight, was also found by levelling ; of which an account is given in Art. 147. It therefore may be considered as the least exceptionable mode of procedure, to deduce the intermediate heights from both those stations ; for which purpose, the following comparison was made, exhibiting the height of the station on Charton Common, both ways.

						Feet.
Height of Nine Barrow Down (149.)			-	-		642
of Black Down	-	-	-	-	-	825
of Charton Common, *deduced from the height of*						
Dunnose	-	-	-	-	-	597
of Butterton	-	-	-	-		1201
of Rippin Tor	-	-	-	-		1545

Height of Furland	-	-	-	-	-	-	585
of Haldon		-	-	-	-	-	811

of Charton Common, *deduced from the height of*
Maker   -   -   -   -   -   568

deduced from that of Dunnose   597

difference   29

Those are the heights resulting directly from the observations. Now, supposing the difference, or the errors, to arise from the mean refractions, and those errors to be nearly the same between every two stations, we shall obtain the corrected heights in the following manner:

                       Feet.

Nine Barrow Down	$649 - 4 =$	638
Black Down	$825 - 8 =$	817
Charton Common	$597 - 15 =$	582
Butterton -	$1201 + 2 =$	1203
Rippin Tor -	$1545 + 4 =$	1549
Haldon -	$811 + 7 =$	818
Charton Common	$468 + 14 =$	582

                                           as in the table.

From those corrected heights, the others to the northward have been deduced. The heights to the westward of Butterton were determined from that of Maker. A mean of two or three results, by using $\frac{1}{11}$ of the contained arcs for refraction, is taken for the height of the station on Mintern Hill.

262. *Secondary Triangles, in which two Angles only have been observed. The first three intersected places were selected for interior Stations, on account of their commanding situations.*

Triangles.	Angles observed.	Distances of the stations from the intersected objects.	
	° ′ ″		Feet.
Pilsdon - Charton Common - Golden Cape	44 6 35 36 59 6	} Golden Cape - {	29848 34533
Rippin Tor - Cawsand Beacon - Great Haldon	68 2 28 41 22 57	} Great Haldon - {	54789 82829
Bolt Head - Maker Heights - Hemmerdon Ball	29 15 10 54 20 9	} Hemmerdon Ball {	82239 49464
Bull Barrow - Wingreen - Noil Windmill	109 12 19 33 45 11	} Noil Windmill {	63692 103255
Bull Barrow - Wingreen - Noil Steeple	22 4 38 111 10 59	} Noil - {	88420 35641
Bull Barrow - Wingreen - Holy Trinity Steeple, Shaftesbury	18 16 15 65 39 45	} Trinity Steeple {	63275 21772
Bull Barrow - Wingreen - St. Rumbold's Steeple, Shaftesbury -	15 45 15 46 55 34	} Rumbold Steeple {	56778 21104
Bull Barrow - Wingreen - Maypowder Steeple	129 15 18 12 31 19	} Maypowder - {	24199 86426
Bull Barrow - Wingreen - Stourhead House	44 25 52 88 31 14	} Stourhead House {	94319 66050

Triangles.	Angles observed.	Distances of the stations from the intersected objects.	
	° ′ ″		Feet.
Bull Barrow - Nine Barrow Down Mr. Frampton's Obelisk	32 25 49 27 41 1	}Frampton's Ob. {	56980 65662
Bull Barrow - Mintern - Mere Steeple -	97 43 51 58 1 14	}Mere - {	88095 108912
Bull Barrow - Mintern - Mrs. Thornhill's Obelisk -	68 44 5 47 19 3	}Thornhill's Ob. {	34902 44145
Bull Barrow - Mintern - Odcombe Steeple	20 37 56 143 59 47	}Odcombe - {	94589 56700
Bull Barrow - Mintern - D Milborne-port Steeple	52 41 35 77 1 36	}Milborne-port {	54098 44107
Bull Barrow - Mintern - D Lord Poulett's Warren House	7 39 0 132 19 30	}Warren House {	8829 49035
Black Down - Pilsden - Portland Light-house	143 32 28 16 12 4	}Light-House - {	63749 135775
Black Down - Pilsden - Naval-Signal-staff on Puncknoll	32 55 8 13 35 5	}Signal-staff - {	25615 59266
Black Down - Pilsden - House in Lambert's Castle	9 2 48 62 47 53	}Lambert's Castle {	74048 13091
Black Down - Pilsden - Lyme Cobb	26 0 41 92 54 15	}Lyme Cobb - {	90349 89815

Triangles.	Angles observed.	Distances of the stations from the intersected objects.
Pilsden Mintern Glastonbury Tor	64 47 55 78 12 22	}Glastonbury Tor { Feet. 127174 117551
Pilsden Charton Common Bridport Beacon, a Sea-mark	40 30 43 62 0 1	}Bridport Beacon { 44332 32616
Pilsden Charton Common Barn on the high land near Sidmouth	15 44 0 45 18 13	}Barn, Sidm. Hill { 39824 15191
Dumpdon Pilsden Naval-Signal-staff on Whitlands	50 52 11 40 22 12	}Signal-staff { 50832 60876
Dumpdon Pilsden Cothelstone Lodge, Quantock Hills	93 52 54 37 51 16	}Lodge { 64521 104901
Charton Common Dumpdon Lord Lisburne's Obelisk on Haldon	61 11 28 91 51 33	}Obelisk on Haldon { 127936 112161
Dumpdon Cawsand Beacon Sir J. de la Pole's Flag-staff, near Shute House	128 45 59 13 59 24	}Flagstaff { 72435 233619
Dumpdon Cawsand Beacon Honiton Steeple	64 18 8 4 0 39	}Honiton { 13650 175852
Dumpdon Cawsand Beacon St. Mary Ottery Steeple	34 20 21 12 27 16	}St. Mary Ottery { 53653 140835

3 D 2

Triangles.	Angles observed.	Distances of the stations from the intersected objects.		
				Feet.
Dumpdon - - Little Haldon - Funnel on Sir R. Palk's Tower, Haldon	17 20 53 69 7 37	} Palk's Tower	{	114716 98347
Cowsand Beacon Little Haldon - D North Bovey Steeple	7 9 50 10 38 19	} North Bovey	{	64319 43141
Little Haldon - Rippin Tor - - Eastern Karn, or heap of stones, on the high ground near Moreton Hampstead	34 8 28 66 14 23	} Eastern Karn	{	52099 91944
Little Haldon - Rippin Tor - - Western Karn, near Moreton Hampstead	37 24 5 69 24 30	} Western Karn	{	54751 35585
Little Haldon - Rippin Tor - Naval-Signal-staff at West Down Beacon	154 35 29 11 28 37	} Signal-staff -	{	46268 99715
Little Haldon - Rippin Tor - - Mr. Woodley's Summer House	5 43 59 81 44 20	} Summer House	{	55462 5598
Little Haldon - Rippin Tor - - Naval-Signal-staff, Berry Head, Torbay	99 46 2 42 35 24	} Signal-staff -	{	62040 90345
Little Haldon - Rippin Tor - - Brixen Steeple	91 52 49 48 37 47	} Brixen - -	{	66070 87993

Triangles.	Angles observed.	Distances of the stations from the intersected objects.	
			Feet.
Little Haldon -	67 8 45	}Ipplepen - {	42675
Rippin Tor - -	44 56 5		55677
Ipplepen Steeple			
Little Haldon -	20 40 42	}Three Barrow Tor{	81460
Rippin Tor - -	185 6 32		35163
Three Barrow Tor, Dartmoor			
Furland - -	71 56 33	}Brent Beacon	68727
Little Haldon -	51 46 15		83180
Ruins on Brent Beacon			
Butterton - -	17 4 21	}Chudleigh -	97302
Rippin Tor - -	136 27 46		41471
Chudleigh Steeple			
Butterton - -	3 37 11	}Signal-staff -	87314
Furland - -	140 5 47		8593
Naval - Signal - staff at Coleton, near Froward Point			
Butterton - -	39 15 6	}Signal-staff -	89129
Furland - -	78 26 47		57561
Naval-Signal-staff, Start Point			
Butterton - -	61 55 7	}Marlborough	64000
Furland - -	48 18 25	*Devon.*	75736
Marlborough Steeple			
Butterton - -	63 40 32	}Signal-staff -	72632
Furland - -	53 24 17		81084
Naval-Signal-staff, near the Bolt Head			
Butterton - -	18 0 46	}Mewstone -	62728
Maker - -	50 17 40		25213
Highest Part of the Mewstone			

Triangles.	Angles observed.	Distances of the stations from the intersected objects.	Feet.
Butterton - -	6 11 21	} Cupola, R. Hosp. {	68709
Maker Heights -	41 49 37		10508
Cupola of the Royal Hospital, Plymouth			
Butterton - -	8 58 35	} St. John's - {	85401
Maker Heights -	122 49 11		15856
St. John's Steeple			
Butterton - -	19 46 39	} Saltash - {	73708
Maker Heights -	75 36 25		25749
Saltash Steeple			
Butterton - -	5 36 20	} Penlee Beacon {	76972
Maker Heights -	96 23 55		7566
Penlee Beacon			
Butterton - -	39 1 33	} Plymstock - {	51259
Kit Hill - -	27 49 38		69143
Plymstock Steeple			
Butterton - -	48 3 55	} Statten Barn {	58906
Kit Hill - -	35 25 31		75599
Statten Barn			
Butterton - -	41 56 57	} Mount Batton {	62687
Kit Hill - -	37 8 33		68738
Mount Batton			
Butterton - -	39 56 31	} Flagst. Plym. Gar. {	59673
Kit Hill - -	34 45 12		67207
Flagstaff in Plymouth Garrison			
Butterton - -	37 21 59	} New Church Steep. {	58399
Kit Hill - -	33 0 38		65058
New Church Steeple at Plymouth			
Butterton - -	37 43 52	} Old Church Steep. {	59524
Kit Hill - -	34 3 59		65081
Old Church Steeple at Plymouth			

Triangles.	Angles observed.	Distances of the stations from the intersected objects.	Feet.
Butterton - - Kit Hill - - *West Chimney of the Governor's House, Plymouth Dock*	37 5 33 39 58 96	} Governor's House {	66558 62479
Butterton - - Kit Hill - - *Flagstaff in the Fort on Mount Wise*	37 6 53 40 43 48	} Flagstaff, Mount Wise	67374 62397
Butterton - - Kit Hill - - *Steeple of the Chapel, Plymouth Dock*	35 14 20 41 25 1	} Chapel, Ply. Dock {	68653 59874
Butterton - - Kit Hill - - *Flagstaff in St. Nicholas' Island*	41 40 8 38 38 52	} Flagstaff, St.Ni.Isl. {	64970 68097
Butterton - - Kit Hill - - *Obelisk at Crimbill Passage*	38 40 39 42 48 20	} Obelisk - {	69376 63809
Butterton - - Kit Hill - - *East Pinnacle on Mount Edgcumbe House*	40 29 28 42 49 3	} Mount Edg. House {	69096 66012
Butterton - - Kit Hill - - *Flagstaff on Maker Tower*	41 54 7 45 25 27	} Maker Tower {	72001 67507
Butterton - - Kit Hill - - *Naval-Signal-staff, near Maker Tower*	41 53 45 45 35 55	} Signal-staff - {	72207 67490
Butterton - - Kit Hill - - *Chestow Steeple*	12 40 29 138 21 13	} Chestow - -	198,522 45738

Triangles.	Angles observed.	Distances of the stations from the Intersected objects.	
	° ′ ″		Feet.
Butterton - -	40 34 1	} Stonehouse -	{ 58310
Carraton Hill - -	23 29 2		95162
Stonehouse Steeple			
Butterton - -	60 48 52	} Puslinch Obelisk	{ 38700
Carraton Hill -	16 41 16		117659
Obelisk at Puslinch			
Butterton - -	41 2 54	} Rame Head -	{ 84846
Carraton Hill -	39 30 40		87594
Rame Head			
Kit Hill - -	116 24 26	} Brent Tor -	{ 43421
Maker Heights -	24 3 10		95419
Brent Tor, near Lydford			
Kit Hill - -	11 30 56	} Block House -	{ 57984
Maker Heights -	46 26 51		15972
Flag-staff of the Block House, near Dock			
Kit Hill - -	4 9 42	} Rame -	{ 74547
Maker Heights -	141 4 43		8409
Rame Steeple			
Carraton Hill -	7 28 15	} Dock-yard Cha-	{ 78468
Maker Heights -	64 48 50	pel - -	11274
Steeple of the Chapel in the Yard, Plymouth Dock			
Carraton Hill - -	7 34 6	} Windmill at Dock	{ 79778
Maker Heights -	71 29 35		11080
Windmill at Plymouth Dock			
Carraton Hill - -	7 31 7	} Statten Battery	{ 97488
Maker Heights -	133 32 55		17199
Battery on Statten Heights			
Kit Hill - -	105 0 39	} St. Stephen's -	{ 44659
Carraton Hill - -	43 47 30	near Saltash.	62330
St. Stephen's Steeple			

Triangles.	Angles observed.	Distances of the stations from the intersected objects.	
Kit Hill - - Carraton Hill - St. Ive Steeple	29 11 14 / 47 42 54	St. Ive -	Feet 25990 16796
Kit Hill - - Carraton Hill - Callington Steeple	42 31 4 / 10 20 54	Callington -	7532 28336
Kit Hill - - Carraton Hill - Linkinborn Steeple	25 20 11 / 28 8 55	Linkinhorn -	19621 17798
Kit Hill - - Carraton Hill - D St Dominic Steeple	121 48 23 / 9 59 38	St. Dominic -	7776 98097
Kit Hill - - Carraton Hill - D South Petherwin Steeple	60 22 24 / 67 55 47	South Petherwin	39475 37027
Kit Hill - - Carraton Hill - South Hill Steeple	19 31 2 / 15 22 32	South Hill -	15493 19522
Kit Hill - - Carraton Hill - Lord Mount Edgcumbe's House, at Empercombe	108 14 2 / 48 46 11	House at Empercombe -	64348 81266
Kit Hill - - Carraton Hill - Northern Sea-Mark on the Hoe	59 59 7 / 42 59 43	Sea-Mark -	66387 87011
Kit Hill - - Bindown - St. Cleer Steeple	39 56 21 / 51 25 10	St. Cleer -	42991 35256
Carraton Hill - Bindown - The Highest part of Brownwilly	130 14 2 / 26 32 44	Brownwilly -	48221 89371

Triangles.	Angles observed.	Distances of the stations from the intersected objects.	
			Feet
Carraton Hill - Bindown - - Cheese Rings	138 42 49 7 21 53	} Cheese Rings {	9773 50300
Carraton Hill - Bindown - - Liskeard Steeple	18 2 57 17 6 59	} Liskeard - {	21739 22685
Carraton Hill - Bindown - - Duloe Steeple	18 6 21 84 32 47	} Duloe - - {	43403 13550
Carraton Hill - Bindown - - Menbeniot Steeple	9 16 26 14 32 34	} Menheniot - {	91502 13806
Carraton Hill - Bindown - - Landrake Steeple	43 17 41 75 46 11	} Landrake - {	47177 33376
Carraton Hill - Bindown - - Naval-Signal-staff at Nealand, near Pol- parrow	22 51 23 129 59 13	} Signal-staff - {	36203 71413
Carraton Hill - Lansallos - - Boconnock Steeple	25 5 53 35 41 57	} Boconnock - {	46079 33495
Carraton Hill - Lansallos - - Obelisk at Boconnock, (Lord Camelford's)	24 4 10 41 27 47	} Boconnock Ob. {	50139 30886
Carraton Hill - Lansall s - - Roach Rock	41 29 10 94 48 32	} Roach Rock - {	99410 66086
Carraton Hill - Lansallos - - Roacb Steeple	42 1 28 94 41 58	} Roach - {	100814 67314

Triangles.	Angles observed.	Distances of the stations from the intersected objects.
		Feet.
Lansallos - Hensbarrow Beacon *Helmen Tor*	21 84 34 46 16 45	}Helmen Tor - { 48412 24633
Lansallos - Hensbarrow Beacon *Mr. Tremaine's Summer House*	37 8 29 70 7 42	}Summer House { 61105 39231
Lansallos - Hensbarrow Beacon *Gorran Steeple*	45 34 10 72 3 29	}Gorran - - { 66624 50008
Lansallos - Hensbarrow Beacon *Naval-Signal-staff on the Deadman*	52 43 25 71 28 51	}Signal-staff - { 71136 59696
Lansallos - Hensbarrow Beacon *Gwineas Rocks*	51 21 9 60 17 27	} Gwineas Rocks, off Mevagissy { 57977 52133
Bodmin Down - Hensbarrow Beacon *Hendellion Steeple*	97 21 30 39 57 45	}Hendellion - { 44851 69455
Bodmin Down - Hensbarrow Beacon *The high Stone on St. Braeg Down*	48 38 46 55 1 58	}Stone, St. Braeg D. { 39924 36571
Bodmin Down - Hensbarrow Beacon *St. Dennis Steeple*	19 28 51 120 37 11	}St. Dennis - { 56722 15359
Bodmin Down - Hensbarrow Beacon D *Lansallos Steeple*	64 55 8 68 45 47	}Lansallos - { 61011 59285
Deadman - - Lansallos - D *St. Veep Steeple*	12 51 38 73 45 53	}St. Veep - - { 67986 15761

3 E 2

Triangles.	Angles observed.	Distances of the stations from the intersected objects.	
			Feet.
Lansallos - - Bodmin Down - D Lanlivery Steeple	26 19 35 33 51 19	}Lanlivery -	{ 39552 31486
Hensbarrow Beacon Deadman - D Gerrans Steeple	30 50 7 106 31 21	}Gerrans -	{ 83901 44858
Hensbarrow Beacon Deadman - St. Michael Carhayes D Steeple	13 56 6 43 10 53	}Carhayes -	{ 48309 17001
Hensbarrow Beacon Deadman - St. Kivern Steeple	31 21 22 128 53 52	}St. Kivern -	{ 136676 91426
Hensbarrow Beacon Deadman - Naval-Signal-Staff at Black Head	29 6 51 133 59 31	}Signal-staff -	{ 146770 99460
Hensbarrow Beacon Deadman - Windmill near Fowey	62 46 29 45 59 37	}Fowey Windmill	{ 45036 55677
Hensbarrow Beacon Deadman - Menabilly House	56 10 33 36 24 22	}Menabilly -	{ 35221 49300
Hensbarrow Beacon Deadman - Old Tower at Polruan	60 28 23 49 6 10	}Tower, Polruan	{ 47561 54749
Hensbarrow Beacon Deadman - Naval-Signal-staff at St. Anthony's Head	30 52 0 116 42 13	}Signal-staff -	{ 98759 56717
Hensbarrow Beacon St. Agnes' Beacon St. Columb Minor D Steeple	31 37 12 28 56 16	}St. Columb Minor	{ 53943 58448

Triangles.	Angles observed.	Distances of the stations from the intersected objects.	
Hensbarrow Beacon St. Agnes' Beacon D Peranzabulo Steeple	11 43 0 31 9 39	}Peranzabulo - {	Feet. 73829 28975
Hensbarrow Beacon St. Agnes' Beacon St. Eval Steeple	57 24 41 35 11 34	}St. Eval - {	56011 81884
Hensbarrow Beacon St. Agnes' Beacon Cubert Steeple	15 2 26 30 37 20	}Cubert - {	69141 25224
Hensbarrow Beacon St. Agnes' Beacon Flagstaff in Pendennis Castle	41 44 14 72 36 24	}Pendennis Castle {	101687 70938
Hensbarrow Beacon St. Agnes' Beacon Windmill near St. Mawes	42 11 25 61 3 38	}St. Mawes' Wind-{ mill -	87286 66985
St. Agnes' Beacon Karnminnis - Karnbury Castle	49 20 11 20 23 49	}Karnbury Castle {	91435 68417
St. Agnes' Beacon Karnminnis - Cupola of the Market House in Redruth	55 59 58 17 46 35	}Cupola in Redruth {	26903 73054
St. Agnes' Beacon Karnminnis - Camborn Steeple	30 57 7 21 45 40	}Camborn - {	39127 54696
St. Agnes' Beacon Karnminnis - Illugan Steeple	31 12 56 10 49 6	}Illugan - {	23718 65490
St. Agnes' Beacon Karnminnis - St. Paul Steeple	40 52 42 117 47 27	}St. Paul - {	110564 81794

Triangles.	Angles observed.	Distances of the stations from the intersected objects.	
	° ' "		Feet.
St. Agnes' Beacon Karnminnis - *Lord de Dunstanville's House*	20 40 33 10 47 12	} Dunstanville House - {	30339 57237
St. Agnes' Beacon Karnminnis - D *Gwinear Steeple*	21 40 44 40 30 44	} Gwinear - {	62144 35390
St. Agnes' Beacon Karnminnis - *Mr. Kneil's Obelisk, near St. Ives*	53 24 45 88 37 48	} Mr. Kneil's Ob. {	79889 39346
St. Agnes' Beacon Karnminnis - *Highest of the Rocks called the Cow and Calf*	141 53 34 20 9 34	} Cow and Calf Rocks - {	94050 169450
St. Agnes' Beacon Karnbonellis - *St. Erme Steeple*	91 43 5 42 10 34	} St. Erme - {	44668 66303
St. Agnes' Beacon Karnbonellis - *St. Allen Steeple*	98 13 52 35 41 11	} St. Allen - {	36816 62462
St. Agnes' Beacon Karnbonellis - *Ludgvan Steeple*	44 12 31 105 49 41	} Ludgvan - {	87573 63169
Karnminnis - Karnbonellis - *Windmill near the Lizard*	41 26 59 93 31 22	} Lizard Windmill {	104413 69440
Karnminnis - Karnbonellis - *Grade Steeple*	40 7 0 160 25 15	} Grade - {	110762 72566
Karnminnis - Karnbonellis - *Ruan Major Steeple*	38 32 27 97 30 19	} Ruan Major - {	102243 64256

Triangles.	Angles observed.	Distances of the stations from the intersected objects.	
	° ′ ″		Feet.
Karnminnis - Karnbonellis - *St. Hilary Steeple*	39 52 32 25 24 25	} St. Hilary - {	33808 50519
Karnminnis - Karnbonellis - *Castle Dennis (Mr. Rogers's Tower)*	10 0 52 7b 13 53	} Castle Dennis {	69233 15749
Karnbonellis - St. Buryan - *Madern Steeple*	9 32 41 33 51 25	} Madern - {	80908 24081
Karnbonellis - St. Buryan - D *Perranutbno Steeple*	60 38 57 49 18 46	} Perranuthno - {	98552 44315
Karnbonellis - St. Buryan - D *Girnhove Steeple*	76 57 1 50 25 43	} Girnhove - {	46355 58583
Karnbonellis - St. Buryan - *Naval-Signal-staff, Park Loughs*	60 25 48 40 43 1	} Signal-staff - {	66344 88458
Pertinney - Karnminnis - *St. Buryan Steeple*	116 12 46 13 40 7	} St. Buryan - {	12751 48411
St. Buryan - Pertinney - *Chapel Karnbury*	23 28 57 58 34 54	} Chapel Karnbury {	10728 5009
St Buryan - Pertinney - *Naval-Signal-staff, St. Leven's Point*	75 36 7 67 31 4	} Signal-staff - {	20094 19169
St. Buryan - Pertinney - *Sennen Steeple*	69 21 10 68 58 0	} Sennen - {	17475 17520

Triangles.	Angles observed.	Distances of the station from the intersected objects.	
Sennen - - Pertinney - - Stone near the Land's End*	106 43 44 7 15 12	}Stone, Land's End{	Feet. 2791 21173
Sennen - - Pertinney - - Longship's Light-house	126 1 11 18 6 39	}Light-house - {	10717 27883

169. *Triangles for ascertaining the Distances of the Eddystone Light-house, from the Flagstaff of Plymouth Garrison, and the Rame-head.*

The ball on the lantern of the Light-house was observed from the stations on Butterton, Kit Hill, and Carraton Hill; and as much uncertainty has heretofore existed, with respect to a knowledge of its true distance from any point in the neighbourhood of Plymouth, observations were made on various arcs of the circle of the Instrument at the two first stations.

The triangles are the following.

Triangles.	Angles observed.	Distances of the stations from the intersected objects.	
Butterton - - Kit Hill - - Eddystone Light-house	66 46 21 64 27 46	}Light-house - {	Feet. 121159 123399
Butterton - - Carraton Hill - Eddystone Light-house	60 5 31 55 52 41	}Light-house - {	121158 126863

* A large rough stone on the right hand, near the path, about 300 yards before you get down to the rocks at the Land's End.

With the distance of the Eddystone Light-house from Kit Hill, and also that of the Flagstaff in Plymouth garrison from the same station, we find the distance from the Light-house to the Flagstaff = 73061 feet;[*] the observed angle being 29° 42′ 34″: and, computing with the *data* obtained from the last triangle, and the third in page 394. with the observed angle at Carraton Hill = 16° 22′ 1″, we get 49435 feet for the distance of the Eddystone Light-house from the building on Rame-head. It may be proper to observe, that the Eddystone Light-house is nearer to the Rame-head than to any other point on the coast.

164. *Triangles for ascertaining the Situations of the Lizard Light-houses, and the Lizard Point.*

Distance from Karnbonellis to Pertinney 101474 feet.

Triangles.	Angles observed.	Distances of the stations from the intersected objects.	
			Feet.
Karnbonellis - Pertinney - - *Eastern Light-house*	78 49 28 42 56 51	Eastern Light- house -	{ 81923 117097
Karnbonellis - Pertinney - - *Western Light-house*	78 40 5 43 0 58	Western Light- house -	{ 81348 116921
Karnbonellis - Pertinney - - *Naval-Signal-staff*	78 8 57 42 28 45	Signal-staff -	{ . 79635 115408
Karnbonellis - St. Buryan - - *Naval-Signal-staff*	71 7 19 45 30 56	Signal-staff -	{ 79645 105873

[*] On referring to the late Mr. Smeaton's Narrative of the Building of the Eddystone Light-house, it will be found, that, from a trigonometrical process, founded on two

From the two last triangles we obtain 79640 feet for the mean
distance between the Lizard Signal-staff and the station on Karnbonellis. Computing with this distance, and also that from the
Western Light-house to the same station, with the observed angle
0° 31' 8", we get 1857 feet for the distance between those objects.

For the purpose of ascertaining the situation of the Lizard Point,
two angles in the following triangle were observed with a sextant,
viz.

Naval-Signal-staff	-	77 4
Western Light-house	-	60 50
Lizard Point.		

These, with the computed distance from the Signal-staff to
the Light-house, give the distance of the Lizard Point from
the {Signal-staff 2419}{Light-house 2700} feet. Hence, the distance of the point
from the station on Karnbonellis is 81085 feet, the angle at that
station, between the Lizard Point and Western Light-house, being
1° 59' 47". With respect to the means by which the situation of
the spot on which Mr. Bradley erected his observatory in 1769,
may hereafter be determined, it will be readily understood from
the following diagram; where E is the Eastern Light-house, W
the Western Light-house, F the Signal-staff, P the Lizard Point,

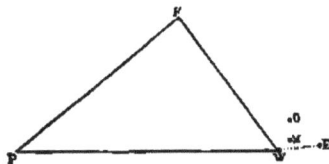

bases measured on the Hoe, among other deductions, he concluded the distance between
the above objects was 73464 feet: being 403 greater than the distance found by the
above computation.

and O the place of the Observatory. The distance between the spot O, and M,* the place where his meridian mark was fixed, we measured and found = 580 feet ; M being 24 feet north of the line joining the centres of the Light-houses.

165. *Distances of the Day-Mark, St. Agnes' Light-house, and other Objects in the Scilly Isles, from particular Stations in the West of Cornwall.* Pl. XXI. †

Observations made at Karnminnis.

Between				Mean.
The station at St. Buryan and the Day-Mark	39	3	22½ ⎫ 22½ ⎬ 23¾ ⎭	23

At St. Buryan.

Karnminnis and the Day-Mark - -	129	52	22 ⎫ 22¼ ⎬	22
Pertinney and St. Agnes' Light-house -	83	59	51½ ⎫ 50 ⎬	51
Flagstaff of the Fort in St. Mary's and Karnminnis - - - - }	134	39	45¾ ⎫ 45 ⎬	45½
Windmill in St. Mary's and Pertinney -	84	23	53½ ⎫ 53 ⎬	53¼

At Pertinney.

St. Agnes' Light-house and Karnminnis -	92	6	20 ⎫ 21½ 21½ ⎬ 23¾ ⎭	21¾

* The person spoken of in Art. 154. as having the care of the Light-houses, pointed out this spot.

† The triangles for this purpose are laid down in a detached position, to shorten the plan.

Between

Day-Mark and Karnminnis - - 148 11 8⅓} 9¼
                                      10¼}

Flagstaff in St. Mary's and St. Buryan - 93 47 18

Windmill in St. Mary's and St. Buryan - 92 26 33

At Sennen.

Day-Mark and Pertinney - - - 145 20 8½} 9½
                                      10 }

St. Agnes' Light-house and Pertinney - 152 43 24 } 24½
                                          24½}

From those observations, result the following triangles, when the necessary corrections are applied for reducing the observed angles to those formed by the chords, *viz.*

Triangles.	Observed angles corrected.	Distances of the stations from the intersected objects.	
	° ′ ″		Feet.
Karnminnis	39 3 24	}Day-Mark -	{190985
St. Buryan - -	129 52 19		{156796
Day-Mark			
Karnminnis	25 15 8	}Day-Mark -	{190989
Pertinney - -	148 11 5		{154551
Day-Mark			
Sennen - -	145 20 7	}Day-Mark -	{137526
Pertinney - -	30 24 7		{154568
Day-Mark			
Sennen - -	152 48 20	}Scilly Light-house	{164010
Pertinney - -	24 21 55		{182199
St. Agnes' or the Scilly Light-house			
St. Buryan - -	83 59 51	}Scilly Light-house	{183096
Pertinney - -	92 6 22		{182915
St. Agnes' Light-house			

Triangles.	Observed angles corrected.	Distances of the stations from the intersected objects.	
			Feet
St. Buryan Pertinney Windmill in St. Mary's	83 24 53 92 26 33	}Windmill -	{172189 171209
St. Buryan Pertinney Flagstaff of the fort in St. Mary's	82 8 18 93 47 18	}Flagstaff -	{174890 173626

The distance from the Day-Mark to Karnminnis, as obtained from the first triangle, is 190985 feet, and by the second, 190989 feet, which differs only 4 feet from the former; and by the second and third triangles, the difference of the distances from the same object, to the station on Pertinney, is 17 feet; which, allowing for the shortness of the bases, must be considered as trifling. We may presume, therefore, that had not the Day-Mark been seen from Karnminnis, but from Sennen and Pertinney alone, the observations from which the angles of the third triangle are derived, would have afforded the means of computing the distance with sufficient precision. In like manner the fourth and fifth triangles seem to prove, that the observations made to St. Agnes' Light-house were sufficiently accurate, as there is a difference only of 16 feet between the distances of the Light-house from Pertinney. The ball on the top of the Light-house was the object always observed; and the Day-Mark being pyramidical, we had the means of making the observations at the different stations to the same point of that building.

166. *Distances of the Objects in the Scilly Isles, (intersected from the Stations in the West of Cornwall) from Sennen Steeple; the Stone near the Land's End; and the Longship's Light-house.*

As the observations made to the Day-Mark, and St. Agnes' Light-house, may be supposed sufficiently accurate; and the ball on the top of the Longship's Light-house was also observed under favourable circumstances, it will be proper to apply the corrections to the horizontal angles, in order to obtain those formed by the chords. Taking, therefore, Pertinney as the angular point, and computing with the following *data, viz.*

Station on Pertinney from $\left\{\begin{array}{l}\text{Day-Mark} & = 75455\frac{1}{2} \\ \text{Scilly Light-house} & = 182807 \\ \text{Longship's Light-house} & = 27883\end{array}\right\}$ Feet. And

the angle at Pertinney, augmented for calculation, between the Longship's Light-house and $\left\{\begin{array}{l}\text{the Day-Mark} & = 11°\ 17'\ 30'' \\ \text{Scilly Light-house} & = 6\ 15\ 25\end{array}\right\}$ We get the distance of

the Longship's Light-house from $\left\{\begin{array}{l}\text{the Day-Mark} & = 127646\ \text{feet} = 24.14 \\ \text{Scilly Light-house} & = 154519\ \text{feet} = 29.06\end{array}\right\}$ Miles.

Calculating also, with the distances of the two other objects in the Scilly Isles, and likewise those of Sennen Steeple, and the Stone near the Land's End from Pertinney, with the included angles at the same station, we get

		Feet.	Miles.
Sennen Steeple from	Day-Mark	= 139521	= 26.43
	Scilly Light-house	= 166255	= 31.49
	Flagstaff in St. Mary's	= 157912	= 29.95
	Windmill in St. Mary's	= 155299	= 29.41
Stone near the Land's End from	Day-Mark	= 135343	= 25.63
	Scilly Light-house	= 162100	= 30.7
	Flagstaff in St. Mary's	= 153744	= 29.11
	Windmill in St. Mary's	= 151138	= 28.63

Of the Scilly Isles, Menawthen is the nearest to the Land's End, being about $1\frac{7}{8}$ miles eastward of the Day-Mark; and the cluster of rocks, called the Bishop and his Clerks, the most remote, being $3\frac{1}{2}$ miles west of St. Agnes' Light-house. Combining, therefore, the above particulars with those distances, we may conclude, that the nearest part of the Scilly Isles is about 24.7 miles from the Land's End, and the farthest nearly 34.

Account of a Trigonometrical Survey carried on in Kent, in the Years 1795, and 1796, with the small circular Instrument. Pl. XXII.

167. Particulars respecting the Instrument.

The instrument used in this Survey was made by Mr. Ramsden; and is about half the size of his large theodolite, or circular instrument, with which we take the horizontal angles, but nearly similar to it in all its parts; consequently a very brief description will be sufficient.

The most material variations in the construction are,

1. The levelling or feet screws. These are below that horizontal movement which serves to direct the lower telescope to any particular object. By this position of the screws, the horizontal circle being once made level, the whole instrument may be moved round without disturbing its horizontality; the levelling screws remaining stationary during that operation, which cannot be done in the large instrument, because the screws are carried round with it.

2. The diameter of the horizontal circle being only half that of the larger one, it follows, that the space between any two dots on the limb, gives double the number of minutes that are contained in the same space on the greater circle: on this account, each revolution in the micrometer screw in the microscope answers to 2′; and the circle on the microscopic micrometer being divided into 60 parts, each division becomes equal to 2″, but for the convenience of notation, they are numbered at every 5th, with 10, 20, &c. to 50, the 60th being marked 1, to denote 1′: the number of seconds

then commencing as before, the whole revolution becomes s'. The revolutions are counted by means of notches on one side of the field in the microscope, in the same manner as in those of the large instrument.

9. This instrument not being intended for determining the direction of the meridian, a vertical semicircle for directing the telescope to the pole star became unnecessary; yet some apparatus was required, whereby small elevations or depressions from the horizon might be ascertained with a tolerable degree of precision. For this purpose, a moveable index, of about four inches long, is made to turn on the horizontal axis of the upper telescope, and so constructed, that by means of a finger screw, it can be fixed firmly in any position. The lower end of this index is furnished with a steel micrometer screw, having a circle on its head, divided into 100 parts, for shewing the fractional parts of a revolution, while other divisions, on a chamfered edge of the index which marks the fractional parts, give the number of revolutions made by the micrometer screw.

The method of finding the value of a revolution of the micrometer head in parts of a degree, &c. was as follows:

A rod, 14 or 16 feet long, was placed horizontally about three quarters of a mile off, and the angle subtended by its ends measured with the instrument in the usual way: the rod was then set up perpendicular at the same place, and the cross wires in the telescope directed to one of its extremities: the telescope was then moved in the vertical plane, by means of the micrometer screw, till the cross wires coincided with the other extremity. In this manner, by counting the number of revolutions, &c. necessary to move the telescope from one position to the other, an angle was measured vertically with the micrometer screw, equal to the former horizontal angle. From repeated trials, the value of a revolution was found equal to 10' 27".

[411]

This instrument, on account of its portable size, may very readily be taken to the tops of steeples, towers, &c. and is, therefore, extremely well adapted to the uses for which it was intended.

Stations. 1795.

168. *Folkstone Turnpike,* the station in 1787.

Hawkinge, about three quarters of a mile from Folkstone Turnpike. This station was chosen for the purpose of having a view of the Belvidere in Waldershare Park, which cannot be seen from the station of 1787.

Dover Castle.

Paddlesworth; about 400 feet from the station of 1787. This new spot was selected, because Hardres Steeple is not visible from the old station.

Waldershare; on the Belvidere in the Earl of Guilford's Park.

On *Ringswold,* or *Kingswould Steeple.*

On a sand hill near the sea shore, between Deal and Ramsgate: this station is denominated *Shore.*

Near *Mount Pleasant House,* Isle of Thanet.

On a rising ground near *Wingham.*

On *Chislet* Steeple.

In *Beverley Park,* near Canterbury.

On Upper *Hardres* Steeple.

Triangles for determining the Distances of the Stations.

169. As the station on the Keep of Dover Castle, in 1787, was directly over the steps of the Turret, a new point was chosen about 6½ feet from the former, where the instrument could stand conveniently: this new point is about 9.8 feet farther from Folkstone

3 G

Turnpike, and 1 foot farther from Paddlesworth, than the point marking the old station.

Feet.

Dover Castle from Folkstone Turnpike 31556 } page 146.
        from Paddlesworth   42563 }

Hence, the new point on Dover Castle from Folkstone Turnpike -   -   -   -   31558.8 } feet.
        from Paddlesworth   42564 }

In order to obtain the distance between Waldershare and Dover
Castle from those new sides, or distances, the three angles of the
following triangle were very carefully taken:

		°	′	″	°	′	″	
{	Dover Castle -	9	49	16	9	49	15	} for compu-
{	Folkstone Turnpike	36	6	31	36	6	30	} tation.
{	Hawkinge -	140	4	16	140	4	15	}
		180	0	3				

The third angles of the two next triangles were not observed:

					°	′	″
{	Hawkinge -	-	-		44	23	30
{	Dover Castle -	-	-		73	53	44
{	*Waldershare* -	-	-		61	42	46
{	Dover Castle -	-	-		62	24	7
{	Paddlesworth (the station of 1787)				32	36	9
{	*Waldershare* -	-	-		84	59	44

By the two first triangles, Dover   Feet.
Castle from Waldershare -   23019.4 } 23020.5 mean dis-
From the latter -   -   -   23021.5 } tance.

And *Hawkinge* from { Dover Castle 28976
                      { Waldershare 31616

N. B. In all the following triangles, the angles at the stations,
or objects, denoted in *italics*, are supplemental, or were not observed. And it is also to be remarked, that whenever Paddlesworth is
mentioned hereafter, the *new station* is to be understood.

Names of stations.	Angles.	Distances.
		Feet.
Waldershare Paddlesworth Dover -	85 2 25 32 53 10 62 4 25	Paddlesw. from { Dover 42239 / Waldershare 37460
Waldershare Paddlesworth Hardres -	57 1 15 69 21 59 53 36 46	Hardres { Waldershare 43548 / Paddlesworth 39035
Dover - Waldershare Ringswold	66 46 45 57 57 24 55 15 51 180 0 0	Ringswold { Dover - 23745 / Waldershare 25743
Waldershare Ringswold Shore -	45 43 8 97 38 32 36 38 20	Shore { Waldershare 42755 / Ringswold - 30883
Mount Pleasant Shore - Waldersbare	40 53 17 111 8 27 27 58 16	Mt. Pleasant { Shore 30635 / Waldershare 60920
Mount Pleasant Wingham - Waldersbare	31 55 12 119 32 5 28 32 43	Wingham { Mt. Pleasant 33459 / Waldershare 37031
Mount Pleasant Chislet - Wingham -	38 32 17 79 25 36—35 62 2 8 180 0 1	Chislet { Mount Pleasant 30062 / Wingham - 21206
Hardres - Wingham - Waldersbare	52 46 14 69 29 1 37 44 55	Hardres from Wingham 39392
Wingham - Beverley Park Hardres -	50 4 0 75 0 0 54 56 4—0 180 0 4	Beverley Park { Wingham 33320 / Hardres 31215

170. *Secondary Triangles.*

Triangles.	Angles observed.	Distances of the stations from the intersected objects.	
			Feet.
Paddlesworth - Waldershare - *Barbam Windmill*	98 28 36 70 22 24	}Windmill - {	37289 24628
Dover - - Waldershare - - *St. Radigund's Abbey*	51 40 11 44 29 40	}Abbey - - {	16196 18160
Dover - - Waldershare - - *Hougham Steeple*	75 13 45 40 31 40	}Hougham · - {	16614 24726
Dover - - Waldershare - - *Gunston Steeple*	32 41 51 17 46 31	}Gunston - {	9111 16193
Dover - - Waldershare - - *St. Margaret's Steeple*	88 19 36 32 34 23	}St. Margaret's {	14144 20817
Hawkinge - - Waldershare - - *Elbam Windmill*	84 50 50 15 3 14	}Windmill - {	8335 31963
Dover - - Ringswold - - *South Foreland Light-house*	39 48 39 28 8 7	}Light-house - {	12081 16403
Waldershare - - Ringswold - - *Upper Deal Windmill*	17 10 7 109 11 7	}Windmill - {	28870 8718
Waldershare - - Ringswold - - *Upper Deal Chapel*	22 20 10 100 38 27	}Deal Chapel - {	30160 11663
Waldershare - Ringswold - - *Lower Deal Windmill*	19 1 31 110 21 19	}Windmill - {	31996 10857
Waldershare - Ringswold - *Deal Castle*	19 28 27 121 2 45	}Deal Castle - {	34689 13493

Triangles.	Angles observed.	Distances of the stations from the intersected objects.	
			Feet.
Waldershare - -	49 26 26	}Windmill - {	22109
Ringswold - -	57 41 19		17648
Norbourn Windmill			
Waldershare -	9 19 40	}Watch-house {	31917
Ringswold - -	125 28 3		7938
Watch-house near the sea shore			
Waldershare -	29 45 47	}Sandown Castle {	38185
Ringswold - -	111 20 13		20351
Sandown Castle			
Waldershare -	12 29 19	}Walmer - {	29491
Ringswold - -	115 33 51		7069
Walmer Steeple			
Waldershare -	15 35 53	}Ripple - - {	24209
Ringswold -	69 33 23		6947
Ripple Steeple			
Waldershare - -	20 45 23	}Waldershare - {	5656
Ringswold -	5 35 50		20552
Waldershare Steeple			
Waldershare - -	16 23 49	}Eastry - - {	25766
Shore - -	21 57 46		19448
Eastry Steeple			
Waldershare - -	35 10 6	}Ash - - {	35750
Shore - -	56 41 26		24639
Ash Steeple			
Waldershare -	28 29 39	}Minster - {	55782
Shore - -	109 15 30		27341
Minster Steeple			
Waldershare -	5 49 2	}Woard - - {	33548
Shore - -	19 37 24		9951
Woard Steeple			
Waldershare - -	13 35 31	}Sandwich - {	98505
Shore - -	59 30 36		10501
Sandwich, bigbest Steeple			

Triangles.	Angles observed.	Distances of the stations from the intersected objects.
		Feet.
Ringswold - Shore - - *Mongebam Steeple*	24 46 49 13 3 56	}Mongeham - { 11379 21098
Ringswold - - Shore - - *Norbourn Steeple*	35 9 0 25 59 2	}Norbourn - { 15450 20909
Ringswold - - Shore - - *Woodnessborough Steeple*	33 7 44 77 48 16	}Woodnessborough{ 32320 18071
Shore - - Mount Pleasant - *Ramsgate Windmill*	41 10 35 47 47 27	}Windmill - { 22695 20179
Shore - - Mount Pleasant - *St. Lawrence Steeple*	96 26 58 54 52 36	}St. Lawrence { 25064 18205
Waldershare - - Mount Pleasant - *Wingham Steeple*	32 2 55 31 1 14	}Wingham - { 35214 36259
Waldershare - - Mount Pleasant - *Goodneston Steeple*	31 12 40 17 58 32	}Goodneston - { 24841 41711
Mount Pleasant - Chislet - - *Birchington Steeple*	77 19 0 22 10 4	}Birchington - { 11500 29735
Mount Pleasant - Chislet - - *St. Nicholas Steeple*	19 36 3 21 19 41	}St. Nicholas - { 16690 15394
Mount Pleasant - Chislet - - *Stormouth Steeple*	16 56 56 33 29 54	}Stormouth - { 21519 11366
Mount Pleasant - Chislet - - *Reculver Windmill*	22 14 40 81 14 59	}ReculverWindm. { 30556 11703

Triangles.	Angles observed.	Distances of the stations from the intersected objects.	
			Feet.
Mount Pleasant - Wingham - - *South Reculver*	69 57 57 51 54 46	} South Reculver {	31012 87017
Mount Pleasant - Wingham - - *Hearne Windmill*	50 51 41 78 50 49	} Windmill - {	42669 33732
Wingham - - Waldershare - *Littlebourn Steeple*	102 34 17 11 3 35	} Littlebourn - {	7752 39442
Wingham - - Chislet - - *Blean Steeple*	58 30 34 88 52 9	} Blean - - {	39329 33544
Wingham - - Chislet - *Wickham Steeple*	59 11 7 24 25 37	} Wickham - {	8824 18926
Wingham - - Chislet - - *Ickham Steeple*	72 8 46 22 6 13	} Ickham - {	8001 20228
Wingham - - Beverley Park - *Bridge Windmill*	47 35 34 44 59 50	} Bridge Windmill {	25584 24628
Wingham - - Beverley Park - *Nackington Steeple*	33 27 20 68 29 54	} Nackington - {	31688 18776
Wingham - - Hardres - - *Chillendon Windmill*	80 53 7 21 53 16	} Windmill - {	15031 39811
Wingham - - Hardres - - *Preston Steeple*	122 1 10 8 3 28	} Preston - {	7220 43572
Wingham - - Hardres - - *Shottenden Windmill*	30 49 24 118 30 8	} Windmill - {	67736 39494

Triangles.	Angles observed.	Distances of the stations from the intersected objects.	
			Feet.
Hardres -	11 35 23	}St. Martin's Wind.{	22943
Beverley Park -	27 48 16		9881
St. Martin's Windmill			
Hardres -	12 11 37	}Harbledown - {	25289
Beverley Park -	39 25 35		8411
Harbledown Steeple			
Hardres -	17 29 59	}Sturry - - {	91691
Beverley Park -	84 9 53		9581
Sturry Steeple			
Waldershare -	24 29 21	}Canterbury Cath. {	54827
Hardres -	105 36 14		23597
Canterbury Cathedral			
Hardres -	40 45 34	}Windmill - {	19347
Paddlesworth -	27 23 18		27458
West-Stone-Street Wind-mill			
Hardres -	31 0 20	}Stelling Windmill {	14081
Paddlesworth -	15 9 20		27924
Stelling Windmill			

Triangles carried over another part of Kent in 1795.

171. On account of the high woody lands to the westward of Hardres and Paddlesworth, the triangles could not be extended in that direction, and therefore the following may be considered as a detached part of the Survey this year.

The Stations were,

> *Westwell Down,*
> *Wye Down,*
> *Brabourn Down,*
> , *Allington* or *Aldington Knoll,* the station in 1787.

Allington Knoll from Tenterden Steeple (triang. xix. p. 144), is 61777¼ feet. The centre of the top of Tenterden Steeple is about 4 or 4½ feet farther from Allington Knoll than the point marking the station in 1787; therefore the distance of the centre from Allington Knoll will be 61782 feet, which is used in the following computations; because, as a flagstaff of moderate height cannot be easily distinguished among the pinnacles at any considerable distance, it was thought it might be sufficiently accurate for the present purpose, to intersect the steeple itself.

179. *Triangles for determining the Distances of the Stations.*

Stations.	Angles.	Distances.	Feet.
Allington Knoll	61 37 46	Westwell D. from { Tenterden	58629
Westwell Down	68 0 16	{ Allington K.	51316
Tenterden	50 21 58		
Allington Knoll	34 37 37	Wye Down { Allington K.	37369
Westwell Down	45 54 19	{ Westwell D.	29562
Wye Down -	99 28 5—4		
	180 0 1		
Allington Knoll	96 15 23	Wye Down { Allington	37360
Wye Down -	54 19 24	{ Tenterden	75603
Tenterden	29 25 13		
Wye Down -	45 8 41	Westwell D. from Wye D.	29566
Westwell Down	113 54 35		
Tenterden	20 56 44		
Allington Knoll	116 49 40	Brabourn D. { Allington K.	26437
Brabourn Down	45 25 31	{ Tenterden	77397
Tenterden	17 44 49		
Allington Knoll	55 11 54	Brabourn D. { Westwell D.	42933
Brabourn Down	93 52 23	{ Allington K.	26415
Westwell Down	30 55 43		

173. Secondary Triangles.

Triangles.	Angles observed.	Distances of the stations from the Intersected objects.		
				Feet.
Wye Down Westwell Down *Ashford Steeple*	42 20 58 59 35 53	Ashford	- {	23922 10023
Wye Down Westwell Down *Brook Steeple*	86 44 28 15 18 43	Brook	- {	7983 30191
Wye Down Westwell Down *Willesborough Steeple*	60 6 18 45 28 29	Willesborough	{	21881 26607
Wye Down Westwell Down *Willesborough Windmill*	58 2 28 41 37 0	Windmill	- {	19916 25413
Wye Down Westwell Down *Kingsnorth Steeple*	58 20 46 65 40 7	Kingsnorth	- {	32498 30360
Wye Down Westwell Down *Shadoxhurst Steeple*	52 19 41 85 50 2	Shadoxhurst	- {	44118 31966
Wye Down Westwell Down *Kennington Steeple*	26 38 18 27 54 54	Kennington	- {	16989 16271
Wye Down Allington Knoll *Great Chart Steeple*	62 23 7 54 24 4	Great Chart	- {	34099 37083
Wye Down Allington Knoll *Westwell Steeple*	96 43 26 33 49 30	Westwell	- {	27384 48851
Westwell Down Allington Knoll *Pluckley Steeple*	97 22 43 20 53 1	Pluckley	- {	20768 57778
Westwell Down Allington Knoll *Eastwell Steeple*	37 55 0 7 17 0	Eastwell	- {	9168 44441

Triangles.	Angles observed.	Distances of the station from the intersected objects.
		Feet.
Westwell Down - Allington Knoll - Charing Steeple	146 22 23 5 24 0	}Charing - { 10211 60085
Westwell Down - Allington Knoll - Allington Sterple	3 15 4 57 34 51	}Allington - { 49609 3333
Brabourn Steeple - Allington Knoll - Lymne Steeple	34 50 49 75 59 12	}Lymne - - { 27443 16161
Brabourn Down - Allington Knoll - Mersham Steeple	33 12 51 45 9 19	}Mersham - { 19136 14784
Brabourn Down - Allington Knoll - Monks Horton Steeple	67 22 25 23 46 14	}Monks Horton { 10657 24405

Operations in 1796, with the small circular Instrument.

174. Stations.

Lydd Steeple ⎫
Allington Knoll ⎪
High Nook ⎬ Stations in 1787.
Fairlight Down ⎪
Goudhurst Steeple ⎪
Tenterden Steeple ⎭ (near the centre of the roof).

Westwell Down, the station in 1795.

Silver Hill, near Robertsbridge. The station is 22 yards S.W. of the Windmill.

Boughton Malherb Steeple.

175. *Triangles for finding the Distances of the Stations.*

Westwell Down from Tenterden Steeple = 58699 feet, (Art. 172.): this used in the following triangle,

Boughton Malherb	81 55 9
Westwell Down -	63 44 8
Tenterden - -	34 20 43

gives the distance from Boughton Malherb to Westwell Down 33409 feet. Also, from this last triangle and the next following, (using 54976.5 feet for the distance from Tenterden to Goudhurst, p. 143.),

Goudhurst -	52 5 44
Boughton Malherb	53 54 20
Tenterden - -	73 59 56

we get 33405 feet for the distance between the same stations: hence the mean, 33407 feet, may be taken for the true distance between Boughton Malherb and Westwell Down. From this latter triangle also, we obtain the distance from Boughton Malherb to Tenterden 53097.2 feet.

Triangles.	Angles.	Distances.	
			Feet.
Goudhurst -	65 29 7		
Silver Hill -	70 32 26	Silver Hill from Goudhurst	40043
Tenterden -	43 58 27		
Fairlight Down from Tenterden 71637.2 feet, (p. 144.)			
Fairlight Down	46 34 5		
Silver Hill -	82 25 8	Silver Hill from Fairlight D.	56174
Tenterden -	51 0 47		

By the two last triangles, we get 52472, and 52481 feet, for the distances of Tenterden from Silver Hill ; the mean of which, 52476.5, we shall hereafter use in determining the distances of the objects intersected from those stations.

For the distances of the stations in 1787, made use of in the following triangles, see Art. 57. The point marking the station on Tenterden Steeple in 1787, is considered as being too near the centre to make any reductions necessary for these computations. The greatest uncertainty in any of the distances, on this account, can be only about 3 or 4 feet.

176. During the operation of this year, the instrument was also taken to the following stations, viz.

> Bidenden Steeple,
> Hartridge,
> Warehorn Steeple,
> Stone Crouch,
> Iden Steeple,
> Brede Steeple.

To determine the distances between these objects, and the stations from whence they were observed, we have the following triangles.

Triangles.	Angles observed.	Distances of the stations from the intersected objects.	
Goudhurst - - Tenterden - - Bidenden Steeple	18 16 4 40 0 12	Bidenden -	Feet. 41097 20040
Goudhurst - - Tenterden - - Hartridge	27 21 34 19 14 19	Hartridge -	19134 38404

Triangles.	Angles observed.	Distances of the stations from the intersected objects.	
	° ′ ″		Feet.
Allington Knoll -	44 16 25	}Stone Crouch - {	51580
Lydd - -	73 7 50		37627
Stone Crouch			
Allington Knoll -	15 46 51	}Warehorn - {	28107
Stone Crouch -	17 18 22		25696
Wareborn Steeple			
Tenterden - -	28 55 46	}Iden - - {	33239
Fairlight Down -	20 42 7		45483
Iden Steeple			
Iden - - -	21 57 0	}Winchelsea - {	21224
Fairlight Down -	17 5 40		26990
Winchelsea Steeple			
Brede Steeple -	67 26 0	}Brede - - {	21755
Fairlight Down -	64 28 0		26979
Winchelsea Steeple			

177. Secondary Triangles.

Goudhurst - -	59 47 4	}Ulcomb - {	56184
Tenterden - -	61 44 12		55123
Ulcomb Steeple			
Goudhurst - -	65 36 50	}Windmill - {	48610
Tenterden - -	52 19 42		36009
Sutton Windmill			
Goudhurst - -	70 48 44	}Chart Sutton - {	46898
Tenterden - -	48 11 12		58717
Chart Sutton Steeple			
Goudhurst - -	91 32 50	}Linton - - {	41690
Tenterden - -	36 54 6		69407
Linton Steeple			
Goudhurst - -	49 11 14	}Windmill - {	40621
Tenterden - -	47 51 2		41468
Headcorn Windmill			

Triangles.	Angles observed.	Distances of the stations from the intersected objects.	
	° ′ ″		Feet.
Goudhurst - -	29 8 0	} Cranbrook -	{ 18239
Hartridge - -	70 10 0		9439
Cranbrook Steeple			
Tenterden - -	94 50 33	} Denenden -	{ 24799
Boughton Malherb	24 7 11		60471
Benenden Steeple			
Bidenden - -	38 47 0	} Staplehurst -	{ 25514
Goudhurst - -	37 0 0		26555
Stapleburst Steeple			
Bidenden - -	33 30 0	} Marden - -	{ 40015
Goudhurst - -	70 42 33		23999
Marden Steeple			
Boughton Malherb	14 39 40	} Frittenden -	{ 36203
Goudhurst - -	17 10 0		31045
Frittenden Steeple			
Tenterden - -	20 46 0	} Windmill -	{ 51527
Silver Hill - -	76 45 52		18768
Brasses Windmill			
Tenterden - -	11 2 0	} Hawkhurst -	{ 44028
Silver Hill - -	42 17 30		12522
Hawkburst Steeple			
Silver Hill - -	72 5 37	} Sandhurst -	{ 16448
Fairlight Down -	17 1 25		53460
Sandburst Steeple			
Silver Hill - -	58 27 19	} Whittersham -	{ 50861
Fairlight Down -	55 42 10		52459
Whittersbam Steeple			
Silver Hill - -	38 49 4	} Peasemarsh -	{ 49016
Fairlight Down -	59 39 33		35602
Peasemarsh Steeple			
Silver Hill - -	82 8 4	} Rolvenden -	{ 98028
Fairlight Down -	36 28 0		63380
Rolvenden Steeple			

Triangles.	Angles observed.	Distances of the stations from the intersected objects.	
			Feet.
Silver Hill - - Fairlight Down - *Beckley Steeple*	42 30 35 35 36 7	} Beckley - - {	33419 38790
Allington Knoll - High Nook - - *New Church Steeple*	46 3 7 36 41 43	} New Church - {	19967 16898
Allington Knoll - High Nook - - *Ivy Church Steeple*	52 3 53 76 5 26	} Ivy Church - {	28691 23256
Allington Knoll - High Nook - - *St. Mary's Steeple*	27 21 0 80 5 0	} St. Mary's - {	23939 11165
Tenterden - - Lydd - - *Playden Steeple*	34 33 5 34 35 48	} Playden - {	40204 40158
Brede Steeple - Fairlight Down - *Icklesham Steeple*	56 0 0 55 1 0	} Icklesham - {	19094 19321
Stone Crouch - Allington Knoll - *Woodchurch Steeple*	55 9 34 32 59 15	} Woodchurch - {	28098 42357
Stone Crouch - Allington Knoll - *Old Romney Steeple*	41 36 38 35 59 39	} Old Romney - {	31037 35070
Stone Crouch - Allington Knoll - *New Romney Steeple*	41 54 7 52 21 33	} New Romney - {	40957 34544
Stone Crouch - Allington Knoll - *Brookland Steeple*	40 47 1 14 44 21	} Brookland - {	15919 40872
Stone Crouch - Allington Knoll - *Orleston Steeple*	20 16 3 29 46 58	} Orleston - {	33121 23308

Triangles.	Angles observed.	Distances of the stations from the intersected objects.	
			Perc.
Stone Crouch - Lydd - - *East Guilford Steeple*	67 14 56 24 46 59	}East Guilford - {	15782 34721
Stone Crouch - Lydd - - *Snargate Steeple*	53 4 1 28 2 7	}Snargate - {	17900 30443
Stone Crouch - Warehorn Steeple - *Snave Steeple*	25 37 0 81 34 0	}Snave - - {	26666 11629
Stone Crouch - Warehorn - - *Appledore Steeple*	9 11 12 6 46 0	}Appledore - {	11016 14925
Warehorn - - Allington Knoll - *Brenzet Steeple*	91 6 0 30 5 41	}Brenzet - {	16476 32852
Allington Knoll - Westwell Down - *Bethersden Steeple*	36 36 26 68 55 44	}Bethersden - {	49701 31762
Allington Knoll - Westwell Down - *High Halden Steeple*	49 12 12 70 39 8	}High Halden - {	55827 44798
Westwell Down - Boughton Malherb - *Lenham Steeple*	17 24 40 64 19 30	}Lenham - {	30424 10101
Westwell Down - Boughton Malherb - *Egerton Steeple*	12 31 21 30 1 45	}Egerton - {	24722 10711
Westwell Down - Boughton Malherb - *Turret on Romden Stables*	42 50 41 71 6 34	}Romden Stables {	34586 24858
Westwell Down - Boughton Malherb - *Smarden Steeple*	37 32 21 84 23 32	}Smarden - {	39104 23850

3 I

Bearings of the Objects intersected in the Survey with the small circular Instrument, from the Parallels to the Meridian of Greenwich; also their Distances from that Meridian, and its Perpendicular.

178. At Folkstone Turnpike, the bearing of the station on Dover Castle in 1787, from the parallel to the Meridian of Greenwich is 65° 50′ 46″ NE. The new point on the Keep is 6½ feet north-eastward from the old one, which will subtend an angle at Folkstone Turnpike of about 38″; therefore the new station bears 65° 52′ 8″ NE. The bearing of the centre of Tenterden Steeple from Allington Knoll, is nearly the same as that of the station in 1787, or 85° 47′ 25″ SW. See page 153, for the bearings and distances whence those in the three following Articles have been derived. But it may be proper to remark, that some of the bearings (and consequently the distances from the meridian and perpendicular) which depend on Goudhurst and Tenterden, will differ a little when obtained from different routes, because the stations in 1787 were not at the centres of the roofs of the steeples. These variations, however, are of little consequence, as the computed latitudes and longitudes which follow, are generally put down to the nearest *second* only.

179. *Bearings and Distances of the Stations, 1795.*

Bearings from the Parallels to the Meridian of Greenwich.				Distances from merid.	Distances from perp.
	°	′	″	Feet.	Feet.
At Folkstone Turnpike.					
Dover - -	65	52	8	NE	309777	194314
Hawkinge - -	29	45	38	NE	276602	194372
At Dover.					
Paddlesworth -	81	30	42	SW	262001	130549
Waldershare -	36	24	53	NW	290111	105788
Ringswold - -	30	21	52	NE	315780	103896
At Waldershare.					
Shore - -	99	54	35	NE	317542	72993
Mount Pleasant -	11	56	19	NE	302713	46186
Wingham - -	16	36	24	NW	279530	70311
Hardres - -	74	21	9	NW	248177	94042
Hawkinge - -	25	17	53	SW		
Ringswold - -	85	37	43	NE		
Near the Shore.					
Ringswold - -	3	16	15	SW		
Mount Pleasant -	28	56	58	NW		
At Mount Pleasant.					
Wingham - -	43	51	31	SW		
Chislet - -	82	23	48	SW	272915	50164
At Wingham.					
Chislet - -	18	10	37	NW		
Hardres - -	52	52	37	SW		
Beverley Park -	77	3	23	NW	247057	62848
At Beverley Park.					
Hardres - -	2	3	23	SE		

Bearings from the Parallels to the Meridian of Greenwich.		Distances from merd.	Distances from perp.
At Allington Knoll.		Feet.	Feet.
Tenterden - -	85 47 25 SW		
Westwell Down =	32 34 49 NW	192300	100795
Wye Down - -	2 2 48 NE	221267	106699
Brabourn Down -	22 37 5 NE	230100	119634
180. *Interior Objects.*			
At Dover.			
St. Radigund's Abbey -	88 5 4 NW	287590	123773
Hougham Steeple -	68 19 22 SW	288338	130451
Gunston Steeple -	3 43 2 NW	303186	115222
St. Margaret's Steeple -	51 54 48 NE	315115	115404
South Foreland Light-House - -	70 10 31 NE	315142	120217
At Waldershare.			
Barham Windmill -	61 0 4 NW	268570	93848
Elham Windmill -	10 14 39 SW	284427	137242
Upper Deal Chapel -	69 17 33 NE	317053	92283
Deal Castle - =	66 9 16 NE	321839	91764
Watch-house near the Shore	85 2 37 SE	321911	108494
Sandown Castle -	55 51 56 NE	321718	84361
Walmer Steeple -	73 8 30 NE	318335	97835
Ripple Steeple -	70 1 50 NE	302864	97520
Waldershare Steeple -	64 52 20 NE	295232	103386
Eastry Steeple -	23 30 46 NE	300890	89162
Ash Steeple - -	4 44 29 NE	293066	70161
Minster Steeple -	11 24 56 NE	301152	51109
Woard Steeple -	34 11 33 NE	308964	78038
Sandwich highest Steeple	26 19 14 NE	307184	71275
Wingham Steeple -	20 6 36 NW	278004	72721
Goodneston Steeple -	19 16 21 NW	281912	82939
Littlebourn Steeple -	27 39 59 NW	271797	70836
Canterbury Cathedral -	49 51 48 NW	248195	70446

Bearings from the Parallels to the Meridian of Greenwich.					Distances from merid.	Distances from perp.
At Ringswold.	°	′	″		Feet.	Feet.
Mongeham Steeple -	21	30	34	NW	311608	95839
Norbourn Steeple -	31	52	45	NW	307620	90706
Woodnesborough Steeple	29	51	29	NW	299690	75796
Near the Shore.						
Ramsgate Windmill -	12	13	37	NE	322348	50813
St. Lawrence Steeple -	7	30	0	NE	320814	48144
At Mount Pleasant.						
Birchington Steeple -	20	17	12	NW	298726	35399
St. Nicholas Steeple -	78	0	9	NW	286388	42717
Stormouth Steeple -	65	26	52	SW	283140	55128
At Wingham.						
The South Reculver -	8	3	15	NW	274343	33659
Hearne Windmill -	34	59	11	NW	260188	42675
Blean Steeple -	76	41	11	NW	241258	61255
Wickham Steeple -	77	21	44	NW	270920	68380
Bridge Windmill -	55	21	3	SW	260129	83719
Nackington Steeple -	69	29	17	SW	249851	81414
Chillendon Windmill -	28	0	30	SE	280588	83582
Preston Steeple -	5	6	13	NW	278888	63120
Shottenden Windmill -	89	42	1	SW	212203	77744
Ickham Steeple -	89	45	57	SW	271530	70344
At Hardres.						
Harbledown Steeple -	74	15	0	NW	241952	69531
Sturry Steeple -	15	26	36	NE	256616	63495
West Stone-street Windmill	33	46	24	SW	236867	109739
Stelling Windmill -	26	1	10	SW	242000	106696
On Westwell Down.						
Ashford Steeple -	24	53	15	SE	200726	118959
Brook Steeple -	63	10	25	SE	219232	114415
Willesborough Steeple -	33	0	39	SE	06795	123107
Kingsnorth Steeple -	12	49	1	SE	59085	130898

Bearings from the Parallels to the Meridian of Greenwich.			Distances from merid.	Distances from perp.
	° ′ ″		Feet.	Feet.
On Westwell Down.				
Shadoxhurst Steeple -	7 20 54	SW	187898	135474
Kennington Steeple -	50 34 14	SE	204867	111189
At Allington Knoll.				
Great Chart Steeple -	52 21 16	NW	190570	121387
Westwell Steeple - -	31 46 48	NW	194206	102508
Pluckley Steeple - -	53 27 50	NW	173509	109639
Eastwell Steeple -	25 17 49	NW	200943	109856
Charing Steeple -	37 58 49	NW	189956	96675
Allington Steeple -	25 0 2	NE	221342	141015
Lymne Steeple -	81 23 44	SE	235911	146454
Mersham Steeple - -	22 32 14	NW	214267	130381
Monk's-Horton Steeple	46 23 19	NE	237603	127202

181. *Bearings and Distances of the Stations, and Interior Objects, intersected in 1796.*

At Goudhurst.				
Boughton Malherb -	54 59 23	NE	159327	95484
Bidenden - -	88 49 3	NE	147434	131748
Hartridge - -	79 43 33	NE		
At Fairlight Down.				
Silver Hill - -	34 28 24	NW		
Iden Steeple - -	32 47 48	NE	167948	180985
Brede Steeple -	14 34 32	NW	137837	197564
At Allington Knoll.				
Stone Crouch - -	57 3 23	SW	176646	172086
Warehorn Steeple -	72 50 14	SW	193078	152330

Interior Objects.

Bearings from the Parallels to the Meridian of Greenwich.		Distances from merid.	Distances from perp.
At Goudhurst.		Feet.	Feet.
Frittenden Steeple -	72 9 28 NE	135897	123083
Linton Steeple - -	15 32 17 NE	117513	92429
Chart Sutton Steeple -	36 16 28 NE	133760	95238
Sutton Windmill -	41 28 17 NE	138537	96172
Ulcomb Steeple -	47 18 3 NE	147636	94495
Headcorn Windmill -	57 53 53 NE	140755	111009
Staplehurst - -	51 49 3 NE	127219	116180
Cranbrook Steeple -	71 3 27 SE	123605	138492
At Fairlight Down.			
Rolvenden Steeple -	1 59 36 NE	145517	155277
Beckley Steeple -	1 7 43 NE	144076	179836
Peasemarsh Steeple -	25 11 9 NE	158462	186401
Whittersham Steeple -	21 13 46 NE	162311	169710
Sandhurst Steeple - -	17 26 59 NW	127281	167618
Winchelsea Steeple -	49 53 28 NE	162954	201230
Icklesham Steeple -	40 26 28 NE	155845	203913
At Allington Knoll.			
Bethersden - -	69 11 15 NW	173476	126377
High Halden - -	81 47 1 NW	164079	136058
Orleston Steeple -	06 30 21 SW	196661	145321
Woodchurch Steeple -	89 57 22 NW	177576	144004
Brookland Steeple -	42 19 2 SW	192417	174257
Old Romney Steeple -	21 3 44 SW	207329	176763
New Romney Steeple -	4 41 50 SW	217104	178464
Brenzet - - -	42 44 33 SW	197637	168163
At Boughton Malherb.			
Benenden Steeple - -	25 12 14 SW	133576	150198
At Silver Hill.			
Brasses Windmill - -	40 7 40 SE	123612	186658

Bearings from the Parallels to the Meridian of Greenwich.		Distances from merid.	Distances from perp.
	° ′ ″	Feet.	Feet.
At High Nook.			
New Church Steeple -	57 43 31 NW	214085	156692
Ivy Church Steeple -	82 52 46 SW	205177	168561
St. Mary's Steeple -	78 53 12 SW	217997	167830
At Lydd.			
Playden Steeple -	85 3 0 NW	169307	187236
At Westwell.			
Lenham Steeple -	69 25 45 NW	165089	87186
Egerton Steeple - -	86 ;8 14 SW	167621	102245
Smarden Steeple -	61 47 14 SW	157848	119261
Turret on Romden Stables	56 18 54 SW	163521	119978
At Stone Crouch.			
Appledore Steeple -	30 33 49 NE	182247	162601
Snave Steeple - -	65 22 1 NE	200830	160997
Snargate Steeple - -	66 35 7 NE	193072	164973
East Guilford Steeple -	6 54 4 SW	174750	187754

182. *Latitudes and Longitudes of Objects intersected in* 1795.

Names of objects.	Latitude.	Longitude east from Greenwich.	
		In degrees.	In time.
	° ′ ″	° ′ ″	m. s.
The Belvidere in Waldershare Park	51 10 53	1 15 39	5 2.6
Ringswold, or Kingswould Steeple	51 11 8	1 22 20	5 29.3
Upper Hardres Steeple - -	51 12 1	1 4 45	4 19
Chislet Steeple - -	51 20 4	1 11 24	4 45.6
St. Radigund's Abbey - -	51 7 56	1 14 44	4 58.9
Hougham Steeple - -	51 6 50	1 15 4	5 0.3
Gunston Steeple - - -	51 9 18	1 19 0	5 16
St. Margaret's Steeple - -	51 9 14	1 22 7	5 28.5
South Foreland Light-House -	51 8 26	1 22 6	5 28.4
Barham Windmill -	51 12 54	1 10 5	4 40.3

Names of Objects.	Latitude.			Longitude east from Greenwich. In degrees.			In time.	
	°	′	″	°	′	″	m.	s.
Elham Windmill - -	51	5	41	1	14	1	4	56.1
Upper Deal Chapel - -	51	19	2	1	22	44	5	30.9
Deal Castle - -	51	13	5	1	23	59	5	35.9
Watch-house near the sea shore	51	12	21	1	23	46	5	35.1
Sandown Castle - -	51	14	18	1	23	59	5	35.9
Walmer Steeple - -	51	15	29	1	23	8	5	32.5
Ripple Steeple - -	51	12	12	1	19	0	5	16
Waldershare Steeple - -	51	11	15	1	16	59	5	7.9
Eastry Steeple - -	51	14	44	1	18	26	5	13.7
Ash Steeple - - -	51	16	44	1	16	34	5	6.3
Minster Steeple - -	51	19	50	1	18	46	5	15.1
Woard Steeple - -	51	15	23	1	20	41	5	22.7
Sandwich highest Steeple -	51	16	30	1	20	15	5	21
Wingham Steeple - -	51	16	21	1	12	38	4	50.5
Goodneston Steeple - -	51	14	45	1	13	36	4	54.4
Littlebourn Steeple - -	51	16	40	1	11	1	4	44.1
Canterbury Cathedral -	51	16	48	1	4	51	4	19.4
Mongeham Steeple - -	51	12	53	1	21	18	5	25.2
Norbourn, or Northbourn Steeple	51	13	13	1	20	17	5	21.1
Woodnessborough, or Woodnesborough Steeple - -	51	15	47	1	18	17	5	13.1
Ramsgate Windmill - -	51	19	49	1	24	20	5	37.3
St. Lawrence Steeple - -	51	20	16	1	23	56	5	43.7
Birchington Steeple - -	51	22	25	1	18	13	5	12.9
St. Nicholas Steeple - -	51	21	15	1	11	47	4	59.8
Stourmouth, or Stormouth Steeple	51	19	13	1	14	3	4	56.2
The South Reculver - -	51	22	47	1	11	50	4	47.3
Hearne Windmill - -	51	21	20	1	8	6	4	32.4
Blean Steeple - -	51	18	19	1	3	4	4	12.3
Wickham Steeple - -	51	17	5	1	10	18	4	43.2
Ickham Steeple - -	51	16	45	1	10	57	4	43.8
Bridge Windmill - -	51	14	35	1	7	55	4	31.7
Nackington Steeple -	51	14	59	1	5	14	4	20.9
Chillendon Windmill -	51	11	32	1	11	19	4	59.3
Preston Steeple - -	51	17	55	1	12	54	4	51.6
Shottenden Windmill -	51	15	41	0	55	25	3	41.7

3 K

Names of Objects.	Latitude.			Longitude east from Greenwich.			In time.	
	°	′	″	°	′	″	m.	t.
Harbledown Steeple	51	16	58	1	3	13	4	12.9
Sturry Steeple	51	17	55	1	7	5	4	28.3
West-Stone-street Windmill	51	10	22	1	1	45	4	7
Stelling Windmill	51	10	51	1	3	6	4	12.4
Ashford Steeple	51	8	56	0	52	18	3	29.2
Brook Steeple	51	9	38	0	57	8	3	48.5
Willesborough Steeple	51	8	14	0	53	52	3	35.5
Kingsnorth Steeple	51	7	3	0	51	49	3	27.3
Shadoxhurst Steeple	51	6	14	0	48	53	3	15.5
Kennington Steeple	51	10	12	0	53	24	3	33.6
Great Chart Steeple	51	8	33	0	49	39	3	18.6
Westwell Steeple	51	11	39	0	50	39	3	22.6
Pluckley Steeple	51	10	30	0	45	14	3	0.9
Eastwell Steeple	51	11	24	0	52	24	3	29.6
Charing Steeple	51	12	37	0	47	44	3	10.9
Allington, or Aldington Steeple	51	5	16	0	57	36	3	50.4
Lymne Steeple	51	4	20	1	1	22	4	5.5
Mersham Steeple	51	7	1	0	55	47	3	43.1
Monks Horton Steeple	51	7	30	1	1	53	4	7.5

189. *Latitudes and Longitudes of Objects intersected in 1796.*

Linton Steeple	51	13	24	0	10	40	2	2.7
Sutton Windmill	51	13	46	0	36	9	2	24.6
Chart Sutton Steeple	51	13	56	0	34	54	2	19.6
Lenham Steeple	51	14	13	0	43	6	2	52.4
Romden Stables	51	8	49	0	42	36	2	50.4
Smarden Steeple	51	8	57	0	41	8	2	44.5
Bethersden Steeple	51	7	45	0	45	10	3	0.7
Rolvenden Steeple	51	3	3	0	37	50	2	31.3
Beckley Steeple	50	59	1	0	47	24	2	29.6
Bidenden Steeple	51	6	55	0	38	23	2	33.5
Headcorn Windmill	51	10	21	0	36	41	2	26.7
Ulcomb Steeple	51	13	1	0	38	31	2	33
Staplehurst Steeple	51	9	30	0	33	9	2	12.6

Names of Objects.	Latitude.	Longitude east from Greenwich.	
		In degrees.	In time.
	° ′ ″	° ′ ″	m. s.
Cranbrook Steeple -	51 5 50	0 32 10	2 8.7
Egerton Steeple - -	51 11 44	0 43 43	2 54.9
Frittenden Steeple - -	51 8 20	0 35 24	2 21.6
Snargate Steeple - -	51 1 23	0 50 10	3 20.7
Snave Steeple - -	51 2 1	0 52 12	3 28.8
Warehorn Steeple - -	51 3 27	0 50 13	3 20.9
Orleston Steeple - - -	51 4 36	0 51 10	3 24.7
Winchelsea Steeple -	50 55 28	0 42 31	2 50
Sandhurst Steeple - -	51 1 3	0 33 4	2 12.3
Whittersham Steeple - -	51 0 39	0 42 10	2 48.7
New Church Steeple - -	51 2 42	0 55 38	3 42.5
Ivy Church Steeple - -	51 0 45	0 59 18	3 59.2
St. Mary's Steeple - -	51 0 52	0 56 28	3 45.9
East Guilford Steeple - -	50 57 40	0 45 21	3 1.4
Appledore Steeple - -	51 1 47	0 47 22	3 9.5
Old Romney Steeple - -	50 59 25	0 53 50	3 35.3
New Romney Steeple -	50 59 7	0 56 22	3 45.5
Playden Steeple - -	50 57 46	0 43 56	2 55.7
Brookland Steeple - -	50 59 51	0 49 58	3 19.9
Iden Steeple - -	50 58 54	0 43 36	2 54.4
Brede Steeple - -	50 56 7	0 35 45	2 23
Benenden Steeple - -	51 3 54	0 34 44	2 18.9
Brasses Windmill - -	50 57 55	0 32 5	2 8.3
Icklesham Steeple - -	50 55 3	0 40 24	2 41.6
Boughton Malherb Steeple -	51 12 51	0 41 34	2 46.3
Peasemarsh Steeple - -	50 57 54	0 41 7	2 44.5
Woodchurch Steeple - -	51 4 51	0 46 12	3 4.8
High Halden Steeple -	51 6 11	0 42 52	2 51.5
Brenzet Steeple - -	50 0 51	0 51 21	3 25.4

www.ingramcontent.com/pod-product-compliance
Lightning Source LLC
Chambersburg PA
CBHW022122020426

42334CB00015B/727